ALSO BY HEATHER ANN THOMPSON

Blood in the Water:
The Attica Prison Uprising of 1971 and Its Legacy

Whose Detroit?: Politics, Labor, and Race
in a Modern American City

(as editor)
Speaking Out: Activism and Protest
in the 1960s and 1970s

FEAR AND FURY

FEAR AND FURY

The Reagan Eighties,
the Bernie Goetz Shootings,
and the Rebirth of
White Rage

Heather Ann Thompson

PANTHEON BOOKS
New York

FIRST HARDCOVER EDITION PUBLISHED
BY PANTHEON BOOKS 2026

Published by Pantheon Books, a division of Penguin Random House LLC, 1745 Broadway, New York, NY 10019.

Pantheon Books and the colophon are registered trademarks of Penguin Random House LLC.

LCCN 2025038701
ISBN 978-0-593-70209-3 (hardcover)
ISBN 978-0-593-70211-6 (eBook)

penguinrandomhouse.com | pantheonbooks.com

Printed in the United States of America
3rd Printing

The authorized representative in the EU for product safety and compliance is Penguin Random House Ireland, Morrison Chambers, 32 Nassau Street, Dublin D02 YH68, Ireland, https://eu-contact.penguin.ie.

For Frank Wilson Thompson Jr.
We miss you every single day.

For Dash Callahan Erb
With you, we can now imagine a better future.

Contents

FEAR AND FURY

Prologue

December 22, 1984

DARRELL CABEY

Things had gone awfully, terribly wrong, but Darrell couldn't understand why. He had just been sitting next to James, smiling as their other friends, Troy and Barry, horsed around a bit farther down the subway car.

It wasn't as if Darrell hadn't noticed the white guy. He definitely had.

To be sure, the man was unremarkable in every way—nerdy-looking, pale, and quiet. Except that he had chosen a seat directly in front of Troy. This was noteworthy. Passengers usually gave teenagers like Darrell and his friends a wide berth.

Also unnervingly, the man was staring straight at Troy and Barry as the two joked, laughed, and occasionally swung around a pole or smiled over at one of the female passengers with a "Hey, what's up?" or a "You got a light?"

But then something shifted. Neither Darrell nor James could hear much over the clatter of the train's wheels, but Troy, still with a smile on his face, was now saying something to the man.

Seconds later, it was as if the air had exploded.

As Darrell looked on in horror, he realized that both Troy and Barry were now crumpled on the floor, immobile, staring blankly at the grimy linoleum.

But why was James on the floor too, bleeding? And why couldn't Darrell just leave? After all, that was what the other passengers were doing—pushing one another toward the doors at the end of the car in their desperation to flee.

For some reason, Darrell could not stand up. He couldn't move. At all. Maybe he was just in shock. Maybe that was why he was still slumped over, unable to get up from the seat that was slick and red.

It was probably best not to dwell on that. Best not to let the panic overtake him. But the paramedics who were hovering over him looked seriously concerned, asking their questions almost too calmly. And then there were the stony-faced cops, standing by the yawning exits of the now mostly empty train car.

Nothing good ever happened to boys like Darrell when the cops showed up.

Even as Darrell and his three friends were carefully laid onto stretchers, then gingerly carried up crumbling and filthy cement subway stairs into waiting ambulances, these victims were becoming the villains.

BERNIE GOETZ

As he darted across the steel tracks of the New York City subway's IRT line, steel-encased lamps dimly illuminated the high concrete walls of the dark tunnel. Bernie Goetz was much closer to a station than he had dared hope.

He stayed low until he reached the end of the platform. Then, he hoisted himself up onto the yellow-painted edge, his eyes scanning for the quickest way out onto Chambers Street.

When Bernie emerged onto the bustling street, few bystanders would have registered such an ordinary-looking man. He was thin, sandy-haired, and kept his head down. He made sure to walk quickly, but not to run. The pale eyes behind his wire-rimmed glasses searched the street for a cab.

He was in luck. Slumping into the backseat of a taxi, Bernie asked the driver to drop him off at 15th Street, where he walked briskly around the corner, into his building, and headed straight to the elevator.

Once in his apartment, he stripped off his thin jacket and fretted about the now-empty gun that sat heavily in the quick-draw holster on his hip. He would need to do something with it. But what? With no good ideas coming to mind, Bernie decided to shower and think this whole mess through.

Suddenly gripped by the overwhelming feeling that he needed to skip town, Bernie dried off, dressed, and threw a few things into a small suitcase. Moments later he was down in the lobby telling the doorman, as nonchalantly as possible, that he would be away for a few days. He had no real plan, but maybe, just maybe, he could lie low for a while before returning to his quiet life. That, after all, was what he really wanted—just to be left alone.

But even as he was pulling out of Olin's Rent-a-Car, anxious to put distance between himself and the gritty city, Bernie Goetz had already become a celebrity. The public didn't yet know his name, but he was being heralded by the local media as a hero.

He was the "Death Wish Vigilante." He was a real-life Charles Bronson. He had stood up to the city's "thugs" as few others had the guts to do.

The Bernie Goetz subway shootings would unveil simmering racial resentments, ones that had been carefully fueled during the Reagan eighties. And they would unleash and legitimize a new era of white racial rage.

This moment would profoundly change America.

PART I

Poisoning the Big Apple

As the 1980s dawned, young people in New York City felt at least a small measure of optimism for the future. It was at least possible that this new decade would turn out to be better than the last, battered as it had been by a global recession.

The punk rock kids in Greenwich Village could be seen irreverently belting out the lyrics of anti-capitalist bands such as The Clash or The Proletariat as they congregated near the arch in Washington Square Park, like so many colorful peacocks, with their hair dyed in outlandish colors and six-inch Mohawks spiking at the top of their heads.

In the South Bronx, teenagers sporting fades and perms were trying to make their mark as well. Whether on the street corner or a city bus, they would find themselves inspiring passersby with the powerful social critique of songs like Grandmaster Flash's "The Message" pumping out of the boomboxes that balanced precariously on slim shoulders or sat on a concrete sidewalk nearby.

Meanwhile, over on Wall Street, young Izod-clad yuppies exuded their own heady self-assurance, perhaps sensing that the 1980s—as embodied by brash business tycoons like Donald Trump—was going to be their decade in particular.[1]

Many other New Yorkers, however, were nowhere near as certain about what the future had in store.

Despite the recent fiscal crisis, many city residents still wanted to believe the claims of the Democratic Party that a "Great Society" might yet be realized, and they worried mightily that the looming Reagan Revolution would take that dream, already too long deferred, and dash it entirely.

Others had instead come out of the seventies suspicious that the Democrats, and liberals more generally, had already done too much, not too little. These overwhelmingly white New Yorkers increasingly worried that overreliance on social programs was fostering dependency as well as damaging the economy. In their view, liberal politicians had also been far too willing to bow down to the demands of the civil rights movement.

Many of these New Yorkers had been lifelong Democrats, ones who themselves had benefited enormously from governmental spending on uplift programs, from the New Deal of the 1930s forward. But the racially tumultuous 1960s, as well as the economic dislocations of the 1970s, had led not a few to agree with the iconic television curmudgeon Archie Bunker when he declared, "If you liberals go on getting your way we're all gonna hear one big loud flush; that's the sound of the USA going down the toilet."[2]

Reagan-era Republicans depended on this mindset, and more specifically on the racial resentments and economic anxieties of this particular group of newly disaffected voters, to put them in the White House in 1980. The party leadership's overarching goal, however, was in fact to slash taxes and to roll back regulations for the nation's wealthiest citizens and businesses—a move that, ironically, would strip cities of what they needed to feel both safe and prosperous, and would only further impoverish their already poorest and most marginalized neighborhoods. Pulling that off would require an ever more dramatic and intentional fueling of white fear and fury.

1

Dreams Dashed

IN 1980, Darrell Eugene Cabey was fourteen years old. He lived in the South Bronx, a neighborhood in New York City that, to presidential candidate Ronald Reagan, represented everything that was wrong with America.

Reagan chose the South Bronx as a campaign stop for exactly this reason.[1] His motorcade arrived on Charlotte Street one scorching day in August, and cameras clicked away as he stood in front of a building on which political street artist John Fekner had scrawled the word "DECAY" in huge orange letters. Another crumbling façade could be seen nearby, where Fekner had painted "BROKEN PROMISES" in an equally loud message of censure and despair. Somberly gazing over the dilapidated lot on which he stood, Reagan told the assembled crowd of reporters and curious residents, in a not-so-subtle rebuke, that "he hadn't 'seen anything like this since London after the Blitz.'"[2]

But this was also the place that Darrell Cabey, known as "Bean" by his family, felt most loved and supported. The Cabey family lived in a small apartment on the twenty-first floor of the Daniel Webster Homes, nestled in the Morrisania neighborhood of the South Bronx. Darrell's mom, Shirley, worked hard to make it feel warm and welcoming. She insisted that he and his brothers help keep the place tidy and she made sure that they had decent meals and treated each other with respect.[3] This was where Darrell and his siblings listened to baseball on the radio and played video games in one of the two bedrooms. Darrell's best friend, Lydell, also lived in this building, and those two always found ways to have fun together too.

President Ronald Reagan speaking on Charlotte Street in the South Bronx.
Photo by Jack Smith/New York *Daily News* Archive via Getty Images

Still, no one who lived where Darrell did, or in any of the many concrete complexes that pierced the sky in this South Bronx neighborhood, would have disagreed with Ronald Reagan's assessment that this part of the city was in bad shape. The apartments were airless and dingy. They were poorly insulated, so that residents sweltered in the summer, and shivered in the winter, kids sometimes having to wear hats and coats inside to stay warm. In the icy winter of 1981, a resident was found literally frozen to death in one of the South Bronx's public housing blocks.[4]

Many of the buildings had also fallen into dangerous disrepair. The elevators clanged and shook ominously and would sometimes stop between floors, leaving residents panicked and uncertain that a maintenance worker would actually be available to respond to the emergency call button they had frantically pushed. From time to time, these lifts stopped working altogether, forcing residents like Shirley Cabey to trudge up seemingly endless flights of stairs with kids on their hips and grocery bags slipping from their hands. Meanwhile, the stairwells themselves were filled with trash, and light fixtures would flicker worryingly, if they hadn't burned out entirely.

The basketball courts and playgrounds just outside the dismal confines of these dwellings could be equally dispiriting. Thanks to cracks and holes in the asphalt, it was easy to trip and fall just trying to dribble the ball or to shred one's skin sliding into a makeshift base.

This, however, had not always been the case.

In the 1920s, the Bronx had been a jewel in the crown of the five boroughs of New York City. The only borough that isn't on an island, in that early decade it boasted beautiful filigreed buildings, lush parks, and spectacular public works with majestic fountains that glittered when lit up at night. Not even Manhattan had anything akin to the Bronx's Grand Boulevard and Concourse, a four-mile stretch of road that was "modeled on the Champs-Élysées of Paris" and featured two roadways—one for automobiles, and a shared one for pedestrians and horse-drawn carriages.[5]

The Bronx drew visitors from the other boroughs and from across the globe, offering exuberant gatherings at Yankee Stadium, exotic animals from all around the world at the Bronx Zoo, and vibrant flowers and foliage in the Bronx Botanical Garden. The borough also boasted two well-respected universities, Fordham and New York University, making it a destination for scholars too.[6]

The "South Bronx" was the rather vague designation bestowed on the southwestern area of the borough, which was more or less "bounded on the north by Fordham Road, on the west by the Harlem River, and on the south and east by the East and Bronx Rivers."[7] It covered approximately three thousand acres of land—a bit over 10 percent of the borough. This part of the Bronx had always been less grand than the more touristy areas, and became even less so when, between 1948 and 1972, it endured the noise, dust, and ugly machinery required to build the Cross Bronx Expressway. This highway bisected the neighborhood and subjected it to inordinate amounts of congestion and pollution and was the first major U.S. highway to run straight through an urban area. It also ran through much of the public housing located there, displacing between forty and sixty thousand residents.[8]

While these housing projects would later be associated with blight and decay, they were once beacons of social aspiration. By the 1950s, the New York City Housing Authority had built five large projects consisting of ninety-six buildings, all intended to provide safe and sturdy housing for primarily white families after World War II. These dwellings, along with access to low-interest housing loans from the federal government and to college classes from the G.I. Bill, made it feasible for a generation of young white families to move up and out of these subsidized units, just as they were supposed to.

When the neighborhood started facing increased grassroots and legal pressures to integrate during the 1960s, the Federal Housing Authority and a federally subsidized highway system made it possible for white residents of the South Bronx to escape to alluring suburban enclaves where they could own their own homes. White flight escalated between 1960 and 1980, and the South Bronx, and many other NYC neighborhoods, underwent a dramatic demographic change as Black and Brown families then moved into these areas.[9]

By the close of the 1970s, Puerto Rican and Black residents predominated in the South Bronx, with an ever-growing Dominican population as well.[10] Over the course of the next decade, a full 39 percent of the people in this part of the Bronx would also be living below the poverty line.[11] The area would, meanwhile, quite literally become a dumping ground for the rest of the city. In time, the majority of New York's commercial waste transfer stations—where trash trucks dumped their loads for compacting—as well as dozens of privately owned salvage yards and recycling centers would be located there.[12]

White flight had proven devastating to the South Bronx, but the damage it wrought had not been inevitable. Had city hall merely continued the same steady infusion of public dollars and had businesses offered the same opportunities for stable employment they had offered the original inhabitants of this area, the fallout from this exodus could have been prevented. But they did not. When a major fiscal crisis then gripped the nation in the mid-1970s, the South Bronx would only continue to be stripped and starved of what remaining resources it had.

This devastating economic crisis was also rooted in ill-fated economic and political choices. A series of oil price shocks in 1973 and more in 1979, as well as stagnating global economic growth accompanied by high inflation—a phenomenon dubbed "stagflation"—had dealt a devastating blow globally. Also important was rising resistance to some of the United States' more extractive policies on the world stage, along with pressures for better and more equal pay at home.[13] Businesses felt their profits being squeezed, and in response, they pulled back on many of their investment plans and slashed jobs.[14]

In urban centers such as New York City, the consequences of this were particularly dire.[15] Thanks to declining tax revenues and the deepening fiscal crisis more generally, NYC was $11 billion in debt by 1975 and unable to meet its obligations to its creditors. To avoid outright bankruptcy, the city had to rely on both state and federal intervention and severely cut back on its spending. Accordingly, it would lay off 38,000 workers, cancel various resident benefits such as free tuition at city colleges, and much more.[16]

For families in the South Bronx, the loss of city jobs as well as this eradication of an educational path out of poverty mattered. In the late 1960s, for example, before the City University of New York (CUNY) system ended free tuition, it had educated a disproportionately high number of first-generation, working-class Black and Puerto Rican students.[17] Indeed, a year after students successfully protested to guarantee every NYC high school graduate a spot in the system without cost in 1969, the percentage of Black and Puerto Rican students had doubled, and by 1976 it had tripled. That year, nonwhite students constituted a full 80 percent of CUNY's enrollees.[18] Reversing this policy thereafter hit these New Yorkers very hard.

Meanwhile, unscrupulous landlords had also begun preying upon the poor residents of places like the South Bronx, with very little oversight from city hall.[19] Landlords' disregard for the needs of their low-income tenants led to serious problems. By the late 1970s, the majority of housing in the South Bronx did not meet even the most basic health and safety regulations. More alarmingly, homes there began igniting in a stunning number of deadly blazes—averaging nearly twelve thousand fires a year.[20]

As historian Bench Ansfield has pointed out, the 1970s "arson epidemic" that engulfed the South Bronx was too often the result of landlords looking to cash in on insurance payouts.[21] As a result of these fires, neglect, and rising rates of poverty, the South Bronx eventually lost a full one-fifth of its housing stock to demolition or abandonment. By the end of the 1970s, city-owned high-rise projects loomed above charred fields with no other dwelling for blocks, like "residential islands on empty landscapes."[22]

This devastation was not simply spatial or abstract; it was felt directly by the neighborhood's residents. Usurious private landlords raised rents and evicted tenants whenever it suited them. Successfully fighting such evictions in court was daunting. As one social worker put it, "Often it was hard to figure out who the landlord was or how to reach him."[23] But fight it the poor still did. They did so via myriad tenant-centered organizations and, as historian Elizabeth Hinton shows, also through open acts of rebellion.[24] Meanwhile, the number of South Bronx residents evicted from public housing would also grow each year of the recession, and they too would resist such displacement.[25]

In fact, people from the South Bronx regularly spoke out against the civic indifference and abuses they now faced. As historian LaShawn Harris has chronicled, they time and again mobilized to demand that their needs be met with the same level of commitment that white residents of this same neighborhood had enjoyed in years past. In one such moment, Harris points out, almost three hundred Bronx families "staged an eight-month rent strike, demanding repairs for windows, washers and dryers, stairwells and hallways, and water-damaged apartments."[26]

NOTABLY, THE CABEYS had not always lived in public housing. In the early years of Darrell's life, the family had lived in the downstairs of a house in Far Rockaway, Queens. Shirley and her husband, Ronald, had moved there in 1965. Though Ronald worked long hours as a truck driver, his earnings made it possible for Shirley to stay home with Darrell and his four brothers. They could go to the beach when it was nice out, and even when it wasn't, she was always encouraging the kids to play outside in their own front or back yards. Their dog, Flocko, loved to run around on the lawn and sometimes, to his family's consternation, even managed to escape for a brief frolic in one of the lush grassy fields nearby.

This family wasn't flush, but they felt financially stable and independent. They owned two cars and loved taking family vacations. Those adventures were especially treasured by the Cabey kids, because their dad was so often away from home. When Ronald's boss retired, he had taken the bold step of going into business for himself, which meant that he was driving his truck longer and later each day. The kids hated having to go to bed before they heard him coming in the front door.

But one night, Ronald Cabey did not come home. That evening in 1973, he stopped at a diner to get something to eat. He chose a seat in a vinyl booth, right next to a window, so that he could keep an eye on his truck. Suddenly, he noticed a stranger hoisting himself behind the wheel.

Ron panicked. His family's entire economic security depended on this vehicle. He ran outside, where the thief was already tearing out of the parking space. Somehow, Ronald managed to jump onto the truck's running board and tried to grab the man inside in order to throw him out of the vehicle. The driver had a gun, but even this did not dissuade Ron.

To the horror of onlookers, however, as the thief turned onto a busy street, he violently wrenched the wheel in an attempt to shake Ron off. At that exact moment, another car was turning into the restaurant's driveway. With a sickening screech, the two vehicles collided, crushing Ronald Cabey between them. He fell to the pavement and died at the scene, as the stolen truck sped away.[27]

Shirley Cabey was devastated. Without her husband's income, she decided to move her family into public housing in the South Bronx, where they would also be closer to her mother.[28] Shirley was only twenty-six years old, a widow with children who were grieving terribly. Darrell was just seven years old when he lost his dad, his dog, and the only home he had ever known. He took his father's death particularly hard, and Shirley tried to get him counseling. She eventually managed to get Darrell to see someone over at Bronx-Lebanon Hospital, but she wasn't sure how helpful it was for her son.[29]

By 1980, the five Cabey brothers and their mother were squeezed into a two-bedroom apartment in the sprawling Claremont Village projects, which included the Daniel Webster Homes. Subsidized housing was a godsend, costing Shirley Cabey only $126.25 a month. And the good news too was that she would eventually land a new state job, working as a food service handler at the Manhattan State Psychiatric Center on Wards Island. She prayed that she would make it past the probationary period customary for all new employees, and that the position would become permanent. Since her husband's death, Shirley also received a monthly Social Security check of $472, which was a great relief as well.[30] The Cabeys were in better shape than most families, and yet the money coming in was still far less than they needed.

2

Secrets and Scars

BERNHARD HUGO GOETZ WAS born at Kew Gardens Hospital in Queens, New York, in 1947. His parents, Bernhard Willard Goetz and Gertrude Karlsberg, emigrated from Germany and met in the U.S., marrying in August 1935 at Central Park's historic Tavern on the Green. They eventually welcomed four children, two girls and two boys, with Bernie being the youngest.

Although his mother was born into the Jewish faith, Gertrude became a Lutheran like her husband, deciding to raise her children in that church.[1] Neighbors and family members alike described Mrs. Goetz as "a gentle, self-sacrificing and subservient woman" and her husband as "a strong, domineering and demanding man."[2]

Although difficult to live with, Mr. Goetz certainly provided a comfortable life for his family. They had first lived in a rather small place on 45th Avenue in Elmhurst, Queens, then moved into "a brand-new home" on Poyer Street before Bernie was born.[3] Bernhard Sr.'s bookbinding business, Mutual Specialty Products, produced everything from photo albums to heavy sample books of drapery and upholstery swatches, and it allowed him eventually to move the family out of the city to a farm in bucolic Red Hook, New York. When Bernie was three, his father moved them again, this time into an unassuming house on Wynkoop Lane in the small town of Rhinebeck, New York.[4]

The success of Bernhard Sr.'s company had also allowed him to purchase several large parcels of land near Rhinebeck on which he decided to operate an additional business, the Silver Lake Dairy. He owned another two-hundred-acre farm near the village of Clinton Corners in Dutchess

County. By the mid-1960s, the Goetz farms were distributing goods to stores across eight counties.[5]

On the surface, the Goetz kids' childhood was idyllic. They spent endless hours outside playing, camping, and learning how to fish and shoot. From a young age, Bernie loved to line up tin cans on a fence or a picnic table and practice felling them with precision. Since Bernie was quite a bit younger than his siblings, who had their own activities and friends, he spent the majority of his time alone. Bernie seemed to prefer this. As his sister Barbara later explained, he was a quiet kid. While he was close to their mother, more so than any of her other kids, she was also busy with her own artistic and philanthropic pursuits. Gertrude wrote poetry, did a great deal of charitable work at the Hospital Guild, and was involved with the local music society.[6]

Bernhard Goetz Sr. wasn't around that much, either. He spent upward of fourteen hours a day in his office, either back in Queens or in one of the outbuildings on Wynkoop Lane, but he nevertheless had great control over what happened in the house. One family member would later describe him not just as stern with his wife but also as a most rigid disciplinarian with his kids, a father who was "very demanding in terms of their behavior and their accomplishments."[7]

Despite being the youngest, Bernie was not exempt from his father's firm hand. If any of the children failed to meet Bernhard Sr.'s expectations, he would yell so loudly the entire household would be frightened. Writer Lillian Rubin's account of Bernie Goetz's early life described how his father would demand that the boy "put in writing what he called a 'memorandum of understanding'—a letter demonstrating that his expectations were understood and promising that there would be no recurrence of the infraction."[8]

One such memo, written by Bernie when he was eleven years old, read: "Dear Mr. Goetz, I am sorry I've been a bad boy. I will be good from now on. I won't yell, write on walls, and make a lot of noise. I will pay attention, I won't jump around, and I'll do what mother tells me. Your son, Bernhard Goetz."[9]

But his father's temperament didn't stop young Bernie from finding his own ways to rebel. In one instance, after being told to be quiet, "he climbed a tree and urinated on an ant below." When that got him in trouble, he defiantly said, "he had, after all, followed instructions. He had been quiet."[10]

This authoritarian upbringing did not bode well for Bernie's ability to socialize and make friends outside of the family. Even going to school offered little respite. He did well academically, winning an essay contest in elementary school and making the honor roll in later years.[11] But according to some of his teachers and former schoolmates, Bernie was often taunted to the point of tears. One classmate recalled that he was usually the last kid picked in gym class, and a neighbor remembered frequently seeing him come home from school crying. "I just felt very sorry for him; he was such a slight, puny little kid," they said.[12]

Meanwhile, though he was harsh with his own children, Mr. Goetz was showing a marked affection toward another young man. When Bernie was ten years old, his father took a business trip to Havana, where he hired seventeen-year-old Octavio Ramos as his tour guide and then, to his family's consternation, brought the boy home with him. Mr. Goetz said simply that he had very much enjoyed taking walks with Octavio as well as swimming with him on that trip, and he now insisted on moving the teen into young Bernie's room permanently—a sure sign of the newcomer's favored status.[13]

Within two years of Octavio's arrival in the Goetz home, the family experienced another unwelcome piece of news. In February 1960, Bernhard Sr. was arrested and charged with sexually molesting two fifteen-year-old boys.[14] He would ultimately be indicted on eighteen counts, which included child endangerment and third-degree assault.[15] Octavio Ramos, for his part, seemed unsurprised by this turn of events. According to him, this was a man who regularly "entertained teenage boys—sometimes at home, sometimes at the farm—and served them alcoholic drinks."[16] One of Goetz's employees also spoke up, having suspected for some time that something was amiss. Her boss always hired teenage boys to work weekends in his factory. In fact, according to her, it had long been "rumored in the community that he like[d] young boys."[17]

This was not the first time Mr. Goetz had come to the attention of the law for his interactions with minors. In 1958, he had been convicted of a misdemeanor after picking up a teenage hitchhiker who lived at a nearby camp for underprivileged kids, taking the boy to a factory on one of his farms, and giving him "a dozen or more shots of cognac."[18]

Hence, when the fifteen-year-olds accused Bernhard Sr. of fondling them and exposing himself at his factory, the local prosecutor believed them.[19] Goetz insisted, as he had with the prior accusations in 1958, that he was being extorted—the boys were trying to shake him down for money.[20] According to the arresting trooper, however, Mr. Goetz had in fact admitted that he'd "let his emotions get away with him and that he went too far with the boys."[21] He had also asked the trooper's advice "on what to tell and how to tell it."[22]

Mr. Goetz required that his children attend every day of his May 1960 trial as a show of support, and thus each child was inundated with "the unpleasant details of the accusations."[23]

Bernie would later describe the experience of his father's trial as "embarrassing," and stated that he "did not feel a great deal of warmth and affection towards his father."[24] Bernhard Sr. was found guilty of eight of the eighteen counts, and the Goetz family became fodder for their small-town rumor mill.

Perhaps in an attempt to shield twelve-year-old Bernie and his sister Denise from the fallout, Bernie's parents shipped them off to school at the Institut auf dem Rosenberg at St. Gallen in Switzerland with little notice or explanation.[25] This was most traumatic for Bernie. According to Rubin, "he clutched at [his mother's] departing figure. 'Mommy, mommy, please don't leave me,' he pleaded tearfully."[26]

Bernie would remain at this school for the next four years.[27]

In the meantime, Mr. Goetz appealed his conviction, getting four counts dismissed on technicalities. A new trial was ordered in 1962 and the DA accepted a plea bargain.[28] Ultimately, Mr. Goetz received a suspended sentence on one charge of disorderly conduct.

In 1964, when Bernie turned sixteen, he felt ready to leave Switzerland and to head to college in America. He had performed well at the Institut, which earned him a letter of recommendation from his counselor for Marist College. Bernie was admitted, and enrolled, but immediately felt in over his head. By November 1964, he had left Marist. According to the dean there, the reason for his departure was that he had "made an abortive attempt to obtain the results of a laboratory test from a faculty office in the chemistry department." According to Bernie, he had withdrawn voluntarily for "personal reasons."[29]

Bernie was adrift. That December, he decided to go back for one more year of high school at Christian Brothers School in Poughkeepsie, New York, hoping that he might become better prepared for college. After that, he headed off to New York University. He would graduate in 1970 from its campus in the Bronx with a major in nuclear engineering and a minor in electrical engineering.[30]

Now a 6-foot-1-inch man, Bernie was ready to enter the workforce. On November 4, 1969, even before earning his degree, Bernie was hired as a test engineer at a company that made nuclear submarines for the U.S. Navy. This was a plum job, and it was one that he might well have kept upon graduation.

Immediately, however, Bernie had begun having conflicts with his superiors. In his view, his bosses were subjecting him to "unacceptable conditions or procedures" that accelerated production at the expense of quality. Things soon grew so tense that he was, in one instance, forbidden from accompanying any naval personnel on an inspection tour. In September 1970, after less than a year on the job, Bernie was fired for "unacceptable performance."[31]

Being dismissed from his job was worrying, considering Bernie could now be drafted to fight in Vietnam. As an NYU student, he had enjoyed a deferment. His job at the submarine company was also considered an "essential" civilian job. But since he'd graduated and was no longer employed, Bernie was required to take the physical examination for the armed services.

Bernie decided, however, that he would do everything he could "to get out of Vietnam," and he would, in fact, beat the system. As he later said with satisfaction, "I'd beat it good."[32] He confessed to having researched "neurotic behavior that would disqualify him" and, after practicing on some psychologists that he met in a draft counseling program, he successfully "feign[ed] mental illness" in his meeting with the draft board.[33] He later boasted that he had shown up for his exam deliberately "unwashed, unshaven and behaving in a neurotic fashion."[34]

But dodging the draft did not help him escape all of life's challenges. After being fired, Bernie had few job prospects, no income, and nowhere to live. He moved in with his parents, now in Orlando, Florida, where they had bought a house in 1963 while he was in high school overseas.

The senior Goetz had over time become a major real estate developer there, eventually building 1,100 tract homes in a subdivision he called Park Manor. Each of these homes sold for between $70,000 and $90,000 (the equivalent of nearly $1 million in 2025), and Bernie Goetz's father was soon very wealthy. He and Gertrude lived in Park Manor themselves, in a "four bedroom, one story structure of stone and brick" that looked out on a lake, had a sparkling blue pool, and sat at the end of a neat cul-de-sac.[35]

Bernie not only lived with his parents; he also worked alongside his father, one of his sisters, and his brother-in-law at the Park Manor Development Company. As with his last job, however, conflicts soon arose. Bernie felt that he cared about the quality of the work more than anyone else did, and worse, as the company engineer, he felt that he was being asked to sign off on shoddy construction.[36]

Perhaps seeking a bit more independence from his family, Bernie married a local woman named Elizabeth Boylan in 1971. Their union would be short-lived, however, ending in divorce in 1975. In later interviews, Elizabeth indicated that the couple harbored no lasting feelings of ill will toward one another—they simply felt it was time to go their separate ways. They did not have children.[37]

Now single, and too often at odds with his father to continue working with him, Bernie Goetz returned to NYC. He rented a small apartment at 211 Thompson Street in Greenwich Village and decided to go into business for himself, starting a company called Electrical Calibration Laboratory, Inc. In this new venture, Bernie would test, repair, and maintain electrical equipment for manufacturing companies locally and across the country. He would never have to answer to another boss.[38]

Though business was never booming, Bernie's income was steady. In April 1977, he moved into an apartment in a twenty-one-story white-brick building at 55 West 14th Street.[39] Irritated by the street noise as well as the "physical graffiti" of the breakdancers beneath his windows, however, Bernie then relocated to a slightly larger apartment in the rear of the building.[40] For $650 a month, he had the place all to himself.[41]

3

Creating Crisis

DARRELL CABEY LOVED his family, but their apartment was so cramped that whenever he could, he headed outdoors. He and Lydell would roller skate and play sports, and though Lydell liked to tease his five-foot-four friend about how terrible he was at shooting hoops, Darrell would just laugh and promise to kick his butt in paddleball, which he preferred anyway. And even Lydell had to admit that Darrell was the far better breakdancer, which was way more impressive than being good at any game.[1]

Breakdancing was, in fact, all the rage in the early 1980s, spreading from its Bronx roots to the rest of the nation thanks to MTV, the cable channel that started broadcasting music videos in 1981, as well as movies like *Breakin'* and *Krush Groove*.[2] According to Lydell, Darrell had amazing agility and control of his body, and had mastered breakdancing long "before it hit Manhattan."[3] When the boys had to be indoors they'd often visit a local arcade, maybe to play Donkey Kong, or would check out a kung fu movie at the nearby dollar theater.

Even with these distractions, however, life was difficult for kids in the South Bronx.

Some of the hardships they faced stemmed, without question, from the brutal economic downturn the nation had just experienced. And yet, history showed that in the normal course of things, the terrible cuts that the fiscal crisis had prompted and the despair it wrought would, in time, end. Once inflation had been reined in, and new global political realities had settled in, the international and domestic economies alike would

A breakdancer spins on a cardboard surface during a dance battle in the Playground 52 public park in the Bronx, summer 1983. Photo by Ricky Flores

recover. New York City could again be solvent. Eventually, it could rehire its unemployed workers and resume providing services to its most needy residents.

But that was not to be. In 1980, America's voters elected a very different president than had been at the helm in nearly fifty years. When Ronald Reagan entered the Oval Office in January 1981, he did so with the explicit goal of upending the way that the government had approached economic growth and social spending since the New Deal.

Ever since Franklin Delano Roosevelt's presidency, ordinary Americans—both die-hard Democrats and those who favored the party of Eisenhower, or later even of Nixon—believed that the government had a duty to protect its citizens from the capriciousness of the market and to assist those who were unable to provide for themselves, whether that be due to their age, their disability, or job scarcity. To be sure, the New Deal had gone nowhere near as far as some other democracies around the world had to rein in capitalism or even to provide for their citizenry. Indeed, the New Deal Democrats very much hoped to save capitalism, not to overhaul it. Nevertheless, this was a fundamental moment of placing the excesses of the rich in check, and it had come thanks to pressure from below.

The notion that a healthy nation required the presence of a social and economic safety net had led to programs such as Social Security, Federal

Housing Authority loans, the GI Bill, and Aid to Families with Dependent Children (AFDC)—all of which had contributed to building strong, albeit overwhelmingly white, working and middle classes in America. Such programs were in fact riddled with discriminatory provisions, but for white Americans there were now myriad new opportunities for social mobility, such as job training programs, the ability to attend college, and more. Such social spending had also helped to provide basic health care and affordable public housing for the elderly as well as the destitute.

In the post–World War II years, and again thanks to the New Deal, white Americans had also become homeowners, secured good union jobs with health and safety protections, and come to rely on the fact that Social Security would allow them to retire.[4]

As the twentieth century wore on, however, these same citizens who had benefited the most from New Deal policies had also begun to forget the role that federal support had played in helping them achieve social mobility and economic security alike. What is more, they never appreciated the extent to which these New Deal–era opportunities—everything from the right to join a union and the ability to get subsidized housing to being able to count on Social Security in their old age—had been difficult if not outright impossible for countless Black and Brown Americans to access.

This lack of equal opportunity was, however, glaringly obvious to those who had been shut out. During the tumultuous 1960s and '70s, civil rights leaders like Martin Luther King Jr., Malcolm X, Fannie Lou Hamer, Cesar Chavez, and Dolores Huerta, as well as countless ordinary people, began taking to the streets to call attention to the absence of equality in America and the damage it had done to so many communities.

Their activism would matter. With the Civil Rights Act of 1964, for example, it became illegal to deny people admission to school, a ride on a bus, or seniority rights on a job based on their race. With the Voting Rights Act of 1965, the franchise was now also shared. And with the Fair Housing Act of 1968, it became illegal to deny someone a home on racial grounds.

These civil rights gains, however, increasingly rankled working- and middle-class white Americans who failed to appreciate their historic and continuing privilege. When legislation meant to rein in racial discrimination was further accompanied by Lyndon Johnson's so-called Great

Society programs, as well as the expansion of programs such as Medicaid and AFDC, it was for many of them a bridge too far.

Indeed, to an increasing number of white Americans, the idea that the Democratic Party would continue to earmark spending on poverty programs—dollars that would go to Americans who did not just seem incapable of escaping poverty but who were also disproportionately (although by no means exclusively) Black and Brown—was outrageous. Those who had not "made it" in America, they suspected, were stuck due to their own limitations as opposed to the persistent effects of racial and gender discrimination. Liberal social welfare programs, they began to argue, had become mere handouts rather than a needed hand up.

Such antagonism toward efforts to effect true equality in America was hardly new. White citizens had violently fought everything from the abolition of slavery to the desegregation of the military, schools, and neighborhoods. Since the earliest centuries in this country they had also utilized threats and violence to keep workplaces all-white too. Even so, between 1932 and 1979, and until their party decided to support civil rights initiatives and fund poverty programs such as Head Start or Upward Bound or legal aid for the poor, countless middle- and working-class white Americans, even the most racially discriminatory among them, had remained staunch Democrats.

That their taxes would now pay for policies and projects intended to level a glaringly uneven playing field—one on which whites alone had always enjoyed the substantial advantage—would leave them looking for a new party.

The problem for the Republican Party, which sought to court these voters, was that the interests of its various constituents were not fully aligned. Wealthy Republicans had always cared most about the fiscal policies of the New Deal—particularly the high taxes that the richest among them were expected to pay toward the broader needs of the nation. But no matter how much disgruntled, particularly working-class white Democrats chafed at racial liberalism, they largely still believed that the well-to-do should be taxed more than middle- and working-class people. They still recoiled from the idea that the rich should run America as they had back during the Gilded Age.

This was, however, a circle that the Republican Party was determined to square. Indeed, party leaders well understood that harnessing the power of white racial hostilities could help them restore the greatest economic privileges to the nation's wealthiest class. It would just take some time.

In 1968, for example, Nixon had successfully convinced a significant number of previously Democratic voters that the Republicans better understood their racial concerns. But while Nixon had not been able to move the needle when it came to reducing taxes for the rich, Reagan managed to appeal to white self-interest and to exploit racial rage to greater success, convincing even some of the most die-hard Democratic Party voters that this was in their interest, also.

Reagan argued that excessive government spending on welfare explained *why* minorities still lagged behind. And taxes should, therefore, be cut for everyone, rather than earmarked for "entitlement" programs. This message resonated with a new breed of voter—the so-called Reagan Democrats—and would ensure the Republican Party's landslide victory in 1980.

Once in office, Reagan knew that his party still had work to do when it came to convincing his newest voters that *all* liberal policies were an utter failure, and thus a robust tax base was no longer required to fund them. One internal memo made this especially clear. It would be a good idea, administration insider Jim Cicconi wrote to top Reagan aides, for the president to continue "questioning the social policies of the past twenty years" whenever he gave a speech, and to continue insisting publicly, albeit in a "low key manner," that " 'a national debate is now occurring' on the social policy of the past twenty years, with hints that a change is needed." Meanwhile, the memo went on, "decreasing government resources" would make "the liberal approach impossible to sustain financially, and dictate that alternatives be tried."[5]

This strategy would pay off stunningly well. The Reagan Revolution would begin reversing decades of Keynesian economic policy and practice. It would dramatically cut taxes for the wealthy by arguing not only that they were unnecessary—the government was too bloated—but also that such cuts would allow business owners to create jobs and improve the economic standing of the nation overall. This "trickle-down" economic thinking would have devastating consequences.[6]

DARRELL CABEY'S FAMILY might not have clocked exactly how Reagan's economic policies represented "a sharp break with the recent past."

In fact, few Americans, even those who voted for Reagan, fully grasped how many federal dollars previously available for food assistance, job training, and health care for seniors and those in poverty would in fact be slashed during his first and second terms. But families like Darrell's would feel these cuts most directly and profoundly. According to urban geographers Sheldon Danziger and Robert Haveman, the Americans hit the very hardest by these cuts were in the lowest mean income group—households headed by women with children. Indeed, as one study made clear, an average mother who worked but, like so many women in the Daniel Webster Homes, made so little that she still needed AFDC, eventually would suffer "a 20% to 30% decline in her monthly income."[7]

Both *El Diario La Prensa* and the *Amsterdam News*, New York City's main Spanish-language and Black newspapers, chronicled these worsening problems along with the community's resistance to them. While it published articles with frank headlines like "CUTS DRIVING POOR TO BREADLINES" (1982) and "HOUSING SHORTAGE 'ACUTE'" (1983), the *Amsterdam News*, for instance, also covered community beautification projects, antidrug campaigns, and other efforts by ordinary people to combat the fallout of evaporating city and federal dollars.[8]

Apart from activism and self-help, voters in the South Bronx also hoped that aid would come from Black politicians such as Jesse Jackson, who was trying to respond to the Reagan agenda with a national campaign, or from the many Puerto Rican and Black New Yorkers who had secured political positions in the wake of the civil rights movement.[9] Such hopes, however, would not be fulfilled. As scholar Keeanga-Yamahtta Taylor put it bluntly, the "lives and deaths" of poor and working-class Black families were really "not a priority for the Black political elite."[10] While the Black middle class overwhelmingly disliked Reagan and clung fervently to the promises of the Democratic Party, too often they, like their white Democratic Party counterparts, blamed the ostensible cultural and moral failings of what was newly being called the "Black Underclass" for the city's many problems.[11]

On the ground, though, this wasn't about personal failings. And places like the South Bronx could not simply be dismissed as mere sites of economic devastation. As hard as things were, the South Bronx remained vibrant in other very important ways. In the park, kids frolicked and teenagers socialized. Old men played games of chess. This was a neighborhood. It had block clubs and community centers, and parents as well as grandparents attended local school functions, hosted wedding and baby showers, and regularly went to church.

The South Bronx was also a place that attracted young musicians from around the country. It was the literal epicenter of beatboxing, the skillful vocal percussions that had also burst on the scene so excitingly in the 1980s. Indeed, to be a teen in the South Bronx meant dreaming of sneaking into one of the neighborhood's many "house parties," where they might catch hip-hop legends DJ Kool Herc or DJ Charlie Chase performing on two turntables plugged into the living room wall. Maybe they'd even see the Bronx phenom Grandmaster Flash one night at a local club.[12]

Of course, the proliferation of house parties and clubs also made many mothers and fathers nervous. The stakes were always high when raising kids, but the usual social distractions of youth seemed especially risky in a place with so few resources. Like all moms and dads, the parents of the South Bronx didn't want their kids to get derailed. They wanted them to grow up to be somebody, to go to college, to get a good job.

Despite the larger forces working against them, countless kids in the South Bronx did just that. The local Black press shouted out some of the most unusual and inspiring stories of triumph, like the kid who managed to make a name for himself as a tennis player despite his dad having been murdered, or the girls whose educational achievements and promise had netted each of them an $8,000 scholarship to a prominent boarding school in Pennsylvania.[13]

TRUTH BE TOLD, Shirley Cabey hoped that her kids would also be able to leave the South Bronx one day. She worried especially about what otherwise might happen to her son Darrell, her shyer and quieter boy, should his horizons not expand. She found herself praying that he might just board "one of the commuter trains that zipped past their apartment every day" and head well outside of this city to make a better life for himself.[14]

Shirley's concern for Darrell had begun to intensify when, at about eight years old, he began struggling in school. It became increasingly clear to Shirley that Darrell had a much harder time with his assignments than other kids did. Eventually, Darrell would be put in a special education program. Shirley hoped this would be a positive change, but she was well aware that it also might sour him on school and make him a target for the savvier boys who lived a faster and more dangerous life in the streets.[15]

For a few years, Darrell's mother didn't have to dwell on these concerns. Her baby-faced son still liked to stay pretty close to home. In fact, she found it sweet when he got involved with a nice girl named Denise and around the same time started to enjoy "dressing, looking good, all that."[16] She took solace as well in the fact that Darrell was a responsible kid who had managed to land a part-time job as a grocery bagger in Harlem. This made it possible for him to help out the family and take Denise on dates every once in a while.[17]

Unfortunately, neither the relationship nor the job lasted very long. The grocery store Darrell worked at, like so many small businesses, was struggling to make ends meet. Paying a teenager so that the checkout process could be more pleasant for its remaining customers was simply a luxury the store could no longer afford, and he lost his job.

With no girlfriend and no money of his own, Darrell seemed to lose his motivation. In the spring of 1984, he decided to drop out of high school.[18] Getting his diploma had seemed ever more pointless the older Darrell got. At seventeen, he should have been graduating, but dwindling school resources and his years in special education classes had set him behind and left him disillusioned.

Reagan-era cuts were leading to dramatic layoffs of school personnel across New York City, including counselors, school nurses, secretaries, crossing guards, and even teachers. This had a particularly deleterious effect on students in neighborhoods like the South Bronx: It meant that there were far fewer support staff equipped to care for their emotional needs, let alone enough instructors to keep them engaged during school hours.[19] Positions for art and music teachers were getting slashed, while after-school programs were also being canceled. Meanwhile, the Parks Department was eliminating its sports teams, and local public libraries were shuttering or operating on a severely reduced schedule.[20]

It was in this grim context that Darrell's friend Lydell also dropped out of school. As Lydell explained, he and Darrell had some notion that they instead might "get a [full-time] job."[21] This hope was, however, naïve. Reaganomics had made it hard even for those with high school diplomas to be employed. Its cuts had hit the public job sector with a particular vengeance and these had been exactly the positions that had provided one of the few paths to stability and self-sufficiency in the South Bronx.

The Nixon administration's Comprehensive Employment and Training Act (CETA), enacted in 1973, for example, had provided public job-training programs and summer employment for low-income teens, jobs that could become more permanent and that at least provided benefits such as health care and pensions.[22] Unfortunately, however, in 1984, Reagan closed down the CETA program altogether and public sector jobs more generally dried up. It was bad enough that almost one-third of Black residents and half of the Latino residents of the South Bronx lost employment during the fiscal crisis of the previous decade. But in the 1980s, these jobs began to disappear altogether, affecting the entire city.[23] Whereas there were 264,000 unemployed New Yorkers in January 1970, by January 1983 there were a full 753,000—a threefold increase.[24]

While the Reagan White House was doing its part to push the narrative of a seemingly intractable "underclass" that was simply refusing to reach for the brass ring of work and personal advancement, the reality was that this president's policies were making it much more difficult for anyone to secure paid, steady, and legal employment.[25]

With fewer opportunities remaining, many felt their only option was to turn to the illegal economy. Lack of job prospects, declining schools, and fewer public places to find enrichment or support meant that young people in the South Bronx had little to do but, as one observer put it, "sit in apartments, or hang out in the street, where they were likely to be tempted by drugs and easy money."[26]

Darrell Cabey still hung out with Lydell in his tiny room, but as he had gotten older, he had also started spending more time several blocks away, in one of the tougher parts of their vast, thirty-building high-rise complex.[27] Over there, near Washington and Third Avenues, a group of young guys gathered regularly. They were brash, cool, and they were always involved in some kind of potentially lucrative hustle, which likely contributed to their allure.[28]

At first, Darrell invited Lydell to join him as he ventured out farther into the neighborhood, but to his disappointment, Lydell remained leery.[29] Darrell had begun experimenting with drugs—mostly pot but, from time to time, coke or angel dust, when it was offered. Lydell didn't like that at all. Still, he didn't give Darrell too much trouble about it, just calling his friend "space face" and hoping that things would soon return to normal.[30]

The good news was that Darrell was only "partying" on occasion. As important, he still had an employed parent, which made it a whole lot easier to resist the pull of the drug economy. Other teens were not so lucky. If their mom or dad did not have stable jobs, or any at all, it was hard to ignore the fact that kids could earn more money by dealing drugs than by working any odd job they might be lucky enough to land. By the mid-1980s, selling coke, and its cheaper derivative crack, was in fact one of the only remaining ways for countless New Yorkers to make money.[31]

The crack trade, however, would have terrible consequences, particularly for neighborhoods in the Bronx. As one local resident said, "The block was nice for a while. . . . Then all of a sudden, the Bronx started to change. . . . People selling drugs on corners. Certain people owned the corners. There were lines of people waiting to buy drugs. They would stand there with ten garbage cans with fires to keep warm. The Bronx was the first to know crack. We were the people to tell others crack was happening in our community and affecting the quality of our lives, our young people. It blew up."[32]

Anyone could see the toll of addiction on this part of the city, which was why Lydell worried about Darrell.[33] One South Bronx priest described it as an "overwhelming flood of really cheap, really potent drugs. . . . And you know, the person who would take it was not really in charge of themselves, because it was the drug taking over them. So, it was an incredibly emotionally devastating period."[34] And it was a problem that soon seemed intractable. Over the next forty years, the South Bronx would come to have "the second-highest rate of drug overdose deaths—34 per 100,000 people—in the country, after West Virginia."[35]

The Bronx was also being ravaged by a new sickness, one that caused many who were addicted to develop horrible lesions and to waste away, growing sicker by the month until they died. In time, it was understood that what was felling so many in this borough and other neighborhoods in New York City—not just IV drug users but many thousands of others, including, disproportionately, gay men with or without any history of drug use—was the human immunodeficiency virus (HIV), which caused a constellation of symptoms referred to as acquired immune deficiency syndrome (AIDS).

Identifying this deadly virus, however, did not mean that federal or state dollars would be put toward mitigating the epidemic it was fast touching off. Community residents in the Bronx were left to cope with the spread of AIDS on their own, periodically protesting and demanding help from city officials, but mostly just doing their best to care for their afflicted loved ones.[36]

The connections between the gutting of social services during the Reagan years, the rise in drug addiction, and the spread of AIDS were direct and profound. It mattered that critical prevention and intervention services, along with health care resources, had become increasingly difficult, if not impossible, to access.[37]

After 1980, parents in the South Bronx were not only struggling to cope with ever-increasing rates of family and child drug addiction as well as the risk of death from AIDS. The social fabric of their community was also being frayed by rising drug-related violence.[38] Here too the link between cuts and chaos was clear. An illegal economy was a dangerous economy, leaving all who were connected to it perpetually vulnerable and desperate.

Gangs, including the Turbans, their rivals the Royal Javelins, and the Savage Nomads, were attracting ever more members who sought both employment and protection on their clearly defined turfs. Within a gang's borders, its piece of the drug trade could be controlled and members could provide for their own families in these dire times.[39] But conflicts always arose. Danger always loomed.

Ronald Reagan would use the violence of the drug trade and the scourge of drug addiction to amplify his broader policy message that individuals, not the government, needed to step up and take responsibility for themselves. In a 1986 address, Reagan declared crack to be "an explosively destructive and often lethal substance, which is crushing its users. It is an uncontrolled fire."[40] He failed to acknowledge, however, that this new crisis was but the result of a desperate and ultimately devastating response to supply-side economics. Instead, his White House would insist on a big-budget PR campaign that simplified the issue: "Just say no" to drugs.[41] Those who failed to do so, the president made clear, would be locked up.

Reagan would eventually enact one of the harshest sets of drug laws in U.S. history, one that would result in unprecedented prison sentences for drug use and sales.[42] The number of people serving sentences of twenty, thirty, forty, and fifty years skyrocketed, as did the percentage of life sentences.[43] Over the eight years of Reagan's presidency, the American prison population nearly doubled, from 329,000 to 627,000.[44] And because the Reagan drug war was enforced much more aggressively among Black and Brown New Yorkers than white, the racial disparity of exactly who was landing in America's prisons was staggering.[45]

Notably, however, far more white New Yorkers, particularly those with money, were buying these drugs and thus were the ones making the trade so lucrative.[46] By 1988, Black people comprised 94 percent of crack-related arrests in Manhattan, even though, according to city health surveys, only 38 percent of users were estimated to be Black. Meanwhile, virtually no arrests were made in wealthier, predominantly white neighborhoods such as the Upper East Side, where cocaine and crack use were also widespread.[47]

Indeed, under Democratic governor Mario Cuomo, New York State had willingly embraced the Reagan administration's War on Drugs and passed its own draconian laws. In November 1988, it became a felony in New York to possess 500 milligrams or more of crack (about five to six vials), a significant decrease from the thirty or more vials previously required to trigger such a serious charge. As important, Reagan's 1986 Anti-Drug Abuse Act set aside only 14 percent of its funding for treatment and prevention.[48] With few resources available to help the addicted get clean, the South Bronx's five police precincts got busier and busier. One of these, the 44th, "went from a 'sleeper' house to one of the most active precincts in the city."[49]

Mothers like Shirley Cabey worried mightily about this new reality. Shirley had begun seeing the police in her neighborhood far more frequently, and suddenly, even her mild-mannered son was in their crosshairs. On two occasions the cops actually took the time to issue Darrell a summons to appear in court for "blocking pedestrian traffic" in a building stairwell.[50] On another occasion, a group of teens, including Darrell, were confronted by armed police in the community center of one of the buildings in the Claremont Village housing projects. The police accused all of them of having committed an earlier theft there, though they never made clear what exactly had been stolen, nor what these youths had to do with the event.

More cops in the South Bronx meant kids like Darrell were being hassled more often in no small part because the cops were literally being incentivized to make "good" arrests—that is, ones that could actually lead to conviction.[51] Because such "good arrests" were not always easy to make, a new departmental premium was placed on bringing in suspected drug dealers.[52]

As two officers from the 44th Precinct explained it to a cop who had recently transferred in, "You're not going to believe this. They're giving us a day off for bullshit narcotics arrests. . . . As a matter of fact, they'll give you four hours off if you bring in an asshole with a hypo!" The new officer apparently "jumped on the gravy train," and accumulated as many days as possible for his "time bank," readily admitting that earning a day off did give him the incentive to nab as many people as possible.[53]

This wasn't to say that residents didn't see a need for public safety. For anyone living in the South Bronx, the violence that came with the illegal drug trade seemed only to be escalating. It felt increasingly unsafe to make even a quick trip to the store or to leave a car or an apartment building unlocked, considering that addicted people were mugging residents or robbing homes for paltry sums of money, and rival gangs used violence to secure their territory. Even Darrell Cabey had been mugged, on one occasion thrown to the ground and robbed while he was high. He suffered a major cut on his head, which alarmed his friend Lydell.[54] Indeed, the rising violence was frightening for everyone.[55]

Capitalizing on this heightened fear, media coverage of crime skyrocketed during the 1980s. As one *New York Post* headline blared as early as 1982, "CRIME IN OUR TOWN: IT'S NEVER BEEN SO BAD."[56] But outlets covering the experiences of the people who suffered this violence most acutely, or asking what they really needed to address it, were hard to come by. Worse, crime reporters too often assumed that those who were at the greatest risk of becoming crime victims were in fact deadly perpetrators.[57]

Rare was the media piece willing to examine the connections between this mounting crime "problem" and the dramatically diminishing social services, let alone how the local community was itself trying to navigate it—not necessarily by calling for even more arrests but rather by setting up mentorship opportunities, gang intervention programs, anti-addiction groups, and more. Instead, the media helped to perpetuate the notion that crime was getting much worse because of a new kind of criminal teen, one who ran in what NYC mayor Ed Koch would call a "Wolf Pack." These new predators' idea of recreation, reporters suggested, was going on violent rampages that they soon dubbed "wilding."[58]

"This wasn't mischief as that word was once used," wrote *New York Post* columnist Pete Hamill.[59] These were animalistic teens who were coming "from a world of crack, welfare, guns, knives, indifference and ignorance. They were coming from a land with no fathers," and they were "driven by a collective fury, brimming with the rippling energies of youth," with "only one goal: to smash, hurt, rob, stomp, rape. The enemies were rich. The enemies were white."[60]

Such views would dramatically shape the way the police treated residents of the South Bronx. As a cop working in the 44th Precinct admitted, the police referred to one particular public housing building as the "jungle habitat," and any kid who lived there was assessed accordingly.[61] In the mid-1980s, when new funding was put toward the creation and then expansion of the Organized Crime Control Bureau's Narcotics Division, officers from the 44th were specifically tasked with looking for "marauding gangs" in the South Bronx. These "gangs," of course, were any group of youths who could be dealing, but could as often be doing little more than listening to music and hoping to meet girls.[62]

For Shirley Cabey and her friends, it was terrifying to think that authorities now just assumed that their kids were joining gangs and committing crimes. There were plenty of stories about kids Darrell's age getting roughed up, even shot and killed, by police officers, and if their families dared to complain, they got nowhere. When police brass asked one South Bronx officer "to do some research on the recent history of police shootings," in advance of a congressional hearing on the subject in 1983, even he was taken aback by what he found. As he put it, "When I looked at the numbers, they were startling."[63]

To Shirley Cabey's undoubted relief, Darrell did not experience any police abuse that she knew of, but he clearly was on the cops' radar. They again accused him of a crime that took place in the Webster Homes—this time an armed holdup, which was a felony that could land him in prison.[64] Even though Darrell had neither a gun nor any stolen property on him or in his apartment, he was arrested.

When she learned of this incident, Shirley was both scared and angry. She confronted Darrell. Was he in any way responsible for this mess? Darrell dissolved into tears as he begged her to believe that he had nothing to do with guns or stealing, period.

Seeing Darrell's fear, and knowing her son, Shirley believed him. But that didn't make her feel much better. Everyone who knew Darrell Cabey had long marveled at his helpful, affectionate, and optimistic nature.[65] But it was hard for boys like Darrell to remain happy or hopeful once they became resigned to a future in which they were always assumed to be thugs. That broke Shirley's heart.

4

Fueling Fear and Fury

BERNIE GOETZ'S NINTH-FLOOR APARTMENT in Greenwich Village boasted three fairly sizable, if slightly shabby, rooms. It was not just his refuge but also his place of business. As such, it less resembled a home than a slightly quirky storage space cluttered with papers, cords, wires, pieces of plastic, and metal objects both large and small. In the living room, a blizzard of invoices, bills, and random notes, and an oscilloscope useful for repairing electrical devices, covered a battered desk. Its drawers overflowed with old phone books and office supplies, and his coffee table was occupied by an energy capacitor—made in 1888 and still in working order.[1]

Bernie enjoyed running his own company from the privacy of his home. Unlike the yuppies who battled the crowded subways every day, trying to get rich on Wall Street, or the squeegee men who camped out at the intersections by the Lincoln Tunnel, trying to make a few bucks, Bernie could do his own thing. He could browse the hundreds of electronics books he'd acquired, or tinker with one of the many electrical contraptions whose exact function would have escaped most people.[2]

Working at home and having his electronics workshop right there was downright convenient. He could, for example, use his oven to bake-dry a piece of equipment he was working on for a client.[3] Even the bathroom had been retrofitted to accommodate his gadgets. A single towel hung limply by the sink, the only sign that Bernie used the room for its intended purpose.[4] For Bernie, this apartment was a refuge from the chaos just outside its windows, which he had covered in stained glass to enhance the home's sanctuary-like feel. The minute he stepped outside, however, any sense of peace evaporated.[5]

Located on 14th Street between Fifth and Sixth Avenues, the 238-unit building in which Bernie lived was one of two high-rises in a fairly commercial area surrounded by clothing stores, furniture outlets, and cut-rate shops. The structure looked stately enough from the outside, complete with a canopy jutting out over the sidewalk, a doorman, and a concierge. But the neighborhood around it, often described previously as a quaint enclave filled with trees, coffee shops, and iconic jazz clubs, had come to seem much seedier.[6] You might still get a good meal at Lush Life over on Thompson and Bleecker Streets, or hear some live music at The Back Fence. But for Greenwich Village residents like Bernie, leaving home now meant encountering too many who were unhoused or addicted.

For many, if not most, New Yorkers, the exact origins of the desperation they saw each day were obscure. Few understood that more than $1.5 billion had already been stripped from city coffers—"cuts in services, and tens of thousands of layoffs of city employees."[7] What was indisputable, however, was that when Greenwich Villagers looked out of their apartment windows, they now saw people shambling past with their feet wrapped in garbage bags to stay dry and their bodies shrouded in filthy clothes. Every time they left the safety of their dwellings, they could not avoid the drug dealers on corners and users in doorways, nor the smell of the rotting garbage that overflowed from city bins or had just been dumped on the street.

Piles of garbage in New York City, December 1981. Barbara Alper/ Getty Images

Thanks to cuts to the Department of Sanitation, trash and litter had become ubiquitous in neighborhoods all over the city, no matter the price of real estate. Blight had also increased as the city's Department of Parks & Recreation was forced to slash its budget. By March 1981, the Parks Department's workforce had dwindled to approximately 2,900 employees, a stark contrast to the 30,000 staff members it boasted during famous urban planner Robert Moses's tenure as parks commissioner. And as parks fell into disrepair, those who used to enjoy them were soon finding them more frightening than serene.[8]

Bernie Goetz was frustrated that city officials didn't seem to care about any of this. Even Mayor Ed Koch, who had previously insisted that he would stay in his one-bedroom unit near Washington Square Park after taking the oath of office, had decided to move uptown to the official mayor's residence, Gracie Mansion, after all.[9] In Bernie's view, men like the mayor had done far too little to, for example, clean up the graffiti that covered nearly every building and billboard in town. And it was as if city officials were just willfully ignoring the people having psychotic episodes, shooting up, and selling sex right in front of his complex.

Of course, the Reagan Revolution's promise that it would remedy all of this—that, as one historian put it, the government could "simultaneously cut taxes, sustain services and reduce the deficit"—had been improbable from the start.[10] Addressing the fallout from the recession of the 1970s by slashing taxes would only make this serious but short-term crisis permanent fiscal policy. The true costs of Reagan's 1981 Economic Recovery Tax Act, his 1982 and 1983 budget reforms, and his Tax Reform Act of 1986 would fall largely to ordinary people, whether they experienced those costs directly, as did Darrell Cabey, or they mostly had to witness the ugly consequences, as did Bernie Goetz.[11]

Notably, just as tenant groups and community organizations came together to deal with the consequences of the Reagan eighties in the South Bronx, where Darrell Cabey lived, so too did various "blight busting" and "neighborhood cleanup" initiatives, as well as "crime watch" groups in Bernie Goetz's neighborhood.

One of these was Villagers Against Crime, Inc. (VAC), which actively patrolled an area between the Hudson River and Washington Street, and from Christopher Street to West 14th. The VAC's particular concern was ridding Greenwich Village of what it said was the new problem of "transvestite prostitution." Working closely with the Sixth Precinct, this organization hoped to remove the new "sleazy" elements of the neighborhood, so that it could remain nice for "the many new families with young children" who lived there.[12]

Like the cops whose policing of the area they sought to augment, and the Reagan administration whose drug war had helped to fund those same cops, VAC exhibited little interest in the reasons why prostitution, drug use and addiction, and crime more generally were on the rise in Greenwich Village. It too had decided that this was largely a matter of morality.

Framing social ills in moral terms had serious costs for NYC, particularly for those suffering the ever-deepening crisis of AIDS. It mattered that just as this epidemic was becoming most acute—with Greenwich Village's main hospital, St. Vincent's, soon housing not only the first but also the largest AIDS ward on the East Coast—New Yorkers were also being bombarded with nostalgia for a mythical past rooted in so-called family values, which, Reagan argued, liberals had eroded, to everyone's detriment. The AIDS epidemic, his administration implied, was, like rising rates of poverty, rooted in poor personal choices. The gay community was also to blame for Gotham becoming Gomorrah.

There was much resistance to this view, as well as to Reagan's refusal to devote resources to the AIDS epidemic so that it might be addressed as the medical crisis that it was. Just as residents of the South Bronx had called for more governmental action and resources, so did countless residents of Greenwich Village also begin to organize and take to the streets to demand attention to this public health emergency.

Absent federal support, ordinary people mobilized with Herculean energy on the ground to provide care to the people who so desperately needed it, for example, establishing the Lesbian and Gay Community Services Center (now the Lesbian, Gay, Bisexual & Transgender Community Center), known to locals as simply "The Center," next to St. Vincent's Hospital.[13] Here, many of the first AIDS advocacy and support groups, such as ACT UP, came together to combat this deadly virus.[14]

By the mid-1980s, however, too many New Yorkers had been actively encouraged to fear both desperation and difference. They had been romanced by the notion that tighter moral control via criminalization might return their city to its ostensibly more wholesome yesteryear. The now-everyday sight of someone ravaged by disease, or experiencing a mental health crisis, or high on drugs, or simply unhoused, which before

A group advocating AIDS research marches down Fifth Avenue during the 14th annual Lesbian and Gay Pride parade in New York, June 26, 1983.
AP Photo/Mario Suriani

might have engendered empathy, now too often elicited anxiety and anger.

This was exactly how Bernie Goetz was experiencing the New York City that he now called home. Bernie's downstairs neighbor, Myra Friedman, recalled that he was "obsessed" with the drug dealers, the "tawdry, bargain stores," and even the pedantic city ordinances that were too often disregarded, like one that mandated the "cleaning of all buildings every twenty years." As Myra explained, she didn't seek out Bernie to discuss such matters, but rather, "I would be returning with a takeout lunch, starving, and he would whip out a document about street peddlers."[15]

Bernie was soon, in fact, on a personal crusade "to clean up the street, pestering city agencies to do something about the litter, the junkies and the homeless."[16] He would regularly write and deliver petitions regarding "what he called inadequate police protection, growing drug abuse and illegal peddlers on the block," and often would register his views about seemingly trivial and temporary problems such as sidewalk obstructions with city officials.[17] So frequently did he file official complaints with the police that he became a familiar face at his local precinct.

Finding limited success through the city channels, Bernie joined his building's own self-improvement group, the Courtney House Tenants Association.[18] He even served as treasurer for a brief period, though working with other people remained difficult for him and tensions often flared between him and other members in the organization. During a September 1980 meeting, after listening to various ideas on how the group might impress upon city officials the seriousness of the excessive trash, houselessness, and drug deals they were seeing, Bernie erupted: "Let's face it; the problem with 14th Street is the Sp—s and N—s and until we deal with that problem we can't deal with any others."[19]

This outburst was followed by stunned silence. His neighbors stared at him in disbelief, and Myra Friedman actually left the room in disgust. Eric Turner, the committee's cochair, was so appalled that he wrote Bernie a personal letter the very next day stating that the committee would not tolerate "the racial slurs and derogatory comments," and that he would be asked to leave the group if he used such language again. "There is no excuse or reason for vigilantism," Turner presciently warned; "it is unlawful and diametrically opposed to the purpose of our organization."[20]

One week later, when someone set fire to an abandoned newsstand on 14th Street—a structure that had seemed to particularly bother Bernie Goetz—Turner was not hesitant to say he was quite certain Goetz was responsible. Turner had seen him near the heap of charred wood and ashes, and was unnerved to hear Bernie say quietly, "I know how to get things done."[21] The New York City Fire Department had been called and arrived fairly promptly, something one could not always count on in this new age of austerity. The battalion fire chief was certain this was a case of arson, but when fire marshals arrived the next day to investigate, mysteriously "they found that the remains of the newsstand had been swept away."[22] If nothing else, Bernie had seemed very pleased with how things had turned out.

In 1981, Bernie Goetz had an experience far more unnerving than coming upon unsightly garbage or an addicted person nodded out on a bench in one of his favorite neighborhood parks. On January 26, he went out to run some errands for his business.[23] As he exited the subway station at Canal Street, carrying a box of items he had just purchased for his shop, he was accosted by three young people.[24]

Bernie fled toward a store he knew on Canal Street called Trans-Am Electronics. He reached the door but found himself pushed up against the plate glass window by one of his pursuers. Sal Alessi, working inside the shop that day, heard Bernie slam into the glass and jumped up to assist him. Alessi could see that he was out of breath and scared.[25] "They took the items I was carrying," Bernie later explained. "I ran out of the subway station up the steps. They came after me." As two of the would-be assailants dropped their stolen goods and fled, a nearby off-duty sanitation officer named Charles Cozza managed to grab the third one, a sixteen-year-old from Brooklyn named Fred Clark.[26]

Clark, however, told police a very different version of events. According to him, the real aggressor had been Goetz. He was so insistent that things had not gone down in the way his accuser described that, totally uncharacteristically for a kid without a lawyer, Clark insisted on filing a cross-complaint against Goetz.[27] Despite Bernie's later claim that he had done nothing wrong, and that "the arresting officer saw [Clark] strike me, knock me down, and he ran into me, knocking me into a plate glass window," Cozza reported that he wasn't really sure what had started the confrontation.[28]

Since a consistent picture of events could not be agreed upon, both Fred Clark and Bernie Goetz spent hours at the police station. To Bernie's disgust, he had to stay for six hours, while Clark was able to leave after only two and a half. Adding to the insult, Bernie was told that the case might be sent to a noncriminal mediation process, sometimes used to resolve nonviolent disputes involving conflicting claims.[29] At that point, he made an offer to the cops—he would lie under oath about what happened, make it juicier, whatever they needed to hear, to make sure Clark was locked up.[30] They did not take him up on it.

Bernie would have to be satisfied with the fact that, like so many Black youths in this decade, Fred Clark would ultimately decide to take a plea deal rather than pin his hopes on the idea that his version of events would sway a jury. To avoid risking a long prison term for robbery, Clark pled guilty to a misdemeanor. He would end up serving four months in Rikers Island.[31] Indeed, plea bargains, ones that were always, as *The Atlantic* put it, intrinsically "tied up with race," would become so commonplace that eventually some 94 percent of felony convictions at the state level, and some 97 percent at the federal level, were obtained via a plea bargain.[32]

Whatever had actually transpired that cold January day, how it had been handled at police headquarters greatly upset Bernie Goetz. Even his doorman could see that this moment had angered Bernie—more so than usual. "Do you believe this?" he said to the doorman. "I spent all this time there and this guy walked out in 2½ hours."[33]

By 1981, Bernie Goetz had decided that he was done waiting on the authorities to do something about the would-be punks that he was now convinced were terrorizing the city. There was no question, he decided, that the incident at the Canal Street station would have gone down very differently if he'd had his gun with him.

Bernie had actually purchased his first gun in 1970, a .38 caliber Smith & Wesson Model 60.[34] But he hadn't had it on him that afternoon on Canal Street, and this frustrating fact plagued him. He decided not only to carry a gun on his person from then on but also that he needed to buy more weapons.

But New York State had some of the nation's strictest gun laws, which had been made even tougher as rates of violent crime rose and citizens demanded legislative action. Possession of a loaded, unlicensed gun in public was a felony that carried a one-year minimum sentence and the possibility of up to seven years in prison.[35]

So, on April 16, 1981, Bernie applied for a pistol permit from the License Division of the New York City Police Department. The process was fairly straightforward. There were three main types of handgun licenses: a "Premises License" issued to a specific address such as a business; a "Carry Business License" for persons who carried large amounts of cash due to the nature of their business; and a "Carry Guard License" for armed security guards.

A successful application needed to show "proper cause" or demonstrate "extraordinary need," which was difficult for an ordinary citizen to do. The reality was, most city officials didn't like the idea of citizens carrying, and at the time, gun advocacy groups such as the National Rifle Association had had difficulty making headway in New York, a northern city with a liberal mayor.

Bernie Goetz's application stated that as the owner of a small business who had to carry merchandise, he was "particularly vulnerable to a robbery attempt."[36] To bolster his bid, Bernie submitted paperwork from an upstate gun shop, Discount Guns, Incorporated, confirming that he had been trained to use a firearm.

It took many months for the application to be reviewed. When he finally got the results, Bernie was disappointed and furious. His request was denied, on the grounds that he had "failed to distinguish himself from others going about their business without the benefit of a license." He was chided for providing "poor documentation of the need," especially since businesses like his were "not prone to robbery." Bernie hired a lawyer to help appeal the decision, first going back to the License Division in May 1982—arguing that its refusal had been "arbitrary, capricious and an abuse of discretion"—and later, filing with the State Supreme Court.[37] Neither appeal was successful.

Perhaps anticipating this failure, or perhaps simply impatient to own another gun, Bernie didn't wait for the appeals to be resolved. In February 1982, he went down to Barrett's Guns, Incorporated, in Orlando, Florida, and bought another .38 caliber Smith & Wesson, this time a Model 36 revolver. If he couldn't buy or carry a gun legally in New York, he could instead visit his family in the Sunshine State and come home with a weapon. In September 1984, shortly after the death of his seventy-eight-year-old father, he paid $400 for two more guns, this time nine-millimeters, from Ken's Firearms, also in Orlando.[38]

There was a certain irony to the fact that Bernie Goetz committed the crime of carrying an unregistered and thus illegal gun in NYC, ostensibly to prevent more crime. And yet, there was no doubt that the number of incidents in which desperate people seeking quick money were targeting others was on the rise. People with addictions to feed and those with no money to feed their families alike had made New Yorkers in every borough feel less safe.[39] Indeed, both Bernie Goetz and Darrell Cabey had experienced a mugging, and a national poll indicated that a full 85 percent of the people it questioned in 1981 said that "they are more concerned about crime now than they were five years ago."[40]

MEANWHILE, HOWEVER, another form of violent crime, one in which white Americans like Bernie Goetz were much less interested, was also showing a particularly alarming upward trend: white-on-Black crime.

In New York City alone, the year 1982 saw a thirty-four-year-old transit worker in NYC named Willie Turks chased down by a white mob shouting racial epithets who then beat him to death.[41] In 1983, a subway graffiti artist named Michael Stewart was also beaten to death, this time by transit cops.[42] The 1984 killing of a woman named Eleanor Bumpurs by a police officer in the South Bronx, as well as the murders of multiple Black residents of Buffalo, New York, apparently by the same assailant, who always used a .22 caliber pistol, terrified New York's Black community too.[43]

All of these acts, and still others, suggested white racial rage was re-emerging as a serious problem in America. And yet, the uptick in the nation's general "crime problem," as explained by politicians and portrayed by the media, was the fault of minorities. As one piece in the *New York Post* noted, an increasing number of white New Yorkers had "recited horror stories of crimes they said had been committed by blacks" and thus "were afraid of blacks."[44] One *Post* reader underscored this sentiment in a letter to the editor: "the prevalence of black crime . . . suggests why some whites would prefer blacks not to enter their neighborhoods."[45]

All of this only added to Bernie Goetz's determination to carry a gun. By 1984, not only did Bernie own four guns, but he had begun carrying an unlicensed weapon at all times so that he could readily flash it at, and perhaps even pull it on, someone who might be a threat.[46]

That opportunity arose when Bernie found himself walking near the north end of Central Park after having taken the wrong train one day. He was looking around nervously, wanting to "get back to civilization," when he noticed two men, one in front of him and one behind. The young man in front was carrying a cane and said, according to Bernie, "Okay motherfucker, give it up." Bernie pulled out his gun. "I was going to shoot him," he later said, "he thought I was going to shoot him . . . but his knees buckled" from sheer terror and "he could hardly walk."[47]

A few weeks later, Bernie saw another young person on Sixth Avenue, someone he later described as a "crazy kid on drugs," who asked him for money. Bernie "got pissed off" and again "pulled out the gun," telling him, "I'm going to blow you away." According to Bernie, the kid "got scared shitless." Later, he admitted that pulling the weapon might have been too much. It was possible, he conceded, that "showing it" would have been "enough to make him run away."[48]

Goetz felt that he had tried hard enough to address the deterioration of the city through the proper systems. He had already filed countless complaints, signed petitions, and joined his tenants association. In 1983 and 1984, he even periodically attended the meetings of an organization called FAB 14, an acronym for "For a Better 14th Street," whose projects included cleaning up the seedy Union Square Park and advocating for community interests in redevelopment plans for the site of the former S. Klein Department Store on East 14th.[49]

But all such efforts produced few results, and this only angered him further.[50] What neither he nor other white middle- and working-class New Yorkers fully grasped was that the deepening civic distress of the

1980s—the rising houselessness, the blight, the terrifying muggings, and the alarming uptick in thefts—was being caused by forces much more structural than simply calling the cops or carrying a gun could address.

What they also missed was that the very same policies that were causing them to feel both unsafe and enraged were meanwhile making it possible for the city's wealthiest residents to earn more money than they had dared hope possible.

5

Profiting from Pain

Americans with the greatest wealth, the preponderance of whom lived in NYC, had for decades been laying the political groundwork that would make the Reagan Revolution possible.[1] They had never liked the tax policies, the regulations on business, or the social welfare policies that had emerged during the New Deal, and they had in fact been fighting against them in myriad ways since the 1930s.

One New Yorker who particularly chafed at governmental policies that he felt were costing him profits or regulating him too much was Fred Trump, a wealthy son of German immigrants. His grandparents had owned vineyards, and his father's economic standing allowed Fred to come through the Great Depression with means and wearing fine suits.[2] He would then go on to make his own fortune over the next several decades, thanks in large part to the federal government's decision to subsidize the construction of housing for so many white Americans during and after World War II. In the course of his illustrious career, he built and managed more than 27,000 apartments in New York City.

Fred Trump steadfastly dodged his own obligations when it came to paying back into that same tax base that had made it possible for the federal government to underwrite and incentivize businesses exactly like his so handsomely. In 1954, he would also find himself under investigation for profiteering by a U.S. Senate committee and again by New York State in 1966. Indeed, as historian Michael Glass notes, he "inflated section 608 mortgages by adding exorbitant fees, and cutting corners during construction, allowing him to pocket millions in FHA-backed mortgage funds."[3] Ensuring his financial legacy would continue, Fred Trump also found ways to pass almost a billion dollars down to his children via loopholes that would allow him to avoid paying a steep gift tax and his heirs to avoid paying premium taxes on their inheritance.

Meanwhile, like many other wealthy business owners who bristled at any new law that might prevent them from discriminating against their employees or customers, Fred Trump also resisted renting apartments to Black New Yorkers, only to find himself sued by the U.S. Justice Department's Civil Rights Division.[4]

The fact that ordinary working- and middle-class white Americans in New York City and across the country had also come to chafe at the idea of following anti-discrimination laws in the 1960s and 1970s would give wealthy Republicans like Fred Trump the wedge they needed to finally dismantle the liberal coalition responsible for the tax and regulatory obligations they had so long despised. They poured money into Republican Party coffers during the 1980 election, and were thrilled with its result.

These wealthiest Americans wasted no time ensuring that they would benefit most from Reagan's policies.[5] Since the New Deal, the richest citizens had been obligated to contribute to the broader social good to the tune of a 70 percent income-tax rate. Under Reagan, their individual tax rate would plummet to 28 percent, with some in fact paying nothing thanks to additional loopholes in the tax code starting in 1981. Corporate tax rates were likewise slashed.[6]

Fred Trump and Donald Trump, undated.
Adam Scull/AP

One New Yorker who took great advantage of those changes was Fred Trump's son, a far more colorful and larger-than-life real estate developer by the name of Donald J. Trump. His father had been lauded by the *New York Post* for his "contribution to the American free enterprise system," and he planned to embrace that ethos even more heartily.[7]

After graduating from the Wharton School of Business at the University of Pennsylvania, Donald Trump began his career developing middle-income housing in Brooklyn and Queens alongside his father. Not long after, he set his sights on Manhattan.

Donald Trump's dream of becoming the king of high-end real estate in the most expensive zip codes of NYC would be immeasurably abetted by the Reagan Revolution. He would, for example, owe fewer taxes on the monies dad Fred Trump had given him for his first large renovation project: purchasing the dilapidated Commodore Hotel on East 42nd Street for cheap and turning it into the newly christened Grand Hyatt Hotel. When the doors opened to this swanky new establishment, the public began to take notice of Trump. And as the 1980s unfolded, he would dramatically expand both his real estate portfolio and his personal fortune. He would, in fact, come to personify the stunning wealth that the Reagan eighties would make possible for those already at the top.

One of Trump's early high-profile developments was a fifty-eight-story mixed-use skyscraper. Located on Fifth Avenue, it would open its doors in 1983 and would serve as both his corporate headquarters and his home. He called it Trump Tower. Trump went on to buy and refurbish a revered address in the Financial District, 40 Wall Street, as well as the Plaza Hotel on Fifth Avenue, which together would cement his presence as one of the city's biggest movers and shakers. But his brand would extend beyond the city, also. He built several hotel-casinos in nearby Atlantic City, New Jersey, including Trump's Castle and Trump Taj Mahal.

According to the mythology of the Reagan eighties, just as the poor deserved their fate, so too did the rich. Indeed, men like Trump were ostensibly proof that the American Dream could be achieved after all, and anyone who didn't realize that dream was simply too lazy to seek it out.

The truth was, Donald Trump had not earned his leg up any more than the Cabey family had earned its bleak prospects. Their respective fates were directly informed by the politics and policies of this new political decade.[8] The dramatic cuts to inheritance taxes and capital gains taxes that both Fred Trump and Donald Trump enjoyed had directly depended on the slashing of funds to public resources such as schools, housing, and health care that harmed families such as the Cabeys.[9] And, of course, such cuts had also dried up the monies needed to keep neighborhoods like Bernie Goetz's pleasant and safe.

Connecting these dots, however, was not easy for those on the ground. Ordinary Americans were not privy to the wheeling and dealing that went on in the halls of power—the hands shaken, the favors called in—and those at the top, the ones who benefited the most from such political and economic wrangling, had every interest in obscuring these machinations. Donald Trump, for example, was loath to call himself a Republican for many years—likely understanding that doing so might hamper his ambitions in a city that, until the later 1990s, saw itself as quite liberal and where Democrats still held key positions in the city's various agencies. He nevertheless took great care to court the Reagan White House throughout the 1980s. In turn, it also courted him.

When invited to a state dinner for the king of Saudi Arabia in February 1985, Trump gushed that he and his then-wife Ivana were two of Reagan's "greatest fans and admirers."[10] The feeling was seemingly mutual. In fact, as Reagan's secretary wrote to them in December 1987, "On behalf of the President, it is my pleasure to send you the enclosed photographs, which were taken during your recent visit to the White House. We hope that you will enjoy having these as mementos of that occasion. With warmest wishes."[11] Trump's first book even included a photograph of him and Reagan, which put him squarely in the then-president's political camp.

Trump was nothing if not shrewd and practical. He might balk at the moralizing of many Reagan Republicans, particularly those in its highly influential Evangelical wing, but he had witnessed firsthand the benefits that the party offered men like him.[12] From the 1980s onward, Trump would, for example, also benefit from the beating that organized labor took. It had become much easier to exploit one's workers, particularly the undocumented among them.[13]

But Donald Trump wasn't merely a businessman, nor was his only concern making money. He was also a showman, one who craved the media spotlight. Trump was a frequent guest on talk shows and he shared his formula for how to become a billionaire in his 1987 book, *Trump: The Art of the Deal.* By the mid-1980s New Yorkers and Americans across the country alike were familiar with his name and had come to admire his curated image as a man who enjoyed the good life—a life that others could also enjoy if they merely followed his advice. Notably, Trump's first how-to book spent thirteen weeks in the number-one spot, and forty-eight weeks total, on the *New York Times* bestseller list. The core of Trump's message to the public, in the books he penned as well as the lavish lifestyle he lived, was simple: Greed is good.

That message was being amplified throughout this decade as well by what Americans watched night after night on TV. Two prime-time television dramas that particularly showcased gaudy wealth and openly celebrated avarice, *Dallas* and *Knots Landing,* premiered as Reagan's campaign was gearing up and when he won the nomination, respectfully. These shows aired weekly and inspired other popular series.

Other shows, like the 1984 hit *Lifestyles of the Rich and Famous*—with its enticing catchphrase "Champagne Wishes and Caviar Dreams"—were also meant to make viewers both envy and admire the rich. Meanwhile, there were comedies, like the ostensibly more edgy *Diff'rent Strokes* (1978–1986), that targeted a more racially mixed audience but offered much the same lesson as *Dallas:* The way out of the "ghetto," if there was one, relied on rich white people. And, of course, no motion picture captured the zeitgeist of this decade more than the 1987 blockbuster *Wall Street.*

Next to Donald Trump, who also made cameo appearances on TV shows like *The Jeffersons* and *I'll Take Manhattan,* perhaps no one better understood the media's role in strengthening not only this new decade's embrace of greed but also its conservative agenda than Australian newspaper magnate Rupert Murdoch. Over time, these two men would come to rely on each other to maximize their profits and to promote their conservative worldview. Murdoch would showcase Trump's lavish and flamboyant personal lifestyle to readers interested in following his exploits, and Trump would eventually depend on Murdoch's ever-growing media empire to boost his celebrity and to eventually build him an almost messianic political following rooted in racial resentment and rage.

But first, Murdoch needed to get a foothold in the U.S. media market.

THIS OPPORTUNITY WOULD come in 1976, when aging New York newspaper icon Dorothy Schiff decided to sell her tabloid, the *New York Post,* to the much younger and deeply ambitious Murdoch for $31 million. This was no ordinary sale. Murdoch's plan was to bring some of his hungriest editors with him and to one day dominate the largest media market in the United States. Never mind that he wasn't from this country, nor that he had only just moved to New York City. Murdoch knew how to attract readers—especially ones who were disgruntled, down-and-out, and frustrated with their own prospects. He had already amassed a fortune bringing splashy and sensationalistic headlines to readers in Australia and the U.K., readers also hit hard by the major recession that had swept the globe in the 1970s and the new and brutal era of austerity that came to their countries as well in the 1980s. They were eager to escape their own lives and to find easy answers to complex social realities. Expanding to the U.S. in the 1970s, especially into a gritty metropolis like New York City, just made sense.

When Murdoch first bought the *New York Post,* it already had a sizable and fairly liberal or at least centrist reader base. For the most part, the *Post* competed with the even more centrist New York *Daily News* for the coins city residents would drop into the many newsstands that dotted NYC streets and filled its hundreds of subway stations.[14] But Murdoch was determined to move his paper's political position rightward and make it the most read tabloid in the nation.[15]

To do so, he would rely heavily on his "star columnist from Australia," Steve Dunleavy. Dunleavy was "cut from a different cloth than most of the columnists working in 1970s New York."[16] He knew how to hit below the belt while also making readers ask for yet another punch to the gut, a skill that other New York reporters had yet to hone. As veteran *New York Times* reporter Jim Rutenberg explained it, Dunleavy was not just "openly right leaning," he was also "way more sensational."[17]

Sensationalism was a key means of building a strong reader base. More specifically, it was the way to pander to, rile up, and even create a very particular new reader demographic: fearful and angry white city residents who, as their personal circumstances grew worse, were increasingly disenchanted with liberal solutions to social problems.

Crime stories would become the *Post*'s go-to way to try to outsell the *Daily News*. The *Daily News* would respond in kind, also by devoting an increasing number of its headlines and columns to even more sensationalized crime-related stories as the 1980s went on.

Always on the hunt for such breaking news, reporters from the *Post* and the *Daily News* spent their days and nights listening to the police scanner and hovering around the second floor of NYPD headquarters, hoping to be first to hear about any particularly dramatic acts of urban mayhem from the many cops who ambled through its corridors.

The *Post* in particular understood the old adage "If it bleeds, it leads." Its reporters knew the power of dramatic headlines that promised the inside scoop on New York's most horrific crimes, most salacious incidents, and the most unsavory elements of living in a city now plagued by the trash piling up on the streets, the graffiti on walls of the subways, and the many drug-addicted and unhoused people sleeping in parks and begging for change.

Dorothy Schiff could not have known that her single sale to Murdoch would set in motion a literal revolution in the way Americans would be informed about the world. The impact of this shift is hard to overestimate. As columnist Calvin Trillin put it mildly, "all it took was some cash to change hands and it was Murdoch's right-wing paper."[18]

The real key to the *Post*'s expanding influence, however, was that it refrained from hard-selling conservative ideas. Instead, it couched them in the language of simply speaking truth to ordinary people. As one March 30, 1993, *Post* editorial explained, the paper was certainly "different from the other dailies in this town," because it refused to bow down

A man sleeping on a New York City subway car in the 1980s.
David Handschuh/New York *Daily News* Archive via Getty Images

to those who would insist on being "Politically Correct." Its main interest was simply to "embrace the concerns and highlight the problems of working- and middle-class New York families."[19]

That Murdoch intended to move the *Post*'s readership to the right politically was nevertheless clear from its conservative explanations of poverty and crime; its regular coverage of hot-button themes such as welfare fraud; and its columnists like Dorothy Rabinowitz and Patrick Buchanan, who took regular jabs at what they called the naïveté, if not downright danger, of liberal values such as progressive taxation.[20]

Buchanan, for example, lambasted the *Post*'s rival paper, the *Daily News,* for allowing its resident "bleeding-heart" columnist, Jimmy Breslin, to dwell on racism in the city and disparage those with more conservative ideas for running the nation.[21] As Buchanan put it in one column, "The knee-jerks on the other side seem to have forgotten who we are. We are Americans—direct descendants of the rebellious forebears, who took up arms and shut down British troops to overthrow the legitimate government, simply because the crown had pestered us with too many niggling taxes without our proper consent."[22]

The paper's writers also tried to influence how New Yorkers first understood the AIDS crisis. As one former writer reflected bluntly, "The *Post*'s editorial pages were predictably homophobic, and its news pages radiated an anti-gay perspective."[23]

The *Post* did its part as well to showcase the Reagan administration's views on these same topics. Indeed, in ways subtle but ultimately significant, the tabloid played an important role in making that group of white Democratic Party voters who might otherwise have been hostile to the fiscal policies of the Reagan Revolution come to see them as necessary and desirable.

Administration officials actively tried to ensure favorable takes on what Reagan was doing in Murdoch-owned papers from the *New York Post* to the London *Times.*[24] They well knew that they needed Murdoch as an ally to remake the political and economic landscape of the country. As Roy Cohn, former attorney for Joseph McCarthy, wrote to top administration officials in 1983:

> I had one interest when . . . I first brought Rupert Murdoch and Governor Reagan together and that was that at least one major publisher in this country (*New York Post*—over one million, third largest and

> largest afternoon; *New York Magazine; Village Voice; San Antonio Express;* Houston Ring papers; now the *Boston Herald;* and internationally influential London *Times,* etc.) would become and remain pro-Reagan. Mr. Murdoch has performed to the limit up through and including today. I enclose the editorials from the three New York papers so you can see how the *Daily News* and *New York Times* blasted the President's speech and how Murdoch's *New York Post* gave its whole Editorial columns to high praise for it. . . . I believe that the total support and loyalty of at least one major publishing chain in this nation is of key importance to the President.[25]

And this strategy worked. How countless New Yorkers would come to see the world around them—through an anti-liberal, socially, racially, and economically conservative lens—had everything to do with the expanding presence of Murdoch's media empire in this period. As media personality Harry Shearer pointed out, it was "hard to find a lot of Reagan supporters" in NYC before "the era of conservative talk radio and conservative television" and, importantly, "The *Post* was really the only place you could reliably turn to for that point of view."[26]

It wasn't simply that Murdoch's paper introduced a right-wing spin on the events that it covered, it was also that at the very moment when New Yorkers were becoming more desperate and fearful, the paper focused on depicting events in anger-producing and divisive ways instead of attempting to relay what had really happened, or why.

As *Post* columnist Dick Belsky shared, "There was a police reporter, who, if there was a murder, might call a cop and say, 'What's going on?' The cop might say, 'We don't have any leads'; the reporter would say, 'Are you ruling out a gay angle?' The cop would say, 'We don't rule out anything. We're still investigating everything.' Then the guy would write a lede like, 'Police are investigating a potential gay angle.' "[27]

As powerful as appeals to homophobia might be, the editors and owners of the *Post* understood that nothing was more divisive than race. Indeed, as former *Post* staffers put it, race "played a disproportionately large role in determining the *Post*'s crime coverage."[28] *Post* reporter and columnist Amy Pagnozzi also noted, years later, that it was remarkable "how little play murders would get if the victim was a Black person."[29]

At the *Post,* it wasn't enough to focus on Black "thugs" and "criminals." Race profoundly impacted every other message about the city that

New Yorkers were being given. As the authors of the oral history *Paper of Wreckage* put it, the "skewed" view of race "seeped from the news pages into other parts of the paper." In this paper, the good guys were "the white and wealthy" and the city's problems, whatever they might be, came from poor Black people.[30]

Apart from these distorted depictions, and the occasional letters to the editor, Black New Yorkers essentially did not exist in the pages of the *Post*. According to Pagnozzi, the paper's photo editor overwhelmingly chose images of white New Yorkers, asserting that "it was impossible to photograph Black people because they didn't come out right."[31] Belsky explained further, "We never really thought about covering the Black community or the Hispanic community. We just covered news."[32]

This was no secret to Black New Yorkers. As civil rights lawyer C. Vernon Mason explained, "over the years, the general sentiment about the *New York Post* in the Black community was that it was the worst in terms of news coverage of Black people, of any of the media outlets. People knew what their content would be, their bias would be, and how they would cover the Black community. Basically, the general sentiment was that they would sensationalize crime."[33]

In a 2001 retrospective on their paper, editors of the *Post* even agreed that its hallmark was how it treated "violent crime, especially when committed by minorities."[34] Notably, the *Post* became the paper for white New Yorkers while the *Daily News* increasingly became the preferred paper for Black New Yorkers.

Playing fast and loose with the real complexity behind the city's greatest challenges and pandering to prejudice would pay off. The *Post*'s circulation soon outstripped that of the *Daily News*, doubling within the first decade of Murdoch's ownership.[35]

To satisfy its readers' seemingly insatiable thirst for salacious stories, and to keep ahead of the *Daily News* by promising the very latest details of a given horror, the *Post* was soon publishing multiple editions a day. Indeed, explained Jim Farber, formerly of the *Daily News*, "There was a period where the [*Post*] was putting out an incredible number of editions per day. You could walk into a subway car, and if there were eight people reading the *New York Post*, every person would have a different front-page headline," all of them extraordinarily sensationalistic and meant to breed skepticism and hostility to particularly liberal politicians and the poor alike.[36]

By 1983, the *New York Post* had become the nation's fourth-largest daily newspaper, with nearly a million readers.[37] When Murdoch added a *Sunday Post* in 1989, for a mere 35 cents, his influence on how ordinary people viewed the country's rightward shift only increased.[38]

Equally importantly, by the mid-1980s, the more traditional media outlets were following the tabloids' lead, also soon playing a major role in turning public concern over drugs, decay, and despair into an all-out crime panic rather than a revisitation of the Reagan Revolution. In 1986 alone, for example, *Time* and *Newsweek* published five cover stories about crack, and more than one thousand articles about the drug appeared in the national news media.

The crime "crisis" was also featured in several high-budget news documentaries that year.[39] One made by CBS, *48 Hours on Crack Street,* had the dubious distinction of being the most-watched crime exposé in television history.[40]

National newscasters as well were soon as good as Murdoch's local reporters at fueling their audience's collective sense of defenselessness. On one occasion, as *NBC Nightly News* anchor Tom Brokaw spoke to viewers about the rise of "crime and the fear that it has spread throughout America," he stressed that "from the smeared subways of New York City to the dusty streets of rural towns, people say they are afraid of the violence, afraid of becoming crime victims."[41] Both TV and print media shared the troubling tendency to avoid any explanations of why this was happening now, and in every major urban center of America.

Rather, as scholars Bruce Johnson, Andrew Golub, and Jeffrey Fagan put it, the media tended to peddle "a seemingly endless supply of unverifiable assertions about crack," as well as "incomplete information derived from police records and individual accounts, often second-hand, collected by reporters."[42] It wasn't that crime didn't matter, nor that drugs such as crack cocaine had not wreaked havoc in the city. The problem was that such stories, and a lack of context, time and again fueled the idea that crime was somehow endemic to "certain" communities, rather than a result of the economic overhauls and the stripping of needed resources that defined this decade.

As reporter John Hart opined on the *NBC Nightly News,* "chances are" every city had a place that "most people would rather not be at night," if they wanted to stay safe. And should one encounter someone from such a place, added criminologist Don Kates, it was better to be prepared to defend oneself. As he put it, "In so violent a society, the only thing citizens can do to protect themselves is buy a gun."[43]

Even those who didn't follow the news could not escape these ever more racially charged messages about the deepening crime crisis. Of course, American literary and popular culture had long been entranced with the theme of vigilante justice, from detective noirs to the Westerns of Hollywood's golden age. But the 1970s and 1980s saw a dramatic uptick in this sort of content. Indeed, the racial justice struggles of the 1960s—and their perceived threat to whiteness, especially in the wake of urban uprisings—had birthed a new and distinctly anti-urban version of this genre.

On the big screen, there was the *Dirty Harry* series (starting in 1971), with its maverick cop protagonist, played by Clint Eastwood, who metes out his own justice to criminals, disdaining civil rights and courts; then *Death Wish* (1974), with its Everyman New Yorker played by Charles Bronson, who becomes "a one-man vigilante squad after his wife is murdered by street punks . . . kill[ing] muggers on the mean streets after dark"; and *Taxi Driver* (1976), with its antihero protagonist driving the decadent, sleazy streets of New York.

All of these films reinforced the message that ordinary people were on their own on America's dangerous streets.[44] Week after week, TV series like *Strike Force* (1981–1982), *Hunter* (1984–1991), and *The Equalizer* (1985–1989) shared these same themes directly into America's living rooms—that the only path to justice was a rogue police officer or a brave citizen taking the law into his own hands.

The urban-vigilante film came of age with a vengeance during the Reagan eighties. The 1980 cult hit *The Exterminator* portrayed an ordinary man who must become a killer himself in order to avenge the death of his best friend, "killed on the streets of New York City."[45] In 1983, audiences cheered aloud for Michael Douglas in *The Star Chamber*, in which a group of judges "frustrated with a legal system gone haywire" decide to hire hit men "to snuff out criminals who escape courtroom justice."[46]

Multiple sequels to *Dirty Harry* and *Death Wish* were released in the 1980s, earning big box office returns. Perhaps no cinematic vigilante was more celebrated, nor evoked more often in popular parlance, than Bronson's *Death Wish* persona. In each subsequent film, the "no-holds barred one-man justice" messaging got bolder and more violent. Even comedies were soon selling the idea that American cities were out of control. The fish-out-of-water story *Crocodile Dundee* (1986), in which an Australian adventurer comes to New York City, featured the tagline "He's survived the most hostile and primitive land known to man. Now all he's got to do is make it through a week in New York." It was the second-highest-grossing film of the year.[47]

Unsurprisingly, the idea that ordinary people needed to rescue their city from predators came to resonate with more New York residents than just Bernie Goetz. One of those for whom this rang true was Curtis Sliwa, the white founder of a citizen "safety patrol" unit called the Guardian Angels, who explained that "the city was completely falling apart" and that citizens were fed up with feeling vulnerable.[48]

And just as Bernie Goetz seemed to see no contradiction when he broke the law to carry unregistered guns in NYC so that he might fight crime, Sliwa's Guardian Angels were not shy about roughing up alleged "criminals," and would quite overtly run afoul of the law in this regard, in their zeal to protect the public from crime. As Sliwa himself later conceded, the group even faked crimes in order to garner public support and build its presence underground.[49]

Curtis Sliwa, founder of the Guardian Angels, on patrol.
Stephen Shamus

Nevertheless, the Guardian Angels freely patrolled the city subway system and Sliwa would become a local celebrity.[50] Even though a detailed study of crime in NYC showed that the Guardian Angels had in fact made no substantial impact on crime rates, their presence in the subway clearly comforted some city residents, who felt better knowing that "a well-muscled young man, wearing a white tee-shirt and sporting a red beret," was on their train and had taken "up his position near the door."[51]

Interestingly, even though the group was founded and run by the white and brashly conservative Sliwa, many of the young people he recruited to do the patrolling were Black and Brown. Wearing the Guardian Angels shirt and their trademark red beret clearly marked them as okay, as non-threatening to fellow passengers.[52]

On one fateful day in December 1984, however, there were no police nor Guardian Angels aboard the 2 train as it hurtled down the tracks headed toward the Chambers Street station with Darrell Cabey, James Ramseur, Barry Allen, and Troy Canty on board. And there was certainly no one to protect them.

PART II

Shooting to Kill

SATURDAY, DECEMBER 22, 1984, was unusually balmy for winter in New York City. There was still a dusting of snow, but that only added to the holiday spirit, which retailers hoped would be good for business. There had already been two recessions since Reagan took office and, even though things seemed a bit better, they were worried. *The New York Times* was reporting that shopping revenue was still likely to "fall short of expectations," with "even Fifth Avenue's merchants feeling the pinch."[1]

There had been a few hopeful signs that the year might end on a higher note. The annual tree lighting in Rockefeller Plaza had taken place a few weeks earlier than usual, and ever since, the mood had felt festive and the streets of Manhattan had been crowded with people window-shopping on the sidewalks and toting bags of gifts. Black Friday sales had also been frenzied as parents jostled to secure the new Cabbage Patch doll for their little kids, or, for their older ones, the new Sony Walkman WM-F8 that boasted a cassette player.[2]

This last Saturday before Christmas was vitally important to local businesses, and many had rolled out glitzy promotions and offered last-minute discounts. That plus the spell of good weather would hopefully do their part to bring in customers in a good mood and ready to spend whatever money they might have.

Plenty of New Yorkers had indeed decided to venture out with shopping lists in hand on that December day, entering subway stations from the top of the Bronx to the bottom of Manhattan. Others bustling through turnstiles and boarding trains were just going about their usual weekend routines—commuting to or from work, heading to see friends, or taking their kids out for the day.

Still others, such as the unhoused people sitting on grates outside the stations, and the various groups of teenagers who could be seen milling about, had no money to spend nor a particular place to go. Nevertheless, they too were happy to take in the glitter of the Christmas lights that decorated storefronts and listen to the familiar and cheerful carols that burst from the doors of nearby restaurants and bars as their patrons came and went.

Good cheer filled the air, even as a bit of drizzle began to fall.

6

An Ordinary Day

For kids from the South Bronx, holidays were complicated. Any tradition that revolved around gift-giving sparked anticipation and excitement but also no small amount of unease. It was hard for their parents to make ends meet even on a regular day. At least there would be days off from school and more time to have fun with friends. This was always something to look forward to.

Three days before Christmas, Darrell Cabey was staying at his grandmother's house, helping to care for her as she battled the flu.[1] Being helpful like this mattered since there was little question that he had been putting both his grandmother Nora Smoot and his mother, Shirley, through a lot lately. There were his run-ins with the cops to consider, as well as the fact that he wasn't in school and had been dabbling in drugs. But Darrell's family had faith in him; they knew that he was trying to figure out his future. And anyone who really knew Darrell understood that he would never do anything that would make his mother seriously disappointed in him.

But lately things had really been hard for this now-nineteen-year-old. He couldn't find a job, and he certainly couldn't afford college, so it was difficult to know how to spend his days. When he had woken up that Saturday, Darrell had initially planned to go home, just to relax and help look after his siblings. He had even started walking in that direction. But the thought of being cooped up in the apartment all day, especially with his little brother's cartoons blaring, slowed his steps. Abruptly changing direction, Darrell headed over to 169th Street and Third Avenue, where groups of teens from his neighborhood tended to gather.[2] He didn't tell his mom about his change of plans. She would just worry.

Knowing how aimless her son now was, and just how much he wanted to fit in with his peers, most definitely did make Shirley Cabey nervous whenever he headed off on his own like this. She was well aware of unpredictable eruptions of violence in their neighborhood as well as the many hard-faced cops who drove through the streets of the South Bronx, or parked for hours outside her building, just waiting to nab kids like her son in order to meet their arrest quotas.

And so, she had put a lot of effort into making her apartment a place where her kids wanted to be. As Shirley explained it, "I bought this stereo, a nice TV, just so's they could listen to their music here, you know, so they'd stay home . . . Lord knows, I tried."[3]

But on the morning of December 22, 1984, none of that sounded good to Darrell. He wasn't so familiar with the particular crowd that happened to be hanging around that day, apart from a guy his age named James Ramseur, whom he had seen around the neighborhood. James was pretty easy to recognize, with his black leather cap always perched atop his short afro. James was standing next to two of his friends, nineteen-year-old Troy Canty and Barry Allen, eighteen.

James Ramseur in the South Bronx.
Getty Images

Barry Allen in his apartment. From *The Confessions of Bernhard Goetz* (MPI Home Video, 1987). Permission from the estate of Darrell Moore.

Troy, Barry, and James had been just as loath to stay inside their crowded, loud, and stuffy apartments. They'd each made their way over to the spot near the bus stop simply looking for something to do too; some escape from the boredom of just watching TV or the drudgery of doing their chores. These teens also lacked a steady job, money, and any real opportunities, and thus, like Darrell, they were floundering with so much time on their hands.

Barry Allen's mother, Mary, was as worried about her son as Shirley was about Darrell, especially since he too was a boy who used to be so optimistic, so happy, but then seemed to lose his way. Barry, a kid who used to talk about what he wanted to be when he grew up, had not even made it past the ninth grade.[4]

Mary's concerns for every one of her children had risen sharply when she lost her job as a switchboard operator. So far her girls, fifteen-year-old Patricia and fourteen-year-old Tanya, were still doing well in school, and her other son, seventeen-year-old Benjamin, was even making straight A's.[5] But Mary was struggling to provide for her family, let alone give them the material things that made being a kid fun. As Barry later remembered, "Growing up, it was just hard. It was rough." His mother "couldn't afford a lot of things" that he needed, let alone wanted. Still, he knew his mother tried. "Like I wanted some Adidas," he recalled, and "she bought me Zips. You know Zips only cost two dollars. Adidas cost like forty-two dollars."[6]

Like Darrell, once he quit school Barry was determined to make his own money. As he later explained it, every time he "came out the house," he felt the need to see "what dudes is doing for money." And that answer too often meant doing something that could get someone into a whole lot of trouble. Barry had observed the "guys over here selling drugs, [and] guys over here breaking in the pinball machines," and it seemed pretty clear that this was what he would have to do too if he was going to have any income. "I start hanging with them, I picked up doing what they was doing," Barry remembered.[7]

When Barry's girlfriend had a baby, his need for extra cash only increased. Everyone knew that neither he nor she was ready to be a parent, but it was too late. Barry's mother could see that her son wasn't coping at all well with his new responsibilities and pressures. He was drifting even further away. She suspected—correctly—that Barry wasn't just selling crack cocaine, but that he was using it himself. Ever since the birth of his son, Jason, Barry had also been doing everything he could to get into a Medicaid-funded drug rehab program. The problem was that the waiting list seemed hopelessly long.

"Just say no to drugs," per Nancy Reagan's dictum, was a difficult proposition when you were already addicted, and cocaine was everywhere. It was even harder to quit if your friends were also using, and Barry's friend Troy Canty, who lived next door to him in another one of Claremont Village's cramped two-bedrooms, had also become mired in addiction. This news would have surprised Troy's dad, Edward, a factory worker who described his son as a kid who did not have a police record and faithfully attended Morris High School, a kid who always talked about "getting a good job and buying a car."[8]

Troy's mother, Eula Canty, had a more clear-eyed view of her son. She appreciated that Troy—the youngest of five siblings, four of them boys—had always been "such a quiet boy." He was a kid who "never gave me no trouble," she was fond of saying.[9] But Eula was well aware that the pull of the city was strong. As she explained, "once the kids get on the streets, they're lost . . . it's mostly the drug problem that turns most of the kids around." It clearly terrified her that, as she put it, drugs were "all over the streets."[10]

As far as Eula Canty knew, her son "wasn't into heroin, just marijuana and cocaine," but this offered her little solace. She fretted, for example, about what might be laced in that weed or coke he was using. "You know," she said, "they don't have no good stuff up here, so who knows what he was taking. It's mixed with Lord knows what."[11] But all Troy's mother could really do was just hope that "things would straighten out for him, that, you know, he'd be alright."[12]

Troy was living closer to the edge than his mom knew. He'd started using cocaine more often, and the potential consequences of this worried him. The good news was that he still had loyal friends who respected him, and he was somehow managing to make enough money to get by. "Troy Canty, he's a thinker," his friend Barry said admiringly. He "[takes] his time with whatever he does. He's thorough."[13] Troy's friend James Ramseur agreed. He had known Troy for about six years and definitely considered him the brains of their group.

For his part, James had his own problems to worry about. Recently, he'd caught a sixty-day sentence for smoking marijuana.[14]

Small and slight, and only weighing about 129 pounds, James lived with his mom and dad in a brick high-rise on the busy commercial corner of Third Avenue and 170th Street. Like Barry and Troy, James had his fair share of encounters with local cops and was always hustling to make money. But he wasn't into hard drugs and he was always cheerful, something that those around him appreciated. James's parents could always count on him to see the brighter side of things, and it was obvious to them that everyone liked him. He had a reputation as a bit of a jokester, which they embraced, although being a fun-loving smart aleck hadn't always won him points with his teachers. In the seventh grade, James also dropped out of school.[15]

Even though James knew who Darrell Cabey was, he had only seen him around for the last year or so and didn't know much about the guy. In a lot of ways Darrell seemed more like a middle schooler, with his baby face and his slightly timid demeanor, but James was nevertheless okay with him joining the group that day.[16] Barry also thought that Darrell seemed awfully young, but he liked his calm presence. "Darrell Cabey," he said, "he's more laid back. He's more like a father."[17]

Once the mild buzz of Darrell's arrival at the hangout spot had passed, the conversation lulled and the dreaded yet familiar restlessness began to infect the collective mood. Not keen on just standing around all day, Troy came up with a plan.

Since none of them had cash, the boys would sneak onto the crowded no. 55 bus heading into Manhattan through the back doors when they opened to let riders out. Once they got to the 149th Street and Third Avenue train station, they would head down, hop the subway turnstile, and take the IRT downtown express 2 train either to Times Square–42nd Street or maybe farther downtown, to Chambers Street. There, they would find a video arcade and make some money by pulling off a maneuver Troy had become really good at—prying open the coin receptacles on the arcade games and pinball machines and pocketing the change.[18] How much they could get for their efforts was unknown, but history showed that they could do all right.

Troy had picked up this particular hustle after stumbling upon a set of generic keys that enabled him and Barry to open most change slots pretty easily. The keys didn't always work, though. Sometimes, Barry later explained, they didn't have the right key for a particular machine, and in those instances, they would use a flathead screwdriver to open the coin box. "What we would do," Barry went on, was "wedge the screwdriver in there and just flick it, like pop."[19] Meanwhile, James would position himself to block anyone's view of Troy and Barry's exploits.

This time, Troy suggested, Darrell would help too. He hadn't brought a screwdriver along, but this wasn't a big deal, Troy assured him. They would give him one of theirs.[20]

None of the boys felt particularly bad about boosting coins from these arcade and pinball machines. Everyone knew that there was no money to be had from doing odd jobs in the neighborhood. At least jimmying coin receptacles wasn't all that risky and didn't physically hurt anyone. The sad truth was that Troy's addiction now required that he get some amount of cash every day, and even if he hadn't needed coke, he reasoned, didn't boys like James or Darrell also deserve to have a bit of money—maybe just to be able to play a couple games of Pac-Man or Centipede, or, say, take a girl to the movies? It was easy to defend, Barry explained. "We just [wanted to] have fun, do things that teenagers do."[21]

Troy added one more step to the plan, though. He knew from past experience that it wouldn't be good for a manager to catch them hanging around a pinball machine without money in their pockets, plausibly waiting to play a game.[22] So, while they were on the bus, or more likely on the long ride on the 2 train, Troy might ask folks if anyone had a few bucks to spare.

Despite Transit Authority rules prohibiting it, panhandling had become a regular feature of New York City life in recent years.[23] And the way Troy saw it, needs must. Sure, it was annoying to be asked for money, but it wasn't easy to get up the nerve to approach complete strangers and ask, either. People might try walking in his shoes for a bit, then they might understand.

IN THE REAGAN EIGHTIES, New Yorkers who had an income, however precarious it might be, didn't seem much inclined to try to understand young people like Troy Canty.

Bernie Goetz was one of those New Yorkers. As Troy and his friends were deciding to head into the city, Bernie was also contemplating a trip downtown. He had been wrangling with a troublesome piece of electronic equipment and, frustrated, had elected to step away from it around lunchtime to go meet some people for a drink.

Given the unseasonable warmth when Bernie ventured out, he wore only a thin blue jacket over his green plaid shirt and blue jeans. Besides, the crowded subway trains were often hot and humid, even in winter. Pushing his wire-rimmed glasses a bit higher up on his nose, Bernie tried to shake off the earlier part of the day.

The fact that Christmas was only a few days away did not lighten Bernie's mood. He wasn't exactly the type to embrace all the holiday folderol. He was more one to brood, especially about what he felt remained wrong with the city. It would have been hard even for him to miss the festive displays in the windows of Macy's and Bloomingdale's in Midtown, or, nearby Washington Square Park festooned in colorful lights. But appreciating any of that also would have required looking past the increasing number of panhandlers on the pavement right in front of those same stores and the many without homes who now huddled on that park's benches.

Unhoused person asleep in Tompkins Square Park, 1989.
Jack Smith/New York *Daily News* Archive via Getty Images

As ever, Bernie kept a wary eye out for anyone who seemed like they might hassle him for change or perhaps run some sort of con as he made his way over to the 14th Street station. Should anything go down, Bernie was now prepared. Despite the useless do-gooding officials running the Licenses and Permits offices, on whom he had wasted nearly two grand in applications, he now had a .38 Smith & Wesson in a quick-draw holster just inside his waistband. Only he knew it was there.

Bernie's weapon was not only easily accessible, but it was also loaded with powerful ammunition: so-called dum dum bullets of two distinct varieties. The first two projectiles he had placed in the chamber were standard load hollow point bullets that would explode on impact. But as deadly as they were, this type of ammunition had slightly less velocity and power than the last three bullets he had loaded right behind them—so-called plus P hollow points with a jacketed nose. These exited the gun much faster and had a more devastating effect on the target.

The order of these bullets was important, not only when it came to having maximum stopping power but also to ensure that the weapon wouldn't jam when Bernie needed it most. It was illegal for him to buy, possess, or use hollow point ammunition in New York City, and, in fact, multiple international treaties prohibited using it, even in warfare, due to the extraordinary damage the bullets could inflict on a human body.

Bernie Goetz, however, was not particularly concerned by this fact.

7

Manhattan Bound

At one in the afternoon on December 22, 1984, as Bernie Goetz was zipping up his thin windbreaker and heading down into the subway station, Troy Canty, Barry Allen, James Ramseur, and Darrell Cabey were boarding car no. 7 of the 2 train headed downtown.

To the other passengers on that subway car, these four teens must have seemed a rather ragtag crew, but hardly an imposing one. They were all skinny, and at five foot six, James was the tallest, with the other boys each standing two inches shorter.[1] Still, the rest of the passengers on the 2 train that day absolutely took notice of the boys. By the 1980s, adults regarded almost any band of loud young people with a bit of wariness, and this group was being particularly boisterous. What's more, these were Black teens, and male to boot, the sort of kids too many people in this city now just assumed were dangerous.[2]

But the quartet would be damned if they would let any glares or suspicious looks ruin their day, deciding instead to continue to yuck it up. They chatted amiably as they spread out in various seats on the subway car, Troy and Barry particularly full of energy. The two would occasionally hop up and say something animatedly to each other, take a twirl around one of the poles, or slap at one of the hand straps that dangled above their heads.

Darrell and James sat a bit farther down, looking on while Troy clowned around and acted as if he hadn't a care in the world, even cockily asking a few of the riders, "How's it going?" or "Got a light?" as they, for the most part, tried studiously to ignore him.

These fellow passengers were a real cross-section of New Yorkers. Like Troy, Barry, James, and Darrell, twenty-six-year-old Garth Reid and his wife, Andrea, lived in the Bronx. They had boarded the train at Gun Hill Road with their baby daughter in a stroller. She was asleep when the couple first sat down on one of the long seats in the middle of the car, but when she awoke from her nap, Garth placed her on his lap and playfully jostled her on his knees.

This was when Garth first noticed the teens, laughing and moving between seats.[3] They were a bit rowdy, but he didn't think much about them.[4] Originally from Jamaica, Garth worked as a computer programmer and attended the Borough of Manhattan Community College on Chambers Street, while Andrea—a native New Yorker—was a part-time model and was studying at John Jay College in the hope of becoming a police officer.[5]

One of the first riders to acknowledge the boys had actually been Josephine Holt, a Black woman who boarded the train at 96th Street and intended to get off at Chambers Street because it was her favorite place to find holiday gifts.[6]

Josephine had grown up in Gastonia, North Carolina, but now lived in the city, working as a maid almost every day of the week over in Fort Lee, New Jersey.[7] She was just glad that today she had enough time after work to head downtown and do some last-minute shopping. Once on the train, Josephine settled in to read her newspaper after having observed the teens farther down the car "laughing loud and talking loud amongst themselves." Then, before she had made it through even one news story, one of them had come over to ask if she had a match. She replied that she didn't, and he moved on. As she went back to her paper, Josephine noticed him talking to another woman and then a male passenger.[8]

Also boarding at 96th Street were two white men, Loren Michaels and Christopher Boucher, who were headed to SoHo to go Christmas shopping. Christopher designed displays at a major San Francisco department store but was visiting his friend Loren, a credit manager and native New Yorker, for the holidays.[9] Loren and Christopher managed to get seats together, down a bit from the four boys, whom they had also noticed "laughing and moving around."[10] As the express train picked up speed, it "became very noisy," so Loren and Christopher stopped conversing and rode in comfortable silence.[11]

An aspiring actress named Mary Gant came aboard the train at 72nd

Street. A white woman originally from Wisconsin, Mary hadn't moved to the city until 1976 but now considered herself a true New Yorker. The train was her main mode of transportation to auditions and her various temp jobs, and she felt more than comfortable taking it. Mary's plan that day was to get off at Fulton Street, south of Chambers, and head over to the bustling South Street Seaport.[12] She sat kitty-corner from both Loren Michaels and Christopher Boucher, who were on her left, and the group of teens, who were down a ways to her right. She noticed them but didn't think much about what they were up to.

When the train hurtled into Times Square–42nd Street, Solitaire MacFoy entered car no. 7 and stood near the doors, carrying two large pieces of plexiglass. Few things fazed Solitaire; he had grown up in West Africa, then went to school in England, and by the time he moved to the U.S. in 1981, he had seen a lot of the world.[13] He noticed the four teens, but decided that they seemed pretty benign, if irritating, in their exuberance. Mostly, Solitaire was making sure that the unwieldy plexiglass he'd purchased for a DIY project in his Brooklyn apartment didn't get messed up by other passengers' wayward feet. As the train headed downtown, Solitaire's thoughts moved to his girlfriend, with whom he was planning to spend time later that day.

When Victor Flores boarded the 2 train at 34th Street–Herald Square, he was preoccupied, wanting to make sure that he got to Brooklyn on time. Although he worked as a cleaner for the New York City Transit Police District 12 in the Bronx, he embarked on the long trip to Brooklyn at least twice a week to help his brother, a building superintendent. To get there, he usually caught the 2 train in the Bronx. Today, he'd been shopping at Macy's in Herald Square and entered the subway feeling a little frazzled, having missed the train just before this one.

As soon as Victor stepped foot into the middle of the car, he too noticed "a lot of noise and talking" at one end, coming from a group of "young black kids," though he was mostly focused on sitting down and taking a breath after his hectic morning.[14] Opening his newspaper, he started to scan the headlines, having no trouble tuning out everyone else around him, including the teens. Victor had come to NYC from Puerto Rico more than thirty-five years ago, and by now he had accepted the chaos of the subway as just part of living in the big city.

None of these passengers took much notice of Bernie Goetz when he shuffled onto the train, head down, at 14th Street. Goetz did not pick a seat far away from the boys, instead choosing a seat directly across from where Troy was standing, diagonal from Barry, and a ways down from Darrell and James, who were seated at the very end, just on the other side of the conductor's cabin in the next car.[15]

Each of the boys immediately took note of this. It was strange enough that this slight, sandy-haired, rather nerdy-looking guy was sitting so close to them, but he also kept staring, looking each of them in the eye. Troy and Barry, the two who had been the most rambunctious since boarding the train, likely found this odd, but perhaps also intriguing. Why was he looking at them? Did he want to start something? Talk to them? They weren't sure.

What they did know was that although they'd greeted several of the passengers, nobody so far had offered them a light, a smile, or even a nod back. Troy decided to speak to the newcomer.

"Hey, what's up?" he said.

The man returned his greeting.

Encouraged, Troy stepped closer, ready to ask if the guy had any money to spare. Even if he said no, it was worth a try. And besides, it was something to make the long train ride pass more quickly.

"Hey, man," Troy said, looking down with a small smile on his face. "How about giving us five bucks?"

The man looked up slowly, coldly, and asked Troy to repeat what he had just said.

Barry, who was standing close to Troy, found the man's response strange and unsettling as he looked on uncomfortably.

James and Darrell, still seated at the end of the car, had been watching the interaction unfold with some curiosity. Neither boy could hear much over the sounds of the train. James thought that Troy might be asking for the time.[16] And while Darrell had no idea what they were saying, the whole situation made him nervous. Troy's brash attitude could be sort of cool, but it could also really piss someone off.

Troy, however, was undaunted. He repeated, "How about giving us five bucks?"

Bernie Goetz stood slowly. He unzipped his jacket and turned as if to retrieve some cash, but instead, he suddenly spun around. Assuming a combat stance, he pulled a gun out of his waistband and began shooting.[17]

8

Bloodbath

DARRELL AND JAMES STARED in fear and disbelief as Troy jolted backward, his chest seeming to explode. As he hit the floor, Troy didn't quite know what had happened. His first thought was that he had been "hit with [a] paralyzer gun," but then he "could feel the blood begin to flow" and his "legs turn numb." He was terrified. He looked over and saw two passengers, women, not too far from him, also on the ground. He feared that they too had been gunned down.[1]

Later, Troy recalled thinking it was like "a scene out of the movie *Death Wish*." The gunman had moved with such cold precision, "slowly and deliberately," like he had "practiced" this scenario "100 times." As Troy explained it, the man had "deliberately" taken "three steps away from [him before] carefully unzipping his windbreaker as his back was turned. . . . Then he whirled around and fired."[2] Worse yet, he wouldn't stop. The man just kept pulling the trigger.

Next to Troy, Barry had relaxed just for a minute, thinking that the white guy was standing up "to get out his money." But suddenly he turned and "went into a crouch, like in a movie," and Barry heard a loud bang.[3] A wave of nausea came over Barry as he watched Troy's chest turn crimson red. He heard, and then saw, his friend falling to the floor, with a look of terror and bewilderment on his face.

In those seconds, all Barry could think to do was flee. But no sooner did he turn his back to the gunman than he heard the terrifying sound of a second shot ring out and felt something tear into his back. As the pain burned through his body, Barry also collapsed to the floor. At first, he didn't understand what had hit him. He too thought that perhaps he had just been tased.[4] But then he realized that he couldn't move his hand. As blood started running down his arm, he really began to panic.

Meanwhile, the man kept shooting.

As Barry fell, Goetz was making his way toward the other two boys, seated about ten feet away. At first, James was too fearful to move. Realizing he was a sitting duck, though, he then decided to try to get out of there, maybe make it into the next car. But just then, another shot rang out. Dizzied by fear, and feeling pain sear through his arm, James registered that he had been the target.

Directly after James went limp, Darrell, at this point also standing, felt a bullet narrowly miss him too. Quaking, he abruptly sat down, head down, and gripped the edge of the seat in terror. He didn't dare even look at the man, hoping against hope that he would just move on. But it was clear the shooter wasn't done. In fact, he was walking toward Darrell, slowly and deliberately.

The man stopped just in front of Darrell, looming over him as Darrell said plaintively, "I didn't do nothing!"[5] But it was as if this man couldn't hear him. In a cold, calm tone, the man raised his gun again and said, "You don't look too bad, here's another," before shooting Darrell point-blank.[6]

WHEN THE FIRST SHOTS were fired, Christopher Boucher thought they might be firecrackers. Perhaps that was what those boys were fooling around with, but it was so hard to tell, with the noise of the subway wheels drowning out other sounds.[7]

When Josephine Holt heard the first shot, she didn't even look up from her paper. Like Christopher, she also thought it might be firecrackers. Maybe that was why the teenager had asked her for a light.[8] Only when she heard an alarmed voice shout out, "Somebody had got shot, somebody had got shot," did Josephine look up and begin to panic herself.[9]

Mary Gant, however, was immediately terrified. Something had just cracked into the air, "the loudest noise [she] ever heard."[10] Her ears began ringing. In the chaos, someone shoved her to the ground where she froze, praying that if that was the sound of a gun, whoever was shooting would assume she was dead. As she let her gaze travel slowly rightward, her fear only deepened. She was looking straight into the eyes of a young Black teenager who was on his stomach, bloody and clearly unable to move. He was staring back at her in sheer terror.[11]

Victor Flores recognized the sound immediately. With a sick feeling in his stomach, he saw a white man "standing with a gun in his hand shooting straight at the kids in front of him."[12] Victor realized that he was in the same line of fire as the first victim. As he later put it, "the kids were frightened, backing off, trying to get away. There was no reason to shoot them. They fell one after another."[13] Without thinking, Victor bolted out of his seat and fled through a door at the end of the car, toward the conductor's compartment. As he ran, he heard the man continue to squeeze off shots and registered the boys' confusion and terror.

Garth Reid could see the teens just a bit farther down being felled—one, two, three, and then the shooter was heading toward another kid, but Garth didn't wait to witness what terrible things might happen next. All he could think about was protecting his baby daughter. He could feel his wife, Andrea, trying desperately to wrench her out of his arms to flee, but he held her firmly, trying to shield her body, and that of his wife, utterly terrified that even standing up might make them more exposed.[14] After deciding to hand her the baby, Garth tried to screen them both as they made their move, fleeing into the next car. In his mind, none of it made any sense. He had not seen any of the boys, who now lay bleeding profusely on the ground, make any threatening gestures, let alone brandish a weapon.

Carrying her baby, Andrea tried to focus only on making it out of there alive, but she could not get the sounds of the shots and the sight of kids trying to get away out of her mind. Overwhelmed, terrified, and sickened as she was, she didn't even process the other passengers between her and the door to the next subway car. Loren Michaels, who was in Andrea's path, felt her slightly trip over him in her haste to get out. He tried to right her as he also bolted to safety.

It was at this moment that Christopher Boucher finally realized something awful was in progress; it hadn't been firecrackers he'd heard. And then, suddenly, he had a clear line of sight on the unfolding nightmare.

One of the teens who'd been laughing and horsing around was now lying facedown on the floor and had clearly been shot. The person who had likely shot him, an unremarkable-looking white guy, was now heading toward the end of the car. Christopher looked on as this man stood over yet another boy with his gun in hand. That teen was sitting down, his hands holding on to the bench, clearly cowering in fear.[15] Christopher watched in horror as the man shot that boy too.

Meanwhile, Loren had been frantically trying to get Christopher's attention so that they could get away from this madness. Shaking, Christopher numbly got up and managed to get himself into the next car.[16]

The remaining passengers, however, stayed, as if glued to their seats, in utter incredulity at the carnage before them. The floor was slick with blood and the air smelled overwhelmingly of copper.

The gunman was now just sitting down, mumbling something to himself, as the subway screeched and shuddered to a stop. Mercifully, someone had finally pulled the emergency brake.

9

Triage

IT HAD TAKEN less than two minutes for the 2 train to leave the 14th Street station where Bernie Goetz had boarded and come to a sudden halt in the tunnel, just shy of Chambers Street. Filled with a deep sense of foreboding, conductor Armando Soler stepped out of his compartment in the train's sixth car.[1] He had heard a rapid series of shots coming from the car just behind his.

Almost simultaneously, terrified riders began bursting into car no. 6. But he could barely make sense of their panicked reports. What he was able to discern from their fragmented gasps was that some kids were being shot in the next car over. But why? he thought. People had no problem coming to him with complaints about other passengers, but he had heard nothing today about disruptive, let alone violent, teenagers.

As he braced himself for what he might find, Armando grabbed his radio and began shouting the code for a weapon on the train, making clear that dispatch needed to send police and ambulances right away.

As he entered car no. 7, a few people were still trying to escape the chaos and confusion. However, there were at least six people not moving at all, sprawled out on the floor and benches. Armando could not process what he was seeing. Some of the people on the ground were severely injured young people. Two more were adults, one of them a Black woman who was lying motionless and the other a white woman, curled up as if trying to make herself small.

As Armando ran to check on these women, a pale and rather serious-looking white guy joined him.[2] He looked upset. As Armando was helping the Black woman, whose identity was never confirmed, the other man hovered over the white woman, seeming distraught that she might have been shot.[3] That woman was Mary Gant, who had been shoved to the floor when the first shots rang out. She was scared, but seemed fine, for the most part.

With these women back into seats, the man who had assisted the conductor also sat down, just across from them. He still seemed unsettled, mumbling something about not knowing why he had just done what he did, and also something about being robbed.[4] It suddenly dawned on Armando that the man who had just been helping must also be the shooter.

Armando was confused. He asked the man if he was a police officer. The man said no. Did he have a permit for the gun that was still in his hand? No, he did not. Jesus, Armando thought. He then asked for the gun, but the man ignored him.

Relatively certain the guy wasn't going to shoot him, Armando resumed his attempts to tend to the victims. It was grim. One of the teens clearly couldn't move. He was unresponsive to Armando's questions and, though he was facedown, blood was pooling rapidly under his chest. Near this boy lay another, his eyes looking glassy. He too had clearly been shot, in the back, it appeared.

Meanwhile, the now-seated Mary Gant tried to calm her breathing and to stop feeling so light-headed. She wanted to get out of this horrible, blood-spattered steel box. When she'd been on the filthy floor, she'd been unable to take in the full extent of what had happened, but the image of the boy on his stomach, so close to her, had been horrifying enough. Their eyes had locked, but in the face of his raw fear, Mary had instinctively looked away. Now that she was safe, this decision haunted her.

No matter how many times she replayed the events that had just unfolded, she couldn't make sense of them. As she had lain on the floor, playing dead, why had the gunman come over to help her? His face had been creased in concern as he asked, "Miss, are you all right? Did I hurt you? Did I hit you?" He had even helped her back into a seat.

More important, Mary wondered, why had this man shot all of those boys? As she recalled, they hadn't been making menacing gestures. In fact, she'd never heard anyone raise their voice in anger or in a threatening manner.

Victor Flores was equally unsettled. He had followed the conductor back into car no. 7 and was bewildered to see the shooter himself kneeling on the floor, gently helping a clearly terrified woman. Just moments before, however, Victor had seen this very same man look carefully into the eyes of one of the injured kids appraisingly, as it to ensure that he had, in fact, hit him.[5]

Another passenger, Arnethea Gilbert, was also finding it hard to make sense of the carnage in car no. 7. She had been riding in the same car as Armando Soler. Like him, she realized something was wrong in the next car over when she'd heard ominous pops and saw people start rushing into her car, faces ashen. In their panic, one of them had actually tripped and fallen right in front of her. Not fully thinking through a plan, Arnethea jumped up and headed into car no. 7 to assist whoever might be hurt.

As soon as she entered car no. 7, Arnethea could immediately see that several teenagers were in grave shape—one slumped over on a bench and three splayed out on the floor. All were motionless. First, she headed toward one of the kids, who appeared to have been shot in the back. This turned out to be Barry Allen. She felt for his pulse and could tell that he was alive and at least somewhat conscious, but clearly in no condition to speak.

Arnethea turned quickly as she heard another boy, his chest soaked red, begin to speak. It was Troy Canty. "Miss, I've been shot through the heart and I'm dying," he said to her, breathing heavily.[6] As she leaned over him, she tried to muster up words that would reassure him. "If you were shot through the heart, I don't think you'd be talking to me," she said with a measure of certainty she did not feel. But he kept speaking, clearly wanting her to know something important. "He shot me for nothing," Troy gasped. "I didn't do anything. I only asked him for five dollars."[7]

With these words ringing in her ears, Arnethea then headed to check on the two teens at the end of the car. One of these young people was slumped over on his seat, his legs sprawled out at a strange angle. This was Darrell Cabey, still conscious but unable to move. As she tried to rouse him, Darrell spoke so quietly she had to lean in to make out what he was saying. Still, she heard him clearly: "I didn't do anything. He shot me for nothing."[8]

While Arnethea and her fellow passengers were busy trying to help the wounded boys, reassuring them as they waited for EMS and the police to arrive, Bernie Goetz quietly got out of his seat and walked slowly over to one of the subway car's sliding doors. Prying it open, and still holding his gun, he jumped down into the darkened tunnel.

For a few panicked seconds he had no idea which way to head. The rows of tracks stretched in both directions and seemed even to crisscross, and who knew where the closest station was. Finally making out a dim glow of light to his left, he bolted. Somehow, he just needed to get back to his apartment and think. He needed a plan.

Meanwhile, back in car no. 7, no one had any idea who he was or where he had gone.

10

Aftershocks

THE FIRST POLICE to arrive on this chaotic and bloody scene were Officers Peter Smith and Dennis Driscoll of the NYPD 1st Precinct.[1] Driscoll made his way straight over to a kid who he noticed worriedly was struggling to breathe. It was Troy Canty. Driscoll did his best to assure and calm the boy and decided to stay right there so that he might assist the paramedics when they arrived. Meanwhile, Smith headed out into the tunnel to try to locate the gunman.[2] The shooter was nowhere to be found, and Smith returned to the car.

When paramedic John Filangeri and his colleagues had managed to lug their bulky stretchers and much-needed medical supplies down into the station, step their way carefully across the tracks, and finally make it up into car no. 7, they were as taken aback as Driscoll had been. They understood that their first order of business was to get the victims' shirts and jackets off so that their wounds could be assessed more carefully. Each teen had a clear entry wound, but not all of them had an exit wound. This was not a good sign.

After efforts were made to address the boys' most critical injuries and to stabilize them with bandages and fluids, it was time to get them ready for transport. Filangeri kept a close eye on the process, making sure that each boy was placed on the stretcher with as little jostling as possible. There was no way to tell the exact path of the bullets, or where they might be lodged in the body, and it was essential to move them carefully so as to avoid further injury.

This, Filangeri knew, wouldn't be easy. First they would have to be

Police officers at the subway shooting crime scene. From *The Confessions of Bernhard Goetz* (MPI Home Video, 1987). Permission from the estate of Darrell Moore.

carried down from the train, the doors of which hovered fairly high above the tracks. Then those same tracks would have to be navigated in the tunnel in order to make it back to the station, where the boys would have to be hoisted up onto the platform. This was all before even arriving at the many stairs that stood between them and the waiting ambulances aboveground.

As the paramedics had been tending to the wounded boys, additional law enforcement had also arrived—officers both from the NYPD and the Transit Authority, because crimes committed on public transportation always involved both departments.

Ideally, their first task would have been to interview the passengers who had just witnessed the shootings. But with the exception of the conductor and riders like Arnethea Gilbert who had stayed to comfort the boys until paramedics arrived, every other passenger was long gone.

Some would later come forward, such as Josephine Holt, who took it upon herself to call the police. She would be interviewed over the phone. Solitaire MacFoy would contact the DA's office directly, after calling the police station and hearing nothing back. Andrea Reid never gave a police statement, but she was approached much later by the DA's office for her account of events. Her husband, Garth, had gone to the police station to try to retrieve the stroller they had abandoned in their haste to escape the subway car, which was likely the only reason they knew she or he had been aboard the train that day.

There was little more for the officers to do but start collecting any physical evidence they could find.

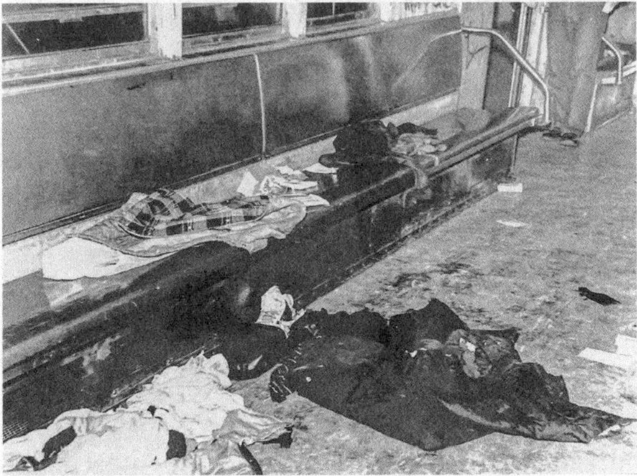

Exhibit photographs of car no. 7, 2 train.

From the papers of Ron Kuby

Eager to try to piece together exactly what had happened here, NYPD Detective Charles Haase began picking his way through the many items that had been scattered across the blood-smeared linoleum and found himself taking particular notice of the clothing that had already been removed from the wounded boys so they could be treated. As he lifted up the jacket that Darrell Cabey had been wearing when he was shot, Haase immediately noticed that it had two holes in it, one clean, the other bloody. Not quite sure what to make of that, he laid it next to another jacket, the reversible navy blue and maroon zip-up that James Ramseur had been wearing, with a bullet hole in the upper left sleeve. Barry Allen's vest, he also observed, had one bullet hole in the back, almost dead center.[3]

Alejandro Torres was the transit cop who had helped paramedics remove the injured boys' shirts and jackets, and what had really caught his attention was not the holes in them but rather what he found inside one of the interior zippered pockets of Darrell Cabey's zip-up: a screwdriver.[4] He then located two more screwdrivers in the pockets of James Ramseur's reversible jacket. Understanding that these screwdrivers might well constitute important evidence, Torres made sure they were bagged and tagged.

AS THE INVESTIGATION INTO the shootings was underway in car no. 7, a caravan of ambulances was rushing the four badly wounded teenagers to local emergency rooms, their prognosis uncertain.

Barry Allen was in bad shape. By the time he had finally been ferried up the last of the subway station's steep stairs, he was having extreme difficulty breathing, indicating the possibility that at least one of his lungs was collapsing. Once his ambulance arrived at Bellevue Hospital's emergency unit, he was rushed immediately into the operating room.

James Ramseur had also been taken to Bellevue, exhibiting equally labored breathing and an alarming pallor. The same bullet that had entered James's arm had also pierced his side, and at this point it was hard to say what damage it had done.

Rather than head to Bellevue, Troy Canty's ambulance sped to the much closer St. Vincent's Hospital. At first glance, this was a strange choice because St. Vincent's had become one of the busiest medical facilities in New York City, and its emergency room was always bursting at the seams—filled with unhoused people suffering from frostbite; with individuals suffering from overdoses; and with too many gaunt New Yorkers flushed with fever and covered in lesions, telltale signs of an AIDS infection. But St. Vincent's was also a major trauma center, and the severity of Troy's injuries meant that time was of the essence.

Troy knew that being shot in the chest at such close quarters was very serious. What's more, the fact that his breaths were shallow and ragged terrified him, no matter the assurances of the kind woman, Arnethea Gilbert, who had kneeled over him. As doctors began inserting tubes into his chest to facilitate respiration as soon as he arrived, his fear only intensified.

Darrell Cabey, however, was in the direst straits. The paramedics had also whisked him to the closer St. Vincent's because they could see that Darrell felt no pain at the site of the injury. This was extremely ominous, as was the fact that his breathing was also dangerously labored. When these EMTs arrived at the emergency room bay they barreled past the many desperate people needing care and handed the wounded teen off to doctors who rushed him straight into the operating room. Darrell was no medical expert, but he seemed to know his situation was grave. He wanted his mother.

UP IN THE BRONX, Shirley Cabey had spent her Saturday wrapping Christmas presents and straightening up the apartment, and she was in a great mood. Just two weeks earlier, she'd received news that her food service job at the mental hospital had become a permanent position. She'd made it through the job's probationary period with flying colors. Now thirty-nine years old, Shirley knew that landing a secure state job in this economy was nothing short of a miracle. Jobs like hers had seemingly dried up overnight, and Shirley could now even imagine accruing a decent retirement fund, which was a pipe dream for most people she knew.

At 9:30 p.m., Shirley vaguely heard an announcement on the TV: "Coming up at ten: Four youths shot on a subway in Manhattan this afternoon. Stay tuned for details."[5] She didn't think much of it, though, as it was now time to make sure her younger kids brushed their teeth and got tucked in for the night.

After finishing the bedtime routine, Shirley headed back into the living room to prepare to turn in herself. But at 10:10 p.m., she heard a knock at her door. This was unsettling. One thing about living in the Webster Homes in the 1980s was that you learned to be leery when someone you didn't know came to your door late at night. But as she peered out of the peephole, she relaxed. It was just her neighbor. Shirley smiled as she unlocked the door.

Was Darrell at home? her neighbor asked. She had just received a call from the Transit Police informing her that her own son had been shot in the city. But her boy was accounted for. Maybe the officers had meant to call Shirley? she ventured nervously. After all, they had similar last names, and Shirley's number was unlisted.

Shirley's mind froze. It was true, she hadn't seen Darrell today. But he was most likely still at his grandmother's house. And, anyway, as far as Shirley knew, he never hung out in Manhattan. Still, she took the small scrap of paper with the number of the transit cop. Numbly, and with mounting dread, she made her way to the phone hanging just above her sofa on the living room wall.[6] After a brief conversation with the officer on the other end, her worst nightmare was confirmed. Darrell had been shot. He was now in an emergency room down in Greenwich Village.

An agonizing thirty minutes later, Shirley was seated in her cousin's car as they raced to St. Vincent's Hospital. Shirley's mother, still recovering from the flu, was in the backseat. As the trio sped past high-rises framed by the night sky, many with Christmas lights twinkling hopefully in their windows, Nora Smoot tried valiantly to persuade Shirley that even if it was their Darrell in the hospital, things might not be that bad. She clung to these words: Her mother had spent twenty-six years working as a nurse's aide. She would know.

Shirley finally arrived at St. Vincent's shortly before midnight, bursting through the doors of the ER with her mother and cousin in tow. When the desk clerk learned that her son was one of the boys who had come in after being shot on the subway, she explained that Darrell was in surgery and Shirley would have to wait to see him. Shirley headed dutifully to a chair, but with each passing minute, her anxiety intensified.

Eventually a doctor came out in scrubs. Shirley couldn't help but notice his somber demeanor. Darrell's situation was much worse than she had anticipated. "Mrs. Cabey," the doctor told her solemnly, "there was nothing we could do. The bullet severed his spinal cord. Darrell will be paralyzed from the waist down. He will never walk again."[7]

It was as if Shirley had been physically struck. All she could manage to ask was whether Darrell knew. No, the doctor mumbled. It would be better for her to explain it to him in the morning. For now, it would probably be best for her to head home, a nearby nurse gently told her. But Shirley didn't want to leave. Home was so far away from her son. Eventually, her cousin and mother persuaded her to come back first thing in the morning. Did she want her mother to stay the night? her cousin asked. No, Shirley said, she needed to be alone, and she still had to tell the other kids what had happened.

The next morning, retracing the steps that her son had taken just the day before, Shirley boarded the M55 bus before switching to the downtown 2 train. She exited at 14th Street, the same station Bernie Goetz had entered to board the train less than twenty-four hours earlier. Standing beside bed no. 4 of the dimly lit ICU, Shirley barely recognized her child, hooked up as he was to hissing tubes and whirring machines that tethered his slight frame to the hospital bed. She would only be allowed a ten-minute visit, the ICU nurses made clear, and that was hardly enough time to make sense of any of this. Still, a part of her might have been relieved. Perhaps Darrell would just keep sleeping and then she might not have to tell him, not just yet, how badly he had been hurt.

As if sensing his mother's presence, though, Darrell stirred, his fingers fluttering weakly as he tried to reach for her. His face slowly contorted as he registered the anguished look in Shirley's eyes. Overwhelmed by the pain he saw there, Darrell began to cry as he looked up at her and whispered, "I'm sorry, Mama; I am so sorry."[8]

11

Victims or Villains

GETTING WORD THAT four Black teenagers from the South Bronx had been gunned down by a white guy on the New York City subway was like Christmas come early for both the New York *Daily News* and its newly determined competitor, Rupert Murdoch's *New York Post.* Both papers hurried to make the most of this dramatic event, no matter how little reporters actually knew about the identity of the gunman or his motives for shooting four people. Subway riders were one of their largest group of readers, and this was a story they would want to devour right away. Indeed, as veteran *New York Post* reporter Cynthia Fagen remembered, "If you went into the subway, everyone was reading a newspaper. It was either the *Daily News* or the *New York Post.*"[1]

The *Daily News* provided the earliest and most dramatic coverage, with front-page headlines that blared "'VICTIM' ON SUBWAY SHOOTS 4," and "A FANTASY COME TRUE: DEATH WISH GUNMAN CAPTURED CITY'S IMAGINATION," and "PREY TURNS PREDATOR."[2] Not to be outdone, the *Post* was soon dubbing the shooter the "Bronson Copycat" and the "Death Wish Gunman" in equally salacious bannered articles. Within days, the *Post* even created a logo to accompany all of the articles on the shooting: a hand holding a gun, against the backdrop of a dark subway tunnel, with the text "Death Wish Vigilante."[3] Over the next few months, these two tabloids would produce an immense volume of increasingly inflammatory reports on this shooting.

What perhaps mattered more than the incendiary headlines or the sheer number of stories both tabloids immediately devoted to this event, however, was the misinformation each was also imparting to the public. The very first piece published by the *Daily News,* for example, claimed that the "men" who had been shot, including "Troy Canty, [age] 25," were all "armed with screwdrivers."[4] Another piece doubled down on its reporting that the teens had been armed, noting that they had actually been "carrying sharpened screwdrivers."[5] Such coverage also showered the shooter with praise. As yet another *Daily News* article insisted admiringly, the gunman was, for New York, "an instant hero, a true-life Charles Bronson, a subway vigilante with his own style of justice."[6]

The *Post's* stories similarly revered the shooter, noting that his "courteous and unrattled style was dramatically similar to that of the character played by [Charles] Bronson." He had, after all, taken the time "to help the hysterical women to their feet and escorted them to another car before fleeing."[7] Meanwhile, the *Post* also noted repeatedly, these young men had "extensive criminal records," and at least one of them, the main offender, Troy Canty, was "twenty-three" and thus was hardly a youngster who was merely horsing around with his friends on the 2 train.[8]

This tabloid also asserted confidently and regularly that the screwdrivers found on the subway teens—sometimes described as "screwdrivers with sharpened tips," or "sharpen[ed] screwdrivers," or as "long, sharpened screwdrivers"—were being brandished first to intimidate and then "to rob" the man who instead shot them.

Even the nation's paper of record, the highly respected *New York Times,* soon jumped on this story line. When its reporters first learned that two of the boys had been carrying screwdrivers, they simply noted it.[9] Soon, however, the paper was also implying that the four Black youths on a NYC subway car had been shot because they had been carrying these "sharpened" screwdrivers.[10] Almost overnight, this detail became so accepted as fact by the national media that even *Time* magazine was reporting on the sharpened screwdrivers.[11] The implication was clear: The ostensible victims in this situation were really the villains.

The information that the teens had been carrying screwdrivers came originally from the NYPD and Transit Authority. At no point, however, did either law enforcement body step in to dispel the rumor that these objects had been sharpened, nor did they ever share the important information that such tools were commonly carried by poor people to jimmy open the coin receptacles in public washing machines, cigarette dispensers, arcade games, and more.

That said, some officers and detectives were unwilling—at least initially—to cast suspicion on the shooting victims themselves. When he finally emerged from the bloodied subway car the night of the shooting, NYPD officer Peter Smith, for example, conceded to a reporter that the gunman "possibly" could have construed the teens' actions as "harassment," but it was his impression that they had just been "fooling around with the guy."[12]

Similarly, the first police officers and detectives from both the NYPD and the Transit Authority who interviewed the wounded boys in the hospital tried to listen to their account of what had actually happened, rather than just assume they deserved their devastating injuries.

Late on December 22, for example, mere hours after the shooting, detectives visited Barry and James, both of them still in the ER with conditions listed as critical, to record their official statements. Still in shock and traumatized, the teens tried their best to recount the events that had, inexplicably to them, led to the eruption of gunfire. The detectives also asked them to describe the shooter, but according to the detective's report, James, at least, "could not give me any description of the perpetrator, stating that he only knows the guy was white."[13] In an additional report filed on this interview, the teens were listed clearly as "victims."[14]

Detectives also headed to St. Vincent's that night to interview Troy Canty and Darrell Cabey, both of whom were out of surgery but still in very bad shape. Troy refused questioning, but Darrell was successfully interviewed, and here too law enforcement seemed to have no doubt that he was the victim; the report they filed explicitly identified Darrell as such. Notably, Darrell had also seemed unable to provide much insight regarding the reason he had been shot. When Detective Richard Commesso asked him when he had become aware that "a rip-off was going to take place," for example, Darrell responded emphatically that he had no idea "what was going down" just before the man started shooting.[15]

The next day, Darrell was interviewed again, this time by Detectives Michael Clark and Daniel Bronte. This exchange yielded them two critically important pieces of new information. First, Darrell stated without hesitation that "the white man then went to shoot me. He missed with the first shot. He then fired a second shot hitting me in the back."[16] He also gave a clear description of the shooter: "a white male in his thirties, with blond hair, Thin Build 5'10–11"." What's more, he went on, the man had "Clear Round Glasses, Jeans, and [was] armed with a silver revolver."[17] Clark and Bronte's report also listed Darrell Cabey as "Victim Gunshot."[18]

Only one day after that, on December 24, however, law enforcement's attitude toward the teens seemed to shift markedly, with neither the NYPD nor the Transit Authority now being willing to just accept their initial statements. On this Christmas Eve, law enforcement higher-ups decided to send Detective Clark back to St. Vincent's, this time with another interviewer—Detective Charles Penelton of the Transit Police—to question Darrell again and to get Troy to talk for the first time.

Darrell didn't tell these detectives anything new that should have made them doubt the initial account, but it was clear that at least Penelton came away dubious. The report that he filed dutifully acknowledged that the statement he had taken from Darrell "was consistent" with that which had been recorded the day before. But whereas those first detectives who spoke to Darrell had designated him as a "victim" on the official police report, Penelton did not follow suit.[19]

Clark and Penelton then went to see if they could get Troy Canty to open up at about 2:10 p.m. that same afternoon. Troy was leery, noting disgustedly, and correctly, that law enforcement had decided this time to send a Black detective, Penelton, hoping that this would put him at ease enough to finally talk.[20] As if on cue, Clark, the white detective, left the room. But Troy was still on heavy pain medicine, "had tubes coming out of his chest going to machines that were sucking blood out of his lungs," and was having a hard time staying awake. Still, he eventually did agree to speak to Penelton.[21] The detective's version of what Troy said that afternoon, however, would in time be hotly contested.[22] In Penelton's view, Troy was no victim—he had provoked his shooter.

MEANWHILE, AND INDICATIVE of how hard it now was for the NYPD to imagine that four Black teenagers could really be innocent in all of this, back at police headquarters a great deal of time was being expended on determining how many crimes each of the teens might have committed before they had boarded that train.

Their efforts were not in vain. In the past few years, the four boys had indeed accumulated a slew of misdemeanor summons for a range of petty offenses—some dating back to October 1981, and others recorded as recently as November 1984. As these were low-level offenses, the officers on the scene had merely issued summonses for them to appear in court. But for poor teenagers in this city, with no means of paying the fines the judge would require if they showed up, skipping such court dates was commonplace. All of these teens had in fact ignored their notices to appear.

Notably, however, no prosecutor had yet asked the court to issue bench warrants for their arrest—until now, less than one week after a man had shot them.

Two judges' decision to hand down a blizzard of bench warrants against these teens—on December 27, 1984, on New Year's Day, and again on January 2, 1985—would have an incalculable impact on the subsequent media coverage of the subway shootings, and in turn, on the way that countless New Yorkers and the nation more broadly would come to understand all that had gone down on the 2 train three days before Christmas.

When Judge Alan Marrus decided to issue a bench warrant for Troy Canty's arrest a mere five days after he had been rushed to the ER, he cited an earlier incident of "breaking into a video game machine at Boyle's Pub" on 23rd Street. According to this warrant, in the course of stealing $14 in quarters, Troy had done "$250 in damage to the machine." He faced charges of larceny and malicious mischief, and should he not now appear in court, he would be arrested.[23]

A few days later, Judge Stanley Katz went even further. It was New Year's Day 1985 and the courts were officially closed, but he nevertheless showed up to issue a collection of ten bench warrants against the teens, each one also stemming from low-level misdemeanors. These included two more warrants against Troy Canty, for "failing to pay a $10 fine for riding between subway cars" (October 1981) and "failing to respond to a summons charging him with subway trespass" (November 1984); three against James Ramseur, for disorderly conduct and marijuana possession (both from February 1984), as well as for failure to answer a summons for subway trespass (May 1984); three for Barry Allen, all for failing to respond to summonses for subway trespass (two from 1983; one from 1984); and two for Darrell Cabey, also for "failing to answer summonses" and "disorderly conduct."[24]

The sudden and aggressive issuing of such warrants was not without controversy. A Manhattan criminal court judge named Edward McLaughlin, who was then tasked with overseeing Troy's case regarding breaking into video machines, simply could not understand why Marrus was so determined to go after the very people that the Manhattan DA's office would most need help from when trying to build a case against the shooter—should they ever find him.

Judge Marrus, however, refused to back down. He argued that Troy's "extensive" criminal record indicated that he "poses a danger to the community."[25] Marrus insisted that Troy Canty should be arrested the instant he was allowed to leave the hospital but also that his bail be set at $1,000—an amount this teen would never be able to pay.

Nowhere in these warrants was there any indication that the boys were violent or dangerous. If anything, the minor charges within them could well have been used to corroborate the boys' claims that their only plan that day had been to jimmy open some arcade machines. Nevertheless, this flood of paperwork would serve only to confirm everything the reporters had already been saying: These were thugs whom the "Death Wish Shooter" had been right to take down. So many warrants were indisputable proof that the shooter had been right to fear for his life.

The fallout from this on the teens themselves was immediate and alarming. Even though they were still in the hospital, under the twenty-four-hour care of nurses and doctors, the boys, as well as their families back in the South Bronx, were soon receiving a torrent of ghastly threats. Callers promised, among other things, that they were "going to come by and 'finish the job.'" In another instance, someone rang the Allen family to say chillingly that they had "heard the good news about Barry being shot." Barry's little sister, who answered the call, was terrified.[26]

And then there was the hate mail that flooded the mailboxes of the boys' families, after both the *Daily News* and the *Post* had published their addresses.[27]

Some of the worst messages came to the Cabeys in the form of "get well soon" and "Merry Christmas" cards. One such festive piece of holiday stationery, addressed "To Darryl Cabey, the cripple N—," expressed the wish that he might "be confined to a wheelchair for the rest of [his] life."[28] Another gaily decorated card addressed to Shirley Cabey read, "I hope your son is crippled for life to remind you that it was your responsibility to raise your child to be a decent human being and not an animal."[29]

Darrell's mother seemed to be a particular target of this vitriol, receiving awful letters such as: "Mrs. Cabey, It's a shame the day you give birth to that no good son [that] the doctor did not choke him with the umbilical cord and kill him."[30] Yet another shrilled, "It's too bad [the gunman] didn't kill the lot, they're all rotten + so are you. . . . [He] is a decent human being pushed to the limit by the likes of your offspring."[31]

This mail wasn't just ugly. Like the phone calls, it could also be downright threatening. One letter addressed to Darrell said coldly, "Your days are numbered. And when your kind are removed from our streets, New York will fulfill its destiny to be the greatest city of all times."[32] Others expressed similar sentiments such as "I am glad Daryl is paralyzed . . . I'm so sorry that the other 3 can't join him," or "I'm sorry he didn't kill you all" (the latter from a "Correction Officer"). Yet another envelope contained only a sticker, with a swastika logo and the words "Deport Sp—s, N—s and Jews!"[33]

Even when it became clear just how much hate they were enduring, neither the boys nor their families garnered much sympathy from their fellow New Yorkers. At the forefront of the public's consciousness, in no small part thanks to the tabloids' coverage of this event as well as the warrants they now faced, was the certainty that Troy, Barry, James, and Darrell were indeed a "danger to the community," and therefore they deserved nothing more than what the shooter had already given them.[34]

Seeing this degree of racism and hatred unleashed on their children and themselves was beyond painful to the families. Just as Shirley Cabey had rushed into Manhattan upon learning that Darrell had been shot, so too had the other boys' parents. They had also been living hour by hour, just hoping that their kids would be all right.

Troy Canty's relatives arrived at St. Vincent's just as bewildered and scared as the Cabeys. On a typical day, Troy would have been getting ready to go to sleep on one of the two sets of bunk beds that had been squeezed into the kids' bedroom at home. Instead, he was in surgery. Troy's older brother Carl just couldn't get his head around it. To be sure, Troy was no saint, Carl would acknowledge to reporters. And he was someone who needed to take drugs to deal with his anxiety.[35] But he was not a thug, and didn't deserve this. Troy's dad, forty-eight-year-old Edward Canty, agreed. There was no way Troy was trying to rob anybody.[36]

At Bellevue, Bessie Ramseur had also been unable to comprehend why this had happened to her son, James. "My son may have been rowdy and loud sometimes, but he never did anything to hurt people," she would insist. Barry Allen's mother, Mary, felt the same disbelief that her son had done anything to warrant being shot. Almost desperately trying to stress this point to reporters, she would even welcome them into her home, pulling out a scrapbook she had made "showing four academic awards her son won in 1978 and 1979."[37]

No matter what these families said or did, however, the press continued to sell its own narrative of the shootings. On some level, these parents and siblings understood exactly what was transpiring, and had little doubt as to why it had been so easy to villainize their loved ones. When asked about the public's reaction to the gunman and victims such as his son, Troy Canty's father didn't hold back:

> I think he's a crazy man. He has to be. But white people don't care too much about blacks. . . . If they get him, they are not going to bother him too much. . . . The kids are black and poor, and [the authorities] will believe everything he says, and nothing the kids say. That's the way it goes. . . . When black people get shot by a white man . . . That's what people will say . . . That they were about to rob someone.[38]

Barry Allen's sister Patricia viewed the situation similarly, though she still couldn't quite fathom how quickly people had sided with the man who had shot her brother in the back. "I am very angry at those people," she said. Those who knew James Ramseur also found the way in which his shooter had been celebrated perhaps predictable but nevertheless hard to process. As one of his close friends said disgustedly, the "people who are praising the gunman are 'sick.' "[39]

To Troy's brother Carl, it was all pretty simple, actually. As he put it, people had just decided that "it was four ghetto kids that wasn't gonna amount to shit anyway. What the fuck are we gonna waste our time with him for?"[40]

Still, this was a hard pill to swallow. Many kids from the South Bronx, including Troy and even Carl himself, had committed their share of petty crimes. But they had never harmed people. Maybe "we was criminals," Carl Canty said sadly, "but not hurting criminals." "I'm not gonna rob you," he continued, "I'ma steal from the supermarket." Sure, some out there were robbing old people, choking people, robbing them, beating them up, taking their money, but Troy just wasn't like that.[41]

There was, however, one person still at large who had very much hurt people. Whether that man could ever be found, let alone brought to justice, remained to be seen.

PART III

A Reckoning Deferred

AMERICANS HAVE ALWAYS loved the excitement of a manhunt, be it watching lawmen try to capture notorious outlaws like Jesse James after the American Civil War, or John Dillinger and the romanticized rebels Bonnie and Clyde during the Great Depression, or the brash Brinks robbers of 1950. Such games of cat and mouse have, in fact, appealed to the public in every decade of American history, and the 1980s was no exception.

This decade also had its share of famous thieves who did their level best to avoid prison. There were the corporate criminals like Charles Keating Jr., who bilked the Lincoln Savings & Loan for personal gain and became the face of a financial crisis costing taxpayers more than $124 billion, and the billionaires like Marc Rich, who bolted to Switzerland to avoid paying more than $48 million in taxes he owed.[1]

The 1980s were, however, pretty good to robbers like these. Marc Rich would never be extradited to face any legal consequences. In fact, years later, he would enjoy a presidential pardon.[2] And the criminal actions of men like Keating had been made possible precisely because regulations on banks and other financial entities had been weakened, making it so much easier to engage in high-stakes deals that could suddenly go so very wrong.

As the "greed is good" ethos took ever greater root, even when the shadiest investments and acquisitions came to light, there seemed to be little interest in making the CEOs in question serve time for their crimes. In 1984, when E.S.M. Government Securities collapsed in scandal to the tune of more than $300 million, no one went to jail.

In the Reagan eighties, even those who had committed some of the most gruesome violent crimes of the decade—men like white supremacist Joseph Christopher, who law enforcement believed had murdered twelve Black people in Buffalo, New York, or white autoworkers Ronald Ebens and Michael Nitz, who beat Chinese American autoworker Vincent Chin to death in Detroit simply because they assumed he was Japanese and thus a threat to their jobs, would be hard to hold to account. Christopher managed to remain off the radar of law enforcement for months, and when he finally was caught, it would take two trials before a conviction stuck. Vincent Chin's killers were at first given probation and a fine, and the federal conviction they finally did receive was ultimately overturned on appeal.

It wasn't that people who robbed or killed or assaulted others weren't going to prison in this decade. The number of Americans serving time had in fact exploded. It was just that those who didn't do so were disproportionately wealthy or at least white. This seemed especially to be the case if they had harmed someone who was Black or Brown. Sometimes these perpetrators escaping justice were lay citizens like Rich, Christopher, Ebens, or Nitz. But they could also be members of law enforcement. Every one of the six cops who were accused in 1983 of brutally beating subway graffiti artist Michael Griffith to death (his injuries were so severe that he arrived at Bellevue Hospital hog-tied and without a pulse) was acquitted.[3]

And so, in the final days of December 1984, what fate might await the man who had gunned down Troy Canty, Barry Allen, James Ramseur, and Darrell Cabey—should he ever be caught—remained a serious question.

12

On the Lam

When Bernie Goetz finally made it back to his 14th Street apartment, somehow managing to get out of the Chambers Street station unseen and to hail a cab, he knew he needed to calm down. A hot shower helped a bit, but he still had to figure out what he should do next. It was only a matter of time, he suspected, before people would come for him. The only plan that seemed to make any sense was to flee New York City, as soon as possible.

Perhaps knowing that driving was less likely to alert law enforcement than buying a plane ticket, he decided to walk over to Olin's Rent-a-Car on University Place around 5:30 p.m. The clerk there, Michael King, noticed that the man standing in front of him was pacing back and forth "like a soldier."[1] He seemed both nervous and in a hurry, but when the man told him that he needed a car for a week—"something heavy with four-wheel-drive that could maneuver in the snow," King didn't question him. He just obliged.[2]

Bernie paid for the car with his American Express card, mumbled that he was late for a meeting, and headed north for Bennington, Vermont, as soon as the car, a blue AMC Eagle, was ready. After arriving, Bernie drove around aimlessly for a while before checking into a nondescript motel. His guard wasn't totally down, though. He gave the clerk an alias—Joseph Adams, the name of a man he had done work for in the past. Bernie wasn't sure why that name popped into his head. It wasn't like they really even knew each other.

Once in his room, Bernie decided it would be best to get rid of his gun, as painful as that prospect was. He disassembled it and drove to a heavily wooded area north of town "where he discarded the gun in the snow, along with the blue jacket that he [was] wearing when the incident took place."[3]

Not at all sure whether the authorities were looking for him, Bernie decided to stay on the move. The next day, he checked into the Follansbee Inn in North Sutton, New Hampshire, just off Interstate 89 and about twenty-five miles west of Concord, New Hampshire. Again, he signed in as Joseph Adams of 959 Morat Street, Red Hook, New Jersey. According to the owner of the inn, Goetz was "very nervous, acting kind of strange."[4] He paid $32.10 in cash for room no. 10, and set off to a store about four miles away where he could purchase a newspaper.[5]

Over the next week, Bernie would travel from hotel to hotel, monitoring local and national news to see what was happening back in New York. To his relief, and astonishment, it did not seem like anyone had a clue that he was the gunman.

Bernie did note, however, that the NYPD had created a Vigilante Task Force, and that an all-out manhunt was underway for the unknown suspect who had shot four people on a NYC subway car. He was surprised that what he had done was being described by papers as an act of vigilantism. But the more he thought about it, the more the description might have resonated. For a while now, Bernie had made it clear to anyone who knew him, anyone who had been paying attention, that he was done with being pushed around.

And yet, Goetz found himself growing increasingly uncertain of how to navigate the aftermath of the shootings. He didn't want to get caught, mostly because he really didn't want to explain himself to idiots who would not understand.

As the days wore on, Bernie grew more careless. He used his own name when he checked into the Mount Sunapee Motel in western New Hampshire on Christmas Eve. There, he even paid with one of his credit cards. When he later checked in at the Ramada Inn in Keene, New Hampshire, he also registered using his own name, but gave a home address in Orlando, Florida.[6] He was, however, careful never to spend too much time talking to any one person.

Despite his efforts, Bernie did make a real impression on at least one person he met—a man named Tom Stotler, the owner of a bookstore over in the White Mountains area of New Hampshire, about twenty-five miles north of Concord. When Bernie wandered into Stotler's establishment, he'd only planned to browse. He didn't have much money on him, the owner recalled. Still, the two struck up a conversation. The Hillside Bookstore had more than its share of conservative books on the shelves, reflecting the right-leaning opinions of its owner.[7]

Goetz, whom Stotler later described as a "scholarly looking man," stood out because "he was interested in books on science and electronics," and also because he mentioned that "he had been in five 'bad incidents' of mugging and harassment in New York."[8] The two men shared similar views on the extent to which cities were going to hell in a handbasket, the problems elitist liberals and urban officials were creating, and how ordinary, law-abiding citizens were being asked to tolerate too much. Stotler, a proud member of a group called Freedom Through Strength, agreed that people in the United States should simply be allowed to arm themselves.[9]

It seemed unlikely that Bernie's newfound friend would turn him in to the authorities, even if he had known his name. And besides, no one in New York seemed to have a clue that he was the subway shooter. Theories about the assailant's identity were in no short supply, and one detective opined there was a real "possibility that the gunman was a cop or a service man," given that his "weapon is believed to have been a .38 caliber revolver, the gun favored by law enforcement agents."[10] But the authorities had no real leads.

They had put out calls to thirteen states to be on the lookout for the mystery shooter, but the description they provided was so vague and nondescript that it was virtually useless. The sketch that accompanied it was no more valuable. The Vigilante Task Force had received numerous tips, but they too were dead ends.

Judging by the letters of support that began pouring into the offices of the *Daily News*, the *Post*, and even the mayor's office, it was clear that a large number of New Yorkers were actually rooting for the gunman to remain at large.

In response to the sketches police had distributed at every subway stop, one letter to the *Post* exclaimed, "Why are they trying to find this gunman so desperately? The police don't look for murderers and rapists this thoroughly, so why harass this gunman? The city should give the gunman a medal, thank him for his help and start fighting the crime that is destroying the city. Bravo for the vigilante—if there were more like you, the city would be a safer place to live in."[11] Fifteen hundred people had in fact used the tip line to express their support for the shooter's actions.[12] As of December 29, according to the *Daily News*, "only about 30 calls have been from people making legitimate attempts to help the police."[13]

One of these calls, however, had been promising. This caller, whose name was never revealed, had seen the sketch of the shooter and said it reminded them of a guy who had been mugged a few years ago—a man who had specifically told this caller that he would "get the n—s" if it ever happened again. The man had even applied for a gun permit in order to be prepared for another such instance. His name, the caller went on, was Bernhard Goetz.

This would prove to be a critical lead. The NYPD task force was able to pull Goetz's gun permit application, and the photograph on the application resembled the sketch. The police finally had a likely suspect.

The next day, the police went to Bernie's apartment. The doorman informed them that Mr. Goetz had gone on a trip, so they put a note on his door, slid one underneath it as well, and stuck another in his mailbox for good measure. Each missive made clear that Bernie should call them immediately upon his return.

Meanwhile, Goetz had decided that he wanted to try going back to his apartment. He had been on the run for nearly a week and knew he couldn't stay gone forever. It seemed possible that he might just get away with all that had happened back on the train, a thought that allowed him to start feeling a bit self-righteous about the whole situation. In those moments it struck Bernie as pathetic, even a bit "funny," that the four Black teens "thought they had him trapped, when in fact they were trapped." They should have known not to approach him when they had no way to "get out," given where they were located on that subway car.[14]

But Bernie was methodical, and he wasn't going home without taking precautions. He called his downstairs neighbor, Myra Friedman, to help chart out a safe return. They weren't particularly close; in fact, she had walked out of their tenants association meeting that time he'd made his racist remarks. But he couldn't think of anyone else. And besides, she was a good listener.

Myra Friedman, in fact, had a bit of a soft spot for Bernie Goetz. Yes, he was odd. And yes, she would try to avoid getting into long conversations with him by the elevator. But notwithstanding his ugly rant at the tenants meeting, she had seen a side of him that some of his detractors in the group had not.

Myra appreciated, for example, that Bernie had paid to have "an unsightly placard removed from the building canopy," with his own money and little fanfare. He had also forked over $300 for new garbage cans to keep the trash to a minimum. What's more, she felt Bernie was kind to the kids in the building, recalling a time she had seen him laughing while lifting a child into the air. Myra fully acknowledged, however, that he was "far less at ease with his adult neighbors."[15]

When Bernie first called her from New Hampshire on the afternoon of December 29, Myra had been taking a nap. To her utter surprise, the first thing he blurted out was "Listen, can you rent a car?" "Huh?" she responded. "Rent a car?" What was he talking about? But Bernie insisted that she hear him out. He hoped that she could meet him in Connecticut, at Exit 6, just off of Route 95 at the Howard Johnson's. Ideally, he went on, she would bring "a couple of Guardian Angels and a tape recorder."[16]

At the mention of the Guardian Angels, Myra felt a frisson of unease go through her. The unknown shooter, the guy who had been all over the news after that recent terrible incident on the subway, had been described, she recalled, as "tall, lanky, and blonde with a thin face and wire rimmed glasses."[17] Had they been talking about Bernie Goetz?

She exclaimed, "You? My God!"

"Yes," Bernie replied. Without pausing, he assured her that it wouldn't be hard to locate someone in the Guardian Angels. "I think they're picketing the mayor's mansion," he said.[18] Still, Myra demurred. This was crazy. She barely knew Bernie Goetz, and here he was asking her to abet a crime. But Myra was a professional writer, the author of a biography of Janis Joplin, and she sensed a story. So Myra kept him talking, and unbeknownst to Bernie, she also began recording the call.

Myra couldn't help but marvel at how her usually subdued and reclusive neighbor now seemed so unhinged, and by turns frightened—on the verge of tears—then outraged and cocky. For her part, she kept trying to persuade Bernie that the best thing he could do was turn himself in. Everyone understood why he'd done what he had, she assured him. Hell, even the cops supported him and didn't think the guys he shot "were innocent."[19]

Myra wasn't just cajoling him. She believed that the public was on his side, and that's how the newspapers made it seem. As one city resident put it in a letter to the editor of the *Post,* "I resent the four thugs being called victims. They are muggers, not victims. If they would've left that man alone, they would be home for the holidays instead of in hospital beds."[20]

This vote of confidence may have reassured Bernie. He had, after all, just run into a deputy sheriff who seemed to recognize him, but then didn't rat him out. In fact, the sheriff had actually said to Bernie that he "should get a medal."[21]

But Bernie was still dubious about surrendering. "Listen, Myra," he kept insisting, "if I don't, if I don't turn myself in, if I don't get caught, I can lead a normal life."[22] Myra persisted. There was no "chance in hell that you're going to do time, Bernhard," she said.[23]

By the end of the call, however, it was clear to Myra that Bernie not only had no plans of going to the police but also had decided to return to New York rather than have her meet him in Connecticut. He was tired of running, he told her. He just wanted to come home, get his mail, write some checks, and do "this and that," what he "normally would be doing." He also needed "a good shower" and clean clothes, and wanted "to straighten up [his] apartment a little bit." He would then leave the city again, he explained. Bernie really hated New York, and he wanted to move for good, but for the foreseeable future, his plan was to head back to New England "until this blows over."[24]

"Just forget this conversation ever took place," Bernie told Myra as he was about to hang up. He then went on to say cryptically that tomorrow he was going to ask her for an important favor so that "maybe, just maybe," he could "get away with [this]."[25]

After the phone call, Myra was in knots. She wanted to give Bernie the opportunity to do the right thing, but she also didn't want to be seen as his accomplice. Later in the day, she learned this was a very real possibility. A local cop with whom she was acquainted intimated that the police were closing in on a possible suspect. And she learned from the doorman that officers had stopped by Bernie's apartment. They'd left notes on his door and in his mailbox and asked that he contact them immediately.

Fearing that these notes might "shock" Bernie when he arrived, and undoubtedly worried that he might spiral in some unpredictable way, Myra slipped up to the ninth floor and pocketed the one on his door. Seeing its words, "Mr. Goetz—please contact the police ASAP," had left her very concerned, so the next morning she took the elevator down to his mailbox and disposed of the copy they had left there too.

Around noon the next day, a Sunday, Myra heard footsteps in Bernie's apartment. As promised, he had returned to the city. By 2:00 p.m., he was knocking on her door in quite a state. He had read the note the cops slipped under his door—the only one she hadn't known about. Myra began insisting once again that the best thing for Bernie to do now was to surrender. "I can't, I can't," he insisted. Why not? she pressed. Because he "could not endure the commotion," he said.[26]

After pacing around Myra's apartment in a frenzy, Bernie abruptly left. Not an hour later, he returned with a folded paper bag containing two guns. He wanted Myra to hold on to them. He made as though to stash them in her bedroom. No, she said emphatically, and instructed him to put the package in her front closet. And then he bolted.

Unsure what to do once Bernie had left, and having no idea where he was headed, Myra fretted, still holding out hope that he was going to the police station. Mostly, she just wanted the guns out of her apartment.

The clerks at Olin's Rent-a-Car were surprised to see Bernie back so soon—the guy had just returned his car earlier that day. "A sudden business deal had come up," Bernie explained, and he asked to rent another car that was also capable of handling snow and icy terrain. He looked better this time, they observed, shaven and dressed in a wool coat with a heavy sweater underneath. But he was still in a real hurry. Taking the keys to a gray Chevy Caprice, Bernie Goetz headed out once more, back to Keene, New Hampshire. It was December 30.[27]

The next morning, Myra received another phone call from Bernie. She again turned on the tape recorder. This time it sounded like he was truly falling apart, with his "anxious breathing" and constant stammering.[28] Mainly, she thought, "He sounded worn and fatigued."[29] What's more, it finally sounded like Bernie was ready to give up. "Probably the best course that I can do is, you know, give myself up to the police here in New Hampshire and just make a deal with the city," he told her.[30]

Myra was glad to hear it, but was now even more worried about the guns in her apartment. "Listen, there is no way that I can get back into your apartment to put that stuff back in?" she almost pleaded. "No," Bernie replied flatly. "First of all . . . because I have the only set of keys, and they're with me. And second, boy, that would really be bad for me, too."[31]

But Myra wasn't about to let the matter drop, even when he tried to reassure her that "the weapon that was used is not in this bag. . . . And there are no bullets in this bag. There's nothing loaded." "Bernie," she pushed, "a grand jury wouldn't believe me, that's all. . . . Could I drop them in the river?" "Oh! That's a good idea," he responded enthusiastically, but immediately began to doubt even this plan. "But here's the thing," he fretted. "Rivers . . . rivers, get dredged." But Bernie then had another idea: "You can take the Staten Island ferry, and just, you know, [dump them] at night."[32]

Myra would do none of those things. Instead, she would contact a well-connected lawyer friend of hers and give him the paper bag containing Bernie Goetz's nine-millimeter and .38 caliber revolvers. In turn, this lawyer would approach Manhattan assistant district attorney Susan Braver, who would interview Myra about her encounter with Goetz a few days later.

Meanwhile, in a small police station in Concord, New Hampshire, Bernie Goetz turned himself in.[33]

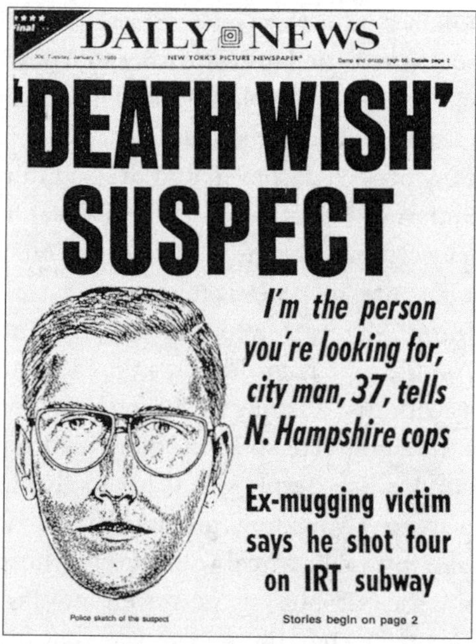

Final

DAILY NEWS

NEW YORK'S PICTURE NEWSPAPER®

'DEATH WISH' SUSPECT

I'm the person you're looking for, city man, 37, tells N. Hampshire cops

Ex-mugging victim says he shot four on IRT subway

Police sketch of the suspect

Stories begin on page 2

Daily News front page, January 1, 1985.
New York *Daily News* Archive via Getty Images

13

Explanations and Obfuscations

On the morning of New Year's Eve 1984, nine days after fleeing the blood-spattered subway car in New York City, Bernie Goetz, wearing a plaid shirt under a brownish leather jacket with faux fur at the collar, walked into the bland brick building that housed the Concord Police Department. He made his way to the front desk and told the watch commander that he was "the person that the police were looking for."[1]

Lieutenant Robert "Bob" Libby was slightly dubious. Nicknamed "the city in a coma," Concord was a town of thirty thousand. Some days were so slow that Libby would spend his entire shift doing administrative tasks like reviewing police reports and processing paperwork for the courts, or just chatting with whichever citizen happened to come by to register a complaint against an irritating neighbor or report a stray dog.[2]

Could the slight, nervous-looking guy standing in front of him actually be the vigilante that the NYPD had been looking for? He sure resembled the sketch that had been circulated, which was no compliment. As a *Time* magazine article memorably described this rendering, it "showed the face of the 'before' figure in comic book ads for bodybuilding devices, the pale visage of the scrawny, bespectacled fellow at the beach who gets sand kicked in his face by the burly bully."[3]

On the off chance that this guy was actually the shooter, Lieutenant Libby decided that he should be formally questioned by his colleague Officer Warren Foote, and right away. Meanwhile, Libby would confer with his chief, David Walchuck, and they would contact the NYPD.

Foote wanted to speak with Bernie in the station's library, perhaps hoping that the quiet, nonthreatening setting might relax him. But that space was being used, so Foote instead took him to a nondescript, empty, carpeted room on the second floor. According to Foote's report, as soon as he was seated, Goetz again blurted out that "he was the one that did the shooting of the four male subjects in the subway in New York City sometime before Christmas."[4] At this point, Foote stopped him to ask if he wanted an attorney present. "No," Bernie said, nor did he need his rights read to him. Foote, however, insisted that Bernie sign the Miranda warning sheet before they went any further.[5]

As Officer Foote was overseeing the signing of this paper, Lieutenant Libby was in his office, trying to get in touch with the right contact at the NYPD. After being put on hold several times, he finally reached Inspector Roark, the head of the Vigilante Task Force. After Libby explained the situation, Roark asked him to keep the guy there. He would send up some detectives to take the suspect's statement.

Libby hung up, admittedly a bit put off by the call. To make sure Officer Foote was fully informed while also questioning Goetz, Libby had asked Roark to share as much intel on the suspect as possible. After all, the man might just decide later to clam up, so they would need to strike while the iron was hot. But no matter how hard Libby pressed, Roark wouldn't divulge much of anything.

To Libby, it almost seemed as if Roark was a fan of Goetz. The only information he had shared on this possible shooter was that he "was a New York businessman, a basically good guy, sort of an electronics wizard." As Libby remembered thinking wryly, "They must do things differently in the big city. It didn't sound to me like they were taking the whole thing very seriously down there. This guy was wanted for attempted murder and he's telling me what a nice guy he is."[6]

Foote did the best he could, considering what little information he had to work with. Over the course of this interview, the suspect seemed relatively relaxed and spoke forthrightly, and Foote took careful notes. They stopped at one point when Bernie, who had earlier said he wasn't hungry, "had the police send out for hamburger, French fries, and a Coke." Otherwise, they talked uninterrupted for two solid hours.[7]

On the day in question, Bernie said that he had been on his way to see some people he knew. His plan was to exit the subway at Chambers Street, but, once on the train, he was approached by a guy who "asked him how he was doing."[8]

Was this greeting threatening? Foote asked him.

No, not at all, Bernie replied. He thought it was funny.[9]

Then "he asked me for five dollars," Bernie continued. Once again, according to Foote's report, "Mr. Goetz stated this in itself was not a threat."[10] Bernie did, however, see "the gentleman's face and noted he was smiling and his eyes were shining." He also said that the guy seemed to have a bulge in his pocket.[11] Did he take that as a potential threat? Officer Foote asked. No, Bernie said, he "did not feel threatened," because he knew the guy "didn't have a weapon."[12]

Although Bernie did not feel on the verge of being robbed, he told Foote that "he already knew what he was going to do." He would lay down "a pattern of gunfire" that would quickly and efficiently take out the teen who had asked him for money, as well as his friends.[13] As Foote's report summarized Bernie's own detailed recounting of the incident:

> He fired at the first subject who was wearing a fur-type jacket at centerbody, he then fired at the second subject in the same fashion, as he had planned to do. He then turned to his right, then shooting the 3rd subject and then the 4th subject. He stated that after firing the four shots he went to check the first two subjects who were now lying on the floor of the subway car. After checking them to see if they were taken care of, he went to the second two subjects, one being on the floor. The other, the 4th being shot, being half sitting half lying on a bench where he was originally. Mr. Goetz stated then that he saw no blood on the subject. At that time, he told the subject, "You don't look too bad here's another," and he shot the 4th subject a second time. Mr. Goetz stated that news media and newspapers stated he fired only four shots. He stated they were wrong he fired five shots.[14]

In his first public account of the shooting, Bernie was matter-of-fact and expressed no guilt. The only time he voiced concern was in reference to a female passenger he was worried had been caught in the crossfire.[15]

Bernie then went on to chronicle the details of his escape. He laid out exactly how he had wended his way through the dark subway tunnel and managed to get back to his apartment within an hour of the shooting.

In the midst of his narration, another Concord policeman, Detective Christopher Domian, interrupted to let Foote know that three detectives and a district attorney were on their way from New York City "to talk to the subject about the incident."[16] Given the extraordinary things that the guy seated before him had just confessed to, Officer Foote decided that it would be a good idea to interview him again, this time on tape. Over the next two hours, while they waited for the team from NYC, Detective Domian questioned Goetz about the shootings. Goetz repeated everything he had already told Foote, and offered even more details.

Meanwhile, it had not been easy for the DA and detectives from NYC to get to Concord. It was New Year's Eve, and thus very chaotic in the city. The drive took about five hours even on a good day, but getting paperwork sorted and waiting in traffic meant that the quartet didn't arrive at the Concord Police Department headquarters until 7:45 p.m.[17]

In charge of the NYPD's investigation was Detective Michael Clark of the Manhattan South Task Force and Deputy Inspector McGowan from headquarters. Representing the New York City Transit Police Department was Detective Dan Hattendorf, and the District Attorney's Office had sent Assistant DA Susan Braver.

By the time a Concord officer finally started the video recorder that would capture Bernie Goetz's official interrogation by this new team, it was 9:40 p.m. In the frame, sitting at the head of a small conference table with his back against the wall, was Goetz, a now most disheveled man, rocking back and forth, hunched over, with his arms wrapped around his body, as if, by drawing further into himself, he might just disappear.[18] He refused to look at the detectives that sat on either side of him. He also studiously ignored Susan Braver, who alternated between standing and sitting at the table's other end.

Bernie insisted with this group as well that he did not want a lawyer present, even after ADA Braver informed him that one of his neigh-

Bernhard Goetz interview with Assistant DA Susan Braver and detectives from the NYPD and New York Transit Authority.
From *The Confessions of Bernhard Goetz* (MPI Home Video, 1987). Permission from the estate of Darrell Moore.

bors, a man named Ralph Naden, had offered his legal services. Naden knew Bernie from the tenants association.[19] No, Bernie repeated. First, he "wasn't going to hide behind this thing," and second, he stammered, "I don't want any hot shit, hot attorney because what, the way how the system works is the attorneys tell you 'don't say this, don't say that' because this jeopardizes you."[20] And besides, he continued, "I can have a far better attorney than Ralph for free and you know it. There are attorneys who would probably pay me money to represent me, because this, this case has notoriety."[21]

While he was rather forthcoming, this did not mean Bernie Goetz would be an easy interview. He had one main point that he wanted to get across, and it wasn't about the shootings. He wanted the investigators to know just how much he hated New York City because of the disaster that it recently had become.

In fact, Bernie hated the city so much that he could barely tolerate the detectives who had just arrived from there. As he put it bluntly, "I just don't trust [unintelligible] in New York City," and, in fact, it bothered him even to "hear a New Yorker speak." "I don't want to be rude," Bernie went on, "but I just don't want to speak to you."[22]

Bernie would eventually get over this prejudice when it came to the male detectives questioning him, but not so much when it came to ADA Susan Braver. His disdain for her, the only woman in the room, was particularly marked. It was as if Bernie saw her as the embodiment of every useless, careerist politician, and suspected that she was more interested in the possibility of using his case to break the glass ceiling she imagined was holding her back, than hearing why he had done what he did. As he sneered at her at one point, "There are so many rules that have been broken. I mean, it's wonderful. It's going to be great for your career, isn't it, miss?"[23]

He would return time and again to his rant against the city and everyone who ran it. As Goetz put it, "the government of New York City is a disgrace. The services are disgraceful . . . the subway system itself is a disaster. The school system is a disaster. The crime system is a disaster."[24] He maintained that he wasn't "hiding behind this thing," by which he meant the shootings. And he had no intention of making any excuses for what he did. But Bernie would rail against them asking him about his motivations in an "intellectual way."[25] Continuing, he said hotly, "Do you know what needs to be resolved here? What needs to be resolved is just a decent level of services." He asked the detectives almost reproachfully,

"Do you know, up here [in New Hampshire], how, how, how nice the people are, how nice the children are?"[26]

It would take some time, but Detective Clark and the others would eventually get Bernie to discuss the matter at hand—did he shoot four teens on the 2 train? And if so, why? While Goetz remained highly erratic throughout the interview, he was very forthcoming with his confessions, which likely surprised both the detectives and the ADA.

Bernie, for example, readily admitted to having procured guns illegally. "I tried to play it by all your rules and say why I needed, I needed the gun," he explained. He noted that he had "tried playing all the games with switching around the money," meaning he had lied on the permit application about the amount of business-related funds he carried on his person to justify carrying a legal gun on the streets of New York.[27] But even this had not worked, he said bitterly. The naïve do-gooders had failed him.

With every confession, Bernie would take the opportunity to rail against "the system" and to condemn any "intellectualizing" of the situation, a pointed jab at the liberals he expected to judge him. But as quick as he was to anger, he would also suddenly seem to feel deeply sorry for himself, saying, "You guys are going to drag me through the dirt and that's okay."[28] Even those moments would, however, be followed up by recrimination.

Still, the admissions kept coming. Over the course of the hours-long interrogation, Bernie Goetz would go so far as to say, "It's disgusting and I was a monster."[29] He acknowledged that what he had done "was vicious."[30] Perhaps most damningly, he called the shooting "attempted cold blooded murder" and stressed that he wasn't denying that, nor did he plan to fight any attempt to hold him responsible.[31] He not only confessed to shooting the teenagers, but would repeat that he hadn't shot them because he had felt threatened. He had already told much of this to Officer Foote, but this interview made it even clearer that his four victims "were just kids kidding around," and that while he could "claim" that this had bothered him, it had not. "Robbery has nothing to do with it," he stated emphatically.[32]

It must have been music to this group's ears to hear Bernie characterize himself as a "monster" and admit to owning illegal guns and attempting "cold-blooded murder." To Braver's and the detectives' astonishment, he would eventually say even more damning things on videotape. As they looked on impassively, Bernie said, coldly and without hesitation:

> If I had more bullets, I would have shot 'em all again and again. My problem was I ran out of bullets. And I was gonna, I was gonna gouge one of the guy's eyes out with my keys afterwards. You, you, you, you can't understand this. I know you can't understand this. That's fine. The reas—, the only reason I didn't do it, was because he had changed his look. . . . My intent was to kill.[33]

As the interview wore on, Bernie Goetz offered additional important details about the shootings that the officials present would not have known otherwise. As he had told Officer Foote hours earlier, he had decided to shoot the teens the very instant Troy Canty asked him for five dollars. In that moment, he had also planned to take out the other boys too. In chilling detail, he went on to explain his thought process as he began firing, including why he had chosen to use specific ammunition:

> You have to have progressively higher loadings for various technical reasons. . . . The [first] bullet comes out at a lower velocity. The next three come out with really higher velocity, so no matter what happens, using progress, you could stop anything. . . . Speed is [also] everything. . . . You just think of speed and the count. . . . It's unimportant to look at what you're firing at. . . . You [just] aim for the center of the mass. You run. You keep moving. All you have to do is to be faster than they are.[34]

Bernie Goetz clearly took pride in the meticulousness with which he had felled the teens. As he put it to his interrogators, "You can accuse me of a lot, of a lot of things, but don't accuse me of being careless."[35] But these detectives continued to push. No matter how detailed and technical Bernie's explanations, they still seemed mystified as to what exactly caused him to unleash such violence.

As if casting about for a rationale, they asked Bernie if he had begun carrying a gun after he was mugged. No, he insisted. The earlier mugging was why he wanted the gun permit but, Bernie stated firmly, that "incident has nothing to do with this."[36] Everything had kicked off because of the way that the guy had approached him about the money. The actual words he had said "meant bullshit." Bernie pulled the gun because of the "smile on [the guy's] face. . . . He was enjoying this." Bernie told the group without hesitating, "And it was at that point I decided I was going to kill 'em all, murder 'em all, do anything."[37]

"Did you feel trapped?" Detective Clark pressed, as if finding it hard to believe that Goetz had intended to admit to cold-blooded attempted murder. "They were going to beat the fucking shit out of me, okay!" Goetz yelled. His frustration was clear: It wasn't about a robbery, he reiterated. "That is all bullshit."[38]

Minutes later, Clark seemed to be trying to throw Goetz another lifeline, and again, he refused to grab it. "I'm trying to see what you were feeling at the time," Clark said. "I was just whistling Dixie, okay?" Bernie responded sarcastically.[39] But then he got more serious, chillingly admitting that he in fact "didn't know they were carrying screwdrivers," and that really had nothing to do with it either. It was enough that the boys were there and that he felt "surrounded."[40] That is why he "laid down the pattern of fire . . . [and] attempted to take them all out. . . . If I had more [bullets], I would have used more."[41]

Indeed, what Bernie wanted to do, he stressed in this interrogation, mincing no words, was "to kill those guys, I wanted to maim those guys, I wanted to make them suffer in every way I could."[42]

But the NYC detectives and ADA interrogating Bernie still weren't fully satisfied. Despite the many details Bernie had offered about his encounter with the teens on the train, his various diatribes about the crisis that had befallen the city had also, time and again, sidetracked them. And, of course, there remained the possibility that he wasn't the shooter at all and was simply seeking attention. So, they kept asking for a more precise chronicle of how the shooting had unfolded, to verify that he was indeed the gunman. Goetz eventually obliged with these even more disquieting specifics.

In reference to Darrell Cabey, Bernie explained that one of the boys pretended that he wasn't with the others to avoid being shot, but Bernie wasn't having it. He shot at him, and "it was funny," but he couldn't be sure the bullet had actually hit him. Bernie said, "I wanted to know if I missed," so he "went to him a second time and looked at him . . . [to see] if I shot him." Still unsure, Bernie recounted, "I said, 'You seem to be doing all right, here's another'" as Darrell jerked his arm up in a failed attempt to protect himself.[43]

Satisfied that Darrell was finally incapacitated, Bernie went to make sure he had indeed taken down the other teenagers. He described going up to the "first guy again, the guy who did the talking, and I was just aware of the keys in my left pocket and I came up to him and I saw his eyes twitching and I saw the fear in his eyes," so Bernie realized it was unnecessary to continue the attack. "You know," he said to the detectives, "things started dissipating."[44]

Bernie still never expressed remorse about the shootings, except, as he had also mentioned to his Concord interrogators, for the moment when he thought he might have shot a woman on the train. "I saw a woman on the left who was lying face down. She was very still. . . . I had forgotten about the count at that point. I thought she, she shouldn't have been hit by shrapnel but she was, or a shot, I had fired several shots there, I didn't know what it was. . . . What can you say to a person, if you've shot an innocent person?"[45]

Bernie had also noticed another woman to his right, who was "just staring blankly ahead." He asked her too, "Are you okay, miss?" But she said nothing. "I asked her again, 'Miss, are you okay?' And she said, 'I'm okay, but I'm not sure about these two here,'" referring to the boys on the floor with bullet wounds. Bernie said he'd told her, "Don't worry about them, they're assholes."[46]

Interestingly, before the interview ended, Bernie also admitted to offenses prior to the December 22 shootings, including that he had "used a gun previously" to scare off people he thought might be after him—other thugs he thought "deserved to die."[47] He also confessed that he'd actually sold guns to other people in New York, guns he had gotten "at cost" whenever he was in Florida.[48]

As erratic as his retelling of events had been, Bernie Goetz remained both arrogant and shrewd. He was, for example, not going to let this interview end without trying to make a deal with the authorities. He promised to turn himself in to police in New York rather than forcing them to extradite him from New Hampshire, but only if the detectives would allow him to drive himself back to the city, go to his apartment, and get his affairs in order. "I have a lot of mail. I have to pay some bills. . . . I just need a few hours in my apartment to straight, to straighten things up. I'll open it up if, for you, I have the keys. I'll show you around."[49]

He went on, "I'm not gonna abuse your trust. I'm not gonna jump out of the window."[50] He was an open book, Bernie tried to assure the detectives. "Do anything you want and you're going to find plenty of dirt. You're going to find, uh, I have marijuana in my apartment,"[51] he admitted. This latter admission was particularly notable for 1985, given that countless people from parts of NYC like the South Bronx were doing major stretches of time in New York State's prison system for marijuana possession. Braver and the detectives, however, seemed unperturbed by this detail, and were more interested in figuring out whether Bernie was actually going to come back to the city willingly or whether they were going to have to file extradition papers.

Stunningly, Bernie continued his attempts to negotiate, even asking the detectives to keep his name out of the media. "Is it possible that my name and address not be released too publicly?"[52] They balked at this request, making it clear that he had been involved in "conduct in New York which would constitute a crime" and that he would, therefore, have to answer those charges in open court.

Bernie then switched gears, suggesting they might want "a couple of days" to "digest" the information he'd just shared, and that he would "voluntarily come back in two days." Ultimately, he decided not to return to NYC that night to be arraigned, claiming "he just didn't want to go back on New Year's Eve."[53]

Since he was unwilling to return to NYC at that very moment, Bernie was officially arrested by New Hampshire police at 1:30 a.m. He was taken to the two-story, sixty-eight-cell Merrimack County jail. By all accounts, his night there was pleasant. He was under twenty-four-hour watch in one of the first-floor cells, segregated from the rest of the prisoners, and was seen "chatting amiably with his guards." At one point, he enjoyed a meal of pot roast, potatoes with gravy, and a vegetable, although, according to a jail spokesman, "He passed up chocolate cake for dessert." While in jail, Bernie received two or three calls from his siblings but only spoke to a lawyer named Jerome Borstein, a friend of his sister's in Tampa, Florida.[54]

The next morning, Bernie was put in a bulletproof vest and taken to the two-story courthouse next door where he was arraigned by Judge Michael F. Sullivan. The courtroom was small and filled with reporters and police officers, with many more waiting outside the building for a glimpse of him.

New Hampshire Assistant Attorney General Andrew Isaac requested and received a bail of $500,000, arguing forcefully that Bernie Goetz "had acted not in self-defense but with premeditation."[55] According to court papers, Bernie had carried out those shootings with "intent to kill" and thus, in that DA's view, any argument for self-defense simply "wouldn't stand up."[56] After being arraigned, he was quietly taken back to the local jail to await transport to NYC the next morning. After all of his attempts to negotiate, Goetz had decided not to fight extradition.[57]

Meanwhile, Susan Braver had been trying to get everything in order so that Bernie might be arraigned as soon as everyone arrived back in New York. She had police search his apartment to ensure they weren't missing any crucial evidence they would need to present this case to a grand jury, as well as to canvas for more witnesses. Braver would herself conduct an extensive interview with his downstairs neighbor Myra Friedman. The DA's office wanted to fill in the blanks regarding all Bernie had told Myra in the week leading up to his surrender and to take a closer look at the guns he had given her.[58]

The confessions Bernie had made late into the night on New Year's Eve—arguably, the most important evidence Braver had procured—were not going to be made available to anyone but the DAs. The New Hampshire judge who arraigned Bernie Goetz had ordered the statements he had given at the Concord police station to be sealed. With the public utterly unaware of all that Goetz had just admitted to, the Manhattan DA's office would soon experience no small measure of backlash for bringing him in. Not a few New Yorkers had already decided that Bernie Goetz shouldn't be prosecuted.

14

Consequences and Costs

AT 8:15 THE NEXT MORNING, January 3, thirteen days after the shooting, police officers woke Bernie Goetz in his cell in the Merrimack jail. Within ten minutes, he was whisked back to the Concord Police Department to await the return of Braver and the NYPD as well as Transit Authority detectives.[1] Upon their arrival, Bernie was ushered into an unmarked blue Plymouth alongside a detective and two other officers. Flanked by a squadron of police cars, he would begin what was ultimately a rather dangerous high-speed ride to the city.

News of Bernie's imminent arrival in New York had been leaked to the press, and scores of reporters had gone to Concord ready to chase the police fleet all the way from New Hampshire to downtown Manhattan, hoping to catch a glimpse of the infamous "Death Wish Vigilante." As one NYPD detective, Jim Levison, remembered, the number of journalists following Bernie Goetz was stunning—a literal "caravan of press cars" clamoring to capture a shot of Bernie entering or exiting the police station and later at the courthouse.[2]

When Bernie finally pulled up outside the rear entrance of Manhattan police headquarters at 1:49 p.m., barricades lined the streets and sharpshooters had been stationed on area rooftops in anticipation of the ensuing spectacle. Though all pedestrian and vehicular traffic had been blocked from the area, the press formed a substantial crowd—at least sixty reporters and photographers surrounded the Plymouth and looked on as Goetz was taken inside the station to be "photographed, fingerprinted, and searched."[3] When he reemerged, they noted his hands were cuffed in front, and that Bernie was "expressionless and silent" before he was ferried over to the Criminal Courts Building for the arraignment.[4]

ADA Susan Braver had feared that this proceeding would be a circus, and her fears were justified. One could barely get close to the courthouse due to the throngs of police trying to maintain order as civilians and reporters from all over the country jostled to get a glimpse of the accused. Still in his now signature leather jacket and plaid shirt, Bernie was accompanied by his new court-appointed attorney, a former judge named Frank Brenner. Bernie stood in the jam-packed courtroom with "hunched narrow shoulders" and "his chin tucked resolutely into his chest" as he waited for the hearing to begin.[5]

The arraignment itself, however, was over rather quickly. ADA Braver presented the state's case as Bernie looked on with a blank expression. But, despite his earlier vows in Concord that he would "plead no contest," Bernie pled not guilty.

Braver requested Bernie's bail be set at $50,000, while Brenner argued that it should be even lower, as his client was unlikely to flee. Presiding judge Leslie Snyder made it clear she found both propositions absurd, given the seriousness of the charges Bernie faced. In her acerbic response to Brenner, she pointed out, "Mr. Goetz did flee the jurisdiction." She then went on to admonish Braver for the "very low bail request," saying, "If Western civilization has taught us anything, it is that we cannot tolerate individuals taking law and justice into their own hands, period."[6]

Andrew Isaac, the assistant attorney general who had originally charged Bernie Goetz in New Hampshire, was also stunned by the low bail request. As he put it, he had seen nothing "that would excuse [Goetz's] use of deadly force."[7] The "flabbergasted" Concord police chief could not believe the bail amount, either. As he said, "You had four counts of attempted murder. We regard attempted murder as a serious offense in this state."[8]

But Judge Snyder was not going to ask for a higher bail than the ADA herself. The matter was settled, making it entirely possible that Bernie could go home. He would only have to cobble together $5,000 to secure a bail bond.[9] For his part, Braver's boss, the head district attorney for Manhattan, Robert Morgenthau, was fine with how the arraignment had played out. Sure, the bail wasn't particularly high, he later acknowledged, but it "was enough to keep him." Morgenthau "didn't want to make a martyr out of the guy," and a high bail would make that a real possibility.[10]

Despite this, it was Bernie, actually, who managed to make himself into something of a martyr by declining to post bail. Following the arraignment, he was remanded into custody and taken to the same notorious New York City jail where his alleged mugger, sixteen-year-old Fred Clark, had landed back in 1981—Rikers Island.[11] When offers began pouring in to post bail on Bernie's behalf, including from a man who showed up with a cashier's check for the full amount, Bernie rebuffed them all.[12]

Unlike Clark, Bernie would not be sent to general population at Rikers. He was taken to the prison hospital, otherwise known as the "celebrity wing," where high-profile prisoners might find some measure of protection. He had not requested protective custody, but it was nevertheless granted to him, with the understanding that at least some New Yorkers—ones far more likely than he to have been policed in NYC, and thus now incarcerated at Rikers—might feel that he had intentionally targeted Troy, Barry, James, and Darrell and exact some sort of retribution.

Bernie, however, barely seemed to register what was happening to him as he was escorted off to this facility. Reporters who attempted to get a statement following the arraignment were disappointed, finding him disoriented and mumbling to himself in ways that no one could make out. That did not stop the press, nor local citizens, from voicing strong opinions regarding what had just unfolded. The *New York Post* had managed to track down Fred Clark, who made it clear that he was largely unsurprised that Goetz had landed in jail, noting that Goetz was clearly "a nervous guy." Still, Clark insisted, that was no excuse for gunning anyone down. It wasn't right, Clark told reporters, to just go "start shooting every Black teen that comes up to you."[13]

Bernhard Goetz leaves court following his arraignment.
Getty Images/Bettman

15

Fallout

THAT BERNIE GOETZ WAS, at least for now, locked up in the hospital wing of Rikers Island likely registered less with the teens he had shot than one might have imagined. At that moment, they had far more important things to contend with.

As James Ramseur's cousins, Chris Sandifer and Michael Lane, explained after having spent time in his tenth-floor room at Bellevue, "He's on a respirator. He's got all these tubes coming out of him. . . . He don't look like James to me. He looks bad." And for what? They wondered. "James was sitting. He wasn't going to rob a man if he was sitting. James never hurt anybody. . . . He did petty larcenies. And nobody ever wanted to hurt James. He wanted to get a job as an emcee. He could make all the girls laugh."[1]

James was indeed struggling. When he had first arrived at Bellevue, it was clear to the ER doctors that the bullet that had torn through his left arm and chest had also ripped into the wall of his stomach and lacerated James's spleen as well as his diaphragm.[2] It would prove impossible to save his spleen or remove the bullet. His physician, the chief surgery resident at Bellevue, Dr. Harry Adler, noted that the bullet had "lodged in the area of his left adrenal gland."[3] Surgeons were able to repair some of the other most badly damaged abdominal tissues and eventually stabilize him.

After surgery, however, James's left lung collapsed and he developed a fever. At first, suctioning out this lung with a bronchoscopy seemed to do the trick—so much so that James discharged himself, against the advice of his doctors. In truth, James wanted to get out of the hospital because he was terrified. He had learned there were now several warrants out for his arrest, and lying in the hospital bed made him feel like a sitting duck for any cop who wanted to come by and slap on the cuffs. The hospital staff had not even been able to prevent detectives from questioning him on the very day he had been shot.

Until the gunman had been located and locked up, James had also been deathly afraid of his assailant coming by to finish the job. Indeed, he had only agreed to talk to a newspaperman because, as he put it, "they have captured the guy."[4]

But James was not in fact well enough to be out of the hospital. Two days later, on the same day that Goetz was being arraigned downtown, James had to be readmitted to Bellevue for another surgery. His small bowel had become obstructed, which posed an entirely new and potentially life-threatening set of complications.[5]

Still, James resisted staying put. On January 13, he discharged himself once again and just five days after that became so ill that he was once more forced to seek medical attention. This time he headed to the ER in the Bronx, where he thought he might be safer. By the time he was admitted there James had developed a serious infection on the left side of his lung cavity.[6] He would remain hospitalized for nine more days.[7]

Bernie Goetz's other victim at Bellevue, Barry Allen, had also endured a great deal since being rushed in by paramedics on December 22. When he first tended to Barry, Dr. Adler immediately noted just how much this slight teen—barely five foot five and, according to his chart, weighing only 110 pounds—was struggling to breathe. Goetz's bullet had hit Barry in his back as he was trying to flee, between his spine and left shoulder blade, and it was apparent to Dr. Adler that blood and pleural fluid had begun to flood his chest cavity. When an X-ray confirmed that Barry's lungs were in extremis, Adler rushed to insert a tube that would drain them, avoiding potentially fatal respiratory arrest.[8]

Thanks to this intervention, Barry not only survived, but he was able to go home just before New Year's Eve, albeit frail and even thinner.[9] But for Barry, some of the worst repercussions from the shootings would be emotional. He found himself particularly haunted by the fact that Goetz had seemed to target his friends. No matter how many times he replayed the day in his head, he couldn't make sense of this. As he would later explain:

I don't know how [he] could have felt threatened. . . . He could have just brandished the gun like, "Boy, you don't want this, get the fuck away." You know I'm saying? I didn't do nothing to this man. . . . Darrell Cabey who's paralyzed, or James Ramseur ain't say nothing to that man.

We was out to rob something—not somebody—something. Why would you try to rob somebody on the train full of people and in broad daylight? If Troy's intentions was to rob this man, bamboozle him, anything, I would have been the first to know. Like we all would've knew what was going down. Troy never gave me a wink, he ain't nod his head, none of that shit.

We was going rob video machines, we needed coins to put in the video machines, that's it. So if he said he asked that man for five dollars, that is what he did. . . . [Instead he] gave us five hot ones. Hot rocks.[10]

Troy Canty had also been shot at close range, right in the chest, and his recovery would also prove challenging. When he arrived at St. Vincent's, Troy was bleeding into his chest cavity, which required immediate surgery. His lung was collapsing, and in order to reexpand it, this fluid had to be drained. Dr. Peter Adams, the on-call physician at St. Vincent's, saw quite clearly on the X-ray just how much damage Goetz's bullet had done. It had entered toward the middle of Troy's chest, then had torn across from right to left through the lung, before finally lodging in his back.[11] Dr. Adams had been able to remove the bullet, but recovery was nevertheless slow, given the chest tubes that had to remain in place to continue suctioning the blood and ensuring no air was leaking from the left lung.[12]

Much like James at Bellevue, Troy felt uneasy being in the hospital. Security was simply too lax. On one occasion, the *Post* had managed to send a reporter "unchallenged into his hospital room" to badger him with questions. The paper detailed how "[the] reporter was referred to an unattended security office, then given Canty's room number, and allowed to take the elevator to his ward. There were no signs of security guards either in the lobby or on Canty's floor." Troy had tried calling for help, even telling a passing doctor, "No one is supposed to bother me."[13] What's more, the hospital staff had also allowed police to question Troy within hours after his surgery and while he was still groggy from the effects of powerful anesthetics.

In fact, none of the boys felt they were being protected as they fought desperately to recuperate. After Barry Allen had received that anonymous call threatening to "finish the job" Goetz had started, the *Post* reported that Bellevue had "beefed up security" and that security over at St. Vincent's was also "said to be tight."[14] Notably, however, this had not stopped its own journalist from getting in.

And yet, being in the hospital had, at least for a time, prevented the boys from facing the many bench warrants Judges Marrus and Katz had suddenly decided to issue. At eight o'clock on the morning when Troy was finally deemed well enough to go home, he was immediately arrested on one of these warrants for the earlier charge of jimmying open a video game machine. He was brought to the courtroom of Judge Edward McLaughlin and sentenced to jail time. The judge, however, then granted Troy parole because with Goetz now caught, the DA's office suspected they would need him in the case they were trying to build against this shooter.[15]

When James was finally stable enough to go home, this time with a doctor's approval, he too was arrested and subsequently sentenced to ninety days in jail for stealing $41 worth of coffee from a Bronx supermarket. He was also scheduled for another court date to answer to charges that he stole "26 packages of Dristan cold tablets from the drugstore."[16] James had boosted bulk coffee and cold medication to resell to people in his neighborhood at a discount. It was a win-win: They got these items for less than they would have in the store, and James got money from each sale.

Darrell Cabey, however, was not at risk of arrest. His condition was so dire that the DA's office had dropped all charges pending against him.

When Goetz was being arraigned on January 3, Darrell was still in the hospital, paralyzed and relying on machines to help keep his chest clear of fluid. Shirley Cabey had watched the coverage of Bernie Goetz's arraignment in anger and despair. Why was this man getting attention worthy of a celebrity? Why was no one speaking about her son's condition? Sure, Shirley had received some opportunistic media requests—a telegram on January 4 from a Chicago-area producer who was interested in purchasing the rights to the boys' story for a possible TV movie, and a telegram on January 7 from a Los Angeles producer who wanted to speak about her son for a nationally televised show called *America Talks Back*.[17] But nothing about these asks suggested to Shirley that Darrell would get a fair shake.

Besides, Shirley was far too busy and emotionally overwhelmed to become the lone spokeswoman for her son. She too needed support. Thankfully, her friends had started a telephone prayer network for her and Darrell, which kept "her phone ringing through most of the day and night."[18] That, at least, helped keep her going. But Shirley was breaking inside. How was she supposed to keep her job, care for her other kids, maintain her home, and somehow still be with Darrell at the hospital down in Manhattan?

The truth was, Shirley Cabey barely had time to dwell even on those logistics. The previous two weeks of her life had constituted a living nightmare, starting with the moment Darrell had finally asked the question that had been flickering so fearfully in his eyes. "Am I going to be alright, Mama?"[19]

No mother would have been able to answer that question without wondering whether she in fact had the strength to do what the doctors had told Shirley she must—make clear to her son just how much damage that bullet had done. Yes, he would be all right, she would need to explain. And, yes, she would be there for him every step of the way. But, she would have to venture, things were going to be very difficult. Darrell was going to need to be strong. And then, with every word likely a razor blade on her tongue, Shirley would have had to forge ahead with the real crux of the matter: Darrell was never going to recover the feeling in his lower body. He was now permanently paralyzed. He would never walk again.

Hearing his mother's quiet voice deliver this news devastated Darrell. He became increasingly withdrawn, soon barely speaking to anyone and no longer acknowledging nurses' requests that he offer an arm for a blood draw or his siblings' questions about how he was doing. His doctors did not shield Shirley from their growing concern.

Darrell's family tried to give him some hope, and to cheer him up. As one reporter explained, his mother had "gone to the hospital every day except Christmas and New Year's Day, when, she said, she gave other relatives a chance to visit Darrell."[20] They too would spend hours trying to help Darrell process what had happened to him, but he remained despondent.

It just didn't make any sense, Darrell would say over and over again. As he told his mother, he had just been "sitting on the other side [of the subway car from Goetz] and did not ask the man for five dollars." As

Shirley, in turn, told reporters, "he said he did not say anything to the man." Despite her attempts to talk it out, to help him get his head around what had happened, Shirley's son was really struggling to come to terms with the altered life he would now lead. In some ways, revisiting it all just made things worse. "He gets angry when he talks about it," Shirley said. It made her mad, too. Goetz had caused irreparable damage when, as she put it bitterly, he "could have done several other things except shoot him."[21]

Even more difficult for Shirley and Darrell was seeing that the public viewed this tragedy as somehow deserved. "It has been so upsetting," Shirley told the *Daily News* in January 1985. "It's hard for me to know how people feel, knowing this man has hurt my boy. He is paralyzed now, and just laying there. . . . If only we could snap our fingers and turn the clock back."[22]

But she could not undo the past, and neither could Darrell, who had taken to staring off blankly as the sound of tubes sucking and machines whirring filled the air around him, day in and day out.

Doctors were soon not only concerned about Darrell's emotional state but also worried about his ability to breathe, even with the help of tubes. Goetz's hollow point bullet had not made a clean exit but left behind massive damage as it traveled through Darrell's body, transecting his spinal cord and decimating the tissue in both his lungs.[23]

This combination—severely damaged lungs along with the spinal shock that patients experience when their spinal cord is severed—had from the start been life-threatening. But spinal cord trauma also meant Darrell's ability to maintain blood pressure and to conduct normal bodily functions, like breathing and coughing out the secretions that accumulated in his lungs, were now severely compromised. Each passing day brought the very real risk that he would contract pneumonia.[24] As important, Darrell was far too weak to fight off such a serious infection. Every time he ran a fever the doctors and his mother alike looked on apprehensively, knowing that his condition could get much more precarious.[25]

On January 8, their worst fears came to pass. A code blue blared loudly in the hallway outside of Darrell's room and, as Shirley looked on helplessly, a throng of doctors and nurses rushed to her son's bed and began working frantically to get him to breathe. Nothing was working. The minutes just kept ticking by.

As it became clear Darrell's infected, fluid-filled lungs were failing, doctors had no choice but to connect him to a respirator to stabilize his breathing and restore his other vital functions. By the time hospital personnel managed to get him breathing again with intubation, Darrell had been deprived of oxygen for far too long.[26]

He slipped into a coma.

"All I kept thinking," Darrell's cousin Aileen later explained, "is he's, he's gonna die. And I just, I just stayed there for a while and just talked to him. I didn't know if he could hear me or not, and just, you know, rubbed his arms and rubbed his head and told him I loved him."[27]

If he were to survive, his doctors explained to the family, Darrell would likely have serious brain damage.[28]

16

Feeling the Love

THE SAME DAY Darrell Cabey slipped into a coma, Bernie Goetz decided he was done with Rikers Island. It was hard being in this terrible jail, even in its hospital wing. The experience hadn't been all bad, though. Since his arrival, Bernie had been inundated with fan mail and had even made some new friends in protective custody.

Among his admirers was famed comedian Joan Rivers, who not only offered to pay Bernie's bail but signed the telegram personally with "love and kisses."[1] He also had the chance to spend quality time with other notorious men, including disbarred lawyer Joel Steinberg (who had beaten his daughter to death) and Emmanuel Torres (who had murdered a recently graduated drama student from Harvard).

Still, he wanted to go home. On Monday, January 7, six days after Bernie was transported to Rikers, his brother, George, now an engineer in Detroit, and his sister Bernice, who was still managing his family's real estate holdings in Florida, paid him a visit with, according to the press, a black attaché case and two garbage bags.[2] The next day, Bernie posted his bond and headed straight back to his Greenwich Village apartment "under a cloak of secrecy." Nevertheless, there were reporters crowded outside his building, hoping to interview him. Bernie slipped in through the back door, "overjoyed to be home."[3]

The next morning, he was supposed to appear in criminal court for a scheduled hearing—one that was ultimately postponed, as the ADA was in the process of presenting evidence to the grand jury. Nevertheless, a throng of supporters stood outside the courtroom waiting for him, their enthusiasm infectious and overwhelming. Bernie Goetz had become a celebrity, and if the press had its way, his fan base was only going to grow.

The porter in Goetz's apartment building noted with amazement that everyone who even remotely knew the man was being "offered money for anecdotes." The porter himself had been offered $500 if he could provide a picture of the inside of Bernie's apartment, and an additional $500 if he let the reporters into the dwelling. The *National Enquirer,* a tabloid known for its sensationalism, had even offered to pay him the unheard-of sum of $30,000 "if the story is good enough."[4]

As one reporter from the *New York Post,* Michael Shain, pointed out, the Goetz story had taken the already "very competitive newspaper war" to a whole new level. Shain had found himself staking out the back of Bernie's building for a full twelve hours only a few days earlier, noting wryly, "There is a lot of loose money floating around on this story, money for access, money for information from cabdrivers, that kind of thing."[5]

It would be the *Post*'s head guy, Steve Dunleavy, who would ultimately get the most coveted scoop. Only two days after being released from Rikers Island, Bernie decided to give Dunleavy his first exclusive interview, a real coup for the paper and for Murdoch personally.

Dunleavy spoke to Goetz in the New Courtney coffee shop, where Goetz was a regular. At this establishment, the owners treated him as a "cherished luminary" and patrons and staff alike wanted him to sign autographs.[6] That day, Bernie was allowed to tell his side of the story, uninterrupted and unchallenged, while eating a toasted sandwich with a side of coleslaw and sipping coffee.[7]

Encouraged by such adulation, especially that coming from reporters at the *Post,* Bernie increasingly felt that he now represented something important. He was one of the few willing to stand on an important principle: The public wasn't going to take it from criminals anymore. As polls indicated, plenty of New Yorkers agreed with him.[8] In one of the first conducted by the *Post*'s rival the *Daily News* in January 1985, almost 50 percent of New Yorkers thought Goetz's actions were justified, and the very next month, a similar Gallup/*Newsweek* poll showed that 57 percent approved, remarkable support by any measure.[9]

By mid-January, while few Americans would have been able to name the four boys he had shot, Bernie Goetz had become a household name. Eighty-six percent of Americans surveyed were familiar with the Goetz case, and in the Northeast, that figure hit 95 percent. His shooting spree had received, according to writer Lillian Rubin, "a level of public attention and awareness that isn't given to most major national events, nor to a presidential election, not even to the Iranian hostage crisis, which dominated the news for 444 straight days a few years ago." Another poll within the state of New York noted that twice as many people had heard of Bernie Goetz as knew the name of their governor, Mario Cuomo.[10]

So popular was Bernie Goetz—so much had he become a hero, a real-life Charles Bronson to the American public, including outside of New York City—that on January 12, 1985, his subway shootings even became fodder for a lengthy skit on *Saturday Night Live,* with comedian Rich Hall playing Goetz.[11]

Myra Friedman, Bernie's downstairs neighbor, was immediately struck by how different Bernie seemed from the last time she'd seen him. His mood was lighter—so much so that he was not even troubled by the mess the police had left when they went over his apartment with a fine-tooth comb. In fact, since his return from Rikers, Bernie seemed almost giddy. It was as if his newfound celebrity had made him feel empowered and now downright enthusiastic to share his less-than-politic views on the city's deterioration and the right to self-defense.

Still, Bernie seemed to be much more comfortable in Myra's flat than his own, where the phone was ringing off the hook. During one visit, Bernie suggested that they order takeout. When the food arrived, he started sharing everything he had been through since they had last spoken. He told Myra that he hadn't actually minded being in Rikers.[12] He enjoyed the meals there and had also gotten to know some new people, mentioning specifically Emmanuel Torres, whose murder of the young aspiring actress Caroline Isenberg a judge had described as being of "Shakespearean proportions in its foul and tragic dimensions."[13] Torres, Bernie told Myra, had even given him a book to read.[14]

What also became clear to Myra was that Bernie was hoping to retrieve the guns he had left in her closet when he was on the run. He told her, "When this thing settles down in a few days, maybe, you, the package, maybe you want to give it back."[15] Nervously, she had to confess that she had turned them over to the DA's office. To her surprise, and great relief, he seemed okay with that.

This didn't mean that Bernie was fully at ease with the impending legal situation that he faced. He was now waiting on a grand jury to decide his fate, and that would have been unsettling to anyone. Myra could hear him pacing night after night in the apartment above hers. And yet, while Bernie might well have been ruminating over the possible outcomes of his case, he was also becoming less and less inclined to take responsibility for anything he had done.

Indeed, though Bernie had insisted when he was first arrested that he didn't want a lawyer, he was determined now to hire not one but two of them.

Many attorneys had offered Bernie their services in the weeks prior, and he had only reluctantly availed himself of two of them: a lawyer named Norman Jacques in New Hampshire, and Frank Brenner, whom the court had appointed during his Manhattan arraignment. But Brenner and Goetz would soon part ways, with the attorney citing differences of opinion with his client regarding how best to defend his actions.[16] Goetz had not been at all pleased when Brenner had gone on the popular television news program *20/20* and intimated that he was considering an insanity defense.[17] Bernie now wanted to hire "one of the top defense teams in the city": Joseph Kelner and Barry Slotnick.[18]

At first glance, Joseph Kelner might have seemed an unlikely pick. He had made his reputation as chief trial counsel for families of the Kent State students slain by members of the National Guard. But, as Kelner explained, he and Bernie shared a most unfortunate but nevertheless "important bond."[19] Kelner had himself been a victim of crime, not once but twice. The first time, he had been held up at gunpoint in the driveway of his Long Island home. The second, he had been strangled, suffocated, and beaten unconscious one day at work.[20] Kelner understood what it felt like to be a mugging victim and he was determined to defend Bernie Goetz.[21]

Barry Slotnick was an altogether different matter. He too was well known, far more so than Kelner. He had become one of the most prominent criminal defense attorneys in the city for defending especially notorious clients such as Meir Kahane, John Gotti, and years later, even the much-feared General Manuel Noriega.[22] Slotnick was not just a lawyer—he was a celebrity in his own right, and in his view, all publicity, even that steeped in controversy, was good publicity.

When he'd first heard about the Goetz shooting, Slotnick had been vacationing in St. Martin with his wife and children.[23] Upon his return, he received a call from Harry Ryttenberg, a journalist he knew who had gotten his start with the *Daily News*. Ryttenberg had subsequently started

Attorney Barry Slotnick discussing the Bernhard Goetz case.
John Roca/New York *Daily News* Archive via Getty Images

his own tabloid news service, one known for its "late night prowlers who roamed the city with police radios and video cameras and responded to bloody crimes and accidents, shot the footage and sold it to the local TV stations who worked by day."[24] This newsman had seen firsthand how insatiable the media's appetite was for anything Goetz-related, and he knew that Slotnick loved the limelight. Ryttenberg minced no words—he was certain Slotnick would want to represent the "Death Wish Vigilante."

At first, Slotnick was dubious. His usual clients were not only high-profile but also high-paying, particularly those like Gotti, who was a member of the Gambino Family, one of the "Five Families" that dominated organized crime in New York City. Bernie Goetz was not that rich, he was clearly a loner, and he was not especially personable. What's more, he had paralyzed a teenager who was now on life support.

That being said, Slotnick decided to at least meet with this potential client. He got into the back of his sleek black Cadillac and had his chauffeur take him straight to Goetz's apartment. Pulling up, he couldn't believe the number of reporters that were camping out—"TV vans, paparazzi, and reporters hoping for a glimpse of the city's man of the moment." That was all he needed to see. "This," he decided right then, "is for me."[25]

No matter how much publicity a case might offer him, however, Barry Slotnick did not represent anyone for free. He was willing to reduce his standard fee of $350 an hour, but he was not going to do this work pro bono.[26] Slotnick would also want to bring another one of the partners he had hired onto the defense team, an anti-corruption lawyer and former hotshot prosecutor by the name of Mark Baker, and that too would be expensive.

Bernie was able to afford Slotnick's services thanks to the steadfast support of some of his neighbors as well as the head of the Guardian Angels, Curtis Sliwa. In fact, on the day he had been arraigned, a group of five men who identified themselves to reporters as "friends and associates of Goetz," including electronics store owner Bernard Goldstein and lawyer Serphin Maltese, held a press conference outside the courthouse to announce that they had formed the Bernhard Goetz Legal Defense Fund.[27] Sliwa was named an honorary member and personally donated $102 to this fund before immediately heading onto the subways to solicit donations on Bernie's behalf.

When the Guardian Angels told passengers that Bernie Goetz was a hero who needed their help, the message resonated. Soon, up to forty envelopes a day were arriving to Bernie's 14th Street apartment mailbox—each filled with cash or checks. The chairman of the state Republican Party, George Clark, gave Goetz $5,000 of his own money because "he too was 'scared of some of the creatures' on the New York City subway."[28] The Firearms Civil Rights Legal Defense Fund, a National Rifle Association group, contributed a whopping $20,000 to the fund.[29]

The higher-ups in the National Rifle Association had also been paying close attention to the public's response to this "Subway Vigilante,"

Curtis Sliwa (left), founder of the Guardian Angels, and Joseph Kelner, attorney for Bernhard Goetz, January 17, 1985.
AP Photo/J. Scott Applewhite

and they were thrilled by what they were seeing. Liberal media outlets like *The New York Times* had never embraced gun culture like southern newspapers had. As NRA lobbyist Richard Feldman put it, this "anti-gun New York media" had always discouraged the NRA from being active in the region.[30] But men like Feldman understood that a profound shift was taking place, one that they intended to capitalize on: Even formerly liberal Americans were coming to see gun ownership as key to their daily personal safety.

Trying to harness this new attitude, the NRA began putting serious resources into its lobbying efforts as well as into trying to influence the outcome of congressional races. Over the course of the 1980s, this organization would move from its association in the public's mind primarily with hunting, sport shooting, and marksmanship to establishing itself as a dominant force in American conservative politics.[31]

In the Bernie Goetz shooting specifically, the NRA saw an extraordinary opportunity "to make a statement about changing the gun laws." It had seen that "the people in New York were very much on the side of Bernie Goetz," which pushed the organization to begin taking out "ads in New York's local papers that read 'Self-protection is Your Right.'" Seeing a positive response, Feldman's boss said to him, most happily, "Richie, I can't believe it. You [were] completely right. These ads are doing fantastic."[32]

With Barry Slotnick as his lawyer, a mailbox full of legal defense cash and fan mail, and now basking in the glow of NRA support, Bernie Goetz had become the man of the hour. He was also a favorite of New York City cops, and he knew it, declaring with a smile, "I took a lot of pressure off those guys." For years after the shootings, officers would continue to greet him with enthusiasm. Years later, one reporter marveled at a "fresh-faced young cop" who was "enthusiastically shaking hands" with Bernie and saying, "Mr. Goetz, pleasure to meet you."[33]

Bernie's rising fame only encouraged him to share his story with as many reporters as possible. He would soon spend hours at a time giving lengthy interviews, always insisting that the city needed men like him, that he had only done what others wished they had the courage to do, and, above all, that he had done absolutely nothing wrong.

17

The Blame Game

As much as Bernie Goetz saw himself as a man for the moment, and as much as the conservative tabloid media had been championing the specific actions he had taken on December 22, 1984, not every reporter in the city, nor every public figure, nor even every ordinary citizen agreed with this positive characterization. Since his fate was ultimately in the hands of a grand jury, and given that he would likely stand trial before a jury of his peers in New York City, such contested views of the "Death Wish Vigilante" mattered.

While the tabloid press and mainstream press alike had almost immediately cast the shootings as a case of a beleaguered ordinary American being preyed upon by a roving band of ruthless teens who unexpectedly, and gratifyingly, got their comeuppance, there were always a few dissenting voices, and one of the most important of these actually wrote for the *Daily News*.

Legendary columnist and longtime white liberal Jimmy Breslin was well aware that his paper was in a fight for its life with Murdoch's *New York Post*. Even so, he found the *Daily News*'s strategy for trying to win this media war distasteful. It too had begun moving rightward and had been trying to out-sensationalize the *Post* in its approach to urban crime. This was particularly true when it came to the paper's coverage of the subway shootings of 1984.

But Breslin was his own man—a reporter known for telling it "like it was," no matter how unpopular that might make him.[1] This was especially apparent in one of the first columns he wrote following the shooting. "As lawlessness was applauded," he wrote, "we, in New York, arrived at the sourest of all moments: when people become what they hate.... Would people now be so jubilant, if the four had been white? Almost nobody wants to hear that question ... [but] the bottom line ... is that people are rejoicing over a 19-year-old kid who will be in a wheelchair for a lifetime. I am sorry, include me out."[2]

In another, less sentimental column, penned several days after the shooting, Breslin asked New Yorkers to consider just how much this subway shooting would cost them—even those who might not particularly care about Darrell Cabey. Think hard, he pressed, about the lifetime of medical care this teenager would need if he lived. Half of this cost, Breslin pointed out, would be covered by the federal government, and 25 percent would be covered by New York State and City—and thus, by New Yorkers themselves.

This cost, Breslin went on, was substantial. "This means that the taxpayers will put up to $1,750,000 to care for Cabey. Or maybe more.... Unless Cabey lives all of the way until he is 90. Then, whether he is at home in the Bronx or in a nursing home, he will have cost the cheering public the sum of $2,135,000." As Breslin put it caustically, "The medical care for Darrell Cabey comes out of the pay checks of the people who said, 'At last!' when they heard of his shooting."[3]

Breslin also did not shy away from what he believed to be the deep racism behind the public's embrace of the shooter. As he put it, "This utterly magnificent rejoicing was done without any knowledge of what went on in the no. 2 subway train on Dec. 22 except that the gunman was white and was harassed by four blacks, and that he shot them." This columnist would even attack the Catholic archbishop of New York, John O'Connor, the alleged "Keeper of Morals for everybody, no matter what their beliefs," because he had remained "totally silent" and not called out his fellow New Yorkers "for what could be considered an unchristian reaction to the shooting."[4]

Perhaps more important, Breslin was one of the few white reporters to actually investigate the incendiary rumor that the boys had been carrying sharpened screwdrivers. As soon as he learned that the screwdrivers found on the boys had not, in fact, been sharpened, Breslin shouted out this fact whenever he had the opportunity to do so, often eliciting extremely hostile reactions from the public.

Going a step further, Breslin also loudly insisted that even if the screwdrivers had been sharpened, this still would not have justified Bernie

Goetz's actions. The fact was, he said, the two boys in possession of the screwdrivers had never approached Goetz. Indeed, the screwdrivers had never even been removed from their pockets, and so the shooter could not possibly have known that they existed, let alone viewed them as a threat.[5]

Breslin would make this point on *The Phil Donohue Show,* a wildly popular daytime talk show, before a highly charged and engaged audience. Also onstage was Curtis Sliwa, and the two sparred throughout the program as to whether the shooting was justified, with the issue of the screwdrivers figuring prominently. As Breslin stated emphatically and unapologetically:

> The screwdrivers never were shown. They were there obviously for thieving, the guys were going to break into these Pacman games and hit subway turnstiles, but they were unsharpened. The press has made it sharpened and each one of them had one, and thereby giving people the vision of these three kids putting the screwdriver in the guy's eyes or something.[6]

The sound of audience members booing, however, would soon drown him out.[7]

But Jimmy Breslin was not alone in his effort to keep some of the media focus on the wounded teens while simultaneously calling out the racial hypocrisy of the public's reaction and dangerous rumor-mongering. Les Payne, the Black editor of another New York tabloid, *Newsday,* aimed to combat this inflammatory narrative as well. He reminded readers who the real victims were in this saga, at times challenging even the writers at his own publication. To those who denied that race had played a role in this shooting, Payne responded pointedly:

> What would've been the public reaction if, instead of what police described as a "golden blonde," a black passenger, say, on the Harlem D train had pulled an unlicensed pistol and shot four black teenagers under the same circumstances? . . . What if the gunman had been black and his victims four white teenagers? . . . In neither hypothetical case would there have been a frenzied lust for blood, and the accompanying embrace, nay, worship, of the subway gunman.[8]

New York's Black press also pulled few punches when it came to calling out the hyperbolic narratives surrounding the shootings and noting how heavily race had influenced the public's reaction to Goetz's actions. This was particularly true for the *Amsterdam News,* published in Harlem, which explicitly called on the white press to treat this event with more distance as well as to offer a more balanced assessment of the victims.

The editors of this paper suggested that all New Yorkers would do well to engage in what amounted to "a thought experiment."[9] Imagine that Goetz was "Black or Puerto Rican. Name him Jones or Suarez. Give him the college degrees and a similar lifestyle. Let him shoot four whites, two of them in the back, for any reason. See what happens to him. You can be sure that it will not be applause."[10]

What's more, the paper argued, contrary to what most white analyses of the Goetz shooting had concluded, this shooter was not simply evidence of how frustrated New Yorkers had become with heightened levels of crime. Rather, what his shootings revealed was just how determined some New Yorkers were to defend violence directed against Black youth in the city.[11]

Though it was less prominent, the left-leaning and avowed radical press was also not shy about calling out the racist underpinnings of this tragedy—arguing that Bernie Goetz's actions had been nothing less than "A Modern Lynching." One paper suggested that the media response to the event was the clearest case of "racism" turning "logic on its head." "Only in a society such as ours where racism permeates every aspect of our lives," observed this piece in the *People's World,* "could the victims of such a shooting be tried and convicted in the press while the perpetrator is glorified as a hero. As of now, there is no evidence that the victims were anything but that—victims."[12]

Meanwhile, New York City leaders—Black, Brown, and white—were also weighing in on the Goetz case. Some tried hard to straddle the fence regarding what this man had done. Initially, liberal mayor Ed Koch publicly condemned the shootings, for example, proclaiming such acts of vigilantism would simply not be tolerated. He even referred to Bernie Goetz's actions as "animal behavior."[13] But in a matter of weeks, Koch had changed his tune. He not only denied saying this but also backed away from the idea that Goetz's shooting even constituted an act of vigilantism.[14]

New York's Democratic governor, Mario Cuomo, a politician known for his staunch anti-death-penalty views even in the face of rising crime rates, was, at least publicly, steadfast in his criticism of Goetz. He pointed out quite heatedly that "people have supported the killing of millions of Jews, the imprisoning of the Japanese—and they thought they were right at the moment when their passion was turned up too high."[15] And yet, when asked to appoint a special prosecutor to investigate the case, Governor Cuomo declined to do so, despite top Republican senators such as Arlen Specter of Pennsylvania supporting the idea.[16] Cuomo was backed in this decision by Republican Alfonse D'Amato, a U.S. senator from New York, who said passionately that "he'd be glad to testify on Mr. Goetz's behalf to help defend him."[17]

Even President Ronald Reagan spoke about Goetz's actions, with similarly mixed messaging. While Reagan acknowledged that acts of vigilantism could lead to a "breakdown of civilization," he nonetheless stated, "I think we all can understand the frustration of people who are constantly threatened by crime and feel that law and order is not particularly protecting them."[18]

Meanwhile, in addition to Goetz defenders like Senator D'Amato, there was at least one prominent leader in the Black community also willing to voice his unqualified support for the shooter: none other than Roy Innis of the Congress of Racial Equality (CORE). CORE had been founded in 1942 on the principles of interracial and nonviolent efforts to promote greater racial equality, but Innis had come to a more hardened perspective. Even before the identity of the shooter was known, Innis proclaimed that Goetz was "the avenger for us," adding that "some black men ought to have done it long before. . . . I wish it had been me."[19]

Knowing that Goetz's fate was being decided by a grand jury, and that he would need the sympathy of Black jurors should he stand trial, Innis went even further in his efforts to publicly support him. Shortly after Goetz had shown up in court for a "black factory worker who had fatally stabbed a candy thief after an altercation at a subway newsstand"—and tried to offer the "weeping" worker a hug—Innis agreed to accompany Goetz to a commemoration for a Black crime victim.[20] They hoped their presence, though wholly uninvited, would be welcomed at "the funeral of a 71-year-old former Harlem school principal who had been shot to death while driving a cab." Instead, both men "were ousted by the family and friends" of the deceased.[21]

Still, having a prominent Black leader stand with Goetz would serve as proof to countless white New Yorkers who supported him that his actions on the subway had nothing to do with race. But Innis's embrace of Goetz meanwhile infuriated New York's other civil rights leaders and organizations. CORE's Brooklyn chapter, which had been particularly active in organizing against police brutality and for community empow-

Roy Innis, of the Congress of Racial Equality, shakes hands with Bernhard Goetz during a news conference in New York.
AP Photo/Bookstaver

erment in the face of city neglect, was so disgusted by Innis that it issued a scathing press release in response to his comments that said:

> Brooklyn CORE wishes to reemphasize the fact of its complete and total dissociation from Roy Innis and the national Congress of Racial Equality. . . . This is a dangerous position for a member of the African-American community to hold in the light of the still-pervasive racism in American society. It is inviting further violent attacks upon black youth as the majority community is all armed with impunity to vent its racism under the guise of personal defense.[22]

Civil rights leaders such as C. Vernon Mason would also speak out loudly against Bernie Goetz and Innis. Mason argued publicly that Goetz was a cold-blooded killer who had flat-out "attempted to murder Darrell Cabey." As he put it, Goetz had "shot him in the back with a dum dum bullet when [Cabey] was several feet away from him and in no way posed any threat to him whatsoever."[23]

When he learned that Innis had "advocated the arming of thousands of people as the solution to street crime," Mason insisted that such sentiments would only make it easier for "a legally competent defendant . . . to kill or perform acts of violence with impunity, contrary to fundamental principles of justice and criminal law."[24]

The radical and controversial civil rights activist Rev. Al Sharpton

C. Vernon Mason speaking on the Bernhard Goetz case. From *The Confessions of Bernhard Goetz* (MPI Home Video, 1987). Permission from the estate of Darrell Moore.

was even more outspoken against Goetz. Sharpton had been ordained in the Pentecostal Church as a child, and while still in high school he had become the youth director of the Southern Christian Leadership Conference's Operation Breadbasket program. He went on to form his own organization, the National Youth Movement, and by the mid-1980s had earned a reputation in the city as a particularly outspoken, uncompromising, and media-savvy racial justice activist.[25] Sharpton not only lambasted Goetz as "a racist" but was also one of the only major civic leaders to visit Darrell Cabey in the hospital, where he prayed with him.[26]

Innis's views on Goetz's actions, and his vocal support for the man himself, also did not land particularly well with ordinary Black New Yorkers. Polling made this clear, as did various interviews with people on the street.[27] As one woman, a museum curator named Kellie Jones, unflinchingly told reporters from a paper founded by the American Nazi Party canvassing the public on Goetz, "I don't think he's a hero. I can understand people being afraid to ride the trains but I don't think they should give him a break because he's a white male who shot four black kids."[28] This point of view was expressed by countless other Black city residents with equal passion to reporters from other papers as well.

The pages of *El Diario La Prensa,* the leading Spanish-language newspaper in New York, also published no shortage of editorials, letters, and news articles expressing grave concern over the glorification of Bernie Goetz. According to one piece in this paper, a young Puerto Rican man had reported how strange it was to come to live in a city and a country where so many whites saw "a hero in Bernhard Goetz." "For this young man," the piece said, "that experience was one of the first lessons he received about the racism that exists in this nation."[29]

Indeed, as Dominican American writer Raquel Cepeda remembered it: "Bernhard Goetz has convinced me that everybody in the city . . . feels that Black and Latino kids are no better than subway tunnel rats. . . . The American Dream for some means a living nightmare for others. In my world, the bogeymen usually get away with murder."[30]

In spite of Black and Brown New Yorkers' widespread hostility toward Goetz, the tabloid and mainstream media nevertheless combed the streets to find quotes from residents of color who were more supportive of him. The reality was, every newspaper counted on selling papers to Black and Brown readers too, and so they worked hard to counter any notion that the press was becoming a mouthpiece solely for white city residents.[31]

For example, when reporters from the *Post* visited the Chambers Street station to ask passengers their thoughts on the Goetz shooting, they zeroed in on young Black men like Kelvin Lastique, whom they quoted as saying that he thought that Goetz was simply reacting to a threat. In fact, Lastique explained, he had thought that Goetz "was guilty" until he'd seen some kids surround another "defenseless man" on the subway and this had changed his mind.[32]

On the national level, the television news media was also committed to showing footage of both the Black and white public who were supportive of the Goetz shooting. *NBC Nightly News* anchor Garrick Utley began one of his broadcasts, for example, by noting that the story of the "mystery man" who took it upon himself to shoot four youths on a NYC subway certainly "says something about our times." Viewers then heard from both a white male neighbor of Bernie's, who stressed that Bernie was just "a regular guy," and a Black female New Yorker who claimed it was "about time somebody protect himself, nobody's protecting us on the subway."[33]

Notably, despite the voices of dissent in the media, including those of Breslin and Payne, and the lack of support from the majority of Black New Yorkers, Bernie's popularity had only increased since he turned himself in. From the letters flooding the tabloids, the polling data, and the effort to fund his legal defense, it was clear that a stunning number of New Yorkers—particularly whites—felt Bernie's actions on the train were justified.

This hadn't escaped the notice of the DA's office, where Assistant District Attorney Susan Braver was preparing to present the case against Goetz to a New York grand jury. The office had received three times as many letters supporting Goetz as those condemning him. This did not bode well.

18

Making the Case

In New York State, felony prosecutions first require an indictment from a twenty-three-member grand jury, made up of randomly selected citizens who reach a decision through majority vote. Whether they might represent potential witnesses (like the teens Goetz wounded) or the defendant in the case (like Goetz himself), defense lawyers are prohibited from participating in these convenings. And, unless the people testifying have already been granted immunity by the prosecutor, this lack of representation can be unnerving. In the case of witnesses, for example, anything they say before a grand jury "could, theoretically, lead to their own prosecution." As one reporter explained, this rule could prove "particularly thorny in the Goetz case, since his four victims had cases pending against them at the time of the shooting."[1]

Discussions regarding which witnesses would in fact be called before the grand jury, especially in a case as high-profile as Bernie Goetz's, always began in the office of the district attorney. As the head DA, Robert Morgenthau would assign the assistant DAs who would present cases to grand juries and trial juries alike. Morgenthau was a formidable legal mind, and with Goetz's taped confessions in hand, he was feeling optimistic about his office's ability to get the indictments it sought. Even though he was not known for his charisma, often in fact described as being rather "wooden" and "formal," few doubted Morgenthau's influence, skills, and power.[2] If anyone could indict Goetz, it would be him.

Morgenthau was a patrician, liberal Democrat who had come to the Manhattan DA's office in 1975, after serving as the United States Attorney for the Southern District of New York. He would ultimately be "elected nine times in succession, usually by landslides and with the endorsement of virtually all the political parties."[3]

Over the course of his career, Morgenthau oversaw the caseloads of more than five hundred lawyers and would be responsible for a staggering 3.5 million cases. He had a hand in shaping the fate of everyone accused of a crime in the city, from "stock manipulators, extortionists, murderers, [and] muggers" to "wife-beaters and sexual predators." By the mid-1980s, Morgenthau was essentially "the face of justice in Manhattan."[4]

Morgenthau was known to be a relentless pursuer of serious indictments for offenses committed against young people and those committed with firearms—each a signature of this case. And yet Morgenthau's very job depended on the will of the voting public. While he was clearly a legal powerhouse, and was putting one of his best, Susan Braver, in charge of presenting the state's case to the Goetz grand jury, it was not clear whether voters would be glad or mad if he did, in fact, manage to throw the book at Bernie Goetz.

The Goetz grand jury would meet over the course of three weeks in January 1985, during which time Morgenthau's office sought to indict the shooter on four counts of attempted murder in the second degree, four counts of assault in the first degree, criminal possession of a weapon in the second degree, and reckless endangerment in the first degree.[5]

As it happened, and in ways that Morgenthau's office had likely underestimated, the outcome of this proceeding would be directly impacted by the barrage of warrants that had been issued by Bronx judges Katz and Marrus against Goetz's victims—Troy, Barry, James, and Darrell—in the immediate aftermath of the shootings.

By the time the grand jury began considering its verdict, all of the teens save Darrell had recovered enough to leave the hospital, only to face these myriad misdemeanor charges. While the bulk of the cases had to do with either jumping subway turnstiles or stealing from video machines, each of the boys nevertheless risked incriminating himself if he took the stand in the grand jury proceeding that would certainly cover similar ground—they had jumped turnstiles and were on their way to jimmy open arcade machines when Goetz had shot them.

Morgenthau's office could have legally immunized the four teens, so that the grand jury could hear what Bernie Goetz had done from the victims' own perspectives. Offering such a deal was, in fact, common practice. Two years earlier, Morgenthau's office had granted immunity to three police officers involved in a similarly controversial case—the fatal beating of a Black graffiti artist named Michael Stewart.[6]

However, according to one of Morgenthau's ADAs, in the case of these teens, prosecutors were "simply not in a position to make an informed decision whether to confer immunity," and thus not doing so "was entirely reasonable."[7] The DA's office decided instead to rely solely on Goetz's recounting of the events in his statements to both the Concord police and to Braver and her law enforcement team from NYC.[8] His own words should easily net the indictments they wanted.

What prosecutors had not considered was how sympathetically this group of grand jurors might view Bernie's demeanor and hear his words on the taped confessions, notwithstanding his chilling admissions. Ultimately, listening to Goetz defend himself for hours—explaining that yes, he had done horrible things, but he had been scared and felt he had no choice—would in fact help them to excuse his actions. Without any testimony from the shooting victims, Goetz's perspective was all they had. Jurors never had the chance to consider what it really meant for, say, Barry to undergo major surgery on his stomach, nor how it felt for James to have a tube placed in his collapsed lung and endure several intensive operations to repair the damage from Goetz's bullet.

The indictments handed down against Bernie Goetz on January 25, 1985, were stunningly minimal. Ultimately, the grand jury, whose composition remained sealed, dismissed all charges relating to the actual shootings and to the injuries he had caused. Bernie would be required to stand trial only for criminal possession of a weapon: one third-degree count for carrying the gun in the subway and two fourth-degree counts for possessing two other guns in his apartment.

Taking no small measure of heat for his failure to indict Goetz on more serious charges, DA Morgenthau defended his office by saying, "We post-mortemed this thing to death." He claimed that he didn't believe it would have made a difference even if prosecutors "had leaned on that grand jury."[9]

To anyone who had been following Goetz's press coverage, it came as no surprise when he subsequently pled not guilty even to the possession charges.[10] The Cabey family, however, was dumbstruck. Shirley had prayed that the grand jury would do the right thing. When asked by a reporter quite directly, "Do you think Bernhard Goetz was justified in what he did?," she was unequivocal. "No. He didn't have to shoot them."[11]

Darrell's cousin Aileen agreed. She had visited him numerous times in the hospital and had seen firsthand "all these tubes and this machine [that] was breathing for him and . . . sucking all this mucus out of him."[12] His fate had seemed irrelevant to this grand jury. And yet, deep down, the families of these wounded teens had never really dared to hope for much more out of their fellow New Yorkers. When asked years later if he had ever believed Goetz would be held accountable, Troy's brother Carl said, "I'm from the street so I already recognize what's going to happen. . . . No. For the gun, not for murder, not for attempted."[13]

It still stung. A lot. As Shirley would later say, hopelessly, "Where's there gonna be any justice? You know, and how could someone have so much hate for somebody that they don't even know?"[14]

19

Not So Fast

As Bernie Goetz celebrated the grand jury's decision, so did others, including Rupert Murdoch's editorial board at the *New York Post,* which wrote without equivocation that "the grand jury's decision is a victory for common sense and self-defense."[1]

Perhaps to the surprise of the press and the DA's office alike, however, a great many others turned out to be infuriated by this outcome. Some took to the streets, such as in a demonstration in front of the Manhattan Criminal Court organized by the All-People's Congress, an activist umbrella organization formed in 1981 by seventy organizations in twenty-two states that had come together to speak out against the ideology and actions of the Reagan administration.[2] At this demonstration, protesters handed out leaflets that read "Goetz is no hero!" and "Protest racist violence against black youth."[3]

Others, like civil rights lawyer C. Vernon Mason, also loudly voiced disgust at the outcome. "The D.A. has demonstrated his total inability to handle this matter," he exclaimed. "Why weren't any of the four youths immunized so they might put their story before the jurors?" Well-known radical lawyer William Kunstler also spoke out publicly. "Nothing could be more heinous and bestial than to fire a second shot into the body of a helpless youth!" He loudly condemned "the failure of Manhattan D.A. Robert Morgenthau in his handling of the case."[4]

Even some more mainstream public figures registered their disgust with this grand jury. Puerto Rican former congressman and previous deputy mayor of NYC Herman Badillo, for example, would go so far as to question the entire grand jury process and to call for its abolition.[5]

Demonstrators protest against Bernhard Goetz outside Judge Stephen Crane's New York courtroom, February 6, 1985.
AP Photo/G. Paul Burnett

Black NYC police commissioner Benjamin Ward, a man who had previously taken great pains to avoid saying anything about the Goetz shootings that might rankle the city's political elite, also spoke out. On February 22, 1985, he stunned his boss Mayor Koch by publicly criticizing the decision of the grand jury. As he stated firmly in *The New York Times,* "Goetz should have been indicted 'for some level of assault,' if not attempted murder," and went on, "You don't shoot two people running away from you and say it's self-defense."[6]

Meanwhile, regular Black and Brown citizens in the city were also expressing their dismay, openly fretting about the kind of message such a weak indictment would send. As a New Yorker named Eddie Sanchez put it, "I think he should be prosecuted, for the simple fact that he used a lethal weapon. If that's the case then everybody could pick up a pistol and run around shooting somebody."[7]

Another resident, Mack Williams, expressed his frustration in an impassioned letter to the *Post:* "If I, as a black man, had shot four white youths in their backs, I might very well be dead. If not, I would definitely be—in the words of the popular rap record—'in jail, without the bail' for virtually no one would be rushing to defend someone who would not be portrayed in the favorable Charles Bronson–like manner as has been Mr. Goetz's."[8]

Letters criticizing the grand jury's decision also arrived at the DA's office from across the country. As Nancy L. Bey from Redwood City,

California, wrote: "Surely there must be a way to bring Goetz to trial for his crime. He has paralyzed a man who may die. HOW CAN IT BE A CRIME TO CARRY A GUN AND NOT A CRIME TO USE IT SO RECKLESSLY? What kind of message is the Grand Jury sending to America? Who are these 23 [people who were] able to obstruct Justice? How many poor and Black people are represented on it?"[9]

Clearly, the DA's office had underestimated not just how difficult it would be to secure a serious indictment against Bernie Goetz but also how many Americans had expected them to do so. Only four days after the grand jury voted not to indict Goetz for attempted murder, the *NBC Nightly News* opined that there might well be "more trouble" in store for the gunman given how many out there were still "determined to see that he doesn't get off easily for shooting 4 black teenagers on a New York subway train."[10]

Some trouble did come for Goetz, and from an unexpected quarter: his neighbor and purported friend Myra Friedman.

In the wake of the indictments, Myra suddenly went public with the two tapes she had made of her conversations with Bernie when he was on the run. The details of these conversations were published in a lengthy *New York* magazine cover piece, and issues flew off the shelves of newsstands across the city. Notably, this magazine was also owned by Rupert Murdoch—and though the piece would prove quite damning to Goetz, it nevertheless stoked the fire of Goetz-mania that Murdoch's other publication, the *Post,* had started. National TV news picked up the story as well, disseminating it across the country.

In the wake of the grand jury's tepid decision, the details of Myra's conversations with Bernie Goetz would prove especially jarring. On her tapes, Bernie had baldly stated that the physical threat posed by the boys was "irrelevant," while also making clear that he had approached the encounter as if he were playing a war game. "Myra," he had said, "in a situation like this, your mind, you're in a combat situation. . . . You are so hyped up."[11] This was the first time that anyone, save the grand jurors, had heard him admit to any of this.

Such details only intensified the ire of those who felt that the DA's office had failed in its efforts to indict Goetz. In response to this new and shocking information, a group of Black and Puerto Rican community leaders and activists requested a meeting with the U.S. Attorney for the Southern District of New York, Rudolph Giuliani, in which they demanded that he open a federal civil rights case against Goetz.[12]

Leading this contingent were Al Sharpton and C. Vernon Mason. Sharpton unabashedly accused the grand jury of being "motivated by racism," while Mason more soberly told the press, "We have come to the Federal Government as black people traditionally have done to seek redress when it is clear that state and local authorities have either failed to act or are incapable of acting."[13] Darrell Cabey, in particular, was central to the case they were hoping the Justice Department would file. As Mason explained, it should "be a suit alleging that [Goetz] attempted to murder Darrell Cabey."[14]

Though Giuliani would agree to "look into" possible federal civil rights charges against Goetz, he doubted this new evidence would provide sufficient proof that the shootings were racially motivated; that Goetz had conspired to violate someone's rights; that he "was trying to stop his victims from using the subway, which would constitute interference with a federally funded activity"; or that he was acting as a public official "under color of law."[15]

What's more, Giuliani warned, "The Federal civil-rights laws in this area give the Federal Government a very limited role." Thus, he did not "want to create public expectation one way or the other." All he could do, he said, would be to "decide whether it is fair, reasonable and appropriate to begin an investigation."[16]

Lacking confidence that Giuliani would in fact file a civil rights case, the families of Troy, Barry, James, and Darrell began searching for some other legal recourse to hold Bernie Goetz accountable. Three of the teens would ultimately decide to bring a civil suit against Goetz. As Al Sharpton told the press, "The families should go as far as they can to recover damages from the injuries their sons received." Simultaneously, Clayton Jones, from the prominent National Conference of Black Lawyers, agreed to offer legal aid to the youths for the various misdemeanor cases each of them had pending against them.[17]

In his civil suit against Bernie Goetz, James Ramseur would be represented by attorney Ron Kliegerman, while Troy Canty ended up at the offices of lawyers Howie Meyer and Scott Greenfield.

As Scott Greenfield knew, his client would not be as easy to represent as some of the other shooting victims because he was the one who had asked Goetz for the money and, as important, the media had systematically portrayed him as a violent criminal.[18] Not long after the shooting, for example, Troy had agreed to speak to the *National Enquirer,* the same tabloid that had dangled the possibility of offering $30,000 to anyone in Bernie Goetz's building who might have a juicy story. He and Barry had both decided to be interviewed by this paper, one notorious for playing fast and loose with the facts, because it had offered to give them each $300.[19]

This was cash that both Troy and Barry desperately needed, but there was a catch. The *National Enquirer* would also insist that they pose, nearly naked, for a series of disturbing photographs with their still-healing and bandaged bullet wounds on full display.[20] Not only did the paper exploit them in this gratuitous manner, but, according to Troy, the reporters then totally twisted everything he and Barry had told them. The piece the *Enquirer* ended up publishing, complete with those haunting images of their injured bodies, made it seem as if they deserved everything they got.[21]

Attorney Scott Greenfield, however, was undeterred. He wanted to help Troy, seeing something naïve and thus heartbreaking about his attempts to stick up for himself with the press. As he would later recall, there was "something surreal about an invisible street kid suddenly becoming a media obsession. . . . But they don't love you. They just want to use you, fit you into the narrative already written. You talk to them and

Barry Allen and Troy Canty photographed for a piece in the *National Enquirer*. Alamy

see something completely unfamiliar on the page. They seemed so nice, so understanding, when you talked. How could they have written something so false, so insulting? How did they make you the villain of your own story?"[22] If nothing else, Greenfield wanted Troy to have some sort of advocate as he navigated such treacherous media waters.

Merely agreeing to represent these boys against Goetz would cause their attorneys their fair share of grief too. The day after filing a case on Troy's behalf, Greenfield was in Albany, arguing a separate case before the New York Court of Appeals. He called his office and discovered the following:

> I had 97 death threats. It turned out that the *New York Post*'s headline that day was "What a Nerve," referring to the filing of Troy's complaint. It inflamed people in a city already on the edge, and they let me know about it. I called my wife and told her not to answer the phone that day. You never know who could find my home number, even though it was unlisted. Plenty of reporters had found me, and if they could, so could the crazies.[23]

The civil case that would ultimately garner the most public attention, however, would be the one filed by Shirley Cabey on behalf of her son, who finally, after one long, terrifying, and uncertain month, had awoken from his coma.[24]

When Darrell Cabey finally regained consciousness, it was immediately clear that he was not okay. It had been bad enough that Goetz's bullet had paralyzed him from the waist down. Now, though, it was clear that his doctors' worst fears had been realized. Darrell had in fact suffered serious brain damage. All of this forced his mother to face a question that had long been troubling her: How would she afford the care her son would require for the rest of his life? Suing her son's shooter for meaningful damages might at least help.

That itself, however, was no easy thing. Shirley knew she would need a lawyer, and a good one. She decided that she would take the subway into Manhattan and approach none other than the famous activist lawyer William Kunstler.

By the 1980s, Kunstler had developed a national reputation for taking on "David and Goliath"–type cases in which serious injustices, particularly those relating to racism or the overreach of law enforcement, had gone unnoticed or unpunished. The more famous of these cases included his work with some of the men who had been charged following the Attica prison uprising in upstate New York in 1971, as well as representing Bobby Seale and the Chicago 7 several years earlier.[25] It also hadn't escaped Shirley's attention that Kunstler had already spoken out against Goetz in the press.

Shirley was in luck. Kunstler was enthusiastic about taking on the case, as was his young associate Ron Kuby. What's more, civil rights attorney C. Vernon Mason, with whom Kunstler sometimes worked, was also game to work with Kunstler on her behalf. As important, the Center for Constitutional Rights (CCR) in New York City, one of the most respected civil rights litigation organizations in the country, was eager to help as well. Both Kunstler and Mason were affiliated with this organization, and not only would it offer the assistance of two more of its attorneys, Randolph Scott-McLaughlin and Betty Lawrence Bailey, but it would also help fund the case. They filed it on January 29, 1985.[26]

Not long after Darrell came out of his coma that February, Kunstler and Kuby took a trip to St. Vincent's Hospital to discuss the case more thoroughly with him. They were taken aback by his condition, and by how little he could remember about "what had happened to him or why."[27] Seeing Darrell's state in the wake of his coma made it clear to both

Lawyers William Kunstler (center left) and Ronald Kuby (center right) talk to media outside their law offices. Bill Turnbull/New York *Daily News* Archive via Getty Images

of them that even if Goetz never paid a price in criminal court, he must be held accountable, at least financially, for the physical and mental damage he had inflicted on this young man.

Kunstler and Kuby decided to sue Bernhard Goetz for $50 million in damages, and Shirley Cabey would need it. With each passing day, she was incurring "enormous medical expenses and needed help to pay the bills."[28] As important to Shirley was the fact that this suit would give her the opportunity to restore her son's reputation. As Kuby later explained it, "she knew her son was fundamentally a good kid. And I think she was just, she was just baffled. . . . She didn't understand how the victim here, her son—who by all accounts never did anything to Bernhard Goetz. . . . How her son became the perpetrator here, and the man who destroyed his life . . . was now a hero?"[29]

Shirley's lawyers felt pretty confident that they would be able to do both—get her the money she needed to support Darrell, and challenge the public's view of him—"because of what Goetz had admitted to police in Concord."[30] Their case, however, would not be allowed to go to trial until the Goetz criminal trial had concluded.

In the meantime, the fact that Shirley Cabey dared to file this suit against Goetz would ignite another barrage of hatred toward her son—and the lawyers who had agreed to help them. One note to Bill Kunstler, from a fellow attorney based in Washington, D.C., called out his "hypocrisy" for taking this particular case: "You proudly defend Black Panthers who assassinate New York City policemen and convicts who murder guards and still you have the unmitigated gall to bring suit against an individual who defended himself from four hoods."[31]

Ron Kuby received similar missives, including one admonishing him "that Civil Rights are NOT solely for N—s and Sp—s, but for Whites as well, Don't be such a bleeding-heart turncoat on your race."[32] Yet another read "Fuck you and that n— Cabey. He should be in a casket along with you."[33]

Such racist vitriol would soon be directed at the DA's office as well. As it turned out, DA Morgenthau wasn't quite done with Bernie Goetz.

20

Pressure Cooker

SINCE HIS OFFICE'S LOSS before the Goetz grand jury, DA Robert Morgenthau had felt enormous pressure to take another run at the subway gunman, especially after the details of his personal calls with Myra Friedman were released. At the end of February 1985, these feelings only intensified when a summary of Bernie's first taped confession, the one he gave to Concord police officer Warren Foote, became public in a most dramatic fashion.

Goetz's detailed and at times damning accounts of the subway shooting, first to Foote and Domian and then to Braver and the NYC detectives, had remained sealed since his arraignment in New Hampshire on January 2, 1985.[1] But as part of the discovery process for the criminal trial, and in an otherwise "routine appearance on the gun charge," the DA's office decided to turn over a discovery package to Goetz's attorneys that included the police report written by Officer Foote that documented all that Goetz had told him about the shooting.[2]

Equally important, this new information was then made part of the official and public proceedings of this case, which in turn made it available to the myriad journalists that regularly combed through any newly filed materials for juicy updates. It was only a matter of time before Bernie Goetz's first ugly confession about the role he had played on that subway car was all over the news.[3]

For Goetz's lawyers, this material was, to put it mildly, an "unsettling surprise." As Slotnick's law partner Mark Baker later recalled, some of the admissions "[were] terribly prejudicial to Goetz." For example, firing a weapon at "someone who was already injured and sitting in a seat," Baker noted, "that's not self-defense."[4]

Many of those who finally had the opportunity to read details from Goetz's own detailed retelling of what had transpired on that train were indeed disturbed by what it revealed.[5] As Police Commissioner Benjamin Ward put it, "he just kind of reminds me of someone who's digging a very deep hole and at some point the sides are gonna collapse in on him, and we're gonna find out a lot more about Bernhard Goetz than maybe we knew in the past."[6] Governor Cuomo stated more guardedly that these revelations seemed to be "significant."[7]

But as much as this reaction to the police report vindicated Morgenthau's original efforts to indict him on a range of serious charges, it also put his office in the hot seat with those who now wondered how the prosecutor possibly could have failed to do so. Goetz's admission that he had attempted to shoot Cabey, a boy who hadn't spoken to him or even been near him, alone should have been enough. And worse, Goetz had also outright admitted that, after he tried to shoot this kid and missed, he then decided to shoot him again, point-blank, while leveling the chilling words, "You seem to be doing all right, here's another."[8]

Because its proceedings were sealed, however, no one knew that the grand jury had already seen this evidence and nevertheless declined to indict him on anything more than having an illegal weapon. Somehow it had not mattered that Goetz had outright admitted that he did not think that he was being robbed, yet already knew what he was going to do. It had not made a difference that he had approached the shooting of the teens with military precision, laying down what he described as a "pattern of fire."[9] And it hadn't seemed incongruent that though Goetz had characterized his own actions as "cold blooded," he did not feel that he had done anything wrong.[10]

Eager to get Bernie's side of the story in the midst of this new controversy, *The New York Times* conducted a two-hour interview with him in his apartment. Although he admitted that he worried that the release of his first statement to the police might elicit "all kinds of negative statements" from people who "are not acquainted with the entire situation," Goetz also didn't deny anything that the report claimed he had admitted to. As the *Times* reported it, he said that Officer Foote's statement was "essentially accurate."[11]

Two weeks after Goetz's admissions became public, Morgenthau issued a press release that raised the possibility of convening a second grand jury. He insisted that his decision had not been "prompted by reaction to the New Hampshire report." Rather, Morgenthau maintained, he had "been considering re-presenting from the day the indictment was voted." The only reason they had not done so already was because, in their view, simply disagreeing with a grand jury determination "[did] not create a legal basis for submitting the case to another grand jury."[12]

Getting fresh eyes on the situation, Morgenthau decided to bring two different assistant DAs onto the case, Gregory Waples and Robert Pitler. Over the years, Morgenthau had come to rely on Waples, who had a reputation for being "a prodigious worker, an excellent investigator and a master at explaining complicated facts to a jury."[13] Pitler, for his part, was unparalleled in the realm of "criminal law, criminal procedure and evidence."[14]

The primary obstacle for Waples and Pitler, as had been the issue for Morgenthau himself, remained that in order for the DAs to present before a second grand jury, there had to be "new evidence or grounds for additional charges."[15]

Those assembled for the press conference that Morgenthau had called could only speculate what this new evidence might be. Most suspected it was the revelation of the Concord police report, especially since Goetz's admissions "could be construed as premeditation." But of course the grand jury had already seen this, and therefore it did not constitute new evidence.[16] It would have to be something else.

As Greg Waples later explained, his office had by then decided "to grant immunity to some of the young men who were shot so that they could testify."[17] Their accounts would provide the DA's office with the new evidence it needed to pursue a second indictment.

But first, the DA's office would have to present this new evidence to the presiding judge, Justice Stephen G. Crane of the main criminal court (oddly called the New York State Supreme Court).[18] The argument that Morgenthau's office would offer Judge Crane was not without irony: The compelling new evidence they had was the testimony of the very individuals who were previously unwilling to testify due to the DA's office's decision to withhold immunity.[19]

In the memorandum of law they submitted in support of their application to convene a second grand jury, prosecutors made clear that the primary factor that had changed since the convening of the first grand jury was the DA's willingness to grant immunity to Troy Canty specifically, because he in particular possessed "significant information about the precise circumstances which apparently precipitated the shootings, and about the shootings themselves."[20]

The DA's office understood this was an awkward argument to make. And yet, its filing explained that "Canty initially refused to be interviewed by a prosecutor," and thus it was in no position to decide immunity.[21]

As it turned out, there had been a reason for Canty's reluctance to speak out, Waples now asserted. His office had learned that "Canty's family [had] received over 50 telephone calls and letters which explicitly threaten[ed] both him and his family. In the wake of these threats, Canty's parents, out of concern for the physical safety and privacy of the family, ha[d] counseled their son not to testify."[22]

But circumstances had changed. Time had passed and now Troy was willing to work with the DA's office, and, in exchange, it was willing to immunize him. In light of this new circumstance, they hoped Judge Crane would "permit resubmission" to a second grand jury because they believed Troy's testimony could prove that Bernie Goetz had indeed committed the more serious charges they had tried to indict him on the first time around—like attempted murder.[23]

The first grand jury had only been able to hear from Goetz himself, they argued. Indeed, Waples maintained, the jurors had taken Goetz's own "unsworn, and possibly self-serving statements to law-enforcement authorities, and to Myra Friedman," a friend and neighbor, to heart. They had, according to ADAs Waples and Pitler, unwittingly been given what amounted to "several hours" of "sympathetic appeals for understanding by the defendant." This had been "the sole evidence of justification," which made it impossible for them to make a fair assessment.[24]

Although it would have been unclear to any reporter exactly which tapes had been played before the grand jury—Domian's, Braver's, Myra Friedman's, or all three—a piece in the *Post* on January 29, 1985, written by none other than Steve Dunleavy confirmed that, according to "a source close to the grand jury," hearing Goetz on tape had, in fact, "had a more positive impact on the grand jury."[25]

Unsurprisingly, Barry Slotnick and Mark Baker vehemently objected to the prosecution's bid to convene a second grand jury. The defense filed its objection with Crane, hoping he would agree that doing so was an outrageous proposition. As Baker stated in a letter, "[T]he neutral court, and not the District Attorney, must make the determination of whether there should be a resubmission."[26]

They would be disappointed. On March 12, 1985, Judge Crane signed an order authorizing Morgenthau's office "to resubmit the previously dismissed charges to a second Grand Jury."[27] The very decision to assemble a second grand jury would incite another deeply contentious battle over whether Goetz would ever truly be held criminally accountable.

21

Second Time Around

Now authorized to re-present their amended case to a second New York grand jury, Morgenthau's team had to ensure that they would, in fact, have testimony from some of the teens Bernie Goetz had shot.

It still would not be possible to hear from Darrell Cabey, as all sides agreed he was in no shape to testify. And the DA's office seemed uninterested in offering Barry Allen immunity to take the stand. So that left Troy Canty and James Ramseur. The fact that these two teenagers would be immunized sparked no shortage of backlash, even though the many charges pending against them were misdemeanors. As one outraged headline in the *New York Post* blared, "THE CRIMINAL GETS IMMUNITY AND THE VICTIM GETS NOTHING."[1] The author of another "Letter to the Editor" in a Russian-language paper published in NYC was incensed that the grand jury would be hearing from "the attacker," Troy Canty, only because he had been granted full immunity—"the 'forgiving' of all his personal crimes. This is absolutely unbelievable!"[2]

On March 18, 1985, a New York grand jury would, for the first time, hear a retelling of the Goetz shooting from the perspective of a victim: James Ramseur. The DA's office felt that James's testimony was particularly important because, like Darrell Cabey, he had been nowhere near Bernie Goetz when Goetz decided to shoot him. James and Darrell had been down at the end of the subway car, and no accounts had suggested they even spoke to Goetz, let alone threatened him or tried to rob him. Just as importantly, several passengers had later come forward and reported that James had been attempting to flee when Goetz shot him.[3]

But perhaps the far more important testimony for this second grand jury to hear was that of Troy Canty on March 21, 1985. In many ways, Troy's actions on the day of the shooting had become the crux of the case. Had he been threatening Goetz? Was he shot only because Goetz was protecting himself?

Absolutely not, Troy insisted during his fifty minutes on the stand.[4]

As he recalled, when Goetz boarded the train, Troy had noticed him right away. The man had sat down and stared directly at Troy and Barry before he had, almost challengingly, "partly unzipped his coat." But Troy was in a good mood that day and was feeling bold and chatty. So, Troy smiled, greeted the man, and then decided to ask him for five dollars. But all that man had to do, Troy insisted, was decline, and "that would've been the end of the matter."[5]

Even if Goetz had been afraid of Troy for some reason, that still didn't explain why he had shot the other boys, Troy made clear. He had been the only one to approach Goetz, "without encouragement" from the others.[6]

It was up to the DAs to ensure that the jurors contemplated not only the testimony of the boys but also what Goetz himself had admitted when he spoke to the various detectives in New Hampshire and confided in Myra Friedman. The boys had not tried to rob him; Goetz had made that perfectly clear. And although he was not concerned they had weapons, he had confessed to wanting to shoot, maim, and even kill the boys long before drawing his gun.

Troy Canty leaving criminal court after his grand jury appearance.
Dan Cronin/New York *Daily News* Archive via Getty Images

The prosecutors also knew that they had to persuade the jurors that, even though screwdrivers had been found in the coat pockets of both James and Darrell, these boys had never brandished them, nor had anyone on the subway that day even known that they possessed these objects.[7] As they would also point out by calling some of the train's passengers to the stand—"old and young, male and female, black, white and Hispanic"—no one in that subway car had been "alarmed or frightened by any of the youths' actions or conduct."[8] If the boys were not a threat, then Goetz had no reason to shoot.

Even so, the question was not simply whether Goetz was justified in pulling a gun. It was about whether he had intentions of harming the boys and even murdering them. The DAs hoped to persuade jurors that he had sought to do both and was "out of control."[9]

No action he took exemplified this more, they argued, than when he turned his gun on Darrell Cabey—not once, but twice. They hammered away at Goetz's own disturbing words: "You seem to be all right, here's another."[10]

If what mattered here was intent, Goetz had admitted that he intended to kill the teens. Prosecutors used his taped confession to show this, particularly the moment when he said if he had been "thinking a little bit more clearly . . . I would have put, put the barrel against [Cabey's] forehead and fired," and that "if I had more bullets, I would have shot 'em all again and again."[11]

This time, the grand jury was receptive to the state's case. On March 27, 1985, after hearing a full seven days of testimony, it handed down a slew of serious indictments including charges of attempted murder (four counts), first-degree assault (four counts), reckless endangerment (one count), and criminal possession of a weapon in the second degree (one count). From the previous grand jury, he was already facing charges for third- and fourth-degree criminal possession of a weapon (three counts), and Goetz would be arraigned on all of these charges on March 28, 1985.[12]

The message was clear—Bernhard Goetz now faced the possibility of doing real time: a maximum sentence of twenty-five years for each of his attempted murder counts, fifteen years each on his four charges of first-degree assault, fifteen years for the charge of criminal possession of a weapon in the second degree, and seven years for the charge of first-degree reckless endangerment. The third- and fourth-degree weapons charges could also net him time, albeit much less.[13]

Manhattan DA Robert Morgenthau and Assistant DA Gregory Waples announce the multicount indictment of Bernhard Goetz on March 27, 1985, at Morgenthau's New York office. AP

Word of these far more substantial indictments set off a new firestorm. Angry missives poured into the "letter to the editor" sections of the tabloids, decrying this "travesty of justice."[14] As M. Purcell from Manhattan said, "since it has been revealed that the four punks who accosted Bernhard Goetz have 19 arrests among them, one would tend to wonder how many felonies they have committed for which they were never arrested."[15]

Letters also flooded the DA's office, some of which were threatening and violent, and it would have been difficult for anyone working there not to feel some measure of concern. As one "citizen" wrote, "Dear District Attorney Morgenthau, my wish is that one of your family has to take the subway some night and gets hers and you get yours next . . . if there is a GOD, you and lawyer cronies and muggies will get yours."[16] Solomon Abbey, from Mount Vernon, New York, wrote to Morgenthau on March 30 to criticize "young, arrogant self-satisfied but stupid assistant Waples" and added, "When you [Morgenthau] or your assistant leave the safety of your cars and do a little walking, the time will come when you get your lumps."[17]

Such letters arrived even from well outside New York State, including from South Carolina (declaring "You could've taken care of the criminals—but you were not taking care of the good, decent, law-abiding citizens of this country—let alone, New York state or city") and from Florida (lambasting the "shit head" DA for going after Goetz, who dared to "defend himself against 4 hoods who had a record of violent crimes before").[18]

Judge Stephen Crane got his share of mail too. Some of it was even supportive, complimenting him as "a credit to our judicial system" for reopening the case and offering opinions on Bernie. ("Mr. Goetz seems like a socially unfit and psychologically unstable individual. . . . It seems [he] could have handled himself differently," wrote Irene Wasserman;[19] "He is not a hero and therefore should not be treated that way," wrote Lisa Robinson.[20])

But most of the mail that landed on Judge Crane's desk was highly critical. As F. Mulrooney wrote, "You know he was right, so just be fair. The hoodlums did not get enough."[21] Lillian Trezza of Flushing, New York, in Queens, accused Crane of coddling the teens. "Goetz is not getting a fair trial," she wrote. "Tired of you defending criminals, these Criminals should be in jail."[22] Frances Mazzuka put forth that sentiment even more boldly: "May I, for one moment ask you how it feels to be part of a lynch mob? Not only are you part of the lynch mob, you are the rope which they will use."[23]

One particularly alarming, and anonymous, letter to Crane read, "Unless all charges against Bernhard Goetz are dismissed . . . and stay dismissed—a substantial quantity of plutonium trichloride (either in aqueous solution or in bulk) will be introduced at several locations into the water supply of New York City."[24]

Of all the letters that flooded the offices of the judge or the DA, however, the number of missives laced with explicitly racist language stood out, and these too came from across the country. One anonymous letter to the judge opined: "One of these things must be true about you: 1. You are n— or part n— 2. Your mother started her whorehouse career in a n— whore house" and that "Mr. Goetz was defending himself against being robbed by N—s. . . . No way these scum can ever be honest or tell the truth."[25]

Another anonymous, aggressively hate-filled letter to Crane declared, "you are such a N— ass kisser that you don't know the difference between a victim and a criminal. There are hundreds of thousands of N—s mugging white riders on subs every year. I don't care if they mug co—s . . . those dirty co—s were looking for trouble—they have committed a lot of hold ups before they attacked Goetz . . . all of those shits should be strung up from a nearby tree. That is the only way to make them behave."[26]

While these writers had been too cowardly to sign their names, plenty of others were willing to own their racist views. A note from Virgil Sams in Brandon, Oregon, ranted that Goetz was being "crucified" and that these legal proceedings proved only "that blacks can get away with ANYTHING."[27] In a letter to Morgenthau, a couple surnamed Katz wrote, "I hope someday that you will be mugged on the street, and your head split open. Maybe you will then think twice about what an injustice you have done to an innocent victim who was attacked by such brutal n—s. You must be a n—r lover."[28]

Bernie Goetz's lawyers ran with this outpouring of outrage. Clearly, there were still many people who supported Goetz and his actions on that downtown-bound 2 train. Slotnick and Baker decided that before things could get any worse for their client, they should take the matter of these new indictments to a higher authority.

22

Last-Ditch Effort

Bernie Goetz's legal team first tried to challenge his new indictments on May 14, 1985, by commencing something called an Article 78 proceeding, in which his lawyers argued that the resubmission of the charges to the second grand jury had been an abuse of discretion on the part of the court.[1] That effort failed.

They tried again on October 14, 1985, this time moving "to dismiss the charges contained in the second indictment alleging, among other things, that the evidence before the second Grand Jury was not legally sufficient to establish the offenses charged . . . and that the prosecutor's instructions to that Grand Jury on the defense of justification were erroneous and prejudicial to the defendant so as to render its proceedings defective."[2]

This latter effort would at least get them somewhere—especially because a few developments had recently taken place that Goetz's lawyers would lean into heavily in order to persuade the judge to rule in their favor.

According to Slotnick and Baker, the second grand jury's decision to indict Goetz on the charge of attempted murder had been influenced less by his own confessions and more heavily by the testimony of James Ramseur, who said he had not spoken to Goetz nor been close enough to threaten him. Hearing from Ramseur directly had mattered. That is, as long as he was an upstanding and credible witness. However, his credibility was now, according to the defense, very much in question.

Back in March, two days before the second grand jury issued its major indictments, a 911 call had been placed by a person who identified himself as Daryl Thompson. According to "Thompson," he had just seen "two persons push James Ramseur, who the caller identified as one of the persons shot by Goetz, into a blue Lincoln automobile and then drive off."[3]

The 911 operator immediately dispatched officers to the apartment where James lived to verify that he was missing. At ten that night, James returned to his apartment and told the officers that he had indeed been "pushed" into a car at 170th and Third in the Bronx and then "taken to some playground in the Bronx where he was forced to get out of the car . . . and a few shots were fired." He was not hit, and so he fled.[4]

According to James, the men who kidnapped him were "two housing detectives, burly white guys" that had been hired by Goetz. The next day, March 26, James helped the police do a sketch of the two Housing Authority cops.[5] The police didn't believe the story and began pressing James, playing the 911 tape for him several times until he admitted that not only had he been the one to make the call but also that the police report he had filed was completely "false." He had done this, he explained, "to test police response when a black person was a crime victim."[6]

The Bronx police charged James Ramseur "with filing a false police report, a misdemeanor punishable by less than one year in jail and a maximum fine of $1,000." He was released with "a summons to appear in court to answer the charge."[7]

But Greg Waples had not shielded the grand jurors from these bizarre events at the time. He had in fact informed them of Ramseur's stunt and made clear to these jurors that he was doing so precisely "for the purpose, for whatever it's worth to you, to evaluate and consider Mr. Ramseur's credibility as a witness." He had not shied away from noting as well that several of the witnesses he called "had previously been convicted of crimes," in case that information was relevant to them when they set about "evaluating their credibility." As he made clear, "You can give it whatever weight you wish."[8]

Still, the defense hoped this would have bearing on their new bid to overturn this jury's decision. If nothing else, it might raise serious doubts in Judge Crane's mind about any testimony James Ramseur had given under oath that had influenced the indictments. But, as their luck would have it, Bernie's lawyers would not have to rely solely on this. Just over a month after they had filed their motion to vacate the indictments against their client, a major and highly inflammatory story by Jimmy Breslin was published in the *Daily News,* and then a cop came forward with some ostensibly new information. The defense was certain that both would greatly help their client.

SINCE DARRELL HAD BEEN admitted to St. Vincent's, his doctors and later his attorneys had protected him from the media. They understood he was in no shape to be interviewed. Their determination to protect him only deepened once it became clear how much cognitive function he had lost since his coma. Going for so long without oxygen, and spending weeks unconscious, had fundamentally changed Darrell. He had suffered notable brain damage.

But in November 1985, Jimmy Breslin managed to gain access to Darrell Cabey's room at St. Vincent's and interviewed him. According to the November 26 piece he published, Darrell had made a very important admission about Bernie Goetz during their chat: Darrell, Breslin alleged, said that not only were his friends all "goin' rob [Goetz]," but they had decided to do this because "they thought he looked like easy bait." According to Breslin, Darrell also told him, "I could see they were going to do that. I said to myself, I don't want to be involved."[9]

Though Breslin acknowledged that Darrell "appeared confused," was "having some trouble speaking," and even that he was clearly disoriented and uneasy whenever Breslin "attempted to ask him about something for a second time," the piece was explosive. The public could focus only on Breslin's assertion that Troy, James, and Barry had in fact intended to "scare" Goetz into giving up his money.[10]

Darrell's attorneys and the DA's office alike were appalled by the piece. They knew from his doctors not only that Darrell's ability to respond or to comprehend was now severely compromised but also that people in his condition tended to say what they thought whoever they were talking to wanted to hear. Darrell could easily have been led to say whatever he felt would make Breslin think he was both helpful and smart.

The public knew none of this medical information, however, nor really did the judge. Thanks to Breslin's piece, therefore, Goetz's lawyers had a new opportunity to introduce even more doubts as to the credibility of Troy Canty and James Ramseur.

The day after Breslin's piece hit newsstands, another equally shocking story broke: a police officer who had been one of the first on the scene of the shooting, Peter Smith, was now claiming that Troy Canty told him that day: "We were going to rob" Goetz.[11] On the day of the shooting, Smith had actually told reporters that the boys had said nothing of importance when he tended to them.[12] But now he was saying he had heard something totally different.

As soon as ADA Greg Waples learned of Smith's claim, he immediately notified Goetz's defense attorney Mark Baker of this development. In a letter dated November 27, 1985, Waples informed him that Smith had brought this claim to the DA's office but that, when pressed, Smith had conceded "that he made no notation of any kind of this important information." Nor had he ever before "disclosed this intelligence to any investigator or supervisor," and he also did not "recall telling any investigator about the statement until he came to [Waples's] office."[13]

Because Waples had found no previous record of Canty's alleged comment, and because Officer Smith had not even recorded such a statement in his own memo book, this was nonsense, as far as he was concerned. Maybe this was simply Smith's way of trying to help Goetz once it was clear the DA was going to go after him full throttle.[14]

This, however, did not stop Mark Baker from arguing that Judge Crane should take Smith's statement seriously, and even consider it to be "new evidence" sufficient to throw out the recent indictments of his client. According to Baker, his office had also received an anonymous call that, to his "somewhat experienced ears, sounded strikingly like a police officer." This caller claimed there had been "several" police reports "bearing highly exculpatory statements" regarding Goetz that were "deep-sixed" by Waples's office. In Baker's view, this demonstrated "all too convincingly—if there was ever any doubt—that [the] defendant's subjective beliefs and his actions in response thereto were more than justified."[15]

For his part, Greg Waples took major exception to the insinuation that the District Attorney's Office or the police had "deliberately suppressed" Smith's statement, or any "other police reports containing purportedly exculpatory information."[16] "[It] is simply untrue," Waples wrote in a letter to Judge Crane:

> I have had a copy of the entire police file since late February 1985 and can attest that nothing has been suppressed. I am equally confident that no reports were suppressed before I became involved in this matter. Nor do I need to dignify Mr. Baker's disappointing attempt, in a letter to the court, to cloak his anonymous rumor monger in the mantle of legitimate mercy, by divining his or her occupation from the sound of a voice over a telephone.[17]

But Waples was savvy enough to understand that any attention given to Smith's eleventh-hour claim could nevertheless derail his hard-won indictments against Goetz. To make matters worse, and to Waples's dismay, Troy Canty had hardly been endearing himself to the public since he'd taken the stand. One day when leaving the courtroom, for example, he had told reporters, "I want to see Bernie Goetz fry."[18]

To ensure the indictments would stick, Waples and Pitler spent a great deal of time crafting their detailed response to Slotnick and Baker's bid. They pointed out that prosecutors had been "scrupulous" in calling the jury's attention to evidence that might undermine James's credibility and told them to take this into account when they deliberated. They pointed out that the judge had known all about this potentially "impeaching evidence" at the time, and thus there was not now any "rational basis for concluding that the new evidence undermined the integrity of that indictment."[19]

With regard to Breslin's claims that the boys intended to rob Goetz, Waples and Pitler insisted this was a total nonstarter unless it was probed further by Cabey's neurologists. As they put it bluntly, if the defense team wanted to make the claim that Darrell was more capable than he actually was, or that he had some critical information to impart despite his well-documented brain injury, then "surely trial . . . is where this testimony should be elicited and this factual dispute resolved."[20]

As for Peter Smith's late-breaking insistence that Troy Canty had admitted to a robbery on the day he was shot, Waples and Pitler scoffed. Smith's claims were utterly unproven and thus they provided zero basis for the judge to vacate the findings of this grand jury.[21] What's more, they argued, absolutely nothing prevented the defense from raising Smith's assertions at trial if they had merit. "It simply cannot be contended," they would insist, "that the integrity of the Grand Jury's deliberations was impaired" simply because Goetz's attorneys fixed on other "potentially impeaching evidence" many months later.[22]

And yet, on January 16, 1986, stunning the city, Judge Stephen Crane would nevertheless side with Slotnick and Baker by dismissing all nine of the most serious charges against Goetz—leaving only the reckless endangerment and gun charges.

Crane went to some lengths to explain his reasoning in a thirty-four-page opinion, one that he drafted four times.[23] The bottom line was that he agreed there had been "prejudicial error" when the prosecution gave its instructions to the grand jury regarding what constituted justification with regard to the shootings Goetz had carried out. The law, Crane insisted, "allows individuals to use deadly force when they have reasonable belief that they are going to be robbed" [and] in the judge's view, Waples "had indeed incorrectly explained that part of the law to the jury."[24]

Crane also made clear that he was troubled by the possibility that any state witness "may have lied to that grand jury."[25] In saying this, he suggested that he too doubted the testimony of James Ramseur and Troy Canty, and the media ran with this suggestion. As *The New York Times* put it, through this decision, Justice Crane implied that "statements before that grand jury by two of those shot now 'strongly appear' to have been perjury." Stating the obvious, it went on, "The integrity of the second grand jury was severely undermined to say the least."[26]

Judge Crane did not fully close the door on the possibility of Goetz facing more serious charges, should they be merited. This, he made clear, would require "the highly unusual step" of convening yet a third grand jury. Although he would be willing to take that step, he was loath to do so in no small part because it would merely prolong "the fierce debate" over vigilantism that had consumed New York City.[27]

Some New Yorkers were ecstatic to hear this news. As one man, Harry Werder, wrote to Crane, "You did a really good job of dropping the charges. Bernhard Goetz had enough. This man should receive a medal rather than the hassle he went through."[28] Another city resident named Birdie Bloch agreed wholeheartedly. "I find myself writing a 'fan' letter for the first time in my life . . . all of my friends and countless numbers around the world are applauding your brilliant decision in this case."[29]

C. Vernon Mason, however, found it "unprecedented that [Crane was] making a judicial decision based on a newspaper account."[30] Police Commissioner Benjamin Ward also expressed his concern about the rescinding of the more serious indictments against Goetz, especially if Officer Smith's claims had factored into this decision. These were "not credible," the commissioner said, and in fact, did "not make a great deal of sense."[31]

Although the commissioner was not explicitly among them, on January 17, 1986, myriad Black leaders responded to Crane's decision by publicly calling "for the charges to be reinstated—either by appeal or through a third grand jury—so that Mr. Goetz could face a public trial."[32] It was simply outrageous, they argued, that the only charges Goetz currently faced were those related to weapons possession and reckless endangerment.

The DA's office could not have agreed more and immediately filed an appeal. They insisted that under the law, self-defense absolutely required "objective reasonableness" and to argue otherwise was to twist or ignore and thus to "proffer a bizarre and totally indefensible interpretation of the legislative intent."[33]

While the DA's office certainly conceded that "the legal and factual issues in this case are complex," nevertheless, all "facts should be fully litigated in a public forum and the question of Goetz's guilt or innocence decided by a jury."[34]

Ultimately, on July 8, 1986, the New York Court of Appeals reversed Crane's highly controversial decision. This highest court in the state had decided that, contrary to Crane's instructions, just because a defendant might have felt they were in "imminent danger," that did not, in itself, justify the use of force. The defendant's perception must also be more objectively "reasonable."[35]

The court further decided that Judge Crane's thoughts on perjury had been speculative and "particularly inappropriate." Indeed, it wrote, "[A]ll that has come to light is hearsay evidence that conflicts with part of Canty's testimony. There is no statute or controlling case law requiring dismissal of an indictment merely because, months later, the prosecutor becomes aware of some information which may lead to the defendant's acquittal."[36]

With this final decision, Bernie Goetz once again faced the litany of charges handed down to him by the second grand jury, including the four counts of attempted murder. In ways he had never expected, however, Bernie was even more popular than he had been before. He was enjoying it immensely, and was seemingly unfazed by the fact that his fate was once again highly uncertain.

Bernie had insisted all along that he actually welcomed his trial. As he told Norma Quarles on *NBC Nightly News* when the second grand jury's indictments were originally announced, "I think that other victims of violent crime will find it easy to understand my reaction . . . hopefully this will bring an end to all the controversy."[37]

His lawyers sincerely hoped that Bernie was right, given that he now faced the possibility of decades in prison. As Barry Slotnick had put it on the same news program, clearly laying the groundwork for how he would try to defend his client in the upcoming criminal case: "Goetz was a victim on December 22nd" and "unfortunately," he still was.[38]

PART IV

Vigilantism on Trial

THE MANHATTAN CRIMINAL COURTHOUSE was an imposing structure. Its granite-and-limestone façade was built in the iconic Art Deco style and rose an impressive seventeen stories. Passersby could easily have mistaken it for an elegant concert hall were it not for the stern-faced police officers, harried attorneys, handcuffed New Yorkers, and rumpled reporters chasing the next lurid headline who populated its corridors.

The building had become so renowned for the high-profile cases taking place in its courtrooms that it actually inspired a popular 1980s sitcom, *Night Court.* The show, which humorously depicted its evening court sessions, became such a hit that fans would often flock to the courthouse's public galleries to observe real cases as they played out.

What the home viewers might not have fully appreciated, however, was the extent to which the cases coming before judges were now so inescapably defined by deep class divisions as well as seemingly intractable racial tension. While "Wall Street is exploding with obscene riches," noted reporter Tim Minton, the rest of the city was suffering economically. And, as important, explained journalist Errol Louis, "if you were black and went into the wrong neighborhood, it would not be unusual for a mob to try and physically attack you."[1]

As the decade of the 1980s had unfolded, acts of white racial violence indeed continued to make the news. Since Bernhard Goetz's shooting of Troy Canty, Barry Allen, James Ramseur, and Darrell Cabey, and as the Goetz legal saga was still playing out, for example, yet another young man, twenty-three-year-old Michael Griffith, was killed—struck by a car—as he desperately fled a white mob that attacked him and his friends near a pizza shop in Howard Beach, Brooklyn.[2]

That incident sparked mass protests in its immediate wake and thereafter. Although three of Griffith's attackers were convicted of manslaughter, a fourth was acquitted, a verdict that enraged many. Protesters took to the streets, some lying down on subway tracks to halt trains at the Borough Hall and Jay Street stations, while others marched through Howard Beach.

By 1986, New York City was completely on edge, not only because of these ever-bolder acts of racist violence but also because it was a metropolis still ravaged by budget cuts, the ongoing crack epidemic, the deepening AIDS crisis, and an ever-escalating drug war. A few years later, director Spike Lee would release his award-winning film *Do the Right Thing*, a searing portrayal of inequality, racism, and rage in 1980s New York City. The film's climactic moments would resonate deeply with the city's most marginalized residents, amplified as they were by the booming sound of Public Enemy's hip-hop anthem "Fight the Power."

Meanwhile, in opposition to one demonstration against the Howard Beach verdicts led by the Rev. Al Sharpton, working-class whites chanted racist slurs and "brandished watermelons to taunt protesters," knowing full well the impact of the now-centuries old racist iconography they were invoking.[3]

It was in this particular context that Bernhard Goetz would finally stand trial for the shootings of the four teenagers back in 1984.

23

Gearing Up for Battle

IT WOULD TAKE nearly two years after Goetz's shootings of Troy, Barry, James, and Darrell for his case to finally get a trial date. In that time, and particularly in the wake of the second grand jury's indictments, the media would continue to devote much of its energy to digging up the wrongdoings of Goetz's victims rather than calling for justice on their behalf.

Sadly, they had quite a bit to work with.

Barry Allen, back home and seemingly on the mend, was now struggling with an ever more serious coke habit and could not find a steady job. This situation was a recipe for another run-in with the law and, sure enough, just shy of nine months after his release from Bellevue Hospital, Barry and one of his friends were arrested and charged with snatching a $150 chain necklace off of a guy they knew in the elevator of their building.[1]

Bernie's defense attorney, Mark Baker, told reporters that not only was his client "not surprised" by Barry Allen's arrest, but he had in fact "predicted" it. As Baker went on, one thing was for sure: "Each of these guys [would end up with] longer records" than his client.[2]

During this two-year interim, James Ramseur had also been arrested, for a far more serious offense.[3] In May 1985, a few months after having faked his own kidnapping during the grand jury proceedings, James was arrested in connection with the assault and rape of a nineteen-year-old he knew named Gladys Richardson, who also lived in the Claremont Village projects.[4] Though James vehemently denied these charges, he was convicted on March 3, 1986. By the time the Goetz trial began, James was already in prison.

Letters to the prosecutors handling Goetz's case indicated how little sympathy the now young men could expect as the trial loomed. ADA Gregory Waples received one particularly sarcastic letter regarding James Ramseur:

> I read in the paper that one of Bernie Goetz's victims has been victimized again.... Poor fellow. I guess some people just have all the bad luck. First, he gets attacked while minding his own business, riding the subway downtown to work, and then he has his virtue violated by a depraved wench. I hope they prosecute that girl to the full extent of the law. This was a premeditated crime if ever there was one. After all, she didn't leave home and go out on the streets carrying that concealed rape equipment without intending to use it at the slightest provocation.[5]

Goetz's other victims, however, were not so easily pigeonholed. Troy Canty, for example, had redoubled his efforts to get clean and was determined this time to succeed. The process had been arduous and uneven, considering the stress of the first and second grand juries, the press scrutiny, and the death threats. But despite all this, Troy had started to make a new life for himself. He had entered a drug rehabilitation center in April 1985 and, by all reports, he was doing well.

That Troy Canty had been able to turn his life around was no thanks to the New York State Crime Victims Board. Each of the teens should have been eligible for compensation from this entity, which reimbursed victims of serious crime for "out-of-pocket expenses, including ... medical or other services necessary as a result of the injury," as well as, even more significantly, "loss of earnings or support resulting from such injury."[6] Troy had applied for these funds, assuming that the extensive, life-threatening wounds he'd suffered after being shot by Bernie Goetz made him eligible. His claim was, however, denied.

As the commissioner of the Crime Victims Board, Diane McGrath, wrote in the Canty decision, "After a thorough review of the file ... it appears that the victim was in the process of robbing the alleged perpetrator at the time he was shot. Therefore, he cannot be deemed the innocent victim of a crime."[7] As the Goetz trial rapidly approached, it was clear that the public had no more interest in these young men's fates than it had on the day they had first been shot. They were not the kind of "victims" the Reagan administration had in mind when it had offered up additional federal funding for the Crime Victims Board. And they certainly were not victims in the eyes of countless ordinary New Yorkers.

In contrast to Goetz's other shooting victims, Darrell Cabey received little media coverage. When Darrell was finally able to go home in February 1986, after more than a year in the hospital, he faced extraordinary hardship. He required around-the-clock care and daily transportation for his visits to a rehabilitation center. His mother still hoped that he might regain his ability to speak clearly, comprehend basic questions and directions, and learn to maneuver the wheelchair that had become a permanent feature of his life.

Based on the media's myriad one-sided pieces on the shootings and their reverberations, it was easy to forget not only that Darrell Cabey was paralyzed for life but also the full range and true seriousness of the charges being leveled against the man who had shot him. It was no small number: four counts of attempted murder, four first-degree assault charges, one charge of reckless endangerment, one charge of criminal possession of a weapon in the second degree, and the charges he was indicted for by the first grand jury—criminal possession in the third degree (for the gun he carried on the subway) and two counts of criminal possession of a weapon in the fourth degree (for the two guns he left with Myra Friedman on December 30, 1984).

The gravity of this pending trial was, however, not lost on Judge Stephen Crane. By December 1986, he had been dealing with this case in some fashion for a long time now, including putting up with the bombastic lawyers who challenged virtually every ruling he made, as well as the rebukes of the appellate court that had overturned his decision to vacate the most serious charges Goetz faced. And then there were the poison-pen letters and telegrams and cards that had filled his inbox. By all accounts, Judge Crane had handled all of this with remarkable calm and good grace, especially when it came to withstanding the ongoing media firestorm.

But with the trial date now set, even he was daunted. Judge Crane was known to spend an extraordinary amount of time preparing, researching the law, and considering every possible angle of every imaginable issue that might arise, well before a given legal proceeding commenced.[8] But no amount of preparation could have softened the reality that this trial was likely going to be both tense and dramatic, assuredly pure theater, no matter on whose docket the case had landed.

Indeed, Barry Slotnick, Goetz's main lawyer, might well have chosen a career on the stage rather than in the courtroom. He was fervent and flashy, and every glance, gesture, and word he uttered was selected for maximum effect. Yet, when it might better serve the interests of his client, Slotnick was also more than capable of presenting his arguments in a calmer, "easy, relaxed manner" and could "effortlessly . . . change his tack and slip into humor, using it to ease tension or as a probing device."[9]

Described by the media as "an unabashed self-promoter [who] views himself as the best criminal lawyer in America," Slotnick was also never shy about calling attention to himself.[10] No matter the occasion, and with particular flair when he knew he would be facing a jury, he insisted on wearing tailored $2,500 suits and being driven into the city from his home in Scarsdale in a chauffeured Cadillac limousine.

This brash attorney's origins were considerably humbler, born as he was to Russian immigrant parents in the Bronx and having a father who worked as a caterer. But Slotnick was always determined to make a bigger mark. He decided on a career in law at a young age, graduating from NYU School of Law at twenty, before he was even old enough to take the bar. When he turned twenty-one and could officially take the exam, he set up shop in lower Manhattan with little more than "a phone number, answering service and maildrop near the courthouse."[11]

Politically, Barry Slotnick was quite conservative. Like many New York Republicans, his hobbyhorse issue was crime, and the need to "[reclaim] the streets of New York City from the criminals and pay more attention to crime victims."[12]

Yet Slotnick was a man of contradictions. As much as he despised crime and would "bristle at being called a 'mob lawyer,'" he hadn't shied away from representing Mafia dons, nor had he refused to defend other high-profile public officials accused of corruption.[13]

Barry Slotnick was nevertheless held in high esteem by some of the city's most powerful legal figures, including the U.S. Attorney in Manhattan, Rudolph Giuliani, who was deciding whether to file a civil rights case against Bernie Goetz. Giuliani considered Slotnick a friend, and described him publicly as "a professional, honest guy."[14]

To Slotnick, who craved the limelight and believed firmly that the city was falling prey to street criminals, defending Bernie Goetz made all the sense in the world—though he did acknowledge this particular client might pose "one of his most difficult legal tests," in no small part because he was known to be so unpredictable.[15]

Although he had first come to represent Goetz alongside lawyer Joseph Kelner, when it came time to litigate the criminal case, he would team up with his law partner, Mark Baker. Baker had a decade of experience as a prosecutor, and the plan was for Slotnick to question the witnesses while Baker would "handle the disputes that arise over legal technicalities," a job that would draw on his expertise "several times during each court day."[16]

"What was unusual about Baker," one Goetz juror later noted, "was his extraordinary powers of observation. He was forever alert and saw absolutely everything, so sharp was his focus and his concentration so strong." Judge Crane later described Baker as "the brains of the outfit."[17]

Slotnick's basic strategy for this case would be to convince the jurors—relying on his talent for sarcasm and hyperbole—that Goetz was not a "Citizen Rambo" or a "raving lunatic," as the prosecution believed, but rather a "fed up" Everyman. Goetz had simply fired his gun to protect himself from the "savages" on the subway.

But as Barry Slotnick well knew, his opposing counsel, Assistant DA Gregory Waples, certainly had the chops to land his client in prison. He had, for example, successfully prosecuted the high-profile, and highly controversial, 1983 CBS murders case, where a man named Donald Nash was charged with the abduction and killing of a federal witness and the deaths of three CBS technicians who attempted to prevent the kidnapping.[18]

And Greg Waples was determined to move heaven and earth to ensure that, like Nash, Bernie Goetz was brought to justice. Having taken on this case following Susan Braver's inability to secure any serious indictments before the first grand jury put pressure on Waples, and made him all the more committed to convicting Goetz of the crimes of which he now stood accused.

Waples's ascendancy to one of the most important legal positions in the city of New York was somewhat unusual. He grew up in Palo Alto, California, and moved to the East Coast to attend Yale, where he majored in American studies. Waples then headed to Columbia Law School and, once a member of the New York Bar, quickly gained the respect of the broader legal community. As one of his fellow Columbia Law grads put it, Greg Waples was "a real superstar" who was "unpretentious to a fault . . . [and] clear-headed and precise and intelligent."[19]

Waples's dream was to be a top prosecutor. Despite a hiring freeze in Robert Morgenthau's office, Waples wrote to him personally and made such an impression that the head DA hired him on the spot. Morgenthau regularly gave Waples some of the trickiest cases, and Waples carried more felony cases than any other assistant DA. The CBS murders had been a real test, with no identifying eyewitnesses nor any discernible motive. From Morgenthau's perspective, Waples had done a stellar job—Nash was not only convicted but also sentenced to one hundred years in prison.[20]

Waples soon became one of Morgenthau's most senior and respected trial lawyers, "an exclusive group" of twelve attorneys who, according to Morgenthau himself, were "able to handle any kind of case" and "handle them extremely well." They did not make a great deal of money; their salaries of $74,500, as one reporter pointed out, were "a fraction of what some of [their] former classmates are earning as partners in major law firms."[21] But a lower salary was fine by Greg Waples.

The truth was that Waples didn't enjoy the limelight and had no desire for a flashy social or personal life. He was actually quite private, which could come off as aloof, even though his friends insisted that he was "a warm person with a wry sense of humor." He liked running and would jog from his apartment on the Upper West Side all the way to work at the DA's office down in lower Manhattan, and otherwise enjoyed competing in marathons, "canoeing, hiking, and tennis."[22]

In terms of personality, style, and physical presence, Waples could not have been more different from Barry Slotnick. Whereas Slotnick would share even the most personal details of his life with the press, Waples would steadfastly avoid all questions about himself or his cases. He regularly refused requests for media interviews, particularly if they had to do with the looming Goetz trial, and he was even known to express "annoyance at some co-workers who have spoken to reporters about him."[23]

Waples also cut a much more modest figure than Slotnick sartorially. Whereas Slotnick was all about three-piece suits and favored a cloying cologne that would linger long after he passed the jury box, Greg Waples carried a basic briefcase and, jarringly, would even walk into the courtroom with an orange backpack slung over one shoulder of his basic blue or black suit.[24] With his tall stature, glasses, and wavy brown hair, he reminded some jurors of Clark Kent.[25]

And while Barry Slotnick remained audacious and loud, Waples was "all business."[26] According to one reporter, Waples employed "more of a 'just the facts ma'am' style that [drew] upon logic and thoroughness." Even in the inherently dramatic CBS murders case, as his opposing counsel recalled, "Mr. Waples delivered an 11-hour summation that was 'all substance.'"[27]

This did not mean that Greg Waples was above appealing to the emotions of the jury. Indeed, this strategy would be key to the case that Waples was meticulously constructing against Bernie Goetz, from his opening statement forward. He understood that his job was to convince the jurors that, no matter what wrongs Troy Canty, Barry Allen, James Ramseur, and Darrell Cabey had done in their lives, and no matter how unpolished they might be, none of them had deserved to be gunned down for asking a man for five dollars.

As another lawyer put it, Waples's unflappable nature made him a logical choice for the Goetz trial because while "someone like Slotnick could shake up most lawyers," he would not rattle Waples. While Slotnick wouldn't go so far as to praise Waples outright, he did concede that Waples had "proven himself quite adequate" in the context of this case.[28] And from Barry Slotnick, this was a compliment of the highest order.

24

Enter the Jury

THE TRIAL IN THE CASE of *The People of the State of New York v. Bernhard Goetz* finally began on December 12, 1986. More than three hundred New Yorkers were called into the chambers of Judge Stephen Crane to be questioned as potential jurors.[1] Those who made the cut would decide the fate of one of the most infamous men in the city—and be the first to see Barry Slotnick and Gregory Waples square off in what would become one of the most publicized trials of the decade.

Selecting the jury would take more than three months.[2] First there was a process of prescreening and then, beginning on March 23, 1987, the formal voir dire, in which attorneys from both sides questioned 135 individuals from the jury pool.[3] This would last for seven weeks, as it could only take place on Fridays because Slotnick was still in federal court for another high-profile legal showdown: *United States v. John Gotti*.[4]

The voir dire also dragged on because it was difficult to find jurors who did not have strong feelings one way or another about the Goetz shootings, given the publicity they had received over the past two years. Too often, a potential juror would make quite clear that they believed either that Goetz should be sent away for a long time or that Canty, Allen, Ramseur, and Cabey should be locked up instead.

The reality was that many of these potential jurors had themselves been mugged. According to one reporter, "When the first 18 potential jurors were seated in the jury box, state Supreme Court Justice Stephen Crane asked how many had been a crime victim. Eleven raised their hands, and five said they had been attacked on a subway."[5]

Prosecutor Waples questioned such candidates with particular intensity. How had they reacted to their ordeal? Were they angry? Were they fearful? He would also push them a bit, trying to gauge their feelings on crime more generally. In Waples's view, it was essential that every juror chosen "accept the fact that if fear turns to anger and you seriously assault someone, that may be a crime."[6]

Slotnick, for his part, wanted to keep any potential jurors who might relate to Bernie Goetz. For those who had been victims of crime, he avoided asking how angry or bitter they might be, simply hoping that a shared experience would work to his client's advantage. He was savvy enough to know that if he asked too many questions, and they admitted too much, the prosecution would nix them.

But even Slotnick understood that one couldn't really know what was on a potential juror's mind. For example, he was convinced that Harlem's *Amsterdam News* had been telling potential jurors "if you're picked for the jury, tell them you know nothing." He was also sure that there were others in this pool, likely fans of the defendant, who would get on the stand and say, "Oh, Bernhard Goetz, who's that? We don't know who he is."[7] To help him navigate this, and to read potential jurors just right, Slotnick hired a jury consultant, a psychiatrist from Oakland, California.[8]

Judge Crane paid little mind to the time this was all taking. He took voir dire seriously, even halting the proceedings at one point after reporters had approached several potential jurors for interviews in order to determine whether this "tampering was significant enough to warrant a mistrial."[9] Only after he had met with the lawyers on both sides did he decide they could continue.

And thus, the horse-trading dragged on.

In fact, in the time it took Slotnick and Waples to agree on who would decide the fate of Bernie Goetz, a great deal had happened in the city, the nation, and the world. New Yorkers had flocked to the highly anticipated premiere of Andrew Lloyd Webber's smash hit *Starlight Express* on Broadway, as well as to the ribbon cutting for Wollman Rink in Central Park—a project that had stalled for years before real estate mogul Donald Trump stepped in and finished the job, with his now trademark self-congratulatory flair and an especially glitzy grand opening.[10]

But they had also seen the horror of Michael Griffith's murder at the hands of the white mob in Howard Beach and learned about the NYPD "Buddy Boys" corruption scandal, in which eleven officers from Brooklyn's 77th Precinct were arrested for robbery, drug trafficking, and extortion.[11] In nearby Philadelphia, another brutal event played out in which elected officials approved the police dropping a bomb on a rowhouse with Black men, women, and children inside, burning them all alive and leaving two full city blocks in ashes.[12] Internationally, there had been troubling news about both the deepening Iran-Contra fiasco and the Chernobyl nuclear reactor explosion.

But finally, on April 7, 1987, a jury panel of twelve and four alternates would take their seats and be sworn in. Of the main jurors, ten were white, two were Black, four were women, and eight were men.[13] Notably, and despite the prosecution's careful questioning, the percentage of crime victims on the final jury was far higher than the overall percentage of New Yorkers who had been touched by crime that year.[14] Altogether, six of the twelve jurors had been victims of crime, and all but three of them said they had a friend or relative who had been victimized.[15]

The jury's foreman, financial analyst James Hurley, had himself been mugged on a subway. Seventy-four-year-old D. Wirth Jackson, the oldest juror, had been the victim of several burglaries, "including one in which an armed intruder threatened his wife and dog."[16] Others of the jurors had never personally been mugged but nevertheless had been impacted by crime in some personal way—thirty-one-year-old Carolyn Perlmuth had been walking with her mother when the older woman was mugged, and twenty-three-year-old James Moseley's previous girlfriend had also been mugged, something that clearly still weighed on him.[17]

Even jurors who had not been victimized or did not know anyone who had been had strong opinions on the proliferation of crime in New York in the 1980s. When asked whether he'd ever been afraid of being assaulted, forty-something bus driver Robert Leach said, "Every time you get on a bus . . . [t]he driver has no chance . . . some kids surround you . . . you're trapped."[18]

What's more, many of the jurors selected expressed that they had a hard time sympathizing with those who committed street crimes like assaults, muggings, or robberies. Sixty-three-year-old Ralph Schriempf, the very last juror chosen, unabashedly "told the court he believes the days of turning the other cheek are 'behind us.'"[19] Michael Axelrod, a thirty-four-year-old telephone technician and speech therapist, stated that he had "no problem with the concept of self-defense."[20] Thirty-two-year-old computer operator Francisco Figueroa seemed inclined to agree. The time he had experienced a burglary, he explained with disgust, “the police hadn’t [even bothered] to show up.”[21]

Mark Lesly, a twenty-something, also had strong views on crime, and more specifically on how to handle such encounters. Lesly was a martial arts expert, and he, like Axelrod, had made clear that he absolutely saw a role for self-defense. Meanwhile, fifty-nine-year-old Catherine Brody, a college English professor who also had been the target of an attempted subway mugging, was not sure how someone should properly react. She had actually resisted her attacker, but in this case, she wanted to hear all of the evidence.[22]

Despite their differing life experiences and varied views on crime and assault, this group of twelve jurors and four alternates would come to form a close bond. Juries in long and highly contentious trials such as this one end up spending hundreds of hours together, both in the jury box listening to testimony as well as in the rather dingy jury room where they were sent whenever the attorneys had to approach the bench. Before the trial was over, a romance would even blossom between two jurors, James Mosely and Diana Serpe.[23]

The jurors had been instructed not to discuss the case, so when they found themselves with downtime in that jury room they would chat about sports and movies, do crosswords and jigsaw puzzles, and play board games. On those particularly trying days when the proceeding had been contentious, emotional, and highly upsetting, that back room would be more subdued, with some jurors, like Catherine Brody, poring over copious notes taken from the jury box, and others, like Diana Serpe, retreating with a good book. Even on a regular day, Serpe usually had a paperback novel in hand.[24]

The men and women of the Goetz jury shouldered a great responsibility. From the voir dire process alone, it was obvious that Gregory Waples and Barry Slotnick were equally determined to win the case. The jurors would have to pay close attention indeed if they hoped to determine which of these men’s extraordinarily different accounts of the events of December 22, 1984, was to be believed. When it came to Goetz’s actions, there would be no middle ground.

25

Making Sense of Madness

On April 27, 1987, the jury assembled in the fifth-floor courtroom of 111 Centre Street to finally begin hearing the case. They, along with a packed crowd of spectators and reporters, would get their first glimpse of Bernie Goetz as he shuffled in, head down, and waited eagerly to hear the prosecution and defense alike lay out the arguments they each planned to make via their opening statements.

Assistant District Attorney Gregory Waples went first, spoke for only one hour, and in that time walked the jury through the events of December 22, 1984, especially the impact of the shooting on Troy Canty, Barry Allen, James Ramseur, and Darrell Cabey, in methodical fashion. He made clear that he intended to "debunk the myth" that Goetz was the victim in this case.[1]

While Waples's opening statement was short, this usually staid and rather dispassionate lawyer was uncharacteristically animated, insisting that Goetz's actions on the train that day had been a "terrifying spectacle."[2] Goetz was not just "very troubled," Waples insisted, but he was also a vicious aggressor, a "sadistic" man who had quite literally tried to "execute" four unarmed teens who, though they "might well have been irritating," had "never posed a threat to him."[3]

What's more, Waples emphasized, Goetz's own statements to the Concord police proved all of this. He himself had admitted to "deliberately" shooting two of the four boys while they "were trying to run away or were in the process of running away from him."[4] Goetz himself had reported the horrifying words he had spoken to his final victim, Darrell Cabey, before shooting him point-blank: "You look alright. Here's another."[5]

Indeed, some of Waples's most impassioned words were saved for his discussion of the costs of this unprovoked bloodshed on Cabey. He described Darrell's "massive injuries," which had "paralyzed [him] from above the waist down," explaining that Darrell would now live "forever in a wheelchair."[6]

Ultimately, Waples called upon the jurors simply to uphold the sanctity of the law itself. To be sure, he conceded, "this case has touched a raw nerve on the American anatomy."[7] But the public's reaction to Goetz's actions had been both alarming and dangerous and had said little good "about ourselves and the society in which we live today."[8] Surely, he almost pleaded, it should not stand that "a self-appointed vigilante" like Goetz was "answerable" only to himself. Surely, it was not okay for him, or any other New Yorker, to simply do what they are "determined to do," despite the rule of law.[9] Why not? If for no other reason, he reminded them, "Providence alone prevented any of the many innocent men, women and children from being killed or seriously injured by the defendant's wild shooting" that day.[10]

Now, Waples said, while looking each juror in the eye, "You are here to decide whether the idea of equal justice under the law, for all people, is a reality or is an empty dream."[11] With those parting words, he returned to his seat.

Bernie Goetz himself took this all in with little reaction, save for periodically breaking into what one juror described as "a hideous grin."[12]

Throughout Waples's statement, Slotnick would periodically erupt, accusing the prosecutor of not making an argument but merely playing on the emotions of the jury.[13] At one point, Judge Crane seemed to agree, cautioning Waples "to stay within the evidence."[14] But as soon as Slotnick had the chance to offer the jury his own opening statement, he too tried to spark jurors' passions and convictions—just different ones than Waples had appealed to.

Slotnick began by comparing the ADA's statement to "a testimonial dinner" for four young men who were in fact "thugs and hoodlums" and "predators of society." These young men "surrounded" Goetz, he claimed, "with the intention to rob him, even admitting it."[15] He then promised to bring witnesses far more credible than any the DA's office might put on the stand, including police officers, all of whom would persuade the jury that Goetz was a "hero."[16]

In fact, Slotnick continued, "We might as well switch tables, because I'm going to prosecute those four . . . [even though] they are not on trial here, for some strange reason, which is not explainable, but Bernhard Goetz is." He then vowed confidently, "You're going to convict them, and acquit him."[17]

As soon as each attorney had finished pitching his case to the jury, the prosecution called its first witnesses.

Waples had decided that his first witness, a graphic artist for the NYPD named Marie Venticinque, was needed to lay the foundation for the testimony to come. She provided the court a scale rendering of the IRT subway car in which Goetz shot the four teens. Entering her drawing as an exhibit was important to Waples, as it allowed him to show the relative positions of Goetz and the four teens, and also, he likely hoped it would prevent Slotnick from arguing for a more sensationalized re-creation of the subway confrontation.[18] Slotnick understood this, and immediately objected to Venticinque's drawing of car no. 7657 being entered into evidence. Waples nevertheless prevailed.[19]

Waples's next witness, John Filangeri, offered some of the first substantive testimony. As the first paramedic to arrive on the scene, he had been a direct, arguably impartial, eyewitness to the aftermath of Goetz's shooting spree. Waples wanted his testimony to focus the jury's attention on Darrell Cabey's extensive injuries on day one. Filangeri had been the first to attend to Darrell and to see how badly hurt he was. This witness made clear that even in those first moments on the train, it seemed likely that Darrell had been paralyzed by Goetz's bullet.[20]

But in cross-examination, Slotnick would try to use Filangeri to the defense's advantage. In the paramedic's report, filed the day after the shooting, he had said that according to Darrell, the other boys were "hassling [Goetz] for some money."[21] Though Filangeri's description was not at all inconsistent with what Troy Canty had always readily admitted, Waples was taking no chances. He knew that Slotnick was trying to imply that Darrell was somehow confirming the boys' intentions to harm his client, and so he asked Judge Crane to exclude the paramedic's account of what Darrell may or may not have said from the jury's consideration as hearsay. Crane said he would take that under advisement.

Filangeri's testimony stretched from the first day into the next. This spirited back-and-forth was riveting—Slotnick's arguments on cross were loud and dramatic, and though Waples tended to be more composed on redirect, he was no less engaging, due to his shrewd appeals to law and logic. These theatrical, often bitter exchanges seemed to barely register with Goetz. At times, he watched Slotnick and Waples intently, but for

Bernhard Goetz (center) and his attorneys Mark Baker (left) and Barry Slotnick (right) outside the courthouse during his trial, April 28, 1987. Larry C. Morris/*New York Times*/Getty Images

the most part, he kept his eyes on his lap, as if the proceedings bored him. As one reporter described it, Goetz mostly "stared into space or at the jury of eight men and four women."[22]

It was not altogether true that this defendant was simply bored or disinterested. It had actually shaken Goetz to hear Waples characterize him as a "walking powder keg" and "a self-appointed vigilante" who had attempted to carry out "a cold-blooded execution." Outside the courtroom, Goetz would admit that hearing himself painted in this way had all been "worse than the subway." He was, however, heartened to see the phalanx of red-beret-clad Guardian Angels right there to offer their encouragement as well as to help him navigate the scores of demonstrators also there carrying signs and shouting "Goetz is a racist, not a hero."[23]

THE NEXT DAY, Waples enjoyed an important victory when Judge Crane ruled that Filangeri's statement about what Darrell told him was indeed inadmissible. Ignoring Slotnick's look of disbelief, the judge stated that the defense "had not established sufficient grounds to make an exception to the hearsay rules of evidence, which generally prevent a witness from recounting statements made by someone else."[24]

After Filangeri, Waples called Detective Charles Haase to the stand. Detective Haase had been one of the first members of law enforcement on the subway after the shooting, and his testimony included photographs that showed scattered clothing on the floor of the blood-smeared subway car, as well as other pieces of physical evidence from the crime scene. The physical evidence included a "deformed" piece of a copper bullet jacket, personally retrieved by Haase from the subway seat closest to Darrell, along with the boys' bullet-holed zip-ups.

Darrell's jacket had two bullet holes, one with blood around it, one without, indicating that one bullet had missed his body but one had not; James's had one hole in the upper left sleeve; and Barry's vest had one hole near the center of the back.[25] Waples would later rely on Haase's testimony heavily, arguing that these items of clothing strongly suggested that Darrell was shot twice and was paralyzed by the second bullet—Goetz's fifth and last—and that Barry and James had both been turning away from, if not outright fleeing, Goetz when the bullets had hit them.

Waples's next two witnesses, Officer Warren Foote and Detective Christopher Domian from the Concord Police Department, also played an essential role in providing the jury critical details about the shooting. With these witnesses on the stand, Waples was able to drive home the fact Goetz had, of his own volition, confessed to shooting the four, had felt no remorse for doing so, and had fled the scene.

Bernie Goetz had even provided Detective Foote with a diagram of the shootings that indicated his recollection of exactly where everyone had been in the subway car when the shooting began.[26] Waples entered this into evidence. More important, however, Foote's colleague Detective Domian had recorded Goetz's statements, and his appearance on the stand allowed Waples not only to play this haunting tape for the jurors but also to give them a transcript of it to read along as they listened to Goetz's words fill the cavernous courtroom.[27]

This moment in the trial was powerful indeed. As *The New York Times* reported, "In the packed, silent courtroom at State Supreme Court, the gallery listened to the scratchy tape broadcast over loudspeakers from 10:40 A.M. until 12:45 P.M.; the judge, lawyers and jurors wore head phones to hear Mr. Goetz's statements . . . [they heard him say] 'I know this sounds horrible, but my intention was to murder them, to hurt them, to make them suffer as much as possible.'"[28]

However, Greg Waples couldn't just assume that this jury would be appalled by what it had read and heard. As the *Times* pointed out, Goetz could have netted himself some sympathy from this recording since, despite his ugly words, he had also sounded "confused but cooperative, polite to the point of meekness, a man who used words like 'darn' and 'yucky.'" He'd even apologized to the Concord policeman interviewing him that "he had parked illegally in front of the police station when he drove up to turn himself in."[29]

Barry Slotnick was counting on the jury to relate to this aspect of his client, especially since Bernie Goetz was not necessarily exuding a warm or likable personality in the courtroom. Indeed, as the audiotape played, Bernie hardly looked up or seemed much to care. Casually dressed in blue jeans and an open-necked pink shirt, he "showed little expression," according to the *Los Angeles Times,* resting his head on his palm for the majority of the day.[30]

While Waples could have just let the jury mull over Bernie's disturbing confession until they reconvened the following morning, he decided instead to end the day by bringing one last witness to the stand—one who would give them even more to consider.

Sally Smithern was the first witness to testify who had actually been a passenger on the train during the shootings. Though she was riding in a car directly connected to the one with Bernie Goetz and the teens, the windows between the train cars had allowed her to watch as the horrifying scene played out. She used a grease pencil to mark her exact position on the diagram provided by police artist Marie Venticinque. Smithern's words to the jury would pack a real punch: "I heard a loud bang which I perceived to be a shot. I saw the hand go like this, in a sweeping motion, and each time it stopped I heard a shot . . . I just knew at least three people had been shot."[31]

When Waples then asked her to show what she had seen, Smithern stood up, swung her arm, and verbalized the "bangs" of Goetz's gun as he emptied it.[32]

Although Barry Slotnick would aggressively cross-examine Sally Smithern, even implying that she had never set foot on this train and that her testimony was therefore fabricated, Waples felt he had nevertheless established some important groundwork in the first three days of the trial. But Barry Slotnick's opening statement had been powerful too. Waples knew he still had a lot of work to do with this jury. Slotnick had, for example, raised the possibility in the minds of the jury that, even if Bernie Goetz had done everything he was accused of doing, those "thugs and animals" on the train had started the dispute. Bernie had only been acting in self-defense. Waples knew that he would have to keep their attention focused on who the real victims were.

And so, Waples decided to let the jury hear directly from the victim whom many considered the most important. On Friday, Troy Canty would take the stand. The jury would go into the weekend with his words—not Goetz's—ringing in their ears.

26

Fumble and Drive

When jurors returned to court the next morning, the room crackled with anticipation. It was Friday, May 1, 1987. Troy Canty, dressed in a light brown suit and a striped tie, walked in quietly and was sworn in.[1] Now twenty-one years old, Troy was still quite slight—5 feet, 7 inches and a mere 140 pounds. He was visibly anxious but doing his best to hide it. It had been nearly a year and a half since he and Bernhard Goetz had laid eyes on each other. The two exchanged no words, only cold stares. For the most part, Troy kept his attention focused on Greg Waples.

Despite the press's tendency to focus on Troy's admittedly less than perfect past, Troy had been feeling good. For the last two years, he had been living in a residential drug facility called Phoenix House in suburban Westchester, New York, and felt his life was taking a new turn. The program expected its participants to obtain a high school diploma, and Troy was on track to do exactly that. His dream was to enroll in the Culinary Institute of America and become a chef.[2]

Today he would hold his head high but also admit to his past wrongdoings, from his heavy use of crack cocaine to his many misdemeanor charges. Mainly, he was there to make sure the jury understood the full gravity of what had happened to him and his friends.[3]

Greg Waples was also on edge. It was risky to put this young man on the stand, and he knew it. Troy had proven to be a wild card, and Waples was painfully aware that Slotnick would try to provoke him to anger. He was also concerned that the jury might well have read the particularly inflammatory piece in the *National Enquirer* for which Troy and Barry had been paid a measly $300 each to strip and show their bullet wounds and that had cherry-picked their words to make them sound aggressive and belligerent.[4]

And Waples had another problem. When Troy had testified before the grand jury in 1985, he had drawn a diagram of where he, his friends, and Goetz had been on the train. Unfortunately, this diagram did not at all square with the positions previous witnesses had just outlined, nor where Goetz had placed himself on his own diagram for Officer Foote.[5] Troy could simply have been confused, especially since he was being asked to recall the minute details of a most traumatic event that had so recently happened. But any perceived inconsistency could well harm the prosecution's case.

Ultimately, the testimony Troy Canty provided was helpful. He stressed that he had not intended to harm Goetz. Yes, he had asked him for five dollars, but he didn't harass him for it, and certainly never threatened him in any way. The money was to be used later in the day, so that when he and his friends boosted the video machines, they would be able to play a few games and "put quarters into the machines to avoid suspicion."[6] As for the three screwdrivers, these were meant for breaking into the machines, not to be used as weapons, Troy said most emphatically.

Troy's harrowing recollection of the shootings, and of seeing his friends bleeding out and crying, was hard to hear. But this testimony did allow Waples to drive the point home to jurors that the teenagers were the victims in this situation, notwithstanding aspects of their lives of which the jury might not approve. Having Troy also report that, despite being shot in the chest and undergoing major surgery to save his life, even the Crime Victims Board had refused to acknowledge that he was the injured party after this event made clear that he had only continued to be victimized after he was gunned down.[7]

Although the *Post* declared that Troy's story of the shooting left the courtroom "spellbound," at least one person present acted as if his words were too unimportant even to listen to.[8] Bernie Goetz studiously shuffled through various papers strewn across the defense table in front of him, and occasionally said something to one of his lawyers, but never reacted to any part of Troy's testimony. Troy occasionally glanced in Bernie's direction, but it was hard to read the emotions he felt when doing so.[9]

Still, Troy Canty's answers to Waples's questions had been clear, unwavering, and contrite when they most needed to be. It was a drastic change from his erratic behavior during the grand jury phases of the case.

None of this sat well with Barry Slotnick. He could see that a chord might well have been struck with the jury and he was eager to remedy this on cross-examination. The following Monday, when court resumed, with great flourish, Slotnick stood up and brought in four large easels on which he perched poster-size photos of the four teens that had been published previously in the *New York Post*.[10] More important, as Mark Baker later explained, "I had my investigator find me the four meanest pictures of these kids he [could]."[11] As one juror recalled, Troy's photo showed "an arrogant sneering ne'er do well with a cocky tilt to his head" and a "scowling and menacing" expression on his face. Slotnick made sure to place this photograph of Troy "smirking, his arms folded across his chest" where jurors could plainly see it.[12]

Slotnick's goal was to ensure that the jury would view Troy as a self-interested con artist and a downright dangerous man, and not be "bamboozled by the current appearance of Mr. Canty, who came to court nattily attired in a suit and tie during three days of testimony."[13] On cross, Slotnick then proceeded repeatedly to note the marked difference between Troy's current appearance and what he had looked like when he

Troy Canty at New York State Supreme Court, May 5, 1987.
AP Photo/Mario Suriani

had preyed on Goetz. "That day on the subway on December 22, 1984, you weren't wearing that nice suit and tie, were you?" Slotnick asked.[14]

Slotnick then implied that Troy was only in rehab because the DA's office felt it would make him look like a more reliable witness. He also wanted to convince the jury that Troy had ulterior motives even testifying that day. He had only agreed to take the stand because he thought it might help him win his own civil suit against Bernie. This was nothing but a shakedown, Slotnick suggested.[15] Troy, however, didn't allow himself to be pushed. When Slotnick asked, "Aren't you interested in the money?" Troy replied, "I am interested, but I'm more interested in justice."[16]

During a particularly damaging exchange between Slotnick and Canty, it also became clear that in the time between the shootings and that day in court, Troy had told at least three different versions of his story. Slotnick highlighted the most important discrepancies when he began quoting Troy's grand jury testimony.

Slotnick also bombarded Troy with questions about his previous illegal activities and looked "stymied" or "highly dubious" anytime Troy answered by saying, "I can't remember" or "I don't recall."[17]

Another part of Slotnick's strategy was to make Troy look like a liar and a brute who had threatened not only Bernie Goetz but many others, including vulnerable women. To demonstrate this, Slotnick had arranged for two women to sit at the front of the courtroom: a middle-aged woman, wearing a blue New York Housing Authority Tenants Patrol jacket and a red turban, and a younger woman who was clearly her daughter.[18] He never identified them by name, but demanded to know if Troy recognized them. Troy denied, repeatedly, that he did.

Slotnick continued to push, asking whether Troy "had ever mugged 'an old lady with a cane.'" Troy looked confused, and insisted that he had not.[19] The lawyer gestured to the younger woman, saying that she'd seen him do so. No, Troy replied emphatically, "She couldn't have seen it because I never did it."[20]

At several points during Slotnick's cross-examination, including at this juncture, Waples jumped up with heated objections and asserted that Slotnick was engaging in grave "misconduct."[21]

Despite Waples's protests and attempts to resurrect his witness's image on the morning of May 5, however, the damage was done. Slotnick had dealt the exact blow he was hoping to. As one reporter put it, "the juxtaposition of Mr. Slotnick's questions and the women's dramatic entrances sent an important message to the jury."[22] In short, Troy Canty must have harmed them in some way, or why else would Slotnick have them there? Troy's tone of voice when he answered any of Slotnick's questions had also done him no favors. As a juror later recalled: "He was mechanical. He had the sound of a guy who has the answers in a test, knowing the answers, the right thing to say, without knowing truly the information."[23]

Reeling from the damage inflicted by Slotnick's cross-examination, Waples regrouped. He still felt that he'd had no choice but to call Troy. There was no question that the jurors needed to hear from the victims, and the most sympathetic one, Darrell, would never be able to testify. So that had left Troy, Barry, and James. He would now call Barry Allen to the stand. But this too quickly backfired.

Waples had not offered immunity to Barry for the second grand jury, and for reasons entirely unknown, he was still unwilling to do so. And so, on the advice of his own counsel (the attorney who was representing him in his separate legal troubles), Barry was not going to cooperate—he planned to invoke his Fifth Amendment privilege to all questions asked of him. Waples well understood that if the jury saw Barry continually take the Fifth when questioned by the prosecution, it could suggest that he had something to hide. This would be deadly. Accordingly, Waples brought Barry before the court, without the jury in the room, to see whether there was another way forward.

Judge Crane could immediately see Waples's quandary. No matter what question was posed to Barry, even in this closed proceeding, he invoked the Fifth, nearly two dozen times. But Crane was finding it hard to be sympathetic. After all, why hadn't Waples granted Allen immunity as he had the other victims? Waples had made it clear that his office had "no interest in pressing criminal charges" related to the events of December 22, 1984, against Barry, so what was going on?[24]

Slotnick also didn't understand what was happening, especially since Allen's testimony would presumably benefit the DA's case. He suspected that Waples was hiding something.[25] Still, Waples wouldn't budge on immunizing Allen. Perhaps this decision had come from higher up in the DA's office, but whatever its origin, it did not serve Waples well in this case.

Meanwhile, Barry Allen's attorney was making no apologies about the fact that his client had refused to testify without immunity. As *The New*

York Times reported, he was concerned that "answering any questions could 'open the door' to further inquiry that could lead to incriminating testimony—whether about the subway incident itself or something entirely unrelated to Mr. Allen's actions that day."[26]

It was still possible, however, for Judge Crane to immunize Barry himself so that he would answer the questions. Slotnick and Baker were maintaining that Allen's refusal to testify would violate their client's constitutional rights as a criminal defendant to face his accusers and naturally suspected that Waples's reasons for withholding immunity could only advantage their client. The jury absolutely had a right to hear from the witness, Slotnick loudly protested. The defense had a right to cross-examine him.

Slotnick's refusal to let this go would pay off. Though Crane insisted it was not "the function of the court to tell the prosecutor which witnesses to call and which witnesses not to call," he would allow Slotnick to call Barry Allen via a so-called missing witness instruction.[27] Slotnick could question Barry, albeit by unconventional means. Ultimately the defense would not call Barry to the stand, but it would still benefit from his original refusal to testify. Crane later agreed to tell the jurors that if they wished to do so they could infer "that Allen's testimony would not have been favorable to the People."[28]

That he could never persuade Barry Allen to testify about being shot as he tried to flee was a major blow to Waples's case—as the *Post* put it, "the second . . . in as many days"—and this day would only get worse from there.[29]

James Ramseur was Waples's next planned witness, one who already had immunity. The young man who walked into the courtroom that day, however, took the jury aback. In contrast to the neatly dressed Troy Canty, James had been brought straight from prison in "dirty dungarees and windbreaker" and seeing him, said legal expert George Fletcher, "it was as though we were all transported back to the subway encounter of December 1984."[30]

Then, rather abruptly, James also refused to testify, in his case as a "protest against a criminal-justice system that . . . wrongly convicted him of rape after the Goetz incident."[31] He would not even place his hand on the Bible. Judge Crane was not pleased, at one point even jumping up and threatening James Ramseur with contempt of court.

James hoped his defiance of the judge would force the jury to ask further questions. What was so important that he would risk doing this? As his attorney, Ron Kliegerman, would explain outside the courtroom, James had been beside himself, "in a dejected state" knowing that he was a crime victim but the justice system had instead wanted to make him the criminal—including "improperly and erroneously" convicting him of rape.[32] Bernie Goetz was the real bad guy here, but James did not know how else to make people see this.

According to Kliegerman, James wasn't wrong. He had been falsely accused and convicted and was now serving a sentence of eight to twenty-five years. It was in fact the negative press attention around James that had given prosecutors the perfect opportunity to seal his fate. As Kliegerman explained to *The Washington Post,* "The [rape] victim did not initially identify Ramseur from police photos," and, in fact, "It was not until six weeks later that she finally reported to the police, after viewing various TV shows and reading about Ramseur in the press and speaking to a lot of people involved in the Goetz case, then she agreed it was Ramseur."[33]

WITH BARRY'S AND JAMES'S testimony having fallen through, all Greg Waples could do was forge ahead with his main eyewitnesses to the crime. To set those up most effectively, though, he first wanted to establish some key facts by calling two transit officers who had responded to the shooting: Richard Reip and Alejandro Torres.

Reip confirmed that no screwdrivers—sharpened or otherwise—were found among the many items that littered the subway car. Torres confirmed that these tools had been in zippered pockets, and that "the zippers were in the closed, zipped up, position."[34] Torres also testified to the boys' conditions when he arrived on the scene. They all "appeared to be in pain" and "they were moaning," he said. Darrell had, he went on movingly, "held onto my arm and asked me to help him and not to let him die." Torres testified as well to having seen "lead fragments and a copper [bullet] jacket" on the seat where Darrell Cabey was shot."[35]

Between May 6 and May 21, Waples would proceed to call eighteen witnesses to the stand, all but four of whom had been on the train when Bernie Goetz shot the boys. Each described the attack as utterly unexpected, uncalled for, and horrifying to watch unfold.

When Victor Flores, who had worked twenty-two years as a cleaner for the Transit Police, took the stand, jurors learned that he had heard four or five shots and that two of the victims had had their backs toward Goetz, like they were trying to flee.[36]

Victor recalled that before escaping into the tunnels, Bernie Goetz had knelt and peered intently at one of the victim's faces to make sure he was truly downed. In disturbing detail, Flores described the condition of the wounded teens as they bled out around him. The heart-wrenching words from one of them had been hard to get out of his mind since that day, and he recounted them to the jury: "He did it for nothing, we were doing nothing."[37]

The train's conductor, Armando Soler, followed Flores on the stand. Soler made it clear to the jury that no one had complained of threatening youths on the train prior to the panicked riders entering his car and the emergency brake bringing the train to a screeching stop. This was significant, he explained, because he was frequently approached by people complaining about the behavior of other passengers.[38]

He also testified to how horrific the scene was that he came upon, and how Goetz had been notably serene, calm, not seeming too excited as he looked out over the wounded teens. Soler confirmed that Darrell Cabey had been in particularly bad shape, slumped over on the seat on the other side of the wall from the conductor cab.

The other passengers were also shaken, Soler stressed. Some of them were frozen in fear on the floor of the car. And like Victor before him, the conductor explained to jurors that Goetz, after so strangely assisting him and refusing to give up his gun, had fled the scene—"by jumping down onto the tracks [where he then] ran between cars."[39]

The conductor's testimony was dramatic, and it would have been difficult for any juror to come up with a reason why he would have fabricated or embellished the grim scene he had come upon. And so, Barry Slotnick approached his cross-examination of Soler a bit differently than the other eyewitnesses: He tried to use the fact that Armando Soler himself had an old arrest record to argue that his testimony was untrustworthy. Though he had no evidence to suggest Soler was violent or even shifty, his implication was clear: Men like Soler were part of the same crime problem overtaking New York City that had pushed Bernie Goetz to take action on that train.

The next testimony came from credit manager Loren Michaels. At the time of the shooting, Loren had been on his way to do some holiday shopping with his friend Christopher Boucher. His account was not nearly as captivating as Soler's, though he did look carefully at the rendering of the subway car and clearly marked passenger locations on its glassine overlay. Loren's markings showed that the boys had not been totally isolated at the end of the car, suggesting that other passengers had not been too afraid to be close by them. In fact, there were people "near them and scattered throughout . . . as people got on and off."[40]

Even more important details would come from the testimony of passengers Garth Reid, Mary Gant, and Arnethea Gilbert.

Garth Reid was the part-time college student from the West Indies who had been riding the subway that day with his wife and their infant daughter. Andrea, his wife, had noticed the boys as they boarded the car. While Garth had been tuned out, getting his daughter settled on his lap as the train lurched along, he testified that though his wife had been nervous about the boys' rowdiness, he had not been scared until the moment the shooting suddenly began.

Garth Reid had seen Goetz, whom he later described as a "regular Mr. Rogers–looking kind of guy," when, to his shock, he heard shooting from his direction. He "saw the defendant firing two shots . . . and then saw the defendant turn and fire additional shots down towards the other end of the car."[41] Reid did not see who Goetz was aiming at when the next shots rang out. By then, he'd been more focused on getting his family out safely.[42]

While he didn't say as much on the stand, where the jury might have considered its importance, Garth later reflected in an interview, "At that time I was saying, is he trying to kill black people? That's what I thought he was trying to do. That was the thing that kind of got me a little bit scared—I wasn't too sure if he was going to shoot all the black people on the train."[43] With these thoughts racing through his mind, he'd become immediately intent on getting his wife and daughter to safety.

As Slotnick had done time and again, such as when he had suggested that Sally Smithern hadn't really been on the train during the shooting, that Troy Canty had mugged an old woman, and that Armando Soler was a disreputable criminal, Slotnick used his cross-examination of Garth Reid to muddy the waters with unproven assertions and allegations. As one reporter put it, Slotnick "repeatedly—and deliberately—phrased questions to call the jury's attention to information that [was] not in evidence."[44]

Waples tried his best to shut down Slotnick's attempts to recast his witnesses' testimony and to suggest "facts" about them for which he offered no substantiation. To a certain extent, he was successful. Over the course of the trial, Slotnick received "several admonitions from the judge in bench conferences out of the hearing of the jury."[45]

But Slotnick was continually willing to risk such censure. In one key instance of cross-examining Garth Reid specifically, Slotnick asked, "Isn't it true that the reason you took notice of these four individuals is because someone said, 'Look at those four punks bothering that man?'"[46] Before Garth could answer, Waples objected, and Judge Crane instructed the defense not to ask questions built on statements that had never been entered into evidence.

Slotnick was undeterred. Challenging Crane, he said tersely, "Judge, you can speak a little louder and the jury can hear you," as if to suggest that the court, not he, had done something inappropriate—in effect undermining him in front of the jury.[47] Crane was taken aback and insisted that this was not the case. "I'm upset with your conduct," he told Slotnick. But Slotnick chose to double down: "I'm upset with your conduct." After a beat, Crane replied in a steely voice, "You know where you can go with that."[48]

Still, Slotnick would not back down. He continued to push his right to ask Reid the question—one that he had already asked, and thus the jury had already heard. Knowing just how much this judge prided himself on being impartial and fair, Slotnick knew he had gone for Crane's Achilles' heel.[49]

And it worked: Crane not only allowed Slotnick to keep this question on the record but also permitted him to repeat it. This victory for the defense would set a critical precedent: If Slotnick just pushed hard enough for something he wanted, he had a good chance of getting it, even if its legal basis was dubious at best.

Refusing to let this derail him, however, Waples called his next eyewitness train rider, Mary Gant. By this point in the trial it was becoming clear that the ADA had a particular strategy regarding which passengers he was calling to testify and in which order. He was carefully alternating between witnesses who had seen the shootings firsthand, and those who had seen, or had personally experienced, the terrible fallout from them. Mary was in the latter category.

Mary had been reading on her journey downtown that day and did not see Goetz's gun being fired. But she had noticed important details about the moments just before Goetz pulled his gun, she had heard the shots, and she had also been one of the two women who had landed facedown on the grimy floor of the subway as the carnage around them unfolded.[50]

Mary had watched the teens as they loudly joked and jostled one another, bouncing from seat to seat. She remembered feeling some "concern" when they looked over at her, but she had not felt threatened, nor did she remotely expect the mayhem that was to follow.[51]

Just before the first shot rang out, Mary happened to glance up from her book. She had noticed two of the teens standing in front of a seated white man. They were holding on to the straps as the train swayed and were saying something to him. A third boy, she thought, was standing away from these two, in the middle of the aisle, and a fourth was still seated down at the end of the train car.[52] No sooner than she had resumed reading, though, the air suddenly erupted with the sound of gunfire. Mary had no time to process what had just happened because someone had shoved her to the floor, where she lay stone-still in fear.

But from her vantage point, trying to play dead, Mary saw more than she wanted to. She recounted how she'd found herself looking straight into the eyes of a boy who was lying on his stomach, unmoving and bleeding profusely. Then, seemingly out of nowhere, she heard the voice of a man asking her if she was okay. She was not, and was even less so when she managed to get back into a seat only to see that the three other teens were badly wounded as well. To her alarm, she also took in that the man who had just spoken to her, the man who apparently had shot those boys, was now seated across from her, seeming "agitated" and "wringing his hands."[53]

From Waples's point of view, Mary Gant's testimony established an important thing for the jury: Only two of the teenagers had ever been near Bernie Goetz.[54]

Again, however, Slotnick would try to turn tainted water into sweet wine for the defense during his cross-examination. Had Mary Gant not, in fact, felt that those young men on the train were "menacing," he pushed. No, she pushed back, she had only been a bit "concerned." But he kept at it. Finally, Mary was willing to say that they were "defiant," which Slotnick took as a win.

Waples dutifully rushed in during redirect to try to mitigate any damage that might have been done by this exchange. Even if Mary had been in any way unnerved by the presence of these teens on the train, was it possible that she was "more apprehensive" of them "than objective facts warranted?" Yes, she admitted that perhaps that was the case.[55]

Just as it had been difficult to shake Mary Gant, so would it prove difficult for Barry Slotnick to undermine the testimony of Waples's next witness, Arnethea Gilbert, the woman who had been in the conductor's car when the shootings took place but had subsequently rushed in to assist the wounded teens.[56]

When she took the stand on May 7, 1987, Arnethea was very clear about what she had seen when she followed conductor Soler into the bloody car and came upon the crumpled bodies of Troy Canty and Darrell Cabey. Both were badly hurt, Troy was clearly terrified that he was dying, and each teen seemed shocked by what had just happened. She recounted for the jury how Troy had said to her that a man had "shot me for nothing . . . [I] didn't do anything only asked for five dollars." Darrell had said with equal bewilderment, "I didn't do anything, he shot me for nothing."[57]

Slotnick went after Gilbert as soon as he had the chance, suggesting that she couldn't have heard the young men correctly.

"[Canty] was mumbling, isn't that a matter of fact?" Slotnick asked.

"No, it's not," Gilbert responded.

"You know you've taken the oath here?" he reminded her.

"Yes," she replied, "I'm very aware of that."

"And you know that if you lie, you could be indicted for perjury?"

"Yes, I know that also."[58]

Arnethea Gilbert was unflappable, so Slotnick tried another tack: questioning whether Darrell Cabey, whatever he might or might not have said, could be trusted.

"He was slurring his words, he wasn't sure of [them], what he was saying?"

"No, he wasn't—"

"You have to wait 'til I finish," Slotnick interrupted her. "We have certain rules here. . . . You have to wait until I finish my question."

Gilbert apologized. Slotnick continued, "He was really slurring his words. He was incoherent, he really didn't know what he was saying to you?"

She adamantly contradicted him. "His words were not slurred. . . . I understood every word completely and fully."[59]

Phrasing it slightly differently each time, Slotnick kept insisting that both teens were unreliable, that "they didn't understand" what Arnethea had been saying to them, and that "they were kind of stunned and incoherent at the time."[60] But she didn't back down. Arnethea had heard them "very clearly, it was not mumbling."[61] As best she could tell, they had understood her just fine, and she'd seen no sign that they were incoherent or unaware of her talking to them.[62]

No matter how hard Barry Slotnick tried to discredit Arnethea Gilbert's account of the teens' reaction to being shot, she refused to budge on what she had seen and heard. Even though it remained to be seen whether the jury could consider these words or if the judge would rule them inadmissable as hearsay, in this moment they had made their mark.

Waples's next witness was Josephine Holt, the passenger who worked as a maid and had been heading downtown to do some Christmas shopping. Importantly, she corroborated much of what Mary Gant and Arnethea Gilbert had testified to. Holt characterized Darrell and his friends as "average kids" who were mostly fooling around, "laughing loud and talking loud amongst themselves."[63] She also felt that when she'd seen two of them talking to Bernie Goetz, they had been standing in front of him "in a non-threatening manner."[64] Even when Waples asked if all four boys had been standing over the defendant, anticipating Slotnick's coming cross-examination, she replied firmly, "No."[65] She had only seen two.[66]

The jury seemed to like Josephine Holt's attitude and blunt answers. When Waples asked whether she had looked in the direction of the "firecracker" sounds, she raised her eyebrows, shook her head and said, "Uh-uh"—there were audible chuckles in the courtroom.[67]

But once again, Slotnick tried to trip up a prosecution witness on cross. Hadn't Holt told the grand jury that the teenagers had been "harassing and bothering people"?[68] Hadn't she said that she had been a bit afraid of these teenagers, and even described them once as "menacing"?[69]

No, that wasn't right, Josephine said. At the very worst, one of the teens might have "said something 'dirty' to one woman."[70] Slotnick then pushed her hard regarding how many people she had really seen standing over Goetz, reminding her, "You were insistent that it was three." Holt had to admit she might have misspoken—"I said three. I was wrong." Trying to score a point, Slotnick responded, "I see" while simultaneously giving the jury "one of his 'can-you-believe-this' looks."[71]

Still, by the time the jury heard from Waples's next witness, the British-educated, West African–born computer programming analyst Solitaire MacFoy, Slotnick might have been frustrated. Notwithstanding Waples's aborted attempt to get Barry and James to testify, the prosecution had so far managed to present a compelling narrative to the jury, one that he was having trouble discounting: that the teens were simply rowdy, not threatening, and that his client had unleashed his weapon on people who had been nowhere near him, and with whom he had had no contact.[72]

On the stand, MacFoy also testified that he "had not noticed anybody threatening anybody."[73] He'd noticed Goetz's face was "calm and bland . . . somewhat calculating" and "without real expression."[74] Waples pushed harder. "Did anybody threaten him?" he asked. "Not that I saw," MacFoy said.[75] What he had seen was Goetz shooting three teens and pointing his gun down at another one who was seated. All of this, MacFoy said, was a "terrible shock."[76]

In his cross-examination, Slotnick tried again to suggest that this was a prosecution witness who had never really been on the train, and, in his case, had only come forward after Darrell Cabey's radical attorney, William Kunstler, had approached him.

That wasn't the case, Solitaire corrected him. Yes, he had some friends who had wanted him to tell the authorities what he had seen that day, one of them being "a friend who knew Mr. Kunstler . . . [who then] spoke with me and urged me to speak with [the DA]."[77] However, he continued, he had in fact already tried to speak with someone about the shooting, having called the police hotline almost immediately after the incident. When he did finally go to the DA, Solitaire said, it was only because the police had never bothered to call him back.

Waples underscored this fact on redirect. He wasn't going to let his opposing counsel suggest that Solitaire MacFoy was but a plant for Kunstler. He decided to call two more witnesses—Solitaire's girlfriend, Ruth Chasek, and his friend David Gilfix—who would corroborate Solitaire's intentions to testify and who confirmed that he had always been very clear about what he had seen.

And so, Slotnick set out to minimize the impact of their testimony. He wasn't subtle about his aims. During his cross-examination of Ruth Chasek, he asked whether one of her reasons for taking the stand was to corroborate the fact that Mr. MacFoy told her that he had been on the train. Yes, she replied.

"To your own knowledge, you don't know whether he was on that train, do you?" he pushed.

"I know he told me," Ruth replied.

"I know that," Slotnick responded tersely. "But I'm asking; to your OWN knowledge, you don't know that?"[78]

WHEN JURORS RETURNED to the courtroom the following Monday, May 11, Waples's focus shifted to expert witnesses who could speak to the carnage Goetz's bullets had caused. He first called Dr. Harry Adler, the emergency room physician on duty at Bellevue Hospital when Barry Allen and James Ramseur first arrived.

As the chief surgical resident at Bellevue's ER, Adler had amassed much experience treating gunshot wounds.[79] His testimony dutifully confirmed where and how the boys were injured, but it also gave jurors insight into what such injuries meant for the boys who endured them.

Adler explained the X-rays of Barry Allen's shoulder and chest to the jury, showing how the bullet fragmented, spreading its damage and causing "injury to some small vessels and soft lung tissue."[80] He explained how fluid had then started to build up in Barry's chest, requiring a tube to be inserted to drain that pleural cavity for days. Even with that extensive intervention, the doctors had been unable to remove the original bullet or any of its many fragments before Barry was finally discharged.

As for James Ramseur, he'd suffered even greater immediate damage that led to long-term complications.[81] At first, his injury, while very serious, had seemed straightforward. James was taken to the operating room for an exploratory laparotomy, a procedure in which the abdomen is opened and any injuries are addressed. But this surgery revealed additional damage to James's tissues that had not been obvious from the outside: a noticeable hole in his stomach, lacerations to his spleen, and a hole in his diaphragm.

While the damage to his other organs would heal, James's spleen had to be removed entirely. The bullet, which had "lodged in the area of his left adrenal gland," could also never be taken out. Complicating all of this too was the fact James kept trying to leave the hospital—fearful that if he stayed put, he would end up arrested and in jail, due to the warrants issued from Bronx County court.[82]

When he was forced to return for more care after the first time he bolted, one of the lobes of his left lung had collapsed, and two days after that, his small bowel became obstructed. Afterward James developed a serious fever, which meant he would have to undergo suctioning of his lungs.

This testimony, as graphic and upsetting as it undoubtedly was for jurors and court spectators to hear, was imperative. It was the first time anyone apart from the victims' families had to contend with what it had actually meant for these teens to have been shot with hollow point bullets at such close range. As Dr. Adler spoke, jurors were forced to ask themselves: What could these teens have done to warrant the damage that Bernie Goetz's bullets inflicted?

Waples did his level best to keep the jury's focus on exactly this point. His last question to Dr. Adler was whether the injuries that James Ramseur suffered could have caused his death, if they had not been treated medically. They well could have, Adler confirmed.[83]

In an attempt to distract from the impact of Dr. Adler's testimony as well as to begin to muddy the waters regarding where which of Goetz's bullets had ended up on that terrible day, Slotnick used his time on cross to ask if it was at least possible that Ramseur's injury had been caused not by one bullet, but by two? (The implication being that none remained in the chamber of his gun for him to take a second shot at Darrell Cabey.) Perhaps it was, the doctor conceded; the bullet that hit Ramseur's arm was "not necessarily" the same one that entered his side.[84]

Slotnick's next move was to direct the jury's attention away from James Ramseur's injuries and instead to get them thinking about the five outstanding warrants for his arrest he'd had on the day he was shot. This tactic was not without irony—Slotnick's very arguments validated James's fears about being treated as a criminal when he was supposed to be recuperating.

But no matter how much his questions pushed Dr. Adler, the physician refused to bite. He stayed focused on James's medical condition. The wounded youth would not be deemed well enough to go home—and stay there—until January 22, a full month after the shooting.

Waples's next two medical experts chronicled the damage Goetz's bullets had inflicted on two of his other victims, Troy Canty and Darrell Cabey.

Dr. Peter Adams was working as an attending physician at St. Vincent's Hospital, board-certified in general and thoracic surgery, on the chaotic afternoon that paramedics rushed in the two most injured teens.[85] He had treated both Troy and Darrell and could enumerate their injuries clearly and dispassionately.

Troy Canty, he explained, had experienced a gunshot to the left side of his chest, just below the nipple. He was bleeding into his chest cavity and immediately required a procedure to both drain the chest wound and also to re-expand his collapsing lung, which itself was in very bad shape. The bullet had torn across and through his lung before lodging in his back. Dr. Adams had been able to remove the bullet, but Troy's recovery was nevertheless slow, given the chest tubes that remained in place to keep the blood suctioned out and to ensure that no air was leaking from the left lung.[86]

ADA Waples asked Dr. Adams pointedly, "[In] your expert medical opinion, were the injuries that Troy Canty suffered potentially life threatening?" Without hesitating, Adams replied that yes, they were.[87]

Waples was even more interested in the jury hearing what Dr. Adams had to say about Darrell Cabey's wounds. It was obvious right away, he testified, that Darrell had come in with the gravest injuries of all the teens. When the bullet entered his body, just above the lowest ribs of his left side, it had ripped through both of his lungs and across the spine—fully severing his spinal cord—before it ended up lodged on the right side of Darrell's body.[88]

With both lungs shredded and filling with blood, Darrell, like Troy, also needed tubes inserted immediately to drain and re-inflate them.[89] But it was the spinal cord injury that had caused Dr. Adams the most concern. Darrell was paralyzed from just above his belly button down to his toes, severely affecting the function of the torso muscles that normally allow for deep breaths and coughing. These bodily functions were crucial for clearing out secretions that build up in the lungs, Adams explained.[90] The biggest risk any patient faces when their lungs can't stay clear, nor expand and contract normally, is pneumonia.

And unfortunately, Darrell did indeed develop significant pneumonia in both lungs, which worsened until, on January 8, 1985, he suffered a respiratory arrest and stopped breathing altogether.[91] Darrell was intubated and connected to a ventilator, but there had meanwhile been a "considerable period" of oxygen deprivation. He went into a coma.[92]

A week later, still unresponsive, Darrell's medical condition grew even direr. He'd developed another serious pneumonia infection, which required the insertion of additional chest tubes for drainage. Darrell was, at this point, in extremis. "Did you expect him to live?" Waples asked Dr. Adams. "I did not, no," he replied.[93]

This question from Waples was vital. This was the first time that the jurors really had the opportunity to consider the ugly aftermath of the shooting for Darrell. Not only had his spinal cord been severed, but it was also now clear that he had nearly died. Even more upsetting, being in a coma for so long, and having been deprived of oxygen beforehand, had a devastating impact on Darrell's "ability to retain full mental faculties."[94]

It was obvious to Barry Slotnick that Dr. Adams's testimony had shaken everyone in the courtroom. At one point, Slotnick even approached the bench—suggesting that Waples was "attempting to prejudice the jury with blood and gore"—and tried, unsuccessfully, to convince Judge Crane to prohibit Adams from going into further detailed descriptions.[95]

Slotnick also attempted to argue that it was unnecessary for Waples's next witness, the neurologist Claude Macaluso, to further chronicle the teen's injuries on the grounds that it would be redundant. "I don't think that really serves a purpose, Your Honor, other than to . . . prejudice and inflame the jury." Judge Crane refused to intervene. He would only agree to give Slotnick "a continuing objection to it."[96]

When Macaluso took the stand, the true fallout from Bernie Goetz's subway rage did come into even clearer focus, just as Slotnick feared it might.[97] Macaluso's credentials were highly impressive, including training at the Memorial Sloan Kettering Cancer Center. He had been a well-respected second-year resident at St. Vincent's Hospital when Darrell Cabey arrived, and his testimony would be hard to refute.[98]

Dr. Macaluso was first called in to assess Darrell's condition on January 9, 1985, one day after he had slipped into a coma and just around two weeks after he was first admitted.[99] Macaluso remembered that evaluation well. At this juncture, Darrell only responded to "deep painful stimuli."[100] He also exhibited "some abnormal posturing" of his extremities, which indicated very bad news neurologically—the respiratory arrest had caused complete lack of oxygen to the brain, and thus a condition called "anoxic encephalopathy," a severe brain injury.[101]

Worse, Macaluso determined that Darrell had entered a "persistent vegetative state."[102] As Macaluso explained it to the jury, "being in persistent vegetative state for over two weeks carries very poor prognosis for recovery and for life."[103] Darrell, the jury was reminded, had remained in this persistent vegetative state for six weeks.

When, against all odds, Darrell did wake up, Dr. Macaluso was tasked with determining his neurological state and, if there had been damage, whether it was permanent and to what degree it would limit his daily activities. According to Macaluso, Darrell had indeed suffered permanent, irreversible damage to the cortex of his brain due to lack of oxygen.[104]

Was Darrell's memory impaired after this experience? Waples asked. Yes, Macaluso confirmed, according to repeated psychological assessments, as noted in the patient's chart, there was "significant memory impairment."[105]

This testimony was of particular significance because many of the jurors would likely remember, and Slotnick would likely remind them of, the *Daily News* column written by Jimmy Breslin on November 26, 1985, in which he had interviewed Darrell while he was undergoing post-coma rehabilitative therapy in the hospital. In this explosive piece, Breslin claimed that Darrell admitted that not only were his friends all "goin' rob" Goetz, but that they had decided to do so because "they thought he looked like easy bait."[106] Even if the jurors had no recollection of this piece, Waples decided to address Breslin's visit to the hospital, and the column, head-on.

Waples hoped to convince the jury that Breslin's conversation with Darrell was not just unsanctioned but also unethical. Macaluso was unable to shed much light on the interview itself, but he did recall asking hospital administrators what was going on. "No one knew about it," he said. Incredulous, Waples asked, "What you're saying is Mr. Breslin just walked in on his own?" "Right," Macaluso confirmed.[107]

Waples then pushed Macaluso on the issue of Darrell's memory. Could he have remembered the shooting? Could he answer questions about it in any reliable way? Macaluso explained that yes, after he came out of the coma, Darrell knew that he had been shot, but "just the fact he had been shot." Eventually, he also spoke again of being "on the subway with some friends, and someone, one of his friends asked for five dollars and the man panicked, started shooting and then he came over to him and shot him."[108]

As sincere as these memories were, Dr. Macaluso said firmly, what they revealed about Darrell's cognitive function was actually quite complicated. Some of what Darrell was processing were the various nightmares and dreams that plagued him, and while these were based on the actual shootings, how they translated into what he was able to recall was not clear.[109] What's more, Macaluso stressed, people with Darrell Cabey's type of brain damage tended to say what they felt people wanted to hear, and could not always distinguish their own memories from information they had been told about themselves.

To drive this point home for the jury, Waples asked, "For example, is it possible for him to assimilate as general memory news accounts which he has been exposed to either on the air, broadcast media or by newspaper?" "I would say yes," Macaluso replied.[110]

In his cross-examination of both Dr. Adams and Dr. Macaluso, Slotnick forcefully suggested that Darrell Cabey's brain injury was exaggerated. Going even further, he argued that Judge Crane should allow him to call Darrell to the stand. "I'd like to show," he said, "that the injury was not so irreparable, and I would like to show, yes, Darrell Cabey is not the sponge that Mr. Waples would like him to be, or brought him out to be, before this jury."[111]

Judge Crane firmly rejected this proposition, and so Slotnick pivoted. He suggested to the jury that Darrell's coma, even if it had resulted in long-term damage, had nothing to do with Bernie Goetz. This sad state of affairs was caused by "perhaps something that occurred in the hospital" while Darrell was under the doctors' care.[112]

Incensed, Waples rose, hotly registering his objection to Slotnick's implication. "I don't think there is any basis for it, Judge," he said. "I'm not aware of any basis for an accusation for negligence, much less gross negligence. Nothing was brought out on direct examination. . . . This is speculation."[113]

On redirect with Macaluso, Waples pointedly asked if there were any measures that could have been taken to prevent Darrell's losing consciousness. Did the doctor believe there had been any "negligence" in not putting Darrell on the respirator earlier? No, Macaluso responded, "his overall medical condition, although grave, was not one which required mechanical ventilation. The patient was awake and talking and alert. And, and his blood gases, which really tell you the amount of saturation of the blood with oxygen, were adequate. . . . I don't believe there was any negligence. It was just an ordinary medical decision."[114]

With the medical condition of Goetz's victims now established, Waples decided to bring Myra Friedman to the stand. Her testimony would also be important to a key aspect of the case Waples was trying to build—that Bernie Goetz possessed illegal guns, not just that he had used them. With her recounting of the various conversations with him, the prosecution felt it would make clear that Bernie had not only fled the scene of the crime he had committed but had also attempted, at various points, to cover up that crime altogether.

Myra seemed to be a most effective witness, confirming these prosecution claims and also making clear how often she had, unsuccessfully, tried to persuade Bernie to surrender.[115] But Barry Slotnick came back at her hard on cross-examination. If anything she had said was true, he suggested, then Myra herself was likely also a guilty party, even a potential accessory to the crime for helping Bernie Goetz. After all, had she not helped him to stash his guns? Perhaps, he went on, she was now helping the prosecution merely to prevent herself from being charged.[116]

Once again, Barry Slotnick had been very skillful in his ongoing effort to plant seeds of doubt with jurors—evidence be damned.

For his part, Goetz could see he was in good hands, no matter how damaging the testimony of so many of Waples's witnesses had been. The previous weekend, he had headed back to New Hampshire for a couple days of rest. He visited with right-wing bookstore owner Tom Stotler and met another like-minded citizen, Robert Sparks. As Sparks told curious reporters: "Goetz is the victim in this case. He's a very defiant person. Having met him, I remain deeply committed to his philosophy and what he did. They are trying to make him a scapegoat."[117]

27

Bombshells and Blowups

IN THE FIRST two weeks of the trial, the Goetz jury had listened attentively as Greg Waples brought eyewitnesses to the stand, people like Garth Reid, who had seen the teens being shot, and those such as Armando Soler and Arnethea Gilbert, who had rushed to assist them in the wake of the shootings. They also heard testimony from the doctors who had cared for Goetz's victims once they arrived at the hospital and in the weeks and months after.

However, for every account the jurors heard that damned Bernhard Goetz, Barry Slotnick had suggested that Waples's witnesses were mistaken, unreliable, or perhaps even criminals themselves. In that latter vein he had attempted to undermine the credibility of dispassionate witnesses such as train conductor Armando Soler and Goetz's neighbor Myra Friedman, a well-respected author.[1] And, of course, Slotnick had also kept intimating that whatever did or didn't happen on the train, these young men had only gotten what was coming to them. They were nothing more than dangerous thugs with long rap sheets who no doubt had been looking for trouble.

But Waples had two aces up his sleeve—two pieces of evidence that he was fairly certain Slotnick would have a hard time explaining away. First, he had an eyewitness who had actually seen Goetz shoot Cabey when he was sitting in a position that no reasonable person could construe as threatening. Second, he had the much lengthier video of Bernie Goetz himself admitting that he had decided to shoot the teens even though, according to him, they had no weapons and were not robbing him. He also still planned to get James Ramseur on the stand so that jurors could hear firsthand from at least two victims.

Waples's star eyewitness was Christopher Boucher, Loren Michaels's friend who had been visiting from San Francisco.[2] Although Boucher had heard the first shots that Bernie Goetz had fired at Troy, Barry, and James—what he thought were firecrackers—he did not actually see them get hit.

In fact, Christopher Boucher only became aware that something more serious was unfolding when a woman who'd jumped up to flee had stumbled over his friend Loren. It was just as Loren was helping the woman right herself that Christopher saw a man, "in his late to early thirties, blondish," standing at the end of the car with a gun drawn.[3]

Waples asked Christopher to confirm that he'd been unaware of the gunman earlier, and then asked, "When you first looked in that direction and saw the blondish man standing, did you see any of the other young men who had been on the train?"

"Yes. . . . One of the men I had noticed earlier was lying on the floor in the aisle, face down, his head was up, looking to the end, looking to the front of the car," Christopher replied.

"In your direction?" Waples asked.

"Yes. One of the other men was slumped in the doorway, on the left side, and those are the only two I'm really positive about. My eyes went directly to the action . . . [the gunman] was standing, looking down at the man in the seat."

Christopher then described how he'd noticed Cabey's "hands like grasping the bench and a frightened look on his face," while Goetz stood "two to three feet" away, pointing the gun, which "he fired into this person" in "just a matter of seconds."[4]

"Did you ever see that person try to get out of that seat?"

"No."

"Did you ever see him threatening Mr. Goetz?"

"No."

"Did he have anything in his hand that you saw?"

"No."

"Is there any doubt in your own mind that you saw a person sitting in that seat when that shot was fired?"

"No, no doubt."

"And how is your eyesight?"

"It is perfect."[5]

Slotnick did his level best to discredit Christopher upon cross-examination. He posited that in the wake of the shooting, before Christopher actually spoke to the police, he had had a few drinks, which might have skewed his judgment or memory. Christopher was firm: He'd only had a drink. Just one.

Undeterred, Slotnick continued, "So, you weren't drunk or inebriated or under the influence of anything when you spoke to this police officer?" Christopher replied clearly, "No. I was not."[6]

Slotnick also tried to imply that there was something untoward in the fact that Christopher's testimony did not exactly match his friend Loren Michaels's regarding the detail that a woman tripped over Michaels, thus allowing Christopher to see the end of the train car, and that he was the one who had it wrong.

"So this woman now falls on Loren and she was a heavy woman, was she not?" Slotnick asked. "No, she was normal built, thin," Christopher replied and, when prompted, described her as "a young black woman . . . carrying a baby in her arms." Slotnick repeated, "So, at the time she was carrying a baby in her arms, and she fell on your friend Loren?," returning to his original question. "Yes," Christopher answered. "Is that correct?" Slotnick needled him—as ever, trying to introduce some doubt into eyewitness testimony.[7]

Despite Slotnick's strategy of taking on every prosecution witness with a mix of sarcasm, incredulity, jab, and insinuation, Christopher Boucher's testimony, the most damning to his client, clearly had made its mark.

Waples hoped that what would seal the deal, however, would be the words of Bernie Goetz himself. On May 13, 1987, Waples would entrance every juror and spectator alike with the videotaped interrogation of Goetz that had been conducted by Susan Braver and representatives from the NYPD and Transit Authority in Concord, New Hampshire—one that had never before been played publicly.[8]

The unveiling of these tapes would constitute one of the most significant moments of the Goetz trial. It would also fuel the nation's seemingly insatiable curiosity about all things related to Bernie Goetz. That night, news stations from coast to coast scrambled to play excerpts of this recording for their viewers too.[9]

The playing of these tapes certainly had the potential to inflame the public anew. That weekend, for example, was the birthday of slain Black activist Malcolm X, and several New York City activist groups, including Whites Against Racism, Solidarity with the Peruvian Revolution, and Gay and Lesbian Liberation, had already been planning to hold demonstrations. A key theme of these protests would now also be the renewed demand to hold Bernie Goetz accountable for the shooting of the four teens.[10]

Since the beginning of the trial, Baker and Slotnick had tried to prevent these tapes from ever being played. Baker was prepared to argue that Goetz had been under duress, having made clear that he didn't want to talk to investigators from New York City, and "at that point, the district attorney should have ceased questioning him under New York and federal constitutional law."[11]

But ultimately, the defense attorneys decided not to fight its admission into evidence. They knew that the jury would want to hear Bernie's own account of events, and there was no way they were going to let him take the stand. As Baker put it, "He was way too much of a loose cannon for that." So, they took a gamble, hoping that their client's obvious psychic pain, as marked by his extreme agitation, might make the jury empathize with him. "Maybe," Baker prayed, "Goetz's humanity would come through on this tape."[12]

Waples was counting on the jury having an opposite reaction to Goetz's rambling, at times coldhearted account of his actions on the train. Still, playing the tapes was risky for him too. After all, the first grand jury had heard the tapes and had ultimately felt for Goetz, just as the defense hoped this jury would. For his part, Judge Crane made clear that he wanted the jurors to treat these recordings as evidence and to focus on what they were seeing and hearing. "I urge you to watch the video because that is what it is there for," Crane told them. "Put your attention there."[13]

This instruction worked to Waples's advantage. He wanted each juror to really sit with Goetz's words, to take in his cold and matter-of-fact tone, and to watch his antisocial mannerisms closely. Even if the jury heard nothing else that Bernie Goetz said, Waples hoped that they would find one line particularly chilling: that he had been "thinking about shooting the four teenagers even before he was asked for money" and that he actually hoped to kill all of them.[14]

To set the stage for the jury to hear these tapes, Waples called NYPD detective Michael Clark and ADA Susan Braver to the stand. They dutifully told the jury how they had traveled to New Hampshire on New Year's Eve and then explained the parameters of their discussion with the suspect Bernhard Goetz. Most importantly, they made clear that Goetz had willingly volunteered the details of the crimes he had committed and even agreed to waive his right to a lawyer, despite being offered counsel on more than one occasion.[15]

A twenty-seven-inch Sony television monitor was then rolled out in front of the jury box. Individual headsets were distributed to each juror, to filter out other potentially distracting sounds in the courtroom, and each of them also had a transcript of the audio in front of them, so they could read Goetz's words while listening to them. Two additional monitors were set up in the courtroom so that spectators could also watch the confession play.

Watching the video confession after only hearing the audio of Goetz's statement was important. The video confession underscored that the more comfortable Goetz got, the more explicit he was about his intention to take the boys out, and the more defiant he became, insisting that he would do it all over again. As one newspaper described it, in the first audiotape Goetz had "seemed turned inward, in an anguished self-appraisal of his actions and values," but in the video, he would appear "far more belligerent and hostile."[16]

As the videotape played, the jury and "more than 100 spectators watched raptly." On a number of occasions, people in the crowd could be heard laughing, either incredulously or finding it humorous each time Bernie Goetz spoke to ADA Susan Braver, for whom, as one reporter there acknowledged, he "seemed to have taken an intense and unexplained dislike."[17]

The jurors, however, did not appear to find even that element of the tape funny. Bernie's words and body language were just too unsettling, particularly when he recounted his actions on the train.

Goetz's words were, at times, chilling. Jurors looked on wide-eyed as he admitted on this tape not simply that what he had done was "cold and ruthless" but that his "intent was to kill 'em," and that he was attempting to carry out "cold blooded murder." He made clear on this recording too that he never thought he was actually being robbed. He thought that the teens were just "kidding around," and he knew they did not have weapons. Even when the one kid had asked him for money, Goetz acknowledged that "at that point pulling the gun would have been enough" but instead he “snapped” because of “the gleam in his eye and the smile on his face.”[18]

The jury also got to hear Goetz describe the care with which he had loaded his gun with bullets that would cause maximum damage before getting on that train, as well as the military precision with which he took out his targets, one by one, once he had “decided” he was going to “kill those guys . . . maim them . . . make them suffer in every way” he could. They also heard him admit that if he had “had more bullets” he “would have shot ’em all again and again,” but since he did not, he “was gonna gouge one of the guy’s eyes out.”[19]

Perhaps most important, though, jurors got to hear Goetz say that the teens did try to flee his gunfire, and that, nevertheless, he had absolutely fired five, not four, shots at them. Goetz had, he said, decided to let these “guys have it,” and so when he fired at a teen who then seemed to be okay, he chose to shoot him again and recalled that the kid had “jerked his arm” up protectively. He also had gone back over to the first kid he had felled to make sure he had really gotten him too. Goetz had his keys at the ready, in order to harm him further, but, as he put it, after looking down at the wounded teen, “I saw his eyes twitching and I saw the fear in his eyes” and saw therefore no need to gouge his eyes out.[20]

Hearing any of the admissions would have been disturbing enough, but when the jurors could actually see the detached steeliness in Goetz’s posture and facial expressions, it was downright haunting. As one juror put it, the filmed statement provided their “only glimpse of the dangerous nature of Goetz’s wrath. Otherwise, we would have never seen evidence of how the meek-looking, mild-mannered individual sitting across from us in the courtroom had been capable of committing the violent acts that he had.”[21]

The tapes were played on Friday, and jurors had the weekend to consider Goetz’s words as well as Christopher Boucher’s eyewitness account of Goetz shooting Darrell Cabey. Significantly, though Slotnick had tried to discredit Christopher’s testimony, Bernie Goetz’s own taped confession corroborated it. What Christopher said he had witnessed was exactly what Bernhard Goetz admitted to doing.

WHEN COURT RESUMED the following Tuesday, May 19, Waples hoped to emphasize this powerful fact by calling Garth Reid’s wife, Andrea—the woman with the baby—to the stand.

Andrea Reid was a striking figure in the courtroom, wearing a black pantsuit, a high-necked metallic gold blouse, and an upswept hairdo. The *Post* took particular notice of "the svelte Bronx woman," never missing a chance to mention her job as a "part-time model."[22]

In many ways, Andrea Reid's testimony had the potential to be as devastating to the defense as Christopher Boucher's.[23] She had also become aware of the shooting only after hearing the first shot, but when she heard it, she immediately began paying attention.[24] Andrea also recounted for the jury that she had seen "two people running away from the gunman who was then on his feet . . . I noticed they were hit and at that moment fall."[25]

Her recollection of events also indicated that the final shot she heard, the one meant for Darrell Cabey, was separate from the ones he fired in quick succession into Troy, Barry, and James and his first attempt to shoot Darrell.[26] This supported the state's contention, and Goetz's own admission, that he had shot at Darrell, missed, and then walked over and shot him again when any possible threat could no longer be alleged.[27]

And yet, Andrea Reid's testimony also presented a handful of problems for the prosecution. She testified, for example, that when she had first seen the teens talking to passengers on the train, she was "afraid because I thought maybe they were going to come over and bother me and my husband."[28] This was music to the defense's ears. And when it was time for Barry Slotnick to cross-examine her, he did his best to persuade jurors that she had been even more fearful than she was now letting on.

Slotnick pushed Andrea Reid hard on cross about previous testimony she had given to the grand jury about the boys' behavior on the train, to suggest that she was now painting the boys in a rosier light. Specifically, he accused her of adding in new details about the shooting this time around to aid the prosecution, as well as failing to include details she had offered up previously that made the teens look bad.

However, Andrea Reid was not easily cowed. She readily admitted that "she may have at times been confused or left out details in speaking about the case," but she also pushed back hard on Slotnick's claim that, for example, she had previously said the boys were "up in [Goetz's] face" and that they had been "standing over" him in a threatening manner.[29] Andrea had never said that more than one boy had spoken to Goetz, she hotly insisted, and what's more, she also had zero memory of saying that "they were up in his face."[30]

Slotnick persisted. Mrs. Reid had indeed said that four boys surrounded Goetz, he said, even suggesting that he had tape of her saying so when two of his investigators had interviewed her at her home. This was an audacious assertion, and one that could well outrage the witness and prosecution both. The notion that Barry Slotnick had surreptitiously recorded a state's witness was itself stunning, but it was also perhaps just a bit of theater, the defense attorney's way of implying that he had some sort of smoking gun that proved she was a liar when he may well have not.

Taped or not, Andrea stuck to the testimony she had just given—insisting that she had not said what Slotnick claimed she had. And so Slotnick offered her an earpiece to listen to the recording herself. She was unimpressed and did not change her position. Because she had been taped without her knowledge, the recording device had been concealed, perhaps in the investigator's pocket, and it was so muffled she couldn't make out what it said.

Moving on swiftly, Slotnick tried a few other tactics to discredit Andrea's testimony. In one of these instances, he reminded Andrea that she wanted to be a cop and asked if she understood how important it was to tell the truth if that was the profession she aspired to. In another, he implied that Andrea's testimony was tainted by the fact that she knew Darrell Cabey's mother, Shirley.

"Has the fact that you met that woman influenced your testimony under oath in this Court in any way today?" he asked. Reid shut him down there, too, pointing out that she had only met Shirley Cabey once before.[31] They happened to be in the same place when Andrea's cousin hosted a crystal party, a gathering similar to a Tupperware party. It was a cursory meeting, Andrea recalled.[32]

Not quite getting the results he wanted, Slotnick once again moved on, deciding to use the rest of the cross-examination of Reid to discredit Christopher Boucher's testimony—specifically the detail he had offered about the woman tripping over Loren Michaels.

"Did you, at any time, fall over another passenger, who was seated in the car, you and your baby?" Slotnick asked.

"Fell over?"

"Yes, or fell on top of?"

"No."

Slotnick's next question must have seemed like a non sequitur. "Does the name Christopher Boucher mean anything to you?"

"No."

"Do you remember," he pressed her, "try and remember; do you remember a white man sitting with a friend of his, and do you remember falling over that man, with your baby in your hands?"

"I remember a white male, yes, sitting where my husband and I were sitting, but, as far as tripping over, I don't recall no one who—I was up at that time because soon as I got up, they left, that's when everybody followed behind."

"So, what you're saying is that you never fell on top of Christopher Boucher or any other white man at that time?"[33]

This detail had nothing to do with whom Goetz shot, or when and where he had shot them. What's more, in her panic to escape, it might not even have registered with Reid whether she had tripped or not. But Slotnick's relentless pushing and his efforts to undermine Christopher Boucher's credibility had nevertheless succeeded in, at least, muddying the waters for the jurors.

It remained to be seen, however, just how much this practiced but substantively thin assault on the credibility of Waples's eyewitnesses would cost the prosecution, and whether Goetz's own words on the tape had answered jurors' most important questions about motivation and impact. Waples was nearly finished. He had just one more witness to call to the stand: James Ramseur.

28

Fighting Dirty

WAPLES HAD WORKED hard to get James Ramseur to take the stand again. Though it could be argued that James had only agreed to return to court because he faced "the prospect of another year in jail" due to the contempt charge hanging over his head if he chose not to make an appearance, return he did.[1] Waples hoped that with James's testimony, the jury would hear directly from one of Goetz's victims who, unlike Troy Canty, had never spoken directly to the shooter, and indeed was nowhere near the man when he was gunned down. There would be an upside for James Ramseur too. If he agreed to take the stand, the judge would vacate his earlier contempt of court charge.

Waples did his best to anticipate anything Barry Slotnick might use to discredit James on the stand, particularly accusations related to the rape and assault of Gladys Richardson but also other things that made this witness and his friends resemble the predators depicted in the *National Enquirer*.

Waples, for example, had taken the time to dig pretty deeply into the Gladys Richardson case, for which James was currently serving time in state prison. James and Gladys had known each other well before the assault, and James was unwavering in his insistence that he was innocent. It didn't appear that Waples really doubted James's guilt, but like James's attorney Ron Kliegerman, perhaps he too found it curious that Gladys had named James well after her brutal attack and in conjunction with the barrage of negative press he had received.

Importantly, Waples had seen evidence that indicated James was not just very upset by Gladys's accusations but also that he seemed genuinely not to understand why she was pointing the finger at him. Over a series of phone calls and at least one letter from prison, James had begged Gladys to tell him why she made these claims against him when, he insisted, he had not done anything to her. Waples managed to procure a copy of the letter James had sent to her as well as the transcripts of their three phone calls made between December 6 and 9, 1985, and the testimony from the Richardson trial.[2]

But while these exchanges raised questions about whether James had been one of her assailants in this case, they also made clear that James had at least been present when others had assaulted Gladys, which hardly cast him in a positive light.[3]

When Waples also looked extensively into the less-than-savory interview that Troy and Barry had given to the *National Enquirer,* one that in its way had also implicated James, he did seem to doubt that it had been aboveboard, and demanded that the paper provide a complete transcript of the conversation. He also requested a copy of the agreement that the teens had signed, in case the tabloid had somehow violated the terms—for instance, with false promises of more money or assurances that this would help their public image. But Waples had no luck. A representative from the paper had written back, tersely, "The National Enquirer, Inc. declines to provide the information which you have requested regarding the interviews with Messrs. Canty and Allen."[4]

Meanwhile, the entire time Waples had been trying to win over the Goetz jury, the *New York Post* had been playing to the court of public opinion in ways that were only energizing the defense and likely encouraged its audacious trial tactics once James took the stand. In a May 16, 1987, piece by the editorial board of the *Post,* headed by Rupert Murdoch himself, Goetz was again held up as the real victim:

> No matter what the . . . jury decides, Bernie Goetz has already been punished for defending himself against four subway muggers armed with screwdrivers. . . . Though his lawyers are working at reduced fees, Goetz is already nearly broke. Two-and-a-half years of protracted litigation—including the cost of investigators, expert witnesses. . . . Meanwhile it is worth noting that James Ramseur, Barry Allen, Troy Canty, and Darrell Cabey would've paid absolutely nothing for their defense if they had successfully mugged Goetz that day.[5]

Even without encouragement from the tabloid press, Slotnick had noticed all on his own that Waples's witnesses could be unpredictable in ways that he could use to his advantage. He was looking forward to this.

On the afternoon of May 19, just after Andrea Reid finished her testimony, James Ramseur was sworn in. He was dressed like "a choir boy," *Post* columnist Ray Kerrison sneered, "in a jacket, blue shirt, red tie, and neatly trimmed hair."[6]

Waples opened his questioning of this critically important Goetz victim by establishing, and therefore preemptively acknowledging, that James was currently serving time at the Attica State Correctional Facility in upstate New York—a move, however, that immediately made his own witness defensive. When Waples asked, "What sentence are you serving?" James initially responded, "For a rape charge that I never committed."[7] Waples repeated the question, and this time James answered more directly but still stonily: "Eight and a third to twenty-five years."

But as Waples went on to introduce the jury to the James Ramseur that had boarded the train that December day, his witness noticeably relaxed and began answering questions quietly, without bravado or suspicion.

Jurors learned that James was a kid who had not gotten past the seventh grade in school, who supported himself and his family by stealing smaller items like coffee or candy and reselling them on the streets. He broke into video machines to get quarters, as the jury well knew, but he also bought items like kitchen knives from wholesale stores in the city and sold them to ladies in his neighborhood or local shopkeepers for a good price.[8]

On December 22, 1984, when James was heading into Manhattan to break into some more arcade machines, he had been shot for reasons he still couldn't quite understand. He remembered seeing Troy talking to a guy on the train—he actually thought Troy might be asking for the time—and suddenly, he found himself on the floor with a bullet embedded somewhere in his body. He had been trying his best to stay away from this man, he explained, when he'd felt his shoulder shatter.

"When I was shot, I seen him, you know, the gun aiming towards me. Looked like it was towards my chest. So, I turned to the side and I just felt it, and I felt the bullet go in my chest," James explained.[9] Waples asked him what he did after being struck, and James continued. "I dived to the floor . . . I just—next thing I heard another shot . . . Darrell Cabey was yelling, 'I didn't do nothing' . . . I could see Goetz was going towards Darrell Cabey."[10]

James testified over the course of two days, and on the stand he still looked very young and seemed unusually shy. His voice was so quiet that, several times, Waples had to ask him to speak louder so the jury could hear his testimony.

While James softly, but vehemently and repeatedly, denied assaulting or raping Gladys Richardson, maintaining that the cops in his neighborhood had been trying to set him up since the Goetz shooting, he never denied being a thief as a teenager or running illegal moneymaking schemes to survive in the South Bronx.[11] Nor did he try to deny that he and his friends were planning on stealing from video game machines the day they were shot, or that he still had multiple misdemeanor warrants out for his arrest. Mostly, he wanted to stress that the shooting had shocked all of them—perhaps Darrell most of all.

When Barry Slotnick began his cross-examination of James Ramseur, it was immediately apparent that his plan was to eviscerate him. He would not rest until he had shown the jury that, as one reporter at the *New York Post* put it, James and his friends were but "hardened, career criminals who hunted in packs, used drugs and preyed on the weak."[12]

Ultimately, Slotnick's cross-examination of James Ramseur proved to be one of the hardest-to-watch events of the entire trial. Slotnick pulled no punches from the very first question.

"You're the same James Ramseur who came here once before and refused to be sworn on the Bible, in fact, waved it away and said you're not testifying, is that correct?" Slotnick asked.

"Yes, it is," replied James.

"And you're also the same James Ramseur who a judge in Bronx County sentenced to eight and a third to twenty-five years, is that correct?"

"Yes, it is."

"And you're the same James Ramseur who was convicted in Bronx County for rape?"

"Yes, it is."

"Robbery?"

"Yes."

"Sodomy?"

"Yes."

"Assault?"

"Yes."

"Possession of a weapon?"

"Yes."

"And you're the same James Ramseur who was convicted for sodomy of a pregnant woman by the name of Gladys Richardson, and caused her eighteen stitches in her anus, is that correct?" Slotnick said icily.

"Yes, it's correct, but I never done the crime," James said.[13]

After this slow and deliberate underscoring to the jury that James was a convicted criminal, Slotnick suggested that he was also a con artist and a pathological liar. The *New York Post* delighted in this, reporting that Ramseur had shown his true colors under questioning, squirming and mumbling unsatisfactory answers that "not a single member of the jury will believe."[14]

And as for his scams, had James not filed a civil suit against Bernie Goetz? Slotnick asked pointedly. Had he not decided to come back to court to testify merely as part of a larger plan to collect $9 million from his civil suit? After all, if Goetz was found not guilty in this case, would it not be exponentially harder to turn a civil trial jury against him further down the line?[15]

Slotnick went on to attack James's credibility, arguing that not only had his gangster behavior and heinous actions landed him in Attica but also that he was the kind of guy to "falsify" his own kidnapping.[16] When James began to explain why he had made this claim, to call attention to the fact that police rarely took crimes perpetrated against a New Yorker like him as seriously as they would if someone accused him of a crime, Slotnick cut him off, coldly reminding him that he was the lawyer and he would ask the questions that he was interested in hearing answers to.[17]

But the topic that Slotnick dwelled on in the most excruciating detail, and kept coming back to, was the rape of Gladys Richardson. "You say you were really not guilty of the rape, robbery, assault, and sodomy; is that correct?" Slotnick said dubiously. "That is correct," James again insisted.[18] Slotnick made it obvious that he found this laughable. He had already suggested to the jury that this was nonsense when he had asked James, "You were tried before a judge and a jury, were you not?"[19]

Just as Barry Slotnick refused to stop asking about the rape, James similarly refused to admit he had committed it. Slotnick kept pushing—not only did James rape Gladys, but he had also been writing and calling her, trying to threaten and intimidate his victim into retracting her story.

That wasn't the way it happened, James insisted, almost plaintively. "Yes, I told her she was lying . . . I wanted to see why she was lying, find out why she was lying—" he began. But Slotnick interrupted him once more and told him, rather than asked him, what his intention had been when writing to Richardson or speaking to her on the phone.[20]

Slotnick fired questions at James so rapidly, without giving him the chance to respond, that with each passing minute on the stand, it was obvious that this witness was getting more and more bewildered, overwhelmed, and frustrated.

Was James the kind of thug who tried to dodge responsibility for the terrible crimes he committed? Slotnick pressed. Had he not snuck out of the hospital rather than take responsibility for the bench warrants he faced?

Again, James tried to explain, for example, that the four warrants had been for petty misdemeanors like turnstile jumping, but before he could even begin to clarify, Slotnick silenced him. "I ask the questions to you, Mr. Ramseur," he again reminded him.[21]

At every turn, Slotnick tried to trip James up on the most minor details, ones that had little bearing on the shooting but had the effect of making him look like he was lying about something significant. At one point during the brutal cross-examination, Slotnick hounded him on the question of whether he had had the screwdriver in his pocket for two days or two weeks. It depended, James tried to explain, because he sometimes landed work at a nearby construction job and frequently needed to carry a screwdriver. This was pure fiction, Slotnick retorted incredulously. He had once again made James's answer seem like but another attempt to dodge responsibility and minimize the danger he had posed to Goetz.

The more Slotnick interrupted James—often peppering him with confusing iterations of the same question—the more flustered he became. When Slotnick accused of him of lying or being manipulative, James could only insist that he always "told the truth."[22] James slowly gave up trying to explain anything. Helplessly, he said, "I know what time it is."[23] It didn't matter how he answered these questions. Goetz was going to be found not guilty.

Eventually, James gave up on cooperating with Slotnick almost entirely. When the lawyer put a document before James, for example, and asked him to read it to "refresh his recollection," he simply refused to do so. "I don't want to see them, you could have just made those up," he said, an indication of how little he trusted this legal proceeding.[24]

The fact that James was completely shutting down on the stand infuriated Barry Slotnick, dismayed Greg Waples, and seemed to utterly befuddle Judge Crane. Crane asked James to explain his refusal to answer Slotnick's questions, to which he replied bitterly, on the verge of frustrated tears, "He's twisting things around. . . . Twisting my stories around."[25] He might say things incorrectly, might have forgotten some details, James choked out, but "I don't [always] remember exactly. . . . I don't remember, I was half dead." Still, he insisted, he always told the truth, even if it didn't make him look so good.

This had not always been the case, James admitted. He had not always been "an honest and truthful person."[26] But when he was actually guilty of a crime, he owned up to it and had even done so in this courtroom.[27] He had not done many of the terrible things Slotnick accused him of, he maintained, including try to rob Bernie Goetz.

"If I was guilty of robbery, I would have told that when I testified," he said emphatically. Slotnick scoffed, before replying, "That could have blown your civil case." No, James retorted. "I would have told the truth."[28]

Though it became increasingly clear that Slotnick's cross-examination was only upsetting James and not particularly adding any new information the jury might need to hear, at no juncture did he cut James any slack. When James suddenly stopped answering altogether, Slotnick angrily demanded that the court "admonish the witness" to respond.[29]

From James's perspective, he had already answered Slotnick's questions in as many different ways as he could. Periodically, he would reengage, verbally pushing back against Slotnick's inquisition, eventually saying outright that he thought what Slotnick was doing was "bullshit."[30]

None of this seemed to rattle Slotnick. Indeed, this seems to have been his plan. As James became increasingly agitated, Slotnick was able to capitalize on the young man's frustration and bewilderment, making him look angry, unstable, and untruthful. And when he then could ask the judge to intervene, that was a bonus. As he appealed to Crane—ever more theatrically—it suggested that even he needed protection from this out-of-control witness. "Your Honor, I don't have to take this abuse, and I ask the Court to intercede," he said at one point.[31] Crane, clearly feeling at a loss, opted again to threaten James with contempt of court for every question that he refused to answer.

But James was far past the point of caring. "I'm tired of him playing games with me," he said. "We not talking about this case. . . . He playing games. He going to ask me about some old bullshit. Take me out of here. . . . I'm ready to cooperate, but he playing fuckin games. Take me out of here; I'm tired of this bullshit. I'm not going to answer this question. If you are going to get me for contempt, go ahead. I'm in jail for something I didn't do. Time isn't going to hurt me."[32]

Rather than let Crane handle the witness, as he had just asked him to do, Slotnick took these responses as an opportunity to additionally undermine James. How dare he use the language he had used in this courtroom? How dare he abuse the "majesty" of this court? When James argued that Slotnick would do the same thing in his position, the lawyer once more brought up Gladys, only sending James into a further spiral.

"See what he's doing," James said imploringly, looking over at the judge. "If it wasn't for those charges, that's all he can use is those charges. He's not talking about the Goetz case, he's talking about some other charges. He's trying to come up with some other bullshit," he said, almost breaking with frustration.[33]

Judge Crane stepped in, but only to say, "I direct you to answer the question, Mr. Ramseur. Do you refuse to answer the question?"

"I refuse," James replied.[34]

The impact on the jury of Barry Slotnick and James Ramseur's dramatic and prolonged back-and-forth was not yet clear—would they see Slotnick as a bully who was belittling one of Goetz's victims? Would it trouble them that the defense lawyer was so clearly trying to overwhelm this young man, who had not even finished junior high, with legal procedure and process that he had little reason to trust? Or would these jurors see James Ramseur as disrespectful and dangerous, a violent rapist and a thief to boot, who deserved it when Goetz shot him?

Based on the press coverage, this day had not gone at all well for the prosecution. After highlighting James's rape charges and noting that he had been held in contempt of court a mere two weeks prior, the *Chicago Tribune* reported that he had become "combative and occasionally flippant."[35] *The New York Times* decided that James had been the problem as well. As its reporter put it:

> The jurors may find it more difficult to purge their memories of Mr. Ramseur's actions. On the two occasions when Mr. Ramseur testified about the wounds he received from Mr. Goetz, he angrily denounced the legal system or the lawyers or both and was ushered from the courtroom by armed guards.[36]

Judge Crane not only oversaw this dramatic removal, but had also said to James, while sentencing him to another six months in prison for contempt, that his "contemptuous conduct . . . conveyed viciousness and selfishness more eloquently than words could."[37]

James Ramseur had been Gregory Waples's final witness. The ugly scene that had unfolded in Judge Crane's courtroom on May 20, 1987, completely shifted reporters', and likely the jurors', focus from the real issue at hand—Goetz's disturbing admissions and the devastating consequences for his victims. Most everyone seemed much more interested now, as one piece in the *Post* put it, in the fact that with seven court officers watching over him closely, "a sneering James Ramseur was sentenced to six months for contempt of court today after refusing to answer questions. . . . He will begin serving the time after completing an 8 to 25 year sentence for rape" and that he had "stood throughout with his arms crossed over his chest. He glared menacingly at the judge when he was let out afterward."[38]

And now, it was Barry Slotnick's turn to call witnesses to the stand.[39]

29

Smoke and Mirrors

DESPITE THE DRAMATIC DAY that the jurors had just witnessed, Judge Crane tried to mitigate its impact on the outcome of the case by ultimately deciding to strike James Ramseur's entire testimony from the record. The jury would no longer be able to revisit it in their deliberations, he announced. "It is no longer any proof in this case for your consideration."[1]

This was a real coup for the defense, and Barry Slotnick knew it. The truth was, to any juror who would have taken the time to really read this part of the court transcript as they sought to reach their verdict, Slotnick might not have looked very good. They could well decide that he had in fact baited a vulnerable young man. But now the specific details of why James had gotten so upset on the stand were gone, even while the image of him furious and cursing clearly would remain in their minds. As Slotnick said openly to a journalist when court had adjourned that day, "His actions are [nevertheless] before the jury. . . . We decided we didn't need to complicate the record with the words."[2]

It was now week five of the trial and the defense's turn to bring witnesses to the stand. Each one had been carefully selected by Slotnick to persuade the jury that Goetz was not a perpetrator but a fearful crime victim. Goetz's reaction to the teens on the train, Slotnick would argue, was not only understandable but utterly unavoidable.

Yet Slotnick had his work cut out for him. As the *Post* articulated it, Goetz's confessions, "filled with violent images and nightmare details, have emerged as a major stumbling block for the defense. . . . [They] must now confront Goetz's searing language head on."[3] What's more, Slotnick would have to address the shooting victims' injuries as well as offer his own, more persuasive, interpretation of the teens' positions and how the bullets had been fired.

He would also have to somehow discredit the eyewitness recollections of the shooting, including the graphic and detailed confession of his own client, in a way that would make sense to jurors who might well privilege the accounts of the parties who were actually on that train as opposed to later theories about what had happened there.

Slotnick's first witness was Charles Cozza, the off-duty Department of Sanitation police officer who, in 1981, witnessed Goetz in the midst of an altercation with sixteen-year-old Fred Clark.[4] According to Cozza, he could not corroborate whether there had been an attempted robbery prior to Clark hitting Goetz, nor if Goetz later required medical attention.[5] He did, however, see an abrasion on Goetz's face, and he believed Goetz when he claimed the group of young toughs had tried to mug him.[6]

On his confession tape, Goetz described this event as a mugging experience that left his knee seriously injured and made him determined to secure a gun permit to avoid the possibility of another such attack. Goetz had been indignant that he had spent hours longer at the police station than his alleged assailant, Fred Clark, and that Clark had had the audacity to accuse him of being the aggressor. Ultimately, Clark—a thug, in Goetz's mind—pled out to a lesser charge.

To underscore how traumatic, and thus formative, this moment had been for Bernhard Goetz, Slotnick then called Dr. Murray Burton to the stand. Dr. Burton had treated Goetz for a knee injury thirteen months after he was assaulted by Clark and his friends, who, Goetz asserted, had hurt his knee when they pushed him into a plate glass window. Dr. Burton had diagnosed Bernie Goetz with a chronic, possibly permanent condition known as chondromalacia, and conceded that such a condition could be caused by trauma.[7] But ultimately, this witness would prove less effective than Slotnick hoped.

On cross-examination, ADA Greg Waples saw an opening and asked Dr. Burton pointedly if "such a condition could be caused by many factors, including physical exercise like aerobics or running."[8] Chondromalacia, jurors needed to know, was often referred to as "runner's knee." The doctor confirmed that yes, it could. In an important follow-up, Waples also made sure that the jury took note of the fact that Dr. Burton testified "that the pain Goetz complained of in March of 1982 had only begun the month before and that after two months of a prescribed exercise regimen, the condition was cured and the knee sound."[9]

While Slotnick's attempt to underscore the brutal physical effects of Goetz's 1981 mugging may have fallen short, his next witness, court stenographer Vincent Palumbo, had the potential to make a bigger impact.[10] While Slotnick felt confident that James Ramseur's time in the courtroom had only benefited his client, he wasn't as sure about Troy Canty's testimony, which was still very much on the record. Vincent Palumbo, he hoped, would provide material to discredit Troy.

The majority of Palumbo's time on the stand was spent rehashing Troy's earlier testimony from the second grand jury in spring of 1985. Slotnick hoped to stress the inconsistencies between Troy's account of the shootings then and now. In 1985, for example, Troy had not been certain whether any of his friends had been seated, nor was he sure where each was positioned in relation to Goetz prior to, or during, the shooting. At that time, Troy had also testified that he was the leader in that group of friends, but when Waples questioned him, two years later, he denied having played that role.

But much of Palumbo's testimony also felt underwhelming, if not outright unhelpful. As one juror later stated, "In some cases I did not find the statements contradictory at all," and whether or not Troy saw himself as the one in charge of the group seemed to be "a rather minor point."[11]

What did seem to matter more to jurors were the inconsistencies that this court stenographer had highlighted regarding how close Troy had been to Goetz. If Troy had been standing very close to Goetz, in his personal space, this could theoretically explain why Goetz had felt threatened enough to pull out his gun. In front of the second grand jury, jurors learned, Troy said Goetz had "taken a couple of steps away" before pulling his gun and had actually described their relative positions as "too close." In this current trial, however, Troy had testified that he had been about "three or four feet away" from Goetz.[12]

At this point, Judge Crane felt the need to weigh in, reminding the jury that the sole relevance of this witness's testimony pertained to Troy Canty's credibility—not the legality of what Goetz did. Slotnick knew this, but he had also managed to tell the jury a version of Canty's encounter with his client in which the latter was being intimidated and had to step back before pulling out his gun. As juror Mark Lesly later wrote, "Slotnick just wanted us to hear it, and so he offered it the only way he could."[13]

The next witness was Peter Smith, the first NYPD police officer on the scene of the shooting and the one who, so controversially, had come forward after the second grand jury, eleven months after the shooting, to change his account of what the wounded teens said to him when he first arrived.[14] According to Officer Smith's later version, Troy Canty had told him, "We were going to rob him. But he shot us."[15]

Slotnick had unsuccessfully tried to use this same "evidence" to vacate the decision of the second grand jury. It had become quickly apparent, however, that Peter Smith had a serious credibility problem. Not only was this new account suspiciously timed, but it was also not supported by his contemporaneous notes nor by the account he'd given to the media on the day of the shooting.[16]

None of this, however, deterred Barry Slotnick from attempting to get substantial mileage from Smith's testimony now. Everyone knew the words of a member of law enforcement could carry a great deal of weight, and the truth was, Peter Smith was affable and handsome. Furthermore, the jurors were in good spirits and willing to hear this new testimony, as they had just been off for Memorial Day weekend.[17]

Smith not only testified that he had heard Canty say that the boys intended to rob Bernie Goetz but also claimed to have reported as much to Detective Michael Clark, the same detective who had gone to Concord, New Hampshire, to take Goetz's confession. He could not recall when, exactly, he had done this—perhaps a week after the incident—but he was mystified as to why there was no paper trail confirming any of this.[18] In any case, he had later filed a police report with a detective named Al Licata, so that should be enough corroboration.[19]

During his cross-examination, however, Greg Waples picked apart every aspect of Smith's testimony, suggesting that he had made all of this up simply to help Goetz. Had he not told a Detective Paar that he was considering calling Slotnick's office to offer him his testimony, just a month after Goetz had been indicted on so many counts, including attempted murder, and right as Slotnick was filing his motion to dismiss every one of these? Was it not the case that, if Smith's new information were true, it would have helped Slotnick's motion to vacate the indictments of the second grand jury? Indeed, had his late-breaking account not, in fact, helped the defense, since Judge Crane had dismissed all of the most serious of these charges, only for them to be reinstated by a higher court?

As for the police report that did exist, the one Smith had filed with Detective Licata, Waples wanted to be sure that the jury understood that Peter Smith did not file it until December 4, 1985—after the Goetz indictment, after Slotnick's motion, and when Waples had already dismissed him as not credible. In that report, he went on, Detective Licata himself had even felt compelled to note that Smith had filed the report only after the DA's office queried whether there was any paperwork corroborating his claim.

Perhaps most damningly, Waples pointed out, Smith's attempt to file a report that differed from his original account meant he was now the subject of an Internal Affairs investigation within the department.[20]

As it would turn out, and likely to Slotnick's dismay, the evening before Smith took the stand, May 27, 1987, WNBC-TV had decided to rebroadcast their original interview with Smith, one that had been recorded less than two hours after the shooting, in which a reporter directly asked Smith what the boys may have said. Waples would run with this too.

"You obviously told that reporter the truth, didn't you?" Waples questioned Smith.

"In substance," Smith replied.

"Did you lie to that reporter, Officer Smith?" Waples asked, more pointedly.

"Somewhat," Smith said.

"Somewhat," Waples repeated. "You are saying you lied to that person deliberately, is that your testimony, sir?"

Over the defense's vociferous objections, Waples entered the twenty-two-second video of the interview into evidence. He reminded the witness—and the jury—exactly what Smith had said back then, quoting his exchange with the reporter: "Question: 'What did the victims have to say?' Answer: 'They just gave me a quick description. He said they were just fooling around with the guy.'" Waples inquired, cuttingly, "As a police officer, even a relatively inexperienced police officer, Officer Smith, you know that there is all the difference in the world between someone fooling around with a guy and someone robbing him, right?" Smith acknowledged that he did.[21]

Thus far, Slotnick's plans for laying out a persuasive defense for his client were meeting with questionable success. Rather than convincing the jury that the shooting victims were in fact the aggressors, as one of the jurors later noted, "By the time Smith was excused from the stand, I no longer felt I could trust his testimony."[22]

Slotnick did not seem concerned. For starters, he had already planted doubts in the jury's mind by questioning Waples's witnesses in the way he had. And besides, he wasn't remotely done presenting his own case.

Slotnick planned to provide the jurors with some sympathetic psychological context for Goetz's shooting spree, and he also planned to call some of the prosecution witnesses back to the stand—anyone he felt he had not sufficiently undermined during cross-examination. Most significantly, however, he had plans to revisit the physical evidence by reenacting the shooting itself, to show Bernie's actions were justified and disprove the idea that Darrell Cabey had been shot in the manner that Waples had asserted he was.

The psychological angle would be challenging. When Slotnick first learned that there was a confession tape, he knew that a jury would need strong guidance in making sense of it from the defendant's perspective. "Tell me how you vote for an acquittal," he later mused, "based upon [this] videotape," especially because the more one heard of it, the worse it got.[23] Now, it was his task to help a jury understand what had led Goetz to shoot these four young men.

To do this, Slotnick was banking on the testimony of Dr. Bernard Yudowitz, a psychiatrist and expert in biological responses to fear and the human nervous system.[24] Like the physicians Greg Waples had called to testify for the prosecution, Dr. Yudowitz was highly credentialed. He was board-certified in three specialties—psychiatry, neurology, and forensic psychiatry—and he was especially knowledgeable about how people reacted to fear. On the stand, he would describe how, when someone was in a fearful situation such as Goetz's, rather than "the mind being in control," human beings tend to go on "automatic pilot," simply reacting to the situation they feel is placing them in danger.[25]

This was critical testimony, and a potential major advance for Slotnick. If Goetz were simply on "automatic pilot," then the issue of whether he had shot the teens because he wanted to teach them a lesson or disregarded their lives was moot. Yudowitz explained that with this sort of "adrenal response," a person has "no conscious control over what is happening" and they simply act to protect themselves from a "threatening situation."[26]

On cross-examination, however, Waples posed a significant question to Yudowitz. Wouldn't responses to fear vary depending on the individual and the circumstances? Yes, Yudowitz answered.

"And you have not examined the defendant in this case?" Waples asked.

"I have not."

"So, your testimony should not be construed by this jury as reflecting in any way an assessment of how this individual defendant responded to stress on December 22, 1984, or on any other date?"

"That is correct," Yudowitz replied.[27]

Whether Waples had been able to neutralize the impact of this defense expert's words was unclear. On the one hand, as juror Mark Lesly later acknowledged, Yudowitz's testimony did provide them with a less damning explanation for why "Goetz would have continued firing at the youths after the physical threat had been thwarted." But, as he also noted, "because the doctor had not personally examined Goetz, my impression when I heard the testimony was that it was inconclusive and certainly did not prove that Goetz was not in conscious control of his actions when he was shooting."[28]

Next, Slotnick decided to go after one of Waples's main witnesses, Andrea Reid. Arguably, he had little choice—only a week earlier she had been an important witness for the prosecution and remained steadfast in her certainty, among other things, that when Goetz shot them, two of the teens were "running away," and also that Goetz's "final shot [was] separate in time by several moments from the first shots."[29]

This last statement mattered tremendously because, if true, it supported the DA's contention, and Goetz's own admission, that he had shot Darrell, missed, and then walked over to shoot him again, when a threat could no longer be alleged.[30]

Of course, Slotnick had already cross-examined Andrea Reid quite relentlessly and had tried hard to mute her impact on the jury. He still felt, however, that he could use her words to his advantage, especially since he really needed to undercut any headway the prosecution may have made in its claim that the teens were doing nothing wrong when Goetz took them down.

Rather than bring Andrea Reid back into the courtroom, however, Slotnick instead called in the investigator who had recorded her in her home, secretly and without her consent. No doubt, Slotnick risked looking underhanded in his tactics. But this was a risk he was willing to take.

When investigator John Barna took the stand, the jurors were once again asked to don headphones. They were also given a transcript of the poorly recorded audio and told to listen carefully to four excerpts from Barna's conversation with Andrea Reid.[31] There were indeed aspects of that tape that would give jurors pause if, in fact, the transcript was capturing the garbled words on it. At one point, for example, Andrea was quoted saying that the youths "were right in [Goetz's] face," sort of "standing over him."[32]

Slotnick's claim that all four of the teens were crowded around his client in a threatening manner was simply not corroborated by this tape. Yet Slotnick persisted, as he'd done before in this trial, in suggesting that a speculative idea was an established fact. In this instance, he asked Barna to clarify how many people Andrea Reid had said were over by Goetz. "I believe she said four," Barna said.[33]

On cross-examination, Waples zeroed in on this claim as sheer fantasy. "She never said anything about four of them," he stated.

"Pardon me?" Barna asked.

"She never said anything about four of them," Waples repeated.

"Yes, she did," Barna insisted. Waples asked him to point out in the transcript where Andrea Reid specified all four boys were standing over Goetz. When Barna failed to do so, Waples sat back down, saying caustically, "I am content with the jury's recollection [of what they actually heard and read]."[34]

Slotnick simply forged ahead. His next objective was to persuade Judge Crane to allow him to reenact the shooting itself. With a staged reenactment, Slotnick felt that he would have the best chance of casting major doubt on the prosecution's portrayal of how this event unfolded. He would also, he knew, have a priceless opportunity to double down on his relentless portrayal of the shooting victims as menaces to society.[35]

Unsurprisingly, there was a fair amount of debate between the defense and the prosecution regarding the possibility, advisability, and feasibility of allowing such a re-creation—and doing so in a manner that would not be unduly prejudicial to either side.

Slotnick wanted two versions of the reenactment: one in the courtroom itself, during which he would call a ballistics expert to testify, and another outside the court, in an actual subway car retrofitted in such a way that the jury could more concretely envision what had happened there.

To further convince Judge Crane that the potential hassle of finding a train that could be made to approximate the original was, sadly, necessary, Slotnick called prosecution witness Detective Michael Clark back to the stand. The detective testified that despite the tragedy that had unfolded onboard that original subway car, it had never been impounded and had been allowed to remain in operation. However, sometime in the past two years, it had been converted to a work train. It was now painted with yellow and black stripes, its seating stripped out, and, most importantly, it had been cut to half of its original size to accommodate a crane.[36]

As he was awaiting final word on whether his out-of-court reenactment would be permitted, Slotnick pressed Judge Crane to at least allow him to turn the courtroom into a mock train. He would need this, he insisted, so that his next witness, a ballistics expert, crime scene reconstructionist, and retired NYPD cop named Joseph Quirk, would be able to rebut Waples's version of events with regard to where the four teens had been positioned during the shootings.

Slotnick planned to bring in actors to play Goetz and the teens. He requested the judge's permission for these stand-ins to sit in the front row while they waited to reenact the encounter between Goetz and those he shot. Waples strenuously objected to this plan, perhaps recalling how poorly it had gone when Slotnick had seated a purported mugging victim in the front row to glare at Troy Canty.

"Can't we use court officers for the purpose?" Waples asked. Slotnick protested, "Your Honor, I have sorted people [of] proper heights, there's a reason I have these four individuals. They have proper heights. They bear a similarity."[37] Whatever Slotnick meant by this likely worried Waples. Apparently, Slotnick "had specifically requested that the Guardian Angels send him four blacks."[38]

In the end, Crane acceded to Slotnick's request.

And so, on Thursday, May 28, 1987, the jury entered the fifth-floor courtroom to find that a large rectangle created out of masking tape had been affixed to the floor in front of the judge's dais. It was constructed to represent the exact scale of the subway car where the shooting took place. Once Slotnick had entered the taped-off "subway car" layout as Exhibit Y, it would remain permanently marked on the floor through the rest of the trial, an ongoing reminder of all that was about to unfold within its boundaries.

Within minutes, this taped stage resembled a gladiator arena, with the jurors jostling in their box to get a better view, leaning forward from the front row or standing up in the back.[39] Then, in what juror Mark Lesly would later dub "a brilliant ploy," a group of menacing-looking members of the Guardian Angels, all Black, entered the room to play the parts of the alleged victims.[40] One of the defense team's own investigators, Frank King, white, was ushered in to play Bernhard Goetz.

The jurors had likely been wondering for a while who King was, since he had been sitting next to Bernie Goetz, every day, right there at the defense table, "feverishly taking notes, scanning documents, and whispering in the ear of the subway gunman."[41] Now, however, this guy was right in front of the jury, surrounded by four menacing young men, trying to defend himself in a macabre make-believe scenario.

The message being sent here did not even pretend to be subtle. "The underlying intention," Lesly went on, "was to give the jury the chance to get the feeling of what four tough guys would look like—even if they weren't huge guys together in one end of a subway car. . . . They definitely produced something of a shock effect."[42]

One *New York Post* piece blared enthusiastically about this dramatic stunt, "PLAY IT AGAIN, BERNIE!" As this article described the scene, "Four Guardian Angels, and a private investigator, mesmerized the jury with a bullet-by-bullet recreation of the shooting. . . . As a spellbound jury looked on" and in "a mix of show, business and legal stratagem," Slotnick had these menacing-looking young Black men "stand in a semicircle around King." Almost giddily the piece went on, "The entire show seemed to infuriate Waples, who jumped to his feet repeatedly, and raised dozens of objections."[43]

He had reason to worry.

Against this exaggerated but seemingly realistic backdrop, ballistics expert Joseph Quirk offered testimony that had the potential to be a real blow to the prosecution's carefully constructed arguments about the case. Quirk asked the quartet of Guardian Angels to place themselves around King, facing him—maintaining that the four teens had surrounded Goetz just this way before he fired. He asserted that "none of the youths had been shot in the back while running away," and even more stunningly, given eyewitness testimony that the jury had heard—including from Goetz himself on the tape—that "Darrell Cabey could not have suffered his paralyzing wound while sitting down."[44]

Darrell, he argued, had not only been standing up and facing Goetz, but he had in fact been hit with the fourth bullet—not the fifth bullet—

that Goetz had fired, and had fallen backward into his seat as a result. The fifth bullet, Quirk insisted, had hit a steel panel, not Darrell. Barry Allen had not been running away but had instead been "standing close to Goetz and had exposed his back by ducking down.[45]

These assertions, if believed, would have totally undermined the prosecution's case. If Darrell had in fact been hit by the fourth rather than the fifth bullet, then the moment Bernhard Goetz had gone over to Darrell and shot him while saying "You don't look too bad, here's another" never happened.

Needless to say, Waples found Quirk's reading of the ballistic evidence utterly preposterous. It did not escape the jurors that during Quirk's testimony "Waples and Slotnick became angrier at each other than at any other point in the trial." Waples had indeed gotten "so infuriated with Quirk's testimony," one opined, "that he let his temper get the better of him."[46]

Waples felt strongly that Quirk was making assertions, and that they were being permitted, with zero evidentiary basis. His hands shook with rage. Even though the answers Quirk had given to Slotnick's questions were, in his view, little more than suppositions offered in response to certain "hypothetical" facts posited by the defense, they might well persuade the jury.[47]

And so, Waples tried mightily to make this exact point to the jurors on cross. Slotnick, however, was ready and repeatedly tried to derail his questioning of Quirk with a "series of frivolous comments" that he "interject[ed] in a sly effort to distract and disrupt [Waples's] train of thought."[48]

Still, the assistant DA did manage to score some points during his cross-examination. For starters, he did a pretty effective job of painting Quirk as a bit of a hack—a defense attorney's "gun for hire" whom no prosecutor would touch with a ten-foot pole. Waples suggested that Quirk was strapped for cash and got him to admit that Slotnick was paying him $1,500 for testifying.[49] He also inquired into Quirk's employment history, and called the jury's attention to his discovery that two people involved with a previous case Quirk had consulted on—a prosecutor and an NYPD ballistics expert—had raised serious questions "concerning [Quirk's] qualifications in the field of firearm examination."[50]

Waples's most dramatic effort to undermine Quirk's testimony involved showing the jury photographs of Barry Allen's actual injuries. Each of these photographs clearly indicated that Barry had been shot in the back. This, he maintained, made Quirk's version of events "physically impossible."[51] Waples even got Quirk to admit that this photographic evidence was completely consistent with a gunshot wound to the back. He conceded that Barry could have indeed "twisted his body, turning to run, when hit."[52]

Furthermore, Quirk admitted that it was possible that "the lateral shot across Cabey's back could have occurred with Cabey sitting down," muddying his earlier assertion that Darrell had to have been standing over Goetz when he was shot.[53]

Slotnick was furious. He called for a mistrial, claiming Waples had ambushed the defense by introducing photographic evidence that had come out of nowhere. He also argued, in what seemed quite a stretch, that these photographs actually impeached Waples's own witness, Dr. Peter Adams, who had testified that the bullet had entered slightly to the left of Barry's spine.

Judge Crane would not grant Slotnick a mistrial, but he did not permit the photographic evidence of Barry's wounds to stay in the record, either.

Notwithstanding Waples's effective cross, having Quirk speak as if he were offering concrete facts about the shootings when he was in fact responding to a series of hypothetical scenarios, offered jurors, as one put it, a "new understanding of the parameters of possibility concerning the shooting of Allen."[54] Slotnick counted on this and would capitalize on it later.

His decision to have threatening-looking young men act out the hypothetical scenarios that Quirk spoke so authoritatively about, and to position these men so close to the jurors, was also highly effective. To be clear, whereas the teens Goetz had shot were, to a one, slight and small, any young man chosen to be a Guardian Angel was welcomed into the group in no small part because he boasted a physique and attitude that would intimidate even the boldest mugger into backing down.

DESPITE THE CLEARLY inflammatory nature of Slotnick's re-creation with the Guardian Angels, after Quirk testified, Judge Crane decided to permit the second reenactment Slotnick had requested. The jury would leave the courtroom and spend some time in a real subway car, one that would look and feel exactly like the car in which the shootings of December 22, 1984, had gone down.

Judge Crane could have insisted that Slotnick instead reference the scale drawings of the IRT subway system car no. 7657 that Waples had admitted into evidence a month ago with his first witness, Marie Venticinque.[55] But Slotnick had pushed. "It's a terrific sketch, Judge," he said, "but it doesn't replace the real thing."[56]

It was crucial to the defense's case, Slotnick maintained, that jurors experience, and really appreciate, Goetz's position in relation to the four teenagers. Even if the jury had experience riding the New York City subway system, not all cars resembled the one that Goetz had been in in 1984.[57]

Judge Crane was persuaded by Slotnick's argument only after making his own visit to the proposed car, during which he was "surprised by several of the spatial relationships inside." He had previously believed, for instance, that the dent made by bullet 4, a spot in the steel panel on the side of the conductor's cab, had been "much higher" than it actually was. Without ever elaborating, the judge later recalled publicly that, during this visit, it had occurred to him "that part of the demonstration" could actually "undercut portions of the defense's case." But Waples certainly didn't see it that way. It was over his strong objections that Judge Crane agreed to what Slotnick began referring to, much to the judge's annoyance, as the "class trip."[58]

This was going to be a very expensive and difficult "trip" to pull off. For starters, the replica train, "consisting of six R-22 model cars . . . and 2 BMT cars," had to be assembled in the Bronx, at the 239th Street station. Then, the cars had to be brought downtown on the 2 line, which meant first heading "to the East New York Station in Brooklyn" and switching them to "a BMT track back to Manhattan and the Chambers Street station."[59]

Then, numerous people would be required to operate this replica train. This reenactment would need "both IRT and BMT motormen on board to negotiate the two different systems." According to authorities, the exact cost of this project was unavailable, nor was it clear who would foot the bill, since everything was ordered by the court.[60]

In advance of their time in the car, Judge Crane laid out clear ground rules for the jurors. "You will have to come to Court and amass here and I will take you to the railroad car where no one can speak to you, you can't speak to anyone else, you can't speak among yourselves and we will bring you back to the courthouse, at which time, I will [again] give you the statutory admonitions I am about to give you now, which is, you must keep an open mind on every issue connected with this case."[61]

On Friday, May 29, 1987, jurors dutifully boarded a minibus outside the courthouse and rode to the nearby Chambers Street station. They had serious matters to consider. Quirk's testimony from the day before, and Slotnick's first reenactment with the menacing Guardian Angels stand-ins, would have been fresh in their minds.

When they arrived at the station, other passengers stepping off the downtown J train looked on curiously, clearly wondering what was going on. At 10:50 a.m., the jurors boarded their specially fitted subway car via a fire door near where it had been parked at an unused platform on the J line.

The members of the jury could not have helped but notice the circus of reporters and photographers who crowded around them, desperate for a quote or a photograph to feed their papers' insatiable appetite for any coverage related to the Goetz trial. So intense was the media presence that day that at least one juror felt "like fish in an aquarium with so many people looking in at us through the glass."[62]

Goetz himself had waived his right to be there, and the only others allowed in the car that day were Judge Crane, Waples, Slotnick, and Baker, along with a smattering of transit officials, transit officers, and a court stenographer.[63] The car itself was in "the same condition" as the model R-22 car in which the shootings had taken place. The train was also, according to the *Post*, "marred by cryptic graffiti like 'to God for me'

Judge Stephen Crane (right) gestures while addressing jurors in the Bernhard Goetz trial, during a visit to a subway car similar to the one in which Goetz shot the four teenagers, May 29, 1987. AP Photo/G. Paul Burnett

and 'chant BMW.'" Attached to this replica was an additional subway car that was intended to approximate the one that conductor Armando Soler and witness Arnethea Gilbert had been in when the shooting began, the one into which passengers had fled.[64]

At 11:05 a.m., the jurors were the only ones remaining aboard the car, whereupon they took a "brief ride," five minutes or so, into an unused tunnel. There, the train stopped for fifteen minutes before returning to the platform.[65] On that short trip, the jurors were "encouraged to sit in the different seats, stand or simply absorb the atmosphere."[66] Though Crane had made it clear that not a word was to be spoken, the jurors nevertheless managed to communicate with one another through hand gestures and meaningful looks. As juror Mark Lesly later explained it:

> We took turns playing the roles of the people who had been on the train; and I remember, for instance, sitting in the "Cabey" seat when another juror—Bob Leach, I think—came up and pointed his finger at me, portraying Goetz. I then demonstrated to him how I thought Cabey might have twisted in the seat to receive the bullet at the proper angle.
>
> I and most of the other jurors made a point of sitting and standing in every position that we remembered somebody testifying to having been in or to having seen someone in.
>
> Although I had for many years been a frequent subway rider, being in this old-style car while contemplating the testimony I'd heard and imagining the situation that Goetz had faced did have a definite effect on me.[67]

What value this trip added to Slotnick's case was not obvious. To be sure, it may have been thrilling to place oneself in a re-creation of the "graffiti-smeared" car where so much drama had played out. It also likely made an impression that so many reporters were clamoring to hear the jurors' take on this highly controversial case. But whether this experience had swayed the jury's opinion on the guilt or innocence of Bernie Goetz was, in the moment, unclear.

Slotnick still had work to do.

THE FOLLOWING MONDAY, the jury returned to court to hear Slotnick's next witness, Dr. Dominick DiMaio, a former New York City medical examiner brought in to augment Quirk's various claims about what the ballistics evidence showed.[68] When Dr. DiMaio took the stand, the Guardian Angels were no longer on tap to reenact things to underscore points being made by Slotnick's witnesses. Waples had drawn the line at any more of these prejudicial theatrics, and convinced Judge Crane to do the same. Instead, DiMaio would analyze a packet of X-rays provided to him by the defense.

Unsurprisingly, DiMaio's testimony lined up with the hypothetical scenarios Quirk had argued, particularly with regard to Darrell Cabey's injuries. His interpretation of the bullet's path through Darrell's body differed from Darrell's doctor's testimony and also what he had read in the medical reports. "It's your testimony," Slotnick queried DiMaio, "that ultimately the bullet went up in an upward path rather than down in a downward path, lateral path?"[69] Yes, his witness concurred. Slotnick then hammered away at the implications of this point.

He asked DiMaio if it was possible that "Mr. Cabey" was shot while sitting down, to which he said no. DiMaio confirmed Slotnick's assertion that there was no position Darrell could possibly have been sitting in that would have been consistent with his injuries; there was "no doubt" in his mind that Darrell had been standing when Bernie Goetz shot him.[70]

Satisfied with DiMaio's assessment of Darrell's injuries, Slotnick moved on to Barry Allen. He asked DiMaio, in several different ways, whether the X-rays were consistent with the notion that Barry had been shot in the back. No, DiMaio again replied with certainty.[71]

But Waples would go after DiMaio most aggressively on cross. He needed to, given DiMaio's unwavering certainty that the prosecution's version of events was dead wrong. As with Quirk, Waples suggested to the jury that everything this witness asserted was based merely on "a hypothetical set of facts" given to him by Slotnick—and scored major points when he got DiMaio to admit as much.[72]

"He could have been three feet [from] the gun and sustained this wound, is that correct?" Waples asked. Yes, DiMaio replied. "Or he could have been ten feet away?" Waples pushed. Again, DiMaio said yes. "In fact," Waples said triumphantly, "you don't know where the defendant was when this wound was inflicted, do you?"[73]

This time around, Slotnick fought back. Much of the case Slotnick was building depended on where the jury believed the teens were when Goetz had shot them. Slotnick continued to insist that Dr. DiMaio's expertise, and his readings of the X-rays, were far more than speculative. He argued that any inconsistencies in DiMaio's opinions about the path of the bullets could be explained by the fact that the train was in motion.

With regard to Barry Allen, for example, Slotnick tried to emphasize that not only the speed but also the "lurching and swaying" of an express subway train could put a person's body in a slightly abnormal stance. Barry could have been in a "position wherein the bullet was slap at an angle and from right to left," Slotnick posited. "Then it would be in direct line to hit the body at an angle." DiMaio confirmed that was correct, and that he had been approximating Barry's position, taking the moving train into account.[74]

But Waples managed to level another hard blow to Slotnick's argument, even accounting for the train's movement. He got DiMaio to agree that it would have been "an extremely lucky event" for Darrell—on a moving train—to have fallen from a standing position into the seat rather than onto the floor, and that it was "most probable" that he had been seated, "as opposed to falling into the seat, in the exact sitting position in which he was found."[75]

In case Waples's nimble questioning had not cast enough doubt on the doctor's testimony, he also went after DiMaio's professional qualifications. First, Waples established that DiMaio, like Quirk, was essentially a witness for hire. In DiMaio's case, he had probably needed this job because, as Waples made clear to the jury, DiMaio had been forced to retire from the Medical Examiner's Office following a mishandled murder case.[76]

Waples's final blow was to bring an actual X-ray viewing machine into court. The machine was set up in front of the jury box, and Waples asked Dr. DiMaio to point out various things with regard to the bullets in the boys' bodies. Eventually he had to concede, "I'm not a radiologist."[77]

Waples's cross-examination of Dr. DiMaio had not been good for Slotnick's case. DiMaio was his second-to-last witness and, as the defense well knew, Waples was planning on bringing rebuttal witnesses to the stand before this case was turned over to the jury. Still, he had a plan. He hoped his last witness, former Transit Police detective Charles Penelton, would turn things around powerfully. If nothing else, Slotnick knew this witness would leave jurors with a bad taste in their mouths about the teens on whose behalf Waples was fighting so hard.

Detective Charles Penelton had been sent along with Detective Michael Clark to re-interview both Darrell Cabey and Troy Canty in the hospital shortly after the shooting. Troy had been reluctant to speak to any cop, and he had suspected, correctly, that Penelton had been sent because he was Black.

Penelton testified to how dubiously Troy had greeted his arrival: "We got to the hospital, Detective Clark left the room, and Mr. Canty said, 'I know why you're here. . . . You're a brother,'" to which Clark had replied, "Yes, I'm a brother. You want to tell me what happened?"[78]

But Troy had still been reluctant to speak to a cop, so much so that Penelton had almost decided to leave. Finally, though, Troy opened up. Their conversation was slow, even disjointed, but Penelton's takeaway—what Slotnick wanted the jury to hear—was that Troy had basically admitted to targeting Goetz.

According to Penelton, Troy told him that when Goetz boarded the train at 14th Street, "We got up and we went over and stood around the white guy."[79] Why him? Penelton had asked. Because, Troy said, "The guy looked soft."[80]

With Troy's character having already taken a number of hits throughout this trial, Waples feared that Slotnick's final witness would cement the jury's view that the teens were the aggressors in the situation, not the victims—despite having been shot.

In a valiant attempt to counteract Penelton's potentially devastating testimony, Waples spent a great deal of time during his cross-examination insisting that Penelton share the lengthier version of his interview with Troy. Waples considered the larger context of the interview important, exculpatory even.

This strategy paid off. Waples got Penelton to admit that Troy had never said anything about robbing Goetz—simply that he had asked him for five dollars. He also made sure to emphasize that this interrogation had taken place while Troy was heavily drugged with both Demerol and Vistaril, as Dr. Peter Adams had already testified. Penelton confirmed that during the interview, Troy was indeed drowsy and kept closing his eyes. "He was talking in such a low voice, such a low audible tone at times, you had to bend down and almost put your ear next to his mouth to even hear, is that correct?"[81] Waples asked. Penelton responded that yes, that had been the case.

Penelton also confirmed that the interview had ended when Troy had fallen asleep. Waples hoped this would convince the jury that Troy had been in no state to give a coherent statement to police, though he was concerned this might not be enough to counteract all that Slotnick had presented the jury with over the last weeks.

AS SOON AS the defense rested its case, Greg Waples called three major rebuttal witnesses to the stand: Dr. Melvin Becker, police officer Dennis Driscoll, and Dr. Charles Hirsch. He also wanted to bring Arnethea Gilbert back to the stand, since Judge Crane had ultimately ruled her earlier testimony regarding Darrell Cabey's words, "he shot me for nothing," hearsay and thus inadmissible. In this case, however, the judge said no.

Nevertheless, most of Waples's rebuttal witnesses were highly effective.

Given the central importance of the teens' positions in the car at the time they were shot—including whether they had been sitting or standing, and whether they had all been crowding around Bernhard Goetz—Waples knew that Dr. Melvin Becker was an especially critical voice for the jurors to hear before they began deliberating.

Dr. Becker wore several hats. He was a professor of radiology at NYU and had been the director of radiology at Gouverneurs Hospital. He was now an attending radiologist at Bellevue as well as at NYU's University Hospital.[82] What's more, he was also a consultant for the chief medical officer of the city of New York.

He had carefully reviewed Barry Allen's medical reports in advance. On the stand, in front of the same X-ray viewing machine where Dr. Dominick DiMaio had stood just a day earlier, Dr. Becker proceeded to make a mockery of the testimony of one of Barry Slotnick's most important witnesses.

With regard to the trajectory of the bullet that had entered Barry Allen's body, Waples asked, "If Dr. DiMaio . . . said that he could tell that this particular bullet was behind the head of the humerus because of its brightness, what would your reaction to that statement be?"[83]

Rather scathingly, Becker replied, "He is using far different criteria than any other radiologist has used in making these definitions."[84] DiMaio's conclusions were not based on scientific fact, Becker said. As far as he was concerned, no knowledgeable and competent radiologist would agree with DiMaio's analysis of the X-rays.

Slotnick must have been seething but did not in fact use his cross-examination to badger Dr. Becker—instead, he asked him to speculate about scenarios that might also have been "possible" and thus could theoretically support Dr. DiMaio's views. He also pressed Becker on whether he himself had ever treated gunshot wounds, which he knew the radiologist had not. None of this, however, resurrected DiMaio's credibility, and this wasn't at all good for the defense.

Waples's next rebuttal witness was NYPD police officer Dennis Driscoll, the first law enforcement officer on the scene alongside his partner, Peter Smith.[85] Waples felt it was essential that the jurors put no stock in Smith's late-breaking, highly charged account of what Troy Canty had said before being carried out of the train.

The good news for Waples was that, during his cross-examination of Smith, he had already managed to raise serious doubts about his veracity. Public reaction to their courtroom exchange made clear that he had been quite effective, with even Police Commissioner Benjamin Ward saying publicly that "he didn't think the officer's statement had the ring of truth."[86] Waples, however, wanted to leave nothing to chance.

Driscoll testified that he, not Smith, had tended to Canty on the train. Not only had Canty never uttered such an admission, but Smith hadn't even been near Canty. He was tending to Barry Allen. Even if Smith had overheard something as important as this purported admission, Driscoll insisted, he certainly would have written that down in his memo book at that time.[87]

The prosecution's final rebuttal witness, the very last witness of the trial, was Dr. Charles Hirsch, the chief medical examiner of Suffolk County, New York. Waples hoped that Dr. Hirsch would also undermine Dr. DiMaio's testimony, specifically when it came to Darrell Cabey's injury, and thus settle the issue of whether Darrell was sitting or standing during the shootings.[88]

Greg Waples wasted no time in asking Dr. Hirsch this question directly. "Doctor, is it possible . . . for that wound to have been inflicted upon Darrell Cabey while he was sitting in a subway seat?" Hirsch replied, "There are countless possible relationships that one could construct between the seated target and the standing assailant."[89] To cement this answer in the jury's mind, Waples pushed, what about Dr. DiMaio's claim that it would have been "impossible" for Darrell to have been seated and shot in the manner he was?[90]

"I disagree," Hirsch answered.

"And how strong is your disagreement, sir?" Waples pressed.

"As strong as I can [make it] because it is, in my opinion, completely false."[91]

Waples likely should have stopped while he was ahead—especially since the jury had just enjoyed some much-needed levity in the midst of his serious questioning of Hirsch. To get the doctor to show the jury exactly where the bullet traveled, Waples had provided him with a Styrofoam mannequin on which to demonstrate. That mannequin, which the *Post* described as "missing arms and legs," and one that "could never have played even a supporting role in a Fifth Avenue window," was also female and busty. All in the courtroom could not help but smile when Waples said "sheepishly" to the judge, "Your Honor, this is not anatomically correct."[92]

But Waples decided once again to push Dr. Hirsch on this point—that Darrell had to have been seated when Goetz shot him that final time—even though this witness had already been very clear this was the most logical scenario given the teen's injuries. As the consummate medical expert he was, however, in response Hirsch had to admit that there was no way, with 100 percent certainty, "to distinguish between those two possibilities," meaning whether Darrell had been seated or standing.

On cross-examination, Slotnick tried his best to make Hirsch "appear to contradict himself," and, stressed that, if anything, this witness supported the defense. As a juror later reflected, "Hirsch could do no more to lend credence to the prosecution's contention about how Cabey was shot, and this was a big weakness in Waples' case."[93]

30

Rewritings and Remonstrations

BY THE TIME Barry Slotnick entered the courtroom to give his closing statement on June 10, 1987, a parade of more than forty witnesses had preceded him. Notably, Bernhard Goetz had not been among them. That fact must have niggled at the jury, since Goetz was a man who had not hesitated to tell his story to any media outlet that might listen. But his lawyers kept him off the stand intentionally. As Mark Baker later put it, Goetz "could not have withstood the intense cross-examination Waples would have mounted against him."[1]

The defense would explain his absence in Slotnick's final remarks: Bernie Goetz had been victimized already, and it was not right to ask him to go through all of this again on the stand. While some worried about Darrell Cabey's family, Slotnick told the jury, "I am worried about, and the system worries about, Bernhard Goetz."[2]

With a microphone in hand like a TV host, due to a bad case of laryngitis, Slotnick began with the sweeping claim that the prosecution had completely failed to present the case that it had promised the jury it would. Slotnick had told the jury on day one that when the trial concluded he would reread Waples's basic opening statement "to show you that even the district attorney, two-and-a-half years after the event, had no idea what this case is about."[3]

That had indeed proven true, he said. Ultimately, Waples had gotten the case "totally wrong" and thus hadn't done the job he needed to do.[4] What the jury must never forget, Slotnick went on, is that in a criminal trial, the onus is fully on the prosecution—on Mr. Waples—to prove its case, beyond a reasonable doubt, not on the defense to prove Goetz's innocence.

The prosecution had failed in this endeavor, Slotnick argued, because of a most crucial fact—none of the unfortunate events of December 22, 1984, would ever have happened had his client not found himself in a terrifying situation from the moment he boarded that train. Bernhard Goetz had been in a good mood, Slotnick said, and he did not "walk on the train hunting. He walked on a train to enjoy some Christmas cheer." The four "predators," in contrast, were taking the train "to go out and plunder decent people in our community."[5]

When Goetz was "surrounded by these four men" he'd "reasonably believed" that they would harm him, Slotnick argued.[6] After all, it had happened before, back in 1981, when he had been assaulted by another group of dangerous thugs, Fred Clark and his friends.

Indeed, Slotnick pointed out, no one has an obligation "to allow yourself to be robbed, beaten, or brutalized." Therefore, his client "had a right to take the action that he did take." These kinds of hoodlums were committed to preying "on the good people . . . the young, the old, the soft looking, the easy bait." This entire saga was a notice that if they were going to do that, "it may backfire on them."[7]

Slotnick also insisted that Goetz was not the only fearful passenger on the train that day. Prosecution witnesses Mary Gant, Josephine Holt, and Garth and Andrea Reid, he baldly asserted, had all said they were "cowering in fear" and "scared to death." Indeed, Slotnick went on, Greg Waples hadn't adequately prepared for his case, because he "didn't know that the Reids were going to tell about the fear that they had" or that Andrea "was going to tell you that she was afraid they were going to come over to her and her child . . . [and] that her first reaction was they got what they deserved."[8]

Slotnick spent a considerable amount of time revisiting Andrea Reid's testimony. In his telling, she was a "sad" witness, one who had lied on the stand because she had been "deathly afraid" of "Cabey."[9] She was also worried, he claimed, that the Cabeys would retaliate if her testimony helped Goetz.[10] Indeed, Slotnick went on, it was a good thing his investigator John Barna had taped her, proving she was lying when she insisted in court that only two of the thugs had been standing.[11]

"There is no question that Bernhard Goetz was surrounded by four people [who] meant him ill," Slotnick maintained.[12] Troy Canty had even admitted that "all of us surrounded him" and that "we tried to rob him,"

Slotnick asserted.[13] "Obviously, you come to realize," Slotnick said as if pained and troubled, that "not all witnesses tell the truth . . . while it's a nice exercise to raise your right hand . . . there are people with vested interests like Troy Canty who lie on the witness stand." That said, there are also "people who do things out of fear at times when they feel justified, and [Mrs. Reid] did what she did out of fear."[14]

The good news, notwithstanding Waples's dishonest or cowed witnesses, was that Slotnick had provided plenty of ballistics and medical evidence to show what had really happened that day—most important, he claimed, had been the testimony of Joseph Quirk and Dr. Dominick DiMaio.

Referencing Quirk's testimony was a subtle but powerful reminder of the reenactments that had served to punctuate his claims—the one in the courtroom, in which menacing-looking Guardian Angels played the shooting victims, as well as the "class trip" to the subway, in which the jurors themselves assumed the roles of the gunman and his targets. Slotnick tried to imply that Waples had fought this second reenactment precisely because he knew it would "negate the theory of this case."[15]

But, Slotnick reminded the jury, Quirk's ballistics descriptions and Dr. DiMaio's medical expertise had made it quite clear that the youths had not been running away, nor sitting helplessly. So clear-cut was DiMaio's testimony, Slotnick asserted, that Waples had been reduced to going all the way to Suffolk County (at the easternmost end of Long Island) to find Dr. Hirsch, and had, he insisted, paid him a lot of money "to come here to testify that it's possible Darrell Cabey could have been sitting down" even though there were thirteen New York City medical examiners he could have brought in instead.[16]

Even as Slotnick took jabs at his opposing counsel, he likely knew that it would still be difficult for jurors to simply dismiss the testimony of prosecution witness Christopher Boucher. Boucher had actually seen Goetz go over to Darrell Cabey to shoot him and had clearly heard a fifth shot. Slotnick took particular care to assert that Boucher was the only witness to insist that there had been a slightly delayed, and deliberate, fifth shot into Darrell Cabey. Everyone else, Slotnick maintained, had heard the bullets fire in "rapid succession."[17] Goetz never paused, and thus did not have the time to walk over to Darrell Cabey and deliver a gratuitous shot at him.

Slotnick had worked hard to lay the groundwork for this. Every time he had questioned someone on the stand about the shots they heard, he always worked into the questioning the term "rapid succession"—in effect getting witnesses to agree without realizing the significance of the words that this was how the shots had happened.[18] By the summation, this phrase had been said so regularly, uncontested, that he could argue it as a ballistic fact in ways that it hardly was.

In fact, Slotnick insisted, "Most of the witnesses that saw Bernhard Goetz after the shooting, after he unloaded his gun, they saw him put it in his waistband, hold it to the side, and that was the end of the shooting."[19] He had shown too, Slotnick maintained, that Christopher Boucher's account of how Darrell was shot "didn't happen" and he had proven this "scientifically."[20]

What's more, Slotnick pressed on, the psychiatrist, Dr. Yudowitz, had made it clear that Bernie Goetz was firing those shots on "automatic pilot," thanks to the adrenaline flooding his system. Once he began shooting, Slotnick argued, Goetz was lost to that moment—his body reacting as prey unconsciously reacts in the face of any serious predator. Why wouldn't jurors believe the facts presented by Quirk, DiMaio, and Yudowitz, especially since the alternative was to believe the version of events presented by career criminals?

Slotnick made sure not to waste his last opportunity to bad-mouth Goetz's victims, repeatedly referring to them as "men"—not teenagers—and painting them as irredeemable predators. Take Troy Canty, for example, a witness who had come to court "all spiffed up in a nice suit telling us things that were absolutely and totally untrue," yet who was such a lowlife that the DA himself had to offer him immunity in order to testify.[21] "Immunity from what?" Slotnick spluttered. "Immunity from panhandling?"[22]

Think about the kind of man Troy Canty really was, Slotnick entreated the jurors. This was a man who was freebasing cocaine every day, and had been "a career criminal" since the age of twelve, someone who had "robbed and shoplifted" his way through life, and had only admitted in front of the jury "to crimes that he had been caught [for]."[23] Slotnick even attributed Canty's longtime failure to get into a drug rehabilitation program to "his character"—"obviously" the same reason, according to Slotnick, that he had failed to get compensation from the Crime Victims Board. "You can infer," Slotnick said, "that if a Crime Victims Compensation Board didn't give Troy Canty any money, it was because they knew he wasn't a crime victim."[24]

Troy Canty was the leader of "this gang of four," and Barry Allen "was second in command."[25] "Let us not kid ourselves," Slotnick admonished the jury, these men "didn't sneak on the back of the bus individually. They did that as group activity."[26]

As for Barry Allen, Slotnick argued that the prosecution had prevented him from even questioning this thug, despite having the power and authority to insist that Allen testify. As he told jurors: "The DA could have and should have called him, but they didn't call Barry Allen and I ask you to hold that against them."[27]

Slotnick was not allowed to refer to James Ramseur's testimony, since the judge had struck that from the record. He had to have faith that the jury remembered this particular Goetz "assailant" being on the stand, and that they had understood him that day to be angry and combative, a man who cursed profusely and who required being dragged out of the courtroom by armed guards.

That left Darrell Cabey, who certainly could have been exempt from the defense's caustic characterizations of the teens in his closing statement. But Slotnick went for the jugular there too. "Don't let anybody kid you," he told the jury. Darrell wasn't some hapless bystander in all of this; he was very much part of the gang that planned to harm Goetz.[28]

Cabey, like the other "men," had been unemployed. He had been kicked out of school and he too was a drug addict, who had been charged with many crimes apart from the one the group was intending to commit against Bernie Goetz.

"These aren't just kids strolling along on December 22, 1984. These are very well organized criminals . . . [they were] organized and worked in group activities with leaders, with true criminal mentality."[29] They had even worn "reversible jackets" to aid in their crimes—this was their uniform. What's more, these muggers knew how to distract their prey with their "signals" and "movements," which is "what they did to Bernhard Goetz."[30] These were seasoned criminals, Slotnick maintained. "They may be young, but unfortunately, they are sophisticated."[31] And they were also shameless: "Each of those people are suing Bernhard Goetz; Troy Canty for, I guess, five million, others, for multiples of eight million. Isn't that shocking? It's scary."[32]

Nothing the prosecution had said or done over the past many weeks of the trial would erase these ugly realities, Slotnick stressed.

But it wasn't enough to claim that the prosecution had fallen down on the job. Slotnick had to address the deeply unpleasant reality that the story he was telling the jury did not align with his own client's account of what had taken place on December 22, 1984.

Goetz himself told the police he never thought that Troy Canty was trying to rob him. He was the one who insisted he had planned to kill these boys from the minute he saw the "smile" on Troy Canty's face. What's more, he had described shooting them methodically, "laying down a pattern of fire." Goetz himself had admitted he wanted to maim them, to gouge out their eyes. When he described the boys' positions on the train, he placed them exactly where Waples's witnesses did. And finally, Goetz himself admitted, on numerous occasions and in times of duress as well as calm, to deliberately shooting Darrell Cabey—to walking over to this guy, after first missing his shot, and shooting him at point-blank range as he sat cowering in his seat.

To account for all of this, Barry Slotnick decided, in effect, to throw his own client under the bus. Where does the DA get his "theories" about the shooting? Slotnick asked the jury. He then answered, stunningly, "He gets his theories from the most unreliable source in the world, the statement of Bernhard Goetz."[33]

Slotnick then set about outlining a most extraordinary theory of how Bernie Goetz himself was this state's most flawed witness:

> Nine days after the event, nine days of pain and suffering, running, nine days later a traumatized, sick, psychologically upset individual walked into a Concord, New Hampshire, police station and made a statement on audiotape, and you heard it. . . . [But] Bernhard Goetz's statement is not trustworthy. Up to the moment of fear, it is trustworthy. Up to the point where [the] body takes over and goes into automatic pilot, the moment of fear, it is trustworthy. After that, it is like every other witness in this case; it is not trustworthy.[34]

After he was "surrounded," Slotnick insisted, Bernhard Goetz did "what was to him a terrible thing." He then became "anguished with pain, anxiety, and all the other horrors that are tended to someone who's truly a victim."[35]

By the time Bernie Goetz arrived at the police station, he was in a post-traumatic state—a fog in which he wasn't remembering things very clearly and was understandably vocalizing things that had not really happened but that he either worried or hoped had—such as taking out some measure of revenge against the thugs who had so terrorized him.

In fact, according to Slotnick, Bernie Goetz had not actually done any of the things that he said he had on the tapes the jury heard. He simply wished that he had done them. Running on "automatic pilot," he had no capacity to remember where his attackers were, let alone what his state of mind had been or even what actions he had taken. And now, maybe the jury could understand why Bernie Goetz had not been asked to take the stand.

This jury, Slotnick said, should find Goetz not guilty on all of the counts of attempted murder looming over him. They should also find him not guilty on charges of reckless endangerment. Now that the jury fully understood why, when, and how he had fired the gun, Goetz could not be construed as recklessly endangering anyone's life on that train.

As for the charges pertaining to the firearms he owned or had used on December 22, 1984, Slotnick claimed, "Bernhard Goetz had no intention to use those weapons unlawfully," and therefore wasn't guilty of even the most minor charges leveled against him.[36]

And so, Barry Slotnick concluded, because the prosecutors had come "in here without a case," this jury could not in good conscience find his client guilty of anything. They must not allow themselves to be swayed by "the very clever argument of Mr. Waples."[37] Now that they understood his client, Slotnick beseeched the jurors with great emotion in his words, "Please let him walk out without a conviction."[38] His client was "angry and he's in pain," Slotnick said. "But Bernhard Goetz did what the law allows."[39] He simply defended himself.

When Slotnick finished his closing remarks at 4:00 p.m., court was dismissed for the day. The *Post,* for one, thought he had done more than he had to in this open-and-shut case. In columnist Ray Kerrison's view, the summation Slotnick had begun at 10:30 a.m. had been "long, laborious, repetitive, and, at times, excruciatingly tedious," despite the fact that he had "kept promising" the jurors, who "sat through it all, glassy eyed, shifting in their seats, frequently yawning," that he was "about to shorten it up, get it over with."[40]

The jurors left the courtroom that afternoon tired, troubled, and silent. The day had been grueling, and tomorrow it would be the prosecution's chance to respond to all that Barry Slotnick had said.

THE NEXT MORNING, Greg Waples arrived ready to sum up his case—clearly, logically, and without fits and starts.[41] His mandate was to address any lingering doubts the jury might have that Goetz had attempted to murder and had viciously assaulted four unarmed teens and, in doing so, had also shot illegal weapons recklessly, all without reasonable provocation. He was eager to start promptly at 8:30 a.m. so that he might push through for the next four hours with little interruption.

Waples began by reminding the jury that they were there to make sure that justice was done. Their verdict would have ramifications beyond this case—the issues at stake were much bigger than one man named Bernhard Goetz. Slotnick, he told the jury, had "in essence" been asking them "to return a verdict that will legitimize the idea that the law does not apply equally to all persons, that some persons are above the law's sanctions, and, worse, that some people are below the law's protection."[42]

Waples barreled on, "Bernhard Goetz, by his own admission, did everything within his power to murder four young men in the subway system shortly before Christmas in 1984. By some stroke of fortune he succeeded in killing none of these young men and he succeeded in maiming only one, but the question before this court is whether the law will hold the defendant accountable for the terrible and irredeemable crimes he committed."[43]

Waples also addressed, directly and up front, any doubts that the jury might have as to whether the shooting victims, particularly Darrell Cabey, were in fact worthy of justice.

> This case cries out for justice. Darrell Cabey cries out for justice. . . . The circumstances surrounding the firing of the last two shots were so different, the shots were so sadistic and unnecessary, as to make any possible claim of justification as to that injury, that attempted murder, almost a cruel joke. . . .
>
> Deep down inside, each of you must know, if you are honest with yourselves, that no matter how much you may sympathize with this defendant, you cannot wink at this "You look all right; here's another," fifth shot, because no reasonable person would have fired that shot or even contemplated firing that shot.[44]

Waples also homed in on Slotnick's attempt to paint the prosecution's witnesses as people who, like Goetz, had been terrified of the boys, and refuted his assertion that any of the passengers had actually testified that all four had surrounded Goetz. Waples reminded the jury that not only had the passengers on the train said clearly that they had not felt endangered by these boys, but some of them, such as Josephine Holt, had even exchanged words with them. Time and again, his witnesses, Waples noted, had said expressly on the stand that they "were not alarmed in the slightest by anything that this group did."[45]

If Bernhard Goetz was as afraid of the teens as his lawyer said he was, Waples pointed out, then why didn't he move to a different seat? "You really should be wondering, folks . . . if he wasn't secretly hoping, if only on a subconscious level, that one of these rambunctious kids would 'make his day,'" to quote Dirty Harry.[46] This choice, the prosecutor went on, "would provide him with some excuse, some pretext that would allow him to draw out that gun and take a lifetime of revenge out on them."[47]

Waples argued that it was not the boys but the shooter who had given the witnesses reason to fear. Andrea Reid's testimony, and even her reluctance to come forward, had more to do with the safety of herself and her baby after she'd seen a man shooting other passengers on the train—a white man shooting Black passengers, as her husband, Garth, had later noted. Solitaire MacFoy had also described December 22 as a "very bad day," but not because of anything the boys did. As he had told the jury clearly, it was petrifying to see "a guy shooting people on the subway, including people who were sitting down in their seats."[48]

Waples also noted that Slotnick had "gambled most of his chips" on trying to present to the jury a certain version of events, one that required them to dismiss the testimony of the many disinterested parties the prosecution had brought in.

Slotnick's experts, who were paid for their testimony, were contradicted by the state's witnesses who had been on the subway. Several, including Victor Flores and Andrea Reid, had clearly testified before the jury that two of the boys were running away from Goetz at the time of the shootings. Several of them had also reported that "Cabey was shot while seated."[49] Other witnesses had heard a sequence of shots that sounded "very deliberate" and "closely bunched together," but not all of them.[50] In fact, not just Christopher Boucher but also Andrea Reid had testified that, as Waples put it, "There was spacing," and thus there was "ample time for the defendant to reflect upon the fact that Darrell Cabey was sitting in the seat, appearing unhurt," as well as to make his way over to shoot him again.[51] This contradicted the defense's argument that Goetz had fired bullets 1 through 5 on "automatic pilot," or that every shot had been in "rapid succession" and thus Darrell Cabey could not have been targeted.

More important, Waples kept coming back to stress, Christopher Boucher had actually seen what happened to Darrell with his own eyes and he too had said, unequivocally, "there was space, a discrete space of time before that last shot was fired."[52]

In a risky move, Waples then acknowledged that the jury could question whether Goetz had really said to Darrell, "You look alright, here's another."[53] But, he argued, "even if the defendant never uttered those words . . . or thought those thoughts," this did not change the fact that he had shot a "seated and helpless" teenager.[54] Indeed, he said pointedly, whether Goetz had said the words out loud or had just thought them in his own head, his "intent was to kill Darrell Cabey, to maim Darrell Cabey, to make him suffer as much agony he possibly could."[55]

If anyone's witness accounts were to be revisited and questioned, Waples argued, it should be Slotnick's. He revisited their red flags methodically, reminding jurors why each should not be trusted. There was Slotnick's investigator John Barna, who had deviously and secretly recorded state's witness Andrea Reid in her own home without her knowledge and then misrepresented what she had actually said to the jury. As Waples put it, "Barna tries to put words on tape because at one point during his examination he said well, she said she was making some kind of reference to four people, when, in fact, the transcript that we all agree is correct, clearly shows that Miss Reid was talking about two people."[56]

And let's not forget NYPD officer Peter Smith, Waples continued, and his utter lack of credibility. Believing Smith's claim that Troy Canty had said they planned to rob Goetz, Waples scoffed, required believing that "when the first white police officer in uniform comes into the car, he suddenly blurts out well, we were going to rob the guy."[57]

Furthermore, Waples noted, Officer Smith's account of this "supposedly important piece of information in one of the most celebrated cases of our time" was contradicted three times over: by his own partner, Driscoll; by the comment he gave to a TV reporter mere hours after the incident; and by his own failure "to make any kind of note whatsoever until one year later."[58]

Just as they should wholly dismiss everything that came out of Officer Smith's mouth, jurors needed also to disregard the defense's other law enforcement witness, Detective Charles Penelton, who had interviewed Troy Canty in the hospital. At the time of interrogation, Canty was under the "powerful effect" of pain medications, which obviously "can cause hallucinations" and "confabulations," and can even "cause people to mis-recall facts that are stored away in their brain."[59] The truth was, there was "no way to know" what Canty was thinking during his conversation with Penelton.[60]

Even if the jurors were inclined to read more deeply into Penelton's statement, Judge Crane had made clear to them that his testimony was only to be considered with regard to Canty's credibility as a witness to the shooting. In no way, shape, or form were the jurors allowed to "consider it as evidence that robbery was, in fact, in progress. That's a difficult thing for you to do," Waples acknowledged, "but you have to do it if you are going to be faithful to your oath as jurors."[61]

Waples took a break from discussing the witnesses who had appeared on the stand to address Slotnick's suggestion to the jury that it should read something nefarious into Barry Allen's absence from the courtroom. Yes, the judge had given the jury permission to infer whatever they liked, but Waples implored them not to assume Allen's testimony would have benefited Bernie Goetz.

"What explanation do you think Barry Allen would have given, concerning how he would have been shot square in the back," he asked, "that would have been helpful to the case of Bernhard Goetz?"[62] Moreover, why would the prosecution prevent Allen from testifying when they had put other flawed victim witnesses like Troy Canty on the stand? Clearly, they had nothing to hide. If Allen's testimony would have helped the defense, then surely Canty's would have likewise supported their case.

Before he would consider his closing statement complete, Greg Waples felt compelled to dispense with the notion that Slotnick's expert witnesses might have proven the prosecution's case wrong. That, in his view, was ludicrous.

First, he emphasized, the testimonies of ballistics expert Joseph Quirk and psychiatrist Dr. Bernard Yudowitz alike had been based on wholly theoretical scenarios. The "expert" opinions they offered were purely speculative. Dr. Yudowitz's "automatic pilot" scenario, for instance, was theoretically plausible, but he had never personally examined Bernie Goetz. More to the point, Waples asked sardonically, how could Goetz have been on "automatic pilot" when he himself made clear that he had "decided" that he was going to "lay down a pattern of fire"?[63]

As for Quirk's testimony on the victims' positions when they were shot, that was sheer fantasy, an opinion completely untethered from any of the evidence already provided not just by eyewitnesses but also the gunman himself.

With even greater energy, Waples tore into the testimony of retired medical examiner Dr. Dominick DiMaio, who had, consciously or unconsciously, "become an advocate for the client that is paying [his] bills."[64] Waples proclaimed Dr. DiMaio an "even more odious example of this misuse of an expert."[65] When the state's rebuttal witnesses, radiologist Dr. Melvin Becker and active medical examiner Dr. Charles Hirsch, had reviewed Barry Allen's X-rays on the stand, they knew how to trace the bullet's path from the middle of his back to its resting point in front of his humerus. When Dr. DiMaio had viewed that same X-ray, he seemed confused and identified a different, and unfeasible, path all on his own.

"Ladies and gentlemen," Waples said, winding up for what he hoped was the knockout blow, "whether [Dr. DiMaio] is deceiving you or whether he is simply incompetent, his testimony, his expert opinion concerning how Barry Allen came to be shot in the path of the bullet through his body is not worth the paper it is printed upon."[66] As for DiMaio's testimony regarding Darrell Cabey, it is "absolutely impossible," Waples said; DiMaio had provided no evidence for his inflammatory and highly consequential claim that Darrell had been standing when he was shot.[67]

But Waples did have evidence that Darrell was not standing when Goetz's bullet paralyzed him—solid, physical evidence—which he suddenly produced most dramatically, as he stood in front of the jury box: Darrell Cabey's bloodied zip-up.

Holding up this jacket, Waples carefully pointed to the two bullet holes that could clearly be seen in its fabric, holes that Detective Haase had described but Joseph Quirk's testimony had completely ignored. Waples identified the higher hole, "in the upper back area," with blood around it, as the shot that had paralyzed Cabey. The other hole, "farther to the front and lower on the jacket," was the shot that had missed.[68]

The courtroom was stunned as Waples then took off his own jacket and put on Cabey's. Wearing this ragged and bloodied garment, Waples then proceeded to demonstrate that DiMaio's contention—that it was the fourth bullet that had paralyzed Darrell Cabey—was a literal impossibility.

The trajectory of the bullet that had missed Darrell, the one that had passed straight through his jacket and had dented the wall behind him, indicated clearly that Darrell had to have still been standing at the time it came at him. This was consistent with Goetz's own testimony that when he first shot him, Darrell was still standing, holding on to a strap farther down the car and trying to "pretend" that he was not any part of what Troy was up to. That meant Goetz's first attempt to shoot Darrell Cabey was, just as he said it was, indeed bullet 4.

As important, Waples went on, the trajectory of the bullet that did hit Darrell, based on the holes in his jacket as well as the location of his paralyzing wound, could simply not have been made unless he was by then seated. Notably, this too was consistent with Goetz's description of standing over Darrell before leveling his last devastating shot.

With a flourish, Waples then sat in a chair and showed that since "the gun, the jacket hole [of the paralyzing shot] and the panel dent" could not be aligned, it was indisputable that the fifth shot, not the fourth, had felled the teen.[69] It was undeniable that Goetz had deliberately hunted him down.

This was simply too much for Barry Slotnick. He spluttered his strong objection to this reenactment, an objection that Judge Crane would take up later and one that would have a consequential impact on the jury's deliberations.

Having delivered his own bit of drama that would stick in jurors' minds, Waples took care not to rely on theatrics alone to make his next, important point. "Maybe this is a tempest in a teapot," he conceded because, ultimately, "it makes no difference to the defendant's guilt of attempted murder . . . whether Darrell Cabey was struck and wounded by the first bullet that was fired at him or the second bullet."[70] The bottom line was that Darrell had been targeted and was now a paraplegic.

The prosecutor wrapped up his summation by returning to his main strategy for convicting Bernhard Goetz: insisting that the shooter himself was the most reliable witness anyone could ask for. Waples appealed directly to the jury: "Why should you disbelieve the defendant's tape-recorded statement?"[71] Literally no one, he said, "can describe what happened . . . better than the defendant himself. . . . The richness of the detail he recalled especially in the audiotaped statement is simply staggering." The only way anyone could offer such detail was if "he lived it," and he had "processed it."[72]

Waples reviewed the many points from Goetz's recorded statements that were corroborated by other eyewitnesses. For one, Goetz consistently said only two teens had ever approached him, Troy Canty and Barry Allen. This assertion was supported by at least three of the prosecution's witnesses, Waples noted. "They saw two persons standing over the defendant before the shots were fired: Josephine Holt saw that; Garth Reid saw that; Mary Gant saw that."[73]

Similarly, Goetz said that he first shot Canty and then Allen, and had explicitly recalled that Allen "was trying to run through this crowd of the subway car."[74] This was corroborated by the prosecution witnesses Victor Flores and Andrea Reid. James Ramseur had also been trying to flee, according to Goetz himself. Ramseur, in his telling, was "trying to climb through the wall of the subway car."[75] Even though he couldn't invoke the testimony, Waples likely hoped that jurors would remember James having said that he indeed tried to flee the gunman.

When it came to Darrell Cabey, Goetz clearly described firing two shots at him, the second shot at close range when Darrell was seated. Therefore, Waples insisted, the prosecution's key witness Christopher Boucher was clearly "not a raving lunatic or a crackpot."[76] Sure, he suggested sarcastically, "is it possible that both of these men, the defendant and Christopher Boucher, had the same vision, the exact same vision, the exact same terrible dream, on December 22nd? Well, that could happen in the *Twilight Zone*, but not here."[77]

Perhaps most important, Waples maintained, Goetz was an entirely reliable authority on the devastation that he had wrought. His confession offered "nearly a dozen and a half major details" that corroborated the testimony of the prosecution's witnesses.[78] This fact, he insisted, "stands as the most convincing proof there can be, I submit, that the defendant was not hallucinating or fantasizing or fabricating when he recalled how he shot at human beings as they were running away from him and how he shot at Darrell Cabey when he was down in his seat."[79]

Even if Goetz had been in some sort of a fugue state, Waples continued, even if his own distress made him less reliable in some moments than others, the synergy between his confession and what other passengers had seen with their own eyes could not be explained away.

Waples knew, however, that it was not enough to determine the events that had transpired on that train car. He needed the jury to really grasp who this guy was—his character.

Goetz was "the perfect example of a person who should not be carrying a gun in New York City," Waples began. He was, Waples insisted, "a deeply suspicious, paranoid individual, intellectually rigid, who's seething inside with suppressed, self-righteous anger, and an individual who is obsessed with crime and his own solutions to problems of crime and disorder in our cities."[80]

Yes, he had been mugged a few years earlier. And that was surely traumatic. But for Goetz, Waples argued, it wasn't so much the mugging, but his indignation about it, that "really tormented and tortured" him.[81] Goetz was obsessed, Waples argued, that the kid who mugged him hadn't received a more severe punishment—so obsessed, in fact, that Goetz tried to lie in order to charge Fred Clark with attempted robbery.

"How presumptuous can one get?" Waples asked.[82] "Here you have a person who is so cocksure about [the] superiority of his own system of values that he presumes that it is right and moral for him to lie, to deliberately fabricate evidence, so that some person who he branded a criminal in his own mind gets the kind of punishment the defendant feels he deserves."[83]

This resentment had caused Goetz to lash out several times, well before that horrific day on the subway. He had admitted to pulling a gun on people on multiple occasions before December 1984. And on the day he shot the boys on the 2 train—contrary to Slotnick's claim that he'd been "happy" to go meet friends for a drink—Goetz himself had admitted that he had been "frustrated" by a project he had been working on. Waples called upon the jurors, "in light of the defendant's self-confessed paranoia about crime and the obsession he has with his personal safety," to ask themselves why he would "deliberately" sit next to four rowdy teenagers. It sure seemed like he was looking for a confrontation.[84]

The costs of Bernie Goetz's fury had been extraordinarily high. These teens were no choirboys, Waples acknowledged, but they were hardly a "gang" of hardcore criminals who deserved the violence that came their way, as Barry Slotnick had suggested. It would be "easy and convenient," Waples told jurors, to simply "shrug their shoulders" and decide that these were "bad kids" who "deserved what they got."[85] But kids who broke into arcade machines to take quarters hardly deserved this brutality, he maintained. And that day on the train, that was the worst of what the boys had planned to get up to.

Troy Canty knew "that there is a big difference between robbing people and breaking into video machines . . . a difference between a felony and a misdemeanor," Waples argued. There was "a big difference between going upstate to prison with murderers and rapists and spending a few weeks on Rikers Island with the boys."[86] In short, Canty was "simply too shrewd to try to rob the defendant in front of a carload of passengers . . . [who] they have been riding with for thirty minutes, conspicuously calling attention to themselves: playing on the bars, pounding on the seats, talking to people, approaching people for matches."[87]

Slotnick's assertion that these boys intended to hurt his client made no sense. Clearly, this was not a robbery. Troy was simply panhandling and, Waples insisted, "the defendant could have refused with no untoward consequences."[88] Furthermore, "from a strictly legal point of view," the boys' intentions didn't even matter. Even if they were going to rob Goetz, that would not have justified this display of "unnecessary and excessive force."[89] It would have justified some degree of response, but it "does not give the defendant the carte blanche to do whatever he wants, whatever he believes is right, to defuse that threat."[90]

More to the point, Waples maintained, "There is really no substantial evidence that this group of persons was intending to rob Mr. Goetz. . . . What about weapons? What kind of weapon is the screwdriver? Well, I would not want a screwdriver put in me. I wouldn't want the point of an umbrella put into me either."[91] But these boys hadn't pulled out the screwdrivers from their pockets. Those were meant for the arcade machines, not Bernie Goetz.

Slotnick had tried to make the case that Goetz had a legal right to try to kill four young men, "not on the basis of what Troy Canty said . . . [or] did, but on the way that Troy Canty smiled." What Troy did that day by approaching Goetz, Waples continued, "was stupid, it was inexcusable, [but] it wasn't criminal."[92]

Waples asked the jury to consider the boys' rights to be free of harm, even if they had dared to ask for money. He asked them to consider "Darrell Cabey's right not to be crippled for life without just cause" and the rights "of the 20 or 15 subway passengers to ride that subway train without being subjected to the terror of the defendant's reckless gunplay."[93] Those rights were important, he went on, because "if the five shots that the defendant fired on December 22nd violated the law, then it violated your rights and everyone's rights, much as it violated the rights of Darrell Cabey and all the people who were in the subway car."[94]

In his final words to the jury, Waples said, "[It] is shockingly clear that what Mr. Slotnick has tried to pass off as a legitimate act of self-defense, was really nothing more than an attempted cold blooded execution." If the jurors agreed that what Bernhard Goetz had done was "excessive, unnecessary, and unreasonable," they must "convict him of the terrible crime that he committed."[95] While even that verdict would "never enable Darrell Cabey to walk another step again," it would at least offer some justice in this case.[96]

With that, court was dismissed for the day and the jury traveled to a hotel in Hell's Kitchen where they would begin sequestration while deliberating. For her part, *New York Post* columnist Beth Fallon voiced concern that Waples's summation had been "brilliant," and she admonished the jurors to "use your heads" when deciding the case.[97]

THE NEXT MORNING, the jurors once more convened in the cavernous courtroom downtown for deliberation instruction from Judge Crane.[98] They listened very carefully as the judge explained exactly what questions they were to consider and how the law should inform their ultimate verdict.

Crane instructed the panel to "decide the facts coolly, calmly, and deliberately without fear, favor, or passion, prejudice, or sympathy."[99] He reminded them that Goetz, as defendant, was "entitled to every inference in his favor that can reasonably be drawn from the evidence." Crucially, "where two inferences may be reasonably drawn from the evidence, one consistent with guilt and one consistent with innocence, the defendant is entitled to the inference of innocence."[100]

Crane also addressed which factors the jury was not permitted to consider in its determination, including the fact that Darrell Cabey had not testified, since for his "absence the People have made adequate explanation," and he had already stricken all mention of James Ramseur's appearance in court.[101]

If they so chose, the jury could consider Barry Allen's absence in their deliberations, and Crane again gave them permission to "draw an inference that Allen's testimony would not have been favorable to the People."[102] The witnesses' criminal backgrounds were also open to consideration, as relevant to the credibility of their testimony—Troy Canty's arrests subsequent to December 1984, for example, or even conductor Armando Soler's arrest record.

Judge Crane also had specific instructions regarding the defendant's confession. The jury must consider whether it was "voluntarily made . . . without coercion or intimidation of any kind" and decide, based on what they knew about Goetz's history and emotional state, whether they felt it was "the result of defendant's own free will and choice."[103]

These stipulations from Crane would prove to be extremely helpful to the defense.

When it came to each of the counts that Bernie Goetz faced—the more serious counts of attempted murder, the lesser charges of reckless endangerment and of illegally possessing the guns—the jury must be certain of his guilt, beyond any reasonable doubt. As important, jurors had to consider both Goetz's intent and the results of his actions. If Goetz had intended to kill the four teenagers, then he could be found guilty of the most serious charges.

Even if the defendant himself believed that he was in peril, that alone was not sufficient to meet the "reasonableness" standard. It was up to the jury to decide "in light of all of the circumstances whether a reasonable person could have had those beliefs."[104] As Judge Crane told them, "a mere preponderance of the credible evidence is not sufficient to prove [the defendant's] guilt in this or any other criminal case."[105]

As to whether Bernie Goetz had been acting in self-defense, he reminded them, that was up to the prosecution to disprove—not up to the defense to prove. This determination hinged, in part, on whether Goetz was being robbed, or thought he was being robbed. It was important to remember the difference, the judge explained: "To constitute robbery, a request or demand for money must be accompanied by both an intent to steal and implicit or explicit threat of force. However, a person who merely asks another for money does not necessarily commit attempted robbery."[106] This distinction could be or not be important, he went on, when "assessing the reasonableness of the defendant's belief that he was about to be robbed."[107]

In other words, it did not necessarily matter if the boys were planning to rob Goetz. Goetz could have "reasonably" thought they were trying to rob him and acted accordingly in "self-defense."[108] Here again, Crane admonished, jurors "should employ the reasonable standard" that he had previously explained to them.

This was a great deal of nuance for any juror to fully wrap their mind around. Under the law, Bernie Goetz might well have been justified in shooting the four boys. But, in order to make this claim, the jury first had to decide whether he had "reasonably believed" that he was being robbed. This in itself must be determined by whether a "reasonable" person would have read the situation as a robbery—regardless of whether or not a robbery was happening—and, like Goetz, think it was "necessary to use deadly physical force to prevent such crime."[109]

Crane put much emphasis on the importance of discerning what Goetz might or might not have understood about the situation he found himself in on December 22, 1984. The fact that jurors were explicitly told that the boys' intent that day was not necessarily relevant—and that the "physical attributes [of] all persons involved, including the defendant" could be considered—might well dash Waples's fervent hope that the jury would spend its time thinking about Darrell Cabey, the one Goetz had inflicted the most serious harm upon.

Judge Crane also acknowledged that each boy's individual situation in relation to Goetz did matter. With regard to "Darrell Cabey alone," Crane instructed the jurors to consider whether Goetz "reasonably believed" that he "was using or was about to use deadly physical force against him." The jury needed to keep in mind that, even if they concluded that Goetz believed himself in danger from one or more of the other boys, that did not mean that he would have been "legally justified in firing his gun" at Cabey.[110]

As Judge Crane wrapped up his at times difficult-to-parse presentation, one that had lasted a full two and a half hours, he reminded the jury that its verdict on each of the counts must be unanimous.

At 1:20 p.m. on Friday, June 12, 1987, the jury left the courtroom to begin deliberations. It was anyone's guess what they would decide.

31

Justifications and Judgment

THE JURY'S DELIBERATION began after a full seven weeks of the trial, and six months to the day since they had walked into the courtroom to begin their service. They were dubbed America's "most closely watched jury" by the *Post,* but they were now sequestered, and were themselves not permitted to read newspapers or watch the nightly news. Throughout the countless hours spent in the jury room, they had been allowed to talk about anything but the case at hand, and it felt good to finally start discussing their perspectives.

Their working conditions were not ideal. They now spent the entire day in the windowless, wood-paneled, beige-painted jury room on the fifth floor of the courthouse.[1] It was long and narrow, with a red-tiled floor, and it was furnished with twelve mismatched chairs arranged haphazardly around a rectangular, chipped Formica table dotted with ashtrays and flanked by two metal wastebaskets, as well as an old coat rack.

But they did get to stay in a hotel each night—one in Manhattan, the others in Queens. When possible, they dined together in the hotels' restaurants and shared laughs after a tense day of deliberation. One of their first hotels was "a really seedy joint on Tenth Avenue and Fiftieth Street in Manhattan called the Clearview," which, rumor had it, "had been the site of a series of homicides where some guy from New Jersey was chopping prostitutes into pieces." Subsequent accommodations were nicer. The jurors particularly liked the Marriott where, on one occasion, they were given permission to go over the usual stipend and above their normal two-drink limit, regardless of the "pricey menu."[2]

Once this group was actually in the jury room, though, it was clear that they had a lot of work to do. On the one hand, the case might have seemed fairly straightforward. The jury had, for example, learned a great deal that might lead them to censure Goetz with a conviction for aggravated assault, if not outright attempted murder. The eyewitness testimonies from other passengers on the train—particularly that of Christopher Boucher, who had seen Goetz double down on his effort to shoot Darrell Cabey—were damning. They had also heard the testimonies of the doctors who had treated the four teens, chronicling the extreme injuries and additional complications caused by Goetz's violence. Most importantly, they had absorbed the recordings of Goetz himself recounting in graphic detail not just what he had done but what he was thinking when he did it.

On the other hand—and this mattered a great deal indeed—it had been abundantly clear ever since the jurors were first questioned and chosen that the majority of them were highly sympathetic to at least the idea that New Yorkers had a right to self-defense. Juror and martial artist Mark Lesly was openly glad that he was better prepared than most to defend himself should the need arise. And as Michael Axelrod had said from the very beginning of the trial, he too was sympathetic to the notion that people should be able to defend themselves.[3]

It was also clear that at least some of the jurors found the victims threatening. One of the alternate jurors actually went to the *New York Post* and reported that all of them had been terrified when James Ramseur had gone on his "rampage" when Barry Slotnick cross-examined him.[4]

According to this alternate juror, a man named Augustine Ayala, whom Crane ultimately decided to excuse from service, "Even though they were surrounded by armed court officers" the jury was "so fearful prosecution witness James Ramseur would 'go berserk' in the court room that they made secret plans to escape. . . . Those petrified jurors formulated a plan among themselves, which they shared with the armed court officers, who stood between them and the menacing witness." What's more, according to the *Post*, Waples's "choice of the agitated, raving Ramseur as a witness for the prosecution, had left the jurors wondering about the prosecutor's judgment."[5]

And yet, the jury was not at all of one mind about whether Goetz's actions on the 2 train had been justified, or even how to go about deciding this question legally. This meant that one of the jury's first tasks would be to set some ground rules for deliberations, starting with reaching an agreement on whether to conduct voting by secret ballot or by voice vote. This was itself contentious.[6] For some, like the more liberal English professor Catherine Brody, it was important that the voting be anonymous. That way, no one could feel guilt-tripped or browbeaten into casting a vote they did not feel comfortable with. At first, everyone seemed to be in favor of secret ballots. But juror Carolyn Perlmuth, an editor from the Upper West Side, was concerned that anonymous voting would obscure who was leaning in what direction, which, in turn, would make it hard to know how close they were to reaching an agreement on the verdict. All votes, she maintained, must be openly declared, and her argument on this matter prevailed.

Deciding how the law should inform their votes would remain its own difficulty. Many of the jurors had entered deliberations with little more than their memories of what they had seen and heard in the courtroom. They had been allowed to take handwritten notes, and Cathy Brody—the professor—had done so, extensively. But that did not diminish the fact that the jury did not have the full transcript of the trial just on hand, nor any of the exhibits right in front of them.[7] While they could ask for anything to be read back to them, or request that an exhibit be brought in, some of the most dramatic pieces of evidence, including the reenactment with the Guardian Angels and the "class trip," could only be remembered—and remembered as each individual juror had experienced them.

To make matters even more challenging, they also did not have a written copy of how Judge Crane had explained the law to them. The jury instructions were difficult to grasp, though this was not entirely the fault of Judge Crane. He had done his best to lay out the legal definitions of terms like "attempted murder," "self-defense," and "reasonable," and the jurors were also permitted to ask for clarification. That was only so helpful, though. They often found that simply having "arcane and convoluted legal phrases read and reread to them" just further muddied the waters.[8]

Thus, the jurors were oftentimes coming up with their own understanding of what constituted "reasonable," and therefore what was or was not illegal for Bernhard Goetz to have done.

A critical example of this concerned the judge's instructions regarding the "reasonableness" standard as it applied to self-defense. When asked for clarification on this point, Judge Crane responded that, legally, even if a defendant was wrong in his assumption that he was facing a threat, the real question at hand was whether that assumption was "reasonable." "Reasonableness," the judge had said, was inherently subjective. One had to think about how other "reasonable" people would have seen the situation. And yet, further complicating the matter, Crane stated that it was not sufficient for this jury to simply put themselves "in [Goetz's] shoes." They were to answer this question of reasonableness "on the evidence that they've heard."[9]

There would be many debates among the jury as they attempted to grasp what Crane had meant by this. If reasonableness was in fact "subjective," which the judge had acknowledged, were they not, in some measure, being asked to put themselves in the shoes of the various players in this case?

Before really wrangling with all of this, though, the jury decided first to see how close or far apart they were on reaching a verdict.

While the majority of jurors were inclined to convict Goetz on some of the charges, at least initially, there was great ambivalence about finding him guilty of anything as serious as assault or murder. In the first vote on the charge of the attempted murder of Troy Canty, for instance, the tally was "four not guilty; and eight abstentions."[10]

Behind the scenes, Barry Slotnick and Mark Baker were only further muddying the waters by revisiting, and at times loudly challenging, what the jury would in fact be allowed to consider as deliberations continued.[11]

Slotnick had taken real issue with Judge Crane's guidelines for understanding self-defense, which said:

> The defendant could not use more force than he reasonably believed necessary. He could not legitimately shoot, for example, if he "reasonably believed" [i.e., should have believed] that he could have repelled any threat without firing his gun, for example, by drawing and displaying his weapon.[12]

He and Baker wanted to remove any suggestion that Bernie "drawing and displaying his weapon" might have sufficiently defused the threat the boys posed. The judge was inappropriately "marshalling the evidence," they claimed, in effect adding an argument that might be made by the prosecutor, rather than simply instructing the jury on the law.

When the jury asked for clarification on a related point, requesting a reading of what the judge had said about the charges regarding "attempted murder and justification," Slotnick seized the opportunity to push for the changes he wanted.

Slotnick not only insisted that the judge remove any reference to Goetz's "displaying his weapon," but also demanded that Crane actually add wording to reference Dr. Yudowitz's "automatic pilot" theory and to mention the bullets being fired in "rapid succession" too.

Astoundingly, and over Waples's forceful arguments against making such changes, Judge Crane acquiesced to most of Slotnick's requests. As one legal expert put it, he "justified this change by claiming that it was merely 'clarifying' the charge."[13]

Judge Crane removed the reference Slotnick did not want to include and sent the following new instruction to the jury:

> In assessing [the defendant's] belief and its reasonableness, you may consider the testimony of Dr. Bernard Yudowitz concerning the operation of the autonomic nervous system and its effect on the firing of a weapon.[14]

Though he declined to include wording to the effect that Goetz had fired his weapon in "rapid succession," the defense lawyers knew that they had secured a major victory and regrouped to push for additional changes to build their very specific version of the case for the jury to mull over.[15]

Altogether, the jury asked the judge for more information a total of six times. Not every request offered an opportunity to influence the jury instructions, but when Slotnick saw the opportunity, he took it.

On the fourth day of deliberation, the jury asked to have testimony about the bullet holes in Darrell Cabey's jacket read back to them—and to see his jacket for themselves, along with "the screwdriver or screwdrivers found in the pockets of that jacket and any other jackets."[16] Slotnick and Baker had strongly objected to this evidence when Waples called attention to it in his closing arguments, and they were clearly worried that it now stood.

They pushed Crane to instruct the jury that it must disregard Waples's demonstration of the bullet holes in the jacket. The defense believed that the jury's understanding of these bullet holes would directly impact whether they believed Waples's argument that Goetz's fourth shot had missed Cabey, leading him to fire his weapon a fifth time in cold blood. They also worried it would discredit Slotnick's arguments that Goetz had been shooting in rapid succession and that Cabey had been inadvertently wounded by the fourth bullet.

Crane again agreed to revise his instructions, offering the jury what legal analyst George Fletcher termed "some gratuitous comments about the likelihood that Waples's thesis was correct." Specifically, Crane instructed the jury to disregard Waples's demonstration because "there was no evidence to support [it]." Instead, they "must rest on inferences from the facts in evidence [that supported two bullet holes], principally the testimony of Detective Haase."[17] Haase was the NYPD detective who had collected and bagged evidence on the subway car, noting the bloodied jackets and the screwdrivers zippered into their pockets.

Furthermore, Crane repeated his previous admonition to the jury that if ever there was evidence that could lead as easily to a conclusion of innocence as to a conclusion of guilt, they must remember that "the defendant is entitled to the inference of innocence." As Fletcher wrote later, "it would have been difficult for the jury not to get the impression that Judge Crane was skeptical about Waples's entire demonstration."[18]

Waples must have been furious. In acquiescing to Slotnick's demands, Judge Crane had dealt a significant blow to the prosecutor's case, gutting one of his most important closing arguments—and at the eleventh hour too. He would have known that the jury would now doubt the ballistics showing that Goetz had deliberately shot Darrell Cabey.

The jury saw none of the back-and-forth that went into these new instructions. As they were dutifully deliberating, Waples himself finally "exploded":

> I think what I just heard was the most one-sided and most unwarranted instruction that I have ever heard given to a jury. . . . It's completely unfair. I made a perfectly proper argument based on the evidence again repeated here and just cannot fathom how Your Honor can give that instruction in good conscience to this jury.[19]

Throughout the deliberation process, Goetz seemed unconcerned about his fate. He sat in the courtroom "nibbling at fruit brought by one of the defense lawyers" to pass the time. He even told one of his Guardian Angel friends, who in turn told the *Post*, that he was "looking to be acquitted," but acknowledged that "he might be convicted on the minor gun charges."[20]

AFTER FOUR DAYS and thirty hours of deliberating, the jury came to a decision. When jurors filed into the courtroom just after 4:00 p.m. on June 16, 1987, the packed room practically vibrated with tension.[21] Entering the courthouse that day had meant navigating a huge crowd of pro-Goetz New Yorkers, blinding flashbulbs, and agitated police officers.

At the defense table, Slotnick looked particularly natty, nicely coiffed, and refreshed, as if he was anticipating a good day ahead. Bernie Goetz, who had been ushered into the courtroom through a private back elevator, sat there in his now signature faded blue jeans and an open-collared white shirt, "his head bowed and a blank expression on his face."[22] At the prosecutor's table, Waples, as usual far less snazzily attired than his opposing counsel, looked grim. The families of Darrell Cabey, James Ramseur, Barry Allen, and Troy Canty were all relying on him to deliver some measure of justice for their sons.

The jurors took their seats, but were looking straight ahead, faces unreadable.

As a hush fell over the room, court clerk Bob Hamkalo asked jury foreman James Hurley whether they had, in fact, reached a unanimous verdict. Yes, he affirmed. Solemnly, Hurley began reading through the sheet on which every charge had been listed and every jury decision had been recorded.

Despite the altered jury instructions and the groundswell of support Bernie Goetz had enjoyed from the minute he'd fled the Chambers Street station, it seemed for a moment that the decisions might go in the state's favor.

On the charge of criminal possession of a weapon in the third degree, the jury found Bernhard H. Goetz guilty.

But then, things started looking grimmer for the prosecution.

On the next two weapons charges: Not guilty.

On three charges of first-degree assault and three charges of the attempted murder of Troy Canty, Barry Allen, and James Ramseur: Not guilty.

The most important charge, the one that everyone somehow understood was the reason many really cared that Bernie Goetz was on trial, was that regarding Darrell Cabey. Was Bernhard Goetz guilty of the attempted murder of Darrell Cabey? Or, at the very least, of assault in the first degree?

"Not guilty," Hurley said firmly to both charges. A collective and audible gasp echoed throughout the courtroom.

Greg Waples looked shell-shocked. Barry Slotnick looked like the cat who ate the canary. Mark Baker was overcome with emotion, tears welling in his eyes. Bernie Goetz, a man who had spent the entire trial largely staring down or slumped over, could be seen smiling faintly.[23]

Goetz was rushed out of the courtroom, securely wedged between the bodies of ten burly court officers, who bundled him into a waiting limousine. Before he sped away into the hot afternoon, his happiness was clear. In front of throngs of reporters, he smiled and said wonderingly, with a "soft" laugh, "How does one ever thank these people!"[24]

As he had following the grand jury verdict, Goetz received a hero's welcome upon returning to his apartment. He told the assembled reporters that he really hoped "some good will come out of this," then went to dinner at the neighboring apartment of a TV news magazine publisher named Allan Horowitz. Over the next days the public's adulation would become so intense that, as Horowitz told the *Post*: "He is sort of like a trapped person with nowhere to go. He cannot go out to buy a paper, he

Court officers push journalists and spectators out of the way as they escort Bernhard Goetz out of New York State Supreme Court, June 16, 1987.
AP Photo/Mario Suriani

can't go to the grocery store. He knows that if he talks to the press, he could make a great deal of trouble for himself."[25]

The jurors, meanwhile, were clearly relieved that this monumental trial had come to a close but also nervous for the media storm to come. As they filed out of the box, they thanked the court officers and judge for the experience of a lifetime and accepted thanks for their service in return. The scores of journalists who had packed into the cavernous courtroom began running outside, prepared to take comments from the jurors and citizens alike.

The scene outside was a madhouse. Most of the crowd that had gathered seemed thrilled with the verdict, but there were still protesters chanting slogans like "Hey, Bernie, have you heard? This is not Johannesburg!"[26]

Into this chaos the jurors soon appeared. They had been rushed down the stairs of the courthouse to board a minibus that would take them to their respective homes. Nevertheless, a "pack of reporters chased us on foot," juror Mark Lesly recalled, and a car full of reporters followed the bus. When jury foreman James Hurley was dropped off at his building in Battery Park City, "several [reporters] jumped out of the car and raced after him."[27]

Mark Lesly found himself loving the spotlight. Upon returning to his own building, he found several reporters waiting for him on the stoop. He gave "dozens" of interviews over "the next several hours," soon made appearances on *Good Morning America* and *The Phil Donahue Show*, and was invited into the studios of both CNN and ABC to discuss the case. Within two days of the verdict, Lesly had also penned the first of three tell-all pieces—for none other than the *New York Post*.

Lesly's first-person reports, based on audiotapes he'd recorded at the end of each trial day, played into more than a few of the *Post*'s established perspectives—namely, sympathy toward Goetz and hostility toward his victims. Lesly had found the victim witnesses "so totally irrelevant to me. They seem to be wasting time." Troy Canty was just a liar, but James Ramseur was "quite pathetic," showing "more bitterness" than Lesly had ever seen in one person.[28]

Lesly later published a book about his experience, in which he recalled, "I found it really exhilarating to be able to communicate through the media to millions of people and believe that they were interested in what I had to say."[29]

Juror Diana Serpe, who lived on the Upper East Side, was also hounded by the press, overwhelmed by her answering machine messages—"I remember the, you know, the blinker light, you'd walk in the room, boom, boom, boom, boom, boom, the blinker light, you know, how many messages? Twenty-seven messages! You know, it was like, Oh my God."[30] Reporters showed up on Diana's doorstep too, "ringing, ring, ringing the buzzer from downstairs."[31]

Other jurors would be invited to appear on the nationally syndicated *Phil Donahue Show* the following week. Through all of this, their phones had been chiming off the hook with reporters, from New York and every other part of the country, seeking insight into how they had come to their verdict.

For its part, even the press seemed at least somewhat astonished at how completely Goetz had been vindicated by the jury and how little time he now might serve. *Washington Post* reporter Margot Hornblower pointed out that "the gun charge carries a maximum penalty of 2⅓ to 7 years in prison, but first offenders generally do not receive jail terms," and Goetz had been acquitted of "charges that could have put him in prison for 50 years."[32]

The Guardian Angels meanwhile felt empowered by the jury's decision. On the day of the verdict, members had filled the courtroom, and when they heard the verdicts, they erupted in cheers and high fives. They understood that their organization would be given even more leeway in their treatment of those they perceived as thugs and bad guys on the subways and streets of New York as a result of this trial's outcome.

Juror Diana Serpe. From *The Confessions of Bernhard Goetz* (MPI Home Video, 1987). Permission from the estate of Darrell Moore.

Others in the city, including Mayor Ed Koch, found the verdict somewhat unnerving. As Koch said, "There may be some who misperceive the case, that might engage in vigilantism."[33] And he was right to worry. Within a month of the verdict, Barry Slotnick himself was attacked by an unknown assailant, for reasons many assumed were related to the role he played in the Goetz trial.[34]

For the families of the shooting victims, this was more than a cautionary tale. On hearing the verdict, Shirley Cabey was so distraught she could barely speak. When she finally managed to muster a comment, she was unequivocal about her takeaway from this verdict: "It gives a license to people who want to shoot black youths." Mostly, however, she just couldn't fathom how any jury could have vindicated Bernie Goetz for permanently paralyzing her son. Darrell had literally said nothing to this man and had been nowhere near him when one bullet changed his life forever.[35]

As Shirley Cabey made clear that this case was ultimately about the value that Americans placed on the lives of Black teenagers, plenty of others agreed.

Shortly after the verdict was read, a national PBS show called *Tony Brown's Journal* devoted "a whole episode to raw reactions from Black Americans" regarding the Goetz verdict. It showcased just how appalled some New Yorkers were.[36] One of the guests was a young woman named Cheryl Wade, who watched the show religiously. (She later recalled, "It was like watching *Soul Train*, you know? You watch *Soul Train* and you watch *Tony Brown's Journal*."[37]) She had been devastated by the Goetz verdict and did not hold back:

> I wonder about those boys on the subway car. I don't know what kind of lives they had. I do remember thinking, I wanna know more about these boys. And I just wondered why there's not more about what happened to them. Why doesn't anybody care that one of them was paralyzed and the others had suffered this physical pain because this man said that he was afraid of them? . . . I remember times when white neighbors were afraid of me even as a ten- and eleven- and twelve-year-old girl.[38]

The jurors themselves took major umbrage any time a racial motive for the verdicts was suggested. While no one on this mostly white jury "favored convicting [Goetz] of attempted murder," some of them insisted that the issue of his fifth shot into Darrell had been "a sticky situation."[39] Others stated even more directly that their "verdict should not be interpreted as having any racial implications because race or racism was in no way a factor in our deliberations or in our decision."[40]

For its part, the *New York Post* had no interest in playing down race, or its view that these Black teens had gotten what they deserved. Under the headline "THE 4 YOUTHS WHO TRIGGERED HISTORIC TRIAL," readers were, once again, regaled with a complete accounting of the boys' criminal records.[41]

What long-term message this verdict might send to America, if any, remained unclear. Four months would pass before Goetz was even sentenced on the gun charge. In the meantime, a new fight broke out regarding how much time, if any at all, he would serve behind bars.

32

Details and Delays

TO JUDGE CRANE'S UNDOUBTED relief, Bernhard Goetz's highly contentious trial had finally ended. But Crane's personal stress was an entirely different matter, and far from over. He still had to decide the fate of the "Death Wish Vigilante," now convicted of criminal possession of a weapon in the third degree, a Class D felony.

Barry Slotnick, for his part, was doing everything in his power to ensure that his client never returned to a cell. He had, for example, ordered an independent psychological evaluation by Dr. Harvey Goldstein, a renowned expert in the field of post-trauma stress and its treatment, to help make the case against any prison time.

As it turned out, Judge Crane would have extra time to navigate this process. Not a month after the trial ended, co-defense counsel Mark Baker fell ill with pneumonia, requiring hospitalization and many weeks of recuperation. In August, Baker formally requested a full six-week adjournment of the sentencing proceedings.[1] Such a long delay clearly benefited Goetz, still out on bail, but Crane was also on board. He strongly felt that he needed time to arrive at a sentence that honored the law as well as the more general expectations and norms regarding what justice should look like.

Meanwhile, Crane had indicated a willingness to accept input not just from lawyers but also from other parties. For example, he carefully read a highly detailed report prepared by the Department of Probation, which included input from evaluations done in the psychiatric clinic the department used as well as a full life history of Bernie Goetz and an assessment of the risks he might pose to the community, alongside a sentencing recommendation. While Crane was not obligated to follow this report's recommendation, it nevertheless carried significant weight.

For their part, the clinicians who had seen Goetz at this clinic did not shy away from noting concerns about the potential risks that Goetz might pose to the community. For one, they noted that Goetz admitted to still carrying an illegal gun for self-defense—"notwithstanding the defendant's statements" to the Department of Probation that, "in the face of his conviction," he would not do so. What's more, recent psychiatric examinations of this defendant had observed him to be "a quietly intense, angry, and fearful individual."[2] They had also found Goetz "to be lacking in a positive and stable self-image, self-esteem, and self-confidence." Further, he very much "sees himself as a 'loser' and a victim." Despite this, he would also suddenly exhibit "hints of grandiosity," and portray himself "as an instrument" of "potential positive societal changes."[3]

More troublingly, and further evidence that Goetz might still be a loose cannon, these clinicians who had contributed to the Department of Probation's report noted that Goetz had recently called the police to claim that some youths were hassling him on Canal Street. When the police told him that they were unable to send him assistance, as there were matters of greater importance to attend to, Bernie responded, "Then I'll have three dead bodies." This statement had prompted the NYPD to send officers to the scene.[4]

Ultimately one of these evaluators diagnosed the " 'defendant as having mixed personality disorder with paranoid features,' " while another offered "a diagnostic impression that trends towards 'borderline personality disorder.' "[5]

The Probation Department had also reached out to Goetz's victims. Because Darrell wasn't up to being interviewed, they spoke with his mother, Shirley. She was "somewhat reluctant to cooperate," and ultimately "offer[ed] no opinion on the matter of sentencing."[6] She did, however, stress that Darrell—after spending fourteen months in the hospital—remained in very bad shape, and required a full-time health care aide at home.

The department spoke as well to now-twenty-one-year-old Troy Canty, who was still working the program in a Westchester County drug rehab facility. Troy largely refused to rehash the incident that led to his injury, but he did discuss the fact that he had been "shot in the chest close to the heart and the bullet was surgically removed." Additionally, he had "sustained five scars which he describes as permanently disfiguring."[7] Unlike Shirley Cabey, Troy was very vocal about what should happen to Goetz: He wanted him locked up.

Neither Barry Allen, serving time in the Elmira Correctional Facility, nor James Ramseur, now serving out his sentence in the Coxsackie Correctional Facility, wanted to talk. Barry outright refused to meet with department representatives, whereas James would only recount his injuries and state that he "was not surprised" that Goetz had been acquitted of nearly all charges.[8]

Despite these troubling psychiatric findings, and the department's discussions with Goetz's victims, the probation report sent to Judge Crane sought to redeem Goetz, rather than ensure that the public was protected from his still-erratic behavior. The report minimized anything unsavory that Goetz might have said or done that had led him to this current position—for example, in the same paragraph where it acknowledged that Goetz had "made four gun purchases" illegally, it also added that he had been "seriously injured" in a 1981 mugging, implicitly justifying his ownership of the weapons.[9]

Its interpretation of Goetz's psychiatric examinations had also been most charitable. Both of his psych evaluators had expressed grave concerns about Goetz's intention to continue carrying a gun, along with his impulse to take matters into his own hands when he became impatient with law enforcement. But the Probation Department's takeaway was that Bernie Goetz had borne many crosses in his life, including the embarrassment of his father's arrest when he was in early adolescence. This, it opined, had likely exacerbated the trauma of having to stand trial himself.[10] He also now had to endure financial worry "as a result of the notoriety accorded him" over the last two and a half years. In fact, the probation report noted, "several of his larger accounts had cancelled their business with him."[11]

Also of note were the times the report called attention to Goetz's racial prejudices but then immediately underplayed their significance. The report openly acknowledged that "the question of racism" had been "raised by some members of the press and community in connection with this crime," and also noted the community meeting in September 1980 when Goetz had proclaimed "the problem with 14th Street is the sp—s and n—s, and until we deal with that problem we can't deal with any others."[12]

But according to the Probation Department, Goetz had explained all of this. With regard to his racially charged outburst, it cited Goetz's frustrations with how little his tenants association was accomplishing, saying it "had become more of a social club than a working organization."[13] As the report concluded, "although it appears that the defendant is not completely free of the racist feelings all too common in our society, our investigation uncovered no evidence to support the conclusion that the events surrounding the . . . offense resulted from racist attitudes on behalf of the defendant."[14]

To further redeem him, this probation report included commentary from Goetz's neighbors, family members, and even his ex-wife. These comments painted a portrait of a friendly, kind, and delightful man, one who would not hurt a fly and didn't have a racist bone in his body. His ex-wife described him as a "humanitarian type of person, kind, gentle and generous." She had even seen him give money to panhandlers on the street.[15] "If there is one thing he is not," the report quoted her as saying, "[it] is prejudiced."[16]

Goetz's lawyer friend who headed up his legal defense fund, Bernard Horowitz, couldn't have agreed more, saying firmly that Bernie was "absolutely opposite of racist." Another friend said that Bernie had "never expressed or showed disrespect to anyone on the basis of race."[17]

Surprisingly, the Probation Department also addressed the crimes for which Goetz was tried, even though he had not been held legally responsible for them—most likely, in aid of its effort to suggest that he was not, in fact, a violent man who needed to be behind bars. The report stressed, for example, that "much of the testimony offered at the trial was conflicting and contradictory as to the events of the shooting, and many aspects remain controversial and unsubstantiated."[18]

Among the controversies, it took the time to note, were the positions of the four teens in relation to Goetz, as well as whether "any of the four men" had been shot in the back.[19] The report also noted the defense's argument that Bernie Goetz had been "tired" and "confused" when he had given his statement to Detective Warren Foote in Concord, New Hampshire, and admitted to approaching Darrell Cabey and saying, "You seem to be alright, here's another." The department pointed out that eyewitness and expert testimony "tended to refute this statement," as did the fact that the shots he had fired had all been in "rapid succession."[20]

However, the report was not so charitable when it came to its opinions about the teens he shot. They were criminals, first and foremost.

The department reiterated the assertion that Troy Canty had been denied compensation from the Crime Victims Board because he was not an innocent victim. In fact, he'd been "in the process of robbing the alleged perpetrator at the time he was shot."[21]

The report pointed out further that even the most sympathetic victim, Darrell Cabey, had gone on the record admitting to columnist Jimmy Breslin that the group "was planning to rob the defendant."[22] And, of course, Barry Allen and James Ramseur were both currently locked up, which spoke for itself, the report continued. It also noted, "All four men have filed civil suits against the defendant."[23]

Ultimately, when it came to the fate of Bernie Goetz, the Department of Probation recommended "a sentence of Probation in lieu of incarceration, with Intensive Supervision." They cited Goetz's zero prior arrests, stressed that he possessed the illegal gun solely for the purpose of self-defense, and reminded the court of his ongoing loss of business and personal standing due to the case's notoriety. There were only two conditions specified for the probation it was recommending: Goetz must receive psychiatric counseling ("in a program approved by" and "for as long as deemed necessary by the Probation Department"), and that he could not continue to possess his illegal weapons. Violation of these conditions would see Goetz immediately incarcerated "for the maximum term allowable for this offense."[24]

No sooner had Judge Crane received this report than its major and most exculpatory conclusions were leaked to the press.[25] This was likely a happy day for Barry Slotnick. He understood just how much pressure the judge was under when it came to Goetz's sentence, and the more information there was out there that suggested Goetz should do no time, the better.

Judge Crane, however, might well have had several reasons to keep the recommendations of Department of Probation staff at arm's length. For starters, a key figure in that department, the head of its union, Wallace Cheatham, had written a letter to *The New York Times* in 1985 "in which derogatory remarks about two of the youths shot with Darrell were contained." Cheatham had also issued a press release in which, influenced by Goetz's case, he urged that probation officers should be allowed to carry firearms.[26] With Cheatham's letter recirculating, questions about the Probation Department's supposedly impartial position as the issuer of recommendations for sentencing could certainly be raised.

Regardless, it would have been unlike Judge Crane to rely solely on this report to make his decision, no matter its potential controversy. He was committed to doing his own due diligence as he mulled over the fairest sentence.

To that end, Crane also carefully read the pre-sentencing memorandum submitted by Shirley Cabey on behalf of her son. Penned by their lawyer William Kunstler, this memo called on the judge to review any report from the Probation Department "with a jaundiced eye," and pointedly reminded Crane of his duty to consider "the incalculable harm to Darrell Cabey and his entire family" that had been wrought by Goetz's illegally owned gun.[27]

This memo argued forcefully that the racial underpinnings of this case must be factored into Crane's sentencing. As their memo pointed out, Goetz had drawn his weapon against other Black people prior to this incident, and there was "ample evidence, both in his own words and those of others," of his hatred of Blacks and Latinos.[28] Kunstler and Shirley Cabey tried to appeal to Crane's noblest sense of duty, writing that they did not believe the judge would administer "the 'slap on the wrist'" predicted by many in the Black community, as it would be an inadequate sentence for Goetz's violent felony offense.

Furthermore, the memo suggested to the judge, whatever he decided would have far-reaching implications. Judges in his position, the memo asserted, had key roles to play in "curb[ing] the tragic virulence that threatens to turn this metropolis into a veritable shooting range, a reincarnation of Dodge City, where all life—whether black, Latino, or white—will be in daily danger." Goetz was the prominent symbol of a frightening prospect, a man who wanted to teach others "how to get the gun out quickly," to shoot first and ask questions later. If the court did not "deal with this defendant with a weather eye on the days and years ahead [it] may well live to rue a decision that imperils us all."[29]

Meanwhile, numerous others were weighing in on how Goetz might best be held responsible for his actions, including organizations hoping he would do community service with them.

The Villagers Against Crime (VAC) community group from Greenwich Village expressed that it would welcome Goetz to work with its court-monitoring project, or perhaps he could serve as a project coordinator. VAC was the local organization that had been created to aid the police in their efforts to lock up prostitutes and "transvestites" in that part of Manhattan. As its founder Robert Rygor wrote, VAC could now offer "an appropriate ending to a story that has been heard around the world" and also show the public, "No, you can't take the law into your own hands, but there are constructive measures citizens can take to make all the members of our community safer from crime."[30] Because the police had a strong relationship with VAC, placing Goetz there would have netted the judge some goodwill with the NYPD.

Another notable offer came from the director of the Department of Volunteer Services at New York University's Medical Center, Mrs. Adell C. Carr, who wrote that her program had a history of comfortably working "with probationers assigned community service" and Goetz was welcome to join.[31]

As these possibilities poured in, Barry Slotnick also made sure that Judge Crane had the full psychiatric report he had ordered for Bernie on hand. He made clear to the judge when handing it over that Crane had better find an alternative to incarceration, because it was Dr. Goldstein's unequivocal opinion that "any custodial or supervisory sentence would be counter-therapeutic" and such an experience would be "devastating" to Goetz's "already exacerbated post-traumatic stress."[32]

OCTOBER 19, 1987, was sentencing day for Bernhard Goetz, and a notorious day in its own right. Later dubbed Black Monday, in this one twenty-four-hour period Wall Street suffered its largest single-day percentage loss in American history, falling 22.6 percent in a sudden and systemic crash that would have worldwide reverberations and take a full two years to see any real recovery from.[33] This was stunning evidence that unfettered capitalism, finance with fewer rules, and an ever-globalizing economy tied to Reaganomics had not just been costly to the poorest Americans; they were jeopardizing the economic stability of the entire world.

While Wall Street investors were in an all-out panic at the New York Stock Exchange nearby, tensions were also at a new high in Judge Crane's chambers even before the formal proceeding could begin.

In a rather stunning move, Barry Slotnick had suddenly decided to file a motion for the judge to recuse himself from the sentencing altogether. Undoubtedly this was Slotnick's last-ditch effort to get a judge who would sentence his client to probation rather than give jail time, or perhaps it was merely a way to put additional pressure on Judge Crane to act in his client's favor, but either way, it caused tensions to go from simmer to boil between these two men.

The core of Slotnick's argument was made subtly but devastatingly. He pointed out that Crane, still serving an interim appointment, was hoping to be nominated to a permanent position on the New York State Supreme Court. Despite its name, this was not the state's highest bench, but it was still a plum judicial appointment. Therefore, Slotnick suggested, Crane was undoubtedly feeling a great deal of pressure to please those with political power in the city. The implication? Slotnick went on. Those higher-ups would want Crane to throw the book at Bernie Goetz, and thus he could not be trusted to render a fair sentence.[34]

Using his now-classic technique, Slotnick made sure to distance himself from the blow he had just leveled—"I think Your Honor would be a credit to the Supreme Court bench," he said—but he nevertheless noted, almost with a shrug, that there were "those who were pointing their finger at the Court," those who felt sending Goetz to jail might be a way "to insure [the] nomination." Mark Baker also chimed in, asking Crane whether he was "trying to curry favor" with those who would help him up the judicial ladder.[35]

Waples was appalled by what he was hearing and felt compelled to speak up with uncharacteristic passion:

> I think I crossed swords with the Court, as the defense has, in the last three and a quarter years. I've been aggrieved by the Court in its rulings either pretrial and during trial. But I view that as water under the bridge. I'm confident the Court can and will pass a fair and just sentence on this defendant. And I'm certainly prepared to have you sentence the defendant.[36]

Obliged to respond, Crane dismissed the defense's suggestions that he was playing politics with this decision as "innuendo and rumor and nothing of any substance," reminding Slotnick that he had remained on the Goetz case for years despite it being "a no-win situation for the judge." Furthermore, he declared heatedly, "Once my personal fortune or my personal future or anything about my own personal interests intrudes on my decision making, I'd better get off the bench entirely. And I honestly believe that it has not."[37]

Ultimately, it was clear that Slotnick had overplayed his hand with the judge. "What hurts here," Crane said, "is that colleagues of mine are commenting."[38] But Judge Crane was not going to recuse himself, and he was going to proceed to render the sentence to which he had already given an extraordinary amount of thought.

With the sentencing hearing about to begin, the courtroom buzzed with excitement. Bernie Goetz was front and center, taking his seat by his lawyers. Several of the jurors also came back to hear the sentence, and the room was packed with reporters and ordinary citizens eager to learn Goetz's fate. It had been four months since his trial concluded, but public interest had not at all flagged. The courtroom was packed with spectators as well as local and national media.

As the proceedings began, a number of people in that courtroom, including the Cabeys' lawyer, William Kunstler, sought to make statements before the sentence was handed down. Judge Crane refused. He had done his research, and the only others who would be allowed to speak were the defense and prosecution attorneys. This, however, did not discourage one determined member of the public in dreadlocks from standing up to shout: "If I can do a mandatory year, he can do a mandatory year!"[39]

Refusing to let anything derail or rush this proceeding, Judge Crane first explained the law that he was obliged to follow, which required a one-year presumptive sentence, "unless the court could find that one was unduly harsh."[40] But he had also taken other important factors into consideration—everything from public safety to what might be the best "deterrent influence"; to what might lend itself best to rehabilitation—which he would soon explain.[41] First, however, he would allow Greg Waples to speak, followed by Barry Slotnick. Additionally, Crane noted, the defendant had "the absolute right to address His Honor on any matter relevant to sentence."[42]

With his time, Waples asserted that he could not recall a single case from his nine and a half years in the DA's office where a defendant this dangerous, "if not to himself, then to other members of the New York community," faced such a light sanction. It would be utterly "incomprehensible" if this court determined that it was "unduly harsh" to give him the year.[43] Even that short a sentence was hard to imagine.

Goetz was a man who chose to obey the laws he liked, Waples continued, and had no compunction breaking those that inconvenienced him or that he did not respect. The only appropriate sentence, the only one that would "have the slightest impact" on Goetz, would be incarceration. "I don't think I'm being vindictive," he concluded. "What I ask, your honor, [is] simply to enforce the law as it was written."[44]

Needless to say, Barry Slotnick spoke just as fervently. Based on the Probation Department's assessment, he claimed, it should be clear that Bernie Goetz was "a rational individual." That report had suggested that "an incarcerative sentence would be harsh, unrealistic and inappropriate." Indeed, Slotnick went on, "I'm asking the Court not to victimize Bernhard Goetz."[45]

But Slotnick did not stop there. He knew Judge Crane's Achilles' heel remained ensuring that the public viewed him as fair-minded, and he unabashedly invoked that same public in making his case: "I'm also asking the Court to understand the feeling of the people out there," he said. Slotnick cited groups he'd recently met with around the city—a gathering of Teamsters, "a political committee," "a charitable group," a group of law students—who had all asked about Bernie Goetz and noted they would hate to see him go to jail. "Judge, ninety-five percent of [the law students] urged me to urge you, and I told them I would, not to send him to jail." Slotnick closed his statement with maximum drama, imploring Crane, "Do not, please don't break the heart of the City of New York."[46]

Bernie Goetz remained silent.

Finally, it was time for Judge Crane to explain how he had come to his decision.

He first recounted the "long and deep consideration" and "extensive research" the Court had undertaken in determining an appropriate sentence. He cited thirty-six written comments from members of the public and institutions—including the Center for Constitutional Rights and "a joint memo from the Congress of Racial Equality and the Second Amendment Foundation." Of these, only eleven called for incarceration, while twenty-five of them "advocat[ed] no jail for the defendant."[47]

While conceding that "obviously no sentence should be based on a poll," and insisting that "the sentence about to be imposed is uninfluenced by these numbers," Crane noted also that ten different community organizations had offered to participate in a "community service sentence" for Goetz. That being said, Crane had some real concerns about community service alone. He was thinking chiefly about deterrence and expressed the view that allowing Goetz to avoid jail entirely would likely "invite others to violate the gun laws who, misguided or not, feel the need to arm themselves without first securing a license."[48]

At last, Crane issued his sentence. Goetz would serve six months in the city penitentiary, and complete 290 hours of community service at the New York University Medical Center, "as a condition of and concurrent with" a five-year probation. During probation, he would be required to participate in psychiatric counseling. He could choose his own provider, but that counselor would be required to periodically report on Goetz's condition and "cooperation with any plan of treatment" to his assigned probation officer. "And lastly, the defendant shall pay a fine of five thousand dollars."[49]

Anticipating strong reactions from both sides, Crane concluded his statement, "Let's not encumber the record any further, my sentence is what it is."[50]

Despite Crane's stern admonition, the courtroom erupted.

Crane's sentence, however mild, would stand. Despite his posturing, Slotnick had to know, as did Judge Crane, that Goetz had gotten off lightly. He owed restitution of only $5,000—a sum that was well within his means. His time in Rikers would also be served in protected custody, the same place he had spent nine days in January 1985. Counting that time already served, Goetz stood to be released after just fifty-one days.[51]

Still, the defense had no intention of accepting it. As soon as Crane delivered the sentence, Slotnick informed him that they had already served the DA's office a notice of appeal and insisted that his client remain free on bail until it was decided by the higher court.[52]

Ultimately, Slotnick's earlier attack on the judge's integrity had apparently netted him exactly what he wanted—a judge eager to avoid further upsetting him. Judge Crane would agree to this request, and Goetz would remain a free man until the appeal had been resolved or until February 16, 1988—whichever came first.[53]

As Bernie Goetz headed back to his 14th Street apartment, Crane clearly remained troubled by the beating that his character had taken on the day he had rendered his sentence. A few weeks later, he gave an interview to the student newspaper at Fordham University, where his wife taught history. Feeling compelled to defend his decision, he explained:

> I needed to impose incarceration for the sake of avoiding making the law a dead letter. It's what we call a factor of general deterrence, one of the five factors that go into sentencing any defendant.
>
> In his particular case, the general deterrent factor was the strongest one in my mind for the sentence I imposed. And if I had followed the urging of Mr. Slotnick . . . that would have invited anybody for

> good motives to carry a handgun contrary to the gun law . . . whatever one might think of the gun control legislation, it is the law, and I am sworn to uphold it.[54]

But while he had followed the law, and had taken vital factors into consideration, Crane made clear that he had paid a high personal price.

> After 7½ weeks of trial, I was exhausted. . . . The sentence, and my preparation for the sentence and the publicity and the leak of the Probation Department report all took a toll on me. I was very, very intense in preparing for the sentence for weeks and weeks and weeks. I thought about it, I researched the law. . . . [It] will be up to the Appellate Division to determine if I acted properly or not."[55]

Crane did have real support, especially from some colleagues. State Supreme Court Justice Michael Dontzin wrote, "Congratulations on your wisdom and good judgment. You will probably get some crazy mail—burn it and keep only the kudos."[56] And even the more mainstream publications seemed to think his sentence had been fair. A *New York Times* op-ed declared, "Six months of jail . . . sends the proper, clear signal: whatever trouble would-be vigilantes think of dishing out to others, they also risk plenty of trouble for themselves."[57] Even the *Daily News* published one sympathetic piece, an outlier, applauding the judge's decision:

> Crane could have slapped him with the seven-year max. Goetz would then have look[ed] like the final victim, a sacrificial lamb on an altar of political opportunism and exploitation. Instead . . . Crane gave a well-considered sentence that should quench the flames of either extreme. Good for him. Good for the rule of law. Good for New York.[58]

Press from well outside of NYC also supported at least the idea of sentencing Goetz to some time. As a piece out of Atlanta put it, "Overly lenient treatment . . . would have sent a dangerous message to potential Goetzes who could turn New York streets into a battleground for carrying unlicensed weapons with the excuse that they were only protecting themselves against the perceived threat of menacing youths, blacks, Hispanics, or any other group they feel uncomfortable around. Chaos would result."[59]

But Crane would also be lambasted, his chambers flooded with nasty missives, many that insulted his morals and integrity or called for his resignation.[60] "Gutless hypocrite," one anonymous critic wrote.[61] Others asserted the rights of "good" and "honest" citizens to self-defense, especially in such a "wicked" city, and characterized Goetz's victims as criminals, thieves, and thugs.[62] Overwhelmingly, the public was upset that Goetz was going to do any amount of time. As Guardian Angels founder Curtis Sliwa told the *Miami Herald*, sending Goetz to prison was tantamount to "throwing raw meat to the vultures."[63]

The media outlets that had vehemently supported Goetz were also outraged, especially the tabloid press. Before the sentencing, Ray Kerrison of the *Post* declared in an op-ed, "The worst justice in the world is selective justice, and that's what we will get if Goetz is put away."[64] The day after the hearing, Kerrison railed against the sentence, as minimal as it was. "Is there a law for black unlicensed gunmen and another law for white unlicensed gunmen? . . . Yesterday, Judge Crane gave the Outlaws a pass. And imprisoned the victims."[65]

The Editorial Board of the *New York Post* was in complete agreement, declaring the sentence "a travesty. The judge apparently accepted the prosecution's claim that 'Goetz is a disturbed man.' . . . [But Goetz] has already paid a steep price for that mistake. Dragged from courtroom to courtroom for nearly three years, his life has been destroyed—it will never be the same again."[66]

Such hostile sentiments were expressed across the country. As a piece in *The Arizona Republic* put it, "Too bad Justice Crane gave so little thought to the encouragement that putting Goetz behind bars will offer the city's mugging community, who represent a far greater peril to New York subway riders than does the occasional passenger who, like the hapless Goetz, is incautious enough to defend himself."[67]

Goetz himself would also eventually weigh in—breaking the silence he'd maintained during the trial and letting people know how he felt about it. When the New York State Rifle and Pistol Clubs gave him a Good Samaritans award in April 1988 for being "one of the most courageous of citizens to defend himself from four horrible animals," Goetz was glad to use this as an occasion to express his gratitude that he had been acquitted on most of the charges but also to lash out at his victims once again. He mocked James Ramseur for "acting like a monkey in court" and Troy Canty for his "champagne memory." He also thanked Barry Allen for "robbing someone in the apartment building where he lived" and Darrell Cabey "for his revealing interview with Jimmy Breslin."[68]

Bernhard Goetz receives a Good Samaritans award from Frank Borzellieri at a New York State Rifle and Pistol Clubs annual luncheon, April 23, 1988. AP Photo/David Bookstaver

Supportive local organizations offered Goetz not only awards but also money to pay his legal bills. The State Rifle and Pistol Clubs, for example, held a fundraiser at an Italian restaurant in Coney Island for Goetz where they were able to add nearly $3,000 to the $10,000 they had already raised.[69] The group's president had also published an opinion piece on Goetz's "harsh" sentence, saying it sent "a dangerously powerful signal to the violent wolf packs who roam New York City as well as to the 'criminal lobby'—those who make excuses for crime and criminals—that predators can rest assured that their victims won't respond with the only effective deterrent there is against depredations: victim gunfire."[70]

AS IT WOULD turn out, Bernie Goetz had a great deal of time to curry the media's favor and to get very comfortable at home. His appeal was not heard by a higher court until July 1988.

On appeal, the core of the defense team's argument was twofold: First, that Crane's jury instructions had been incorrect, and second, that he had "abused [his] discretion as a matter of law" in determining that jail time "was not 'unduly harsh,'" by "virtually ignoring" the expert advice of Dr. Goldstein that incarceration would be harmful to Goetz.[71] Moreover, the appeal asserted, the split sentence Goetz had been dealt was "inherently illegal," and therefore, the sentence would need to be revised even if the Appellate Division were to agree with the judge's decision.

In their reply brief, the DA's office argued vociferously that the appellate court should not rule in favor of the defense, even though it conceded that the split sentence was indeed illegal and that the jury instructions had been incorrect. Still, the prosecutors argued, none of this mattered because defense counsel had not objected to these issues at the time or on the record.

At the time Crane gave his instructions, this brief pointed out, the defense had not challenged his missive to the jury that they "must" convict "if the prosecution established beyond a reasonable doubt each of the elements of the gun charge. And they had to have done so in order to raise this matter on appeal."[72] What's more, the prosecution's reply brief went on, that original jury charge had in fact been both "legal and logical tradition."[73]

Ultimately, the appeal would backfire on the defense. In November 1988, the Appellate Division, First Department, announced that it would uphold Goetz's conviction of gun possession and that it had not found any "abuse of discretion" by Judge Crane. The court did agree with the defense on one point: Goetz would need to return to court for resentencing. But the reason why was bad news for their client. Judge Crane had assigned Goetz a jail term of only six months, the appellate court stated, but New York State penal law clearly required a minimum jail term of one year for the charge of illegal possession of a weapon, third degree.

Now, instead of spending fewer than sixty days in jail, given the time he had already served, Goetz faced closer to 350 days, "barring an extraordinary reprieve." Such a reprieve, however, was not totally out of the realm of possibility, especially if Goetz's team had their request granted for "conditional release after 60 days," or if they decided to take their appeal to an even higher court.[74]

On January 13, 1989, Bernie Goetz was resentenced to one year at Rikers Island. He took the opportunity in this proceeding to finally speak before Judge Crane.[75] "This case," he said matter-of-factly, "is really more about deterioration in society than it is about me."[76] Picking up steam, Goetz "complained that Darrell Cabey had previously been arrested for robbery and released on bail. He also accused the prosecutor in his trial of acting 'very irresponsibly.'" As he put it, "Gregory Waples, uh, seems to be concerned that society needs to be protected from me. And, uh, I don't believe that's the case. Society needs to be protected from criminals."[77]

Barry Slotnick was not pleased with his client's words. He told him sotto voce to "sit down."[78] The last thing he needed was for the judge to see how little remorse this man actually had for his actions. Shortly thereafter, Bernie Goetz left the courtroom to begin his sentence in protective isolation in the hospital wing of Rikers. His bid for early release was denied. Ironically, in March 1989, now twenty-three-year-old Barry Allen would also find himself locked up in the North Facility on Rikers Island after again being arrested, this time for stealing $58 from a man in the Bronx.[79]

Deep down, Barry Slotnick likely felt relieved. The outcome could have certainly been much worse for his client, given the toll his actions had taken on the boys he had shot. And Greg Waples, as dispirited as he was, was never entirely persuaded that this verdict was really a "validation" of Goetz's actions by this jury. He remained convinced that "there were a number of jurors who were deeply troubled by what went on." Still, he felt responsible for what had happened. "Given the jury instructions in our constitutional system," the onus was on him to prove his case "beyond a reasonable doubt," and, as he saw it, "I just hadn't met my burden."[80]

In many ways, this had been an anticlimactic end to a roller-coaster ride of a case, one that left New Yorkers with many questions. Many simply didn't understand how Bernie Goetz had been found guilty of anything. Still others, particularly those who had prayed for some measure of justice on behalf of the four unarmed teen victims he had gunned down, couldn't fathom how he had not been convicted on all counts. Reflecting this rage and despair, Black writer, poet, playwright, and political activist Amiri Baraka wrote:

> The only reason our lives are made tragic by poverty & ignorance & repression is white supremacy. . . . If Goetz can carry a gun, the African American people must consciously arm themselves against racial violence sanctioned by the state![81]

One juror, Mark Lesly, would help shine some much-needed light on how this case had ended as it did.

33

Postmortem

HOW HAD A JURY of twelve that had listened to Gregory Waples lay out a powerful, nearly two-month-long case on behalf of Goetz's shooting victims—including tapes of Goetz himself explaining that he not only had meant to harm those boys but had actually intended to kill them—concluded that Goetz was not guilty of anything more than carrying an illegal gun?

This question likely plagued prosecutor Greg Waples. He had always assumed that Goetz's own words were "by far the most powerful evidence in the prosecution's arsenal." Still, he had known that everything would hinge on corroboration, which was why he had called so many witnesses to the stand. Was it simply the case that, as Waples said in an interview years later, Barry Slotnick had done a "very effective job of persuading the jurors that there was at least reasonable doubt as to the accuracy of those statements"?[1]

As the jurors themselves began sharing the behind-the-scenes discussions that had led to such a stunning verdict, the answer became disturbingly clear: This was a group of New Yorkers that fundamentally related more to Goetz than they did to the boys he shot.

But this was deeply ironic. These were jurors who either had been touched by crime themselves (the majority of them) or had been in situations where they could easily imagine being a victim (the remainder). And yet, it was Goetz to whom they related—they had ultimately empathized with the man who had shot unarmed teens as they cowered and tried to flee. Clearly, when this jury imagined what a victim looked like, it wasn't boys like Troy, Barry, James, and Darrell.

This was a group of people searching for any explanation that would make the man wielding the gun the crime victim, and the horrific act of violence he carried out something other than what the shooter himself admitted it was.

Helping make this happen, and ultimately drowning out the concerns of at least two jurors less inclined to sanction what Goetz had done, was Mark Lesly, who proudly embraced the nickname he had earned by the trial's end: "Barry Jr." Not only did Lesly admire Slotnick, but he seemed to have developed a special rapport with him early on, when questioned during voir dire, over their shared love of sports.[2]

This highly public case had an outsized impact on Mark Lesly's life, thrusting him into the limelight in ways he had never imagined possible. One year later, he wrote his own memoir, *Subway Gunman: A Juror's Account of the Bernhard Goetz Trial.* This was not the only book to be written about the case, but it was the only one in which an actual Goetz juror laid bare what had gone on behind the scenes, and he did so most unselfconsciously.[3]

According to Lesly's memoir, he had initially leaned toward Goetz's guilt. Others, like D. Wirth Jackson, a seventy-four-year-old retired engineer, insisted loudly that "he was not convinced Goetz had intended to murder the youths. Goetz had no motive . . . despite the statements [he] had made in New Hampshire."[4] Lesly tried to talk Jackson out of this position, before eventually agreeing that Goetz was, in fact, not guilty. "There was then a heated discussion," Lesly recalled, "with me arguing that the intent was present as I had believed all along. Searching for a way to convince Jackson, however, I devised an argument that in fact did the opposite, and I wound up deciding that I had been wrong."[5]

The discussions were contentious at some times, agreeable at others, and at still others, pure grandstanding. Sometimes, it wasn't clear exactly who was on trial here, Goetz or his victims.

As juror Diana Serpe later recalled, "It was very hard to keep it straight [that] it was Goetz that was on trial, [when] often the discussions had the boys on trial. You know . . . that's how it would appear, how the conversations would get twisted. It's like, well, wait a minute. They're not on trial. You know, Goetz is, so we need to separate some of that and, uh, kind of focus on his actions."[6]

Eventually, the question of Goetz's guilt or innocence with regard to Darrell Cabey in particular took center stage. As Lesly explained it, "Our deliberation on count eleven [concerning the attempted murder of Darrell Cabey] took up about twenty percent of our total time and overlapped with discussions of the other assault counts quite [a] bit." Lesly had been willing to argue "to acquit Goetz for the assault of Canty, Allen, and Ramseur," but even he "felt that the Cabey assault was different."[7]

As far as Lesly was concerned, everything hinged on whether Darrell had been "shot as part of a single burst of gunfire," or if Goetz had taken the time to shoot him twice, after noticing the first shot had missed. If the former were true, then Goetz was not guilty, because he had faced a "verified threat." If, however, he had taken the time to reflect on his actions, "and to reassess his situation," that was a different matter—"Goetz should be found guilty of that crime."[8]

The other jurors tended to agree that this was the crux of the matter: Did Cabey get hit "while standing in front of his subway seat, then fall backward into the seat as a second bullet fired at him missed, striking the wall of the conductor's cab? Or was he missed by the first volley and then cold-bloodedly and unjustifiably shot while cowering in his seat?"[9]

It would seem that the testimony of Christopher Boucher should have decided this question, along with Waples's dramatically donning Darrell's jacket during his closing statement. But, according to Mark Lesly, the jurors had problems with Boucher's account.[10] He personally wondered, for example, whether Boucher had really seen what he said he did, or was only trying to help the teens because he was gay—also a "minority."[11] For his fellow jurors, however, Lesly would craft, quite proudly, his own well-argued rebuttal of the prosecution's version of this most serious shooting to discredit him.

To Lesly, the "most glaring" problem with Christopher Boucher's account was that Cabey was still seated, with Goetz "two or three feet directly in front of him, with his right arm extended and crooked at the elbow, the gun held slightly above the waist." According to Lesly, Boucher "did not see Cabey jerk his arm, twist, or flinch in any way" when Goetz fired his weapon. If his account were correct, "there also would have been an audible separation between the fourth and fifth shots," which "had not been noticed by any of the eight other eyewitnesses who had testified before us."[12]

Since Waples's reconstruction corroborated what Boucher had seen, the jury had to contend with that. They asked to see Darrell's jacket again, as well as the screwdrivers found in its pockets.[13] Lesly commandeered the evidence, then did his own dramatic reenactment. He donned the jacket, putting the screwdrivers in its pocket to see where he thought the offending bullet may have hit, and whether Cabey would have been seated or standing, holding a strap above his head.

Lesly followed his own theatrics by passionately arguing his own theory:

> Cabey could have been standing in front of his seat, facing the aisle, and been hit by the fourth shot that Goetz fired. That shot could have been the one that paralyzed him. As he was falling backward into the seat, Goetz's gun could have fired again. The fifth bullet could have passed through the left side of his jacket, just forward of his chest, and then struck the panel "more or less flatly," leaving the dent on the conductor's cab wall.[14]

Lesly insisted to his fellow jurors, including English professor Catherine Brody, who he could see remained dubious, that his reenactment had proven that Goetz was in fact innocent of having targeted Cabey deliberately. He had acted in the heat of being under threat.

Lesly also had a ready answer for any juror who might wonder how Darrell could have been threatening Goetz, given his position on the train, and the fact that he had not brandished a weapon nor spoken a word to him. "According to the judge's charge, we were to take the physical attributes of all persons into account," he said.[15]

Based on his own martial arts experience, which he said suggested that even someone's body could be a weapon—but notably not on any information presented in the trial itself, by either side—Lesly drew his own conclusions and argued persuasively for them. As he put it, "any one of the youths could have beaten Goetz in a fight."[16] Darrell Cabey could, Lesly insisted, have injured Goetz severely using only his hands on "two pressure points at the base of the skull where a person can be killed if hit by a blow."[17]

Lesly didn't rest there, arguing as well that the DA's accounting of the teenagers' positions on the train had been incorrect. He believed that "Ramseur was shot while in front of Goetz, not off to Goetz's right, meaning that either three youths"—not two, as most witnesses said—"had been standing around Goetz before he fired, or that Ramseur's and Allen's positions were reversed." All of this, of course, called Cabey's positioning into question as well.[18]

And yet, there remained the testimony of Bernhard Goetz himself, which would have been difficult for even the most defense-oriented juror to explain away. This testimony, for example, made jurors like Cathy Brody, Carolyn Perlmuth, and Erniece Dix leery of clearing Goetz on the most serious charges he faced.

The jury would in fact clash quite a bit over Goetz's words, not only those he uttered on his taped confessions but also what he had said to virtually everyone he spoke to—including his neighbor Myra Friedman—between the day of the shootings and the beginning of the trial. Ultimately, the jurors questioned Friedman's credibility, with at least one of them, Robert Leach, suggesting that she had her own agenda. Specifically, as another juror explained, Leach raised the possibility that she might have "concocted the story about [Goetz's] guns with the intent to sell a feature article—which she did in *New York* magazine for $4,000."[19]

Prosecutor Greg Waples had erroneously assumed that Goetz's explanations of his own actions would be concerning to jurors like Lesly—or, at the very least, would push them to try to answer, with other evidence, the core question his words posed: Was Bernie Goetz a man "with a score to settle . . . who held the entire city of New York in contempt . . . who had decided to take the law into his own hands?" Or was he "a frightened, confused, bitter man" whose life "had been irrevocably changed," who was expressing "internal turmoil, guilt, self-deprecation [and] self-directed rage?"[20]

Lesly's and juror James Moseley's answer to this—the one most sympathetic to Goetz—would prove effective in bringing most of the other jurors around to the same understanding. But not all of them.

Catherine Brody, for example, "proved the hardest to persuade." In virtually every vote, and throughout the deliberation process, not only was she "the staunchest undecided" juror, but according to Lesly, "quite often she was the last to be swayed."[21] To Lesly's clear annoyance, Brody could be quite persuasive herself. Brody was very articulate, and she often spoke for several of the less vocal members of the jury. According to Lesly, Erniece Dix, a twenty-three-year-old who worked as an administrative aide in the city Youth Department, often waited for Brody to be convinced before making up her own mind—and the reservations that Brody voiced were clearly those that Dix also felt.[22]

WHEN GOETZ'S TAPED ADMISSIONS and justifications were first played, they had in fact deeply troubled every juror. As Diana Serpe later admitted, the tape "was incriminating, completely incriminating." But having Slotnick's interpretation of Goetz's state of mind during the interrogation later hammered home by jurors such as Moseley and Lesly definitely changed opinions. The tape would, in fact, end up vindicating Goetz. He had been traumatized; there was no question. As Serpe came to see it, his "previous mugging was very important" when it came to understanding his reaction to these youths. As James Moseley persuasively put it in one interview, "Just being mugged, just going through the ordeal of getting beat up, is very humiliating." Even worse, in this case, "They went free."[23]

Their experience on the replica subway car also helped jurors sympathetic to the defendant. As Serpe later recalled:

> One of the other jurors . . . came and put his hand up on the, um, the bar and was just standing above me as I sat in the seat and I'm thinking, Oh my God, how, how could I get, if I wanted to run, how could I get out? . . . You know, he's over me. The other side had an armrest on it. So, it would be impossible to really get away quickly. And that was really, that made a big impression on me to realize that how intimidating that is.[24]

Juror Michael Axelrod concurred. "Mr. Goetz was not a vigilante, he was a sad, frightened man," he told the *Los Angeles Times*; he was "trapped on the train."[25]

Juror James Moseley. From *The Confessions of Bernhard Goetz* (MPI Home Video, 1987). Permission from the estate of Darrell Moore.

Furthermore, jurors like Mark Lesly were eager to reiterate another one of Slotnick's positions: that Goetz had not just been on fear-induced "automatic pilot" when he shot the teens, but he was clearly in an "adrenal haze" when he finally recounted his story. Goetz's confession was the hindsight version of his actions—an embellished one because, psychologically, he felt the need to claim more ownership and control over a situation where he'd felt he had absolutely none. By this reading, for instance, he only admitted to deliberately shooting Darrell Cabey because he actually "wished he'd put his gun to Cabey's head and fired." He'd said he had "wanted to gouge Canty's eyes out with his keys" only because "he was expressing the rage he felt for the way in which his encounter with the youths had turned his life upside down and for the emotional turmoil he was suffering as a result."[26]

Overall, the jury had decided that this had been a man who "was exhausted and clearly distraught." He had been on the run for nine days and had been carrying the weight of the incident during this time, not to mention having to "go through his story three times with police."[27] As Diana Serpe later put it, "as far as walking over to one person and saying, 'You look all right, here's another,' I don't believe those words were ever uttered. On the whole I believe that he thought later, 'That would have sounded good, I should have said that.'"[28] Once they discounted this part of Goetz's confession, it seemed easy to also discount all of his recollections, including that his victims had tried to flee.

Notably, it had been prosecutor Greg Waples himself who nodded to the possibility that Goetz had embellished his confession when it came to what he actually said to Darrell Cabey and what he wished he had. As legal scholar George Fletcher put it, "that concession . . . was a major mistake because that encouraged the jury's skepticism about whether the confession was believable."[29]

This analysis was, perhaps, unduly hard on the prosecution.

Far more than any prosecutorial misstep, it was thanks to the extraordinary lengths Barry Slotnick had gone to provide the jury with an alternate, more sympathetic narrative, one that would allow them to see up as down and down as up, that would ultimately find the jurors explaining away Goetz's many damning explanations and justifications for his actions with astonishing alacrity.

Even when it came to Goetz's tale of shooting Cabey, the jury decided that his own account of what had happened was simply not credible. "What concreted it for us," Moseley explained, was "Slotnick's tale of the ballistics. If [Cabey] was shot on his left side, Bernie Goetz had to have been not over him but where he had been originally, over to his left. Boucher could not have seen what he said he saw or [the] shot would not have been to his left."[30] That was all the "reasonable doubt" the jury needed to acquit Goetz.

Ultimately, Lesly explained, the jury "disliked" Waples's contention that "Goetz was taking out a lifetime of revenge on his victims" and that he was an "emotional powder keg," because they felt that he was the opposite. He was both rightfully fearful and furious. In their view, Bernie Goetz had, in truth, been a remarkably patient man. As Lesly put it, he "demonstrated a 'long fuse,' by carrying a gun every day for three years and not using it."[31]

But even as the jurors finally agreed on which version of events to believe, they still had to wrestle with the law—particularly when it came to what constituted a "reasonable" response to the threat Goetz faced. They had to decide if Goetz had the right to shoot or if he should more reasonably have just shown his gun.

The jury would debate whether Goetz "faced the threat of deadly force" until the bitter end. As had been the case for the entirety of the deliberations, Catherine Brody held out the longest on the charge of assaulting Cabey. But the group hounded her, with Lesly going so far as to insist that "at the moment when Goetz started firing it was from Cabey that [Goetz] had the most to fear." He and others would urge Brody at least to concede that there was a chance that the threat the youths posed could "have resulted in Goetz's death."[32]

Finally, Brody reluctantly agreed that there was too much reasonable doubt to support a conviction based on either how Goetz shot Darrell Cabey or a nagging belief that the shooting of four unarmed youths on a subway train was not a reasonable act.[33]

The key part of Crane's instructions that jurors heard, as Cathy Brody remembered it, was that it didn't matter whether Bernie Goetz had actually been in mortal danger back on December 22, 1985. What they needed to decide was whether it was "reasonable" for him to believe that he was. As James Moseley would later put it, "We pretty much all agreed that, you know, it was reasonable for Bernhard Goetz to think that he was, his life was threatened potentially in this situation. The way the charge read, almost the only thing you could come up with is that, you know, well then he's not guilty."[34]

After Lesly and Moseley finally persuaded Cathy Brody that "it was impossible to prove that Goetz had harbored an intent to commit murder," the jury could, with ease, "unanimously [find] Goetz not guilty of all four of the attempted murder charges . . . [and] the assault charges . . . and ultimately offer a guilty decision only on the most minor gun charges."[35]

By Lesly's own admission, this jury had stepped over the line in its deliberations by positing theories to justify Goetz's actions. In one such instance, as Lesly candidly said:

> Despite all of the judge's admonitions against speculating on facts not in evidence, we surmised that perhaps, since we knew from the tapes that Goetz had been reading and listening to news reports about the shootings, Goetz might have learned of Boucher's version and concocted his story as a result. I have since learned that Boucher's version was not reported until he testified before the grand jury; so not only were we wrong to speculate, but we drew a conclusion that was absolutely false.[36]

As juror Carolyn Perlmuth also later mused, "People were coming up with the wildest scenarios as reasons for doubt."[37]

Similarly, the jury had on several occasions interpreted the law not as the judge had instructed in his charge to them but as they themselves had argued it. According to legal scholar George Fletcher, "Justice Crane defined intent to mean nothing more than 'having the conscious aim or objective' of bringing about a particular result," which meant that the jury would not have to attribute any particular malevolence to Goetz in order to decide that he had intended the outcome he received.[38] But "the jurors had another way of thinking about the intent to kill."[39]

Again, Lesly was instrumental in pushing forth this particular definition. Initially, he argued that "anytime you point a handgun at somebody, with hollow point bullets no less, that's attempting to murder somebody." Later, he would change his mind. He "became convinced that unless there was a clear motive to murder, there was no intent to kill." He didn't buy his own interpretation of Waples's argument, that Goetz's motive was revenge, and thus, he decided there was no clear motive.[40]

As Fletcher noted, "Mixing the issues of motive and intent" had serious consequences, namely the jury's embrace of a moral rather than legal "conception of intent." This is what ultimately led juror Carolyn Perlmuth to discount Goetz's own confession. To her, "it was obvious that if you shoot someone, you run the risk of killing someone. [Goetz] was aware of that possibility but [I] don't think he identified that one thing as what he wanted by shooting them."[41]

Perlmuth could personally relate to Goetz's experience. She had been with her mother when she was mugged and at the time "she just felt fear." Later, she admitted, "I really felt that [I] wanted to kill the guy. . . . This did influence me [in the deliberations]."[42]

This was also how Diana Serpe came to dismiss Goetz's confession. In her case and in the case of other jurors, and in ways utterly beyond what they had been instructed to consider, this jury "incorporated Goetz's purpose of defending himself into their analysis of his intention under their various conceptions of intent."[43]

All of this had been of particular consequence when it came to the jury's decision on what had happened to Darrell Cabey. If Bernie Goetz did not "intend" to paralyze Darrell, then he was not guilty of having done so, they reasoned.[44] Such thinking allowed the jury's eventual consensus on the general issue of justification, leading them to render not guilty verdicts on the most serious charges Goetz faced and to easily dispense as well with his charge of criminal possession of a weapon in the second degree. Goetz had only been carrying a weapon in case he needed it to defend himself. There was no "unlawful purpose."[45]

This jury simply could not accept that Bernhard Goetz, by his own admission, had a longstanding problem with authority and had been contemplating ways to even the score between himself and anyone who might even think about trying to accost him on a city street or subway. Neither did it seem to figure into its deliberations that long before encountering Troy, Barry, James, and Darrell, he already had a track record of both buying guns illegally and of pulling these weapons on other Black New Yorkers.

Goetz's hostile views of the city, his racist diatribes at earlier community gatherings, and his confession to wanting to maim and kill, as well as the fact that one young man would live the rest of his life brain-damaged and in a wheelchair while three others had also had their lives destroyed by Goetz's actions, did not seem to matter either.

The jury had been able to overlook these aspects of the case and had been unable to see Goetz as a threat to the public not because Barry Slotnick had presented a better case than Greg Waples. It was not because of weaknesses in, or limitations of, the law that these factors were ultimately irrelevant. Nor was it necessarily a consequence of the way Judge Crane had ultimately instructed the jury.

These details were not enough to convict Bernie Goetz because in 1980s New York, even a strange, antisocial, gun-wielding loner like Goetz was more sympathetic to these jurors—a slice of mainstream New York and America both—than four unemployed Black teenage dropouts trying to survive and somehow thrive in that same city and country.

Ultimately, this jury could not see Goetz as a vigilante or a predator because they did not see the young Black people he had shot as victims.

Conservative commentator and talk show host Geraldo Rivera would later sum it up as a "sense of us against them." According to Rivera, the mood in NYC toward these teens, and the communities they belonged to, was "You're not gonna keep this city from us. You're not gonna keep my wife scared. You're [not] gonna keep my kids scared. [Goetz is] the man that we need. . . . He's the Superman. He's the hero and, you know, the fact that [Darrell] was paralyzed, that he was shot at point blank range, was almost irrelevant to the vast majority of New Yorkers outside of a very small percentage of black moms."[46]

Barry Slotnick could not have agreed more. As he later explained, "The jury got it."[47] Indeed, they so identified with this white Everyman that juror Mark Lesly described the minimal sentence Goetz received—on the lesser charges that he and his fellow jurors had been willing to convict him on—as being "quite harsh."[48]

Despite the many times that Greg Waples had reminded the court that the actions of four Black boys were not on trial, it was impossible not to consider the reverse situation. As Darrell Cabey's civil trial lawyer Ron Kuby most bluntly asked and then observed:

> What black defendant in the history of this country ever got a jury like this? . . . [Goetz] gives a confession on video tape after surrendering himself and the jury disregards it saying, "He was nervous, he was disturbed, and so we are going to disregard his confession." And there was [even] an eyewitness that corroborates most of that confession, [but] the jury says, "Well there are some inconsistencies so we are going to disregard the testimony of that eyewitness." No black defendant in the history of this country ever got a jury like this.[49]

NYPD Police Commissioner Benjamin Ward was also taken aback. "I have never [in] all my legal history heard of a judge changing his charge to the jury three times in one case." But Crane did, and therefore, Ward said, the jury got it wrong—and "when juries are wrong, the judge has an obligation to set aside the verdict, but [Crane] did not."[50]

But as the majority of the eyewitnesses in this case had made clear, the boys Goetz gunned down had not tried to rob him. The cumulative testimony of eyewitnesses described a scene in which Goetz may have had reason to be irritated, and maybe even nervous, given his past mugging and subsequent ideas about Black youth writ large. But at no point did Goetz have reason to think that his life was threatened.

That didn't matter. As Carolyn Perlmuth put it, "Nobody thought he was guilty from the beginning."[51]

While he was not typically a fan of the DA's office, even famed radical defense lawyer William Kunstler found himself reaching out to Greg Waples shortly after the sentence was rendered. He offered Waples support, writing, "You were fighting forces so primordial that even if Christ, Mohammed and Buddha had entered the courtroom and demanded guilty verdicts, they would have been hard to come by."[52]

It was Kunstler along with his young law partner Ron Kuby who would now take center stage in what had become an uphill and years-long effort to secure some measure of justice for the boys that Bernie Goetz had gunned down way back on December 22, 1984.

Now that the criminal trial had ended, Kunstler and Kuby could finally take Darrell Cabey's suit against Bernie Goetz to civil court. This lawsuit, which Shirley Cabey had filed on his behalf in 1985, had spent years in limbo while the criminal proceedings were underway. During this prolonged wait, Darrell's legal advocates had been preparing for the moment when their client's story would finally be heard. In fact, they could not wait to get on with it.

PART V

Justice Served Cold

By the late 1980s, everyday life in America had come to feel like a trip through the looking glass—both thrilling and terrifying, depending on who you were.

Youth from the suburbs, those who drank Long Island Iced Teas and spent summers driving to the Jersey Shore with Bon Jovi blasting, still dreamed of the glitzy life they could have if they just moved to a NYC loft. Hip-hop anthems like Bobby Brown's "My Prerogative," as well as the audacious lyrics and personal style of Salt-N-Pepa, Madonna, and Janet Jackson, were doing their part to inspire city kids as well to chase bigger and bolder lives.

And yet, so much that had been promised to their generation—the success as well as the excess—was starting to unravel. The greed-induced savings and loan crisis, Michael Milken's brazen securities fraud scandal, and unwelcome nosebleeds that came from the life of clubs and cocaine signaled the beginning of the end.[1] Debt was accumulating, interest rates were rising, and a new recession surely loomed.

Meanwhile, Reagan's War on Drugs also escalated dramatically with the Omnibus Anti-Drug Abuse Act of 1988. Despite the name, this legislation did little to alleviate suffering, instead introducing but more criminalization—mandatory minimum sentences for first-time crack offenses, provisions denying benefits to individuals convicted of drug offenses more generally, and worse. At the state level, prison populations had only continued to soar, as did rates of addiction and crime.

In fact, the more the drug trade had been criminalized during the

1980s, the more violent it had become, just as had been the case when alcohol was outlawed during Prohibition.[2] Of the 414 homicides that took place in New York City from March through October 1988, nearly 40 percent "involved territorial disputes, assaults to collect debts, robberies of drug dealers, and similar circumstances." Of those drug-related murders, 84 percent involved cocaine in some form, and nearly 60 percent specifically involved its most heavily criminalized derivative, crack.[3]

Other crimes, especially those that were both brutal and highly racialized, had also continued to make the headlines. In 1989, two particularly violent incidents—the vicious murder of sixteen-year-old Yusef Hawkins by a mob of white teens, as well as a horrific attack on a white female jogger in Central Park purportedly by a group of Black teens—would inflame passions, stoke prejudices, and further fuel the rise of the conservative media. As it turned out, Bernie Goetz's shootings had unleashed and normalized a new era of racialized rage.

Over the course of the next decade, the drug war would only intensify, racial tensions would escalate, and while few were paying attention, the wealthy would set about reshaping the city in unprecedented ways, through both criminalization and gentrification.

Meanwhile, the city courts would see an explosion of cases—not just criminal cases, but increasingly also those filed by New Yorkers seeking financial remedy for rights that had been violated, harms that had been caused, or contracts that had been breached.[4]

The civil courts were in fact the last hope of those New Yorkers whose faith in the criminal court system had been utterly betrayed.

34

In for a Penny

Although Bernie Goetz did not succeed in overturning his guilty verdict for illegal gun possession, his decision to appeal had allowed him to stay well away from any prison cell for several years. During that time, he tended to hole up in his 14th Street apartment—not because he was hated but because he was beloved and always mobbed for autographs and accolades.

On one occasion, Bernie thrilled his fans and the media alike when he unexpectedly stepped out onto a rear balcony of his apartment building, peered over with a camera at his eye, and snapped a photo of the crowd below. A cheer went up before Goetz promptly headed back inside.[1] Another time, when he received the Good Samaritans award celebrating him, a group of bikini-clad women who called themselves "Bernie's Girls" showered him with attention.[2]

That said, Bernie was not lacking for company or support even within the familiar surroundings of his gadget-filled apartment. In its ongoing coverage of Bernie's post-trial life, the *Post* reported that his neighbors dropped by regularly with meals and "words of encouragement." On at least one occasion he opened his door to nine members of the Guardian Angels, led by Curtis Sliwa himself, who was there to remind Goetz "that the people are behind him" and "we have a headquarters right nearby" should he need anything.[3]

Meanwhile, over at the 14th Street subway station, less than a hundred feet from where Bernie lived, the man selling subway tokens was so pleased about the verdict that he had "scrawled on a message board in his booth 'Goetz Acquitted!'"[4]

Bernhard Goetz poses with some of "Bernie's Girls" in Queens.
AP Photo/David Bookstaver

The Goetz verdict had been a hot "conversation on the playgrounds and corners" of the South Bronx's housing projects. Shirley's neighbors were as upset by the outcome as she had been and were generous with their love and support. When she went out, the *Post* reported, Shirley Cabey would get a hug or see heads shaking in disbelief and sympathy. One neighbor who lived in her building asked a journalist, "How can you not convict Goetz for shooting Darrell twice? Goetz had a malicious intent to hurt him. That is not self-defense."[5]

Darrell's grandma, Nora Smoot, had always known that Goetz would somehow get off "scot-free," she told the *Post*. Though she too was appalled by the verdict, she counseled her family to leave it in God's hands because he was the ultimate jury. She had faith that "God would take care of us and Goetz."[6] And while Darrell had shown no real emotion when she told him of the verdict, in his characteristic fashion, he did express worry about what it would mean for his mother. He knew how much it upset her when the press crowded around their building.

But although Shirley felt like the system "only works one way," it did not break her. She had agreed with her mother that "what verdict he don't get down here, he will get when he meet his master upstairs. So, I'm not worried. I'm not worried." That said, Shirley also had a plan for making sure that Goetz would face the true costs—emotional and financial—of what he had done to her son in this lifetime.[7]

As Bernie Goetz was basking in the glow of his celebrity, Darrell was being transported to a rehabilitation center every day of the week for physical therapy. On the weekends, he took a break from this routine and tended to stay in the apartment with his siblings, watching horror movies on video.[8] Attending to Darrell's intense medical needs, while continuing to raise the rest of her kids, put a significant emotional and financial strain on Shirley Cabey.

In January 1985, when Shirley had been forced to quit her highly coveted state job to take care of her son, she'd still had Medicaid, as well as the Social Security checks she received for being a widow. Her rent was also subsidized. But providing for her family was expensive. Reaganomics may have promised that it would curb inflation and reduce the cost of living, but prices had continued to rise, while cuts to benefits had only deepened. Even before Darrell was shot, 46 percent of Americans polled by the Pew Research Center in March 1983 had said "their personal financial situation had gotten worse."[9]

For all of these reasons, Shirley, like Troy Canty, had been deeply relieved to learn about the Crime Victims Board. Due to the law establishing the board, she could potentially receive reimbursement for "out-of-pocket expenses, including indebtedness reasonably incurred for medical or other services necessary as a result of the injury upon which the claim is based," as well as, even more significantly, "loss of earnings or support resulting from such injury."[10]

Shirley Cabey had also applied for these funds back in January 1985, one week after Darrell fell into a coma.[11] She hoped the process would be rather straightforward: Her son had suffered a catastrophic injury at the hands of a NYC resident and, as the rules clearly outlined, this body could award financial support to "victims of crime," or to "a parent, guardian, brother, or sister of a child victim of a crime."[12] But when the board issued its decision on December 12, 1985, nearly a year after the incident, Shirley was profoundly disappointed. The claim was closed "without prejudice," to be reconsidered only after the criminal case against "the alleged perpetrator" Bernie Goetz had been decided.[13]

The board would take nearly a full year after the criminal trial ended to review the claim, following up with Shirley on June 23, 1988. This time, the ruling was even more upsetting. Not only did it determine that Darrell was ineligible to receive funds, but it also claimed that Darrell was no more a victim than Troy Canty was. He had, the board maintained, "contributed to the infliction of his injuries and was not the innocent victim of crime."[14]

Unwilling to give up, Shirley enlisted the aid of William Kunstler, the attorney who was already working on a civil suit against Goetz on Darrell's behalf, to appeal the decision. In a written statement and at an in-person hearing in December 1988, Kunstler articulated the many ways that Darrell had not been the aggressor in the encounter with his assailant and had, in fact, been targeted by him—as Goetz himself had corroborated.

On February 7, 1989, one month after Goetz was resentenced to a full year in jail, the Crime Victims Board made its final determination: Darrell Cabey would not get a dime. It had taken umbrage at "some of the 'facts' that Shirley Cabey was alleging in her appeal, including that Goetz had shot Darrell twice and that Darrell was not, himself, a criminal."[15]

According to the board's written decision, it appeared "from all evidence" that Darrell "certainly had the propensity to participate in the crime that was perpetrated on Bernhard Goetz." The board identified the four teens as "criminals acting in concert when they attempted to rob Mr. Goetz" because they were "travelling together." Therefore, Darrell's injuries were the result of his own conduct, and he "was not the innocent victim of a crime."[16]

There was much irony here. The Crime Victims Board was ostensibly comprised of some of the most victim-sympathetic New Yorkers in city government, yet they were clearly biased against Darrell and the other boys who'd been injured by Goetz. It could not be ignored that the board had been additionally funded by the Reagan White House as a way to deal with the crime crisis in America, as the federal government saw it.[17] And, of course, the members of this board were immersed in the same New York tabloid media environment as Mark Lesly and the other jurors in Goetz's criminal trial.

While it was true that crime was on the rise generally, the media tended to obfuscate or ignore two key facts. The first was that some of the most egregious crimes—homicides, for example—had "lower rates of commission by African Americans than European Americans through most of our nation's history," according to a report by the esteemed National Academies. Second, Black and Brown Americans were becoming increasingly likely to experience crime from rage-filled whites, as had Darrell. As one analyst noted, there had in fact been "a dramatic increase in bias related crimes since 1985."[18]

IN 1989, HOWEVER, one particularly violent crime would blind much of the nation to these troubling realities. One evening in April, a twenty-eight-year-old white woman named Trisha Meili was assaulted while jogging in Central Park, beaten and raped so violently that she fell into a coma for twelve days. Although it took police several days to piece together her movements that night, they wasted little time in apprehending a group of Black and Latino teens who had been in the park around the time of the attack. The police succeeded in coercing "confessions" out of all the boys, who came to be known collectively as "the Central Park Five."[19]

While these teens would be exonerated decades later, at the time there was no public ambivalence about locking them up and throwing away the key. Riding—and fueling—the racially charged calls for the Central Park Five to be behind bars for life, real estate mogul and NYC personality Donald Trump paid $85,000 to place full-page ads in four papers, including the *Daily News,* calling for the return of the death penalty in New York. This had been terrifying, one of the accused recalled. "I knew that this famous person calling for us to die was very serious. . . . We were all afraid. Our families were afraid. Our loved ones were afraid. For us to walk around as if we had a target on our backs."[20] Surprising no one, this group of fourteen-, fifteen-, and sixteen-year-olds were all found guilty of charges including attempted murder, assault, and sodomy.[21]

A mere four months after the attack on Trisha Meili, another brutal crime took place, one that was also vicious but would make far less of a mark on the nation's narratives about crime and punishment. That August, a mob of nearly thirty white individuals, armed with baseball bats and a gun, attacked sixteen-year-old Yusef Hawkins along with his younger brother and two friends in Brooklyn's Bensonhurst neighborhood. Hawkins was shot and killed by one of the attackers, but there would be no full-page ads calling for the return of the death penalty, nor any media commentary suggesting that he had been attacked by "animals." City officials nevertheless feared that this time a full-scale riot might erupt. As they well knew, too many Black New Yorkers had by then lost all faith that any justice for Hawkins might be had in the courts, particularly in the wake of the Bernie Goetz trial.

Only reinforcing this lack of confidence, just a month after Hawkins's vicious murder, Bernie Goetz was released from prison after his stunningly short sentence. As the *Post* reported: "Prisoner 78900316" had dined on a "final supper in the Brooklyn House of Detention for Men

Protest against the killing of Yusef Hawkins by a mob of white teens from Bensonhurst, Brooklyn. Photo by Ricky Flores

Bensonhurst residents hold up watermelons to mock Black protesters who took to the streets of this largely white neighborhood following the acquittal of Keith Mondello in the shooting death of sixteen-year-old Yusef Hawkins, May 19, 1990. Photo by Ricky Flores

[of] pork chops, potatoes, collard greens, fruit, and Kool-Aid." Before being transferred to this facility, at Rikers Bernie had earned $42 for three weeks of work in the prison radio shop. He spent half of this money in the commissary, so now he was returning home "$22 richer, a polished chess player—and an angry man."[22]

Perhaps motivated by the public's reaction to the so-called Central Park Five and the killing of Yusef Hawkins, and likely angry that Bernie Goetz was already out of jail and enjoying a comfortable transition back into society, Shirley Cabey and Bill Kunstler refused to give up fighting for Darrell's right to receive compensation from the Crime Victims Board. They filed a case against the board that then involved the New York State Attorney General's Office.[23] In Kunstler's view, racism and classism had "played an enormous role" in the public's understanding of Darrell's situation—from the jurors in the criminal case, to white people in general, to this board specifically—and he was going to fight it.[24]

Throughout this long and complex battle, Darrell's medical records had been newly scrutinized and affidavits had been entered, from Shirley Cabey as well as various board members about how they had come to their original conclusion.

Angelo Petromelis, who had worked for the board for more than two decades, had authored the Cabey decision. In his affidavit, Petromelis noted that the board had questioned from the beginning whether Darrell was really a crime victim. Since the jury had acquitted Goetz of all but one charge—essentially declaring that the shooting "was not a crime but rather a justifiable act," regardless of the serious, permanent injuries it had caused Darrell Cabey—it was a seemingly simple choice for the board to reject the claim.[25]

Ultimately, however, none of Kunstler's efforts on Shirley and Darrell's behalf paid off. The state Attorney General's Office determined that Shirley's complaint against the board was "unsubstantiated and without foundation."[26] She would get nothing.

This was a major blow for Shirley and the Cabey family. The bashing of Darrell's character in the press had been hard to take; the hate mail flooding her mailbox had been terrifying. But the Crime Victims Board's unequivocal acceptance of the view that Darrell Cabey was responsible for his own paralysis emphasized just how important Goetz's acquittal in court had been. It forever legitimized his actions—officially, and on the record—because in its opinion, her son had, in effect, asked for this violent reaction. In commenting on the board's decision, the *Post* reminded its readers that only "a blameless crime victim can seek reimbursement."[27]

At least Shirley had had the foresight to file that civil case against Bernie Goetz back in 1985, one that could net her monetary damages for what he had done to Darrell. According to the tabloids, however, Goetz was now broke. As one *Post* columnist bemoaned, "He hasn't worked much since the incident. His only suit is the one he wore to the trial," and he even lived in a rent-stabilized apartment.[28] But it seemed possible that he had money squirreled away somewhere.

At the very least, Shirley hoped that the civil trial would allow her son's story to be told in open court, and thus, his name could be cleared. But if any of these hopes were to materialize, the trial would actually have to happen.

35

A Different Kind of Case

WAITING ON THE civil suit to wend its way through the system was its own excruciating process. Ultimately, it would take more than a decade for the case that Shirley Cabey had filed on behalf of her son to come to trial.

For starters, each of the shooting victims who had sued Bernie Goetz was forced to wait until the criminal court case was resolved. That took four years. Second, the rules of evidence are different in civil court. The inciting event of the case is of less importance than what happened as a consequence of that event, meaning that the plaintiff's and defendant's legal teams had to go through a tedious and time-consuming process of gathering and analyzing medical and financial records, as well as trying to take the deposition statements of anyone who could speak to the question of damages or lack thereof.

What's more, for years, Goetz had tried to have all of the cases filed against him by the teens consolidated into just one, which Darrell's attorneys fought. But despite Kunstler's strident objections to linking his client with the other two plaintiffs, Troy and James, arguing that doing so would cause "overwhelming prejudice" against Darrell, Judge Edith Miller would accede to Goetz's request a few years later.[1] Goetz's real goal was to get the case dismissed altogether, and five years later he would achieve at least partial victory in that regard.[2] Troy Canty's case would be dismissed on September 11, 1995, for "failing to move forward in any proactive way."[3] A week later, on September 18, James Ramseur's case was also dismissed, likely for similar reasons, as he had filed without legal support.[4]

Darrell Cabey's attorneys, Kunstler and Kuby, would stay the course. The suit they filed in January 1985 had asserted that Darrell had suffered damages that were remediable under the law, due to the "serious and imminent bodily harm" that Goetz had intentionally caused him, thereby violating Darrell's civil rights.[5] The suit also cited the harm done by "numerous death threats and other hate mail," providing examples such as:

> "I'm glad Daryl is paralyzed he need to sit his black ass in a wheelchair for the rest of his life. I'm sorry that the others can't join him."
>
> "I guess you won't be break dancing anymore. Don't worry, if you're a good boy, I'll buy you a pair of roller skates."
>
> "Beware, there is another nut out there who may just harm your family to I am not kidding try me."[6]

There would be myriad legal and logistical challenges to keeping this case alive, and at least in the early years, they had help from attorneys Randolph Scott-McLaughlin, Betty Lawrence Bailey, and C. Vernon Mason of the Center for Constitutional Rights—as well as funding from the CCR itself. This group of lawyers divided the many early aspects of trial preparation, including case research, preparing for depositions, and reviewing transcripts from the various criminal proceedings, all while those were still taking place.

The rules of a civil trial allowed the plaintiffs' lawyers more freedoms than the DA had been allowed in the criminal trial. As attorney Ron Kuby explained later, "We could talk about it with the press, [and] could get access to information that we might not otherwise have through the discovery process."[7] Goetz's confession would also be admissible in a civil case, which was good news for the plaintiffs since, as Kuby put it, he "had been absolutely loquacious in his various confessions. So, we had a good body of material."[8] More important, they could compel Bernie Goetz himself to take the stand as a witness and cross-examine him in front of a jury.

Years later, Greg Waples still wished that he had been able to get Goetz on the stand, that he "had been able to say, 'Your Honor, the people call Bernhard Goetz as our last witness.'" As he recalled, "I believed in my heart of hearts that if Bernie were called as a prosecution witness, he would affirm the accuracy of everything that he said in the audio tape [and] in the videotape." Barry Slotnick seemed to agree that it would have been a game changer. When asked, "Would you [have] let him testify as a prosecution witness?" he replied, "Of course not."[9]

Bill Kunstler and Ron Kuby had other advantages compared to Greg Waples, specifically because the criminal case had preceded theirs. Thanks to Waples, who had promised to "safeguard" all of the physical evidence and testimonies from the criminal trial, Kunstler and Kuby had Waples's thorough argument in front of them as they prepared to go to court.[10] They began to consider what additional material might prove useful, who to consult—and what questions to ask them—both in depositions and on the stand.

What's more, Darrell Cabey's lawyers had chosen to file in Bronx County rather than in New York County, where the borough of Manhattan was located, which clearly unnerved Goetz. He was eager to get the trial over with, but only if he could change the venue back to Manhattan, where he felt more confident in the jury he might face.

The *New York Post* was firmly on his side in this regard. There was no question, one of its articles opined, that this venue indicated that William Kunstler was "planning to employ an ugly courtroom strategy. He obviously intends to play upon racial tensions to secure a hefty settlement for his client."[11]

Bernie had tried once before to get the case into a Manhattan courtroom, with no success. Among other things, he claimed to be "too fearful to ride [the] subway" and could not afford to take a "taxi to the Bronx from his Manhattan residence." Kunstler immediately fought back, insisting that Goetz's arguments for venue change were "entirely specious."[12] Indeed, he wrote sarcastically, if Goetz had "any fears whatsoever" about riding the D train to 161st Street, "just two blocks from the courthouse," Kunstler was "sure that the Guardian Angels, who have pledged to support him, will furnish guards to ensure his safety as undoubtedly will Brooklyn CORE which has made the same assurance."[13]

The judge hearing these motions ruled that the trial would stay in the Bronx. While it was true that the demographics of the Bronx meant that the prospective jurors were more likely to be Black and Latino, it was also logical and customary to file a civil case where the plaintiff, not the defendant, resided.

Bernie, however, was unwilling to let this go. Failing to see the irony that he was seeking to change venue because he wanted a jury with more whites, he would continue to insist that it was "intolerable" and "unconstitutional" for him to be tried in a county chosen for its "racial composition."[14] But the judge ultimately assigned to this case, Judge Barry Salman, would not budge. It was clear to him that it would be a much greater hardship for Darrell Cabey to commute into Manhattan than for Goetz to come into the Bronx. The trial would stay in the Bronx.

36

Tit for Tat

HAVING FAILED TO dismiss the case that Darrell Cabey had filed against him or move it back to Manhattan, Bernie Goetz opted for a strategy of obstruction. The *New York Post* heralded this decision with the headline "NO-SHOW BERNIE STARTS 50M STIR."[1] He began by refusing all attempts for the plaintiff to get him into a deposition. He would move on to suing his suers, and finally, he would do everything in his power to further discredit Darrell Cabey.

Goetz particularly resented having to answer to Darrell's attorneys in a deposition setting. As he well knew, depositions were essential in civil cases. It was at this stage where each side could get information they would need to argue their cases most effectively when the trial began, and in that sense, it resembled the discovery process in a criminal trial. But every time they tried to depose him, Bernie steadfastly refused to cooperate. Darrell's attorneys were able to get him into just two depositions over ten years, and both times it required no small measure of legal strong-arming to get him to show up.

The first of these depositions took place in April 1985. This process had become so fraught that Judge Salman, who had to issue an order for Bernie's compliance, also decided to preside over the deposition in order "to cut the garbage," as Ron Kuby put it.[2] Scott-McLaughlin and Mason handled this deposition, with the main goal being to establish some key pieces of information related to the monetary damages they would be seeking on Darrell's behalf.

This required, among other things, establishing where Goetz in fact lived and worked (NYC or Florida), as well as the nature of his assets. They already knew that he'd inherited a substantial sum of money from his late father, Bernhard Sr., and that he was listed as a vice president of one of the family companies in Florida. Other than confirming that he had residential addresses in both Florida and New York, and that his apartment was full of furniture, equipment, and gadgets of little obvious value, this first deposition was not particularly illuminating, at least on the monetary questions.[3]

On the other hand, in the process of questioning Bernie about where he actually resided, Scott-McLaughlin and Mason had at least been able to get him on the record regarding his longstanding fixation on crime and blight. Bernie talked about the various neighborhood improvement organizations he'd joined in the past, such as the Courtney House Tenants Association and FAB-14.[4] He also revealed that he had signed as many as ten petitions "in connection with issues involving the 14th Street area."[5]

It wasn't long before Darrell's attorneys requested that Bernie sit for a second deposition. He would fight this one even more vigorously—and largely without the help of his original legal counsel, Joseph Kelner. While Kelner had stepped away from Bernie's criminal defense, he had, for a time, agreed to help him in this civil matter.

Goetz claimed that he had decided to fire Kelner, but court records indicate that the attorney petitioned to be let off the case in 1988 after representing Bernie for three years, and after having "performed voluminous services" on his behalf. Kelner stated that his client had been wholly "uncooperative" and often was "unavailable," making it impossible for him and his associates to do the job being asked of them.[6] From that point on, Goetz's primary representation in the legal wrangling leading up to the civil trial would be himself.

It would take a full five years and eventually the threat of legal sanctions to get Bernie Goetz into another deposition. In their paperwork, Kunstler and Kuby cited his "repeated failure to appear for deposition," and called his claims that both "medical and financial hardship" were preventing him from appearing "absurd."[7] In January 1990, Goetz, now undergoing radiation treatment for testicular cancer, insisted that he could not attend a deposition. But since he was making that argument while in Judge Salman's very courtroom, the judge ruled that he could in fact be deposed.[8]

Not until September 24, 1990, would Darrell's lawyers finally have another opportunity to question the defendant under oath. This round, however, proved quite valuable to their case.[9]

By focusing their questions on Bernie's actions leading up to the shooting, they confirmed that he was prone to using racial epithets and did so without apology. For example, Kuby asked Goetz, did he say at a local community meeting "The only way we are going to clean up the street is to get rid of the sp—s and n—s?" Goetz bluntly responded, "Yes I did."[10]

Their line of questioning about the shooting itself proved to be even more damning. Because the scene on the train was "somewhat of a blur," Bernie said, he couldn't be sure of "their exact positions," with one exception: "The only person I know the exact position [of] was the person I fired the last shot at."[11]

Everyone in the room looked stunned. This was not a man offering up a confession in a fugue state after days on the lam, saying what he only wished he had done in the moment. As it turned out, and as Greg Waples had maintained at the criminal trial, Goetz was an entirely reliable witness to his own actions on the day he shot four teens on that downtown-bound 2 train.

In this deposition, Goetz continued to explain that the last person "did not appear to be seriously injured," and so he had "walked directly in front of that person, put the gun in his ribs, and pulled the trigger again with the words, 'you don't look too bad, here's another.'"[12]

"What was that?" Kunstler asked pointedly, to ensure that Goetz's words would be crystal clear on the transcript.

"I fired again with the words, 'You don't look too bad, here's another,'" Goetz repeated.[13]

As they left this proceeding, Darrell's lawyers could barely contain their disgust. "I hope the jurors in that trial wake up screaming in the night when they read this," Kunstler exclaimed, reminding everyone how "defense attorney Barry Slotnick [had] argued at Goetz's criminal trial that his client 'fantasized' making that statement in the subway car."[14]

Once again, Bernie was headline news, at least sort of. Whereas the Associated Press wrote, "Subway gunman Bernhard Goetz's sworn version of the day he shot four teens . . . drastically contradicts the defense that won him acquittal on attempted murder charges in 1987," the *New York Post* downplayed this stunning revelation by burying the story, first

Bernhard Goetz points to his back in Bronx State Supreme Court in New York, indicating where he shot Darrell Cabey.
AP Photo/Charles Arrigo

in a small column on page 8 of its September 25, 1990, edition and then by reprinting the AP story days after it circulated, and well inside the paper, under its own small-font headline, "Goetz Flips His Version of Subway Shooting."[15]

For his part, Goetz seemed unconcerned by the stir he had caused, largely preoccupied as he still was with finding a way to go after Darrell's lawyers. Perhaps seeking an opening to get the civil trial postponed—or canceled altogether—Goetz first made multiple attempts to file disciplinary charges against the Cabeys' lawyers with the state of New York. For example, he filed a series of disciplinary charges against Kuby and Kunstler that cited a poem Kunstler had published that Bernie felt had slandered him, as well as separate television appearances in which Kunstler and Kuby had each commented on ongoing civil litigation (which, in a civil trial, is not unethical or illegal).[16]

Ultimately, however, Goetz's attempts to take on his opponents in this manner did not net him much. The Departmental Disciplinary Committee quickly rejected Bernie's poetry complaint but did review the television appearances. Only one claim, regarding a statement Kunstler had made on a local show in which he said "Goetz went patrolling the subway for two years waiting for trouble," actually got a hearing in committee. Kunstler defended himself with the arguments that his utterances had been factual, and that they were protected by the First Amendment. The body hearing the complaint ultimately agreed that Kunstler's statement was "not actionable by this committee."[17]

Undaunted, on January 9, 1990, Bernie went on to file a civil suit seeking a total of $40 million in compensatory and punitive damages from eight defendants—Darrell and Shirley Cabey and their entire legal team.

Notably, when it came to Bernie's turn in the civil courts, the tabloid media would give him a measure of grace not afforded to the teens he had shot when they had taken legal action against him. For example, after Goetz's victims sued him, the *Post*'s editorial board called for aggressive efforts to initiate major tort reform in the state but completely ignored the fact that Bernie had in turn filed numerous cases against them.[18]

In this filing, Goetz demanded $5 million each from Kunstler, Kuby, Darrell Cabey, Shirley Cabey, the Center for Constitutional Rights, and "attorneys Betty Lawrence Bailey, C. Vernon Mason, and Randolph Scott-McLaughlin, formerly or at that time associated with that organization."[19]

The allegations in this suit were wide-ranging and included that Kunstler et al. were engaged in "malicious prosecution" and abuse of the legal system by filing a lawsuit that "they knew or should have known . . . was frivolous and non-meritorious." The defendants had conspired to "defraud" Goetz, the suit continued, by presenting Darrell "to the public and the press" as "a mental vegetable" (with the additional note that "The 'mental vegetable' claim . . . is unsubstantiated and is false"). Finally, it stated that the defendants had inflicted "serious emotional distress" on Goetz via their lawsuit, their fraud, and their "false, malicious, libelous and slanderous representations [of Goetz] to the public and the press."[20]

In the same suit, Goetz claimed to have been both libeled and slandered—in court memoranda, in a poem published in the *Amsterdam News,* and in interviews with the press. He also provided a list of "misrepresentations," including:

> That Goetz was a walking time-bomb and a racist.
> That Goetz was a coward when he did not have a gun.
> That Goetz did not show up for a deposition because he was a coward.
> That Goetz had no intention of answering the lawsuit filed by Darrell Cabey.[21]

When the defendants responded with their own motion to dismiss, Goetz was not deterred. He was convinced that the Cabeys could afford to be sued because "a wealthy organization"—the Center for Constitutional Rights—was paying their legal expenses. He himself was "virtually without funds" and "did not inherit $140 thousand." He also declared that Kunstler was "a millionaire who sends his children to private school and owns a house in Greenwich Village in New York City and a coop in Condado, Puerto Rico," notwithstanding the fact that Darrell's lawyers' finances had no bearing on whether Bernie Goetz would owe him damages.[22]

A few years later, when none of his prior legal moves had borne fruit, Bernie decided to sue Kunstler and the publisher of his recent autobiography, in which he discussed the Goetz shootings and case.[23] Kunstler's *My Life as a Radical Lawyer* (1994) clearly enraged Goetz. He sued for $30 million, claiming "that passages in the book injured his 'good name, reputation, feelings and public standing.'" He took particular umbrage at Kunstler's characterization of him as being "paranoid" and having "venomous feelings against black people."[24]

In response, Kunstler and Kuby issued a press release quoting Goetz's September 1990 deposition, in which he admitted to stating that "the only way we are going to clean up this street is to get rid of the sp—s and n—s" at a building meeting, noting that "most people would find that statement venomous." They successfully filed a motion to dismiss on the grounds that "Truth is a defense."[25]

Thwarted in every attempt to undermine the civil suit against him, Goetz decided to go for the jugular. As a defendant representing himself, he was in fact empowered legally to demand discovery and take depositions, and so he would insist on deposing Shirley Cabey as well as the young man he had stood over and shot, her son Darrell.

It was perhaps ironic that Bernie would try to use the deposition process that he had resisted at every turn to his own advantage. But in his view, a deposition would be the best way to reveal exactly how "damaged" Darrell Cabey really was, since the lawsuit hinged on whether Goetz was responsible for Darrell's current condition. In fact, Bernie Goetz decided to make Darrell's mental and physical disabilities—specifically the idea that Darrell was somehow faking the severity of his condition—a cornerstone of his defense.

37

Dirty Tricks

BERNIE HAD BEEN taunting all of his victims well before he turned his attention so singularly to Darrell, as was clear when he had received the Good Samaritans award and had "shot from the lip" and "sarcastically thanked the four youths he wounded"—James Ramseur, specifically, for "making a monkey out of himself in court"—to the applause of the group assembled. When the *New York Post* had covered that event back in 1988, under the rather gleeful header "GOETZ TAKES AIM AT 'VICTIMS' AGAIN," the paper noted that Bernie had been thanked at this event for "courageously wasting [those] four criminals."[1]

Now, though, Goetz began targeting Darrell Cabey specifically for, as a piece in the *Post* put it, perpetuating the "charade" designed to shield him from his own legal liability.[2] The UPI news service picked up on this unseemly legal strategy, distributing an article to hundreds of newspapers nationwide that described how "Subway gunman Bernhard Goetz" claimed that "one of the four youths he shot is not the 'mental vegetable' he claims to be and his fifty million dollar lawsuit should be dismissed and his lawyer disbarred."[3] The *Post* also ran its own piece with the rather charged but straightforward headline "GOETZ: VICTIM ISN'T A 'MENTAL VEGETABLE.'"[4]

Darrell's lawyer Ron Kuby could only marvel at Goetz's gall and vitriol. As he put it, "From the beginning of the case Bernhard Goetz has manifested a murderous and sadistic hatred of Darrell Cabey."[5] William Kunstler likewise identified Goetz's contention that Darrell's mental status was a "fraud" as Goetz's particular hobby horse.[6]

Bernie wanted to prove this contention via a deposition, but therein lay the rub. If Darrell was in fact mentally incapacitated, he could not be deposed.

Of course, during the criminal trial, not only had expert witnesses for the prosecution testified that Darrell was unfit to take the stand, but neurologist Dr. Claude Macaluso had also been clear that "there is no way to determine when, if ever, [Darrell's] conditions will improve." Indeed, in Macaluso's medical judgment, trying to involve Cabey in any legal proceeding would be "potentially dangerous," because it "could cause him to further withdraw mentally and could jeopardize the progress that Mr. Cabey has made thus far." What's more, it was highly "unlikely that Mr. Cabey would be able to understand the proceedings."[7]

In the ensuing years, Darrell's post-coma brain trauma had not much improved. It was hard to imagine that Bernie Goetz would be able to compel him to sit for a deposition. Not to mention, from the perspective of Darrell's lawyers, how obscene it would be for him to be questioned by the man who had paralyzed him for life.

To ensure that he would be able to do exactly that, Bernie had a plan.

Unbeknownst to anyone, in 1989, Bernie Goetz had hired a private investigator named Harry Katz to find some dirt on his now-archnemesis, Darrell Cabey. Specifically, he asked Katz to come up with a way to catch him in the act of faking his injuries.

Darrell had been going to the United Cerebral Palsy Center (UCPC) daily for rehabilitation services since shortly after he came home from the hospital. The more skills he could learn to control his wheelchair, feed or bathe himself, or even potentially change his own catheter, the more likely he would be able to care for himself when Shirley was no longer alive. With his rehabilitation plan, there was also hope that he could regain some of his cognitive abilities and learn to speak more clearly.

To start, however, the wish list was much more basic. Darrell needed to relearn how to execute the simplest tasks—like taking a drink on his own—because the damage to his spinal cord had left his arm movements spastic and unreliable.

To that end, Shirley was deeply grateful for this resource. A bus picked Darrell up outside his apartment complex in the Bronx and took him to the facility, where he would spend "hours doing simple repetitive tasks—sometimes successfully, sometimes not." As Shirley explained, in this building, Darrell was "learning new things all over again," and although he was definitely making strides, their daily lives were by no means "the same" as they had been.[8]

Meanwhile, Bernie Goetz's investigator, Katz, had come up with a few schemes to "prove" that Darrell was a fraud. The first involved impersonating a physician and calling Darrell on the phone at the UCPC, surreptitiously recording him, to see if he could trip him up.[9]

"Hi Darrell, how are you? This is Dr. Schwartz," Katz opened, and then proceeded to pepper the obviously confused young man with questions, ranging from "You know what I heard on the radio today?" to "Uh, they said that Bernhard Goetz has less than two months to live. He's going to die from the cancer. What do you think about that?" to "You know how long it's been already since you got shot? I think it's been, what is it, three years?" to what did Darrell's friends call him, and what did he have for lunch?[10]

Perhaps frustrated by the fact that this yielded him nothing of value, Harry Katz then decided to secrete himself outside of the Daniel Webster Homes, where Darrell still lived, and follow him to the rehabilitation center. Katz then entered the building under the guise of seeking a placement for his brother, "Robert," who was too afraid to come to the center. He began questioning staff, other patients, and Darrell himself, all the while video-recording these interactions for delivery to Bernie Goetz.

On this tape, staff and patients alike tried genuinely to help Katz, oblivious to the fact that they were being baited and conned.[11] Over the course of his visit, Katz asked everyone—from Carlos the workshop manager to other disabled persons—a barrage of odd questions, though it was obvious that he was not actually listening to anyone's attempts to assure him that his brother would absolutely be well taken care of, that people were friendly, that he had nothing to fear, and that the food was pretty good too.

Katz's actual goal was to slowly work his way to the area where Darrell sat in his wheelchair, dressed neatly in a sweater and slacks. His hair was cleanly cut, and he was looking curiously at Katz with a hesitant smile on his face. Once more, tape still running, Katz opened the conversation with the same questions he had been asking everyone else. Darrell tried his best to follow what this man was asking and to give him responses that would please him, and to offer reassurances that his brother would be treated well at this facility.

"He was afraid to come, he said. He's afraid." Katz stuttered nervously, "Should, should, should my brother Robert be afraid?"

"I don't think so," Darrell replied, smiling reassuringly but also obviously uncertain why he was being queried.

"Is anybody gonna hurt him?" Katz pushed.

"Not that I know of." Darrell's smile faltered a bit.

Katz searched for ways to keep the conversation going. "Is, is it, are all the teachers, nice and everything? And you think it's a nice place?"

"Yes," Darrell answered, more happily. And then, inviting the other man to feel at ease, he offered, "Check it out yourself. Don't be afraid."[12]

As Katz kept talking, the conversation became increasingly one-sided, and Darrell's answers started to echo Katz's questions. He asked if the teachers were lazy or hardworking, and Darrell simply answered, "Hardworking."[13]

Eventually, Katz began to probe Darrell on current events, asking him about New York City's incoming mayor, David Dinkins, and the mayor he had just succeeded, Ed Koch.

"Did you like Koch? Did you like Koch?" Katz wheedled.

"He was alright . . . He was [unintelligible]," Darrell said uncertainly.

"And how long was Koch mayor for?" Katz pressed.

"For about four or five years?" Darrell asked hesitantly.[14]

"Yeah, for a long time," Katz said, before turning to another disabled man sitting next to Darrell and asking his opinion on the matter. "Melvin?" he asked. Melvin responded, "Twelve years." To which Darrell asked hopefully, as if now knowing the answer Katz wanted to hear, "Twelve years?"[15]

Katz also asked him about the current mayor, Dinkins. "What do you think about Mayor Dinkins? Will he be a good mayor?" To which Darrell could only say, "I wouldn't know." "You know what I predict?" Katz pushed. "I predict he's gonna be an even better mayor than Mayor Koch." "Well, that remains to be seen," Darrell replied, as though it was a stock phrase he'd heard before.[16]

Bernie Goetz considered Katz's tape a smoking gun. He hoped it would persuade Judge Salman to order Darrell to sit for a deposition, and in order to move that process along, Goetz pulled a media-savvy stunt: He held a press conference on the front steps of city hall in Manhattan to announce the existence of the eight-minute tape.[17] Bernie insisted that, contrary to attorney Ronald Kuby's claim to reporters that Darrell "has extremely limited ability to form memories at all, and he's incapable of distinguishing between a general memory and something he has seen on

T.V.," Darrell was "no vegetable."[18] A few days later, Goetz also went public with the audiotape in which Katz had posed as "Dr. Schwartz" when calling Darrell on the phone.[19]

As expected, the *New York Post* showcased Goetz's recordings with two bold headlines, "TAPES SHOW CABEY CAN TESTIFY: GOETZ" and "GOETZ SAYS 2ND TAPE PROVES CABEY FIT TO TESTIFY."[20]

Judge Salman was less than pleased with these antics. He sternly chided Goetz for the unscrupulous way he had obtained the videotape, and ordered him and Katz to stay away from Darrell from then on.[21] As to Goetz's deposition request, Salman declared that he would decide this matter only after securing his own expert evaluation of plaintiff Darrell Cabey, one that would be added to another evaluation submitted the week before by Cabey's lawyers. That assessment had also been conducted by an expert to assess his "ability to provide testimony either in court or by deposition."[22]

For the plaintiffs, Dr. Wayne Gordon, director of the Center for Rehabilitative Medicine at Mount Sinai Medical Center, had examined Darrell Cabey on May 8, 1990, in order to determine the extent of his mental fitness to be questioned in any legal proceeding. Dr. Gordon's evaluations lasted two hours and employed two diagnostic tools—the Galveston Orientation and Amnesia Test (GOAT), which determined a patient's "orientation to time," and the Dementia Rating Scale (DRS), which assessed a patient's "Attention, Initiation/Perseveration, Construction, Conceptualization, and Memory."[23]

The doctor noted that Darrell "was friendly and cooperative," but nevertheless, his scores on both tests indicated a "profoundly impaired mental status." In fact, compared to patients diagnosed with severe senile dementia of the Alzheimer type (SDAT), Darrell's scores were "markedly below those with SDAT."[24]

The details behind Darrell's aggregate scores were sobering. He could not "follow two successive commands, e.g., 'open your mouth and then close your eyes,'" nor could he "copy a square or correctly write his name." He was also unable to "describe the ways in which pairs of simple objects, e.g. 'orange–banana' were alike, even when primed." When asked, Darrell did not know "the day of the week, date, month or year, nor the name of the president, governor, or mayor." And finally, "he was unable to read a list of simple words, or discriminate between words or figures he had been presented from those he had not."[25]

In short, Dr. Gordon concluded, Darrell's "state of severe disorientation and profound cognitive dysfunction would undermine both the validity and reliability of any information he might be able to provide."[26]

In light of these findings, on May 15, 1990, Darrell's attorneys filed a detailed protective order on his behalf to try to head off the deposition, reminding the court that despite Goetz's claims to the contrary, Darrell was still a "crippled and brain-damaged youth whose life he [had] destroyed" and it would be "indecent" for the Court to permit Goetz's proposed deposition.[27]

Unfortunately, this bid to protect their client failed.

JUDGE BARRY SALMAN HAD deemed Gordon's report insufficient to disqualify Darrell from sitting for deposition, which is what led him to call for a second opinion. On June 14, 1990, the court paid for another expert, Dr. Martin Lubin, to evaluate Darrell's mental acuity. Lubin conferred with Dr. Macaluso directly and reviewed "voluminous" records from St. Vincent's Hospital. He also visited the UCPC to speak with staff and meet Darrell in person.[28]

Dr. Lubin's report noted that when Darrell was accepted into the rehab program offered by the UCPC, he had been "tested and found to function in the range of mild retardation." They had created a rehabilitation plan for him accordingly and tried to teach him how to do the basic skills of daily living. Eventually, he was allowed to work in "a sheltered workshop" where he tried to learn "how to take telephone messages."[29]

UCPC staff told Lubin that Darrell "came to work regularly and on time, was responsible, and posed no behavioral difficulties." And, when Dr. Lubin conducted his own assessment, he would indeed find Darrell most affable. But he also found a young person whose speech was thick, whose vocabulary was "primitive," and who "could not recall simple items of information that were repeatedly reinforced such [as Lubin's] name or the date."[30]

What was more, Dr. Lubin noted, Darrell clearly did not know the answers to questions posed to him, even though his desire to be cooperative and polite led him to "sometimes signify that he [did]." For example, when Lubin asked Darrell about the events that had led to his injury or those pertaining to his civil suit against Goetz, he seemed only able to agree to whatever details Lubin had offered. On his own accord, Darrell "could neither provide the name of his attorney, Mr. Kunstler, or the name of the defendant, Mr. Goetz, nor what he was suing for."[31]

Rather mystifyingly, however, Lubin's report to the court declared the question of whether Darrell was competent to be deposed by Bernie Goetz "a very difficult one for me to resolve." His own tests clearly indicated that Darrell's "ability to think and recall [was] very poor." Yet, his report nevertheless concluded that "perhaps" Darrell had "greater ability than the examination conducted by Dr. Gordon" had indicated, and therefore, that he "would probably have the ability to comprehend" should he appear in court.[32]

The court should bear in mind, Lubin conceded, that Darrell's testimony might be of limited value, since he was likely to retain anything asked of him for only "a brief time" and everything would need to be "reinforced." For example, he might have to be told "that he was there in connection with his trying to obtain money for having been injured."[33]

Still, Dr. Lubin understood "why an adversary might wish to pursue this." And so, he suggested to Judge Salman, maybe Darrell could be questioned, bearing in mind that whatever testimony was gleaned should be viewed as that of "a young child."[34]

Judge Salman reviewed Lubin's conclusions and, astonishingly, sided with Goetz. He ordered Darrell Cabey to sit for a deposition across from the man who had gunned him down six years earlier. As the *New York Post* crowed, "GOETZ GETS OK TO QUIZ CABEY IN 50M SUIT."[35]

This court-mandated proceeding took place on September 26, 1990, but it would not work to Bernie Goetz's advantage. Darrell was unable to answer any of the questions that Bernie asked, which seemed to both fluster and embarrass him. Several times when he could not remember something, he said ruefully, "I'm sorry." This only infuriated Goetz, who left the proceeding doubling down on his claim that Darrell Cabey was "faking being a mental vegetable."[36] As he put it to *The New York Times*, "Many years ago I tried to escape the draft and did something similar. But I think I did a much better act."[37]

Goetz was so unsatisfied with Darrell's responses in this first deposition that he demanded another one.

In an affidavit to Judge Salman, he argued that Darrell had "willfully" refused "to answer the deposition questions." He claimed that Darrell had done so "in direct violation" of the judge's discovery order, which directed the plaintiff to answer the defendant's questions to the "best of his ability."

The way Bernie saw it, when he had finally been able to question Darrell, "the examination lasted only 30 minutes" because the young man had faked his performance. Both Dr. Gordon's report and Ron Kuby's contentions of brain damage remained, Goetz asserted, "nonsense."[38]

Judge Salman took all of this under advisement, not inclined to simply rubber-stamp Bernie's request. In the meantime, he would allow Bernie to take the deposition of Darrell's mother, Shirley Cabey.

38

On the Offensive

When Shirley Cabey's attorneys informed her that she would have to sit for a deposition and that the person questioning her would be Goetz himself, it must have been hard to believe. It had been bad enough that her son had had to endure such questioning. Now the man who had paralyzed her child was coming for her too.

But as quiet, private, and reserved as Shirley Cabey was, she was also strong in ways that Bernie Goetz had perhaps underestimated. On June 18, 1991, she was more than prepared to hold firm in defense of her son as she sat across a table from the man who had caused her so much pain.[1]

Thanks to paralegal Harry Katz's research, Goetz entered this deposition with a wealth of information at his disposal: various facts and innuendos that had been gathered by combing through original police reports, paperwork from Shirley's applications to the Crime Victims Board, and even, somehow, a piece of paper indicating that Shirley had signed a form consenting for Darrell to be evaluated at a Bronx hospital department of psychiatry where she had taken him to get support as a child.

As the proceeding began, it was immediately clear that Goetz intended to paint her as little more than an unemployed welfare mother. Maybe he'd even get her to admit that she was trying to scam him on behalf of her criminally minded and mentally ill—not disabled—son.

Shirley, however, was undaunted. No matter how hard Goetz came at her, she pushed right back. This was clear from their very first exchange. "How may I refer to you, as Shirley?" Goetz asked. "Mrs. Cabey," she coldly answered.[2]

When Goetz asked about her employment status, she said pointedly, "I was employed at the time Darrell was shot, yes. But since he's been home, I haven't been able to go back to work because I have to take care of my son. . . . During the week, from Mondays to Fridays, he goes to United Cerebral Palsy, downtown, until five o'clock. He comes in, I give him his dinner, he's in his room, we watch TV or whatever."[3]

Shirley also took the opportunity to point out how much family help was needed for Darrell's care. Whenever he wanted to go outside, she said, "he cannot go out alone. His brother takes him out or the home attendant takes him out."[4]

Goetz then, rather abruptly, inquired if Darrell's brothers had "a reputation for crack dealing." Shirley responded icily that that would be "very surprising to me."[5]

Goetz was also determined to get Shirley to admit that her son had a history of being unstable, even violent. "Is it true that you threw Darrell out of the apartment a few weeks before he was shot?" he asked.[6] No, she said firmly.[7]

Hoping to show that Darrell Cabey's current and coma-related mental limitations were, in fact, longstanding, Goetz pivoted to ask if Darrell had ever been enrolled in special education. Shirley readily admitted that, yes, when he was about eight, Darrell had started at an elementary school for kids with learning disabilities.[8]

Ron Kuby jumped in to object, seeing what Goetz was trying to do. To Kuby's displeasure, the judge accepted Goetz's explanation for asking the question—that "Darrell may have had previous medical conditions that [were] unrelated to him being shot. Or Darrell may have had a history of violence."[9]

So, Goetz continued asking if Darrell had a learning disability.[10]

"I think that's what it was . . . a learning disability," Shirley replied.

But then, Goetz went even further. "Could it have been for violent conduct?" he persisted.[11]

"No," she said most emphatically.[12]

Unperturbed, Bernie Goetz moved on, trying to establish that any injury Darrell might have suffered back on December 22, 1984, had been his own fault. Shirley was not having it.

"Did you ever hear Darrell say words to the effect that his companions were going to rob me on the train?" the defendant asked.

"No," she answered.

"Did you ever hear Darrell say words to the effect that I looked like easy bait?"

"No."

"Did you ever hear Darrell say words to the effect that I looked like I had money?"

"No."

Goetz then asked if her son had ever watched him on television, and Shirley acknowledged that he had. "He did not know who he was [watching].... During the course of the trial, he wanted to know, he wanted information, he wanted to know... why was he involved with all of this."[13]

"Does Darrell follow the news on this case?" he persisted.

"Darrell is trying to live from day to day," she responded sardonically.[14]

Goetz questioned Shirley about her son's memory, his ability to carry on a conversation, and his jobs at the Cerebral Palsy Center. He even asked her bluntly: "Did any of your attorneys ever advise you or Darrell that Darrell should fake or misrepresent his condition?"[15]

But no matter how hard he pressed Shirley to reveal a different version of herself or her son, one that Bernie Goetz was deeply wedded to, she remained firm in her and Darrell's integrity.

Ultimately, however, he would push her too far. Shirley Cabey ended up storming out.[16]

STILL SEEKING A SECOND DEPOSITION of Darrell Cabey, Bernie Goetz hired a third expert, Dr. Jason Brown, to review Darrell's medical records. Despite Goetz's claims otherwise, he had in fact found the resources to fight this civil suit.

Much of that funding came from none other than the National Rifle Association.

In 1978, the NRA had created the Firearms Civil Rights Legal Defense Fund to provide funds for "civil defendants who have used handguns in self-defense," and for lobbyists proactively challenging gun laws. In one year, the fund paid more than $500,000 for such self-defense cases and lobbying efforts. This same fund had contributed to Goetz's criminal defense in the 1980s, and in the early 1990s it gave another $20,000 to his civil case.[17]

This infusion of cash had allowed Bernie to hire Harry Katz and Dr.

Jason Brown. He tasked Dr. Brown with going over both Dr. Wayne Gordon's and Dr. Martin Lubin's reports with a fine-tooth comb, as well as closely assessing the depositions of Darrell Cabey and Shirley Cabey, to determine if Darrell was faking his disability or if his mother had coerced him to do so. Most controversially, he would ask Brown to include in his evaluation a close look at Harry Katz's videotaped conversation with Darrell Cabey from December 1989.[18] Unlike the earlier doctors, however, Brown would not get to do an in-person evaluation with Darrell.

Even though he had never actually met Darrell Cabey, Dr. Brown's review of the prior competency assessments significantly weakened Cabey's lawyers' attempts to prevent another one-on-one deposition. He was "suspicious" of the experts' findings and made sure to point out that Dr. Lubin had already suggested that Darrell's abilities were "greater than in Dr. Gordon's examination."[19]

According to Dr. Brown, Dr. Gordon's report showed that Darrell's comprehension of digits was significantly impaired—and such an "impaired digit span is one of the more common symptoms of malingering." Darrell's inability to write his name was also "very unusual," and, in Brown's experience, this phenomenon was "simply not seen in cases of head injury." Additionally, Dr. Brown expressed skepticism that Darrell could not "recognize words previously seen," because that indicated "an impairment of recognition memory." He was dubious, he said, because such recall "is often fairly good even in amnestic cases."[20]

Notably, he had completely disregarded the well-documented effects of spinal shock—which included exactly these outcomes and which no one disputed Darrell had experienced.

And then there was Harry Katz's tape. Officially, Dr. Jason Brown claimed that he did not put much stock in this tape. He did note, however, several instances that he felt clearly illustrated Darrell's cognitive disabilities, such as the times Darrell tried to answer Katz by repeating his questions. He also pointed out the "slight dysarthria" in Darrell's speech, a motor disorder that presents as slurring and difficulty forming words after damage to the nervous system. In Brown's view, the tape did support Goetz's suspicions. Darrell had, when prompted, "recalled the name of the current and past mayor and had knowledge of the time schedule at [the center] and meals." What is more, Brown pointed out, Darrell never responded to the questions by saying "I don't know" or "no."[21]

In his final assessment, Dr. Brown concluded that although "Mr. Cabey probably does have some degree of cognitive impairment as result of the cardiopulmonary arrest and the resultant anoxic encephalopathy," he was not persuaded it was as serious as had been assumed. In fact, he agreed that they should be "very suspicious of malingering or exaggeration" on Darrell's part.[22]

Whether or not this additional report swayed Judge Salman remains unclear. But he did decide that Bernie Goetz could depose Darrell Cabey one more time, on June 9, 1993.[23] By the time this second deposition came, multiple reporters were all there vying to witness it firsthand in the courtroom.

When the defense demanded that reporters be let into the proceeding, Darrell's lawyers pushed back strongly at the idea of their disabled client becoming a spectacle.[24] Before allowing the deposition to begin, Ron Kuby demanded to know "How many individual reporters we are talking about? . . . If you are talking about one reporter, that is one thing, if you are talking about ten, it is something else."[25]

There were in fact nineteen reporters waiting outside, from tabloid papers to several television stations. They crowded around Darrell as he arrived in his wheelchair, began the difficult process of entering the courtroom, and tried to navigate close to the bolted-down table where the questions would be asked. Judge Salman held the line at admitting only one reporter into this proceeding. But Bernie Goetz was allowed to choose the reporter—Andrea Peyser of the *New York Post*.[26]

No sooner had the stenographer poised her hands over the keyboard than Bernie began peppering Darrell Cabey with a familiar, aggressively framed question: "Did any of your attorneys ever advise you to misrepresent your medical condition or ability to remember?"[27]

When he could not get the answer he hoped for, he asked again.

Eventually, after a full thirty minutes of badgering, Judge Salman called a halt to the deposition. As Ron Kuby recalled that moment, "It became clear to the judge after very few minutes that Darrell Cabey was incapable of responding to Goetz. Between his presentation as an eight-year-old and his consistent inability to remember anything, it was not a very long deposition."[28]

The *New York Post*, in Bernie's camp as always, ran a sympathetic report of what it described as a "reunion between the shooter and the thug":

> From across the wood-paneled courtroom, Bernhard Goetz addressed the young man in the wheelchair like an old friend. "Darrell," Goetz said in his gentlest voice. "I'm going to ask you some questions. Take as much time as you want to answer . . ."[29]

But to Bernie Goetz, this deposition was even more infuriating than the first. Darrell was now "acting" as if "he could not even understand the questions being asked of him, let alone being able to answer them." This was just more evidence of "Darrell Cabey's continued defiance of this Court's order for him to cooperate with the Defendant's questioning of him regarding the events in this case," Goetz claimed. Bernie Goetz would go on, unsuccessfully, to seek sanctions against Darrell Cabey.[30]

Years later, when asked to reflect on this series of depositions, Ron Kuby could still only shake his head in disgust. "I don't know if Goetz genuinely believed somehow Darrell Cabey was faking all of this . . . that Goetz didn't do the catastrophic damage that he did. I don't know if he knew it, [or] he just wanted to be as cruel as possible. . . . Whether that appealed to some part of Goetz's sick mentality, I don't know."[31]

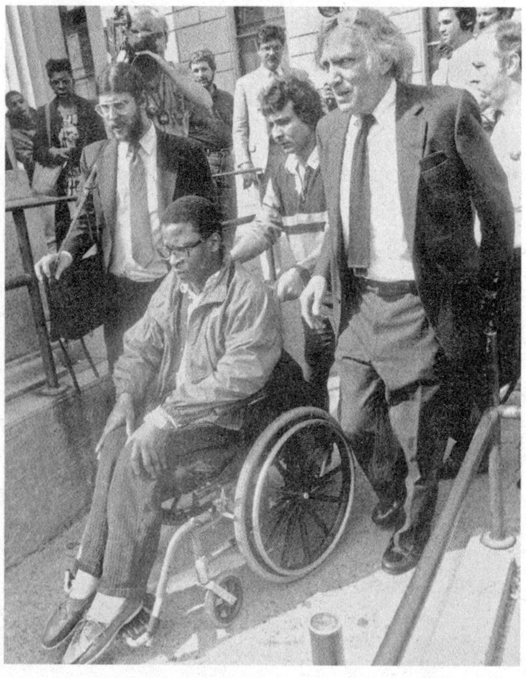

Darrell Cabey leaving Bronx County Courthouse with attorneys Ron Kuby and William Kunstler.
John Pedin/New York *Daily News* Archive via Getty Images

Two years would pass, with little movement in the civil case. Goetz would continue to try to have the case dismissed, while Darrell's lawyers would keep pushing for a trial date.

Meanwhile, New York City itself was becoming a very different place. Still reeling from the economic fallout from the Reagan eighties, white New Yorkers had nevertheless just elected a Republican to the mayor's office. Under this new leadership, the Big Apple would only grow more racially polarized, more heavily policed, and more economically stratified. Indeed, for New Yorkers like Shirley and Darrell Cabey, the stakes of winning the civil trial against Bernie Goetz were getting higher and higher with each passing year.

39

Old Wine, New Bottles

IN THE FALL of 1993, Rudolph Giuliani unseated Democratic incumbent David Dinkins, becoming the second Republican mayor of New York City since 1945.[1] This was the same Rudy Giuliani that, as U.S. District Attorney, had been asked to file a civil rights case against Bernhard Goetz on Darrell Cabey's behalf. Notably, he had declined to do so, ultimately declaring in the ten-page report his office had produced that any description of this man as a "vigilante" was "simply not supported by the known facts." Giuliani made clear that he believed "Goetz acted out of fear—justified or not—that he would be harmed."[2]

Observing the Goetz saga had led Giuliani to understand that the path to Gracie Mansion was paved with disaffected white voters. He had first tried to get there in the 1989 mayoral race, but that bid fell short.

Giuliani lost that election to Dinkins, who had just bested Mayor Ed Koch in the Democratic primary. The brutal fallout from the 1980s—the cuts to services, the AIDS crisis, the drug war, as well as the racial rage that had led to the killing of Willie Turks, the shooting of Darrell Cabey and his friends, and the violent deaths of Michael Griffith, Eleanor Bumpurs, and Yusef Hawkins—had rallied the Black community. White progressives had stood with them to elect Dinkins, the first Black mayor in the city's history, in hopes of reversing the damage done by the Reagan Revolution.

Dismay at the treatment of Black citizens and how they had fared under Reagan had in fact put Black mayors into office across the country in the 1980s and 1990s—in Philadelphia, Boston, Chicago, Atlanta, and many other cities.[3] Some would stay there for multiple terms. Dinkins, however, would not be one of them. When Rudy Giuliani finally won the mayor's office in 1993, it was by a razor-thin margin.

Essential to his victory had been the *New York Post*. It had, in effect, been helping to build his base since the Goetz shootings.

By championing an ordinary white guy like Goetz, and repeatedly asserting that his life had fallen apart because of the Black thugs Troy Canty, Barry Allen, James Ramseur, and Darrell Cabey, the *Post* had been able to offer white working-class New Yorkers who also had endured the fallout of Reaganomics a simplistic, knee-jerk, deeply self-interested, and highly racialized narrative for understanding their personal plight as well. What the city needed? A candidate like Rudy Giuliani, who would finally take on the criminals and the con artists.

On the tenth anniversary of Goetz's shooting spree, the *Post* insisted that New Yorkers owed Bernie "a debt of gratitude," because he had "awakened the elites," men like Giuliani, to the "reality" that "ordinary people feel an enormous sense of frustration in the face of random, violent crime."[4]

As the *Post*'s city hall bureau chief David Seifman later noted, Giuliani and the *Post* were, in fact, "on the same philosophical wavelength most of the time. Especially when it came to crime."[5] As *Post* reporter Eric Fetterman also noted, "The *Post*'s audience became . . . Giuliani voters."[6]

Tough-on-crime Republican Giuliani was a particular favorite of white Staten Islanders, many of whom had, under Dinkins, strongly considered seceding from New York City entirely. Their grassroots campaign to that end, as well as their collective support for Bernie Goetz and the white mobs accused of killing Black New Yorkers like Griffith and Hawkins, had galvanized this Republican base, and votes from this borough were essential to Giuliani's narrow victory.[7]

Giuliani's win had also depended most heavily upon the militant support from the white rank and file of the NYPD. On one notorious occasion, he spoke at a police rally that drove over four thousand officers into such a frenzied fury that they marched to city hall and blocked the Brooklyn Bridge.[8] His campaign also helped to spread rumors that the city's polling stations might be compromised, filled with fraudulent liberal voters whose ideas posed a direct threat to the law-and-order policies the city needed. To combat this "threat," Giuliani hired scores of off-duty cops, firefighters, and corrections officers to "monitor" polls in Manhattan, Brooklyn, and the Bronx on election day.[9]

Unsurprisingly, one of Giuliani's most important decisions after his

1993 victory would be who to hire as his new police commissioner. He would poach a man who was making a name for himself nationally as an innovative and aggressive crime fighter: Bill Bratton. Bratton, in turn, would completely overhaul the way that New York City was policed, and heavy-handed policing would become Giuliani's calling card as mayor.

Rudy Giuliani's victory over Dinkins was, he decided, a mandate to totally remake New York City.[10]

Giuliani understood that it was the petty crimes that particularly upset his constituents, wealthy and working-class alike. They hated the poor kids who jumped turnstiles. They feared the unhoused adults who panhandled. They were infuriated by the "squeegee men" who, uninvited, cleaned their windshields and asked for tips when they were stopped at a red light. And they were disgusted by the unemployed youths who spray-painted graffiti on buildings and trains.

Unlike Dinkins, however, Giuliani was uninterested in the root causes of blight or crime—the reasons why so many New Yorkers were, by the close of the 1980s, in such bad shape that they had to beg or hustle. Instead, Giuliani promised to police the city's way out of the crisis.

That he would be able to do just that was thanks in no small part to a Democrat who had won the White House the year before, William Jefferson Clinton. The same year Giuliani took over Gracie Mansion, President Clinton, also seeking to curry favor with disaffected white voters, had signed one of his first major legislative efforts into law: the Violent Crime Control and Law Enforcement Act of 1994. This was the largest crime bill in U.S. history, allocating $1 billion for policing, punishment, and prisons—including plans to put 100,000 new police officers on the street, to provide "the largest-ever expansion of the Federal death penalty to cover 53 offenses," and to earmark a stunning $800 million "in one-time prison construction costs."[11]

Unprecedented numbers of Americans—including New York City residents—had been arrested and imprisoned during the Reagan eighties, but thanks to this crime bill, that number would skyrocket during the Clinton '90s. Over the course of the 1990s, the prison population in the United States would increase from the already staggering 774,000 to 1.38 million.[12]

In line with the Clinton administration's anti-crime efforts and the wishes of many New Yorkers, Giuliani and Bratton would embrace the "Broken Windows" theory of policing. Back in 1982, criminologists James Q. Wilson and George L. Kelling had introduced the idea that reducing lesser "nuisance" crimes such as fare evasion, vandalism, and panhandling would in turn prevent more serious and dangerous crimes like robbery and assault.[13]

This theory, a call for more aggressive policing of even the most minor misdemeanor offenses, would enjoy the same popularity—with certain New Yorkers—as had Bernie Goetz's 1984 act of vigilantism. Both spoke to a collective frustration with blight, with drug dealers, with visible poverty, and with rising crime rates. When asked why his theory had resonated so resoundingly in NYC, its architect, James Q. Wilson, said, "It may simply indicate that there are no more liberals on the crime and law-and-order issue in New York, because they've all been mugged."[14]

Wilson's theory would have serious consequences for those who experienced its implementation firsthand. The NYPD was given the green light to arrest New Yorkers for the most minor, albeit sometimes unsavory, public acts. In turn, the plight of these New Yorkers worsened, thanks to the fines they subsequently owed and the jobs they lost or could not procure because of their criminal records. Notably, this intense crackdown did not prevent acts such as Goetz's from happening again, as was clear from the horrifying acts of white racial violence that made headlines in this decade too.

Meanwhile, Commissioner Bratton would augment Broken Windows with another new approach to policing New York City—this one more methodical, and ostensibly scientific, known as "CompStat." CompStat would use computers, mapping, and statistical analysis to determine where crimes might be more likely to happen and then concentrate law enforcement in those areas.[15] CompStat had received particular legitimacy thanks to Harvard's Kennedy School of Government, which conducted research on the program and held seminars and workshops for police brass. Just like the theory of Broken Windows, CompStat was soon being utilized by police departments in large cities across the country.

This embrace of the idea that policing and technology could together solve the nation's crime problem would not bode well for neighborhoods hoping instead for a reinvestment in jobs and social programs. Even more dollars flowed to law enforcement. Over the course of the 1990s, crime rates across the U.S. had, in fact, begun to decrease—notably so. Scholars and the media scrambled to understand what was soon being dubbed the "Great Crime Drop."[16] Was this decline really due to saturating the poorest neighborhoods with police officers to arrest and imprison unprecedented numbers of Americans?

Pundits were divided on the answer, but all, when pressed, had to acknowledge that crime rates were trending downward in cities that had adopted aggressive crime-fighting methods like CompStat—as well as in cities that had not. Moreover, the crime rate had actually been in decline well before Giuliani and other like-minded mayors took office, and it had also begun to drop across the world.[17]

Nevertheless, white and more conservative-leaning New Yorkers—those who had especially welcomed the clearing out of "riffraff" from glittery cities like Gotham—absolutely credited decreasing crime rates to the punitive policing methods that were causing ever greater harm to city residents without jobs or stable housing.

That such New Yorkers were so vulnerable to Giuliani's aggressive policing approach was in no small part due to what had been happening at the federal level. To be sure, the Reagan Republicans had begun the dramatic overhaul of countless New Deal–era policies that had provided safety nets for generations of Americans. And later Republican leaders like President George H. W. Bush had continued that ideological and economic revolution. But it was in fact the Democratic administration of Bill Clinton that would take it to a whole new level.[18]

First, Clinton's Violent Crime Act of 1994 criminalized the poor more harshly than either Reagan or Bush had. Then another sweeping piece of legislation, the Personal Responsibility and Work Opportunity Reconciliation Act (PRWORA) of 1996, enacted the most dramatic cuts to resources for the poor since the New Deal and set the most stringent limits on aid for shelter and food since Lyndon Johnson's Great Society.[19] All of this would prove devastating on the ground.[20]

When PRWORA replaced the Aid to Families with Dependent Children (AFDC) program with the new Temporary Assistance for Needy Families (TANF) program, for example, it fundamentally altered the structure and delivery of public assistance. Welfare caseloads lessened, but the number of children living in extreme poverty—defined as a household income below 50 percent of the poverty line—increased, with a particularly pronounced impact on Black and Brown families.[21]

New York State did amend one of the most draconian provisions of PRWORA, which had imposed a lifetime ban on individuals with felony drug convictions from receiving anything from the Supplemental Nutrition Assistance Program (known colloquially as food stamps) or TANF benefits for other necessities such as housing. But the fallout from the PRWORA and Violent Crime Act together was nevertheless profound and disturbing. Record numbers of children in NYC lost their parents to prison, unprecedented numbers of adults were rendered unemployable due to having a criminal record, and countless families also lost access to subsidized housing and food.[22]

Clinton's presidency would substantially fortify the Reagan Revolution by making it clear that neither its cultural assumptions nor its economic logic would be reversed, even by the opposing political party. Although Clinton raised the top income tax rate early in his presidency, the richest Americans would still benefit markedly from Clinton's dramatic deregulation of the financial sector, cuts to capital gains, and passage of the North American Free Trade Agreement (NAFTA). In turn, ordinary people saw stagnant or declining economic security, particularly as manufacturing jobs moved overseas in droves.

In New York, Mayor Giuliani would also pander to the financial desires of Manhattan's wealthiest whites and pave the way for them to flourish as no mayor had since the Gilded Age.

Among those who seized and ran with the Giuliani moment was Donald Trump, whose reputation as a flamboyant real estate developer had only grown throughout the 1980s. His ability to attract press coverage and align himself with political power would only be augmented during the new mayor's time in office.

Indeed, Trump's glitzy developments—and the tax abatements and incentives that made them possible—exemplified the shift in city policy priorities. In 1995, Trump used tax breaks from Giuliani's Lower Manhattan Revitalization Program to acquire and renovate 40 Wall Street and further cater to the luxury market. His project to build Trump World Tower at 845 United Nations Plaza did not receive a direct tax abatement but did benefit from the Giuliani administration's zoning flexibility, as well as its particularly relaxed oversight for large luxury developments.

As more of the city was gentrified, and his own financial and cultural cachet grew, Trump's real estate portfolio offered a vision of exclusivity and security that seemed to be the realization of all that Reagan's "greed is good" ethos and Giuliani's law-and-order agenda had promised. Trump was soon appearing regularly at city hall events and White House galas alike—he and other wealthy Americans had been adopted across party lines, just as the Reagan agenda had been. As a Trump employee astutely pointed out in a letter to President Clinton, the two men "[had] much in common: age, broad vision for the future and most importantly, the resources and desire to make America bigger and better than it already is."[23]

"The Donald," as the press had dubbed him, had become a culture warrior on behalf of this new moment of tax cuts, aggressive policing, and gentrification. His face, and stories about his glamorous life, were routinely splashed across the pages of New York City's tabloids. He was the particular darling of the *New York Post,* still the signature publication in Rupert Murdoch's conservative media empire that loved Trump's messaging, even as Murdoch himself found Trump to be a bit crass.[24]

Trump's and Giuliani's favorable coverage in the *Post* had mattered. Both had insisted that gentrification was good, that the city would be better off if the "undesirables" were locked up, and that wealthy businessmen knew how to run the city better than did the liberals of yesteryear. This messaging was wrapped in repeated and not-so-subtle racial messaging and had seduced not a few white working- and middle-class New Yorkers, even as it had actually delivered so few material or economic results.

Ultimately, Giuliani's voters and Trump fans alike—all overwhelmingly white—were by the mid-1990s willing to divert ever more funding to the police if that meant they might end up in nicer, cleaner neighborhoods, or that they might have a more lavish lifestyle one day. It was Giuliani's aggressive policing and mass incarceration that had made it possible to "Disney-fy" seedy areas of the city like Times Square, and to clear out other districts to make them ripe for real estate developers like Trump. Of central importance, also, was keeping white working-class neighborhoods white.

As long as racial ideology distracted New York's white voters from the fact that the city's now almost two-decade-long retreat from social spending primarily and overwhelmingly benefited the wealthy, all was fine.

But, of course, slashing taxes at the top, unleashing the police, and incentivizing gentrification had not solved the city's problems. This newly aggressive policing of public space, for example, absolutely did "clean up" New York City, particularly where its most affluent citizens worked and dined. But making some parts of the city much more pleasant had not addressed the city's poverty, its drug crisis, and its additional ills that had only intensified since the Reagan Revolution began. Those same problems had simply been relegated to, and indeed actively contained within, a few very specific Manhattan and outer-borough neighborhoods, like the South Bronx.

Darrell Cabey's mother, Shirley, understood this. She could only hope that the civil case she had filed on behalf of her son would offer her help that her city would not. And now, that case was finally ready to go to trial.

40

Going It Alone

TWO MONTHS BEFORE Darrell Cabey's suit was finally due to go to court, on November 27, 1995, his case was thrown into limbo by the unexpected death of attorney Bill Kunstler at the age of seventy-six. The *Post* ran an article on his passing, not missing the opportunity to disparage him even in death, describing him as the "radicals' champion" who had represented "New York terrorism suspects."[1] Just a few years earlier, one of its columnists had described him also as a "guilty white leftist who apologized for blacks charged with violent crimes by calling them 'victims' of American racism."[2]

For Kunstler's junior law partner, Ron Kuby, this news had been an utter gut punch. As he later explained, it was "just a huge tragedy for the American people, for Bill's friends and family, for me. . . . And for the Goetz case." With the trial date now set, "emotionally, financially, [and] logistically," this was a terrible blow.[3]

In addition to Darrell's case, Kuby and Kunstler were, together, in the midst of preparing for two murder cases that were about to go to trial and were still overseeing scores of other cases that they had taken on over the previous months and years. To make matters worse, Randolph Scott-McLaughlin, C. Vernon Mason, and Betty Lawrence Bailey, lawyers who had originally joined with Kunstler and Kuby when they had filed the suit on Darrell's behalf back in 1985, had since stepped away. According to Kuby, Mason had "lost interest after only about a year or so," and over time, the other two lawyers went on to work on other important cases.[4]

Not only was Kuby now short on manpower; he also had no money. In the wake of Kunstler's death, the Center for Constitutional Rights, with which Kunstler had been affiliated, as had Mason, Scott-McLaughlin, and Bailey, decided that it could no longer support Kuby's work on this civil suit. The CCR had been paying for things such as "deposition transcripts and exhibits and experts," Kuby explained. "This wasn't a huge amount of money, even by the standards of the time. But it was, you know, money that we were using."[5]

Ron Kuby was also all too aware that he was a criminal defense lawyer and lacked experience in a civil courtroom. Not only did the rules of evidence differ between criminal and civil cases, but so did the burden of proof. Whereas criminal defense lawyers have no burden of proof—their job is to pick apart the prosecution's case to create reasonable doubt—civil lawyers have to prove their case by presenting the evidence that substantiates the harm.

The timing of all of this could not have been worse. With a tremendous amount of trial prep still to do, Kuby wrote a panicked request for more time to prepare.[6]

Bernie Goetz, meanwhile, may well have hoped that Kunstler's death would end this litigation once and for all. He too was trying to navigate this case solo, acting as his own lawyer, and like Kuby, he had much to do before trial. And by all accounts, Goetz was falling down on the job.

As Kuby explained in his motion to move the trial date back, he needed this extension not just because he had lost his law partner but also because of things that he still needed from his opposing counsel—Bernie Goetz. "Mr. Goetz," he wrote, "was to subpoena the New York County District Attorney's file and exhibits in this matter, and to notify me when this was done . . . so that we might begin the process of contacting witnesses who are scattered all over the country." As important, Kuby also pointed out, the "decade-long delay between the filing of the lawsuit and today" was also down to Goetz.[7]

When Judge Salman agreed to move the trial date to April 11, 1996, both parties likely breathed a sigh of relief. Goetz would have time to get an actual lawyer, a man named Darnay Hoffman who'd been referred to him by his notorious friend and chess partner back at Rikers, Joel Steinberg. And Kuby would be able to bring on two young attorneys, both former interns, to help him prepare—Daniel Perez and Daniella Korotzer.

Kuby found himself feeling much more optimistic about his prospects when, just two weeks before the trial was scheduled to begin, Bernie Goetz accepted an invitation to appear on NBC's popular news show *Dateline,* hosted by charismatic anchor Stone Phillips. On that March 31, 1996, episode, Goetz apparently couldn't hold back from sharing his thoughts about young Black New Yorkers, and Black people in general.

In this *Dateline* special, Goetz expressed the view that "society is better off without certain people," and said to host Phillips that the only question was whether "they should be killed, or locked up, or used in a forced labor system."[8] The teens Goetz had shot, he then made clear, were exactly those sorts of people.

Just to be certain of what his guest was saying, Phillips asked him, "Do you think what you did was a public service?"[9]

"I think yes. . . . [W]hat I did, I'm not ashamed of at all. Perhaps that's a good way of looking at it—a public service," Goetz replied.[10] Indeed, he also said, turning himself in to the authorities had been a mistake.

Goetz continued to regale Phillips with insights into the shootings he had carried out now more than a decade earlier. He readily admitted to having "decided" from the moment he came in contact with the teens that he "was going to kill them all before they could do anything." Once again, Phillips pressed him: "Were you more afraid because they were Black?" "Possibly yes," Bernie answered.[11]

He also admitted that he had shot Darrell Cabey and that his bullet had paralyzed the teen. This time, however, and in direct contradiction to his last deposition, Goetz insisted that he had felled Darrell with his first shot and had only imagined, or wished he had said, the infamous words, "You look alright, here's another." He clearly remembered the major stir it had caused the last time he had veered from the way Barry Slotnick had accounted for this statement in the criminal trial.

Before the episode ended, Bernie Goetz had admitted as well to having used the terms "n—s" and "sp—s," although he suggested that this was only because he had been using "angel dust and marijuana" and had been "stoned at the time."[12]

Ron Kuby was far from surprised that Goetz held the unsavory views he had spouted here on national TV. Kuby was stunned, however, that Bernie had professed to them again so recently. These comments would be a godsend to Kuby in the trial. He too had been interviewed for the *Dateline* piece, and with regard to Goetz's admission about his drug use, Kuby had said sardonically, "Well, angel dust, pharmacologically, has a lot of effects. But as far as I know, racism isn't one of them."[13]

THE BRONX COUNTY COURTHOUSE—a nine-story building at the corner of 158th and Grand Concourse, two blocks from iconic Yankee Stadium—was a world of poor people and of government, two things for which Bernie Goetz had no love. Whereas his neighborhood of Greenwich Village had grown whiter and wealthier over the course of the 1990s, the Bronx had grown ever poorer and more racially diverse.[14] The scores of people hustling and bustling in and out of this building—which housed virtually every municipal department, from the marriage bureau to the borough president's office—were far more representative of Darrell Cabey's New York than Bernie Goetz's.

The presiding judges there, however, including Barry Salman, were still overwhelmingly white. They oversaw many thousands of cases filed in this jurisdiction each year, from incidents involving motor vehicles to medical malpractice, all in which the damages sought by the plaintiff were over $50,000.

Judge Salman was a New Yorker through and through. He had attended City University of New York's Hunter College and had received his JD from St. John's University School of Law in 1965. Originally elected to the New York City Civil Court, in 1990 Salman began a fourteen-year-term on the Bronx Supreme Court.

The judge wasn't perfect—a few years earlier he had been censured for misusing campaign funds "to buy a car phone and a camcorder, and to make political contributions"—but he generally showed good judgment in the courtroom.[15] In Ron Kuby's estimation, Salman's rulings in the case thus far had largely been fair, aside from allowing Goetz's depositions of Darrell Cabey.

And for ill or good, Salman was a judge that cared about transparency—which meant that he was open to the idea that the entire trial be televised. The previous year, Americans had watched beloved football hero O.J. Simpson stand trial for the brutal killing of his wife, Nicole Brown Simpson, and her friend Ron Goldman. The fact that the Simpson case centered on a Black male defendant and a white female victim was, in the view of corporate media types, television gold. Likely hoping that the public's seemingly insatiable interest in all things Bernie Goetz would net the same viewership as the O.J. trial, emerging cable channel COURT TV successfully sought to broadcast his civil trial.

COURT TV had a similar origin story to Rupert Murdoch's Fox News, which would go on the air at the end of the year. Like Murdoch, COURT TV's backer and founder, billionaire John Malone, was also politically conservative and had decided to found a media company, called Liberty Media, to spread this messaging. Driven by Malone's libertarian economic philosophy, fierce belief in consolidation, and desire for tight capital control and freedoms, Liberty Media's holdings would eventually include not just COURT TV but also the SiriusXM Group, the QVC shopping channel, Starz, Live Nation Entertainment, and even the DirecTV satellite television company.

Despite a disconcerting habit of looking directly at one person while speaking to someone else entirely, Judge Salman seemed comfortable in front of the cameras in his courtroom throughout these proceedings. Being filmed, Kuby felt, was probably not a bad thing when it came to ensuring that any judge would be both patient and fair.[16]

The other person who was probably quite happy about the TV cameras was Bernie Goetz's new lawyer, Darnay Hoffman.

Hoffman seemed, at first glance, an unlikely choice to be assisting Goetz in any capacity. He was the son of a Broadway actress and had been trying to make it as a television producer, but late in life he decided to go to law school. Hoffman had virtually no trial experience, but he loved to play the part. He favored snazzy suits and ties and lived on the Upper West Side with his current (and third) wife, a socialite who hailed from a wealthy family.

But Hoffman's involvement with Goetz did make a certain kind of sense. Anything having to do with Bernie Goetz was sure to shine the media spotlight on Hoffman, and he was hungry to make a name for himself.

In fact, Hoffman had no qualms about media attention garnered through associations with persons who were more infamous than famous. His wife was none other than Sydney Biddle Barrows, also known in the press as the "Mayflower Madam," who had been indicted in 1985 for running a million-dollar-a-year call-girl operation from an Upper West Side apartment.[17] And he had gone to law school in no small part because he hoped to carve out a niche for himself as a legal advisor on notorious cases and then pitch them to Hollywood as dramatic TV movies. That is why Hoffman regularly visited Joel Steinberg in Rikers—a man he knew originally because Steinberg had handled Hoffman's divorce from his first wife before he was disbarred for committing murder.[18]

So, Hoffman was thrilled when Bernie asked him to head up his civil case. No matter that he had tried only one case before this one, and even then, not as the lead lawyer. His plan was to soak up the Goetz limelight in this trial, win the case, and then pitch his story of triumph to film and TV. An upside for Goetz, as Ron Kuby noted wryly, was that "Darnay Hoffman was working for free if not actually financing the case himself."[19]

Hoffman was in fact so eager to show his moves in court that he largely gave away his trial strategy to his opposing counsel before it even started. Hoffman's plan, as he made clear in various conversations with Kuby's team, was to put Goetz himself on the stand, so the jury could "get to know him, and to like him." He was confident that Goetz wouldn't alienate the jury with, say, comments like those he had recently shared on *Dateline*. Further, Hoffman had big plans to dazzle this jury in other ways. He wanted to try to get Mayor Giuliani on the stand, thinking that if a man of the mayor's standing had already dismissed the notion that Goetz had been in any way motivated by racial bias, so too could these jurors.[20]

Alternatively, he said he might bring in Dr. Yudowitz, the expert witness who had argued that Goetz had simply been on "automatic pilot" at the time of the shooting. Or perhaps Andrea Reid, Troy Canty, James Ramseur, and maybe even Shirley Cabey—they would all make his client look good.[21]

Ron Kuby would not let himself be psyched out by this showboater. As Kuby later reflected, "I was always confident in our ability to prove the case."[22] Kuby was representing Darrell Cabey, and in his mind, there was no other way to see it: Goetz had permanently injured a kid who had literally done nothing to him. The only way Goetz could have assumed that Darrell was with the guy who had asked him for five bucks was simply because he too was young, and Black, and on that same train.

Optimally, Kuby would have had another experienced and ideally high-profile civil lawyer on this case, but he wasn't in the position to hire one. But Perez and Korotzer would be all he needed. As he remembered, "They were really important parts in all of this. That is, each one of them would take a piece of the case. And be responsible for it. So, I mean, while I had overall responsibility for everything, I didn't have to do everything. . . . It was, you know, fabulously helpful."[23]

Equally helpful was the fact that Darnay Hoffman was also completely new to the civil suit game.

41

Relitigating the Past

THE JURORS WALKED slowly to their seats in the Bronx courtroom of Judge Salman on April 10, 1996, almost nine years to the day from the start of Goetz's criminal trial. COURT TV cameras were in the room, capturing every utterance for broadcast to a national public. The two men and four women on this civil jury, chosen from a pool of about four dozen Bronx residents that morning, seemed eager to be a part of this historic proceeding. Neither Bernie Goetz, now forty-two, nor Darrell Cabey, now thirty, had been in the room when they were selected.[1]

The fact that no one on this jury was white—four Black and two Latino jurors, with three Latino and one Black alternates—was loudly noted by the press covering this trial.[2] Whereas few press outlets intimated that the majority-white jury picked in the earlier criminal trial was incapable of being fair in their assessment of Goetz, most now suggested, both subtly and overtly, that this jury would certainly side against Bernie Goetz because he was white and Darrell was Black.

As one *New York Times* reporter described the scene:

> The plaintiff's lawyer, the one with the long graying ponytail, addressed the largely nonwhite panel of prospective Bronx jurors yesterday with an easy familiarity. Smiling sympathetically, he asked them whether they thought there should be fewer guns on the street and if they had ever been discriminated against. More often than not, he got the answers he sought: Yes and yes.[3]

This was a point that Goetz's lawyer also wanted to highlight. Darnay Hoffman felt that the jury didn't like him much, and as he told this same reporter during a break, this was likely because "the other guy has the home court advantage."[4]

It was, however, Hoffman's frat boy air as well as his manner of asking questions that actually failed to ingratiate him with the jury. He exuded an arrogance, exemplified in his attire, which included a loud "Nicole Miller tie decorated with sharks and legal books,"[5] and it also did not help that Hoffman's every word to this jury suggested with a wink and a nod that he "got it"—they would be biased against his client.

For his part, Ron Kuby wasn't at all certain that a jury of color was going to favor his client over Goetz. As he well knew, Black and Brown juries in the Bronx weren't afraid to be tough on crime too—particularly as the 1980s and 1990s wore on.[6] And besides, Ron Kuby was also white. Kuby understood that his client would have to be particularly sympathetic in order to win any damages in a crime case, no matter the race of the victim or perpetrator. Indeed, it was likely that Kuby internally winced at the uphill battle he faced when a potential juror he and Hoffman questioned earlier that day had reported that he had been mugged four times, twice on the subway.[7]

This did not mean that Ron Kuby would shy away from arguing that this case was about racial violence. He pulled no punches when he delivered his opening statement on April 11, 1996, and began by reminding the jury of Goetz's long history of using racial epithets, along with his habit of making highly offensive remarks to reporters, including in his most recent *Dateline* interview.[8]

Kuby promised to present a case that would allow the jury, unhesitatingly, to "impose the highest possible damages on Goetz, to punish his cruelness, his racist violence, and to deter other people" from mimicking his actions. As he finished pointedly, "Mr. Goetz shot these kids because he could. It is up to you to tell him he can't."[9]

Darnay Hoffman opened with a very different argument. "I believe Darrell Cabey put himself in that wheelchair by being with those three men, by trying to rob Bernie Goetz," he told the jury. His client, he said proudly, had turned out to be "their worst nightmare." And now, he said incredulously, "Darrell Cabey is in court, asking you to make him a millionaire, make him one of the richest men in America."[10]

If these jurors wanted to make a point here, Hoffman insisted, they should "send a message" to "'criminals' like Cabey." In doing so, they would be doing their part in "stopping the madness."[11] Poking at their presumed inherent racial bias, he also challenged the jury: "Can you take the heat? 'Yeah, I let Bernie Goetz off'? Can you take the pressure? Can you leave here with that weight?"[12]

It was then Kuby's turn to start proving his legal arguments before this jury. He began on April 12, 1996, with a metaphorical bang. His first witness would be Bernie Goetz himself. From Kuby's perspective, if calling Goetz to the stand "wasn't going to do it, then calling a whole bunch of other witnesses, [wasn't] going to do it either."[13]

Indeed, Kuby had always planned to "prove the case through Goetz's own mouth." He was even more certain than prosecutor Greg Waples had been before him that "the more you hear this guy, the more you're repulsed by him. The more he talks about what he did, the less sympathy there is for him. The more he describes the shooting, the more revulsion you feel and the more he describes his background, the more unhinged he sounds."[14]

To lay this groundwork, Kuby first regaled the jury with Goetz's entire taped confession as well as a recording of the highly inflammatory *Dateline* interview he had done with Stone Phillips. When the bulky television set was wheeled before the jury box and Kuby pressed play, the courtroom was deadly quiet. Unlike in the criminal trial, the jurors had not been given a transcript. Kuby wanted them to focus not only on the words Goetz said but also how he said them.[15]

Kuby's case hinged on whether Bernie had recklessly and willfully shot, and thus rendered permanently disabled, Darrell Cabey. In this trial, as he would later put it, "the liability" depended not just on Goetz's actions that day but more on the consequences of them for Darrell Cabey's life.[16]

Bernie Goetz walked slowly over to the witness box wearing his usual white button-down. As he took his seat, he and Darrell glanced at each other uncomfortably, but Goetz seemed to studiously avoid his gaze thereafter. For her part, Shirley Cabey sat "stoically" behind her son's wheelchair in the very front of the courtroom as Bernie's testimony began.[17] While it was likely terribly difficult for Shirley to hear Bernie Goetz's recounting of how he had gunned down her son, she knew how important it was that he not hold back. He did not disappoint.

In one of the trial's most riveting exchanges—captured in living color by COURT TV—Ron Kuby confronted Goetz with every admission that

Darrell Cabey awaiting Bernhard Goetz's testimony in State Supreme Court in the Bronx, April 12, 1996.
AP Photo/Ralph Ginzburg

he had made to the police in 1984, along with the many objectionable opinions and boastful remarks he had shared with the press in the decade that followed. This was a risky tactic. At any point, Goetz could deny that he had said something, attempt to minimize its meaning, or in the worst-case scenario, embrace the defense that Barry Slotnick had handed him—that he might have "wished" he had done the terrible things he said he did but not actually done them.

Instead—often with a sneer or a small smile on his face—Goetz would admit, embrace, and even appear to double down on everything he had already confessed to doing to Darrell Cabey back in 1984 and every racialized defense he had offered since.

Ron Kuby aimed especially to show jurors that Bernie Goetz was a coldhearted and violent man who felt little remorse for the horrific things he had done or said, and who had a particular vendetta against Black and Brown New Yorkers.

"Isn't [it] right," Kuby pressed, that Goetz had said in an interview "it would've been a lot better had Shirley Cabey had an abortion"?[18]

Yes, Goetz affirmed, and then elaborated, unprompted: "It would probably be better than the present status quo we have today."[19] As these words hung in the air, Darrell's mother and grandmother glowered at him.[20]

Was it not also the case, Kuby continued, that Goetz had a habit of pulling his gun on panhandlers to frighten them, long before he'd shot the boys on the train? Once, had he not said that someone he pulled a gun on "deserved to die"? To which Goetz responded, "Uh, well he was acting like such an asshole I did say that and I felt it at the time."[21]

"And why did he deserve to die, Mr. Goetz?" Kuby prompted.

"Because he was acting like a total asshole," Goetz responded.

"And in your view, people that you perceive to be assholes should be killed?"

"Well, in many cases, it might make the world a better place."[22]

The courtroom then erupted, some spectators shaking their heads in incredulity, others laughing as if stunned. In the bedlam Judge Salman was forced to call for a recess.[23]

Even the news reporters seemed astonished by Goetz's responses on the stand, ones that Darnay Hoffman seemed too flummoxed to redirect or try to shut down.[24] Indeed, as his client kept saying one incriminating and distasteful thing after another, Hoffman stayed largely silent.[25] Goetz admitted that it was the look on Troy Canty's face, and specifically his smile, "that set me off." When Kuby asked whether he had "thought about gouging out the wounded youth's eyes with his keys," Goetz replied matter-of-factly, "I could have—it was a thought that crossed my mind."[26]

"And is it also fair to say that at that point you decided you were going to 'Kill them all, murder them all,' do anything?" Kuby continued.

"I snapped," Goetz replied, with a smile.[27]

With these words echoing in the jurors' ears, and with the image of Goetz's chilling smirk fresh in their minds, Ron Kuby wanted to ensure that the jury heard the testimony of Christopher Boucher next, the train passenger who had seen Bernie Goetz stand over Darrell Cabey and shoot him in cold blood. Unfortunately, Boucher, though still a very young man, had died three years earlier.

Kuby had fretted about the best way to make sure the jury could still hear Boucher's eyewitness account. As Kuby well understood, Boucher's testimony alone "confirmed so much of the account that Goetz gave but later disputed."[28] He could, of course, have the court reporter read Boucher's earlier testimony into the record, but he knew that doing so risked a dry rendering of testimony that in fact had been both passionate and believable.

As if he was taking a page from Slotnick's theater playbook—and perhaps even inspired by the COURT TV cameras—Kuby hatched a plan

Bernhard Goetz on the stand in the civil trial, April 12, 1996.
Reuters

that would require appealing to Darnay Hoffman's ego and his earlier aspiration to be an actor. As Kuby would later recall, he approached Hoffman and said, "Look man, rather than just having a court reporter read it, why don't I retain somebody to be the witness. And then I will read the questions, on direct, from the transcript, [and then you can] read the cross-examination from the transcript on cross. . . . The jury will know it's not the same person, but at least it'll be better. It won't be as boring."[29]

Hoffman was intrigued by this proposal, as Kuby hoped he would be. "You know," Kuby would later recall, "I work with what I have. I've got a television producer here, [so] we'll make it like for TV. And I thought that Darnay would really like it too, not just for the optics, but because he could impersonate Barry Slotnick." Darnay Hoffman, Kuby said, "stupidly agreed."[30]

For this stunt, Kuby asked one of his friends if he might enlist the help of her husband, Peter McCabe, who was an actor. Not only was McCabe "magnificently talented," in Kuby's opinion, but he also "looked a lot like you'd expect Chris Boucher to look [and] the age was the same, the face was [also that of a] handsome young man." For all the jury knew, he also "could be gay."[31]

All Peter had to do was "go over the transcript a few times before he [got] up there and he would sound great." And he did. To Kuby's delight,

Hoffman's generally lackadaisical approach to trial preparation meant that he did not adequately prepare for his own role in the reenactment. All he had to do was read what Barry Slotnick had actually said to this witness back in the criminal trial. He just had to play this lawyer to the hilt. According to Kuby, however, Hoffman "just kind of winged it" and missed every opportunity to discredit Boucher."[32]

Having quite masterfully presented Christopher Boucher's eyewitness account to the jury, Kuby's next challenge was conveying the gravity of Darrell's medical condition and the challenges he was facing as a young man who was paraplegic and had brain damage.

RON KUBY AND his team had pored over thousands of pages of Darrell's medical records, and the tale they told was deeply distressing. The records documented the terrible post-coma nightmares he suffered due to his anoxic encephalopathy as well as other extremely difficult times for Darrell during the fourteen months before he was finally permitted to go home.[33]

On February 8, 1985, for example, these medical records indicated that Darrell "continue[d] to be very agitated."[34] Then on February 11, 1985, although he was still in bad shape, some better news was reported—Darrell was "responding to his mother's voice."[35] But things went downhill again on February 23 because Darrell's temperature was spiking in an alarming fashion. By March 8, 1985, the doctors were disturbed to see that he was still "only able to name 3 of 5 objects" in one of the tests they had administered.[36] The emotionally devastating aspects of Darrell's brain trauma were also clearly indicated on this chart. As Dr. Macaluso firmly noted but three days later, "It is my opinion that he should not be pushed to perform beyond his capabilities. This could have a negative effect by frustrating [the] patient. He needs constant reassurance."[37]

Darrell's medical records would reveal some particularly poignant moments to Kuby, as well. A note on his chart from March 12, 1985, stated that "He smiles and shows affection for the family." Another note, from March 18, 1985, said that Darrell should only "be 'gradually and gently' informed as to events leading to his hospitalization that he wants to know. Family would be the most appropriate people to clarify this for him."[38]

The court recessed for the weekend, and the plaintiffs would take that time to continue to familiarize themselves with this record as they prepared their questions for two of Darrell's doctors, Dr. Adams and Dr. Macaluso. Some of the material they would present on Monday would reiterate details the criminal jury had already heard. But the focus this time was on what, exactly, Darrell's pain and suffering had felt like in real time.

The stakes must have felt particularly high for Kuby and his team. Outside the courtroom, Goetz was continuing to insult the Cabey family in ways difficult to understand. On Friday evening, for example, he had gone on Guardian Angels leader Curtis Sliwa's talk show and said, "It would be better if [Darrell] weren't in a wheelchair or if I had killed him that day."[39]

On Monday morning, April 15, 1996, Dr. Peter Adams, one of Darrell's attending physicians at St. Vincent's, took the stand and would be questioned by Kuby's associate, Daniel Perez.[40] As a physician who performed both general and thoracic surgery, Dr. Adams understood just how serious Darrell's situation was from the moment he came into his ER. He also knew all that he endured as he fought to live.

Darrell had to undergo significant surgical procedures, Dr. Adams confirmed. He had a hole in both of his lungs, which "produced damage, a lot of damage to the lung itself, there was some bleeding, and collapse of both."[41] As important, his blood pressure would plummet, putting his body into profound shock. "In other words," Adams explained, it "looks like he has no blood pressure. . . . We used to call this spinal shock" and its consequences were dire.[42]

Spinal shock, in turn, created a host of issues for Darrell in addition to paralyzing him, he went on. Because of the nerve damage from his paralysis, for example, even breathing was very hard for Darrell to manage. As Dr. Adams put it, "You can't clear your secretions, you can't cough, you can't do these things and you tend to get accumulation of these secretions in the area of your airway, windpipe."[43] In turn the lungs begin to fill and get "contaminated by the mucus."[44]

Is that also painful? Daniel Perez asked.

"No one likes to choke to death, it's discomforting not being able to breathe comfortably," Adams replied.[45]

And, so, Darrell periodically needed help to clear his lungs.

"When they mechanically go into your lungs, does that cause any pain or discomfort?" Perez went on.[46]

Without missing a beat, Dr. Adams replied, "You bet."[47]

Worse for Darrell, his lungs had been shredded by Goetz's bullet and were already collapsing. With Perez's guidance, Adams went on to explain the dire effects of Darrell's collapsed lungs. Not only were blood and fluid filling them, but his inability to cough easily even when they were drained meant that he risked severe pneumonia. Darrell got this serious infection and worse, went on to develop an abscess in his chest called empyema. In cases such as Darrell's, Adams continued, "you can give them four buckets of antibiotics and it won't get better."[48]

When Darrell grew sicker and sicker and eventually went into respiratory arrest, the process of resuscitating him had also been brutal. As Dr. Adams told the jury, they had to give Darrell both a tracheotomy and a bronchoscopy due to the abscess that had formed between his lung and ribs on the right side of his chest. This abscess had filled the cavity with pus, "like a big boil," and had to be drained to eliminate that source of infection. In order to do this, they had performed a rib resection, creating a hole large enough that the infected material could escape through. Several months later, since the infection persisted, they were forced to do a procedure called a decortication. They "[took] away the lining of the lung and the inside of the chest" to encourage the lung to re-expand.[49]

Again, Perez asked if the procedures were painful. "Oh, yeah, sure," Adams replied.[50]

Even when he finally came out of his coma, Darrell's injuries meant that he would remain in pain on a daily basis, Adams revealed. While he was given medication to manage it, his loss of nervous control of many of the organs in the lower half of his body, including his bladder, intestines, and blood vessels, created additional discomfort by periodically sending his body into wrenching spasms—where his muscles would suddenly "contract very hard or sometimes . . . relax very hard," making his condition most unstable.[51]

The jury also learned the details of the devastating sacral decubitus ulcer that had formed on Darrell's lower back from lying down for so long, the tracheostomy tube that would be in place for months, the invasive nasogastric tube that he also had to endure, and the serious pain that had come with all of these assaults to the body.

Finally, Perez asked Dr. Adams how bad things had been for Darrell Cabey on the whole. He was in "critical, critical condition," the doctor stressed. "Did you expect him to recover?" Perez asked.[52] After he had gone into respiratory arrest, the doctor said, he had been "very much in doubt."[53]

When Dr. Peter Adams stepped down from the witness box, the mood in the room was somber indeed. Hearing the graphic and disturbing details of the shooting's aftermath on Darrell in the days, months, and now years thereafter had been devastating. But Ron Kuby was not finished driving this point home. Next, he brought to the stand Dr. Macaluso, another of Darrell's doctors, the neurologist who had previously testified at the criminal trial to the extraordinary costs of the shooting on Darrell's cognitive abilities.

With virtually no pushback from Darnay Hoffman, Dr. Macaluso offered at times even more graphic and heartbreaking medical testimony, much of which he had already provided in an affidavit to the court.[54] Dr. Macaluso was also intimately familiar with Darrell's condition. He had been Darrell's doctor on the day he went into respiratory arrest and became comatose, entering a "persistent vegetative state" for more than a month.[55] He'd also been there when Darrell eventually opened his eyes and moved his arms, and he was the first doctor to note the extent of his brain damage.

Dr. Macaluso laid out how Darrell Cabey had been deprived of oxygen and made clear that the long-term fallout from this had been devastating. "This brain damage," he explained, "resulted in a significant impairment of cognitive functioning" including a loss of memory from the time of the shooting until he came out of his coma.[56] When he finally woke up, "He was able to speak . . . but with slurred speech."[57] He could remember things periodically, but these memories would quickly disappear because he now had significant memory impairment. He could move his upper body, but with a complete lack of coordination in his arms.

Darrell had difficulty retaining new information, challenges coping with stress, and significant cognitive impairment. By the time he emerged from this coma, he was no longer able even to write his own name.[58]

Macaluso had always been blunt in his assessment of Darrell's prognosis, writing earlier that there was "no way to determine when, if ever, the abovementioned conditions will improve."[59] He hadn't grown any more optimistic. As it stood, Kuby was hoping that the jury would see that Darrell had been left, even all these years later, with the mental capacity of an eight-year-old due to the injuries he had sustained.[60]

And, of course, Darrell still could not walk. This fact was not lost on the jury as he sat before them during this trial, slight and sad, having been wheeled into the courtroom and placed awkwardly in a more open space where he could at least see what was going on in the trial.

As the jury processed the disturbing testimony provided by both Dr. Adams and Dr. Macaluso, the day's testimony, mercifully, came to an end.

THE NEXT MORNING, the jury would hear directly from Darrell's mother, Shirley Cabey. She took the stand on Tuesday, April 16, and Ron Kuby hoped that the jury would take this opportunity to really listen to her more intimate and familial perspective on all that had happened to her son.

Shirley Cabey had been reluctant to testify. As Kuby's other assistant on the case, Daniella Korotzer, said, she remained an "intensely private person." Nevertheless, Shirley ultimately agreed to share her story. In a voice that reporters described as "so soft she could have been talking to herself," she chronicled for the jury how drastically Goetz's actions had changed their lives over the last eleven years.[61]

Tearfully, this "short, stout woman," as *The New York Times* described her, explained that even the most basic daily tasks and everyday routines were "an arduous chore."[62] Life had never been easy—she had been a widow since Darrell was seven years old—but after Goetz had shot her son, it became, at times, almost unbearable.

As journalist Adam Nossiter reported, caring for Darrell took up almost all of her time. "This was her life now."[63]

As important, the road taken even to arrive at this challenging, albeit consistent, daily routine had been extremely difficult to travel. Darrell had been in the hospital for over a year. He had undergone multiple major surgeries and endured immense physical pain. And then, there was the terrible moment he had stopped breathing altogether and gone into a coma. Even when, by the grace of God, Darrell had managed to survive respiratory arrest, the brain damage he had been left with was profound. It had taken "months, months" before her son could even talk. And though he did get better, he was never the same.[64]

"He repeats himself," Shirley explained. At times, she would see him responding to people's questions inappropriately simply because he knew he should respond, and also because "he [didn't] want people to think he's stupid."[65]

As Shirley testified, she refused to even acknowledge Goetz. Instead, she kept her gaze affixed to her son's face, his expression hard to read. Shirley was almost wistful as she described the kid Darrell had been before the shooting. Her son had certainly faced a number of challenges. He had a learning disability, and he didn't finish high school. But, she insisted, he was also a normal and happy and kindhearted kid, one who "liked going to the movies and enjoyed dressing sharply and admiring himself in the mirror."[66]

Now, her son "spends his days at a center with other victims of paralysis" doing menial tasks such as "putting pens together."[67] He didn't have friends, a detail that really seemed to break her heart. Night after night, he sat in front of the television alone, watching "others run and jump and live on TV."[68]

Shirley Cabey's testimony was brief, but it was powerful. As she spoke, Bernie Goetz "sat up straight in his seat" but showed "no reaction as he heard Mrs. Cabey's description."[69] His lawyer, Darnay Hoffman, seemed unsure of how to proceed. To badger a broken woman on cross-examination would clearly have been in poor taste, and in spite of his desire for the limelight, even he did not seem to have the stomach for it.

As Hoffman explained "testily" to the reporters who chased him to the elevators, asking why he had not questioned her, "Quite frankly, lawyers are part of the human race." Further, he continued, "Mrs. Cabey, obviously, is still very upset and quite understandably so." Hoffman acknowledged that "her son was very grievously injured, and I think that everyone can see that Mrs. Cabey is deserving of a great deal of sympathy."[70]

WHEN RON KUBY CALLED his last witness to the stand, it must have seemed almost superfluous. The last three witnesses had gutted everyone who had listened to their testimony, especially as it had followed Goetz's own sneering embrace of the violence he had perpetrated and the pain he had caused Darrell.

But Kuby was not taking any chances. On April 17, he called radiologist Dr. Charles Hirsch to the stand as his last witness. Hirsch was the chief medical examiner of Suffolk County, New York, whom Greg Waples had called as his own last rebuttal witness in the criminal trial. By 1996, Dr. Hirsch was the head medical examiner for the city of New York and was also employed by the medical school of New York University, where he served as both a professor and chairman of the department of forensic medicine and a professor of pathology. His credentials were impeccable and unimpeachable.

Kuby's assistant Daniel Perez would handle this questioning, as he had done for Dr. Adams.[71] In graphic and chilling detail, Dr. Hirsch made clear to the jury that Darrell was seated when Bernie Goetz stood over him and shot him, with one devastating bullet, at very close range. He again testified to all of this with a high degree of "medical certainty" before describing the devastation Bernie Goetz's fifth hollow point bullet had wrought.[72] This bullet had struck Darrell in the back, just below his left shoulder blade. It grazed one of his ribs before it perforated his spine, leaving a trail of metal particles in its wake and a large number in the spine itself, before it "came to rest on the right side of his body."[73]

After his spinal cord had been "essentially transected," Darrell had suffered "an immediate loss of voluntary control of his muscles below that level."[74] There was no doubt that Goetz's bullet had done all of this.

It was now time for Darnay Hoffman to put on a robust defense.

Remarkably, however, he did not bring in any of the many witnesses he had originally planned to, save one. In fact, to the utter surprise of all parties assembled, he would call only two witnesses to the stand—his "star" witness, the popular and bombastic news columnist Jimmy Breslin, and Bernard Yudowitz, the rather sour psychiatrist now famous for the "automatic pilot" defense that had allowed Barry Slotnick to explain away why Bernie Goetz had exacted such violence when he had defended him in criminal court.

Jimmy Breslin had remained nothing short of a New York institution, a man whom many New Yorkers liked and trusted—Kuby included. Kuby viewed Breslin as "a really decent guy—a man on the side of the little guy, and of justice and fairness."[75] Breslin had even given a beautiful tribute at Kunstler's funeral the year before.[76]

All of that said, when it came to his client Darrell Cabey, Kuby felt that Breslin had stooped unforgivably low. Breslin was the reporter who interviewed Darrell in his hospital room without legal counsel present and published a piece on him that had touched off a media firestorm back in November 1985. At that point, Kunstler and Kuby's services had already been retained by the Cabey family, and neither of them had any idea that this interview was going to take place. In Kuby's opinion, "Jimmy Breslin knew damn well that if he had contacted me or contacted Bill, we would say no."[77]

As Curtis Sliwa would explain on his talk radio show, Breslin had savvily decided to get past hospital security by approaching Darrell's mother. "Unlike other journalists who had queued up" and were turned away, with Shirley at his side, Jimmy Breslin was "given the red carpet treatment."[78]

This interview had proved devastating for the Cabey family. Not only did it make major headlines, but it likely played a role in Goetz's criminal acquittal. In one of the most read columns he wrote for the *Daily News*,

Breslin had relayed that Darrell told him the boys had indeed planned on robbing Goetz, because he looked like "easy bait."

Breslin's wide readership had no way of knowing Darrell was hardly a reliable narrator of his own history. As detailed in Dr. Macaluso's medical notations, at the time of Breslin's visit, Darrell was unable to recall the events of that day and was almost desperate to understand what had placed him in the hospital. And Breslin's readers didn't seem to care that during their interview Darrell was slurring his words, was hard to understand, and at times seemed confused—details all pointed out by Breslin himself. This article had done significant damage to Greg Waples's case and now threatened to do the same to Ron Kuby's.

Kuby was determined to ensure that this would not happen. When Hoffman finished with the witness, Kuby put aside his personal affection for Jimmy Breslin, whom he had described as "a personal hero . . . [since] before I even became a lawyer. I mean, my dad introduced me to his first book, *The Gang That Couldn't Shoot Straight*."[79] His cross-examination of Breslin was one of the most contentious and dramatic moments of the entire televised trial.

He began his rebuttal by reminding the jury that while Jimmy Breslin was "a fantastic reporter. And may he live and write and report forever," he was no neurologist. When it came to assessing Darrell's memory, they would have to trust the expert, Dr. Macaluso, over Breslin.

In response, Jimmy Breslin said, rather heatedly, that he "stood by his reporting."[80] He insisted that he had no dog in this fight and maintained that he "equally dislike[d] both sides" in the case.[81] Ultimately, the jury did not seem moved one way or the other by Breslin's testimony. It had been fun to watch this legendary figure in action, and the jurors had even chuckled as he sparred with Kuby. But if anything, the exchange had advantaged the plaintiff rather than the defense, since nothing conclusive was established and it devolved into a "he said, he said" type of situation.

Undoubtedly feeling rather deflated, considering his glory moment in front of the cameras had not gone as planned, Darnay Hoffman dutifully called his second and final witness, Dr. Yudowitz, to the stand. With this witness he would attempt to persuade the jury, as Barry Slotnick had done before him, that Bernie Goetz had been in the midst of an adrenaline fugue and had no idea who or what he was shooting at. It was Hoffman's hope that the jury would see, at the very least, that the damage Bernie inflicted on Darrell Cabey was not malicious or intentional.

Should Hoffman lose this case, this could, at least theoretically, mitigate against an outrageous damages award.

Although Dr. Yudowitz's testimony was a virtual repeat of the claims he had made during the criminal trial, it seemed to land less successfully this time around. After Goetz himself had readily admitted just a few days prior that he'd intended to shoot, kill, and even maim Darrell Cabey and his friends, Yudowitz's argument must have seemed wholly implausible.

As important, perhaps, was that it seemed like Hoffman himself didn't much believe in his own client. At the very least, he hadn't done the work to offer a plausible defense on his behalf. As one paper put it, Hoffman had all the time he needed to mount his own case, but "by lunchtime he had shut it down."[82] The press was completely baffled that Hoffman had not done more to stand up to Darrell Cabey's lawyers. But as he said to one outlet, "A weak offense is often a strong defense," perhaps attempting to sound like everything had gone to plan. When asked if he had felt out of his league in this proceeding, Hoffman tried to laugh off the accusation, saying, "Not at all, if anything, I am very much in my league."[83]

Judge Salman announced that it was now time for each side's closing statements. The jury was slated to return the next day, Friday, April 19, to hear Kuby's and Hoffman's remarks, but both lawyers asked to have the weekend to regroup, and the judge granted their request. Court would resume the following Monday.

NEW YORK'S CONSERVATIVE media outlets—print and radio—had been revisiting this now more than ten-year-long debate over whether Goetz was in fact responsible for the fact that Darrell Cabey would live the rest of his life paralyzed and cognitively compromised. The answer was clear, as far as the editors of the *New York Post* saw it: "Cabey's injuries were grievous, but he deserves little sympathy. People who choose a life of crime risk having to pay a price. Indeed, a verdict for Cabey would only serve to send one more signal to law-abiding New Yorkers that the legal system tends to provide 'justice' for criminals—not their victims."[84] This was, of course, more than a little ironic, considering that Bernie Goetz, not Darrell Cabey, was a convicted criminal.

Ron Kuby found himself arguing against this exact viewpoint when he appeared on Curtis Sliwa's morning talk show on WABC Radio on Saturday, April 20, 1996. Both Kuby and Sliwa loved to spar, and when Sliwa invited him to discuss the civil case on air, Kuby was more than game.[85]

The central issue for Sliwa, as it was for most of white New York, was whether Darrell Cabey had provoked Goetz, or whether Goetz had in fact targeted him with that gratuitous and deadly fifth shot. "Did he go back to Darrell Cabey? Did he shoot him again? Nobody seems to know, like we get different answers from different people," Sliwa said.[86]

Goetz had admitted back in 1985 to targeting Darrell and his friends, something he had just confirmed again on the stand in the civil trial. Kuby found Sliwa's desire to deny this almost laughable. "He never denied this account!" Kuby retorted—not then, not since, not now! But Sliwa just couldn't accept it.[87]

Momentarily suspending his obvious disbelief, Sliwa entertained Kuby's premise. Perhaps Goetz had purposefully gone over to Cabey and delivered the shot that would sever his spine. But why was Cabey on the train in the first place?

Before answering Sliwa's loaded question, Kuby would first turn to Goetz's own admissions:

> According to Bernhard Goetz, Curtis, you know . . . before you can shoot somebody, they have to do something to you. I asked Mr. Goetz, I said in a 1992 deposition, I said, question: "What specifically, to the best of your recollection, did Darrell Cabey do?" Answer, "He was part of the group." "Did he ever raise his hand?" "No." "Did he ever raise a fist?" "No." "Did he ever threaten you?" "No." "Did he ever speak to you?" "No, no, no." . . . So whatever was on Darrell Cabey's mind, which I contend we will never know because of the brain damage . . . Darrell Cabey didn't do anything, and he didn't say anything, and he didn't deserve to get shot down.[88]

When faced with these facts, Sliwa pivoted. He tried to fall back to the argument of self-defense and the trauma Goetz sustained from his past mugging in 1981. As he recounted how Goetz was "savagely mugged" at the Canal Street station, Kuby shot him down once more. "Of course, this is part of the mythology that Bernhard Goetz has created," Kuby replied. "But you know, the fact is, when Bernie Goetz had a chance to get on the witness stand and to tell the jury this, tell the jury about this horrible mugging, [he didn't]."[89]

Still undeterred, Sliwa went down an entirely new, highly inflammatory path. Had he not been shot, Darrell Cabey "probably would have been doing time for the shotgun robbery of a young man," Sliwa claimed.[90]

Kuby would not stand for this wild speculation, and dove into his own dramatic and embellished version of events. "Curtis. Curtis, what? . . . You don't know that at all," he said. "The system never got a chance to work because . . . [Bernie Goetz], while buying illegal drugs, while stoned out of his mind with an illegal handgun, decided to dispense some summary justice and became a hero to the bigots and fools out there."[91]

Passions now running hot for both men, Curtis Sliwa responded, "I'll give him a medal. In fact, I would say . . . 'Hey Bernie, the only problem? Your aim was off.' . . . Ron Kuby, playing the race card as you so often do. Feeling though that you are correct in doing so. . . . We will . . . await the jury's findings."[92]

ON THE DAY of closing statements, Darnay Hoffman would fail to make an argument in defense of Bernie Goetz anywhere near as powerful, or as impassioned, as the one Sliwa had made over the weekend on his radio show. On Monday, April 22, 1996, Hoffman told the jury that they must simply, as one paper put it, "look beyond his client's much-publicized racist beliefs and focus more on his state of mind at the time of the shooting."[93]

In fact, in the course of his defense, Hoffman had offered the jury a "bunch of maybes," which hardly amounted to a compelling argument. "Does anyone really believe that those youths were just panhandling?" he jeered. "Do you really think he had any choice but to use that gun?" he went on.[94]

In an attempt to find some common ground with each juror, he acknowledged that they were in a terrible position. He was essentially asking them to ignore their "feelings" about the defendant's character "or lack of character." He went on to admit, "I mean, Bernie made that hard. There's no question about it. He came in here and he sat on your heads as jurors. He made it tough for you. I mean, clearly, your instinct is just to sock it to him."[95]

Ultimately, Hoffman brought more energy to his closing statement than he had offered the entire rest of the trial. He even dragged in a lectern to more theatrically deliver his remarks, and brought some oversized images of Goetz's other victims into the courtroom in a strange attempt to replicate Barry Slotnick's criminal defense. His problem was he didn't have much to work with. He kept trying to pander to what he assumed were the jurors' thoughts about his client—at one point calling him "a clown." But in the end, he was basically pleading with them to not rule against Bernie Goetz.[96]

It was then Ron Kuby's turn. Not only did he replay parts of Bernie's own confession tape to remind the jury of his "character," but he also insisted—in an oration that at times resembled a civil rights speech from an earlier era—that the case could not be clearer. It had become personal, he also noted. By now, Ron Kuby had known Shirley and Darrell for eleven years. He had helped them navigate the legal and personal difficulties that had befallen Darrell thanks to Bernie Goetz's "racist" and "violent" acts.[97] What the jury was about to do really mattered.

Kuby looked each juror in the eye as he gestured to a stack of papers on the table. "These are Darrell Cabey's medical records. You want to talk about vicious?" he asked. "You want to talk about being hurt? You want to talk about going to the hospital? Permanent pain? What did Darrell Cabey do to Bernhard Goetz? Nothing. What did Bernhard Goetz do to Darrell Cabey? He shot him in the back."[98]

He walked them through Goetz's many ugly admissions to remind them that this shooter had intended to cause everything that had befallen Darrell Cabey. With regard to Hoffman's supposed star witness, Jimmy Breslin, he suggested that Breslin wasn't a vicious guy, but that he was simply mistaken about what Darrell Cabey had been capable of remembering at the time of his interview.

More to the point, Kuby went on, even if his friend Troy Canty had asked Bernie Goetz for five dollars, Darrell Cabey did not deserve the horror that followed. He would need assistance for the rest of his life, and he was entitled to be paid damages. "Award enough in punitive damages," he told them passionately, "that you bankrupt every other bigot with a gun out there."[99]

ON TUESDAY, April 23, 1996, the Bronx jury found Bernhard Goetz liable for all that happened to Darrell Cabey as a result of being shot on December 22, 1984. After deliberating for less than five hours, these jurors would indeed "sock it to him" when it came to damages.[100] The jury was unanimous, which was significant. In New York City civil court, it would have only taken five out of the six jurors to side with the plaintiff. In this case, all of them did. The jury read its determination out loud as TV cameras rolled:

> As to claims of Assault and Battery: Do you find that Defendant intended to shoot Darrell Cabey?
> YES 6–0
> Was Defendant justified in his shooting of Plaintiff Darrell Cabey?
> NO 6–0
> As to claims for Intentional Infliction of Emotional Distress: Do you find that Defendant's conduct was so shocking and outrageous that it exceeded all reasonable bounds of decency as an average member of the community would tolerate?
> YES 6–0
> Do you find that Defendant recklessly acted with the intention to cause Plaintiff severe emotional distress?
> YES 6–0
> Do you find that Defendant so acted to cause Plaintiff such emotional distress?
> YES 6–0
> Was the Defendant justified in his actions?
> NO 6–0

As for damages, the jury brought down the hammer. The breakdown was $2.2 million for pain and suffering, $15.8 million for future pain and suffering, and $25 million in punitive damages. Darrell Cabey and his family were entitled to a total compensation of $43 million.

This number stunned the media. As the *NBC Nightly News* broadcast opined ruefully, "Goetz may have been his own worst enemy during the trial," because this "verdict was a stunning defeat." As reporter Rehema Ellis then noted, "His lawyer says Goetz will not appeal today's verdict," and therefore, "we should tell you that under New York State law, up to 10% of Goetz's earnings for the next 20 years must go to the victim to pay off" this damages award.[101]

The *New York Post* and other conservative media outlets made their outrage at the verdict well known, painting it as a race-based attack on

Ron Kuby raises his fist in celebration as he leaves the Bronx State Supreme Court, April 23, 1996.
AP Photo/Kathy Willens

common sense, but this Bronx jury wasn't having it. As juror Elba Torres put it, race was irrelevant. What had mattered to her was that the defendant had readily admitted to committing the most callous acts, deliberately shooting Darrell Cabey when he was "cowering in fear." "That," she insisted, "was unfair."[102]

For his part, however, Goetz seemed confident that the outcome of this civil suit wouldn't impact him much at all. He hadn't even shown up to hear the verdict. As one editorial mused, it was as if Goetz had been "empowered by his support from right-wing talk-show audiences."[103]

42

Duck and Weave

IN A CRIMINAL TRIAL, everyone waits with bated breath for the sentencing phase, which can at times happen at a later date. Similarly, in a civil case, the actual damages awarded a plaintiff might be decided later in another "damages phase." In the case of Darrell Cabey's civil trial, however, the decision had been made immediately.

This was good news for the Cabey family—this jury's verdict was the end of an excruciatingly long fight to be heard. As Shirley told reporters, "I feel relieved that it's over. . . . It's not a dream where I'm jumping for joy. But I'm happy the rest of the world knows my son didn't do anything."[1] It meant they could also begin, at least in theory, to secure the resources Darrell would need to manage his physical and mental disabilities in the future.

Deep down Shirley knew that her chances of seeing $43 million were slim to none. And Ron Kuby had made clear to reporters just after the verdict was announced that "This case was never about money."[2] It was, he later opined, "about the necessity to expose Bernhard Goetz as the racist would-be murderer that he is despite public perceptions."[3]

But the truth was, the money did matter. Financially, Shirley could not be more stressed. Ron Kuby and his associates assured her that even if Goetz only had a few resources, some of them would go to Darrell. This was a relief. "If I get some—hey, my son sure could use it. . . . Anything I get sure will be worthwhile."[4]

The question was, how "few" assets did Bernie Goetz actually have? In every deposition, Goetz remained vague regarding his financial connections to his family's business in Florida. While he conceded that he was an acting vice president, Darrell's attorneys never got clarity as to how much money this venture netted him. It had also remained unclear how much he made from his own business, Electrical Calibration Laboratory, Inc. One thing was certain, however—every attempt they made to access his funds would disappoint.

Goetz had inherited $140,000 after the death of his father, but there seemed to be no evidence that these funds remained anywhere where they might be transferred to Darrell.[5]

Still, Kuby kept trying. "We did a first round discovery, and Goetz simply had no assets," he recalled.[6] But that did not mean he would not eventually accrue assets or that some would not eventually be found. The judgment against Goetz was good for the next twenty years. If he came into any family money, Darrell would come into that same money. If he won the lottery, Darrell would also win the lottery. And so, Kuby closely monitored Goetz's finances for years.

Meanwhile, Goetz continued to dodge any questions regarding his financial status from Darrell's attorney until, once again, Ron Kuby was forced to legally compel him to reply. At 8:30 p.m. on December 29, 1998, just over fourteen years to the day after he shot Darrell, Ron Kuby served Goetz with a subpoena.[7]

As this document noted, Bernie Goetz owed Darrell Cabey "45,699,208.00 together with interest thereon from January 3, 1997." Goetz was put on notice that any "false swearing or failure to comply with this subpoena" would immediately place him in contempt of court. He was told that he had seven days to "answer in writing under oath" all outstanding questions regarding his finances. This required listing every payment made over the past two years to Goetz personally, or to his businesses, as well as "all debts owed" to him personally, or to his businesses, including the date, amount, and purpose of each figure.[8]

Understanding that, at 9 percent interest, the amount of money he owed Darrell Cabey was growing ever larger, Bernie Goetz had already tried to get out of his debt by filing for bankruptcy.[9] To do this, he'd had to submit his own financial disclosure, which insisted that he had only about $17,000 in assets, including "a $320 wardrobe, some electronic equipment, a pet chinchilla and guinea pig valued together at $130, and about $500 in cash."[10]

Goetz said that he also owed "a $1 million liability for an unfulfilled book contract and $16 million in unpaid lawyers' bills" in addition to the damages due to Darrell Cabey. The book contract, dated 1985, would have to be broken so that he could "sign a new, seven-figure deal he hopes to get with a new publisher." Of the legal fees, he owed Barry Slotnick alone a cool $6.5 million.[11]

That Bernie Goetz's response to losing to Darrell Cabey was to file for bankruptcy should not have been a surprise. The 1980s had made it easier than ever for both persons and businesses to avoid debt thanks to a major overhaul of the bankruptcy code. This had both streamlined the process by which bankruptcy could be declared and established different ways to do so—Chapters 7 and 13 for individuals and Chapter 11 for businesses.

The number of bankruptcies in America had in fact skyrocketed in the 1980s—especially after the decade's two major recessions, one in the earliest years of Reaganomics and the second with the crash of 1987.[12]

As important, however, was the fact that the wealthiest Americans had played a big role in destigmatizing bankruptcy in the Reagan eighties. Bankruptcy could, some high-profile corporate figures had argued, be essential to doing business. Indeed, in the 1990s, perhaps no major wealthy figure was more essential in rebranding bankruptcy as the sign of a savvy entrepreneur than New Yorker Donald Trump. Trump's companies had filed Chapter 11 in relation to his massive Trump Taj Mahal Casino in 1991 and then to his baby, the Trump Plaza Hotel, in 1992.

However, this Hail Mary move, it would turn out, was not a simple win for Bernie Goetz, any more than it had been for the countless other ordinary people in the 1980s and 1990s who had tried to address their mounting debt via the bankruptcy courts. And his case was more complex than most. As a general legal matter, intentional torts such as the one facing Goetz were not dischargeable under bankruptcy law. As Judge Cornelius Blackshear of United States Bankruptcy Court made clear to Bernie, "the jury award could not be dismissed by a declaration of bankruptcy. Legal fees, however, were discharged."[13]

Ron Kuby felt that this was at least some good news. As he put it, "When you cause injury to another person, not just financial injury, but physical or mental injury, you don't get to write it off."[14] He remained worried, however, that Goetz would find other ways to wriggle out of paying Darrell Cabey even one dollar.

Still, Kuby wouldn't give up. In time, he even hired a law firm—

Fishman and Neil—to help recover monies owed to the Cabey family.[15] But eventually, even he had to admit defeat. As the years went by, it seemed increasingly clear that they were never going to get so much as a nickel out of Bernie Goetz. Continuing to go after funds that he refused to disclose or to hand over was itself becoming too costly. It was time to cry uncle. But damn, did it sting. As Kuby suggested to one reporter, Goetz was choosing to "live in voluntary squalor" rather than do the right thing by Darrell Cabey.[16]

The day that he gave Shirley this sobering news, Kuby tried to stress the positive. "We accomplished what we set out to do," he reminded her. "We held Bernie Goetz to account, money or no money."[17]

"She was very quiet," Kuby recalled, and, he could tell, "deeply hurt."[18]

Shirley Cabey's profound disappointment, and her deep skepticism that fairness might finally win the day, would be shared by countless other New Yorkers, particularly those who had continued to struggle as the 1980s had become the 1990s, and as politicians such as Clinton and Giuliani had only doubled down on the fear-mongering and escalated the income inequality of the Reagan eighties.

What few could ever have predicted, however, was that this was just the beginning. The greed-is-good ideology; the trickle-down and social-safety-net-slashing economics; the get-tough-on-crime policies of those earlier decades would truly come of age over the next three.

They also could not have expected how, once again, Rupert Murdoch's conservative media company would be essential to the normalization and celebration of all of this.

BY THE 1990S, Murdoch's media empire did not rely solely on the *Post* to spread its conservative views and to reshape politics as well as culture. For a time, Murdoch had actually been forced to sell the paper, and even when he got it back, countless Americans had already begun turning to cable television and to cable news channels like CNN to make sense of the world around them. And so, Murdoch decided to conquer that market too.[19]

In fact, the world of print and television media had undergone its own revolutionary changes over the course of the late 1980s and into the 1990s.[20] With the rise of cable television, and the advent of the internet, entirely new possibilities for engaging audiences arose. Rupert Murdoch understood the possibilities of the digital revolution far better than any of his rivals, and he had the means to capitalize on it. He recognized not only that "the screaming front-pages that are part of the time-honored tradition of big-city newspaper battles" needed now to "be underscored with special urgency," but also that pandering to readers' basest instincts in order to dominate print media was too limited a goal.[21]

By the mid-1990s, Murdoch began to imagine an entire news channel that would do for viewers what the *Post* had done for readers. He wanted to give this new audience a way to make sense of the dismay they felt at the declining wages, the lack of city services, and the blight and crime, one that would turn anger toward the people suffering even more than they were.

When Rupert Murdoch premiered Fox News in October 1996 to an eager audience of 17 million cable subscribers, it was but six months after Bernie Goetz's loss to Darrell Cabey in that civil courtroom in the Bronx. Of course, Murdoch's newspaper, the *New York Post,* had played a crucial role in presenting Darrell's win to many white New Yorkers as pure graft, and as punishing a man who had already suffered enough. But in the wake of that trial, and with Fox News, it became possible for Murdoch to blast this sort of conservative messaging not just to New Yorkers but to all Americans.

Notably, Rudy Giuliani had made all of this possible. As Newsmax Media CEO Chris Ruddy pointed out:

> When Fox News launched they had problems because they couldn't get into New York City. Time Warner owned the whole franchise and they also owned CNN. [Its liberal owner] Ted Turner was hell-bent on stopping that. [*Post* columnist] Eric Breindel is the guy that got Rudy to go and put Fox on a public access channel. That broke the blockade and Fox News got on all the other systems.
>
> Had they not had the *New York Post,* and had Eric not been so aligned with Rudy I don't think they would have gotten that.[22]

When Fox News began broadcasting from its "hub in Midtown Manhattan at New York City's Rockefeller Center," few people could have predicted just how significant it was that the same narratives regarding poverty, race, crime, blight, sexuality, and so much more, which had been fed to New Yorkers by way of the splashy headlines and stories of the *Post,* would now be fed to America through the even splashier medium of twenty-four-hour television news.[23] This would change history.

PART VI

The Rebirth of White Rage in America

IN 1996, Darrell Cabey's victory against Bernie Goetz in civil court was met with elation and surprise but also no small measure of skepticism in the South Bronx. And rightly so. The 1980s and the 1990s had been unbearably bleak for Black and Brown New Yorkers. True, there was now a Democrat in the White House, and he had certainly courted civil rights leaders and the Black vote more generally. But just as Darrell Cabey's Bronx courtroom win had not changed his fate, neither did the election of William Jefferson Clinton reverse the Reagan Revolution nor undo the serious damage it had done.

The economic and cultural overhaul that had taken place during the Reagan eighties had clearly mattered more than anyone appreciated at the time. The overt and celebrated abandonment of the many in favor of the few had wreaked havoc on lower-income America. The cementing of the idea that poverty and racial disparities stemmed from laziness and lack of a moral compass, rather than from lack of opportunity, had devastated the nation's already most marginalized citizens. So had the notion that safety would come through more criminalization. And the fact that the success of all of this, of the Reagan Revolution itself, had depended upon the deliberate stoking of white racial resentment, as well as on the slow normalization and relegitimization of white vigilante fury, would leave an indelible stain on the nation and compromise its very future.

Indeed, in the four decades that followed Bernie Goetz's act of vigilante violence, incidents in which white citizens decided to take justice into their own hands became not only more commonplace but also more acceptable under the law. From firearm violence to brutal physical assaults on the part of both individuals and mobs, cops and ordinary citizens, Americans would come to feel that they could act upon their fear or their fury with impunity.[1]

The twenty-first century did bring some important moments of pushback against this slow but sure embrace of guns and greed as well as other destructive legacies of the Reagan Revolution. Ordinary people would win important economic and social justice victories against the unfettered prerogatives of the rich and unchecked racial fury alike with the Occupy Wall Street and Black Lives Matter movements; the election of Barack Obama to the presidency of the United States was also a dramatic rebuke of the ugly path the country had been on.

But the Obama years proved to be a fleeting reprieve and would, in fact, touch off altogether new levels of white fear and fury.

The white racial rage of the Obama years would be cultivated by the media in unprecedented ways. Rupert Murdoch's conservative media empire had entered the 2000s more powerful, and less tethered to the truth, than ever before, and its messaging was now being promulgated as well by countless other, and even more incendiary, right-wing outlets.

This was the historical context within which Donald J. Trump would become the next president. It was the economic and cultural landscape that made his ascent to the White House not just possible but perhaps inevitable.

Beginning in 2017, and with ever more resolve as his second term began in 2025, President Trump would set about dismantling the final vestiges of the New Deal and the Great Society—an outcome that Ronald Reagan had dreamed of, but even he had not imagined possible.

Perhaps more prescient than most was singer Billy Joel in his 1989 chart-topper "We Didn't Start the Fire." It was he who explicitly shouted out the lived costs of the Reagan eighties, from "homeless vets, AIDS, crack [and] hypodermics on the shore" to Bernie Goetz himself. And the refrain of this song eerily summed up the endless reverberations of that tragic decade:

We didn't start the fire
But when we are gone
It will still burn on, and on, and on, and on, and on, and on, and on, and on.[2]

43

Hearts and Minds

Not long after Ron Kuby went on Curtis Sliwa's conservative WABC talk radio show in 1996, just before the Bronx jury decided Bernie Goetz's fate in civil court, Kuby accepted a years-long cohosting stint with Sliwa in this most coveted morning talk show time slot.[1] The show's audience loved listening to right-wing guys like Sliwa take on bleeding-heart liberals like Kuby, but after eight years Kuby would abruptly be booted, with executives meanwhile hiring so-called Shock Jock Don Imus, who had recently made headlines for his racist comments about the Rutgers women's basketball team.[2]

As Kuby explained, "WABC was always right-leaning, but [for a time] there were many independent and left voices." Eventually, they were all "purged, leaving only me."[3] And soon, not even him. Curtis Sliwa remained on the air and became even more of a local celebrity. He spoke a language that appealed to the city's disaffected residents in the same way that Rupert Murdoch's media empire had, first capturing their interest and loyalty in the *New York Post* and then, by 1996, offering them even more unabashedly conservative viewpoints via its ever-expanding Fox News network.[4]

From the outset, it was clear that the Fox News Channel was going to grow, and grow rapidly. In its first quarter in 1997, it was averaging approximately 46,000 viewers in prime time. Twenty-three years later, in 2020, the network was averaging 3.6 million prime-time viewers—a stunning increase of more than 6,300 percent. That same year, according to Nielsen Media Research, Fox News Channel was averaging 1.9 million daytime viewers, the highest day and prime-time audiences in cable news history.[5]

Just as the *Post* sought to be seen as mainstream rather than avowedly right-leaning, Fox News presented itself as "Fair and Balanced," implying that its views were neither controversial nor conservative. They were factual, and frankly, mainstream. As one writer noted, this was a brilliant marketing move. It suggested to viewers that so-called traditional media outlets "were biased," whereas conservative views were bias-free and un-ideological.[6]

Fox News' 1996 starting lineup of shows included *Hannity & Colmes* (1996–2009), in which Sean Hannity presented the conservative viewpoint while cohost Alan Colmes provided the liberal perspective. In time, the liberal counterpoint virtually disappeared from Fox's content too. By January 2009, Colmes was gone, and Hannity was hosting his own program, lambasting any politician or policy that might be too soft on immigration or crime or the "lazy" poor.

In fact, *Hannity* became the network's top show, eventually boasting 4,397,000 viewers, a whopping 788,000 of whom were in the key voting demographic of ages twenty-five to fifty-four.[7] This made *Hannity* the highest-rated program in cable news history. Sean Hannity's knee-jerk, take-no-prisoners approach to the deeply complex challenges his viewers faced had quickly proven to be a winning formula.

Early Fox shows such as Hannity's were soon joined by others, including *The O'Reilly Factor* (1996–2017), which branded itself as the source for "no spin news," as well as *The Ingraham Angle* (2017–present), which featured the same perspective but with a female host. While "moderately conservative" men were Fox's primary demographic between 1996 and 2000, the channel's viewership would become younger and more female over time.[8]

On November 14, 2016, *Tucker Carlson Tonight* (2016–2023) premiered. This program soon boasted the network's second-largest audience, a stunning 4,368,000 viewers, and it was clear that right-wing media's impact on the hearts and minds of Americans could no longer be dismissed as niche.[9] As Fox News Media CEO Suzanne Scott noted, "this ratings milestone" meant that Fox had become "the destination for news and opinion in America."[10]

Alongside the steady supply of print stories in the *New York Post* that decried affirmative action, welfare, crime, government spending, and the lazy poor, Fox News offered a glitzy visual medium viewers could watch at the end of a long day, only reinforcing their steadily more conservative take on the world around them.

The synergy between the *New York Post* and Fox News was not at all coincidental. As a later exposé on the network reported, from the very beginning, founder Murdoch's intention was to have his new network "follow the unapologetically lowbrow model of the tabloids that he published," and to appeal even more to a "working-class audience." He would do that by providing them not just politics but also escapist entertainment and sports. At a fancy dinner hosted by the chairman of the Federal Communications Commission under President Bill Clinton, Murdoch pitched the idea of reaching "football fans" on the local Fox affiliate stations to expand his audience and to build the Fox brand familiarity and loyalty—something that became possible in the early 1990s because he had just purchased the rights to broadcast NFL games on a regular basis.[11] It soon just made sense to watch your news, whenever you liked, on the same network brand where you watched your favorite teams play.

It was significant that Fox presented itself as a mainstream network, one that aimed to entertain audiences rather than bore them with stuffy news programming or liberal excuses for the unsettling realities they were seeing on the streets. Its messaging could be dealt out in a casual manner at any time of the day, delivered conversationally and consistently, regardless of the media market or which party's president happened to be in the White House.

But Murdoch's media empire was most committed to the Republican Party and had been since Reagan took office back in 1981.[12] Over time, it would also become even more important to the Republican Party, as Murdoch's Fox News Network, specifically, was essential to the building of its increasingly conservative voting base—an ever-more-cynical group of overwhelmingly white Americans—providing these voters a constant feedback loop of resentment and rage.[13]

As Taylor K. Reade observed in her history of Fox, the network and the Republican Party became inexorably entwined. "On one hand," Fox was soon a channel expected to "amplif[y] Republican ideas and policies to its large audience base," Reade wrote. In turn, Fox was granted special "access to key political figures and insider stories" that would substantially "enhance its journalistic offerings."[14]

And the access was remarkable. Fox News cofounder Roger Ailes had not only previously served as a media consultant for Republican presidents Nixon, Reagan, and George H. W. Bush, but Fox's personalities and commentators—people such as Tony Snow, John Bolton, Bill Shine, Ben Carson, and Pete Hegseth—would all go on to play powerful roles in

Republican administrations. Sean Hannity himself would become deeply embedded in Republican White House strategizing and messaging. As scholar Nicole Hemmer noted, Fox became "the closest we've come to having state TV."[15]

As the twenty-first century began to unfold, Fox News' influence on the American electorate was hard to overestimate.[16] In 2008, for example, Republican presidential candidate John McCain and vice presidential candidate Sarah Palin appeared on Fox News over 150 times; in 2016, presidential candidate Donald Trump appeared on the network over 250 times; and in 2020 Trump and his vice president Mike Pence made over 300 appearances on the platform, ensuring that the incumbent party's messaging reached American voters and made them passionate about turning out to the polls.[17]

Viewers were drawn to Fox News for many of the same reasons readers had originally flocked to the *New York Post*'s journalism in the 1980s: its sensational and simplistic analyses of complex social and economic issues, and its willingness to use misleading or exaggerated sound bites to elicit outrage appealed to audiences.

As important, its journalistic style was still steeped in racialized fear and, over time, had an increasingly tenuous relationship to truth. From Tucker Carlson touting the "Great Replacement" theory of whites being on the verge of extinction and reporting on the alleged violence of Black Lives Matters protests to the network's promotion of conspiracy theories about election fraud and lies about climate change and the coronavirus, Fox News was changing history with its broadcasts.[18] As the 2000s wore on, the Murdoch empire would create an audience ever more hungry for these narratives that affirmed viewers' suspicion that liberals, Black and Brown Americans, and undocumented immigrants were all out to undermine the best that this country was or could be, as well as fueled a growing number of conspiracies and mistruths that assuaged their sense of dislocation and despair.

Murdoch was not the only one to see the potential of this angry white, conservative audience. Other cable TV channels and online media offerings such as Newsmax, OutKick, and Rumble, as well as personalities such as Steve Bannon and Alex Jones, would capitalize on this rage and mobilize it as well, albeit sometimes grudgingly, toward Republican Party candidates.

44

Politics and Prejudice

IN 1997, one year after Goetz's loss in civil court, Republican Rudy Giuliani was still enthusiastically supported by both Wall Street and white working-class voters and managed to win a second term as New York City's mayor. As one poll noted, Giuliani had a 68 percent approval rating; 70 percent of New Yorkers were satisfied with life in the city and 64 percent said conditions had improved compared to four years previous. In response to an open-ended question about Giuliani's appeal, "45 percent of respondents [wrote that] the Mayor's record on crime/drugs is what they like most about him, followed by 25 percent listing positive leadership and 18 percent listing his overall record."[1]

Giuliani's second win was an indicator of just how "mainstream" conservative ideas about urban governance had become, even in a city like New York. His tough-on-crime policies had even earned him endorsements from longtime Democratic stalwarts, including LGBT groups, labor unions, and also *The New York Times*.[2] His opponent, Manhattan borough president Ruth Messinger, seemed to understand what Giuliani's victory portended. As she said in her concession speech, "Tonight, we lost a battle but the war goes on. . . . Our schools still don't work . . . and they are still worth fighting for. We gave it everything we had."[3]

Giuliani's crackdown on crime only continued with his second term. In the 2000s, record numbers of arrests were made possible by the embrace of a policing tactic called "Stop and Frisk." Broken Windows policing had ensured that existing laws even for very minor infractions were aggressively enforced. CompStat disproportionally concentrated police officers in the city's poorest Black and Brown communities. It was Stop and Frisk, however, that arguably led to the most serious criminalization of Black and Brown New Yorkers. In 2011 alone, the NYPD stopped and frisked 685,724 citizens, markedly and disproportionately nonwhite.[4]

This new law-and-order policy was widely supported by white New Yorkers who had by now fully and unapologetically bought into notions of innate Black and Brown criminality. It was also supported by developers who saw it as a boon to gentrification efforts. The newly draconian approach to drug addiction, mental illness, and lack of income and housing security, however, only increased the devastation of the city's poorest neighborhoods. Indeed, certain areas of the city were soon dubbed "million dollar blocks" to signify the extraordinary costs of placing an entire urban neighborhood under some form of correctional control—especially locking them up in the state's now seriously overcrowded prisons.[5]

In spite of this, when Rudy Giuliani prepared to leave office in 2001, he was not viewed as a politician who had exacerbated income and racial inequality. He was applauded and embraced as the leader who had turned Gomorrah back into the glittery wonder of Gotham.

In the eyes of many white New Yorkers, in fact, Giuliani was a savior. He had been there to stand up against the thugs, criminals, and welfare cheats, just like Bernie Goetz had two decades earlier. Giuliani was also a hero. After the horrific 9/11 attack on the World Trade Center, he was additionally lionized as someone willing to stand up to any Muslim "terrorist" on behalf of his constituents. In 2001, *Time* magazine named Giuliani "Person of the Year."[6]

Bernie Goetz, who had mostly spent the years since his loss in civil court out of the media spotlight, agreed that Rudy Giuliani had done a good job during his time in office. He might have demurred from the Giuliani administration's major investment in Stop and Frisk, considering how it ensnared people involved in low-level drug deals, and Bernie was a fan of marijuana. But this policy rarely affected people who looked like him.

In fact, when Giuliani had run for his second term, Bernie Goetz publicly commented that he felt the other candidates were completely unfit for the job. As he put it, NYC Public Advocate Mark Green was "just a typical liberal lawyer," civil rights activist Al Sharpton was "a flimflam minister," and Democratic councilwoman Ruth Messinger "pander[ed] to the left wing that put me on trial." Once again, Goetz reserved particular vitriol for the powerful woman in this mix. Referring to Messinger, he told *The New York Times*, "I'm ashamed of my Jewishness because of her."[7]

After the civil trial, the tabloid media, which still lapped up any news it could find on Bernie Goetz, had started depicting him as a peaceful vegetarian who fed the squirrels in Union Square Park. For his part, however, Goetz had not abandoned his more draconian views on how society's ills should be addressed.[8] For example, he remained quite open about his opinion that the AIDS epidemic had made NYC city safer by "getting rid of the [worst] elements of society."[9] He also made clear that he was drawn to squirrels because they "can be ferocious," and because "they can really go a little bit crazy. It doesn't take a lot" just like "it doesn't take a lot for people, either."[10]

He was also not willing to step fully out of the public view. Even before Giuliani had reached his two-term limit in office, Goetz had in fact decided that maybe he himself would make a better mayor. After all, he had strong views about what the mayor of the city might push for, including "the death penalty for the first violent sexual offense" and better pay for "firemen, police, and correction officers."[11] Word that Goetz might formally enter the race for the 2001 election was greeted with bemusement, surprise, and some measure of admiration, if not outright respect.

According to *New York Post* reporter Andrea Peyser, Goetz's entry into the mayoral race showed that "the thugs no longer run the city unchallenged." To be sure, he was "one of the most unlikely celebrities of the century . . . a 36-year-old subway passenger [who,] minding his own business, was transformed against his will into a case and a cause." But, argued Peyser, he was also a good guy who rescued "needy animals"—he had a squirrel, chinchillas, and "a little mouse who's running around the apartment."[12]

But whereas news that a "peaceful animal lover" was hoping to court "the anti-crime vote" and also welcome the endorsement of "the pro-vigilante party" in order to become mayor of NYC generated no small measure of media incredulity when Bernie Goetz first flirted with the idea in 1998, when he actually entered the race in 2000, few eyebrows were raised.[13] Goetz had, in his way, become an Everyman in the New York City of the 2000s; the idea had been normalized that mayors were expected to ensure that a person using a gun for self-defense would be protected and that the legal system would go after the "real" criminals.[14] Goetz was not to be feared, he was just a quirky guy. As the *Los Angeles*

New Yorker Joe Spinelli (left) asks independent mayoral candidate Bernhard Goetz for an autograph after signing Goetz's ballot petition to run for mayor, August 11, 2001. AP Photo/Chad Rachman

Times reported about this mayoral candidate, he'd even "quit smoking marijuana after 'a family tragedy' . . . the death of a pet squirrel."[15]

The Republican leadership, however, favored conservative billionaire Michael Bloomberg over an unpredictable, and not wealthy, oddball like Goetz. On election day, Bernie received only 1,049 votes, whereas Bloomberg got 744,757—the majority being from the city's elite as well as its white working-class voters in Staten Island and Queens. With this mandate, Bloomberg would only double down on Giuliani's tough-on-crime and pro-business policies.[16]

In keeping with this new era in which a former vigilante could become a candidate for public office with lovable animal sidekicks, Bernie Goetz could also end up arrested for marijuana possession and escape any consequences whatsoever. In 2013, Bloomberg's final year in office, Goetz was arrested "for peddling $30 worth of pot to an undercover female cop" outside of his apartment, as Larry Celona of the *New York Post* explained.[17]

In an eerie reprise of his 1984 arraignment for the subway shootings, reporters swarmed Goetz's car as he was driven to Manhattan Central Booking. Cops surrounded him to shield him from the paparazzi and, according to one reporter, "screamed at news photographers and reporters to get across the street."[18] Goetz was "held overnight Friday" due to his previous weapons conviction.[19]

Once again, in fact, the media downplayed Bernie Goetz's actions as foolhardy at worst, but not criminal. As *New York Post* reporter Laura Italiano described the interaction, Goetz "had been lamely hitting on the young undercover narcotics cop" when he was arrested. This "cute undercover" had no idea who the " 'creepy old man' was who chatted her up in Union Square Park" before he "allegedly" sold her drugs. As important, according to Italiano, Goetz had only given her "a small amount of pot."[20] The article also mentioned, yet again, his pet squirrels.

When word got out about Goetz's arrest, he once more enjoyed tremendous public support. One citizen was quoted in the *Post* exclaiming, "Oh, come on, they arrested him for that? It's just pot, they should let him go." This same person went on to opine, disgustedly, "People will now probably say he shot those kids because he was high."[21]

The *Post* did in fact offer Goetz the opportunity to clear up any possible suspicion that he had been high on the subway that day and thus misinterpreted the situation. Under a headline that blared "BERNIE GOETZ: I WASN'T HIGH IN 1984," an "exclusive" *Post* interview asked Goetz point-blank whether he had been stoned at the time of the shootings, to which he replied, "What an odd question! Of course not!" There was no way anyone could have "perform[ed] as good as that, with shooting," he continued, if they were stoned.[22]

As for the marijuana charge, Goetz rejected a plea deal for ten days of community service and demanded an outright dismissal or a jury trial. He claimed he had been framed, suggesting that he just wanted to get high with a pretty woman and "take it from there," but she had insisted on paying for the pot.[23]

Goetz's proclamation of innocence paid off. In the same city where record numbers of Black and Brown people were languishing for months and even years in jail awaiting trial on marijuana charges, Goetz would spend only one night in lockup. His case was dismissed altogether after prosecutors missed the ninety-day window in which they were required to try him.

This irony did not escape reporters, nor did the deeper contradiction that four young men had paid a much higher price for asking Goetz for five dollars than he did for shooting them, and now even for dealing dope. Goetz could apparently do whatever he wanted with impunity. One such reporter asked Goetz if he ever thought about Darrell Cabey, all these years later. "I never think about Darrell Cabey," Goetz replied. "Now I just feed squirrels in the park. Why would I ever think about him?"[24]

45

Saying Their Names

In 2013, at the same time fifty-nine-year-old Bernie Goetz had so publicly dismissed Darrell Cabey, Darrell himself had still not received any money to help finance his ongoing care from the man who had shot him. He had by now lived nearly thirty years paralyzed—fully reliant on a wheelchair and totally dependent on his aging mother, who herself depended on what public resources remained available after the cuts of the Reagan 1980s as well as the Clinton and Giuliani 1990s.

The truth was that by the 2000s, a whole lot of Americans were finding it hard to cope with the now-decades-long impacts of trickle-down economics. No longer could people grit their teeth and bear the brutal cost of this abandonment of public services to pay for ever-increasing tax breaks for the rich, as well as a now unprecedentedly punitive system of policing and prisons. Crisis once again loomed in America.

The financial collapse of 2008 was perhaps the first real wake-up call to those who had been pushing trickle-down economics that they, maybe, had overplayed their hand, hurting not just the poor and even the middle class but also the economic stability of the entire nation. As the Federal Reserve's annual report of that year explained, "The U.S. economy weakened markedly," and over the course of 2008 "the turmoil in financial markets intensified, credit conditions tightened further, and asset values continued to slump." The U.S. labor market also "worsened significantly" and "nearly all major sectors of the economy registered steep declines."[1]

The origins of this crisis were twofold—the end of a short but dramatic housing boom in the United States that had been based in no small part on predatory lending practices in the mortgage industry, and, relatedly, the fact that vital regulations that had long existed for the financial sector had been so dramatically rolled back. In short, Wall Street entities such as Goldman Sachs and Lehman Brothers Holdings had been getting richer under every administration since Reagan's, and now they largely did whatever they pleased to make money.

The 2000s had in fact been defined by the high-risk lending practices of the mortgage industry, which included the issuance of risky subprime loans to those purchasing or refinancing homes.[2] The financial institutions bundled these loans into mortgage-backed securities, then sold them to investors worldwide. When housing prices suddenly began to decline, and loans became due on properties that were now worth less than that same loan, American homeowners and small landlords defaulted on their mortgages en masse. This not only decimated families, but it also led to significant losses for financial institutions. The latter triggered a global financial crisis.

In the mass recession that followed, 3.8 million American families lost their homes to foreclosure, a stunning level of evictions and houselessness that had not been seen since the Great Depression.[3] In 2008, household net worth fell by $11 trillion, or about 18 percent of the market, marking the largest year-long decline on record.[4]

This massive economic downturn also meant the United States would lose nearly 8.7 million jobs, causing a dramatic spike in unemployment.[5] The crash wiped out the bank accounts of middle- and working-class Americans alike. But for the poor, already struggling with an ever-shrinking safety net and too little affordable housing, it was catastrophic.

To the shock of those with plenty to spare, ordinary people eventually began taking to the streets. By 2011, the Occupy Wall Street movement had burst onto the scene in major cities across the nation. New York City was the epicenter of that uprising.

Inspired by anti-austerity movements springing up across Europe, the Canadian activist group Adbusters proposed a peaceful occupation of Wall Street, the symbolic heart of global finance. This call was a match to kindling for an America that had been suffering under Reaganomics for three decades. On September 17, 2011, about one thousand protesters gathered at Zuccotti Park in New York City's Financial District to criticize the ever-growing wealth gap, stagnant wages, and corporate greed and influence.

Two months later, Occupy Wall Street encampments that condemned the "Top 1%" had also sprung up in Philadelphia, Detroit, Kansas City, and Los Angeles, and on November 17, 2011, tens of thousands of protesters marched in New York City.

That very same top 1 percent, which had benefited from the dismantling of regulations and a progressive tax code alike for decades, expected such demonstrations to be reined in. They would not be disappointed.

From the moment they stepped into the streets, the NYPD, the FBI, and the Department of Homeland Security put extraordinary pressure on the Occupy Wall Street protesters, even releasing a "Special Coverage" report decrying "disruptive effects on transportation, commercial, and government services." FBI agents surveilled the Wall Street encampment, and the NYPD arrested hundreds. In one event that took place that October, the Brooklyn Bridge protest, 768 people were arrested in a single afternoon.[6]

While the charges against Occupy protesters were generally dismissed, it was nevertheless a chilling marker of the dividends that the Reagan era's vision of a law-and-order America had in fact paid to those most invested in it.

That the police would be called upon not just to help maintain the economic status quo in the 2000s but increasingly also to protect the privileges and power of the nation's white residents over those who lived in its Black and Brown neighborhoods was becoming clear as well. In this decade, racialized violence was celebrated rather than censured, legitimized rather than deemed illegal.

To be sure, assaulting and killing Black and Brown citizens with impunity had a long history in America.[7] But due to the relentless activism of everyday people in communities of color across the country, and eventually of large institutions like the NAACP, grassroots organizations such as the Student Nonviolent Coordinating Committee (SNCC), the Black Panther Party, and Brooklyn CORE, it came to be understood that ad hoc acts of racialized violence were, at the very least, extralegal.

While such ugly acts of vigilantism never disappeared, the principle that they were incompatible with the rule of law had increasingly taken root as the twentieth century unfolded. Such brutality—be it carried out by ordinary white citizens or by agents of the government such as the police or prison guards—was never sufficiently censured or reined in, but by the close of the 1960s, it was not something to applaud, nor was it lawful.

In 1980s America, however, there had been a marked uptick of incidents in which disaffected white citizens, ordinary people like Bernie Goetz who weren't card-carrying members of the KKK or other avowedly supremacist groups, unleashed their rage on Black and Brown people, and on fellow whites with whom they disagreed politically. And the conservative media outlets had covered this rebirth of white rage as needed and long overdue. The Goetz shooting had garnered the most dramatic local and national coverage, but the myriad individual and mob acts of vigilantism that followed it would be equally embraced by the press and politicians alike.

Meanwhile, police violence in neighborhoods like the South Bronx had also been on the rise, incentivized as it was by Reagan's ever-escalating War on Drugs. As cops in the 44th Precinct had explained, they were facing new pressure to make more arrests, which, too often, led to the harassing and roughing up of city residents with the fewest resources to resist. Police killings in the neighborhood had also increased. As one officer from the South Bronx had conceded in 1983, "When I looked at the numbers, they were startling."[8]

The 1990s and early 2000s saw more of the same as Reagan's policies were embraced, expanded on, in fact, even by Democratic President Clinton. From the 1991 police beating of Rodney King in Los Angeles to the horrific 1997 incident in NYC in which Abner Louima, a thirty-one-year-old security guard, was viciously beaten and sodomized while in police custody, extralegal violence by the police remained ubiquitous and unchecked.[9]

Most significantly, however, both police killings and those meted out by ordinary white citizens were slowly but surely being legitimized in law as well. It would take several decades for this new era of extralegal and vigilante violence to be legally codified almost everywhere. But the Goetz case was essential in cementing the notion that it was all right for at least some people to use firearms if they felt at all threatened. And that was just the beginning. Black and Brown New Yorkers would reel from the lack of justice not just for Goetz's victims but also thereafter for Michael Stewart, Michael Griffith, Yusef Hawkins, and so many more.[10]

One 1985 ruling by the U.S. Supreme Court regarding police officers' use of deadly force was significant to that end. *Tennessee v. Garner,* a case that intended to place clear limits on the police's use of such force, had also ended up codifying, and arguably therefore legitimizing, police killings of even unarmed citizens. In effect, it offered the possibility of legal cover for cops who resorted to such force in the course of an arrest. Now officers could argue that they had indeed followed the law—they had used lethal force on a suspect only because he or she had tried to flee, or because the officers had feared a significant threat to themselves or the public.[11] Of course, any victim here—anyone who might have refuted an officer's claim that they were running or resisting—was already dead.

In numerous state-level cases in the 1980s, the self-defense argument was netting acquittals for ordinary citizens as well. Again, perhaps the most public and dramatic case had been *People of the State of New York v. Bernhard Goetz,* but its verdict had sent a crystal-clear message to the American people, and to judges across the country: If a citizen reasonably felt threatened, even if they were not in fact being threatened, deadly force could be used.

Meanwhile, the National Rifle Association had begun pouring more and more dollars into the political arena, making it easier for Americans to buy and to use guns however they liked. These efforts paid off when, in 2005, the state of Florida made history by enacting the nation's first formal "Stand Your Ground" law, which made it even easier for ordinary citizens to claim self-defense, just as Bernie Goetz had done twenty years earlier.[12] Stand Your Ground laws would proliferate across the country over the next decade, in effect removing the requirement—dating back to English Common Law—that one must first attempt to escape a threatening situation before resorting to the use of deadly force.[13]

The NRA was also instrumental in 2008 in getting a case heard before the U.S. Supreme Court, *District of Columbia v. Heller*. Thanks to the court's decision, an individual's right to own a gun purely for the purpose of self-defense was both affirmed and protected.[14] Overnight it became much easier for people not just to own and use a gun for personal self-defense but also to be exonerated should they in fact kill someone. As one article on this ruling observed, there is "no questioning the momentous change *Heller* wrought."[15]

In reality and on the ground, this ruling and Stand Your Ground laws more generally were deeply discriminatory because they favored and protected the violent acts of a very specific swath of Americans. A 2013 study by the Urban Institute found that in states with Stand Your Ground laws, homicides with white shooters and Black victims were deemed justifiable 17 percent of the time, compared to 1 percent when the roles were reversed—a disparity of 94.12 percent.[16] By 2023, thirty-eight out of fifty states would have such laws on the books.

Just as a deepening, and utterly unbearable, economic crisis had ignited a groundswell of outrage and activism, eventually so too would the rise in the number of killings of Black citizens without consequence.

The 2012 killing of seventeen-year-old Trayvon Martin, a Black high school student who was shot to death by a man named George Zimmerman, would spark outrage across the country.[17] Although Zimmerman was dutifully arrested and charged with second-degree murder for deciding to "take him out" before the police arrived, he was acquitted due to Florida's robust Stand Your Ground law. And notably, like Bernie Goetz before him, Zimmerman had hardly lived his own life free of encounters with the law that might well have landed him in prison.[18]

News of this not-guilty verdict touched a collective nerve with Black Americans as nothing had done since the killing of fourteen-year-old Emmett Till back in 1955. As in Till's case, there was zero indication that Trayvon Martin had done anything to threaten his killer other than simply being a young Black teenager. Another new movement pushing back hard at the now decades-long fallout from the Reagan Revolution was soon born.

IN 2013, in the wake of the George Zimmerman acquittal, three Black women, Alicia Garza, Patrisse Cullors, and Opal Tometi, came together, and brought others together, under the clarion call of "Black Lives Matter" to demand an end to the extraordinary racist violence scarring the nation. A year later, when white police officers killed unarmed Black teenager Michael Brown in Ferguson, Missouri, and a Black father, Eric Garner, who was selling loose cigarettes in New York City, it was clear that this movement was only going to grow in numbers and passion.[19] Thousands of protesters were turning out in the streets, driven by social media the same way they had been during the Occupy Wall Street protests.

The subsequent deaths of Freddie Gray in Baltimore and Sandra Bland in Texas, both in 2015; Philando Castile in Minnesota in 2016; and many others whose names never became as familiar would spark another wave of protests across the country. This was a decentralized and community-based movement that would only grow over time. Scholar-activist Kimberlé Crenshaw's manifesto *Say Her Name* would also powerfully raise awareness in this moment—specifically with regard to the record numbers of Black women who also had been killed. It was vital, she argued, that their lives be honored too.[20]

By 2016, the media and politicians alike could sense that something new was in the air. The American public had been coming out in droves: First people had mobilized against Wall Street greed and the financial despair so many felt after thirty years of trickle-down economics. And then they rose up against the consequences of three decades of punitive crime policies as well as rising rates of racialized civilian or state violence toward Black and Brown citizens.

This was a critical juncture in American history. Even though there had only been a doubling down on the Reagan Revolution since Reagan left office, this vision of America's future was no longer guaranteed. The Occupy and Black Lives Matter (BLM) movements signified a growing grassroots rejection of that status quo.

Perhaps no single moment signaled this more than the landslide victory of America's first Black president, Barack Obama, in 2008. This triumph of a Black Democrat running against two powerful white Republicans—first John McCain, then Mitt Romney in 2012—laid bare just how fragile conservative hegemony in the United States had become, even with the market saturation of right-wing media.[21]

Obama had promised on the campaign trail and throughout his two terms in office that he would work actively to respond to policies of the previous decades. He insisted that he had heard the voices of the ordinary people who had suffered from those same policies, whether they had joined an Occupy Wall Street encampment or had been clamoring for reforms of the criminal legal system and an end to white violence when they had taken to the streets in a Black Lives Matter protest.

The Obama White House's success in addressing the catastrophic consequences of decades of a "hands off Wall Street" approach to the nation's economy as well as the fueling and legitimizing of racial rage and injustice would be a mixed bag.

On the one hand, this administration's response to the near collapse of the entire financial sector in 2008 was but a bailout of Wall Street. But while Obama did save companies like Goldman Sachs from collapse, his American Recovery and Reinvestment Act (ARRA)—a $787 billion stimulus package—also provided critically needed funding for infrastructure, education, and renewable energy projects.[22]

Meanwhile, in a pointed rebuke to the idea that the government did not have a role to play in economic regulation, the Obama administration also passed the Dodd-Frank Wall Street Reform and Consumer Protection Act, which established new regulations and oversight mechanisms for the financial system and created an entire governmental bureau to protect consumers from corporations' greed.[23]

In response to the devastating fallout from Reagan-era criminal justice policies, particularly in the area of the drug criminalization that had reached crisis levels during the Clinton years, Obama and his attorney general Eric Holder also initiated a number of legislative reforms. None of these would roll back mass incarceration or rein in racialized violence, and the Obama years would meanwhile oversee a record number of deportations. This administration's rectifications would nevertheless signify the first even minor interruption of the federal embrace of domestic policing and prisons since 1980. The Fair Sentencing Act of 2010, for example, reduced the sentencing disparity between crack and powder cocaine offenses from 100:1 to 18:1, eliminated the mandatory minimum sentence for simple possession of crack cocaine, and retroactively reduced sentences for thousands of incarcerated people.[24]

The Obama administration's Clemency Initiative then granted freedom to over 1,900 incarcerated individuals, mostly nonviolent drug offenders serving disproportionately long sentences, and worked closely with the Department of Justice to identify federal prisoners eligible for sentence commutations.[25] They also put forth a ban that prohibited the use of solitary confinement for juveniles serving time in federal prison and placed limits on how solitary confinement could be used for adults in federal custody.

In an attempt to address what it considered a primary cause of incarceration, drug addiction, Obama's White House called for treatment rather than punishment, albeit too often still within a criminal legal framework. For example, it increased funding for drug courts and diversion initiatives that directed individuals into various mandatory programs instead of prisons.[26]

This administration also recognized the nation's embrace of criminalization and vigilantism over the previous three decades as a particularly racialized project. On March 23, 2012, President Obama stood before the nation and expressed his deep sympathy, called for a thorough investigation, and said somberly, "If I had a son, he'd look like Trayvon."[27] This statement infuriated many, but the backlash did not stop Obama from speaking out once more after Zimmerman's acquittal. "Trayvon Martin could have been me thirty-five years ago," he said, and proceeded to call out the crisis of racial profiling and discrimination.[28]

As the BLM movement gained momentum, this administration cautiously embraced its energy. After Michael Brown was killed in Ferguson, Missouri, and that city became ground zero for BLM activism, Obama personally invited BLM leaders to the White House and praised their efforts. His intention was to "bring young Black Lives Matter protesters together with long-time leaders from the civil rights movement." According to White House officials, this event was the "first of its kind."[29]

In addressing police violence against Black citizens more generally, Obama called it a "specific problem that is happening in the African American community that is not happening in other communities."[30] But in an attempt to avoid alienating more conservative Americans, and the police themselves, the president emphasized that the protests were not anti-police but rather aimed at accountability and fairness. To that end, he called for a President's Task Force on 21st Century Policing in 2014 to improve police practices and rebuild trust between law enforcement and communities of color.[31] He also encouraged police departments to adopt body cameras and provided funding for their implementation.

This administration also restricted the transfer of certain military-grade equipment (such as grenade launchers and armored vehicles) to local law enforcement and expanded federal investigations into police departments accused of misconduct. The Obama Department of Justice slapped several cities with consent decrees, including Ferguson, which had seen months of uprising after Michael Brown was killed, as well as Baltimore, which had also erupted in the wake of Freddie Gray's killing.[32]

Just as Obama's efforts to respond to the economic crisis by saving some of its most offending institutions netted him criticism from the right and left alike, so too did his administration's efforts to address mass incarceration, as well as to balance support for BLM with support of law-abiding police officers.[33]

The truth was that this administration had not cracked down on Wall Street nearly enough. The 1970s, the tax breaks, loopholes, and the lack of regulations it still enjoyed were appalling. Stark income inequality, declining wages, and lack of opportunity still defined America. The same could be said of its attempts to rein in white racial rage, be it on the part of prison officials, police officers, or men like George Zimmerman. On the ground, too much had remained the same.

But these stark realities, as well as the very real disappointment on the part of economically and racially marginalized Americans about the pace of change—if they felt changes were happening at all—did not compare to the ire of the wealthy, who were threatened by even very subtle economic shifts and incited by Obama's audacity to challenge their privileges and the benefits of their status. The Occupy Wall Street movement had been threatening enough; it had struck a powerful chord even with disaffected working-class whites who had been drifting to the right. It mattered that Obama was now encouraging this way of thinking. That was unacceptable.

But the wealthiest Americans could also see that having a Black president who in any way supported BLM, and who publicly rebuked the white civilians and cops alike who said they were only "protecting" themselves in their neighborhoods and on city streets, might save their trickle-down dreams. Handled correctly, any possibility of the 99 percent continuing to stand together across racial lines could likely be stopped in its tracks.

Indeed, those who had felt optimistic about the nation when Barack Obama won the presidency had underestimated three things: the power of racism, the power of the rich, and the power of the mainstream right-wing media to recapture the attention and stoke the racial self-interest of white working- and middle-class Americans. This demographic that had listened up as Occupy grew, and that had found itself attracted to the anti–Wall Street platforms of politicians like Bernie Sanders and Elizabeth Warren, simply had to be reminded that the economic pain they were suffering was caused by Black people, by immigrants, and by eight years under the leadership of a Black president. They too could be rich, if these groups were put in their place and if the White House was white again.

By 2016, the nation's conservative political elites, in direct partnership with the conservative media empire built by Rupert Murdoch and a growing number of alt-right-wing conspiracy media outlets, had kicked into high gear. The nation's future hung in the balance. Once again, as it had not been since 1980, the presidential election that year would be a critically important referendum on what exactly this country stood for.

46

Referendum

THE PRESIDENTIAL ELECTION of 2016 would turn out to be the first of two historic referenda on how Americans understood, and wanted to respond to, a number of pressing issues—chief among these, the economy and the seemingly intractable problem of race in America.

Fearing that the Obama years had potentially cost it its remaining white working-class base, the mainstream Democratic Party faced a clear choice. It could embrace the anti–Wall Street energy that had led to Occupy and hope that a desire to realize higher wages, to expand access to education and housing and health care, and to make a dent in income inequality in America would provide covering fire while they also sought to address racial violence and injustice. To do this would mean nominating someone like Bernie Sanders or Elizabeth Warren for president.

Or, the Democrats could decide to renounce the explicitly anti–Wall Street politics of the more progressive wing of their party as but the pipe dreams of socialists and decide deliberately to mute Obama's acknowledgment that America had a systemic race problem, in order to both assuage the economic concerns of wealthy donors and hopefully win back any white working-class voters who could not accept a Black president, let alone his willingness to address white violence.

Hillary Clinton was the establishment candidate party strategists would end up counting on to thread this needle. After all, they reasoned, Black voters had liked her husband, notwithstanding the way they had been betrayed by both the PRWORA and the Violent Crime bill. And

Wall Street had done really well by him too. What's more, the Democratic Party would be putting the first woman in the White House on the heels of the first Black man, so hopefully even the progressive wing of the party would see this as a win.

Far more effectively than the Democrats, however, the most ambitious and savvy members of the Republican Party understood the deeper significance of both the Occupy movement and the Black Lives Matter movement. In response, they would choose a most strategic path forward: The party would do what it needed to do, rhetorically at least, to court those who had been drawn to Occupy's economic message and then continue to pander to the basest racial resentments among them, all while, in fact, enacting an even more pro-business policy agenda.

This strategy was, of course, not new. Paying lip service to those who were suffering the worst fallout from trickle-down economics, while passing laws that favored the wealthy and fanning the flames of racial fear and fury to do it, was by now a tried-and-true formula. This time, however, the lip service would have to come across even more loudly, and the race-baiting would be even more virulent and overt.

The candidate who would most capitalize on this strategy and count on it, first to become the Republican Party's nominee for president and then to take the White House, would be none other than New York's very own white Wall Street billionaire, Donald Trump. That this would be the new face of the party left more traditional Republicans and virtually all Democrats utterly gobsmacked.

They should not have been.[1]

ALTHOUGH MANY IN the national Republican Party had been focused on finding a candidate from its bench of party stalwarts, and New York's conservative political elites had hoped that Rudy Giuliani, post-9/11 hero and America's mayor, or even Mike Bloomberg might break onto that roster, anyone paying attention would have noticed that by 2000, Donald J. Trump had already decided that a guy like him should actually be running the country.

Throughout the 1980s and into the 1990s, Trump had remained mostly a local NYC celebrity. But he had always craved national recognition and adoration. It was to the nation that he had pitched his books on becoming a successful real estate mogul, and he actively courted the attention lavished on him by national and local tabloids alike—from his splashy lifestyle to his dramatic divorces, first from Ivana Trump in 1992 and then from Marla Maples in 1999.

Always a media hound, Trump hit gold in 2004 when his wildly popular reality television show, *The Apprentice,* premiered on NBC. Each week, viewers from across the country were bombarded with the message that businessmen, no matter how ruthless they might be, were to be admired and emulated. In a move that glorified the total and unilateral power of the employer over the employee and suggested that such power was a prerequisite for success, he would eliminate any contestant who displeased him with his signature catchphrase "You're fired."

Ordinary people seemed to love anyone who was both bombastic and uncompromising, and Trump understood this. Had they not cheered on every audacious stunt Bernie Goetz's lawyer Barry Slotnick had pulled in his criminal trial? Had they not loved Goetz and his outrageous assertion that the world would have been better off had Darrell Cabey never been born?

Trump also understood the importance of wooing this "Everyman" demographic if he wanted to expand his own celebrity and one day run the country. To that end, Trump would dabble in professional wrestling, appearing in WrestleMania's 2007 *Battle of the Billionaires.* In 2013, he was even inducted into the WWE Hall of Fame's celebrity wing.

But as well known as Trump was, his exact political affiliation had always been a bit mysterious. Like his buddy Giuliani, Trump had by and large refused to be pigeonholed. While he was always willing to stoke the fears and resentments held by those who leaned conservative, he also loved being included in the circles of the more liberally oriented New Yorkers who attended the high-end clubs and turned a blind eye to his infidelities.

Indeed, Donald Trump had flirted with the Reagan White House and Clinton White House alike. He had registered as a Republican in 1987, but by 1999 he had become a member of the Independence Party, which was the New York state affiliate of the political party that Texas businessman Ross Perot had formed in 1995, the Reform Party.

In 2000, Trump decided to run for president as the Reform Party candidate. He announced his intention to run on the *Larry King Live* show and he outlined his platform in a book titled *The America We Deserve.*[2] Though it wasn't met with the same success as his business books, on its pages Trump clearly put forward the idea that the country should be run by the wealthy and run like a business, not a charity. His brazen call for the reinstatement of the death penalty in the wake of the arrest of the boys wrongly accused of raping the jogger in Central Park had already pointed to the manner in which he would address matters of race as well as crime and punishment.

While he received only 1 percent of the vote in 2000, Trump forged ahead. In 2001, he joined the Democratic Party and considered running for the presidency in 2004. By 2009, he had changed his party affiliation back to Republican. And in 2011, Trump decided to forgo party affiliation altogether and considered another run as an independent. Accordingly, he published a new book, *Time to Get Tough: Making America #1 Again*.[3] That said, the press that published this book, Regnery, was an avowedly conservative publishing company—a self-proclaimed counterweight to what it perceived to be the too-liberal publishing and media industries.

By 2012, Donald Trump was determined to run, and this time he would do so as a registered Republican.

It was the Obama years that particularly lit a fire in Trump and made him certain that he should be America's answer to the outrageous attacks on the prerogatives of corporations and white people alike.

But Trump faced some real challenges if he hoped to unseat the Democratic Party. Occupy Wall Street's grassroots rebuke of Reaganesque economic policy had been vast and deeply felt. And as much as racially conservative working- and middle-class whites may have hated the fact that the president was Black and a man who publicly condemned cops and vigilante citizens, Obama had also championed and succeeded in passing the Affordable Care Act, which had dramatically expanded access to health care, reduced its costs, widened Medicaid eligibility, and prohibited insurance companies from denying coverage for preexisting conditions. Due to this law, over 20 million previously uninsured Americans now had health coverage.

But as Trump alone grasped, there was a way to square this circle. There was a way to take people who benefited from Obama's policies and make them hate not just him but the entire Democratic Party. Trump would turn to his buddy Rupert Murdoch's Fox News Network to start convincing ordinary viewers—who had landed there either because they liked the politics or simply because the Fox channels had become their go-to to get their news and sports—that Obama was "a disaster" who was ruining this country in ways that should scare them.[4]

Between 2011 and 2015, Trump appeared multiple times as a guest commentator on the increasingly popular Fox News morning show *Fox & Friends*.[5] As journalist David Freedlander noted astutely, Trump had learned a great deal from watching Rudy Giuliani race-bait his way to an illustrious political career. He saw firsthand that one could, in concert, "harness racism," embrace "say-anything recklessness," and exploit the twenty-four-hour news cycle of conservative media to court a particular kind of white voter—one who was down on cities and government officials alike. Both men had seen how the bitterness of that particular voting bloc had caused them to rally around Bernie Goetz from the minute he was arraigned.[6]

In fact, Trump drew most audaciously and deliberately from the tabloid tradition that had made a celebrity of Goetz. His misleading, if not outright false, pronouncements about Obama blared from screens much like the headlines of the *Post* had decades earlier with regard to Black teens like Troy Canty and James Ramseur. Obama wasn't even American!, Trump insisted. Obama was a Muslim!, Trump asserted. Obama was part of the terrorist organization ISIS!, Trump claimed, all without blinking an eye. Fox anchors egged him on while Fox viewers admired his stunning assertions as brave, no-holds-barred truth-telling.

Meanwhile, and most importantly, Trump was also courting his peers among the wealthiest Americans. He decried regulation. He insisted that the tax code was unfair. He suggested that government was inefficient and needed to be run as they would run their companies.

Indeed, Donald J. Trump had hit on an extraordinarily effective political strategy. To the down-and-out white working class, he would be the guy willing to take on race-obsessed liberals and the Wall Street pirates, both. To the nation's richest, he would be the operator who would get government off of business's back and make Wall Street even wealthier. To be both would require finesse and no small measure of moxie.

More specifically, it would require a willingness to exaggerate, to obfuscate, and to peddle misinformation and outright lies—all things that the meteoric rise of Rupert Murdoch's *New York Post* and Fox News had demonstrated were not just entirely acceptable but a winning formula.[7]

It would prove to be effective for Trump, as well. On November 8, 2016, Donald J. Trump was elected the forty-fifth president of the United States.[8]

47

Fury Unfurled

Trump's electoral victory was immediately greeted by a plummeting stock market, with everyone feeling uncertain what having such an erratic and divisive personality at the helm would mean for one of the world's most important economies. However, not long thereafter, the market began a stunning rise, soon to levels not seen in the previous five years, as America's rich and their global counterparts realized the possibilities of his win, from deeper tax cuts to even more deregulation and other, equally pro-business policies.

In this particular domain, the new president did not disappoint. His 2017 Tax Cuts and Jobs Act further reduced corporate taxes, offering even greater benefits to wealthy corporations and individuals. And there were other dramatic benefits for them alone, such as the fact that only a business's U.S.-generated income would be taxed, not the money it made overseas.

Overall, thanks to this act, the graduated corporate tax structure was replaced with a flat 21 percent corporate tax rate.[1] More important, the effective tax rate that was already at the historically low range of 16 percent in 2014 became as low as 9 percent in 2018. Indeed, according to the Government Accountability Office, "about half of all large corporations had no federal income tax liability" whatsoever.[2]

Meanwhile, this new presidential administration would significantly weaken many things that companies hated and working-class people desperately needed. Trump rolled back Occupational Safety and Health Administration (OSHA) regulations that made workplaces safer; he stacked the National Labor Relations Board (NLRB) with pro-business appointments to weaken workers' ability to organize for better wages and health benefits in their unions; he stepped away from policies like the Clean Air Act and Clean Water Act that protected worker and public health. He even blocked Obama-era policies that would have expanded overtime pay eligibility, depriving millions of workers of additional pay and protections.

But of tremendous significance was the fact that few people were paying attention to these changes. Indeed, from the moment that he took office, Trump's public energies were expended on pandering to white racial rage.

While Trump was taking the financial hopes and dreams of the Reagan Republicans to new heights, the media's attention was fixed on his most racially inflammatory policy initiatives. Rather suddenly, for example, Trump put forth Executive Order 13769 and subsequent orders that became known as the "Muslim Ban," which dramatically restricted entry into the United States from several predominantly Muslim countries.

He also called for a "zero tolerance" immigration policy, one that would result in migrant families being separated at the border and children being corralled in camps. He additionally repealed the Deferred Action for Childhood Arrivals (DACA) program, and meanwhile engaged in unapologetically racist rhetoric more generally—referring to Caribbean and African nations as "shithole countries" and continually repeating claims about Latino criminality and about the "horrible" and "corrupt" U.S. cities that had large Black populations.

All of this served to divert attention from the policies that were substantially deepening already devastating income inequality in America. It also signaled to any white individuals or groups that had been itching to lash out at those who didn't look like them that it was open season.

RIDING HIGH AND feeling empowered with Donald Trump in the Oval Office, a bouillabaisse of white extremist groups from around the country decided to hold a "Unite the Right" rally in Charlottesville, Virginia, on August 11, 2017, the day that the city planned to remove a statue of Confederate General Robert E. Lee from Emancipation Park.[3] During Obama's two terms in office, these groups had been mobilizing against his administration and who supported him—the Black Lives Matter movement in particular.

On that hot Virginia day, several hundred white nationalists, neo-Nazis, and members of the Ku Klux Klan congregated in the park. They proudly waved the Confederate flag, displayed Nazi symbols, and shouted overtly racist and antisemitic slogans, phrases like "Jews will not replace us" and "White lives matter." That night, the assembled group lit torches and proceeded to march straight through the campus of the University of Virginia.[4]

This choice of location was not accidental. Despite his own Ivy League education, Donald Trump mocked and disparaged the "elites" who both taught at and attended America's universities. These institutions had also become a target for white resentment and rage. White working-class families that could no longer afford to send their children to college were told that this was the fault of the liberal elites who ran universities, as opposed to the decades-long stripping of financial aid and other measures that had made obtaining a college education possible for so many in the 1960s and 1970s.

That night, violence broke out on the UVA campus between Unite the Right demonstrators and the counter-protesters they hoped would materialize. By the next day, as skirmishes spilled into the city itself, Charlottesville looked like a battleground. Suddenly, a white vigilante attending the rally decided to turn his vehicle into a deadly weapon. James Alex Fields Jr. deliberately drove his car into a crowd of counter-protesters, killing a thirty-two-year-old white woman named Heather Heyer and injuring thirty-five other people.[5]

President Trump's response was notable. He was willing to condemn "hatred, bigotry, and violence on many sides," but he refused to explicitly denounce the white supremacists. Later, he would argue that there had actually been "very fine people on both sides," suggesting a moral equivalency between white supremacists and those who opposed them.[6]

Charlottesville proved to be a turning point. The Trump administration began effectively to endorse acts of vigilantism and white supremacy, all while failing to address the continuing crisis of police violence against unarmed Black citizens.

But Trump did not speak for all Americans. The Obama presidency had been a strong rebuke to the politics of austerity and racism that had become so normalized over previous decades, and its mark was not easily erased. A number of violent acts against unarmed Black citizens during Trump's first term revealed a nation sorely divided.

While the Trump agenda had successfully redirected much of the anti–Wall Street sentiment that had animated the Occupy movement, its race-baiting rhetoric and policies would only intensify the energy that had led to the Black Lives Matter movement. In February 2020, three white civilians chased and shot a Black man named Ahmaud Arbery while he was jogging in a suburban Georgia neighborhood. After video footage of the confrontation was made public in May 2020, cries for justice went up nationally. Eventually, Arbery's killers would be convicted of murder and hate crimes.

At the end of May, another unarmed Black man was killed—this time by police. George Floyd of Minneapolis died while being arrested for a misdemeanor.

In many ways, Floyd's death was no different from countless others that had preceded it. But that was precisely the point. An untold number of police killings of Black arrestees had taken place over the years, and efforts to prevent them had been virtually nonexistent.

The murder of Floyd would be the catalyst for a movement that made the Black Lives Matter protests of the Obama years seem mild. Throughout the summer of 2020, thousands of people took to the streets to condemn violence against Black and Brown people in all fifty U.S. states and in over sixty countries, making it one of the largest protest movements in the twenty-first century.[7]

In the same way conservatives had marshaled the mainstream media, which had played an essential role in winning over the hearts and minds of viewers, activists from the Occupy and Black Lives Matter movements had also capitalized on the power of social media to build community and to mobilize.

Inspired by the ways in which protesters had used internet platforms like Facebook, YouTube, and Twitter to demand political reform, greater personal freedoms, and an end to authoritarian rule in the Arab Spring, so too did Americans use videos, hashtags, and social media posts to raise awareness of the ubiquity of racialized violence and to organize protests against it.[8]

In the case of George Floyd's death, from the minute police officers initiated their arrest, bystanders began recording the encounter on their cell phones. One particular video, which showed an officer suffocating Floyd by kneeling on his neck for over nine minutes, went viral.[9] The protests set in motion by this gruesome and gratuitous act were clear in their demands: Police reform was not enough. The police needed to be defunded and utterly abolished, so that funding for law enforcement could be reallocated to social services, education, and jobs—resources that, protesters argued, would reduce crime and increase public safety far more than policing ever could.[10]

The dramatic show of Black, Brown, and white activism against police violence, during what would later be called "George Floyd Summer," would only fuel Trump's ire and, in turn, the racial rage of his carefully curated base of supporters. White supremacist groups now felt that the president himself had their backs.[11]

Over the course of George Floyd Summer, existing far-right organizations such as the Oathkeepers and the Proud Boys—already well known for confrontational tactics with those they considered enemies—saw increased activity and membership.[12] Emerging extremist groups like the Boogaloo movement, whose members openly carried firearms and were prepared to carry out what they felt was a much-needed second Civil War, were emboldened to move their activities offline and into the real world.

These groups did not shy away from violence. According to a report by the Center for Strategic and International Studies (CSIS), not only did 2020 see a notable increase in activities attributed to far-right groups, but there was also a significant rise in incidents of domestic terrorism.[13] When the FBI released its hate crime statistics for 2020, it specifically noted an increase in bias-motivated incidents. While not all of these hate crimes were linked to organized extremist groups, this data reflected a broader trend of rising racial rage during that year.[14]

The connection between the Trump administration's messaging and the escalated activities of these groups was direct and profound. The chatter on conservative networking platforms and channels like 4chan, Parler, and Telegram made clear that, as *The Washington Post* had reported, "Trump appeared to give permission for attacks on protesters." White supremacist group the Proud Boys even began wearing shirts and hoodies emblazoned with the words PROUD BOYS STANDING BY, in reference to a comment that the president had made suggesting that they be at the ready in the event he should need them.[15]

Right-wing activists on the ground had become increasingly committed to Trump and to resisting any potential challengers to the racial status quo. On August 2, 2020, a white seventeen-year-old named Kyle Rittenhouse traveled from his hometown of Antioch, Illinois, to the city of Kenosha, Wisconsin. Kenosha had just erupted in another wave of anti–police violence protests after an officer shot a Black man named Jacob Blake.[16]

Armed with an AR-15-style rifle, Rittenhouse shot and killed antiracist protester Joseph Rosenbaum. Two other protesters were also caught in the crossfire as they tried to get Rittenhouse to drop his gun. Twenty-six-year-old Anthony Huber hit Rittenhouse in the head with his skateboard, but he was killed by another of Rittenhouse's bullets. Twenty-six-year-old Gaige Grosskreutz pulled out a handgun, but Rittenhouse shot him in the arm and then fled.[17]

Rittenhouse faced five very serious counts—first-degree intentional homicide for the murder of Anthony Huber, first-degree reckless homicide for the murder of Joseph Rosenbaum, attempted first-degree intentional homicide in the case of Gaige Grosskreutz, and first-degree recklessly endangering safety. Much like Bernie Goetz and George Zimmerman had before him, Rittenhouse asserted that he had acted in self-defense. Despite the fact that his actions horrified so many across the country, the jury found him not guilty, even after watching a video of the violence he had exacted on the two unarmed men.[18]

By the end of 2020, the message was clear: Almost four decades after Bernie Goetz had shot Darrell Cabey, James Ramseur, Barry Allen, and Troy Canty, vigilantism had become both morally and legally acceptable. In 2021, *PBS NewsHour* questioned this notion, wanting to hold on to the idea that "Rittenhouse's treatment and trial [had] defied norms," but the sad truth was that it had not, at least in terms of its outcome.[19]

Rittenhouse's vindication was music to the ears of the many conservatives who had funded his legal defense. The *New York Post*'s Michael Goodwin reported that Rittenhouse supporters "erupted in cheers" when the verdict was read, celebrating "a ringing victory for gun rights and self-defense."[20] To these individuals, prosecutors had "overreached," ignoring that crime was surging and ordinary citizens were frightened and frustrated at a lack of police protection. "Then and now," Goodwin stated, "the breakdown of public safety carries consequences."[21]

Most important, Donald Trump openly stood with this vigilante and celebrated his acquittal. Trump appeared on Fox News' most popular show, *Hannity,* to not only criticize the prosecution's handling of the case but in fact endorse Rittenhouse to its millions of viewers as "really a nice young man."[22] Rittenhouse was even invited to meet Trump at his Mar-a-Lago resort in Palm Beach, Florida.

As in 1980s New York City, this dramatic vindication of vigilantism had material consequences. According to one nonpartisan group tracking guns in America, The Trace, between 2020 and 2022 almost 60 million guns were purchased and yearly gun sales were "running at roughly twice the level of 15 or 20 years ago."[23] As one *New York Post* piece put it bluntly, "Those trends mean Kyle Rittenhouse likely won't be the last private citizen to step into the public space abandoned by law enforcement."[24]

Donald Trump's ever-expanding and increasingly emboldened base of supporters quickly convinced him that he deserved a second term, but his intention to remain in the White House was hardly guaranteed. His presidency had been rocked not only by the racial tension of 2020's protests, but by the global COVID-19 pandemic and its devastating impact on the U.S. Trump had politicized even this public health crisis as yet more fodder for the simmering resentment, rage, and political extremist ideas of his base.

But this same crisis, accompanied as it was by both financial devastation and police brutality, also made his opponents even more determined to unseat him. In the closest election in recent history, Donald Trump lost the 2020 presidential race to Joseph R. Biden, who had served as Obama's vice president.

This Democratic victory, as Obama's had been in 2008, was an emphatic public disavowal of much of the ideology and policy that undergirded the intentions of the Republican Party. And, just as Obama had done when he moved into the Oval Office, Biden set about trying to undercut the worst of those policies and undermine the most hateful rhetoric that Trump had seeded in his first term.

In 2021, for example, the Biden White House celebrated when the House of Representatives passed the George Floyd Justice in Policing Act. Though the bill was ultimately stalled in the Senate and never became federal law, it was a dramatic difference from the front-facing attitudes of Trump's administration. The Biden administration also saw a major win as corporations seemed to again understand the importance of, or at least willingly complied with, internal efforts to promote diversity, equity, and inclusion, and even to donate funds to external organizations engaged in racial justice and related causes.

In 2021, President Biden also expanded a set of income transfers "that led to strong reductions in child poverty." According to experts, "whether using the Supplemental Poverty Measure (SPM), relative poverty measures, or an absolute poverty measure, the U.S. child poverty rate in 2021 was at its lowest level since at least 1967."[25] These transfers, part of the American Rescue Plan Act (ARPA) signed into law on March 11, 2021, had also temporarily increased the Child Tax Credit, raising it from $2,000 per child to $3,600 per child under age 6 and $3,000 per child ages 6 to 17.[26]

The Child Tax Credit was enormously helpful for poor families living in places like the South Bronx, even if they made too little income to owe taxes. They were still in fact eligible for this credit, which could be used to pay for necessities like food and utilities. Such a credit would have made a huge difference to the five Cabey kids and their mother back in the day.

Despite these strides—ones that, to be sure, had not aimed to disrupt the most important prerogatives and advantages enjoyed by the wealthiest Americans that the progressives in his party had continued to call out—Biden was swimming against the political current. Not only was the right more emboldened than ever, but individuals within his own party also pandered to this impulse. Indeed, serious pushback from Republicans along with top Democrats like West Virginia's senator Joe Manchin would mean the income-assistance provisions of 2021 would not stick. As a result, the child poverty rate would double and return to being higher than in most other high-income countries.[27] The Supplemental Poverty Measure would jump from 5.2 percent in 2021 to 17.8 percent and 19.5 percent in 2022 for Black and Latino children respectively, compared to 7.2 percent for white children.[28]

Biden's presidency had been a remarkably tepid response to the continued fallout from the Reagan Revolution. But it had also gotten off to a precarious start. For the first time in American history, the transfer of power had not been executed peacefully. The 2020 election was a clear referendum on the identity of America. So high were the stakes that Donald Trump began sowing the seeds of distrust in the American electoral process itself so that if he lost his reelection campaign, no one would trust the results.

After losing the presidential race, Trump insisted that the election had been fraudulent and demanded that his allies refuse to certify Biden's win. Simultaneously, he riled up the most conservative and militant members of his base to deputize themselves and right the election's outcome by literally storming the U.S. Capitol. This was an extraordinarily violent and historically unprecedented effort to prevent Biden from being recognized as the forty-sixth president of the United States.

At the center of this unsuccessful attack on both the election and its results was a race-baiting, fear-mongering, and rage-generating information machine. What had started as Rupert Murdoch's attempt to dominate the tabloid media space in 1980s NYC had transformed into a powerful nationwide apparatus that informed white Americans' understanding of their interests and how best to fulfill them. That Fox News' messaging relied on sensationalism rather than verifiable facts to build its loyal viewer base should have surprised no one. That was its origin story.

This media strategy would pay off for Trump most dramatically four years later, in another bitterly contested presidential election.

In 2024, Donald Trump would not only win a second term, but the most extreme right-wing conservatives in the Republican Party would also take the House and the Senate. The passionate but still rather ideologically disparate conservatism that had put him into the White House the first time had matured, solidified, and become fully uncompromising by 2024.

To watch Fox News on the eve of the 2024 "battle for the White House" was to believe that the main problems the country faced were not, in fact, severe income inequality, child poverty, the disappearance of affordable housing, racial discrimination, racialized violence, the environment, declining education rates, and rising mortality rates for pregnant women. The problems that required the president's utmost attention, viewers were told, were transgender youth, immigrants who were rapists and murderers, the war on tradition and masculinity, and liberals.[29]

This slanted coverage was motivated by profit and politics alike. In early 2024, Fox News had been forced to pay out nearly $800 million to avert a trial in a massive defamation lawsuit that would have "exposed how the network promoted lies about the 2020 presidential election."[30] But it had been worth it. In a deposition in that suit, Fox chairman Rupert Murdoch said, under oath, that it had been purely a business decision to give the election lie so much airtime. He admitted "that he chose not to keep election deniers such as Rudy Giuliani off the air even though he had the power to do so" and that Fox made a considerable sum by giving conspiracy theorists like MyPillow entrepreneur Mike Lindell so much advertising time. As he put it, "It is not red or blue; it is green."[31]

The Fox News Media division of the Fox Corporation, which in 2018 had launched an on-demand streaming platform called Fox Nation for its most committed viewers of Fox News, was but a small part of the misinformation and racialized rage machine that had consumed conservative American media by the 2024 election. Others, such as Newsmax, would be so shameless in their promulgation of literal lies that they also would have to pay out millions in settlements—Newsmax specifically agreed to pay $67 million to settle a defamation suit over fraudulent claims about the 2020 election.[32] By then, Trump had already gotten himself banned from Twitter due to the sheer volume of his false claims and contentions. In response, he simply created his own platform called Truth Social, on which he could say whatever he wanted to without being fact-checked.[33]

Although Truth Social's numbers fluctuated, by January 2025 it boasted approximately 6.3 million active users.[34] Meanwhile, Trump advocate Elon Musk finalized his purchase of Twitter on October 27, 2022. [35] In a controversial move, Musk renamed the platform "X." Under his ownership, X was flooded with countless inflammatory and unverified posts. On the eve of the 2024 election, the platform reported having over 600 million monthly active users.[36]

Those voices, those views, had mattered far more than anyone had predicted . . . except, of course, those who had been slowly but most deliberately riling them up for the previous five decades.

Within the first weeks of Trump retaking office, it was clear that the agenda that Ronald Reagan had brought to the White House in his presidency to reestablish the economic policies and social norms of the Gilded Age was finally on its way to being fully and finally realized.

At his inauguration, Trump was flanked by the three richest men in America—Elon Musk, Jeff Bezos, and Mark Zuckerberg—men whose degree of wealth made that of their Gilded Age counterparts look meager in comparison, and whose fortunes had been amassed, in no small part, due to the Republican Party's fifty-year effort to protect the nation's richest citizens.

With the ascendancy of Donald Trump to a second term, any remaining doubt that the rule of law was conditional at best and thoroughly optional at worst—at least for the nation's wealthiest citizens and any white citizen who decided they had the right to take the law into their own hands—also had been settled.

48

Reaping What Was Sown

One of President Trump's first acts upon taking office in 2025 was pardoning the men and women who had stormed the U.S. Capitol on January 6, 2021. They had collectively terrorized his political opponents, shown an utter disregard for the rule of law, and killed a police officer. This pardon sent a widespread and resounding message. That messaging mattered more than even the stunned public might have understood at the time.

Back in 2016, presidential candidate Donald Trump had asserted on the campaign trail that he could shoot someone on Fifth Avenue and "not lose any voters."[1] In 2021, he congratulated Kyle Rittenhouse for having killed anti-racist protesters and then being vindicated by a jury.[2] But these troubling incidents were part of a much larger picture. By 2024, exactly forty years after Bernie Goetz was lauded as a hero and absolved in NYC, ordinary, day-to-day white citizens—even if they weren't right-wing zealots—had come to understand that should they decide to take the law into their own hands, they would most likely get away with it.

Indeed, this through line, running from the America of President Donald Trump back to the moment Bernie Goetz pulled out his .38 Smith & Wesson and gunned down four teens from the South Bronx, was laid bare in a particularly brutal way on May 1, 2023.

On that otherwise beautiful spring day, a white military vet from a New York City suburb named Daniel Penny was riding the uptown-bound F train when an unhoused street performer by the name of Jordan Neely began making a disturbance in Penny's subway car.[3] Thirty-year-old Neely was known by many New Yorkers for dressing up like Michael Jackson and mimicking his famous moonwalk in the hopes that passersby would give him a dollar or two. This time, though, he was far too depressed and desperate to do much more than beg passengers for spare change.[4]

That day, Jordan Neely utterly broke down. He stood in the middle of the subway car yelling in anguish that he was tired, that he had no food, no water, and no home. His tortured outbursts made more than a few others in the car nervous. From Penny's account, Neely was threatening the lives of other passengers if they refused to help him, and Penny felt compelled to act. Something about the sound of Neely's zipper hitting the floor when he threw his coat onto the ground, and something about watching this distraught man pick trash up off the floor and begin throwing it at people, drove Penny to grab Neely in a choke hold, which he held for six long minutes until Neely died.

In an eerie reprise of the Goetz shootings, just shy of forty years earlier, countless New Yorkers rallied behind Penny. They hailed him as the hero that NYC needed. This time, though, the perpetrator had not even felt the need to escape into the tunnels to dodge the authorities. He did not even have to argue that he had felt that his life was in jeopardy when he killed Jordan Neely. He said that he was protecting others. What's more, he seemed calm, utterly unconcerned that he faced any possibility of prison.

This was a nation that had become stunningly comfortable with ordinary men—men like George Zimmerman, Kyle Rittenhouse, and now Daniel Penny—choosing to become real-life Charles Bronsons. This was a nation that had endorsed the idea that ordinary citizens had the right to mete out extralegal punishment and to engage in spectacles of public vengeance. Long gone seemed the days when one could imagine a jury outcome like that which Ahmaud Arbery's killers had experienced. That outcome, it turned out, was but a blip on the graph of the previous four decades.

And as he had expected, on December 9, 2024, a Manhattan jury acquitted twenty-six-year-old Daniel Penny of negligent homicide, almost forty years to the day since Bernie Goetz had fired his gun on Troy Canty, Barry Allen, James Ramseur, and Darrell Cabey.

Just as the testimony of multiple eyewitnesses in the Goetz case, who stated they had not felt threatened by the boys, had failed to sway the jury's decision, it would not matter to the Penny jury that multiple eyewitnesses, including journalist Juan Alberto Vázquez, insisted that Jordan Neely had never posed a lethal threat.

And just as it would prove irrelevant that Goetz himself had admitted on tape that his violent act had nothing to do with robbery—it was merely the "shine" in Troy Canty's eyes and the "smile" on his face that made him want to maim these boys, even kill them—it had not mattered that Daniel Penny had been recorded as fellow passengers voiced their fears that he was long past immobilizing Jordan Neely and was now certain to kill him.

In the NYC of the 1980s, Darrell Cabey was not allowed to be the vulnerable teen that he was. He was declared to be a thug, rather than a sweet and well-liked kid from the South Bronx who had lost his father to a terrible crime. He was said to be an animal rather than an ordinary boy whose hardworking, widowed mother, Shirley, did her best to raise him despite the challenges posed by rapidly diminishing social safety nets. He was deemed a vicious criminal, rather than understood as an ordinary New Yorker with limited job prospects and no money, one who had hoped on December 22, 1984, three days before Christmas, to go downtown with some guys from the neighborhood and maybe come home with a few bucks in his pocket.

In the NYC of the 2020s, Jordan Neely was also publicly reviled. Neely was not understood as a child who had grown up without secure housing, at times living in shelters, but nevertheless closely bonded to his mother, Christie. He was not empathized with as a teenager whose life completely fell apart at age fourteen when his mom was brutally murdered. Nor was he applauded for being a young man who, against all odds, had found some joy entertaining folks dancing and singing like the King of Pop, using the money he earned to pay for haircuts and other basics for his foster siblings. He was never recognized as a young man in despair—someone who could not earn enough money to find a stable home or attend to his struggles with mental health.

Just as Shirley Cabey had done, Neely's father, Andre Zachary, turned to the civil courts to find some measure of justice. He filed a wrongful death claim against Penny just days before he was acquitted. For Zachary, one central question burned: Did Penny put his son in that choke hold for too long? Should he have let go? Penny's lawyer immediately filed to have the suit dismissed, arguing, just as Goetz and his attorneys had nearly five decades earlier, that if there had been any "injuries or damages," they "were caused in whole or in part by the culpable conduct, negligence, carelessness, and lack of care on the part of Plaintiff."[5]

In the United States of 2024, however, few doubted that this argument would win the day. Men like Daniel Penny were now legally protected in all ways that mattered.

By 2024 not just ordinary citizens but the president-elect of the United States himself, Donald J. Trump, treated Penny like a national hero.

As soon as the not-guilty verdict was announced, Donald Trump asked his vice president–elect, J.D. Vance, to invite Penny to join them in their box suite for the Army-Navy football game. With photographers snapping pictures, Trump greeted Penny with open arms. He had already weighed in on Neely's death, noting that people like Penny were "in great danger" when they rode the subway, but now the message was much clearer in support of Penny's actions. As Vance put it, "Daniel's a good guy, and New York's mob district attorney tried to ruin his life for having a backbone. . . . I hope he's [now] able to have fun and appreciate how much his fellow citizens admire his courage."[6]

Eighty-year-old Bernie Goetz could not have agreed more.

Goetz had hardly retired from the public eye. In 2021, he had chimed in with his opinion on the Rittenhouse case, on Fox News, of course. Goetz opined that Rittenhouse was only being tried at all "to satisfy a mob." According to Goetz, Rittenhouse's trial was "a political trial like mine was." This was simply a kid who had the right to take measures to defend himself when threatened. "Someone has already hit you with a skateboard, and someone else is pointing a gun at you and they are shouting that they are going to kill you. You also have a gun; wouldn't you start pointing your gun at them?" he told the Fox commentator interviewing him.[7]

Fox reminded its audience that Goetz had faced a similar threat—invoking, four decades after it had been debunked, the myth of the "sharpened screwdrivers" that the four teens had "with them at the time."[8]

Bernie Goetz was also called upon to comment on Penny's trial. His anti-government hostilities had only deepened since the 1980s, and he was most vocal about the problem of governmental "overreach"—especially when it came to marijuana laws as well as mandates intended to prevent the spread of the COVID-19 virus. He decried the latter and insisted, as Fox News broadcasters also did, that politicians were lying about the dangers of the virus. As he put it, it was all "bulls—t about wearing a mask, and the social distancing."[9] Daniel Penny's indictment was just another example of too much Big Brother. Prosecuting Penny had been, in Goetz's view, "BS" and, like his own case, it summed up all that was wrong with New York.[10]

Elaborating on this point in the *New York Post,* Goetz went on, "what the Penny case has in common with my case is, it's all BS," and that this is what happened under "states with left wing government." Goetz felt that Penny, much like himself, was merely shedding "light on the high crime in New York and that New York City was failing as a city, and also the government here was simply not addressing crime at the time," and ignoring those who were "preying on the rest of the population."[11]

By 2024 this perspective was utterly mainstream. It was clear by now that the decade of the 1980s had mattered to the future at every level. Bernie Goetz's decision to take his fury out on the most vulnerable people he encountered had been fueled and vindicated by a racial rage that would continue to percolate. This is what would make it possible for men like George Zimmerman to walk free so easily after killing boys like Trayvon Martin. It is what would allow Kyle Rittenhouse to evade prison and become a folk hero. It would also make Trump's ascendancy to the White House possible and ensure that his supporters could do anything they wanted to do to keep him in power. And it would guarantee that Daniel Penny did not serve a day in prison for killing Jordan Neely.

49

Requiem

By 2025, so many Black and Brown Americans had been violently assaulted or killed due to a white racial fury that was now both fully unleashed and totally legitimized that, as podcaster Katie Puckrik said wonderingly, it often felt like "an incomplete list" to name all who died at the hands of white vigilante justice.[1] But there were some names, she went on, that the nation was forced to know:

> The man who fatally shot Trayvon Martin in Florida a few years ago, Zimmerman, George Zimmerman, I'm thinking about Kyle Rittenhouse hunting and killing Black Lives Matter protesters. Those three men who hunted and killed Ahmaud Arbery, who was jogging through a neighborhood, those recent shooting attacks on teenagers who ding-dong the wrong front doorbell, or those Texas cheerleaders who got into the wrong car, and now Jordan Neely, who was killed in a choke hold.[2]

Did these murders, she mused, not add up to an overwhelming "trend towards vigilantism"? Was it not the case that today people in America "are just like, well, I don't like the look of this guy, I feel vaguely discomfited, and I am going to take their life?"[3]

As writer Roxane Gay put it even more bluntly,

> It is a simple fact: White people—both men and women—feel wholly empowered to police and adjudicate the behavior of Black people as they see it. While white women tend to weaponize the police against

> Black bodies . . . white men have been emboldened to take the law into their own hands, oftentimes with deadly results. Ahmaud Arbery, Trayvon Martin, and Jordan Davis, were all killed by white men who deputized themselves as law enforcement, judge, jury and executioner.[4]

Indeed. And, for every nationally recognized case of vigilantism, there was a much lesser-known case.[5] By 2025, much of America had heard about Kyle Rittenhouse and Daniel Penny, and some may have even remembered that it was the Bernie Goetz shootings that had set a dangerous precedent for these more recent extralegal killings.

But there were so many other cases they had likely never heard of, such as the landlord in NYC who assaulted an unhoused man lying on the ground outside the subway station at Chrystie and Grand Streets in Manhattan. When that terrified man tried to defend himself by grabbing a piece of wood, the landlord hit him until he fell backward, blood gushing from his face, and "slammed his head into the subway station railing." The victim was hospitalized with facial and skull fractures and required a ventilator to breathe.[6]

Even though the assailant admitted that he had gone after this man "because he was haunted" by an unrelated murder of one of his tenants two years earlier, Manhattan DA Alvin Bragg decided not to prosecute him.[7]

Between 1985 and 2025, fists and firearms once again, like in previous centuries, became the go-tos for citizens and cops alike. Indeed, in the autumn of 2025, when Donald Trump began ordering masked ICE agents into urban neighborhoods populated by poor Brown and Black residents across the country, and when those same agents began summarily rounding up, assaulting, and disappearing countless of these same residents in the name of "protecting" America from criminals, the legacy of the Bernie Goetz shootings, like the Reagan Revolution itself, had truly come of age.

As news media personality Geraldo Rivera mused about all that had unfolded over the previous decades, "you had Charles Bronson. And you had the Death Wish movies where that whole notion of vigilantism as heroes had been developed. So, it was very, very easy for the white population particularly" to relate to vigilantes like Bernie Goetz. Goetz had become a hero, he went on, "in the sense that everybody invested in him . . . unless you were the parent of a black teenager."[8] Over time, it became accepted, and much easier, to be just like Goetz.[9]

But the costs of all of this were so much higher than imagined.

THE FAMILIES OF Troy Canty, Barry Allen, James Ramseur, and Darrell Cabey had borne these consequences acutely. But from December 22, 1984, onward, their voices and their lived experience had been dismissed. The suffering these boys endured was virtually erased from mainstream media narratives and collective memory.

Troy Canty was the youngest child of five, with older siblings Carl, Bobby, Veronica, and Eddie. His father, Edward, was a factory worker, and his mother, Eula, proudly described him as a child who "never gave me no trouble." As a teenager, Troy would light up when he "spoke about getting a good job and buying a car."[10] He had aspirations for his life, but he was also a young person simply trying to navigate the difficult waters of adolescence and find his way in one of the poorest boroughs in NYC, at a time when jobs were disappearing and drugs were dominating the economy.

Before Troy became an adult, he had developed a deep addiction to cocaine. Worse, he was freebasing, which, as his brother Carl noted, "is hard to kick."[11] But Troy's family had not given up on him, and neither had his friends. They admired Troy—he was the thinker in the group; and as one of them said, he always took "his time with whatever he does. He's thorough."[12] He still had a future. That is, until he boarded the 2 train three days before Christmas in 1984.

Troy's family, particularly Carl, had appreciated prosecutor Greg Waples's efforts to humanize him. Carl, who was twenty-one at the time of the shootings, knew firsthand what Troy had been through in life, and who he was. It was obvious to anyone who met Troy that he was smart, not just "criminal minded" as the media made him out to be.

Sure, Carl conceded, his brother "was busting the pinball machines," but he "didn't rob or sold drugs or nothing." He was just a normal kid. Things had taken a turn when Troy had "started smoking weed when he was around twelve," and it had been even more consequential when he got into crack. After that, his life "started getting worse and worse."[13] But that didn't make him hardcore.

After all, as Carl pointed out, "People from the ghetto have to make their own world." With their father having left their mother when they were young, finding a way to make money was not just optional—it was a necessity. As Carl put it, "You have to step up and be able to be responsible for things that you wasn't ready to be responsible for. So, you have to become basically a criminal, but you gotta be a good criminal."[14]

At the end of the day, Carl maintained, Troy was a hustler. He would "[buy] wholesale items, like perfume and toys," and then sell them on the street at a markup. When the wildly popular Transformers toys came out, for example, Troy "would pay like two dollars getting ten" and then walk through Harlem selling them to "ladies in the store."[15]

From the moment that Troy Canty was shot, he and his family were treated not as victims of a crime but as the vilest of criminals. Hateful letters flooded into the mailroom of their Claremont Village high-rise and their phone jangled ominously every night, each member of the Canty family terrified to pick it up because death threats so often followed. Troy himself was berated and belittled in the courtroom, and he had been called a monster by the media before he had even turned twenty years old. And as media support for his assailant grew, particularly in the wake of Goetz's legal vindication, Troy grew even more discouraged by the challenges life threw his way.

Following the trial, Troy Canty racked up a string of petty offenses as he sought to feed his lingering habit. Eventually, with help, he ended up in a drug rehabilitation center in Peekskill, New York. Being in rehab for eighteen months gave Troy the opportunity to work in a car wash and start learning to become a mechanic. He also met the woman that he would later marry.[16] And this was everything.

But it wasn't all that his life could have been. And deep down, Troy knew this. When he came home from rehab, he decided to go totally off the grid. He was no longer willing to share his story because in his experience, the media never failed to distort his words. White people would always believe what they wanted to believe. He would always be the guy with the sharpened screwdriver that had never actually existed. His brother Carl understood why Troy had no interest in talking to anyone about his life—"New York is a racist world," Carl said bluntly, and his brother was done trying to persuade the public of this obvious fact.[17]

Barry Allen's fate was much bleaker. When his mother, Mary, had lost her job as a switchboard operator, his family's financial hardship deepened, he dropped out of school, and he gravitated with ever greater pull to the drug economy. When his girlfriend then had a baby, his financial needs intensified, and the risks of making money by breaking into video machines and selling cocaine seemed less and less important. So did his concerns about using. That is, until he turned eighteen. By then, Barry wanted to get clean, but the possibilities for getting help seemed elusive. When he was shot on the 2 train, he hadn't given up on the idea of drug rehab, but he wasn't quite sure how to make it happen.

The shooting did as much emotional as physical damage to Barry Allen. While he was recovering, Barry feared the threatening phone calls he received in the hospital, and he felt scared as well as angry and utterly helpless every time he heard his siblings speak of the vicious calls that were also coming to the house.[18] He wanted a better life but didn't know how to get one. He wanted his son, Jason, to see him as a good guy, but even with a bullet wound in his back, the public only viewed him as thug and predator.

And then came the grand jury proceedings. The first grand jury had been unwilling to hold Bernie Goetz accountable for his actions, and while the second grand jury had been more amenable, Goetz was nevertheless vindicated at trial. In this process, the DA hadn't even been willing to give Barry immunity from possible charges so that he might have testified against his assailant.

Barry continued to spiral downward. He couldn't find a job. He never could find help to kick his drug habit. But he still needed to support himself and his kid, and to help provide for his siblings.

In the years after he was shot, Barry would end up serving time for two robberies, including for snatching that chain worth only $150 and another time for stealing a little more than $50.[19] He would spend almost a decade of his life in and out of prison, and wouldn't be released for good until 1995.[20] But this would not prove to be the new lease on life that it could have been. The years of poverty, drug use, and abysmal health care while incarcerated had taken their toll. Barry Allen died within a decade of coming home.[21]

For their part, James Ramseur's parents had imagined a totally different life for their son and for his good friend Barry, whom he had known for six years by the time they boarded the 2 train that fateful day in December. Sure, raising kids in a high-rise on a busy commercial corner of the South Bronx had not been easy on the Ramseur family. And it was true that James had felt so disillusioned with school that he stopped attending at the age of twelve.[22] But James was funny and optimistic. And no matter how loud or rowdy her son was, his mother, Bessie Ramseur, remembered that he had never done anything to hurt anyone.[23]

But hope for the future, especially for one's children, was damned hard to hold on to in the South Bronx of the Reagan eighties. In that decade, the infrastructure of Ramseur's neighborhood would be decimated. The Ramseur home at 3670 Third Avenue, located in one of the poorest zip codes in NYC, would remain in desperate need of repairs, and their skinny son, James, would have stunningly few prospects as he entered adulthood. Even ten years earlier, there had at least been some reason to be optimistic about what might lie ahead in neighborhoods like his.

But it was being shot that really destroyed James's life. James could never fully understand why he, not Bernie Goetz, was being painted as a horrible person by reporters, by the television media, by those who sent him hate mail, by the cops who interviewed him in the hospital, by Barry Slotnick on the stand, and ultimately by a jury that refused to hold his assailant responsible for shooting him. James hadn't even talked to this man on the subway. He was nowhere near him. Somehow, though, it was acceptable for this man to shoot him down. Somehow, people felt he even deserved it.

In the wake of the shootings, James's life imploded even more spectacularly than either Troy's or Barry's. James grew increasingly bitter, angrier, and more fatalistic. His sad attempt to convince the public that he had been kidnapped was a desperate plea for empathy that had, ultimately, been disastrous. As had the fact that he ended up being arrested for a brutal crime against a young woman—one that he maintained he was innocent of to the end. He would eventually get out of prison, but at that point, it was too late for him to imagine a better life for himself.

On the twenty-seventh anniversary of the shootings, forty-five-year-old James Ramseur checked into the low-budget Paradise Hotel on Boston Road in the Bronx. He swallowed a handful of prescription pills, lay down on the bed, and was discovered dead the next morning.[24] It appeared that James had deliberately overdosed. He had paid up front, made sure he had his ID on his person so he could be readily identified, and had received no visitors. When the hotel staff discovered his body, they immediately called his sister Brenda. She rushed to the seedy room and confirmed it was him. James Ramseur had spent twenty-five years in prison, and seventeen months after he finally was able to come home, he had clearly found no future waiting for him in the South Bronx.[25]

Shirley Cabey, too, would find few reasons to stay in this neighborhood in the aftermath of the shootings. It was a stark contrast to how she felt when she first moved her young kids into the Daniel Webster Homes. To the new widow, life had felt daunting but not without hope. When her job at the psychiatric hospital became permanent, she even had reason to feel some real excitement for the future, even though the neighborhood in which she was trying to raise her family was being ravaged by unemployment, drugs, and police brutality. But when Bernie Goetz paralyzed her son Bean, it was a blow from which she never really recovered.

Shirley had tried her best to convey to the public just how costly Goetz's act of rage had been for her family. She had fought to make sure everyone knew that her son was not the criminal in this ordeal. She had weathered every setback to make sure that Goetz would at least be held accountable in a civil courtroom, even if he had been acquitted in criminal court. And that jury's verdict had mattered to Shirley. She would never see a penny from Goetz, but she was finally able to tell her story in that civil trial. Before then, Shirley simply had to endure the way Goetz and the media spoke about her child.

This had been difficult for her. She had no way to respond, no real access to the media that mattered, when Goetz, for example, told reporters that she "should have had an abortion rather than give birth to Darrell, and that the shooting of her son was a public service."[26]

But then, it was all over. The civil trial had ended. Goetz went on with his life in Greenwich Village, feeding squirrels, dealing weed but doing no time, and continuing to tinker with the electronic gadgets that filled his apartment. Her life and Darrell's life, however, had been frozen in time.

Every day, Shirley had to get her son dressed. She had to check him for bed ulcers, assist him with his bodily and hygienic needs, and make sure that she gave him a thorough bathing every Saturday. As she had told the Bronx jury in a quiet voice, "He basically needs help for everything."[27] Meanwhile, the television and the radio had become Darrell's constant and only companions. He still loved watching and listening to the Yankees. And he still loved to hear music, even though the days when he and Lydell used to clown around break dancing and playing sports must have been painful to recall, if he could recall them at all.

Shirley remained fiercely protective of her son. Eventually, she decided to move her family out of the South Bronx to Spring Valley, New York, and away from a city that was a daily reminder of the ugliness, the injustice, and the racism that had led to her son's condition. As one of Darrell's closest relatives shared with podcast host Leon Neyfakh, "She was done with the city. If we weren't going out there to visit Grandma or go to the swap meet or fish market or something . . . She's like, no, she just wants to move outta this city. She couldn't stand it. She hated it. . . . She could care less for the Bronx."[28]

Just under two decades after moving to Spring Valley, Shirley became ill. This was the moment that she had feared most—what would happen to her son when she could no longer care for him? When Shirley died in September 2015, Darrell had thankfully already been settled into a care facility. He still had his siblings, including a younger sister born in 1990 named Raven, and they were a blessing. But as the years unfolded, he still missed his mother. As his sister said fondly, "He love eating food, period. Nice home-cooked meals, especially food that reminds him of Mommy, forget about it. Mac and cheese, lasagna and everything."[29]

Darrell also still thought about that terrible moment back in December 1984. At least, his sister thought he did, even though he still seemed a bit uncertain about what exactly had happened. As Raven Cabey said wistfully, "It's sad. It's sad because [Goetz] still hasn't got his just dues. . . . This person, this person's still living life, selling weed to cops and stuff and feeding squirrels. Sounds pretty good to me." Meanwhile, she couldn't imagine her brother ever wanting to set foot in the city again, not even to "take a family trip to the Bronx Zoo."[30] She was pretty sure if he was asked, "he's gonna sit in silence and not say nothing. And that's the answer right there for me."[31]

NEW YORK CITY HAD betrayed Darrell Cabey, James Ramseur, Barry Allen, and Troy Canty. In fact, when America took the dramatic turn that it did during the Reagan eighties, slowly abandoning the hard-won policies and programs that had reduced poverty, expanded voting rights, improved health care, and increased equality of opportunity more generally, it betrayed all of its citizens.

The Reagan Revolution's determination to undo all that had been gained since the New Deal and thanks to the civil rights era was in many ways remarkably effective, especially for those who had launched it and those who really led it. But its long-term costs were staggering for everyone else.

Indeed, as inequality and desperation had deepened between 1980 and 2025, it had required an altogether new level of fact distortion, even more unabashed pandering to privilege, and a more intentional stoking of racial resentment and rage to persuade so many ordinary white voters that it still made sense to give away their own hard-won rights, opportunities, and economic security. Continuing to sell the brutal trickle-down economics of the long Reagan Revolution would now require not just a conservative press but a rage- and race-baiting misinformation media machine. Such was needed to translate the brutal fallout of this dramatic political and economic turn in such a way that any anger it might spawn would be directed not at those who were actually responsible for it but rather at those who suffered it most acutely.

This was a new age of fear and a fury so strategically curated that it would put American democracy itself in the gravest danger.[32]

But misinformation does not always triumph. And the ideas that the wealthy few deserve more power and resources than everyone else and that white racial rage should be legitimized and normalized have always been pushed from above, but they have also always been contested and resisted from below. Indeed, throughout American history, and against extraordinary odds, ordinary people have time and again come to recognize their common interests. They have successfully worked to lessen income inequality, to repel racism, and to insist as well that this nation actually provide equality of opportunity and ensure that there is equal justice under the law.

And as history has also shown, those who have the least also have the least to lose. Ordinary Americans, in fact, have every reason to resist the rage and every incentive to come together to fight for a society in which there is a real future, a just future, for everyone's children.

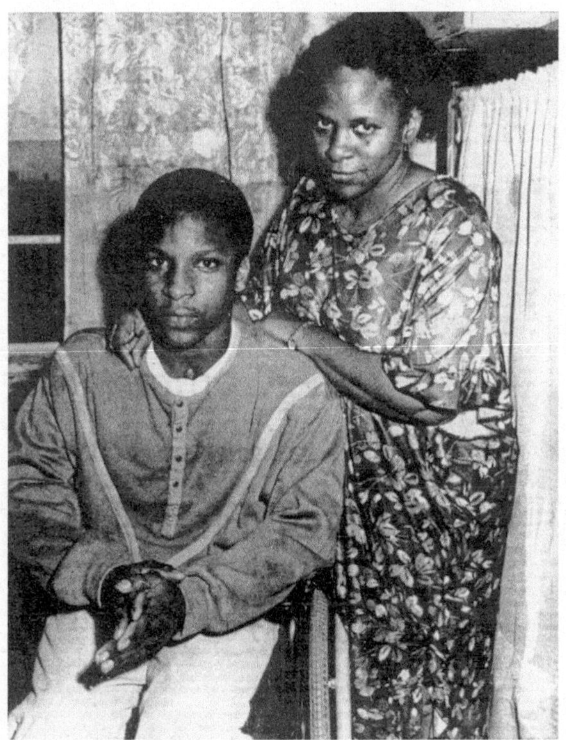

Darrell and Shirley Cabey in their apartment in the South Bronx circa 1997. Unknown

Acknowledgments

In 2023, I was deep into writing another book—one I still intend to finish. But that November, I realized I needed to pivot. Donald J. Trump was on track to become president of the United States again and, as a historian, I needed to understand this.

By then, Trump was under criminal indictment in four separate cases. He had already been found liable for sexual abuse and defamation, and for financial fraud, in two civil trials. His supporters had already stormed the U.S. Capitol in the most violent collective assault on the federal government in American history. Those who hadn't been there in person nevertheless fully endorsed the effort to return him to power—by any means necessary.

Many of his backers were poor and working-class white voters—often criticized for failing to see that he was in fact making their lives harder. But some of his most important supporters were Americans of extraordinary wealth and privilege who understood exactly what he could do for them. They too would go to unprecedented lengths to secure his return to the White House in 2024. Their money, and their power to shape the nation's cultural and social landscape, especially through the media, would prove decisive.

So too would the racial rage that had been unleashed with such a vengeance, and had so easily been normalized and legally vindicated, during the preceding decades.

But when did this political tide *really* turn? And what *actually* was the relationship between the legitimization of white racial rage and the simultaneous ascent of America's wealthiest citizens to a level of riches not seen since the Gilded Age?

Thanks to my wonderful agent, Susan Ginsburg, and my editor, Edward Kastenmeier, I was able to dive into these questions when they felt most pressing. Susan has been my anchor over these past few years. Her calm, her assurances, and her steadfast advocacy have meant everything. I am so lucky to know her. Edward has been in the trenches with me as well, shaping this book as he has my others, and always pushing me toward the clearest and strongest version of my work. I am humbled by the time and care he has given to these pages.

I am also deeply indebted to Lisa Lucas, who immediately understood the urgency of these questions and championed this new project from the very beginning. Lisa remains one of the most extraordinary author advocates, and one of the most beautiful human beings, I know.

This book could not have made it over the finish line without four remarkable people: Emily Giglierano, Lisa Kwan, Allyson Moralez, and Jackie Lauer. Emily's sharp editorial eye, tireless labor to make sense of the nonsensical, and readiness to drop everything to meet a deadline were gifts beyond measure. I owe her little girl a trip to the park. Lisa's close readings, unflagging optimism, and above-and-beyond commitment to the manuscript absolutely sustained me. Ally and Jackie were my lifelines—hunting down photographs, wrangling source notes, and lifting me up when I most needed it. I am also so grateful to Michiko Clark and Julianne Clancy at Pantheon, as well as to Suzanne Williams of Shreve Williams and to Caitlin Corcoran of C3 Creative, whose efforts to ensure that this book reaches readers have been nothing short of amazing.

I also could not have written this book without the remarkable generosity of so many who encouraged this project and shared their insights, sources, and research leads, as well as access to countless boxes of documents. My deepest thanks to Leon Neyfakh; David Pedersen; Alberto Toscano; the archivists at the New York Historical, at the Municipal Archives, and at the Ronald Reagan Presidential Library; and the remarkable women at the Whiting Foundation, as well as to those who juried the Whiting Creative Nonfiction Award of 2024. Thanks also to the Carr-Ryan Center for Human Rights at Harvard University, to William Sturkey, Karen Tani, Naomi Murakawa, the students and faculty at Penn's and Princeton's workshops, and to Austin Lukondi, Kat Brausch, Alvin Hill, Robin Collier, and the late Darrell Moore.

A special thanks here as well to Darrell Cabey's lawyer Ron Kuby. Without his astonishing kindness and generosity, this book would quite literally not exist.

My deepest gratitude goes to the many scholars, filmmakers, and journalists whose work on this period, on these politics, and on the places within this book, including, but of course not limited to, Kathleen Belew, Nicole Hemmer, Kathryn Brownell, Kim Phillips-Fein, Julian Zelizer, Bruce Schulman, LaShawn Harris, Bench Ansfield, Reiko Hillyer, Lynne Novick, and Chenjerai Kumanyika.

Meanwhile, and as always, my friends have been a godsend—cheering me on and believing that I could pull this off. I could not be the person, or the historian, that I am without each of them. Bryant Simon has been my sounding board for every book I've written, and it is always thanks to him that I finally reach the "aha" moment that makes it clear what the story is that I am really trying to tell. Elizabeth Hinton, Julilly Kohler-Hausmann, Donna Murch, Kalie Gross, Kelly Lytle Hernández, Keeanga-Yamahtta Taylor, Karen Cox, Danielle McGuire, and Melanie Newport remain my core "history peeps" and close friends, inspiring me on every page that I write. And then, of course, there are the guys in that group from whom I always learn so much—David Goldberg, Simon Balto, Robert Chase, Max Felker-Kantor, Carl Suddler, and Khalil Gibran Muhammad. To Gary Gerstle I owe a special thank-you, as he is also always there, so steadfastly in my corner these many decades later, making me a better scholar.

Meanwhile, as I wrote this book, my History Studio family—Jim Downs, Erica Armstrong Dunbar, Becky Nicolaides, and Caitlin Parker—has served as a constant reminder to me that bringing history to life is essential. My Carceral State Project family—Matt Lassiter, Stephen Cassidy Jones, and Katie Pieper—also reinforce that truth every day.

No paragraph could possibly be long enough to thank my family for their patience, support, and love during my long absences as I researched, wrote, and edited. Agnes, I so miss you, and promise I'll be there soon for this new chapter in our lives. Andre, thanks for always being there to help the Thompsons, all of us, hold it together. Saskia, you are not just my sister but also my comrade-in-arms, and I am grateful beyond words for your instinctive knowledge of exactly what I need and what needs to be done. Dillon, I remain in utter awe of every dream you have realized, and I am prouder of you than I can possibly say. Truly. Caitlin, you are so amazing, and have made me so happy over these past two years—from pulling off that surprise birthday, to your beautiful wedding, to the moment you arrived with news of the baby. Wilder, you are the best of what a human being can be; I am endlessly proud of you and wish the world were more like you. Ava, you are my heart and my inspiration—braver, smarter, more determined, and funnier than I will ever be. You've got this. Isabel, your creativity and vision are rare, and the work you do is so important. You've also got this. Shawn, thank you for also being my kid; you've already moved mountains, and I know you will climb many more. Kamilah, I am so grateful to you because your strength and warmth inspire me every day. To Dan, Carrie, and Brynne, I am so very thankful that I am part of your family too. Brynne, you are brilliant and on your way to amazing things. You've got this too.

Mom, your strength is beyond anything I can fathom. I love you and am so grateful for everything you did to make me believe that I could do this. Kathy, I am here for you—always—and love you so much.

And Jon, you are my strength, my rock, my life. I could never do any of this—any of it—without you. I love you so deeply, but that, actually, doesn't even begin to cover it.

Notes

PART I · POISONING THE BIG APPLE

1. Dylan Gottlieb, "Yuppies: Young Urban Professionals and the Making of Postindustrial New York," PhD diss., Princeton University, 2020.
2. *All in the Family*, episode 24, "Archie the Liberal," March 5, 1977, CBS.

1. *Dreams Dashed*

1. Kenneth T. Jackson, ed., *The Encyclopedia of New York City*, 2nd ed. (New Haven, CT: Yale University Press, 2010), 1149.
2. Jill Jonnes and Nilka Martell, *South Bronx Rising: The Rise, Fall, and Resurrection of an American City* (New York: Fordham University Press, 2002), 333.
3. As described through interviews with Shirley Cabey and Darrell's cousin in: Lillian B. Rubin, *Quiet Rage: Bernie Goetz in a Time of Madness* (New York: Farrar, Straus & Giroux, 1986), 64–65; Leon Neyfakh, *Fiasco: Vigilante*, podcast transcript, episode 3, "Four Teenagers," Prologue Projects, Audible Originals, July 27, 2023.
4. For a rich account of life inside public housing in the South Bronx, see: LaShawn Harris, *Tell Her Story: Eleanor Bumpurs & the Police Killing That Galvanized New York City* (Boston: Beacon, 2025).
5. Randol Contreras, *The Stickup Kids: Race, Drugs, Violence, and the American Dream* (Berkeley: University of California Press, 2012), 37.
6. Ibid., 38.
7. Jackson, *Encyclopedia of New York City*, 1213.
8. Ibid., 228, 1213; Adam Paul Susaneck, "Segregation by Design," TU Delft Centre for the Just City, 2024, https://www.segregationbydesign.com/.
9. John H. Mollenkopf, *The Contested City* (Princeton, NJ: Princeton University Press, 1983); Paul A. Jargowsky, *Poverty and Place: Ghettos, Barrios, and the American City* (New York: Russell Sage Foundation, 1997); Lance Freeman, *There Goes the 'Hood: Views of Gentrification from the Ground Up* (Philadelphia: Temple University Press, 2006).
10. New York University Institute for Civil Infrastructure Systems, *South Bronx Environmental Health and Policy Study: Phase I Report*, New York: Robert F. Wagner Graduate School of Public Service, New York University, September 2002; Clara E. Rodríguez, *Changing Race: Latinos, the Census, and the History of Ethnicity in the United States* (New York: New York University Press, 2000).
11. New York University Institute for Civil Infrastructure Systems, *South Bronx Environmental Health and Policy Study: Phase I Report*, Also see: Rodríguez, *Changing Race*.

12. Jackson, *Encyclopedia of New York City*, 65, 1053. Notably, the now mostly low-income, Black and Brown communities of the South Bronx did not just accept that their neighborhood had become a dumping ground for the rest of the city. A number of grassroots community organizations such as Groups Against Garbage (GAGs), for example, worked hard to ensure that the city would not just assume it could relegate its waste to this part of the Bronx as the next decade unfolded. Their battles with the city and those of tenant organizations alike usually were doomed. By the close of the 1970s the South Bronx had become a place both easily exploited and happily ignored by those with means and power. Indeed, the faster that ethnic whites abandoned the area between the 1960s and 1980, and the higher the number of Black and Latino New Yorkers that moved into the South Bronx in their wake, the truer this became.
13. One of these policies was the "Bretton Woods System," which fixed other currencies to the U.S. dollar, convertible to gold. This allowed the U.S. to run large deficits and export inflation, especially as the Vietnam War dragged on, while countries in the Global South were pressured to maintain currency stability and service debts in dollars. Meanwhile, U.S. corporations regularly extracted oil, minerals, and agricultural commodities from Latin America, Africa, and the Middle East under favorable investment terms (tax breaks, profit repatriation rights, etc.). This in turn led to local movements to control natural resources. The 1971 Algerian oil nationalization and 1972 Chilean copper nationalization were two key instances of this. Finally, there were major uprisings in countries such as Cuba, Nicaragua, and Angola where locals disliked the U.S. backing of local dictators. Most important in the 1970s was the 1973 OPEC oil embargo, which reinforced dollar supremacy and deepened developing countries' dependency on foreign exchange to pay for oil imports. Such countries began defaulting or restructuring their debts, leading to the so-called Third World debt crisis. Robert Barsky and Lutz Kilian, *A Monetary Explanation of the Great Stagflation of the 1970s*, Working Paper 7547 (Cambridge, MA: National Bureau of Economic Research, February 2000); Andrés Solimano, "Stagflation in the 1970s, Globalization, and the Financial Crisis of 2008–2009," in *A History of Big Recessions in the Long Twentieth Century* (New York: Cambridge University Press, 2020).
14. James R. Crotty, *The Effects of Increased Product Market Competition and Changes in Financial Markets on the Performance of Nonfinancial Corporations in the Neoliberal Era*, Working Paper 44 (Amherst, MA: Political Economy Research Institute, October 11, 2002); David M. Gordon, "Stages of Accumulation and Long Economic Cycles," *Review of Radical Political Economics* 12, no. 4 (1980): 1–26; Thomas E. Weisskopf, "Radical Political Economy in Recent Decades," *Review of Radical Political Economics* 47, no. 4 (2015): 436–49; Robert Brenner, "The Origins of Capitalist Development: A Critique of Neo-Smithian Marxism," *Review of Radical Political Economics* 6, no. 2 (1974): 1–22; Samuel Bowles and Herbert Gintis, "The Crisis of Liberal Democratic Capitalism: The Case of the United States," *Review of Radical Political Economics* 12, no. 3 (1980): 1–26.
15. Kim Phillips-Fein, *Fear City: New York's Fiscal Crisis and the Rise of Austerity Politics*, (New York: Metropolitan Books, 2017).
16. Stacey M. Kean, *The New York City Financial Crisis: Important City, State and Federal Considerations* (Washington, DC: Congressional Research Service, Library of Congress, 1976); Contreras, *The Stickup Kids*, 43.
17. For a powerful look at how access to free education changed the lives of Black young people in California too, see: Donna Murch, *Living for the City: Migration, Education, and the Rise of the Black Panther Party in Oakland, California* (Chapel Hill: University of North Carolina Press, 2010).
18. Elaine Velie, "The Overlooked Student Protest That Changed College Admissions," *Hypoallergenic*, July 18, 2023; "1970–1977 Open Admissions—Fiscal Crisis—State Takeover," CUNY Digital History Archive (CDHA), American Social History Project/Center for Media and Learning; Stephen Brier, "Revolution at CUNY: The 1969 Student Strikes," *Radical Teacher* 80 (2007): 18–26; Adriana Villavicencio, "The Broken Promise of Urban High School Reform: When Rhetoric Trumps Reality," *Urban Education* 48, no. 3 (2013): 363–94.

19. Carolyn McLaughlin and David Gómez, *South Bronx Battles: Stories of Resistance, Resilience, and Renewal* (Berkeley: University of California Press, 2019), 64.
20. Contreras, *The Stickup Kids*, 42.
21. Bench Ansfield, *Born in Flames: The Business of Arson and the Remaking of the American City* (New York: W. W. Norton, 2025); Bench Ansfield, "Born in Flames: Arson, Racial Capitalism, and the Reinsuring of the Bronx in the Late Twentieth Century," *Enterprise & Society* 23, no. 4 (2022): 923–27.
22. Peter L'Official, *Urban Legends: The South Bronx in Representation and Ruin* (Cambridge, MA: Harvard University Press, 2020), 75; Jackson, *Encyclopedia of New York City*, 1213.
23. On the long history of landlords' abuses and public housing as well as the role of private real estate racism in creating housing inequality and homelessness, see: Rhonda Y. Williams, *The Politics of Public Housing: Black Women's Struggles Against Urban Inequality* (Oxford, UK: Oxford University Press, 2004); Lisa Levenstein, *A Movement Without Marches: African American Women and the Politics of Poverty in Postwar Philadelphia* (Chapel Hill: University of North Carolina Press, 2010); Richard Plunz, *A History of Housing in New York City* (New York: Columbia University Press, 2016); Thomas J. Main, *Homelessness in New York City: Policymaking from Koch to de Blasio* (New York: New York University Press, 2016); Ella Howard, *Homeless: Poverty and Place in Urban America* (Philadelphia: University of Pennsylvania Press, 2013); Alice O'Connor, *Poverty Knowledge: Social Science, Social Policy, and the Poor in Twentieth-Century U.S. History* (Princeton, NJ: Princeton University Press, 2001); Matthew Desmond, *Evicted: Poverty and Profit in the American City* (New York: Crown, 2016); Luis Ferré-Sadurní, "The Rise and Fall of New York Public Housing: An Oral History," *New York Times* online, July 9, 2018; Ben Austen, *High-Risers: Cabrini-Green and the Fate of American Public Housing* (New York: HarperAcademic, 2019); Keeanga-Yamahtta Taylor, *Housing for Profit: How Banks and the Real Estate Industry Undermined Black Homeownership* (Chapel Hill: University of North Carolina Press, 2019), Destin Jenkins, *The Bonds of Inequality: Debt and the Making of the American City* (Chicago: University of Chicago Press, 2021).
24. As Hinton makes clear, poor and working-class urbanites across the country have always engaged in dramatic acts, including arson, as their own coherent and collective response to civic abandonment and abuse. See: Elizabeth Hinton, *America on Fire: The Untold History of Police Violence and Black Rebellion Since the 1960s* (New York: Liveright, 2022).
25. "1,000 Families Evicted from Housing Projects," *New York Times*, December 27, 1989, B4.
26. Harris, *Tell Her Story*, 47.
27. Rubin, *Quiet Rage*, 66.
28. "Darrell Cabey: Did One Tragedy Lead to Another?," *Democrat and Chronicle* (Rochester, NY), March 24, 1985.
29. "Consent Form for Treatment of Minors," October 28, 1980, Department of Psychiatry, Bronx-Lebanon Hospital Center, Papers of Ron Kuby; Fact Sheet, October 28, 1980, Department of Psychiatry, Bronx-Lebanon Hospital Center, Papers of Ron Kuby.
30. William M. Kunstler to Messrs. Gennaro A. Fischetti, George L. Grobe, Jr., and Ms. Diane McGrath, Commissioners of the Crime Victims Board, December 8, 1988, Papers of Ron Kuby.

2: *Secrets and Scars*

1. Bernie was baptized in the fifth grade: "Goetz Baptized," *Poughkeepsie Journal*, November 26, 1958, 34.
2. Probation Department Sentencing Report Dossier, "Departmental Sentence Recommendation with Supporting Reasons," 30, September 14, 1987, Case No. 8704982—Bernhard Hugo Goetz, Manhattan Adult Investigation Branch, New York City Department of Probation, Papers of Ron Kuby. Various documents within this Department of Probation sentencing dossier are unnumbered. The page numbers provided here are based on the author's pagination of the entire scanned dossier.

3. Ron Marzloc, "Before the Gun, Goetz Was a Toddler in Elmhurst," *Queens Chronicle*, December 21, 2023.
4. Cynthia Fagen, Peter Moses, and Malcolm Balfour, "The Vigilante's Untold Life Story," *New York Post*, January 3, 1985, 2–3.
5. Robert D. McFadden, "Goetz: A Private Man in a Public Debate," *New York Times*, January 6, 1985, A1.
6. Probation Department Sentencing Report Dossier, 6.
7. Ibid.
8. Lillian B. Rubin, *Quiet Rage: Bernie Goetz in a Time of Madness* (New York: Farrar, Straus & Giroux, 1986), 51.
9. Ibid.
10. Ibid.
11. "Goetz Winner at Rhinebeck," *Poughkeepsie Journal*, April 3, 1959, 10; "Rhinebeck Central School Publishes Honor Roll," *Poughkeepsie Journal*, March 27, 1960, 6B.
12. Rubin, *Quiet Rage*, 54.
13. Ibid., 85.
14. Probation Department Sentencing Report Dossier, 19.
15. "Trial Begins in Morals Case," *Poughkeepsie Journal*, May 16, 1960, 20.
16. Rubin, *Quiet Rage*, 109.
17. Ibid., 114.
18. Ibid., 109.
19. McFadden, "Goetz," A1.
20. "Police Seek Pair Who Robbed Rhinebeck Man," *Times Record* (Troy, NY), October 29, 1960, 9.
21. Rubin, *Quiet Rage*, 112.
22. Ibid., 109.
23. "Trial Begins in Morals Case," *Poughkeepsie Journal*; Probation Department Sentencing Report Dossier, 20.
24. Probation Department Sentencing Report Dossier, 20.
25. McFadden, "Goetz," A1.
26. Rubin, *Quiet Rage*, 124.
27. Probation Department Sentencing Report Dossier, 23.
28. "Man to Appeal Morals Case," *Poughkeepsie Journal*, January 22, 1960, 12; "Haver to Argue New Motions for Goetz," *Poughkeepsie Journal*, May 29, 1960, 4B; "Court Reverses Goetz Conviction," *Poughkeepsie Journal*, October 6, 1962, 7.
29. Probation Department Sentencing Report Dossier, 23.
30. Ibid.
31. Ibid.
32. Myra Friedman with Michael Daly, "My Neighbor Bernie Goetz," *New York*, February 18, 1985, 34–41, Papers of Ron Kuby.
33. McFadden, "Goetz," A1.
34. Probation Department Sentencing Report Dossier, 27.
35. McFadden, "Goetz," A1.
36. Probation Department Sentencing Report Dossier, 25.
37. Ibid.
38. McFadden, "Goetz," A1.
39. Ibid.
40. Sally Banes, "Physical Graffiti: Breaking Is Hard to Do," *Village Voice*, April 22, 1981.
41. McFadden, "Goetz," A1.

3. *Creating Crisis*

1. "Darrell Cabey: Did One Tragedy Lead to Another?," *Democrat and Chronicle* (Rochester, NY), March 24, 1985.
2. This form of dancing began to take off among Black and Brown young people in urban neighborhoods in the late 1970s. The nomenclature stemmed from the new form of danc-

ing to a certain section of a hip-hop song or beat called the break. See: Abiola Sinclair, "'Beat Street': Authentic Look at Bronx Breakers," *New York Amsterdam News*, June 9, 1984, 22.

3. "Darrell Cabey: Did One Tragedy Lead to Another?," *Democrat and Chronicle*.
4. For important histories on the New Deal, its greatest beneficiaries and limitations, and its eventual fracturing, see: Steve Fraser and Gary Gerstle, eds., *The Rise and Fall of the New Deal Order, 1930–1980* (Princeton, NJ: Princeton University Press, 1989); Thomas J. Sugrue, *The Origins of the Urban Crisis: Race and Inequality in Postwar Detroit* (Princeton, NJ: Princeton University Press, 1996); Heather Ann Thompson, *Whose Detroit?: Politics, Labor, and Race in a Modern American City* (Ithaca, NY: Cornell University Press, 2001); Matthew J. Countryman, *Up South: Civil Rights and Black Power in Philadelphia* (Philadelphia: University of Pennsylvania Press, 2006); Lisa McGirr, *Suburban Warriors: The Origins of the New American Right* (Princeton, NJ: Princeton University Press, 2001); Bruce J. Schulman, *The Seventies: The Great Shift in American Culture, Society, and Politics* (New York: Free Press, 2001); and Matthew D. Lassiter, *The Silent Majority: Suburban Politics in the Sunbelt South* (Princeton, NJ: Princeton University Press, 2006). For an important debate on how progressive, comprehensive, or enduring the core ethos of the New Deal actually was, see: Jefferson Cowie and Nick Salvatore, "The Long Exception: Rethinking the Place of the New Deal in American History," *International Labor and Working-Class History* 74, no. 1 (Fall 2008): 3–32, and Nancy MacLean, "Getting New Deal History Wrong," *International Labor and Working-Class History* 74, no. 1 (Fall 2008): 49–55.
5. James Cicconi to Donald Regan and Michael K. Deaver, "Follow-Up on Black Strategy," February 12, 1985, Ronald Reagan Presidential Library, Simi Valley, California. Cicconi served as a special assistant to Reagan and to White House chief of staff James A. Baker III from 1981 to 1985.
6. As writer Jonathan Mahler put it about NYC specifically, "A city that had once aspired to provide a safety net and a foothold to all of its residents" would eventually "become a gladiatorial arena for those with the biggest appetites, the loudest voices, and the most outsized ambitions." Jonathan Mahler, *The Gods of New York: Egotists, Idealists, Opportunists, and the Birth of the Modern City: 1986–1990* (New York: Random House, 2025), 14.
7. Sheldon Danziger and Robert Haveman, "The Reagan Budget: A Sharp Break with the Past," *Challenge* 24, no. 2 (May/June 1981): 5–13.
8. "Study: Cuts Driving Poor to Breadlines," *New York Amsterdam News*, July 24, 1982, 3; Fred Silverman, "The Sad Case of Bronx Hospital," *New York Amsterdam News*, February 26, 1983, 13; J. Zamgba Browne, "Housing Shortage 'Acute,'" *New York Amsterdam News*, November 26, 1983, 3, 39; Joyce Hauser, "The Bronx Is Desolate—But It's Banana Kelly Improvement," *New York Amsterdam News*, February 7, 1981, 14–15; Simon Anekwe, "Groups Urge Adequate Health Care for Poor," *New York Amsterdam News*, December 12, 1981, 16; J. Zamgba Browne, "Woman Says City Thwarts South Bronx Rehab Effort," *New York Amsterdam News*, February 6, 1982, 58; Simon Anekwe, "$1M Goes to Bronx; Pierce: 'Be Grateful,'" *New York Amsterdam News*, May 8, 1982, 53; Simon Anekwe, "S. Bronx Prison Plan Irks Groups," *New York Amsterdam News*, September 17, 1983, 9; J. Zamgba Browne, "Sharpton on Anti-Drug Campaign," *New York Amsterdam News*, November 8, 1986, 32; Abiola Sinclair, "Community Calls for Jihad Against Crack and . . ." *New York Amsterdam News*, February 28, 1987, 30; Stan Lundine, "Drug Demonstration Area in the City Set," *New York Amsterdam News*, July 29, 1989, 13.
9. Jackson in fact sought the Democratic Party's nomination for president in both 1984 and 1988. His "Rainbow Coalition" would not, however, get the nod of the party's more conservative and centrist wings. Manning Marable, "Jackson and the Rise of the Rainbow Coalition," *New Left Review* 1, no. 149 (January/February 1985): 3–44. Meanwhile, the Bronx was represented by Puerto Rican congressman Herman Badillo, to whom many looked to take on the worst of Reagan's cuts despite his own increasingly conservative leanings. He would eventually switch to the Republican Party in the 1990s and in 2006 pen a major rebuke of liberal politics and policies: Herman Badillo, *One Nation, One Standard: An Ex-Liberal on How Hispanics Can Succeed Just Like Other Immigrant Groups* (New York: Sentinel, 2006).

10. Joshua Guild, George Derek Musgrove, Benjamin Talton, Keeanga-Yamahtta Taylor, and Leah Wright Rigueur, eds., "Special Issue: The Black 1980s," *Journal of African American History* 108, no. 3 (Summer 2023): 356. This new political moment is defined, according to these scholars, "by a unique racial regime characterized by the rise of the New Right (and the Democratic Party's concurrent shift to the right) and the emergence of a new Black political class that was increasingly disconnected from the interests of Black workers and the poor," and they have dubbed it "the Black '80s." For a deep dive into the complex politics of this moment, see the introduction to this special issue.
11. There is a vast literature from the 1980s on the "Black Underclass." The more notable conservative white scholars writing on this include: Douglas G. Glasgow, *The Black Underclass: Poverty, Unemployment, and Entrapment of Ghetto Youth* (Hoboken, NJ: Jossey-Bass, 1981) and Charles Murray, *Losing Ground: American Social Policy, 1950–1980* (New York: Basic Books, 1984). Black conservatives writing on this include Thomas Sowell, *The Economics and Politics of Race: An International Perspective* (New York: William Morrow, 1983). Black Democrats' notable books on this subject include: William Julius Wilson, *The Truly Disadvantaged: The Inner City, the Underclass, and Public Policy* (Chicago: University of Chicago Press, 1987). A notable radical Black critique of such theories is Manning Marable, *How Capitalism Underdeveloped Black America* (Boston: South End Press, 1983). Historian Danielle Wiggins argues that the exact reasons why Black civil rights leaders and elected officials took what appeared to be neoconservative views of what was happening to the Black community in the 1980s were complicated and were actually rooted in deep-seated liberal notions about the best way to bolster the Black community in the face of austerity. Danielle Wiggins, *Black Excellence: Atlanta and the Making of Modern Black Liberalism* (Philadelphia: University of Pennsylvania Press, 2025).
12. On the history of hip-hop, see: Jeff Chang, *Can't Stop Won't Stop: A History of the Hip-Hop Generation* (New York: St. Martin's, 2005); Murray Forman and Mark Anthony Neal, eds., *That's the Joint!: The Hip-Hop Studies Reader,* 2nd ed. (New York: Routledge, 2011); Tricia Rose, *Black Noise: Rap Music and Black Culture in Contemporary America* (Hanover, NH: University Press of New England, 1994).
13. Marie Moore, "Two South Bronx Sisters Receive $8,000 Scholarships," *New York Amsterdam News,* November 27, 1982, 8; J. Zamgba Browne, "Youth Realizing Tennis Goal Despite Dad's Death," *New York Amsterdam News,* August 5, 1989, 12.
14. Larry McShane, "For One Goetz Victim, Suffering Won't End," *Los Angeles Times,* January 8, 1995.
15. "Darrell Cabey: Did One Tragedy Lead to Another?," *Democrat and Chronicle.*
16. Lillian B. Rubin, *Quiet Rage: Bernie Goetz in a Time of Madness* (New York: Farrar, Straus & Giroux, 1986), 68; McShane, "For One Goetz Victim, Suffering Won't End."
17. Rubin, *Quiet Rage,* 68.
18. Complaint for Compensatory and Punitive Damages and Permanent Injunction, 1–24, *Darrell A. Cabey, by his legal guardian and proposed conservator, Shirley Cabey v. Bernhard Hugo Goetz,* No. 6747-1985 (Sup. Ct. Bronx Cnty, January 30, 1985), Papers of Ron Kuby.
19. Carolyn McLaughlin and David Gómez, *South Bronx Battles: Stories of Resistance, Resilience, and Renewal* (Berkeley: University of California Press, 2019), 266.
20. Ibid, 53.
21. Rubin, *Quiet Rage,* 68.
22. McLaughlin and Gómez, *South Bronx Battles,* 104.
23. Ibid., 44, 102.
24. United States Bureau of Labor Statistics, *Monthly New York State and New York City Employment and Unemployment Reports,* 1989–1996, raw data (New York: Middle Atlantic Regional Office, 1989–1996).
25. For more on the dawning of this created and deeply racialized crisis and the damaging narrative that was spun to justify it, see: Donna Murch, "Toward a Black Working-Class History of the Long 1980s," Special Issue: The Black 1980s, *Journal of African American History* 108, no. 3 (Summer 2023): 425–66.
26. McLaughlin and Gómez, *South Bronx Battles,* 53.

27. "Darrell Cabey: Did One Tragedy Lead to Another?," *Democrat and Chronicle.*
28. Rubin, *Quiet Rage,* 69.
29. Ibid.
30. Ibid., 70.
31. Bruce D. Johnson, Andrew Golub, and Jeffrey Fagan, "Careers in Crack, Drug Use, Drug Distribution, and Nondrug Criminality," *Crime & Delinquency* 41, no. 3 (1995): 281.
32. McLaughlin and Gómez, *South Bronx Battles,* 50.
33. For an intimate look at the costs of the drug war in this borough, see: Adrian Nicole LeBlanc, *Random Family: Love, Drugs, Trouble, and Coming of Age in the Bronx* (New York: Simon & Schuster, 2004). For an extraordinary and beautiful memoir on the family and personal price paid even well outside of the Big Apple, see: Mitchell Jackson, *Survival Math: Notes on an All-American Family* (New York: Scribner, 2019).
34. Todd Bookman, "Addiction, Compassion, Race: Looking Back at the Crack Epidemic," *The Pulse,* Philadelphia, WHYY-FM, February 22, 2016, NPR.
35. Ginia Bellafante, "In the Bronx, Heroin Never Went Away," *New York Times,* March 23, 2017.
36. "Let Us Fight AIDS Campaign Launched," *New York Amsterdam News,* May 30, 1987, 14; Richard S. Jones, "Say Students Have AIDS," *New York Amsterdam News,* August 22, 1987, 4; Beny J. Primm, "Don't Deny Addicts' Right to Treatment," *New York Amsterdam News,* May 20, 1989, 15. For more on the Black community's response to the AIDS crisis more generally, see: Cathy J. Cohen, *The Boundaries of Blackness: AIDS and the Breakdown of Black Politics* (Chicago: University of Chicago Press, 1999); Dan Royles, *To Make the Wounded Whole: The African American Struggle Against HIV/AIDS* (Chapel Hill: University of North Carolina Press, 2020).
37. U.S. Congress, House of Representatives, Select Committee on Narcotics Abuse and Control, U.S. Congress, "Preliminary Staff Study—Drug Abuse in New York City Schools," 95th Cong., 1st Sess., January 1977, H. Doc 95-1-7, 1–6.
38. For a particularly powerful and local account of what the coming of crack meant on the ground, see: Donovan X. Ramsey, *When Crack Was King: A People's History of a Misunderstood Era* (New York: One World, 2023).
39. Jill Jonnes and Nilka Martell, *South Bronx Rising: The Rise, Fall, and Resurrection of an American City* (New York: Fordham University Press, 2002), 237.
40. Bookman, "Addiction, Compassion, Race."
41. Max Felker-Kantor, *DARE to Say No: Policing and the War on Drugs in Schools* (Chapel Hill: University of North Carolina Press, 2024).
42. Specifically see the Comprehensive Crime Control Act of 1984 as well as the Anti–Drug Abuse Act of 1986, which, among other things, introduced mandatory minimum sentences for drug offenses, particularly those involving the sale of cocaine, as well as much harsher penalties for the cultivation, possession, and sale of marijuana. This also filled the jails. For more on the explosion of jail populations in preceding decades, see: Melanie D. Newport, *This Is My Jail: Local Politics and the Rise of Mass Incarceration* (Philadelphia: University of Pennsylvania Press, 2022); Nicole Gonzalez Van Cleve, *Crook County: Racism and Injustice in America's Largest Criminal Court* (Stanford, CA: Stanford University Press, 2016).
43. Ashley Nellis, *Still Life: America's Increasing Use of Life and Long-Term Sentences* (Washington, DC: The Sentencing Project, 2017), 7.
44. Elizabeth Hinton, *From the War on Poverty to the War on Crime: The Making of Mass Incarceration in America* (Cambridge, MA: Harvard University Press, 2016), 6.
45. For the ways in which the post-1965 embrace of War on Crime ideas and policies bolstered both the numbers of and the legal access afforded to members of law enforcement as they policed communities and carried out Reagan's drug war, see: Hinton, *From the War on Poverty to the War on Crime.* For the long history of the criminalization and incarceration of Brown people, and its relationship to immigration politics, see: Kelly Lytle Hernández, *City of Inmates: Conquest, Rebellion, and the Rise of Human Caging in Los Angeles, 1771–1965* (Chapel Hill: University of North Carolina Press, 2017).

46. Drug use rates across racial lines are remarkably similar, but with the white population being exponentially larger than, say, the Black population in New York City in 1980 (60.72% versus 25.23% in NYC and 80% versus 11.5% nationally), and wealthier, their dollars drove the illegal drug trade. U.S. Bureau of the Census, *1980 Census of Population, Volume 1: Characteristics of the Population, Chapter A: Number of Inhabitants, Part 34: New York,* PC80-1-A34 (Washington, DC: U.S. Government Printing Office, 1982), Table 6; National Institute on Drug Abuse, *National Household Survey on Drug Abuse: Main Findings 1985* (Rockville, MD: U.S. Department of Health and Human Services, 1987).
47. Craig Reinarman and Harry G. Levine, eds., *Crack in America: Demon Drugs and Social Justice* (Berkeley: University of California Press, 1997), 19–20.
48. Johnson, Golub, and Fagan, "Careers in Crack," 275.
49. John F. Timoney, *Beat Cop to Top Cop: A Tale of Three Cities* (Philadelphia: University of Pennsylvania Press, 2010), 20. For the longer history of policing in New York City and race, see: Marilynn S. Johnson, *Street Justice: A History of Police Violence in New York City* (Boston: Beacon, 2004); Robert J. Kane and Michael D. White, *Jammed Up: Bad Cops, Police Misconduct, and the New York City Police Department* (New York: New York University Press, 2012); Michael F. Armstrong, *They Wished They Were Honest: The Knapp Commission and New York City Police Corruption* (New York: Columbia University Press, 2012); Clarence Taylor, *Fight the Power: African Americans and the Long History of Police Brutality in New York City* (New York: New York University Press, 2018); Matthew Guariglia, *Police and the Empire City: Race and the Origins of Modern Policing in New York* (Durham, NC: Duke University Press, 2023); Shannon King, *The Politics of Safety: The Black Struggle for Police Accountability in La Guardia's New York* (Chapel Hill: University of North Carolina Press, 2024); Chenjerai Kumanyika, *Empire City: The Origins of the NYPD,* podcast, episodes 1–9, Wondery, 2024.
50. Selwyn Raab, "All 4 Teens Shot by 'Vigilante' Had History of Criminal Arrests," *Sun Sentinel* (Fort Lauderdale, FL), January 10, 1985, 6.
51. Timoney, *Beat Cop to Top Cop,* 20.
52. For important histories of policing of other major American cities such as Los Angeles and even smaller locales that also led up to this, and resistance to such, see: Simon Balto, *Occupied Territory: Policing Black Chicago from Red Summer to Black Power* (Chapel Hill: University of North Carolina Press, 2019); Max Felker-Kantor, *Policing Los Angeles: Race, Resistance, and the Rise of the LAPD* (Chapel Hill: University of North Carolina Press, 2018); Elizabeth Hinton, *America on Fire: The Untold History of Police Violence and Black Rebellion Since the 1960s* (New York: Liveright, 2021).
53. Timoney, *Beat Cop to Top Cop,* 20.
54. Rubin, *Quiet Rage,* 70.
55. Yolanda M. Scott, *Fear of Crime Among Inner-City African Americans* (New York: LFB Scholarly Publishing, 2001), 32.
56. David Seifman, "Crime in Our Town: It's Never Been So Bad," *New York Post,* February 27, 1982, 2.
57. For the origins of this fear-stoking, see: National Criminal Justice Information and Statistics Service, *Crime in the Nation's Five Largest Cities: National Crime Panel Surveys of Chicago, Detroit, Los Angeles, New York, and Philadelphia,* advance report (Washington, DC: Law Enforcement Assistance Agency, April 1974), i–29; New York City Police Department Street Crime Unit, *An Exemplary Project: New York City Police Department Street Crime Unit,* by Andrew Halper and Richard Ku (Washington, DC: National Institute of Law Enforcement and Criminal Justice, 1975); Kim Phillips-Fein, *Fear City: New York's Fiscal Crisis and the Rise of Austerity Politics* (New York: Picador, 2017).
58. Nancy Gibbs, "Wilding in the Night," *Time,* May 8, 1989; Victor M. Rios, *Punished: Policing the Lives of Black and Latino Boys* (New York: New York University Press, 2011).
59. Pete Hamill, "A Savage Disease," *New York Post,* April 23, 1989, 4. For a close study of how dependency and criminality were linked, moving the country rightward, see: Julilly Kohler-Hausmann, *Getting Tough: Welfare and Imprisonment in 1970s America* (Princeton, NJ: Princeton University Press, 2017).

60. Hamill, "A Savage Disease," 4. For the longer history of how Blackness itself has been criminalized nationally and in NYC specifically, see: Khalil Gibran Muhammad, *The Condemnation of Blackness: Race, Crime, and the Making of Modern Urban America* (Cambridge, MA: Harvard University Press, 2010); Carl Suddler, *Presumed Criminal: Black Youth and the Justice System in Postwar New York* (New York: New York University Press, 2019); and Douglas Flowe, *Uncontrollable Blackness: African American Men and Criminality in Jim Crow New York* (Chapel Hill: University of North Carolina Press, 2020).
61. Timoney, *Beat Cop to Top Cop*, 38.
62. Ibid., 45.
63. Ibid., 32.
64. Rubin, *Quiet Rage*, 69.
65. Ibid., 70.

4. *Fueling Fear and Fury*

1. Bernhard Hugo Goetz Deposition, 98, April 8, 1985, Papers of Ron Kuby.
2. Ibid., 101.
3. Ibid., 103.
4. Ibid., 102.
5. Myra Friedman with Michael Daly, "My Neighbor Bernie Goetz," *New York*, February 18, 1985, 35, Papers of Ron Kuby.
6. Robert D. McFadden, "Goetz: A Private Man in a Public Debate," *New York Times*, January 6, 1985, A1.
7. Stacey M. Kean, *The New York City Financial Crisis: Important City, State and Federal Considerations* (Washington, DC: Congressional Research Service, Library of Congress, 1976); Andy Logan, "Déjà Vu," *New Yorker*, July 14, 1991, 69; Randol Contreras, *The Stickup Kids: Race, Drugs, Violence, and the American Dream* (Berkeley: University of California Press, 2012), 154.
8. Jordan Paige, *One Percent for Parks? A Historical and Current Overview of the Parks Budget*, New York: New York City Independent Budget Office, June 22, 2023.
9. Marion Nestle, "How I Ended Up Living in Ed Koch's Famous Greenwich Village Apartment," *The Atlantic* online, February 12, 2013.
10. Alan Brinkley, "Reagan's Revenge—As Invented by Howard Jarvis," *New York Times*, June 19, 1994, 26.
11. Sheldon Danziger and Robert Haveman, "The Reagan Budget: A Sharp Break with the Past," *Challenge* 24, no. 2 (May/June 1981): 5–13.
12. Villagers Against Crime, "Application and Budget to Be Recognized as a Neighborhood Crime Fighting Organization," August 1, 1985, Folder 23, Box 7, Series II, Justice Stephen G. Crane Papers on the Bernhard Goetz Trial and Other Cases, MS 3152, The New York Historical, New York, NY.
13. Sarah Schulman, *Let the Record Show: A Political History of ACT UP New York, 1987–1993* (New York: Farrar, Straus & Giroux: 2022), 7.
14. Communities were also mobilizing on the ground to have the disease recognized and treated in extraordinary ways. Tamar W. Carroll, *Mobilizing New York: AIDS, Antipoverty, and Feminist Activism* (Chapel Hill: University of North Carolina Press, 2015); Dan Royles, *To Make the Wounded Whole: The African American Struggle Against HIV/AIDS* (Chapel Hill: University of North Carolina Press, 2020); Schulman, *Let the Record Show*. See especially Jafari Allen's contributions in Jafari Allen, N. D. B. Connolly, Bill Fletcher Jr., Elizabeth Hinton, and Keeanga-Yamahtta Taylor, "Roundtable: Defining the Black 1980s," Special Issue: The Black 1980s, *Journal of African American History* 108, no. 3 (Summer 2023): 347–68.
15. Friedman with Daly, "My Neighbor Bernie Goetz," 35.
16. Richard Stengel, "A Troubled and Troubling Life: Who Is Bernhard Goetz, and Why Did He Do What He Did?," *Time*, April 8, 1985, 35–38.

17. McFadden, "Goetz," A1; Plaintiff's Memorandum of Law in Support of Motion for Remand, *Darrell A. Cabey, by his legal guardian and proposed conservator, Shirley Cabey v. Bernhard Hugo Goetz,* No. 6747-1985 (Sup. Ct. Bronx Cnty., 1985), Papers of Ron Kuby.
18. Plaintiff's Memorandum of Law in Support of Motion for Remand, 85 Civ. 1383.
19. Probation Department Sentencing Report Dossier, "Departmental Sentence Recommendation with Supporting Reasons," 14, September 14, 1987, Case No. 8704982—Bernhard Hugo Goetz, Manhattan Adult Investigation Branch, New York City Department of Probation, Papers of Ron Kuby. Various documents within this Department of Probation sentencing dossier are unnumbered. The page numbers provided here are based on the author's pagination of the entire scanned dossier.
20. Ibid, 15.
21. Ibid.
22. Jimmy Breslin, "The Gunner Grows Smaller as the Facts Mount," New York *Daily News,* January 3, 1985, 6, Papers of Ron Kuby.
23. McFadden, "Goetz," A1.
24. Stengel, "A Troubled and Troubling Life," 35–38.
25. Hear this account of the 1981 mugging in Leon Neyfakh, *Fiasco: Vigilante,* podcast, episode 1, "Fear City," Prologue Projects, Audible Originals, July 27, 2023.
26. McFadden, "Goetz," A1.
27. Ibid.; Bernhard Hugo Goetz Deposition, 81–83.
28. McFadden, "Goetz," A1; Bernhard Hugo Goetz Deposition, 81–83.
29. McFadden, "Goetz," A1.
30. Bernhard Goetz, statement to Detective Chris Domian and Officer Warren E. Foote, Concord (NH) Police Department, December 31, 1984, 26, Papers of Ron Kuby.
31. Ibid.
32. Emily Yoffe, "Innocence Is Irrelevant," *The Atlantic,* September 2017.
33. McFadden, "Goetz," A1.
34. Probation Department Sentencing Report Dossier, 19.
35. Ronald Sullivan, "Self-Defense as Defense: Unwritten Law for Gun Users," *New York Times,* August 20, 1988, 29.
36. Probation Department Sentencing Report Dossier, 9.
37. Ibid., 10.
38. Ibid.
39. More billboards began springing up on the walls of subway platforms as well as on city streets warning New Yorkers about the ever-present threat of criminals in their midst. As one of these read: "Scuse me, while you're standin' there . . . here's 5 ways not to get mugged." Featured in Jen Carlson, "Tourist Shares Awesome Old-School Photos of 1980s NYC," *Gothamist* (New York, NY), April 1, 2014.
40. This information came from a major poll conducted by NBC and the Associated Press in 1981: *NBC Nightly News* (listed as *NBC Evening News*), "Poll / Crime #518053," reported by John Chancellor, aired July 20, 1981, Vanderbilt Television Archives.
41. Barbara Basler, "Black Man Is Killed by Mob in Brooklyn: Attack Called Racial," *New York Times,* June 23, 1982.
42. Elon Green, *The Man Nobody Killed: Life, Death, and Art in Michael Stewart's New York* (New York: Celadon Books, 2025).
43. LaShawn Harris, *Tell Her Story: Eleanor Bumpurs & the Police Killing That Galvanized New York City* (Boston: Beacon, 2025); *NBC Nightly News,* "Buffalo, New York / Murders of Blacks #507337," reported by Jessica Savitch, aired Saturday, October 11, 1980, Vanderbilt Television Archives.
44. Neil Scognamiglio and Gene Ruffini, "Neighborhood of Hate and Shame," *New York Post,* December 22, 1986, 5.
45. Daniel Mercer, letter to the editor, *New York Post,* December 30, 1986, 16.
46. Video Statement of Bernhard Goetz, transcript, December 31, 1984, to ADA Susan Braver, Det. Dan Hattendorf, and Det. Michael Clark, Concord, New Hampshire, Papers of Ron Kuby.

47. Ibid.
48. Ibid.
49. James Sheehan, "Union Square Is Ready to Bloom . . . and Boom," *The Villager* (New York, NY), March 7, 1985.
50. Plaintiff's Memorandum of Law in Support of Motion for Remand, 85 Civ. 1383.

5. *Profiting from Pain*

1. For a study that examines 1980s census data for the 100 largest U.S. cities, including New York City, see: Alan Berube and Thacher Tiffany, *The Shape of the Curve: Household Income Distributions in U.S. Cities, 1979–1999*, Living Cities Census Series (Washington, DC: Brookings Institution, August 2004), 10.
2. Natasha Frost, "The Trump Family's Immigrant Story," *History.com*, last modified February 17, 2025.
3. Michael Glass, *Cracked Foundations: Debt and Inequality in Suburban America* (Philadelphia: University of Pennsylvania Press, 2025).
4. *United States v. Fred C. Trump, Donald Trump, and Trump Management, Inc.*, No. 73-1529 (EDNY, filed October 15, 1973, closed June 10, 1977).
5. For more on the rise of Reagan and its connection to conservatism and the wealthy, see: Richard C. Elling, "Ideology and Reform: The Political Foundations of Reagan's Social Policy," *Polity* 21, no. 4 (1989): 655–84; Special Issue, "Governing in the Age of Reagan," in *Governance: An International Journal of Policy, Administration, and Institutions* 6, no. 4 (October 1993), Special; Gary Gerstle, *American Crucible: Race and Nation in the Twentieth Century* (Princeton, NJ: Princeton University Press, 2001); Donald T. Critchlow, *The Conservative Ascendancy: How the GOP Right Made Political History* (Cambridge, MA: Harvard University Press, 2007); Bruce J. Schulman and Julian E. Zelizer, eds., *Rightward Bound: Making America Conservative in the 1970s* (Cambridge, MA: Harvard University Press, 2008); Thomas Frank, *The Wrecking Crew: How Conservatives Rule* (New York: Metropolitan Books, 2008); Meg Jacobs and Julian Zelizer, *Conservatives in Power: The Reagan Years, 1981–1989: A Brief History with Documents* (Boston and New York: Bedford/St. Martin's, 2010); Daniel T. Rodgers, *Age of Fracture* (Cambridge, MA: Belknap Press of Harvard University Press, 2011); Paul Pierson, *Dismantling the Welfare State? Reagan, Thatcher, and the Politics of Retrenchment* (Cambridge, UK: Cambridge University Press, 1994); Kim Phillips-Fein, *Invisible Hands: The Businessmen's Crusade Against the New Deal* (New York: W. W. Norton, 2009); Special Issue, "Reagan and the Transformation of American Government," in *Journal of Policy History* 18, no. 3 (2006); Sean Wilentz, *The Age of Reagan: A History, 1974–2008* (New York: Harper, 2008); Daniel Yergin and Joseph Stanislaw, *The Commanding Heights: The Battle for the World Economy* (New York: Simon & Schuster, 1998); Julian E. Zelizer, ed., *The Reagan Presidency: Pragmatic Conservatism and Its Legacies* (Lawrence: University Press of Kansas, 2009).
6. *Historical U.S. Federal Individual Income Tax Rates & Brackets, 1862–2021* (Washington, DC: Tax Foundation, August 24, 2021).
7. "Trump's Empire Takes Root in Brooklyn and Queens," *New York Post*, June 18, 1985, 27.
8. Of course, the families to which they had been born also mattered immeasurably. Whereas Darrell Cabey's mother depended upon public housing, Donald Trump had been born to a wealthy real estate developer who, in turn, paved the way for his son. Fred Trump had also benefited from government largesse—he became stunningly wealthy thanks to governmental support for the construction of postwar housing. What's more, charges of tax evasion, real estate discrimination, and the fact that he was known to use racial slurs and had even been arrested in his younger years at a Ku Klux Klan march in Queens, New York, did not cost him anything.
9. R. D. Plotnick, "Changes in Poverty, Income Inequality, and the Standard of Living in the United States During the Reagan Years," *International Journal of Health Services* 23, no. 2 (1993): 347–58.
10. Donald John Trump to President Ronald Reagan and Mrs. Reagan, February 13, 1985,

"Donald Trump" Folder, WHORM: Alpha File, Ronald Reagan Presidential Library, Simi Valley, California.

11. Linda Faulkner to Donald and Ivana Trump, December 1, 1987, "Donald Trump" Folder, WHORM: Alpha File; see also: Kathy Osbourne to Linda Faulkner, June 17, 1988, "Donald Trump" Folder, WHORM: Alpha File.
12. For more on the connection between the rise of conservatism and Evangelicalism, see: Kevin M. Kruse, *One Nation Under God: How Corporate America Invented Christian America* (New York: Basic Books, 2015).
13. For more on the fate of labor in this era, see: Thomas Geoghegan, *Which Side Are You On?: Trying to Be For Labor When It's Flat on Its Back* (New York: Farrar, Straus & Giroux, 1991); Nelson Lichtenstein, *State of the Union: A Century of American Labor* (Princeton, NJ: Princeton University Press, 2002); Joseph A. McCartin, *Collision Course: Ronald Reagan, the Air Traffic Controllers, and the Strike That Changed America* (New York: Oxford University Press, 2011); Nancy MacLean, *Freedom Is Not Enough: The Opening of the American Workplace* (Cambridge, MA: Harvard University Press, 2006); Nelson Lichtenstein, *A Contest of Ideas: Capital, Politics, and Labor* (Urbana: University of Illinois Press, 2013); Ruth Milkman, *Immigrant Labor and the New Precariat: Latino Workers in the United States* (Cambridge, UK: Polity Press, 2015); Nancy MacLean, *Democracy in Chains: The Deep History of the Radical Right's Stealth Plan for America* (New York: Viking, 2017); Kurt Andersen, *Evil Geniuses: The Unmaking of America: A Recent History* (New York: Random House, 2020); Gary Gerstle, *The Rise and Fall of the Neoliberal Order: America and the World in the Free Market Era* (New York: Oxford University Press, 2022).
14. For more on the battle for market dominance between these papers, see: Mike Jaccarino, *America's Last Great Newspaper War: The Death of Print in a Two-Tabloid Town* (New York: Fordham University Press, 2020).
15. Murdoch was no newbie when it came to dominating a media market. He already owned the London tabloid *The Sun,* which had a huge readership, and he would hedge his bets in NYC by also, for a time, owning controlling shares of the New York Magazine Company, publisher of *New York* magazine; *New West,* its California equivalent; and *The Village Voice,* New York City's alternative weekly paper. Susan Mulcahy and Frank DiGiacomo, *Paper of Wreckage: The Rogues, Renegades, Wiseguys, Wankers, and Relentless Reporters Who Redefined American Media* (New York: Atria, 2024), 15.
16. As quoted in this extraordinary account of the Bernhard Goetz shooting: Leon Neyfakh, *Fiasco: Vigilante,* podcast transcript, episode 2, "If It Bleeds," Prologue Projects, Audible Originals, July 27, 2023.
17. As quoted in Neyfakh, *Fiasco: Vigilante,* episode 2, "If It Bleeds."
18. Calvin Trillin interview, in Mulcahy and DiGiacomo, *Paper of Wreckage,* 38.
19. "A New Beginning," *New York Post,* March 30, 1993, 17.
20. Dorothy Rabinowitz, "Explaining Away Subway Muggers," *New York Post,* January 18, 1985, 45.
21. Patrick J. Buchanan, "Rejoicing in His Success Is a Sign of Moral Health," *New York Post,* January 1, 1985, 4.
22. Ibid.
23. Charlie Carillo interview, in Mulcahy and DiGiacomo, *Paper of Wreckage,* 317.
24. As Reagan personally wrote to Murdoch early in his first term, "It is a pleasure to congratulate the *New York Post* on its 180th anniversary and to extend my greetings in the pages of this special anniversary edition to your staff and to your readership. . . . A free press is essential to the pursuit of that truth and to the human freedom it engenders." Larry Speakes, Memorandum, "Courtesy Call and Photo with Charles Douglas-Home," July 6, 1983, "White House Staff Memoranda" Folder, Box 4, James A. Baker Collection, Ronald Reagan Presidential Library; Ronald Reagan to Rupert Murdoch, December 10, 1981, "White House Staff Memoranda" Folder, Box 4, James A. Baker Collection.
25. Roy M. Cohn to Hon. Edwin Meese III, Hon. James A. Baker III, Hon. Michael K. Deaver, January 27, 1983, "White House Staff Memoranda" Folder, Box 4, James A. Baker Collection.
26. Harry Shearer interview, in Mulcahy and DiGiacomo, *Paper of Wreckage,* 313–14.
27. Dick Belsky interview, in Mulcahy and DiGiacomo, *Paper of Wreckage,* 50.

28. Mulcahy and DiGiacomo, *Paper of Wreckage,* 148.
29. Amy Pagnozzi interview, in Mulcahy and DiGiacomo, *Paper of Wreckage,* 148.
30. Mulcahy and DiGiacomo, *Paper of Wreckage,* 150.
31. Amy Pagnozzi interview, in Mulcahy and DiGiacomo, *Paper of Wreckage,* 149.
32. Dick Belsky interview, in Mulcahy and DiGiacomo, *Paper of Wreckage,* 149.
33. C. Vernon Mason interview, in Mulcahy and DiGiacomo, *Paper of Wreckage,* 148.
34. Felix et al., eds., *The Post's New York,* 214.
35. According to *The New York Times,* the *Post*'s circulation went "from 400,000 to nearly one million in the early 1980s." Douglas Martin, "Roger Wood, a Brazen New York Post Editor, Dies at 87," *New York Times,* November 5, 2012.
36. Jim Farber interview, in Mulcahy and DiGiacomo, *Paper of Wreckage,* 245.
37. Mulcahy and DiGiacomo, *Paper of Wreckage,* 355.
38. Felix et al., *The Post's New York,* 172.
39. Bruce D. Johnson, Andrew Golub, and Jeffrey Fagan, "Careers in Crack, Drug Use, Drug Distribution, and Nondrug Criminality," *Crime & Delinquency* 41, no. 3 (1995): 281.
40. Ibid., 275.
41. *NBC Nightly News,* "Special Segment (Crime and Fear) #542207," reported by Tom Brokaw and John Hart, aired February 8, 1985, Vanderbilt Television Archives.
42. Johnson, Golub, and Fagan, "Careers in Crack," 275.
43. *NBC Nightly News,* "Special Segment (Crime and Fear) #542207."
44. Jefaud, "The Best Vigilante Movies," IMDb (blog), October 29, 2011.
45. Ibid.
46. "*The Star Chamber* Plot," IMDb (blog), accessed July 31, 2025.
47. "Domestic Box Office for 1986," Box Office Mojo by IMDbPro, accessed June 23, 2025.
48. Curtis Sliwa interview, in Mulcahy and DiGiacomo, *Paper of Wreckage,* 147.
49. Michael Brooks, "Stories and Verdicts: Bernhard Goetz and New York in Crisis," *College Literature* 25, no. 1 (1998): 82.
50. For more on the Guardian Angels, see: Dennis Jay Kenney, *Crime, Fear, and the New York City Subways: The Role of Citizen Action* (Westport, CT: Praeger, 1986). See also: Brooks, "Stories and Verdicts," 77–93.
51. That study was Kenney's *Crime, Fear, and the New York City Subways.* See also: Brooks, "Stories and Verdicts," 77–93.
52. For more on the history of the Guardian Angels, including how they had been dubbed the "ghetto boy scouts," see: Reiko Hillyer, "The Guardian Angels: Law and Order and Citizen Policing in New York City," *Journal of Urban History* 43 (2017): 886–914; Joe Merton, "The Guardian Angels: Anticrime Activism and 'Popular Neoliberalism' in Crisis-Era New York City," *Journal of Social History* (July 22, 2025): 1–24.

PART II · SHOOTING TO KILL

1. Winston Williams, "A Festive Fifth Avenue Christmas," *New York Times,* December 16, 1984, F1.
2. Although the fervor of parents shopping for Cabbage Patch dolls had cooled somewhat in 1984 (compared to outright riots the year before), there was still a great rush to purchase them on Black Friday. On the start of this craze, see: "The Strange Story of the Cabbage Patch Kid Riots of 1983," *ABC Eyewitness News,* November 18, 2022.

6. *An Ordinary Day*

1. Lillian B. Rubin, *Quiet Rage: Bernie Goetz in a Time of Madness* (New York: Farrar, Straus & Giroux, 1986), 70.
2. Testimony of James Ramseur in Trial Transcript, 7038, May 19, 1987, Folder 5, Box 10, Series III, Justice Stephen G. Crane Papers on the Bernhard Goetz Trial and Other Cases, MS 3152, The New York Historical, New York, NY.
3. Rubin, *Quiet Rage,* 31.
4. Margot Hornblower, "Wounded Youth Denies Intent to Rob New York City 'Subway Vigilante,'" *Washington Post,* January 11, 1985, A3.

5. Ibid.
6. Interview with Barry Allen in prison, in *The Company You Keep,* written and directed by Adrian Liang (New York: Stone Age Films, 2018), animated documentary short.
7. Ibid.
8. Phillip Messing, "Bitter Dad: He'll Get Off Easy," *New York Post,* December 26, 1984, 2.
9. Rubin, *Quiet Rage,* 33.
10. Ibid., 29.
11. Ibid.
12. Ibid., 33.
13. Interview with Barry Allen in prison, *The Company You Keep.*
14. It is unclear from the record whether he served this time in a facility or at all before December 22, 1984. Testimony of James Ramseur in Trial Transcript, 7036.
15. Testimony of James Ramseur in Trial Transcript, 7033.
16. Ibid., 7039.
17. Interview with Barry Allen in prison, *The Company You Keep.*
18. Testimony of James Ramseur in Trial Transcript, 7036.
19. Interview with Barry Allen in prison, *The Company You Keep.*
20. Testimony of James Ramseur in Trial Transcript, 7042.
21. Interview with Barry Allen in prison, *The Company You Keep.*
22. "2 Gang Members Shot by the Vigilante Tell All," *National Enquirer,* January 1985, Papers of Ron Kuby.
23. Fox Butterfield, "New Yorkers Growing Angry over Aggressive Panhandlers," *New York Times,* July 29, 1988, A1.

7. Manhattan Bound

1. Lillian B. Rubin, *Quiet Rage: Bernie Goetz in a Time of Madness* (New York: Farrar, Straus & Giroux, 1986), 56.
2. Phillip Atiba Goff et al., "The Essence of Innocence: Consequences of Dehumanizing Black Children," *Journal of Personality and Social Psychology* 106, no. 4 (April 2014): 526–45; Andrew R. Todd et al., "Does Seeing Faces of Young Black Boys Facilitate the Identification of Threatening Stimuli?," *Psychological Science* 27, no. 3 (December 2016): 1673–84.
3. Testimony of Andrea Reid in Trial Transcript, 7011–15, May 19, 1987, Folder 5, Box 10, Series III, Justice Stephen G. Crane Papers on the Bernhard Goetz Trial and Other Cases, MS 3152, The New York Historical, New York, NY.
4. Ibid., 6937.
5. Ibid., 6933, 6954.
6. Testimony of Josephine Holt in Trial Transcript, 6307–8, May 7, 1987, Folder 1, Box 10, Series III.
7. Ibid., 6305.
8. Ibid., 6310.
9. Testimony of Christopher Boucher in Trial Transcript, 6830–32, May 13, 1987, Folder 4, Box 10, Series III.
10. Ibid., 6833.
11. Ibid., 6835.
12. Mark Lesly with Charles Shuttlesworth, *Subway Gunman: A Juror's Account of the Bernhard Goetz Trial* (Latham, NY: British American Publishing, 1988), 113.
13. Testimony of Solitaire MacFoy in Trial Transcript, 6362, May 7, 1987, Folder 1, Box 10, Series III.
14. Testimony of Victor Flores in Trial Transcript, 5872–5931, May 5, 1987, Folder 12, Box 9, Series III.
15. Richard Stengel, "A Troubled and Troubling Life: Who Is Bernhard Goetz, and Why Did He Do What He Did?," *Time,* April 8, 1985.
16. Testimony of James Ramseur in Trial Transcript, 7049, May 19, 1987, Folder 5, Box 10, Series III.

17. Bernhard Hugo Goetz Deposition, 18–27, April 8, 1985, Papers of Ron Kuby; Ed Magnuson, "Up in Arms over Crime: As the Goetz Case Showed, Americans Are Fearful and Angry," *Time*, April 8, 1985.

8. *Bloodbath*

1. "2 Gang Members Shot by the Vigilante Tell All," *National Enquirer*, January 1985.
2. Ibid.
3. Ibid.
4. Interview with Barry Allen in prison, in *The Company You Keep*, written and directed by Adrian Liang (New York: Stone Age Films, 2018), animated documentary short.
5. Testimony of James Ramseur in Trial Transcript, 7057, May 19, 1987, Folder 5, Box 10, Series III, Justice Stephen G. Crane Papers on the Bernhard Goetz Trial and Other Cases, MS 3152, The New York Historical, New York, NY.
6. Officer Warren E. Foote, Concord (NH) Police Department, Police Supplemental Report 027331, at 8, January 2, 1985, Papers of Ron Kuby.
7. Testimony of Christopher Boucher in Trial Transcript, 6838, May 13, 1987, Folder 4, Box 10, Series III.
8. Testimony of Josephine Holt in Trial Transcript, 6315, May 7, 1987, Folder 1, Box 10, Series III.
9. Ibid.
10. Testimony of Mary Gant in Trial Transcript, 6237–53, May 6, 1987, Folder 13, Box 9, Series III.
11. Mark Lesly with Charles Shuttlesworth, *Subway Gunman: A Juror's Account of the Bernhard Goetz Trial* (Latham, NY: British American Publishing, 1988), 114.
12. Ibid., 98.
13. Richard Stengel, "A Troubled and Troubling Life: Who Is Bernhard Goetz, and Why Did He Do What He Did?," *Time*, April 8, 1985.
14. Testimony of Andrea Reid in Trial Transcript, 6986, May 19, 1987, Folder 5, Box 10, Series III.
15. Lesly with Shuttlesworth, *Subway Gunman*, 160.
16. Testimony of Christopher Boucher in Trial Transcript, 6842, 6843, 6857, May 13, 1987, Folder 4, Box 10, Series III.

9. *Triage*

1. Testimony of Armando Soler in Trial Transcript, 5941–76, May 5, 1987, Folder 12, Box 9, Series III, Justice Stephen G. Crane Papers on the Bernhard Goetz Trial and Other Cases, MS 3152, The New York Historical, New York, NY; "*People v. Goetz* Trial Transcript Notes: Witnesses, Exhibits and Their Significance," 4, n.d., compiled by Legal Team of Ron Kuby, Papers of Ron Kuby.
2. Victor Flores testified to this. See description in Mark Lesly with Charles Shuttlesworth, *Subway Gunman: A Juror's Account of the Bernhard Goetz Trial* (Latham, NY: British American Publishing, 1988), 99.
3. One author, George Fletcher, suggested that this woman was Josephine Holt, but Holt herself testified that she didn't leave her seat until she left the train for good. Testimony of Josephine Holt in Trial Transcript, 6315, May 7, 1987, Folder 1, Box 10, Series III. See also: George P. Fletcher, *A Crime of Self-Defense: Bernhard Goetz and the Law on Trial* (Chicago: University of Chicago Press, 1988), 194.
4. Lesly with Shuttlesworth, *Subway Gunman*, 102.
5. "*People v. Goetz* Trial Transcript Notes," 3.
6. Testimony of Arnethea Gilbert in Trial Transcript, 6273, May 7, 1987, Folder 1, Box 10, Series III; Esther Pessin, "The Judge in the Bernhard Goetz Trial Today Refused . . . ," May 7, 1987, UPI Archives.
7. Testimony of Arnethea Gilbert in Trial Transcript, 6274.
8. Ibid.

10. Aftershocks

1. Testimony of Peter Smith in Trial Transcript, 7486–7585, May 26–27, 1987, Folder 8, Box 10, Series III, Justice Stephen G. Crane Papers on the Bernhard Goetz Trial and Other Cases, MS 3152, The New York Historical, New York, NY.
2. Testimony of John Filangeri in Trial Transcript, 4910–5033, April 27–28, 1987, Folders 7–8, Box 9, Series III; testimony of Dennis Driscoll in Trial Transcript, 8325–52, June 5, 1987, Folder 12, Box 10, Series III.
3. Testimony of Charles Haase in Trial Transcript, 5066–68, May 5, 1987, Folder 12, Box 9, Series III; "*People v. Goetz* Trial Transcript Notes," n.d., 1, compiled by Legal Team of Ron Kuby, Papers of Ron Kuby.
4. Testimony of Alejandro Torres in Trial Transcript, 5862–63, April 28, 1987, Folder 8, Box 9, Series III; "*People v. Goetz* Trial Transcript Notes," 3.
5. Lillian B. Rubin, *Quiet Rage: Bernie Goetz in a Time of Madness* (New York: Farrar, Straus & Giroux, 1986), 90.
6. Ibid., 91–92.
7. Ibid., 33.
8. For an insider view of Shirley's harrowing time learning that her son had been shot, and this quote, see Rubin, *Quiet Rage*, 94. For another recap, see: Paul Tharp, "'I'm Sorry, Mom,'" *New York Post*, January 11, 1985, 3.

11. Victims or Villains

1. Leon Neyfakh, *Fiasco: Vigilante*, podcast transcript, episode 2, "If It Bleeds," Prologue Projects, Audible Originals, July 27, 2023.
2. Reuben Rosario et al., "'Victim' on Subway Shoots 4," New York *Daily News*, December 23, 1984, 3; "A Fantasy Come True: Death Wish Gunman Captured City's Imagination," New York *Daily News*, January 1, 1985; Murray Weiss et al., "Riders Cheer Gunman: They'd Give Him a Medal," New York *Daily News*, December 25, 1984, 3; Murray Weiss and Don Singleton, "Prey Turns Predator," New York *Daily News*, December 30, 1984, 6.
3. Neyfakh, *Fiasco: Vigilante*, "If It Bleeds."
4. Rosario et al., "'Victim' on Subway Shoots 4," 3.
5. Peter McLaughlin and Don Gentile, "Finest to Flood the Subways: 1,350 Cops Added After Vigilante Shootings," New York *Daily News*, December 24, 1984, 3.
6. Weiss et al., "Riders Cheer Gunman," 3.
7. Ransdell Pierson, "Movie That N.Y. Cheered," *New York Post*, December 24, 1984, 2.
8. Chris Oliver and Leslie Gevirtz, "The Victims: We Wanted $5 to Play Video Game," *New York Post*, December 24, 1984, 3; Charles Lachman et al., "'Death Wish' Victim Threatened in Hospital," *New York Post*, December 26, 1984, 2; Richard Esposito and Paul Tharp, "Vigilante Victim Is Sitting Duck," *New York Post*, December 27, 1984, 2.
9. Robert D. McFadden, "A Gunman Wounds 4 on IRT Train, Then Escapes," *New York Times*, December 23, 1984, 1.
10. David E. Sanger, "The Little-Known World of the Vigilante," *New York Times*, December 30, 1984, 6.
11. "Vigilante: New York's Subway Hero," *Time*, January 7, 1985.
12. Testimony of Peter Smith in Trial Transcript, 7673, May 26–27, 1987, Folder 8, Box 10, Series III, Justice Stephen G. Crane Papers on the Bernhard Goetz Trial and Other Cases, MS 3152, The New York Historical, New York, NY.
13. Detective McCormack, NYPD, Police Report, "Investigate Two Men Shot, Bellevue Hospital," December 22, 1985, Folder 13, Box 6, Series II, Justice Stephen G. Crane Papers on the Bernhard Goetz Trial and Other Cases, MS 3152, The New York Historical, New York, NY.
14. Detective Al Licata, NYPD, Police Complaint, "Subject: Assault, Subway, Gunshot, Four Victims. Statements Made by Allen and Ramseur to Det. McCormack," December 22, 1984, Folder 13, Box 6, Series II, Justice Stephen G. Crane Papers on the Bernhard Goetz Trial and Other Cases.
15. Detective Richard Commesso, NYPD, Police Complaint, December 22, 1984, Papers of Ron Kuby.

16. Detectives Michael Clark and Daniel Bronte, NYPD, Police Complaint, December 23, 1984, Papers of Ron Kuby.
17. Commesso, Police Complaint.
18. Clark and Bronte, Police Complaint.
19. Detective Charles Penelton, NYPD, Police Complaint, December 24, 1985, Papers of Ron Kuby.
20. Ibid; Testimony of Charles Penelton in Trial Transcript, 8215–16, June 5, 1987, Folder 12, Box 10, Series III.
21. Testimony of Charles Penelton in Trial Transcript, 8218.
22. Penelton, Police Complaint.
23. Patrice O'Shaughnessy et al., "Twelve Counts on Wounded 4," New York *Daily News,* January 3, 1985, 3, Papers of Ron Kuby.
24. Ibid.
25. Troy would in fact be arrested as soon as he was discharged. James too would recover only to receive a ninety-day jail sentence for the 1983 theft of $41 worth of coffee from a Bronx supermarket and would also face another court date to answer to charges that he stole cold medicine to resell. Seeing her brother now facing jail time greatly upset his sister Gayle, who accompanied him to court. James leaned over to her there and whispered that he was okay. Peter Moses, "Goetz Victim Gets Jail in Theft," *New York Post,* February 20, 1985, 42. On Troy Canty's court dealings, see: Mike Pearl and Marc Kalech, "Shot Teen Arrested—Freed Without Bail," *New York Post,* January 2, 1985, 5; Richard Esposito, "'My Brother Preys on Subway Riders to Pay for Drugs,'" *New York Post,* January 3, 1984, 5; Patrice O'Shaughnessy et al., "Twelve Counts on Wounded 4," *Daily News,* January 3, 1985, 3, Papers of Ron Kuby.
26. Lachman et al., "'Death Wish' Victim Threatened in Hospital," 2.
27. Weiss and Singleton, "Prey Turns Predator," 6.
28. "A Friend" to Darryl Cabey, January 2, 1985, Papers of Ron Kuby.
29. "A Sympathizer" to Shirley Cabey, December 31, 1984, Papers of Ron Kuby.
30. "A Fed Up Citizen" to Shirley Cabey, January 16, 1985, Papers of Ron Kuby.
31. "A Fed Up Citizen Who Dares Not Leave Home for Fear of Your Son's Ilk" to Shirley Cabey, January 10, 1985, Papers of Ron Kuby.
32. John P. Neilsen to "Teenager Cabey," January 2, 1985, Papers of Ron Kuby.
33. Swastika sticker sent to Cabey family, January 12, 1985, Papers of Ron Kuby; "A Retired N.Y.C. Correction Officer" to Darrell Cabey, January 13, 1985, Papers of Ron Kuby.
34. Pearl and Kalech, "Shot Teen Arrested," 5.
35. Esposito, "'My Brother Preys on Subway Riders to Pay for Drugs,'" 5.
36. Oliver and Gevirtz, "The Victims: We Wanted $5 to Play Video Game," 3.
37. Ibid.
38. Phillip Messing, "Bitter Dad: He'll Get Off Easy," *New York Post,* December 26, 1984, 2.
39. Ibid.
40. Neyfakh, *Fiasco: Vigilante,* podcast transcript, episode 3, "Four Teenagers," Prologue Projects, Audible Originals, July 27, 2023.
41. Ibid.

PART III · A RECKONING DEFERRED

1. Robert D. McFadden, "Charles Keating, 90, Key Figure in '80s Savings and Loan Crisis, Dies," *New York Times,* April 2, 2014; Douglas Martin, "Marc Rich, Financier and Famous Fugitive, Dies at 78," *New York Times,* June 26, 2013.
2. Rich would be pardoned by President Bill Clinton. Martin, "Marc Rich."
3. Elon Green, *The Man Nobody Killed: Life, Death, and Art in Michael Stewart's New York* (New York: Celadon Books, 2025).

12. *On the Lam*

1. Mary Ann Giordan, "He Was Pacing Back and Forth," New York *Daily News,* January 2, 1985, 3.
2. Ibid.

3. Officer Warren E. Foote, Concord Police Department, Police Supplemental Report 027331, at 8, January 2, 1985, Papers of Ron Kuby.
4. Deborah Orin, "Flight of the Fugitive," *New York Post,* January 3, 1985, 4; Richard Sisk and Tony Burto, "N.H. Cops Tracing Goetz Moves," New York *Daily News,* January 4, 1985, 12–13.
5. Orin, "Flight of the Fugitive," 4; Sisk and Burto, "N.H. Cops Tracing Goetz Moves," 12–13.
6. Orin, "Flight of the Fugitive," 4.
7. Bernhard Hugo Goetz Deposition, 56–58, April 8, 1985, Papers of Ron Kuby.
8. Tony Burton, "City 'Out of Control,'" New York *Daily News,* January 3, 1985, 30.
9. Nora Bonosky, "NY Gunner's Rightist Links," January 19, 1985, 1, Folder 9, Box 27, Collection REC0073, Bernhard Goetz closed case files, New York County District Attorney records, The New York City Municipal Archives, New York City Department of Records and Information Services, New York, NY.
10. Charles Lachman et al., "'Death Wish' Victim Threatened in Hospital," *New York Post,* December 26, 1984, 2.
11. Sherry Saunders, letter to the editor, *New York Post,* December 31, 1984, 18.
12. "Bernie Goetz, the Subway Vigilante—*Only in New York*—Episode 1," YouTube video, created by Heath Benfield, uploaded March 8, 2019, PIX11, 2019, video clip.
13. Murray Weiss and Don Singleton, "Prey Turns Predator," New York *Daily News,* December 30, 1984, Papers of Ron Kuby.
14. Foote, Police Department, Police Supplemental Report 027331, at 9.
15. Myra Friedman with Michael Daly, "My Neighbor Bernie Goetz," *New York,* February 18, 1985, 36, Papers of Ron Kuby.
16. Ibid.
17. Ibid.
18. Ibid.
19. Ibid.
20. Irene Kelly, letter to the editor, *New York Post,* January 1, 1985, 18; Pamela Siegfried, letter to the editor, *New York Post,* January 1, 1985, 18.
21. Friedman with Daly, "My Neighbor Bernie Goetz," 37.
22. Ibid.
23. Ibid., 38.
24. Ibid.
25. Ibid.
26. Ibid.
27. Giordan, "He Was Pacing Back and Forth," 3.
28. Friedman with Daly, "My Neighbor Bernie Goetz," 39.
29. Ibid., 40.
30. Ibid., 39.
31. Ibid.
32. Ibid, 40.
33. Ibid., 41.

13. *Explanations and Obfuscations*

1. Murray Weiss and Richard Sisk, "Suspect in IRT Shootings Walks In and Surrenders," New York *Daily News,* January 1, 1985, 3; Lillian B. Rubin, *Quiet Rage: Bernie Goetz in a Time of Madness* (New York: Farrar, Straus & Giroux, 1986), 15.
2. Leon Neyfakh, *Fiasco: Vigilante,* podcast transcript, episode 2, "If It Bleeds," Prologue Projects, Audible Originals, July 27, 2023.
3. Richard Stengel, "A Troubled and Troubling Life: Who Is Bernhard Goetz, and Why Did He Do What He Did?," *Time,* April 8, 1985, 35–38, Papers of Ron Kuby.
4. Officer Warren E. Foote, Concord Police Department, Police Supplemental Report 027331, at 1, January 2, 1985, Papers of Ron Kuby.
5. Officer Warren E. Foote, Concord Police Department, Miranda Warning Waiver, December 31, 1984, Papers of Ron Kuby.
6. Rubin, *Quiet Rage,* 17.

7. Tony Burton and Richard Sisk, "'I'm Your Man': N.H. Cops Unruffled by Visitor," New York *Daily News*, January 1, 1985, 5.
8. Foote, Police Supplemental Report 027331, 2.
9. Ibid.
10. Ibid., 3.
11. Ibid., 7.
12. Ibid., 3.
13. Ibid.
14. Ibid., 4.
15. Ibid.
16. Ibid., 6.
17. Testimony of Michael Clark in Trial Transcript, 6901–5, May 13, 1987, Folder 4, Box 10, Series III, Justice Stephen G. Crane Papers on the Bernhard Goetz Trial and Other Cases, MS 3152, The New York Historical, New York, NY.
18. Video Statement of Bernhard Goetz, transcript, December 31, 1984, to ADA Susan Braver, Det. Dan Hattendorf, Transit and Det. Michael Clark, Concord, New Hampshire, Papers of Ron Kuby; testimony of Michael Clark in Trial Transcript, 6901, 6918–22.
19. Frank Faso et al., "50G Bail Set for Suspect in IRT Shooting," New York *Daily News*, January 4, 1985, 1, 8.
20. Video Statement of Bernhard Goetz, 44.
21. Ibid., 51.
22. Ibid., 1.
23. Ibid., 39.
24. Ibid., 8.
25. Ibid., 35.
26. Ibid., 46
27. Ibid., 24.
28. Ibid., 8.
29. Ibid.
30. Ibid., 11.
31. Ibid., 19.
32. Ibid., 11.
33. Ibid., 19, 22.
34. Ibid., 28, 29.
35. Ibid., 28.
36. Ibid., 20.
37. Ibid., 27.
38. Ibid., 28.
39. Ibid., 29.
40. Ibid., 37
41. Ibid., 38.
42. Ibid., 18.
43. Ibid., 30.
44. Ibid., 31.
45. Ibid.
46. Ibid.
47. Ibid., 24.
48. Ibid., 22.
49. Ibid., 44.
50. Ibid., 50.
51. Ibid., 51.
52. Ibid., 44.
53. Faso et al., "50G Bail Set for Suspect in IRT Shooting," 1, 8.
54. Richard Sisk, "'It Had to Be Done,' Suspect Tells Guard," New York *Daily News*, January 2, 1985, 3.
55. *NBC Nightly News*, "New York City Subway Shootings / Goetz Arraignment #539787," reported by Tom Brokaw, aired January 8, 1985, Vanderbilt Television Archives.

56. Richard Sisk, "Goetz Agrees to Come Home to Face Charges in IRT Shooting," New York *Daily News,* January 3, 1985, 3; Deborah Orin et al., "Human Barricade: Security Is Air-Tight as Vigilante Returns," *New York Post,* January 3, 1985, 4.
57. Concord Police Department, Arrest Report 027331, December 31, 1984, Papers of Ron Kuby; Brief for Appellant at 4, *The People of the State of New York v. Bernhard Goetz,* 501 N.Y.2d 326 (1986), Folder 2, Box 4, Collection REC0073, Bernhard Goetz closed case files, New York County District Attorney records, The New York City Municipal Archives, New York City Department of Records and Information Services, New York, NY.
58. Testimony of Michael Clark in Trial Transcript, 6919.

14. *Consequences and Costs*

1. Deborah Orin et al., "Human Barricade: Security Is Air-Tight as Vigilante Returns," *New York Post,* January 3, 1985, 4.
2. Leon Neyfakh, *Fiasco: Vigilante,* podcast transcript, episode 2, "If It Bleeds," Prologue Projects, Audible Originals, July 27, 2023.
3. Orin et al., "Human Barricade," 4.
4. Ibid.
5. Richard Stengel, "A Troubled and Troubling Life: Who Is Bernhard Goetz, and Why Did He Do What He Did?," *Time,* April 8, 1985, 35–38, Papers of Ron Kuby.
6. Frank Faso et al., "50G Bail Set for Suspect in IRT Shooting," New York *Daily News,* January 4, 1985, 1, 8.
7. Richard Sisk, "Goetz Agrees to Come Home to Face Charges in IRT Shooting," New York *Daily News,* January 3, 1985, 3.
8. Richard Sisk, "Goetz' Bail Surprises N.H. Cops," New York *Daily News,* January 5, 1985, 5.
9. A full decade earlier at least one accused drug dealer's bail was set at $5 million, and a few years after the Goetz shootings the majority of the kids accused in the "Central Park Jogger" case were denied bail altogether.
10. Sam Roberts, "Morgenthau Says Goetz Case May Go to 2d Grand Jury," *New York Times,* March 1, 1985, 1.
11. Because Fred Clark was a minor when he was accused of mugging Bernhard Goetz, his full record is not open to the public. Some sources suggest that he was allowed to mediate that case and not serve any time; others suggest that he pled to a misdemeanor and also went to Rikers Island. It remains unclear which it was. One source reported, "Clark pleaded guilty to misdemeanor assault charges and served four months of a six month sentence." Frank Faso et al., "Backfire from Gun Bid," New York *Daily News,* January 4, 1985, 3.
12. Richard Esposito, "Mug Victim Tries to Bail Out Vigilante," *New York Post,* January 4, 1985, 15.
13. Philip Messing, "Mugger: 'Sorry I Drove Him to Buy Gun,'" *New York Post,* January 17, 1985, 4, 33.

15. *Fallout*

1. Jimmy Breslin, "Why Shoot Him? It's $5 Question," New York *Daily News,* December 25, 1984, 6.
2. Testimony of Harry Adler in Trial Transcript, 6478, May 11, 1987, Folder 2, Box 10, Series III, Justice Stephen G. Crane Papers on the Bernhard Goetz Trial and Other Cases, MS 3152, The New York Historical, New York, NY.
3. Ibid., 6481.
4. Jared McCallister et al., "Relieved, Not Bitter," New York *Daily News,* January 1, 1985, 4.
5. Testimony of Harry Adler in Trial Transcript, 6481.
6. Ibid., 6484.
7. Ibid., 6483.
8. Ibid., 6476.

9. Ibid., 6477–78.
10. Interview with Barry Allen in prison, in *The Company You Keep,* written and directed by Adrian Liang (New York, NY: Stone Age Films, 2018), animated documentary short.
11. Testimony of Peter Adams in Trial Transcript, 6525, May 11, 1987, Folder 2, Box 10, Series III.
12. Ibid., 6508.
13. Richard Esposito and Paul Tharp, "Vigilante Victim Is Sitting Duck," *New York Post,* December 27, 1984, 2.
14. Charles Lachman et al., "'Death Wish' Victim Threatened in Hospital," *New York Post,* December 26, 1984, 2.
15. Peter Moses, "Goetz Victim Gets Jail in Theft," *New York Post,* February 20, 1985, 42. On Troy Canty's court dealings, see: Mike Pearl and Marc Kalech, "Shot Teen Arrested—Freed Without Bail," *New York Post,* January 2, 1985, 5; Richard Esposito, "'My Brother Preys on Subway Riders to Pay for Drugs,'" *New York Post,* January 3, 1984, 5; Patrice O'Shaughnessy et al., "Twelve Counts on Wounded 4," New York *Daily News,* January 3, 1985, 3.
16. Moses, "Goetz Victim Gets Jail in Theft," 42.
17. M. J. Siegal to Daryl [*sic*] Cabey, January 4, 1985, Papers of Ron Kuby.
18. Paul Tharp, "'I'm Sorry, Mom,'" *New York Post,* January 11, 1985, 3.
19. Lillian B. Rubin, *Quiet Rage: Bernie Goetz in a Time of Madness* (New York: Farrar, Straus & Giroux, 1986), 100.
20. Keith Moore et al., "Victim's Mom Not Bitter," New York *Daily News,* January 11, 1985, 3.
21. Ibid.
22. Ibid.
23. Testimony of Peter Adams in Trial Transcript, 6516.
24. Ibid., 6517–18.
25. Lachman et al., "'Death Wish' Victim Threatened in Hospital," 2.
26. Testimony of Peter Adams in Trial Transcript, 6518–21.
27. Aileen Clark as quoted in Leon Neyfakh, *Fiasco: Vigilante,* podcast, episode 1, "Fear City," Prologue Projects, Audible Originals, July 27, 2023.
28. Testimony of Peter Adams in Trial Transcript, 6520–24.

16. Feeling the Love

1. Leon Neyfakh, *Fiasco: Vigilante,* podcast transcript, episode 2, "If It Bleeds," Prologue Projects, Audible Originals, July 27, 2023.
2. Peter Christopher and Chris Oliver, "Goetz Kin Flies Here for Jailhouse Huddle," *New York Post,* January 7, 1985, 13.
3. Myra Friedman with Michael Daly, "My Neighbor Bernie Goetz," *New York,* February 18, 1985, 41, Papers of Ron Kuby.
4. William E. Geist, "Covering the Case of Bernhard Goetz," *New York Times,* January 12, 1985, 25.
5. Ibid.
6. Steve Dunleavy, "Goetz Talks to the Post," *New York Post,* January 10, 1985, 33.
7. Lillian B. Rubin, *Quiet Rage: Bernie Goetz in a Time of Madness* (New York: Farrar, Straus & Giroux, 1986), 101.
8. James Patterson and Benjamin Wallace, *The Defense Lawyer: The Barry Slotnick Story* (New York: Grand Central, 2021), 31.
9. WABC-TV/New York *Daily News* Poll: Subway Shooting Follow-Up Poll (Cornell University, Ithaca, NY: Roper Center for Public Opinion Research, 1985); Gallup/*Newsweek* Poll #1985-85064: Bernhard Goetz Case, Gallup Organization (Cornell University, Ithaca, NY: Roper Center for Public Opinion Research, 1985).
10. Rubin, *Quiet Rage,* 78.
11. *Saturday Night Live,* season 10, episode 10, "Green Room Cold Opening," performed by Billy Crystal and Rich Hall, aired January 12, 1985, NBC, skit.

12. Friedman with Daly, "My Neighbor Bernie Goetz," 41.
13. Marcia Chambers, "Life Term Imposed in Rooftop Slaying of Aspiring Actress," *New York Times,* August 6, 1985, 1.
14. Friedman with Daly, "My Neighbor Bernie Goetz," 41.
15. Ibid.
16. Marsha Kranes, "Goetz' Lawyer Quits," *New York Post,* January 14, 1985, 5.
17. George P. Fletcher, *A Crime of Self-Defense: Bernhard Goetz and the Law on Trial* (Chicago: University of Chicago Press, 1988), 103.
18. Kranes, "Goetz' Lawyer Quits," 5.
19. Mike Pearl et al., "DA to Goetz—You Can Still Face Grand Jury," *New York Post,* January 15, 1985, 5.
20. "Goetz Gets New Lawyers; One Was Mugged Twice," *Los Angeles Times,* January 14, 1985, A2.
21. Pearl et al., "DA to Goetz," 5.
22. Alex Steinberg, "Barry Slotnick—Defense Attorney, Legal Eagle," *Vassar Spectator* 8, no. 2 (October 1989): 12–16.
23. *92Y American Conversation,* "Revisiting the Trial of Bernie Goetz—92nd Street Y," YouTube video, featuring Mark Lesly, Geraldo Rivera, Thane Rosenbaum, Barry Slotnick, and Gregory Waples, uploaded February 13, 2014, The 92nd Street Y, New York and Fordham University School of Law.
24. Burt Kearnes, "Harry Ryttenberg Died," *Tabloid Baby* (blog), December 20, 2006, https://tabloidbaby.blogspot.com/2006/12/harry-ryttenberg-died.html; Patterson and Wallace, *The Defense Lawyer,* 9–10.
25. Patterson and Wallace, *The Defense Lawyer,* 30–31.
26. E. R. Shipp, "A Tenacious Slotnick Faces Biggest Test," *New York Times,* May 16, 1987, 33.
27. Richard Esposito, "Mug Victim Tries to Bail Out Vigilante," *New York Post,* January 4, 1985, 15; Richard Esposito, "Helpful Lawyer's House Is Robbed," *New York Post,* January 4, 1985, 2–3.
28. Rubin, *Quiet Rage,* 77.
29. Jan Hoffman, "Fund Linked to N.R.A. Gave $20,000 for Goetz's Defense," *New York Times,* April 16, 1996, 1.
30. For the media frenzy surrounding the Goetz shooting as well as the boon that it was for the NRA, see: Neyfakh, *Fiasco: Vigilante,* episode 1, "Fear City."
31. Jill Lepore, "Battleground America," *New Yorker,* April 23, 2012; Scott Melzer, *Gun Crusaders: The NRA's Culture War* (New York: New York University Press, 2009).
32. Neyfakh, *Fiasco: Vigilante,* episode 1, "Fear City."
33. Larry McShane, "10 Years Later, Goetz Faces Suit," December 19, 1994, *The Record* (Woodland Park, NJ), A4, Papers of Ron Kuby.

17. The Blame Game

1. Richard Esposito, *Jimmy Breslin: The Man Who Told the Truth* (New York: Crime Ink, 2024).
2. As quoted in James Patterson and Benjamin Wallace, *The Defense Lawyer: The Barry Slotnick Story* (New York: Grand Central, 2021), 37–38.
3. Jimmy Breslin, "Bite the Bullet for Subway Gunmen," New York *Daily News,* December 27, 1984, 6; Michael Brooks, "Stories and Verdicts. Bernhard Goetz and New York in Crisis," *College Literature* 25, no. 1 (1998): 77–93.
4. Jimmy Breslin, "Color Us White and Brutal on This Black Day," New York *Daily News,* December 31, 1984, 6.
5. Ibid.
6. As quoted in Leon Neyfakh, *Fiasco: Vigilante,* podcast transcript, episode 2, "If It Bleeds," Prologue Projects, Audible Originals, July 27, 2023.
7. George Maksian, "CBS Crushes Primetime Rivals," New York *Daily News,* January 9, 1985, 22.
8. As quoted in Lillian B. Rubin, *Quiet Rage: Bernie Goetz in a Time of Madness* (New York: Farrar, Straus & Giroux, 1986), 103–4.

9. Brooks, "Stories and Verdicts," 86.
10. "The Vigilante," *New York Amsterdam News,* January 19, 1985, 12, as quoted in Brooks, "Stories and Verdicts," 86.
11. Ibid.
12. "NY Subway Shooting a Modern Lynching," *People's World* (Chicago), January 12, 1985, Folder 9, Box 27, Collection REC0073, Bernhard Goetz closed case files, New York County District Attorney records, The New York City Municipal Archives, New York City Department of Records and Information Services, New York, NY.
13. Douglas O. Linder, "The Trial of Bernhard Goetz: An Account," Famous Trials: Accounts and Materials for 100 of History's Most Important Trials, University of Missouri, Kansas City, School of Law, https://www.famous-trials.com/goetz/133-home, accessed October 15, 2025.
14. *NBC Nightly News,* "New York City / Goetz, Koch Interview #539906," reported by Tom Brokaw, aired January 25, 1985, Vanderbilt Television Archives.
15. As quoted in Rubin, *Quiet Rage,* 10.
16. *NBC Nightly News,* "New York City / Goetz #542247," reported by Tom Brokaw, aired March 1, 1985, Vanderbilt Television Archives; Sam Roberts, "Morgenthau Says Goetz Case May Go to 2d Grand Jury," *New York Times,* March 1, 1985, 1.
17. *NBC Nightly News,* "Commentary (Goetz Case) #539733," reported by Tom Brokaw and John Chancellor, aired January 17, 1985, Vanderbilt Television Archives.
18. "The President's News Conference," January 9, 1985, Ronald Reagan Presidential Library, Simi Valley, California; "Asked About Goetz, Reagan Cites the Law," *New York Times,* January 10, 1985, B3, Papers of Ron Kuby.
19. Rubin, *Quiet Rage,* 10.
20. Richard Esposito, "Subway Avenger Breaks Down in Tears," *New York Post,* February 25, 1985, 5; Margot Hornblower, "Backlash Hits 'Vigilante,'" *Washington Post,* March 1, 1985, A2.
21. Hornblower, "Backlash Hits 'Vigilante.'"
22. Sam Pinn, press release (re: Roy Innis), 1985, Independent Brooklyn CORE, Inc., Papers of Ron Kuby. For more on Brooklyn CORE's key demonstrations, including against the policies of the New York Department of Sanitation in the early 1960s, see: Bob Adelman photographs of Brooklyn Congress of Racial Equality (CORE) demonstrations, New York University Special Collections, Center for Brooklyn History, Brooklyn, NY.
23. *NBC Nightly News,* "New York/Goetz #539978," reported by Tom Brokaw and Norma Quarles, aired January 29, 1985, Vanderbilt Television Archives.
24. C. Vernon Mason, "Let Justice Flow Like Water," *New York Amsterdam News,* July 12, 1986, 12, Folder 10, Box 27, Collection REC0073, Bernhard Goetz closed case files.
25. Rev. Al Sharpton, The Wyatt Tee Walker Social Justice Society of Preachers & Prophetic Witnesses Celebration, Virginia Union University, accessed June 25, 2025, https://www.vuu.edu/wyatt-tee-walker-social-justice-society-of-preachers-prophetic-witnesses/rev-al-sharpton.
26. Patrice O'Shaughnessy et al., "Twelve Counts on Wounded Four," New York *Daily News,* January 3, 1985, Papers of Ron Kuby.
27. "From what you know about the [Bernhard Goetz] case so far, do you tend to approve or disapprove of Goetz shooting four youths on a New York subway?" (Washington, DC: Gallup Organization, February 28–March 1, 1985); NBC News/Wall Street Journal Poll: New York City (Cornell University, Ithaca, NY: Roper Center for Public Opinion Research, 1987), dataset, DOI: 10.25940/ROPER-31094695.
28. Michael Hardy and Warren Liebesman, "Media's Big Lie About Subway Shootings Exposed," *National Alliance* (New York, NY), January 18, 1985, 3, Papers of Ron Kuby.
29. Evido De la Cruz, "Goetz Siempre Fue una Bomba de Tiempo," *El Diario La Prensa,* April 17, 1996, 2.
30. Raquel Cepeda, *Bird of Paradise: How I Became Latina* (New York: Atria, 2014), 62, 108.
31. Brooks, "Stories and Verdicts," 86.
32. "The *Post* went to the Chambers St. subway stop—where Goetz shot four youths—and asked: What do you think of verdict?," *New York Post,* June 17, 1987, 4, Folder 11, Box 27, Collection REC0073, Bernhard Goetz closed case files.

33. *NBC Nightly News*, "New York City Subway Shootings #535200," reported by Dennis Moore and Garrick Utley, aired December 31, 1984, Vanderbilt Television Archives.

18. Making the Case

1. Ed Magnuson, "Up in Arms over Crime," *Time*, April 8, 1985.
2. Robert D. McFadden, "Robert Morgenthau, Longtime Manhattan District Attorney, Dies at 99," *New York Times*, July 21, 2019.
3. Ibid.
4. Ibid.
5. Marcia Chambers, "Grand Jury Votes to Indict Goetz Only on Gun Possession Charges," *New York Times*, January 26, 1985, 1.
6. S. O'Brien, draft on Bernie Goetz, January 15, 1985, Papers of Ron Kuby.
7. Memorandum of Law at Part 80, *The People of the State of New York v. Bernhard Goetz*, 502 N.Y.2d 577, Indictment no. 0476/85 (1985).
8. Brief for Appellant at 5, *The People of the State of New York v. Bernhard Goetz*, 501 N.Y. 2d 326 (1986), Folder 2, Box 4, Collection REC0073, Bernhard Goetz closed case files, New York County District Attorney records, The New York City Municipal Archives, New York City Department of Records and Information Services, New York, NY.
9. Sam Roberts, "Morgenthau Says Goetz Case May Go to 2d Grand Jury," *New York Times*, March 1, 1985, 1.
10. Brief for Appellant at 5, *The People of the State of New York v. Bernhard Goetz*, 326.
11. Leon Neyfakh, *Fiasco: Vigilante*, podcast episode, episode 3, "Four Teenagers," Prologue Projects, Audible Originals, July 27, 2023.
12. Ibid.
13. Carl Canty, conversation with author, March 26, 2024.
14. Neyfakh, *Fiasco: Vigilante*, episode 3, "Four Teenagers."

19. Not So Fast

1. Editorial Board, "Bernhard Goetz Verdict: A Victory for Common Sense," *New York Post*, January 26, 1985, 18.
2. All-People's Congress Collection Papers, 1970s–1981, Accession #959, The Walter Reuther Library of Labor and Urban Affairs, Wayne State University, Detroit, MI.
3. All-People's Congress, "Goetz Is No Hero!," leaflet, 1985, Papers of Ron Kuby.
4. Statement of the Center for Constitutional Rights, February 28, 1985, Papers of Ron Kuby.
5. Marcia Chambers, "U.S. Attorney Meets with Blacks over Request for Inquiry on Goetz," *New York Times*, January 30, 1985, 6.
6. Leon Neyfakh, *Fiasco: Vigilante*, podcast transcript, episode 3, "Four Teenagers," Prologue Projects, Audible Originals, July 27, 2023.
7. Michael Hardy and Warren Liebesman, "Media's Big Lie About Subway Shootings Exposed," *National Alliance* (New York, NY), January 18, 1985, 3, Papers of Ron Kuby.
8. Mack Williams, letter to the editor, *New York Post*, January 31, 1985, 34.
9. Mrs. Nancy L. Bey to District Attorney Robert Morgenthau, January 28, 1985, Folder 9, Box 27, Collection REC0073, Bernhard Goetz closed case files, New York County District Attorney records, The New York City Municipal Archives, New York City Department of Records and Information Services, New York, NY.
10. "U.S. Prosecution of Goetz Sought," *New York Times*, January 29, 1985, 3; *NBC Nightly News*, "New York/Goetz #539978," reported by Tom Brokaw and Norma Quarles, aired January 29, 1985, Vanderbilt Television Archives.
11. *NBC Nightly News*, "New York City/Goetz Follow-Up #541735," reported by Tom Brokaw and Norma Quarles, aired February 11, 1985, Vanderbilt Television Archives.
12. Chambers, "U.S. Attorney Meets with Blacks," 6; *NBC Nightly News*, "New York City/Goetz Follow-Up #541735."
13. "Possible Civil Rights Charges Against Goetz Studied by U.S.," *Washington Post*, January 28, 1985, A5; Chambers, "U.S. Attorney Meets with Blacks," 6.

14. *NBC Nightly News,* "New York/Goetz #539978."
15. "Possible Civil Rights Charges Against Goetz Studied by U.S.," *Washington Post.*
16. "U.S. Prosecution of Goetz Sought," *New York Times,* January 29, 1985, 3.
17. Paul Tharp, "Families of Shot Teens to Sue Goetz," *New York Post,* January 3, 1985, Papers of Ron Kuby.
18. Scott Greenfield, "Remembering Troy," *Simple Justice: A Criminal Defense Blog,* November 13, 2017.
19. Margot Hornblower, "Wounded Youth Denies Intent to Rob New York City 'Subway Vigilante,'" *Washington Post,* January 11, 1985, A3.
20. The series of photographs taken and published by the *National Enquirer* included numerous ones of them nearly naked with their wounds on display. Only the one of them fully clothed is included here, as the others are both gratuitous and exploitative.
21. Hornblower, "Wounded Youth Denies Intent," A3; Greenfield, "Remembering Troy."
22. Greenfield, "Remembering Troy."
23. Ibid.
24. Claude Macaluso, "History and Progress Notes," St. Vincent's Hospital and Medical Center of New York, March 8, 1985, Papers of Ron Kuby.
25. For more on the Attica trials, see: Heather Ann Thompson, *Blood in the Water: The Attica Prison Uprising of 1971 and Its Legacy* (New York: Pantheon, 2016).
26. Complaint for Compensatory and Punitive Damages and Permanent Injunction, 1–24, *Darrell A. Cabey, by his legal guardian and proposed conservator, Shirley Cabey v. Bernhard Hugo Goetz,* No. 6747-1985 (Sup. Ct. Bronx County, January 30, 1985), Papers of Ron Kuby.
27. Neyfakh, *Fiasco: Vigilante,* episode 3, "Four Teenagers."
28. See account in Kunstler autobiography *My Life as a Radical Lawyer* (Secaucus, NJ: Carol, 1994) as pertinent to a later civil defamation suit: *Bernhard Goetz v. William Kunstler and Carol Communications, Inc.,* 164 Misc. 2d 557, 625 N.Y.S.2d 447 (1995).
29. Neyfakh, *Fiasco: Vigilante,* episode 3, "Four Teenagers."
30. See account in Kunstler, *My Life as a Radical Lawyer,* as pertinent to a later civil defamation suit.
31. Daniel J. Popeo to William Kunstler, February 8, 1985, Papers of Ron Kuby.
32. "An American" to Ron Kuby, March 15, 1985, Papers of Ron Kuby.
33. Letter to Ron Kuby, April 10, 1996, Papers of Ron Kuby.

20. *Pressure Cooker*

1. Eli Teiber and Philip Messino, "Goetz Confession Barred," *New York Post,* January 18, 1985, 4; Sam Roberts, "Morgenthau Says Goetz Case May Go to 2d Grand Jury," *New York Times,* March 1, 1985, 1.
2. Marcia Chambers, "Goetz Spoke to One Youth, Then Shot Again, Police Say," *New York Times,* February 28, 1985, 1; George P. Fletcher, *A Crime of Self-Defense: Bernhard Goetz and the Law on Trial* (Chicago: University of Chicago Press, 1988), 5.
3. Teiber and Messino, "Goetz Confession Barred," 4.
4. Leon Neyfakh, *Fiasco: Vigilante,* podcast transcript, episode 4, "Anti-Hero," Prologue Projects, Audible Originals, July 27, 2023.
5. "Leaks from the Videotaped Confession of 'Death Wish' Gunman," January, 18, 1985, UPI Archives.
6. Neyfakh, *Fiasco: Vigilante,* episode 4, "Anti-Hero."
7. Roberts, "Morgenthau Says Goetz Case May Go to 2d Grand Jury," 1.
8. Video Statement of Bernhard Goetz, transcript, 30 December 31, 1984, to ADA Susan Braver, Det. Dan Hattendorf, Transit Police, Det. Michael Clark, NYPD, Concord, New Hampshire, Papers of Ron Kuby.
9. Ibid., 28.
10. Ibid., 19.
11. Chambers, "Goetz Spoke to One Youth," 1.
12. Roberts, "Morgenthau Says Goetz Case May Go to 2d Grand Jury," 1.

13. E. R. Shipp, "Goetz Prosecutor: Intensity and Talent," *New York Times*, May 30, 1987, 33; "Robert M. Pitler Memoriam," New York State Law Revision Commission, accessed June 27, 2025.
14. Shipp, "Goetz Prosecutor," 33; "Robert M. Pitler Memoriam," New York State Law Revision Commission.
15. Roberts, "Morgenthau Says Goetz Case May Go to 2d Grand Jury," 1.
16. Ibid.
17. *92Y American Conversation*, "Revisiting the Trial of Bernie Goetz—92nd Street Y," YouTube video, featuring Mark Lesly, Geraldo Rivera, Thane Rosenbaum, Barry Slotnick, and Gregory Waples, uploaded February 13, 2014, The 92nd Street Y, New York and Fordham University School of Law.
18. Roberts, "Morgenthau Says Goetz Case May Go to 2d Grand Jury," 1.
19. Affirmation in Support of Application to Resubmit Charges to the Grand Jury at Part 80, *The People of the State of New York v. Bernhard Goetz*, 502 N.Y.2d 577, Indictment no. 0476/85 (1985), Folder 2, Box 1, Collection REC0073, Bernhard Goetz closed case files, New York County District Attorney records, The New York City Municipal Archives, New York City Department of Records and Information Services, New York, NY; Memorandum of Law at Part 80, *The People of the State of New York v. Bernhard Goetz*, 502 N.Y.2d 577, Indictment no. 0476/85 (1985), Folder 1–2, Box 2, Collection REC0073, Bernhard Goetz closed case files.
20. Memorandum of Law at Part 80, *The People of the State of New York v. Bernhard Goetz.*
21. Ibid.
22. Affirmation in Support of Application to Resubmit Charges, *The People of the State of New York v. Bernhard Goetz.*
23. Memorandum of Law at Part 80, *The People of the State of New York v. Bernhard Goetz.*
24. Ibid.
25. Steve Dunleavy, "Secret Tape Swayed Goetz Grand Jury," *New York Post*, January 29, 1985, 5. Slotnick also felt that the tape had been helpful and assumed it was the Friedman tape. He had by now seen the police report, but had not yet heard the taped confession his client had made to Braver. Michael Coakley, "Jury to Hear Goetz Testify on N.Y. Subway Shootings," *Chicago Tribune*, March 26, 1985, 4.
26. *The People of the State of New York v. Bernhard Goetz* at Part 81, 68 N.Y.2d 96, Indictment No. 1914/85 (1986), Folder 12, Box 6, Series II, Justice Stephen G. Crane Papers on the Bernhard Goetz Trial and Other Cases, MS 3152, The New York Historical, New York, NY.
27. Brief for Appellant at 5, *The People of the State of New York v. Bernhard Goetz*, 501 N.Y.2d 326, (1986), Folder 2, Box 4, Collection REC0073, Bernhard Goetz closed case files.

21. *Second Time Around*

1. Sub-headline in Bernhard Goetz, "My Story," *New York Post*, March 22, 1985, 5.
2. Letter to the Editor, *The New Russian Word* (New York, NY), April 19, 1985, Folder 10, Box 27, Collection REC0073, Bernhard Goetz closed case files, New York County District Attorney records, The New York City Municipal Archives, New York City Department of Records and Information Services, New York, NY.
3. Brief for Appellant at 5, *The People of the State of New York v. Bernhard Goetz*, 501 N.Y.2d 326, (1986), Folder 2, Box 4, Collection REC0073, Bernhard Goetz closed case files.
4. Chris Oliver and Mike Pearl, "Grand Jury Mulls Bid to Let Goetz Delay Testimony," *New York Post*, March 22, 1985, 5.
5. Affirmation in Support of Application to Resubmit Charges to the Grand Jury at Part 80, *The People of the State of New York v. Bernhard Goetz*, 502 N.Y.2d 577, Indictment no. 0476/85 (1985), Folder 2, Box 1, Collection REC0073, Bernhard Goetz closed case files.
6. Brief for Appellant at 13, *The People of the State of New York v. Bernhard Goetz*, 501 N.Y.2d 326, (1986), Folder 2, Box 4, Collection REC0073.
7. Affirmation in Support of Application to Resubmit Charges to the Grand Jury at Part 80, *The People of the State of New York v. Bernhard Goetz.*

8. Brief for Appellant at 10–11, *The People of the State of New York v. Bernhard Goetz,* 501 N.Y.2d 326, (1986), Folder 2, Box 4, Collection REC0073, Bernhard Goetz closed case files.
9. Affirmation in Support of Application to Resubmit Charges to the Grand Jury at Part 80, *The People of the State of New York v. Bernhard Goetz.*
10. Brief for Respondent at 18, *The People of the State of New York v. Bernhard Goetz,* 73 N.Y.2d 751 (1988), Folder 5, Box 12, Collection REC0073, Bernhard Goetz closed case files.
11. Ibid.
12. Ibid.
13. Margot Hornblower, "Grand Jury Indicts Goetz on Attempted-Murder Counts," *Washington Post,* March 27, 1985.
14. "Second Grand Jury Is 'Travesty of Justice,'" *New York Post,* April 5, 1985, 24.
15. M. Purcell, letter to the editor, *New York Post,* April 5, 1985, 24.
16. "A citizen" to Robert Morgenthau, April 1985, Folder 9, Box 27, Collection REC0073, Bernhard Goetz closed case files.
17. Solomon Abbey to District Attorney Robert Morgenthau, March 30, 1985, Folder 9, Box 27, Collection REC0073, Bernhard Goetz closed case files.
18. "A Good American! Law Abiding!" to District Attorney Robert Morgenthau, January 21, 1985, Folder 9, Box 27, Collection REC0073, Bernhard Goetz closed case files; Robert York from Jay, Florida, n.d., Folder 10, Box 27, Collection REC0073, Bernhard Goetz closed case files.
19. Irene Wasserman to Stephen Crane, March 21, 1985, Folder 1, Box 6, Collection REC0073, Bernhard Goetz closed case files.
20. Lisa Robinson to Stephen Crane, n.d., Folder 1, Box 6, Collection REC0073, Bernhard Goetz closed case files.
21. F. Mulrooney to Stephen Crane, March 23, 1985, Folder 1, Box 6, Collection REC0073, Bernhard Goetz closed case files.
22. Lillian Trezza to Stephen Crane, March 23, 1985, Folder 1, Box 6, Collection REC0073, Bernhard Goetz closed case files.
23. Frances Mazzuka to Stephen Crane, March 22, 1985, Folder 1, Box 6, Collection REC0073, Bernhard Goetz closed case files.
24. Anonymous to Stephen Crane, March 30, 1985, Folder 1, Box 6, Collection REC0073, Bernhard Goetz closed case files.
25. Anonymous to Stephen Crane, April 30, 1987, Folder 2, Box 6, Collection REC0073, Bernhard Goetz closed case files.
26. "A Concerned Good Citizen" to Stephen Crane, October 15, 1987, Folder 2, Box 6, Collection REC0073, Bernhard Goetz closed case files.
27. Virgil Sams to Robert Morgenthau, January 23, 1986, Folder 7, Box 27, Collection REC0073, Bernhard Goetz closed case files.
28. M. and L. Katz to Robert Morgenthau, March 27, 1985, Folder 9, Box 27, Collection REC0073, Bernhard Goetz closed case files.

22. *Last-Ditch Effort*

1. *The People of the State of New York v. Bernhard Goetz,* 501 N.Y.2d 326 (1986), Opinion, Argued May 28, 1986, Decided July 8, 1986.
2. Ibid.
3. Statements by Gregory Waples, Assistant District Attorney, and Angela Torregosa, Grand Jury Reporter, *The People of the State of New York v. Bernhard Goetz,* 502 N.Y.2d 577, Indictment no. 0476/85 (1985).
4. Ibid.
5. Testimony of James Ramseur in Trial Transcript, 7078–85, May 19, 1987, Folder 5, Box 10, Series III, Justice Stephen G. Crane Papers on the Bernhard Goetz Trial and Other Cases, MS 3152, The New York Historical, New York, NY.
6. Statements by Gregory Waples, Assistant District Attorney, and Angela Torregosa, Grand Jury Reporter, *The People of the State of New York v. Bernhard Goetz.*

7. Selwyn Raab, "A Man Goetz Shot Is Charged with Faking Own Abduction," *New York Times,* March 27, 1985, 8.
8. Statements by Gregory Waples, Assistant District Attorney, and Angela Torregosa, Grand Jury Reporter, *The People of the State of New York v. Bernhard Goetz.*
9. Jimmy Breslin, "Shooting Script," New York *Daily News,* November 26, 1985, 5–6, Papers of Ron Kuby.
10. Ibid.
11. Gregory Waples to Mark Baker, November 27, 1985, Folder 2, Box 4, Collection REC0073, Bernhard Goetz closed case files, New York County District Attorney records, The New York City Municipal Archives, New York City Department of Records and Information Services, New York, NY.
12. Officer Peter Smith, NYPD, Police Complaint Report 16768, January 4, 1985, Papers of Ron Kuby.
13. Ibid.
14. Ibid.
15. Letter from Mark Baker to Stephen Crane as referenced and quoted from, in Letter from Gregory Waples to The Honorable Stephen Crane, December 6, 1985, Prosecutor's Correspondence, Folder 8, Box 13, Collection REC0073, Bernhard Goetz closed case files.
16. Letter from Gregory Waples to The Honorable Stephen Crane, December 6, 1985.
17. Ibid.
18. Associated Press, "'Vigilante' Jury Is Upheld; Teen: 'I Want to See Bernie Goetz Fry,'" *Sun-Sentinel* (Fort Lauderdale, FL), March 20, 1985, 3A, Folder 9, Box 27, Collection REC0073, Bernhard Goetz closed case files.
19. Reply Brief for Appellant at 29, *The People of the State of New York v. Bernhard Goetz,* 73 N.Y.2d 751 (1988), Folder 2, Box 2, Collection REC0073, Bernhard Goetz closed case files.
20. Ibid.
21. Ibid.
22. Ibid. at 28.
23. *The People of the State of New York v. Bernhard Goetz* at Part 81, 68 N.Y.2d 96, Indictment No. 1914/85 (1986), Folder 12, Box 6, Series II, Justice Stephen G. Crane Papers on the Bernhard Goetz Trial and Other Cases, MS 3152, The New York Historical, New York, NY; Frank Faso and Joseph McNamara, "DA Will Appeal Decision by Judge to Clear Goetz," New York *Daily News,* January 18, 1986, 3.
24. Faso and McNamara, "DA Will Appeal Decision by Judge," 3.
25. Ibid.
26. Robert D. McFadden, "Justice Drops All Major Charges Against Goetz in Shooting on IRT," *New York Times,* January 17, 1986, 1.
27. Ibid.
28. Harry Werder to Stephen Crane, January 17, 1986, Folder 1, Box 6, Collection REC0073, Bernhard Goetz closed case files.
29. Birdie Bloch to Stephen Crane, January 18, 1986, Folder 1, Box 6, Collection REC0073, Bernhard Goetz closed case files.
30. Richard J. Meislin, "Morgenthau to Appeal Ruling on Goetz," *New York Times,* January 18, 1986, 31.
31. Ibid.
32. Ibid.
33. Reply Brief for Appellant at 2, *The People of the State of New York v. Bernhard Goetz.*
34. "Statement of Manhattan District Attorney Robert Morgenthau Regarding the Dismissal of the Goetz Indictment," press release, January 17, 1986, Papers of Ron Kuby.
35. *The People of the State of New York v. Bernhard Goetz,* Opinion.
36. Ibid.
37. *NBC Nightly News,* "New York/Goetz #542599," reported by Roger Mudd and Norma Quarles, aired March 27, 1985, Vanderbilt Television Archives.
38. Ibid.

PART IV · VIGILANTISM ON TRIAL

1. "Racial, Economic Divide in '80s New York Preceded Central Park Case: Part 1," segment in "One Night in Central Park," ABC 20/20 documentary, *ABC News*, aired May 22, 2019.
2. Charles J. Hynes and Bob Drury, *Incident at Howard Beach: The Case for Murder* (New York: Putnam, 1990).
3. Sam Roberts, "Racial Attack That, Years Later, Is Still Being Felt," *New York Times*, December 18, 2011.

23. *Gearing Up for Battle*

1. Esther Pessin, "Goetz Says His Alleged Victim Was 'Stupid' to Commit Crime," October 31, 1985, UPI Archives.
2. Ibid.
3. Patricia O'Shaunessy and Robert Carroll, "Goetz Victim Held in Rape," New York *Daily News*, June 29, 1985, 3.
4. *NBC Nightly News*, "New York City/Ramseur #544413," reported by Roger Mudd, aired June 28, 1985, Vanderbilt Television Archives.
5. This letter was sent to Greg Waples's office, typed by one J.T. Brown, but its header suggests that Brown also intended to send it to the Letters to the Editor section of the *San Francisco Chronicle*. There is, however, no evidence he actually did. Folder 7, Box 27, Collection REC0073, Bernhard Goetz closed case files, New York County District Attorney records, The New York City Municipal Archives, New York City Department of Records and Information Services, New York, NY.
6. Affidavit at 2, *Shirley Cabey, as the mother and guardian of Darrell Cabey v. The Crime Victims Board, Executive Department, State of New York*, No. 13054/89 (N.Y.S.2d, September 7, 1989), Papers of Ron Kuby.
7. Probation Department Sentencing Report Dossier, "Departmental Sentence Recommendation with Supporting Reasons," September 14, 1987, Case No. 8704982—Bernhard Hugo Goetz, Manhattan Adult Investigation Branch, New York City Department of Probation, Papers of Ron Kuby. Various documents within this Department of Probation sentencing dossier are unnumbered. The page numbers provided here are based on the author's pagination of the entire scanned dossier.
8. Mike McLaughlin, "Judging the Goetz Case," *the paper* 18, no. 12 (November 13, 1987): 1–9, Folder 27, Box 7, Series II, Justice Stephen G. Crane Papers on the Bernhard Goetz Trial and Other Cases, MS 3152, The New York Historical, New York, NY.
9. Mark Lesly with Charles Shuttleworth, *Subway Gunman: A Juror's Account of the Bernhard Goetz Trial* (Latham, NY: British American Publishing, 1988), 15–16.
10. E. R. Shipp, "A Tenacious Slotnick Faces Biggest Test," *New York Times*, May 16, 1987, 33.
11. Ibid.
12. Ibid.
13. Ibid.
14. Ibid.
15. Ibid.
16. Ibid.
17. Lesly with Shuttleworth, *Subway Gunman*, 15–16.
18. Shipp, "A Tenacious Slotnick Faces Biggest Test," 33.
19. Ibid.
20. "The CBS Murders: The Trial of Donald Nash," University of Virginia Special Collections and Archives, accessed July 3, 2025.
21. Shipp, "A Tenacious Slotnick Faces Biggest Test," 33.
22. Ibid.
23. Ibid.
24. Ibid.
25. Lesly with Shuttleworth, *Subway Gunman*, 15–16.
26. Ibid.

27. Shipp, "A Tenacious Slotnick Faces Biggest Test," 33.
28. Ibid.

24. *Enter the Jury*

1. George P. Fletcher, *A Crime of Self-Defense: Bernhard Goetz and the Law on Trial* (University of Chicago Press, 1988), 86.
2. For the long journey of the court's jury selection, see: Trial Transcript, 1–4712, December 12, 1986–April 7, 1987, Boxes 8–9, Series III, Justice Stephen G. Crane Papers on the Bernhard Goetz Trial and Other Cases, MS 3152, The New York Historical, New York, NY.
3. Fletcher, *A Crime of Self-Defense,* 87.
4. *92Y American Conversation,* "Revisiting the Trial of Bernie Goetz—92nd Street Y," YouTube video, featuring Mark Lesly, Geraldo Rivera, Thane Rosenbaum, Barry Slotnick, and Gregory Waples, uploaded February 13, 2014, The 92nd Street Y, New York and Fordham University School of Law.
5. Philip Lentz, "Goetz Jury Selection Puts Attitudes About Street Crime on Trial," *Chicago Tribune,* March 29, 1987, 22.
6. Ibid.
7. *92Y American Conversation,* "Revisiting the Trial of Bernie Goetz."
8. Fletcher, *A Crime of Self-Defense,* 88.
9. Mark Lesly with Charles Shuttleworth, *Subway Gunman: A Juror's Account of the Bernhard Goetz Trial* (Latham, NY: British American Publishing, 1988), 15–16.
10. Charles McGrath, "The Rink," *New Yorker,* December 1, 1986, 30.
11. Mike McAlary, *Buddy Boys: When Good Cops Turn Bad* (New York: Open Road Media, 1987).
12. For more on the bombing of the MOVE organization in Philadelphia, see Mike Africa Jr., *On a Move: Philadelphia's Notorious Bombing and a Native Son's Lifelong Battle for Justice* (New York: Mariner Books, 2025); Richard Evans Kent, *MOVE: An American Religion* (Oxford, UK: Oxford University Press, 2020); Michael Boyette and Randi Boyette, *Let It Burn: MOVE, the Philadelphia Police Department, and the Confrontation That Changed a City* (New York: Quadrant Books, 2013); and forthcoming comprehensive history of this event by author. On the Iran-Contra affair, see: Malcolm Byrne, *Iran-Contra: Reagan's Scandal and the Unchecked Abuse of Presidential Power* (Lawrence: University Press of Kansas, 2017). On the Chernobyl nuclear disaster, see: Adam Higginbotham, *Midnight in Chernobyl: The Untold Story of the World's Greatest Nuclear Disaster* (New York: Simon & Schuster, 2019).
13. Esther Pessin, "Selection of Jury Clears Way for Goetz Trial," April 8, 1987, UPI Archives; "List of Jurors in Goetz Case," April 8, 1987, UPI Archives.
14. According to a survey conducted in New York State in 1988, respondents reported that approximately 10.3 percent of households had at least one member victimized in a crime committed in their neighborhood during the prior year. Bureau of Justice Statistics, "A Survey of Public Opinion Volume I: Crime, Neighborhood Safety and Responses to Crime," by Sharon E. Lansing, Office of Justice Systems Analysis, NCJ 128505 (New York: Division of Criminal Justice Services, December 1988): 1–31.
15. Pessin, "Selection of Jury Clears Way for Goetz Trial."
16. Lesly with Shuttleworth, *Subway Gunman,* 15–16.
17. Ibid., 16.
18. Ibid.
19. Pessin, "Selection of Jury Clears Way for Goetz Trial."
20. Lesly with Shuttleworth, *Subway Gunman,* 16.
21. Ibid.
22. Ibid., 15.
23. Ibid., 46.
24. Ibid.

25. *Making Sense of Madness*

1. Opening statement of Gregory Waples in Trial Transcript, 4713–4898, April 27, 1987, Folder 7, Box 9, Series III, Justice Stephen G. Crane Papers on the Bernhard Goetz Trial and Other Cases, MS 3152, The New York Historical, New York, NY.
2. Ibid.
3. E. R. Shipp, "Goetz Prosecutor: Intensity and Talent," *New York Times*, May 30, 1987, 33.
4. Opening statement of Gregory Waples in Trial Transcript, 4713–4898.
5. Ibid.
6. Ibid.
7. Ibid.
8. Ibid.
9. Ibid.
10. Shipp, "Goetz Prosecutor: Intensity and Talent," 33.
11. Opening statement of Gregory Waples in Trial Transcript, 4713–4898.
12. Mark Lesly with Charles Shuttleworth, *Subway Gunman: A Juror's Account of the Bernhard Goetz Trial* (Latham, NY: British American Publishing, 1988), 28.
13. Shipp, "Goetz Prosecutor: Intensity and Talent," 33.
14. Lesly with Shuttleworth, *Subway Gunman*, 27.
15. Opening statement of Barry Slotnick in Trial Transcript, 4713–4898, April 27, 1987, Folder 7, Box 9, Series III.
16. Ibid.
17. Ibid.
18. Testimony of Marie Venticinque in Trial Transcript, 4898–4909, April 27, 1987, Folder 7, Box 9, Series III; "*People v. Goetz* Trial Transcript Notes: Witnesses, Exhibits and Their Significance," n.d., 1, compiled by Legal Team of Ron Kuby, Papers of Ron Kuby.
19. Ibid.
20. Testimony of John Filangeri in Trial Transcript, 4910–5033, April 27–28, 1987, Folders 7–8, Box 9, Series III; "*People v. Goetz* Trial Transcript Notes," 1.
21. Detective Miller, NYPD, 1st Precinct Detective Unit, Police Complaint—Follow Up—"Interview with Paramedic; John Filangeri," December 23, 1984, Papers of Ron Kuby; testimony of John Filangeri in Trial Transcript, 4910–5033; "*People v. Goetz* Trial Transcript Notes," 1.
22. John J. Goldman, "Goetz Called 'Powder Keg' as Trial Opens," *Los Angeles Times*, April 28, 1987, 4.
23. Ibid.
24. Kirk Johnson, "Goetz Judge Blocks Attempt to Use a Victim's Statement," *New York Times*, April 29, 1987, 3.
25. Testimony of Detective Charles Haase in Trial Transcript, 5034–5109, April 28, 1987, Folder 8, Box 9, Series III; "*People v. Goetz* Trial Transcript Notes," 1.
26. Testimony of Officer Warren Foote in Trial Transcript, 5110–44, April 28–29, 1987, Folder 8, Box 9, Series III; "*People v. Goetz* Trial Transcript Notes," 2.
27. Testimony of Detective Christopher Domian in Trial Transcript, 5145–95, April 29, 1987, Folder 9, Box 9, Series III; "*People v. Goetz* Trial Transcript Notes," 2.
28. Kirk Johnson, "Goetz Account of Shooting 4 Given on Tape," *New York Times*, April 30, 1987, B1.
29. Ibid.
30. Bob Drogin, "Recording Played at Trial in Subway Shootings of Four: 'Intention Was to Murder,' Goetz Says on Tape," *Los Angeles Times*, April 30, 1987, 18; "Admitted Intentions in Tape Played at Trial: Goetz Told of Wanting 'to Murder,'" *Los Angeles Times*, April 30, 1987, 18.
31. "Admitted Intentions in Tape Played at Trial," 18.
32. Ibid.

26. Fumble and Drive

1. Bob Drogin, "Says He and Companions Didn't Attempt Robbery: Victim Denies Goetz Allegation of Threat," *Los Angeles Times,* May 2, 1987, 24; Margot Hornblower, "One of Youths Shot by Goetz Testifies About Words, Glances on Subway," *Washington Post,* May 2, 1987, A4.
2. Esther Pessin, "One of Four Young Blacks Wounded by Subway Gunman," May 1, 1987, UPI Archives.
3. Testimony of Troy Canty in Trial Transcript, 5294–5816, May 1, 4, 5, 1987, Folders 10–12, Box 9, Series III, Justice Stephen G. Crane Papers on the Bernhard Goetz Trial and Other Cases, MS 3152, The New York Historical, New York, NY.
4. Testimony of Troy Canty in Trial Transcript, 5407, May 1, 1987, Folder 10, Box 9, Series III.
5. Testimony of Troy Canty in Trial Transcript, 5769, May 5, 1987, Folder 12 Box 9, Series III.
6. Kirk Johnson, "Goetz Shooting Victim Says Youths Weren't Threatening," *New York Times,* May 2, 1987.
7. Testimony of Troy Canty in Trial Transcript, 5673, May 4, 1987, Folder 11, Box 9, Series III.
8. Mike Pearl and Doug Feiden, "5 Bullets in 5 Seconds—Then Screams," *New York Post,* May 2, 1987, 5.
9. Drogin, "Says He and Companions Didn't Attempt Robbery," 24.
10. Testimony of Troy Canty in Trial Transcript, 5390–91, May 1, 1987, Folder 10, Box 9, Series III.
11. Leon Neyfakh, *Fiasco: Vigilante,* podcast transcript, episode 5, "Reasonable People," Prologue Projects, Audible Originals, July 27, 2023.
12. Mike Pearl and Doug Feiden, "Jury's Job—To Find the Real Troy Canty," *New York Post,* May 2, 1987, 5
13. E. R. Shipp, "A Tenacious Slotnick Faces Biggest Test," *New York Times,* May 16, 1987, 33.
14. Kirk Johnson, "Goetz Account of Shooting 4 Given on Tape," *New York Times*, April 30, 1987, B1.
15. Ibid.
16. Mike Pearl, "Shouting Drama as Goetz Lawyer & Victim Lock Horns," *New York Post,* May 4, 1987, 9.
17. Shipp, "A Tenacious Slotnick Faces Biggest Test," 33.
18. Mike Pearl, "Showdown! Goetz' Victim Face to Face with Accuser," *New York Post,* May 5, 1987, 7.
19. Shipp, "A Tenacious Slotnick Faces Biggest Test," 33.
20. Associated Press, "Goetz Victim Denies He's a Mugger," *Windsor Star,* May 5, 1987, 5.
21. Shipp, "A Tenacious Slotnick Faces Biggest Test," 33.
22. Ibid.
23. Mark Lesly, "Diary of a Goetz Juror," *New York Post,* June 19, 1987, 5.
24. As recounted by Crane in Crane Decision re: Allen Missing Witness charge, 3, June 5, 1987, Folder 18, Box 7, Series III, Justice Stephen G. Crane Papers on the Bernhard Goetz Trial and Other Cases.
25. Closed testimony regarding Barry Allen when he took the Fifth: Trial Transcript, 5979–6013, May 5, 1987, Folder 12, Box 9, and then regarding judge's ruling about whether to grant him immunity and how/if the jury could consider his nontestimony, 6631–64, May 11, 1987, and 7560–90, May 26, 1987, Folder 8, Box 10, Series III, Justice Stephen G. Crane Papers on the Bernhard Goetz Trial and Other Cases.
26. Kirk Johnson, "Behind the Scenes at the Goetz Trial: A Fierce Legal Battle over a Witness," *New York Times,* May 11, 1987, B2.
27. Associated Press, "Judge Refuses Immunity for Youth Shot by Goetz," *Washington Post,* May 11, 1987, A3.
28. Jury Charge in Trial Transcript, 9138, June 12, 1987, Folder 17, Box 10, Series III.
29. Mike Pearl and Doug Feiden, "Goetz Victim No. 2 Clams Up," *New York Post,* May 6, 1987, 7.
30. George P. Fletcher, *A Crime of Self-Defense: Bernhard Goetz and the Law on Trial* (Chicago: University of Chicago Press, 1988), 130.

31. Margot Hornblower, "Youth in Goetz Cases Refuses to Testify: Surprise Move Draws Contempt Citation," *Washington Post,* May 5, 1987, A3.
32. Ibid.
33. Ibid.
34. Testimony of Richard Reip in Trial Transcript, 5827, May 5, 1987, Folder 12, Box 9, Series III; direct quote from: "*People v. Goetz* Trial Transcript Notes," 3.
35. Testimony of Alejandro Torres in Trial Transcript, 5862–3, May 5, 1987, Folder 12, Box 9, Series III; direct quote from: "*People v. Goetz* Trial Transcript Notes," 3, as also quoted in Lesly with Shuttleworth, *Subway Gunman,* 52.
36. Testimony of Victor Flores in Trial Transcript, 5881–83, May 5, 1987, Folder 12, Box 9, Series III; "*People v. Goetz* Trial Transcript Notes," 3–4, as also quoted in Lesly with Shuttleworth, *Subway Gunman,* 99.
37. Ibid.; "Goetz Victim Won't Testify," *Jersey Journal,* May 6, 1987.
38. Testimony of Armando Soler in Trial Transcript, 5858–59, 5956, 5966–7, May 5, 1987, Folder 12, Box 9, Series III; "*People v. Goetz* Trial Transcript Notes," 4.
39. Ibid.; direct quote from Lesly with Shuttleworth, *Subway Gunman,* 102.
40. Testimony of Loren Michaels in Trial Transcript, 6060, May 6, 1987, Folder 13, Box 9, Series III; direct quote from: "*People v. Goetz* Trial Transcript Notes," 4.
41. People's Summation in Trial Transcript, 8861, June 11, 1987, Folder 16, Box 10, Series III.
42. Testimony of Garth Reid in Trial Transcript, 6128, May 6, 1987, Folder 13, Box 9, Series III; "*People v. Goetz* Trial Transcript Notes," 5.
43. Leon Neyfakh, *Fiasco: Vigilante,* podcast transcript, episode 1, "Fear City," Prologue Projects, Audible Originals, July 27, 2023.
44. Shipp, "A Tenacious Slotnick Faces Biggest Test," 33.
45. Ibid.
46. Ibid.
47. Ibid.
48. Testimony of Garth Reid in Trial Transcript, 6128; "*People v. Goetz* Trial Transcript Notes," 5; Shipp, "A Tenacious Slotnick Faces Biggest Test," 33.
49. Ibid.
50. Testimony of Mary Gant in Trial Transcript, 6237, May 6, 1987, Folder 13, Box 9, Series III; "*People v. Goetz* Trial Transcript Notes," 5.
51. Ibid.
52. Ibid.
53. Ibid.
54. People's Summation in Trial Transcript, 8946.
55. Testimony of Mary Gant in Trial Transcript, 6237; "*People v. Goetz* Trial Transcript Notes," 5.
56. Testimony of Arnethea Gilbert in Trial Transcript, 6273, May 7, 1987, Folder 1, Box 10, Series III; "*People v. Goetz* Trial Transcript Notes," 5.
57. Ibid.
58. Testimony of Arnethea Gilbert in Trial Transcript, 6276.
59. Ibid., 6277.
60. Ibid., 6280.
61. Ibid., 6278.
62. Ibid.
63. Testimony of Josephine Holt in Trial Transcript, 6309, May 7, 1987, Folder 1, Box 10, Series III; "*People v. Goetz* Trial Transcript Notes," 5.
64. Testimony of Josephine Holt in Trial Transcript, 6323–24.
65. Ibid., 6318.
66. Ibid., 6309; People's Summation in Trial Transcript, 8947, June 11, 1987, Folder 13, Box 9, Series III.
67. Larry Nathanson, "Goetz Witness 'Heard Sound, Didn't Look,'" *New York Post,* May 7, 1987, 5.
68. Testimony of Josephine Holt in Trial Transcript, 6323; "*People v. Goetz* Trial Transcript Notes," 5.

69. Testimony of Josephine Holt in Trial Transcript, 6334.
70. Ibid., 6342.
71. Lesly with Shuttleworth, *Subway Gunman,* 120.
72. Testimony of Solitaire MacFoy in Trial Transcript, 6345–55, May 7, 1987, Folder 1, Box 10, Series III.
73. Ibid., 6357.
74. Ibid., 6352.
75. Mike Pearl and Doug Feiden, "Witness: Goetz Opened Fire Before Being Threatened," *New York Post,* May 8, 1987, 13.
76. People's Summation in Trial Transcript, 8888, June 11, 1987, Folder 13, Box 9, Series III; also see testimony of Solitaire MacFoy in Trial Transcript, 6363, 6355, 6351–52.
77. Testimony of Solitaire MacFoy in Trial Transcript, 6366, 6374.
78. Testimony of Ruth Chasek in Trial Transcript, 6403, May 7, 1987, Folder 1, Box 10, Series III.
79. Testimony of Harry Adler in Trial Transcript, 6471–6503, May 11, 1987, Folder 2, Box 10, Series III.
80. Ibid., 6477.
81. Ibid., 6478–88.
82. Ibid., 6481.
83. Ibid., 6488.
84. Mike Pearl and Doug Feiden, "MD: Goetz Victim May Have Been Shot Two Times," *New York Post,* May 11, 1987, 13.
85. Testimony of Peter Adams in Trial Transcript, 6504–52, May 11, 1987, Folder 2, Box 10, Series III.
86. Ibid., 6509.
87. Ibid., 6512.
88. Ibid., 6516–17.
89. Ibid., 6517.
90. Ibid., 6519.
91. Ibid., 6519–20.
92. Ibid., 6521.
93. Ibid., 6524.
94. Ibid., 6521.
95. Ibid., 6522–23.
96. Ibid.
97. Testimony of Claude Macaluso in Trial Transcript, 6553–6616, May 11, 1987, Folder 2, Box 10, Series III.
98. Ibid., 6555.
99. Ibid., 6556–57.
100. Ibid., 6553–6616; "*People v. Goetz* Trial Transcript Notes," 6.
101. Testimony of Claude Macaluso in Trial Transcript, 6553–6616; "*People v. Goetz* Trial Transcript Notes," 6.
102. Testimony of Claude Macaluso in Trial Transcript, 6574.
103. Ibid., 6576.
104. Ibid.
105. Ibid., 6553–6616.
106. Jimmy Breslin, "Shooting Script," New York *Daily News,* November 26, 1985, 5–6, Papers of Ron Kuby.
107. Testimony of Claude Macaluso in Trial Transcript, 6590–91.
108. Ibid.
109. Ibid., 6593–96.
110. Ibid., 6596.
111. Lesly with Shuttleworth, *Subway Gunman,* 198.
112. Testimony of Claude Macaluso in Trial Transcript, 6560–61.
113. Ibid.

114. Ibid.
115. Esther Pessin, "Bernhard Goetz' Neighbor Today Testified She Urged the Frantic . . . ," May 12, 1987, UPI Archives.
116. Testimony of Myra Friedman in Trial Transcript, 6623–26, May 11, 1987, Folder 2, Box 10, Series III.
117. Mike Pearl and Doug Feiden, "Goetz Finds Peace in Rural Hideaway," *New York Post,* May 11, 1987, 13.

27. Bombshells and Blowups

1. Testimony of Myra Friedman in Trial Transcript, 6623–26, May 11, 1987, Folder 2, Box 10, Series III, Justice Stephen G. Crane Papers on the Bernhard Goetz Trial and Other Cases, MS 3152, The New York Historical, New York, NY.
2. Testimony of Christopher Boucher in Trial Transcript, 6820–96, May 13, 1987, Folder 4, Box 10, Series III.
3. Ibid., 6839.
4. Ibid., 6841.
5. Ibid., 6852.
6. Ibid., 6870, May 13, 1987, Folder 4, Box 10, Series III.
7. Ibid., 6862.
8. From *The Confessions of Bernhard Goetz,* directed by Darrell Moore (Orland Park, IL: MPI Home Video, 1987), VHS.
9. Ibid.
10. Anne Groer, "Goetz on Trial Tape: Shootings 'Savage,'" *Orlando Sentinel,* May 14, 1987, A1.
11. Leon Neyfakh, *Fiasco: Vigilante,* podcast transcript, episode 5, "Reasonable People," Prologue Projects, Audible Originals, July 27, 2023.
12. Ibid.
13. Mark Lesly with Charles Shuttleworth, *Subway Gunman: A Juror's Account of the Bernhard Goetz Trial* (Latham, NY: British American Publishing, 1988), 145.
14. *NBC Nightly News,* "New York City / Goetz Trial #556475," reported by John Chancellor, aired May 4, 1987, Vanderbilt Television Archives.
15. Testimony of Michael Clark in Trial Transcript, 6716–33, May 13, 1987, Folder 4, Box 10, Series III.
16. Kirk Johnson, "Jury Watches an Angry Goetz on Tape," *New York Times,* May 14, 1987, B1.
17. Margot Hornblower, "Intended to Gouge Eye of Teen, Goetz Tape Says: 'My Problem Was I Ran Out of Bullets,'" *Washington Post,* May 14, 1987, A3.
18. Video Statement of Bernhard Goetz, transcript, December 31, 1984, to ADA Susan Braver, Det. Dan Hattendorf, Transit Police, Det. Michael Clark, NYPD, Concord, New Hampshire, Papers of Ron Kuby.
19. Ibid., 19.
20. Ibid., 30–31.
21. Lesly with Shuttleworth, *Subway Gunman,* 153.
22. Doug Feiden and Mike Pearl, "'Goetz Youths Got Their Due'—Rider," *New York Post,* May 19, 1987, 14; Ray Kerrison, "Prosecution Witness Helps Goetz Instead," *New York Post,* May 20, 1987, 9.
23. Testimony of Andrea Reid in Trial Transcript, 6931–7015, May 19, 1987, Folder 5, Box 10, Series III; "*People v. Goetz* Trial Transcript Notes: Witnesses, Exhibits and Their Significance," n.d., 7, compiled by Legal Team of Ron Kuby, Papers of Ron Kuby.
24. Testimony of Andrea Reid in Trial Transcript, 6943–45, 6949–52.
25. People's Summation in Trial Transcript, 8888, June 11, 1987, Folder 13, Box 9, Series III; see also testimony of Andrea Reid in Trial Transcript, 6944–45, 6949.
26. Testimony of Andrea Reid in Trial Transcript, 6944–45, 6949–52.
27. Ibid., 6951–52.
28. Ibid., 6984.
29. Ibid., 6957.

30. Ibid., 6973, 6994–99.
31. Ibid., 7013.
32. Ibid., 7011–15.
33. Ibid., 6987.

28. Fighting Dirty

1. Philip Lentz, "Goetz Victim Tells Court He Tried to Run," *Chicago Tribune,* May 20, 1987, 6.
2. Mitch Garber to Assistant District Attorney Gregory Waples, January 20, 1987, Folder 1, Box 14, Collection REC0073, Bernhard Goetz closed case files, New York County District Attorney records, The New York City Municipal Archives, New York City Department of Records and Information Services, New York, NY.
3. Testimony of James Ramseur in Trial Transcript, 7092–97, May 19, 1987, Folder 5, Box 10, Series III, Justice Stephen G. Crane Papers on the Bernhard Goetz Trial and Other Cases, MS 3152, The New York Historical, New York, NY.
4. Gerson A. Zwelfach to Gregory Waples, November 24, 1986, Folder 2, Box 14, Collection REC0073, Bernhard Goetz closed case files.
5. Editorial Board, "Goetz Has Already Paid a Heavy Price," *New York Post,* May 16, 1987, 14.
6. Ray Kerrison, "Prosecution Witness Helps Goetz Instead," *New York Post,* May 20, 1987, 9.
7. Testimony of James Ramseur in Trial Transcript, 7030–7130, May 19, 1987, Folder 5, Box 10, Series III.
8. Ibid., 7120.
9. Ibid., 7055.
10. Ibid., 7055–58.
11. Lentz, "Goetz Victim Tells Court He Tried to Run," 6.
12. Ray Kerrison, "Goetz DA Betrayed Us All," *New York Post,* June 15, 1987, 3.
13. Testimony of James Ramseur in Trial Transcript, 7069–70, May 19, 1987, Folder 5, Box 10, Series III.
14. Ray Kerrison, "'Victims' Back in the Line of Fire," *New York Post,* May 21, 1987, 7.
15. Testimony of James Ramseur in Trial Transcript, 7071, May 19, 1987, Folder 5, Box 10, Series III.
16. Ibid., 7077.
17. Ibid., 7074.
18. Ibid., 7076.
19. Ibid., 7070.
20. Ibid., 7094.
21. Ibid., 7105.
22. Ibid., 7125.
23. Testimony of James Ramseur in Trial Transcript, 7151, May 20, 1987, Folder 6, Box 10, Series III.
24. Ibid., 7211.
25. Ibid., 7151.
26. Ibid., 7237.
27. Ibid., 7235.
28. Lentz, "Goetz Victim Tells Court He Tried to Run," 6.
29. Testimony of James Ramseur in Trial Transcript, 7239, May 20, 1987, Folder 6, Box 10, Series III.
30. Ibid.
31. Ibid.
32. Ibid., 7251.
33. Ibid., 7272–76.
34. Ibid.
35. Lentz, "Goetz Victim Tells Court He Tried to Run," 6.
36. Kirk Johnson, "Testimony of Youth Goetz Shot Is Thrown Out," *New York Times,* May 29, 1987, A1.

37. Ibid.
38. Mike Pearl, "Sneering Ramseur Gets 6 Months for Contempt," *New York Post,* May 22, 1987, 9; Mike Pearl and Doug Feiden, "Sneering Ramseur Gets 6 Months for Tirade," *New York Post,* May 23, 1987, 7.
39. Pearl, "Sneering Ramseur Gets 6 Months for Contempt," 9; Pearl and Feiden, "Sneering Ramseur Gets 6 Months for Tirade," 7.

29. *Smoke and Mirrors*

1. Kirk Johnson, "Testimony of Youth Goetz Shot Is Thrown Out," *New York Times,* May 29, 1987, A1.
2. Ibid.
3. Mike Pearl and Doug Feiden, "Goetz Judge Returns to Scene of the Crime," *New York Post,* May 26, 1987, 16.
4. Testimony of Charles Cozza in Trial Transcript, 7419–35, May 21, 1987, Folder 7, Box 10, Series III, Justice Stephen G. Crane Papers on the Bernhard Goetz Trial and Other Cases, MS 3152, The New York Historical, New York, NY; "*People v. Goetz* Trial Transcript Notes: Witnesses, Exhibits and Their Significance," n.d., 7–8, compiled by Legal Team of Ron Kuby, Papers of Ron Kuby.
5. Notably, in the piece for the *Post* (in which the reporter got his name slightly wrong too), Cozza said that he had been in "a pizza parlor on Canal and Varick when someone ran in and told me that a man was being beaten. I ran out and saw Goetz on the ground. One kid was on top of him beating him pretty badly. The other two kids were kicking Goetz while the other beat him. I grabbed the kid on top of him, threw him over the hood of a car and put handcuffs on him. The other two ran away . . . his face was bloody, and had cuts all over it. But Goetz kept saying 'what about the other two? How are we going to get the other two?" He did not give this level of detail on the stand. Joanne Wasserman, "I Saved Vigilante," *New York Post,* January 8, 1985, 7.
6. Testimony of Charles Cozza in Trial Transcript, 7424–28; "*People v. Goetz* Trial Transcript Notes," 7–8.
7. Testimony of Murray Burton in Trial Transcript, 7440, May 21, 1987, Folder 7, Box 10, Series III; "*People v. Goetz* Trial Transcript Notes," 8.
8. Testimony of Murray Burton in Trial Transcript, 7442–43; "*People v. Goetz* Trial Transcript Notes," 8.
9. As quoted re: Trial Transcript pages 7442–3 in "*People v. Goetz* Trial Transcript Notes," 8.
10. Testimony of Vincent Palumbo in Trial Transcript, 7445–60, May 21, 1987, Folder 7, Box 10, Series III; "*People v. Goetz* Trial Transcript Notes," 8.
11. Mark Lesly with Charles Shuttleworth, *Subway Gunman: A Juror's Account of the Bernhard Goetz Trial* (Latham, NY: British American Publishing, 1988), 181.
12. Ibid.
13. Ibid.
14. This story first broke in early December 1985 on local TV station WNBC. Smith's claims were not supported by the report he filed at the time. See the testimony of Peter Smith in Trial Transcript, 7486–7585, May 26–27, 1987, Folder 8, Box 10, Series III; "*People v. Goetz* Trial Transcript Notes," 8.
15. Peter Kerr, "Officer Says Man Goetz Shot Told Him of a Robbery Plan," *New York Times,* December 10, 1985, B2.
16. Letter from Barry Slotnick to Judge Stephen Crane, December 10, 1985, Folder 1, Box 14, Collection REC0073, Bernhard Goetz closed case files, New York County District Attorney records, The New York City Municipal Archives, New York City Department of Records and Information Services, New York, NY; Letter from Gregory Waples to Judge Stephen Crane, December 6, 1985, Folder 8, Box 13, Collection REC0073, Bernhard Goetz closed case files.
17. Lesly with Shuttleworth, *Subway Gunman,* 181.
18. Slotnick asked Smith: "After December 22, 1984, that is the date of the incident; after December 22, 1984, when you told Detective Clark that you had been told by one of the

people on the floor of the car, 'We were trying to rob the white guy and he shot us,' after that incident, after you told that to Detective Clark, which is the same day; am I correct?" Smith answered in the affirmative. Testimony of Peter Smith in Trial Transcript, 7610, 7617–23, May 27, 1987, Folder 9, Box 10, Series III.

19. Officer Peter Smith, NYPD, Police Complaint Report 16768, January 4, 1985, Papers of Ron Kuby.
20. Gregory L. Waples to Mark M. Baker, November 27, 1985, Folder 8, Box 13, Collection REC0073, Bernhard Goetz closed case files; Detective Al Licata, NYPD, Police Complaint—Follow Up—"Interview with PO Peter Smith," December 4, 1985, Papers of Ron Kuby.
21. Testimony of Peter Smith in Trial Transcript, 7675–76, May 27, 1987, Folder 9, Box 10, Series III.
22. Lesly with Shuttleworth, *Subway Gunman,* 188.
23. *92Y American Conversation,* "Revisiting the Trial of Bernie Goetz—92nd Street Y," YouTube video, featuring Mark Lesly, Geraldo Rivera, Thane Rosenbaum, Barry Slotnick, and Gregory Waples, uploaded February 13, 2014, The 92nd Street Y, New York and Fordham University School of Law.
24. Testimony of Bernard Yudowitz in Trial Transcript, 7689–7704, May 27, 1987, Folder 9, Box 10, Series III.
25. Ibid., 7693–96, 7702–3.
26. Ibid., 7695.
27. Ibid., 7703–4, 7702–3.
28. Lesly with Shuttleworth, *Subway Gunman,* 191.
29. Testimony of Andrea Reid in Trial Transcript, 6951–52, May 19, 1987, Folder 5, Box 10, Series III; Brief for Respondent at 9–10, *The People of the State of New York v. Bernhard Goetz,* 73 N.Y.2d 751 (1988), Folder 5, Box 12, Collection REC0073, Bernhard Goetz closed case files.
30. Testimony of Andrea Reid in Trial Transcript, 6951–52; Brief for Respondent at 9–10, *The People of the State of New York v. Bernhard Goetz.*
31. Testimony of John Barna in Trial Transcript, 7705–27, May 27, 1987, Folder 9, Box 10, Series III.
32. Ibid., 7718.
33. Lesly with Shuttleworth, *Subway Gunman,* 192.
34. Ibid.
35. Lawyers for Darrell Cabey explained this portrayal in an internal memo as follows: "Defense Counsel apparently sought to avoid [the diagram drawn by Marie Venticinque] in favor of more dramatic representations, such as calling burly Guardian Angels to simulate the scenario in one instance, and [trying to take] the jury on a field trip to a similar subway car." "*People v. Goetz* Trial Transcript Notes," 1.
36. Esther Pessin, "Goetz Confession to Be Shown Jurors," May 13, 1987, UPI Archives; testimony of Michael Clark in Trial Transcript, 7731, May 27, 1987, Folder 4, Box 10, Series III.
37. Colloquy before Judge Crane in Trial Transcript, 7741–42, May 28, 1987, Folder 4, Box 10, Series III.
38. George P. Fletcher, *A Crime of Self-Defense: Bernhard Goetz and the Law on Trial* (Chicago: University of Chicago Press, 1988), 129.
39. Mike Pearl and Doug Feiden, "Play It Again, Bernie!," *New York Post,* May 28, 1987, 3.
40. Lesly with Shuttleworth, *Subway Gunman,* 199.
41. King was actually a legendary private investigator in NYC and, according to the *Post,* he was "working today for Goetz' lawyer, Barry Slotnick, uncovering crucial bits of evidence that he says were overlooked by the district attorney." Mike Pearl, "Bernie's Mystery Gumshoe," *New York Post,* May 13, 1987, 7, 22. As the *Daily News* also noted, one of King's main jobs in this case was to make sure that Bernie Goetz didn't "pop off to the press after a day's court proceedings." He would field any questions while making sure to usher Goetz into a car as soon as possible. Larry Sutton, "The Man Who Keeps Bernie from Media," New York *Daily News,* May 13, 1987, 15.

42. Lesly with Shuttleworth, *Subway Gunman,* 199.
43. Pearl and Feiden, "Play It Again, Bernie!," 3.
44. Testimony of Joseph Quirk in Trial Transcript, 7772–73, 7787–90, 7798–99, May 28, 1987, Folder 10, Box 10, Series III.
45. Ibid., 7770; Lesly with Shuttleworth, *Subway Gunman,* 199.
46. Lesly with Shuttleworth, *Subway Gunman,* 200.
47. Waples makes this point; see: Testimony of Joseph Quirk in Trial Transcript, 7772–73, 7787–90, 7798–99, May 28, 1987, Folder 10, Box 10, Series III.
48. Lesly with Shuttleworth, *Subway Gunman,* 202.
49. Ibid.
50. Testimony of Joseph Quirk in Trial Transcript, 7839, 7849, 7875, May 28, 1987, Folder 10, Box 10, Series III.
51. Ibid., 7872; Lesly with Shuttleworth, *Subway Gunman,* 204.
52. Testimony of Joseph Quirk in Trial Transcript, 7898, May 28, 1987, and 7995–97, June 1, 1987, Folder 10, Box 10, Series III.
53. Ibid., 7778, May 28, 1987.
54. Lesly with Shuttleworth, *Subway Gunman,* 204.
55. Testimony of Marie Venticinque in Trial Transcript, 4898–4909, April 27, 1987, Folder 7, Box 9, Series III; "*People v. Goetz* Trial Transcript Notes," 1.
56. Testimony of Marie Venticinque in Trial Transcript, 4898–4909; "*People v. Goetz* Trial Transcript Notes," 1; Lesly with Shuttleworth, *Subway Gunman,* 215.
57. Lesly with Shuttleworth, *Subway Gunman,* 215.
58. Ibid., 216.
59. Kirk Johnson, "Goetz Case Jury Takes Short Trip on the Subway," *New York Times,* May 30, 1987, 35.
60. Ibid.
61. Crane instructions on train in Trial Transcript, 7883, May 28, 1987, Folder 10, Box 10, Series III.
62. Lesly with Shuttleworth, *Subway Gunman,* 217.
63. Crane instructions on train in Trial Transcript, 7886, May 29, 1987, Folder 10, Box 10, Series III.
64. Mike Pearl and Doug Feiden, "Goetz Sits Out Jury's Ride Back in Time," *New York Post,* May 30, 1987, 4.
65. Johnson, "Goetz Case Jury Takes Short Trip on the Subway," 35.
66. Ibid.
67. Lesly with Shuttleworth, *Subway Gunman,* 216.
68. Testimony of Dominick DiMaio in Trial Transcript, 8045–8208, June 1–2, 1987, Folders 11–12, Box 10, Series III.
69. Testimony of Dominick DiMaio in Trial Transcript, 8061, June 1, 1987, Folder 11, Box 10, Series III.
70. Ibid., 8074, 8076–77, 8092, June 1, 1987, Folder 11, Box 10, Series III.
71. Ibid., 8088.
72. Ibid., 8033.
73. Ibid., 8134, June 2, 1987, Folder 12, Box 10, Series III.
74. Ibid., 8158.
75. Ibid., 8170–71.
76. Ibid., 8181–87, June 2, 1987, Folder 12, Box 10, Series III.
77. Lesly with Shuttleworth, *Subway Gunman,* 207.
78. Testimony of Charles Penelton in Trial Transcript, 8210, June 5, 1987, Folder 12, Box 10, Series III.
79. Testimony of Charles Penelton in Trial Transcript, 8319.
80. Ibid., 8211.
81. Ibid., 8317.
82. Testimony of Melvin Becker in Trial Transcript, 8274–77, June 5, 1987, Folder 12, Box 10, Series III.

83. Ibid., 8283.
84. Ibid.
85. Testimony of Dennis Driscoll in Trial Transcript, 8326, June 5, 1987, Folder 12, Box 10, Series III.
86. Esther Pessin, "One of the Four Youths Gunned Down by Subway . . .," May 26, 1987, UPI Archives.
87. Testimony of Dennis Driscoll in Trial Transcript, 8329–32.
88. Testimony of Charles Hirsch in Trial Transcript, 8325–52, June 8, 1987, Folder 12, Box 10, Series III.
89. Ibid.; Lesly with Shuttleworth, *Subway Gunman,* 212–14.
90. Testimony of Charles Hirsch in Trial Transcript, 8325–52; Lesly with Shuttleworth, *Subway Gunman,* 212–14.
91. Testimony of Charles Hirsch in Trial Transcript, 8325–52; Lesly with Shuttleworth, *Subway Gunman,* 212–14.
92. Mike Pearl and Doug Feiden, "Last Witness Grilled in Goetz Case," *New York Post,* June 8, 1987, 5.
93. Testimony of Charles Hirsch in Trial Transcript, 8325–52; Lesly with Shuttleworth, *Subway Gunman,* 213.

30. Rewritings and Remonstrations

1. Mark Lesly with Charles Shuttleworth, *Subway Gunman: A Juror's Account of the Bernhard Goetz Trial* (Latham, NY: British American Publishing, 1988), 220.
2. Defense Summation in Trial Transcript, 8789, June 10, 1987, Folder 15, Box 10, Series III, Justice Stephen G. Crane Papers on the Bernhard Goetz Trial and Other Cases, MS 3152, The New York Historical, New York, NY.
3. Defense Summation in Trial Transcript, 8635.
4. Ibid.
5. Ibid., 8814.
6. Ibid., 8685.
7. Ibid., 8688.
8. Ibid., 8712.
9. Ibid., 8789, 8711.
10. Ibid., 8713.
11. Ibid., 8788.
12. Ibid., 8643.
13. Ibid., 8698.
14. Ibid., 8790.
15. Ibid., 8668.
16. Ibid., 8671.
17. Ibid., 8707, 8790, 8810, 8647, 8660.
18. According to legal expert George Fletcher, this tactic was remarkable, an "emergent pattern," in Slotnick's questioning of all witnesses. Over time this phrase got cemented as fact in the jury's minds. See: George P. Fletcher, *A Crime of Self-Defense: Bernhard Goetz and the Law on Trial* (Chicago: University of Chicago Press, 1988), 122.
19. Defense Summation in Trial Transcript, 8661.
20. Ibid., 8667.
21. Ibid., 8679.
22. Ibid., 8689.
23. Ibid., 8690.
24. Ibid., 8692.
25. Ibid., 8693–94.
26. Ibid., 8693.
27. Ibid., 8711.
28. Ibid., 8693.

29. Ibid., 8695.
30. Ibid., 8696.
31. Ibid., 8695.
32. Ibid., 8681.
33. Ibid., 8461.
34. Ibid., 8662.
35. Ibid., 8674.
36. Ibid., 8817.
37. Ibid., 8818, 8819.
38. Ibid., 8818.
39. Bob Drogin, "Goetz Lawyer Urges Jurors to Ignore Client's 'Ravings,'" *Los Angeles Times,* June 11, 1987, 24.
40. Ray Kerrison, "Boring Barry's Snooze Bulletin," *New York Post,* June 11, 1987, 13.
41. People's Summation in Trial Transcript, 8824–9082, June 11, 1987, Folder 16, Box 10, Series III.
42. Ibid., 8826.
43. Ibid.
44. Ibid., 8847.
45. Ibid., 8937.
46. Ibid., 8942.
47. Ibid., 8943.
48. Ibid., 8888.
49. Ibid., 8896.
50. Testimony of Andrea Reid in Trial Transcript, 6944, May 19, 1987, Folder 5, Box 10, Series III; People's Summation in Trial Transcript, 8895.
51. Testimony of Andrea Reid in Trial Transcript, 6944; People's Summation in Trial Transcript, 8895.
52. People's Summation in Trial Transcript, 8895.
53. Waples actually said more specifically that "in all probability the defendant uttered those words only to himself and probably not even mouthing the words, but saying them in his own mind as he squeezed the trigger a fifth time." George P. Fletcher, *A Crime of Self-Defense,* 175.
54. People's Summation in Trial Transcript, 8895.
55. Ibid., 8891.
56. Ibid., 8891–92.
57. Ibid., 8958.
58. Ibid., 8960.
59. Ibid.
60. Ibid., 8956.
61. Ibid.
62. Ibid., 8902–3.
63. Ibid., 8977.
64. Ibid., 8878.
65. Ibid., 8880.
66. Ibid., 8881.
67. Ibid., 8873.
68. Ibid.
69. Lesly with Shuttleworth, *Subway Gunman,* 254–55; People's Summation in Trial Transcript, 8871.
70. People's Summation in Trial Transcript, 8852.
71. Ibid., 8855.
72. Ibid., 8857.
73. Ibid., 8859.
74. Ibid.
75. Ibid., 8865.

76. Ibid., 8866.
77. Ibid., 8865.
78. Ibid.
79. Ibid., 8920.
80. Ibid., 8926.
81. Ibid., 8931.
82. Ibid., 8931.
83. Ibid., 8842.
84. Ibid., 8827.
85. Ibid., 8952.
86. Ibid., 8953.
87. Ibid., 8952, 8953.
88. Ibid., 8950.
89. Ibid., 8950–51.
90. Ibid., 8954.
91. Ibid., 8970.
92. Ibid., 8829.
93. Ibid., 8830.
94. Ibid., 8832.
95. Ibid., 9011.
96. Ibid.
97. Beth Fallon, "'Jurors Use Your Heads,'" *New York Post,* June 12, 1987, 9.
98. Jury Charge in Trial Transcript, 9083–9292, June 12, 1987, Folder 17, Box 10, Series III.
99. Ibid., 9127.
100. Ibid., 9131.
101. Ibid., 9138
102. Ibid.
103. Ibid., 9150.
104. Ibid., 9220.
105. Ibid., 9154.
106. Ibid., 9229.
107. Ibid., 9232.
108. Ibid., 9214, 9236.
109. Ibid., 9234.
110. Ibid., 9221.

31. Justifications and Judgment

1. Tim McDarrah and Doug Feiden, "Jury Still Grappling with Fate of Bernie," *New York Post,* June 15, 1987, 3.
2. Mark Lesly with Charles Shuttleworth, *Subway Gunman: A Juror's Account of the Bernhard Goetz Trial* (Latham, NY: British American Publishing, 1988), 284.
3. Ibid., 15–16.
4. Lucette Lagnado, "Snarling Ramseur Had Us Terrified—Juror," *New York Post,* June 13, 1987, 5.
5. Ibid.
6. George P. Fletcher, *A Crime of Self-Defense: Bernhard Goetz and the Law on Trial* (Chicago: University of Chicago Press, 1988), 188.
7. Ibid., 180.
8. Ibid., 188.
9. Leon Neyfakh, *Fiasco: Vigilante,* podcast transcript, episode 5, "Reasonable People," Prologue Projects, Audible Originals, July 27, 2023.
10. Lesly with Shuttleworth, *Subway Gunman,* 278.
11. Fletcher, *A Crime of Self-Defense,* 188.
12. Ibid., 189.

13. Ibid.
14. Jury Charge in Trial Transcript, 9126–9265, June 12, 1987, Folder 17, Box 10, Series III, Justice Stephen G. Crane Papers on the Bernhard Goetz Trial and Other Cases, MS 3152, The New York Historical, New York, NY; Fletcher, *A Crime of Self-Defense*, 190.
15. Fletcher, *A Crime of Self-Defense*, 190.
16. McDarrah and Feiden, "Jury Still Grappling with Fate of Bernie," 3; Doug Feiden and Tim McDarrah, "Goetz Jury Asks to See Testimony of 2 Witnesses," *New York Post*, June 16, 1987, 7.
17. Fletcher, *A Crime of Self-Defense*, 191.
18. Ibid.
19. Ibid.
20. Feiden and McDarrah, "Goetz Jury Asks to See Testimony of 2 Witnesses," 7.
21. Jury Verdict in Trial Transcript, 9467–9505, June 16, 1987, Folder 20, Box 10, Series III.
22. Margot Hornblower, "Jury Exonerates Goetz in 4 Subway Shootings: New Yorker Convicted of Weapon Possession," *Washington Post*, June 16, 1987, A1; Fletcher, *A Crime of Self-Defense*, 198.
23. Hornblower, "Jury Exonerates Goetz in 4 Subway Shootings," A1; Fletcher, *A Crime of Self-Defense*, 198.
24. Mike Pearl and Doug Feiden, "Goetz: It's Been Hell," *New York Post*, June 17, 1987, 1–3.
25. Gene Ruffini, "Goetz 'Doesn't See Himself as a Winner,'" *New York Post*, June 18, 1987, 5.
26. Hornblower, "Jury Exonerates Goetz in 4 Subway Shootings," A1.
27. Lesly with Shuttleworth, *Subway Gunman*, xvi.
28. Mark Lesly, "James Ramseur Comedy Hour Was No Laughing Matter," *New York Post*, June 20, 1987, 8.
29. Lesly with Shuttleworth, *Subway Gunman*, xvii.
30. Leon Neyfakh, *Fiasco: Vigilante*, podcast transcript, episode 6, "Damages," Prologue Projects, Audible Originals, July 27, 2023.
31. Ibid.
32. Hornblower, "Jury Exonerates Goetz in 4 Subway Shootings," A1.
33. Ibid.
34. This expression of violence was unnerving even to his trial opponent, Greg Waples. Waples had been heading out on vacation but felt the need to reach out to Slotnick before he left. He wished him well, and, only half in jest, he also wrote, "Where I am going, the bears have never heard of Bernhard Goetz. If they eat me, then, it will be because I taste good, and for no other reason. The rest of the world should be as sensible." Gregory Waples to Barry Slotnick, July 13, 1987, Folder 2, Box 14, Collection REC0073, Bernhard Goetz closed case files, New York County District Attorney records, The New York City Municipal Archives, New York City Department of Records and Information Services, New York, NY.
35. Hornblower, "Jury Exonerates Goetz in 4 Subway Shootings," A1.
36. Neyfakh, *Fiasco: Vigilante*, episode 6, "Damages."
37. Ibid.
38. Ibid.
39. Hornblower, "Jury Exonerates Goetz in 4 Subway Shootings," A1; Lesly with Shuttleworth, *Subway Gunman*, xviii.
40. Ibid.
41. Charles Carillo, "The 4 Youths Who Triggered Historic Trial," *New York Post*, June 17, 1987, 20.

32. *Details and Delays*

1. Mark Baker to Judge Stephen Crane, August 10, 1987, Folder 2, Box 14, Collection REC0073, Bernhard Goetz closed case files, New York County District Attorney records, The New York City Municipal Archives, New York City Department of Records and Information Services, New York, NY.

2. Probation Department Sentencing Report Dossier, "Departmental Sentence Recommendation with Supporting Reasons," 2, September 14, 1987, Case No. 8704982—Bernhard Hugo Goetz, Manhattan Adult Investigation Branch, New York City Department of Probation, Papers of Ron Kuby. Various documents within this Department of Probation sentencing dossier are unnumbered. The page numbers provided here are based on the author's pagination of the entire scanned dossier.
3. Ibid., 28.
4. Ibid., 30.
5. Ibid., 29.
6. Ibid., 7.
7. Ibid.
8. Ibid., 8.
9. Ibid., 10.
10. Ibid., 20.
11. Ibid., 26.
12. Ibid., 14.
13. Ibid.
14. Ibid., 1.
15. Ibid., 20.
16. Ibid., 21.
17. Ibid., 15.
18. Ibid., 12.
19. Ibid.
20. Ibid., 17.
21. Ibid., 13.
22. Ibid.
23. Ibid., 14.
24. Ibid., 2.
25. Mike Pearl, "Goetz Needs a Shrink, Not Jail," *New York Post,* September 24, 1987, 7; Patrick Clark and Joseph McNamara, "No Jail for Goetz, Probation Urges," New York *Daily News,* September 24, 1987, 5.
26. Pre-Sentencing Memorandum Submitted on Behalf of Darrell and Shirley Cabey, 1–13, *The People of the State of New York v. Bernhard Goetz,* 68 N.Y.2d 96, Indictment No. 1914/85 (September 28, 1987), Papers of Ron Kuby.
27. Ibid.
28. Ibid.
29. Ibid.
30. Robert Rygor, president of Villagers Against Crime, to Stephen Crane, August 6, 1987, Folder 23, Box 7, Series II, Justice Stephen G. Crane Papers on the Bernhard Goetz Trial and Other Cases, MS 3152, The New York Historical, New York, NY.
31. Mrs. Adell C. Carr, director of Department of Volunteer Services, New York University Medical Center, to Judge Stephen Crane, August 25, 1987, Folder 23, Box 7, Series II, Justice Stephen G. Crane Papers on the Bernhard Goetz Trial and Other Cases.
32. Brief for Appellant at 17, *The People of the State of New York v. Bernhard Goetz,* 73 N.Y.2d 751 (August 25, 1988), Folder 2, Box 13, Collection REC0073, Bernhard Goetz closed case files.
33. Donald Bernhardt and Marshall Eckblad, "Stock Market Crash of 1987," *Federal Reserve History,* November 22, 2013.
34. Sentencing Remarks, *The People of the State of New York v. Bernhard Goetz* at Part 81, 68 N.Y.2d 96, Indictment No. 476/85 & 1914/85 (October 19, 1987), Folder 25, Box 7, Series II, Justice Stephen G. Crane Papers on the Bernhard Goetz Trial and Other Cases.
35. Ibid.
36. Ibid.
37. Ibid.
38. Ibid.

39. Kirk Johnson, "Goetz Given 6-Month Term on Gun Charge," *New York Times,* October 20, 1987, A1.
40. Mike McLaughlin, "Judging the Goetz Case," *the paper* 18, no. 12 (November 13, 1987): 1–9, Folder 27, Box 7, Series II, Justice Stephen G. Crane Papers on the Bernhard Goetz Trial and Other Cases.
41. Stephen G. Crane to Mr. Martin F. Corn, February 23, 1989, Folder 29, Box 7, Series II, Justice Stephen G. Crane Papers on the Bernhard Goetz Trial and Other Cases.
42. Sentencing Remarks, *The People of the State of New York v. Bernhard Goetz* at Part 81, 38.
43. Ibid., 6.
44. Ibid., 21.
45. Ibid., 30.
46. Ibid., 36–37.
47. Ibid., 50.
48. Ibid.
49. Ibid., 54.
50. Ibid., 67.
51. Ronald Sullivan, "Goetz Is Given One-Year Term on Gun Charge," *New York Times,* January 14, 1989, 1, Papers of Ron Kuby.
52. Sentencing Remarks, *The People of the State of New York v. Bernhard Goetz* at Part 81, 57.
53. Kirk Johnson, "Goetz Given 6-Month Term on Gun Charge," *New York Times,* October 20, 1987, A1.
54. McLaughlin, "Judging the Goetz Case," 9.
55. Ibid.
56. Justice Michael Dontzin to Stephen Crane, October 20, 1987, Folder 27, Box 7, Series II, Justice Stephen G. Crane Papers on the Bernhard Goetz Trial and Other Cases.
57. "Justice for Bernhard Goetz," *New York Times,* October 20, 1987, A34.
58. "Jail for Goetz: Firm and Fair," New York *Daily News,* October 20, 1987, 26.
59. "Goetz Deserves Jail Time for His Crime," *Atlanta Journal,* October 13, 1987.
60. Stanley Lane to Judge Crane, October 19, 1987, Folder 27, Box 7, Series II, Justice Stephen G. Crane Papers on the Bernhard Goetz Trial and Other Cases.
61. Rose Katz to Stephen Crane, October 19, 1987, Folder 27, Box 7, Series II, Justice Stephen G. Crane Papers on the Bernhard Goetz Trial and Other Cases.
62. Kathleen A. Colotta to Stephen Crane, October 20, 1987, Folder 27, Box 7, Series II, Justice Stephen G. Crane Papers on the Bernhard Goetz Trial and Other Cases.
63. Joe Starita, "Sentenced to Six Months in Jail, Five Years Probation," *Miami Herald,* October 20, 1987.
64. Ray Kerrison, "Media's Hounds of Hypocrisy Bay for Bernie's Blood," *New York Post,* October 6, 1987, 13.
65. Ray Kerrison, "Judges Signal: Free the Punks, Jail the Victims," *New York Post,* October 20, 1987, 13.
66. Editorial Board, "Injustice for Goetz," *New York Post,* October 20, 1987, 26.
67. "A Message for the Muggers," *Arizona Republic,* October 21, 1987, A18, Folder 27, Box 7, Series II, Justice Stephen G. Crane Papers on the Bernhard Goetz Trial and Other Cases.
68. Elaine Rivera, "Goetz Ridicules Teens He Shot; Receives 'Citizen Award,'" *Newsday,* April 25, 1988, 3.
69. Ibid.
70. Gerald Preiser, "Goetz Sentence Sends a Dangerous Message," *New York Times,* October 31, 1987, 26.
71. Brief for Appellant at 6, *The People of the State of New York v. Bernhard Goetz,* 73 N.Y.2d 751 (August 25, 1988), Folder 2, Box 13, Collection REC0073, Bernhard Goetz closed case files.
72. Brief for Respondent at 24, *The People of the State of New York v. Bernhard Goetz,* 73 N.Y.2d 751 (1988), Folder 5, Box 12, Collection REC0073, Bernhard Goetz closed case files.
73. Ibid. at 27–51.

74. Susan Milligan, "Lock Up Goetz, Says the Court," New York *Daily News,* November 23, 1988, 12.
75. For Judge Crane's handwritten draft version of his resentencing statement, see: Folder 28, Box 7, Series II, Justice Stephen G. Crane Papers on the Bernhard Goetz Trial and Other Cases.
76. Leon Neyfakh, *Fiasco: Vigilante,* podcast transcript, episode 6, "Damages," Prologue Projects, Audible Originals, July 27, 2023.
77. Ibid.
78. Ibid.
79. "Goetz and One of His Shooting Victims Jailed at Same Facility," March 7, 1989, UPI Archives.
80. *92Y American Conversation,* "Revisiting the Trial of Bernie Goetz—92nd Street Y," YouTube video, featuring Mark Lesly, Geraldo Rivera, Thane Rosenbaum, Barry Slotnick, and Gregory Waples, uploaded February 13, 2014, The 92nd Street Y, New York and Fordham University School of Law.
81. Amiri Baraka, "If Goetz Goes Free Black People Must Arm Themselves!," *Unity* (Oakland, CA), June 15–17, 1987, 3, Papers of Amiri Baraka, Auburn Avenue Research Library on African American Culture and History, Atlanta-Fulton Public Library System, Atlanta, Georgia.

33. Postmortem

1. *92Y American Conversation,* "Revisiting the Trial of Bernie Goetz—92nd Street Y," YouTube video, featuring Mark Lesly, Geraldo Rivera, Thane Rosenbaum, Barry Slotnick, and Gregory Waples, uploaded February 13, 2014, The 92nd Street Y, New York and Fordham University School of Law.
2. Mark Lesly with Charles Shuttleworth, *Subway Gunman: A Juror's Account of the Bernhard Goetz Trial* (Latham, NY: British American Publishing, 1988), 436.
3. See, for example, Michael D. Knox with Mike Walker, *The Private Diary of an O.J. Juror: Behind the Scenes of the Trial of the Century* (Beverly Hills, CA: Dove Books, 1995). The book offered an insider look at the trial of famed accused football icon O.J. Simpson. Similarly, a book on the Goetz trial such as Lillian B. Rubin, *Quiet Rage: Bernie Goetz in a Time of Madness* (New York: Farrar, Straus & Giroux, 1986), and a short film, *Confessions of Crime: Bernhard Goetz—The Subway Shooter,* directed by Stuart Goldman (New Canaan, CT: Total Content Digital, 2017), documentary short, were released.
4. Lesly with Shuttleworth, *Subway Gunman,* 280.
5. Ibid., 278.
6. Leon Neyfakh, *Fiasco: Vigilante,* podcast transcript, episode 6, "Damages," Prologue Projects, Audible Originals, July 27, 2023.
7. Lesly with Shuttleworth, *Subway Gunman,* 300.
8. Ibid.
9. Ibid.
10. Ibid., 306–11.
11. Ibid., 242.
12. Ibid., 307.
13. Ibid., 301.
14. Ibid., 305.
15. Ibid., 290.
16. Ibid., 291.
17. Ibid., 298.
18. Ibid., 286.
19. Ibid., 276–77; George P. Fletcher, *A Crime of Self-Defense: Bernhard Goetz and the Law on Trial* (Chicago: University of Chicago Press, 1988), 182, 184.
20. Lesly with Shuttleworth, *Subway Gunman,* 310.

21. Ibid., 280.
22. Ibid., 281.
23. *The Confessions of Bernhard Goetz,* directed by Darrell Moore (Orland Park, IL: MPI Home Video, 1987), VHS.
24. Leon Neyfakh, *Fiasco: Vigilante,* podcast transcript, episode 5, "Reasonable People," Prologue Projects, Audible Originals, July 27, 2023.
25. Bob Drogin, "Goetz Faced 'Deadly Threat,' Jurors Say," *Los Angeles Times,* June 18, 1987, 20.
26. Lesly with Shuttleworth, *Subway Gunman,* 295.
27. Ibid., 294–95.
28. *The Confessions of Bernhard Goetz,* directed by Darrell Moore.
29. Ibid.
30. Ibid.
31. Lesly with Shuttleworth, *Subway Gunman,* 317.
32. Ibid., 312.
33. Ibid.
34. Neyfakh, *Fiasco: Vigilante,* episode 5, "Reasonable People."
35. Lesly with Shuttleworth, *Subway Gunman,* 282.
36. Ibid., 311.
37. Fletcher, *A Crime of Self-Defense,* 183.
38. Ibid., 185.
39. Ibid., 186.
40. Ibid.
41. Ibid.
42. Ibid., 187.
43. Ibid.
44. Ibid., 192.
45. Ibid., 197.
46. *92Y American Conversation,* "Revisiting the Trial of Bernie Goetz—92nd Street Y."
47. Ibid.
48. Lesly with Shuttleworth, *Subway Gunman,* 320.
49. *The Confessions of Bernhard Goetz,* directed by Darrell Moore.
50. Anne E. Murray, "Judge Was Wrong to Flip-Flop Charge to Jury: Ward," *New York Post,* June 18, 1987.
51. Bob Drogin, "Goetz Faced 'Deadly Threat,' Jurors Say," *Los Angeles Times,* June 18, 1987, 20, 5.
52. William M. Kunstler to Gregory Waples, June 24, 1987, Folder 2, Box 14, Collection REC0073, Bernhard Goetz closed case files, New York County District Attorney records, The New York City Municipal Archives, New York City Department of Records and Information Services, New York, NY.

PART V · JUSTICE SERVED COLD

1. Lynn Emmerman and Jon Van, "Cocaine Confronts a Challenge as Yuppiedom's Drug of Choice," *Chicago Tribune,* June 23, 1985, 1; Connie Bruck, *The Predators' Ball: The Inside Story of Drexel Burnham and the Rise of the Junk Bond Raiders* (New York: Simon & Schuster, 1988); Kenneth J. Robinson, "Savings and Loan Crisis, 1980–1989," Federal Reserve History, last modified November 22, 2013.
2. Indeed, when Prohibition was repealed, the number of murders in cities plummeted. See: David S. Jacks et al., *Urban Mortality and the Repeal of Federal Prohibition,* Working Paper 28181 (Cambridge, MA: National Bureau of Economic Research, December 2020).
3. P. J. Goldstein et al., "Crack and Homicide in New York City, 1988: A Conceptually Based Event Analysis," *Contemporary Drug Problems* 16, no. 4 (Winter 1989): 651–88.
4. The number of civil suits generally increased in the 1990s, particularly in the area of civil rights. Specifically, the number of civil rights complaints filed in U.S. district courts increased from 18,922 in 1990 to 43,278 in 1997. Bureau of Justice Statistics, "Civil Rights

Complaints in U.S. District Courts, 1990–2006," by Tracey Kyckelhahn and Thomas H. Cohen, Bureau of Justice Statistics Special Report, NCJ 222989 (Washington, DC: U.S. Department of Justice, August 2008): 1–12. Debt collections and eviction cases, as well as employment discrimination cases, also proliferated in the court system in this decade.

34. *In for a Penny*

1. Sonia Reyes, "Hounded by the Press, Bernie Snaps Back," *New York Post,* June 18, 1987, 2.
2. Douglas Martin, "Love of Guns, and Applause for Goetz," *New York Times,* April 25, 1988, B3.
3. Sonia Reyes et al., "Holed Up Bernie Has Angels on His Shoulders," *New York Post,* June 19, 1987, 4.
4. Sonia Reyes, "A Tale of Two Neighborhoods," *New York Post,* June 17, 1987, 24.
5. Ibid.
6. Randell Pierson and Sonia Reyes, "Acquittal Was No Surprise to Victims' Relatives," *New York Post,* June 17, 1987, 21.
7. Leon Neyfakh, *Fiasco: Vigilante,* podcast transcript, episode 6, "Damages," Prologue Projects, Audible Originals, July 27, 2023.
8. Larry McShane, "For One Goetz Victim, Suffering Won't End," *Los Angeles Times,* January 8, 1995.
9. Richard C. Auxier, "Reagan's Recession," Economic Conditions, Pew Research Center, December 14, 2010.
10. Affidavit at 2, *Shirley Cabey, as the mother and guardian of Darrell Cabey v. The Crime Victims Board, Executive Department, State of New York,* No. 13054/89 (N.Y.S.2d, September 7, 1989), Papers of Ron Kuby.
11. Crime Victims Board—Claim Form, January 14, 1985, Papers of Ron Kuby; Geraldine Jordan to Shirley Cabey, January 14, 1985, Papers of Ron Kuby.
12. Affidavit at 2, *Shirley Cabey, as the mother and guardian of Darrell Cabey v. The Crime Victims Board, Executive Department, State of New York.*
13. Angelo Petromelis to Shirley Cabey, December 12, 1985, Papers of Ron Kuby.
14. Amended Decision, to Ms. Shirley Cabey, from Angelo Petrolemis, Crime Victims Board, Claim #77883 on Behalf of Darrell Cabey, June 23, 1988, Papers of Ron Kuby.
15. Procedural history summarized in Petition Pursuant to Article 78, CPLR, Supreme Court of the State of New York County of New York, *Shirley Cabey, as the mother and guardian of Darrell Cabey, Petitioner v. The Crime Victims Board, Executive Department, State of New York,* Respondent (May 30, 1989), Papers of Ron Kuby.
16. Ibid.
17. Blair Ames, "A Brief History of the Victims of Crime Act," Safe Communities, U.S. Department of Justice, Office of Justice Programs, October 11, 2024.
18. Howard Pinderhughes, "The Anatomy of Racially Motivated Violence in New York City: A Case Study of Youth in Southern Brooklyn," *Social Problems* 40, no. 4 (1993): 478–92; *Homicide Rates in the U.S., 1900–2006,* National Academies of Sciences, Engineering, and Medicine.
19. Olivia B. Waxman, "President Trump Played a Key Role in the Central Park Five Case. Here's the Real History Behind *When They See Us,*" *Time,* May 31, 2019.
20. Oliver Laughland, "Donald Trump and the Central Park Five: The Racially Charged Rise of a Demagogue," *Guardian,* February 17, 2016.
21. Sarah Burns, *The Central Park Five: The Untold Story Behind One of New York City's Most Infamous Crimes* (New York: Vintage, 2012); *When They See Us,* created by Ava DuVernay, aired May 31, 2019, Netflix, 2019, television miniseries.
22. Esther Pessin, "'Angry' Goetz Leaving Jail," *New York Post,* September 19, 1989, 14.
23. Verified Answer at 4, *Shirley Cabey, as the mother and guardian of Darrell Cabey v. The Crime Victims Board, Executive Department, State of New York.*
24. William M. Kunstler to Messrs. Gennaro A. Fischetti, George L. Grobe, Jr., and Ms. Diane McGrath, Commissioners of the Crime Victims Board, December 8, 1988, Papers of Ron Kuby.

25. Verified Answer at 4, *Shirley Cabey, as the mother and guardian of Darrell Cabey v. The Crime Victims Board, Executive Department, State of New York.*
26. Ibid.
27. "Goetz Victim Loses Compensation Bid," *New York Post,* July 13, 1988, 17.
28. Jerry Nachman, "Subway Shooter Living Kafka's 'Trial,'" *New York Post,* February 24, 1988, 13.

35. *A Different Kind of Case*

1. Memorandum of Law in Opposition to Motion to Consolidate, 1–5, *Darrell A. Cabey, by his legal guardian and proposed conservator, Shirley Cabey v. Bernhard Hugo Goetz,* No. 6747-1985 (Sup. Ct. Bronx Cnty., July 8, 1987), Papers of Ron Kuby.
2. Notice of Entry, Order & Judgment, *Troy Canty v. Bernhard Goetz,* No. 2790/85 (N.Y.S.2d, September 11, 1995), Papers of Ron Kuby; Notice of Entry, Order & Judgment, *James Ramseur v. Bernhard Goetz,* No. 18631/90 (N.Y.S.2d, September 18, 1995), Papers of Ron Kuby.
3. Notice of Entry, Order & Judgement, *Troy Canty v. Bernhard Goetz.*
4. Notice of Entry, Order & Judgement, *James Ramseur v. Bernhard Goetz.*
5. Specifically, the suit highlighted rights guaranteed by the Fifth, Sixth, Eighth, Thirteenth, and Fourteenth Amendments. Complaint for Compensatory and Punitive Damages and Permanent Injunction, 1–24, *Darrell A. Cabey, by his legal guardian and proposed conservator, Shirley Cabey v. Bernhard Hugo Goetz.*
6. Ibid.
7. Leon Neyfakh, *Fiasco: Vigilante,* podcast transcript, episode 6, "Damages," Prologue Projects, Audible Originals, July 27, 2023.
8. Notice of Entry, Order & Judgement, *Troy Canty v. Bernhard Goetz;* Notice of Entry, Order & Judgement, *James Ramseur v. Bernhard Goetz;* Neyfakh, *Fiasco: Vigilante,* episode 6, "Damages."
9. *92Y American Conversation,* "Revisiting the Trial of Bernie Goetz—92nd Street Y," YouTube video, featuring Mark Lesly, Geraldo Rivera, Thane Rosenbaum, Barry Slotnick, and Gregory Waples, uploaded February 13, 2014, The 92nd Street Y, New York and Fordham University School of Law.
10. Memorandum of Law in Opposition to Motion to Consolidate, 4, *Darrell A. Cabey, by his legal guardian and proposed conservator, Shirley Cabey v. Bernhard Hugo Goetz.*
11. Jerry Nachman, "Subway Shooter Living Kafka's 'Trial,'" *New York Post,* February 24, 1988, 13.
12. Memorandum of Law in Opposition to Motion to Consolidate, 1–5, *Darrell A. Cabey, by his legal guardian and proposed conservator, Shirley Cabey v. Bernhard Hugo Goetz.*
13. William M. Kunstler to Hon. Edith Miller, November 9, 1987, Papers of Ron Kuby.
14. Memorandum of Law in Opposition to Motion to Consolidate, 1–5, *Darrell A. Cabey, by his legal guardian and proposed conservator, Shirley Cabey v. Bernhard Hugo Goetz;* Supplemental Affirmation in Support of Motion for Sanctions and in Opposition to Motion to Dismiss, 1, *Darrell A. Cabey, by his legal guardian and proposed conservator, Shirley Cabey v. Bernhard Hugo Goetz.*

36. *Tit for Tat*

1. "No-Show Bernie Starts 50m Stir," *New York Post,* December 2, 1989, 7.
2. Ron Kuby, conversation with author, July 29, 2024.
3. Bernhard Hugo Goetz Deposition, 97–118, April 8, 1985, Papers of Ron Kuby.
4. Ibid., 61, 75.
5. Ibid., 79.
6. Request to Withdraw as Counsel, Affidavit, *Troy Canty v. Bernhard Goetz,* No. 2790/85 (N.Y.S.2d, May 19, 1988), Papers of Ron Kuby.
7. Supplemental Affirmation in Support of Motion for Sanctions and in Opposition to Motion to Dismiss, 1, *Darrell A. Cabey, by his legal guardian and proposed conservator,*

Shirley Cabey v. Bernhard Hugo Goetz, No. 6747-1985 (Sup. Ct. Bronx Cnty., 1990), Papers of Ron Kuby.

8. William M. Reilly, "Goetz Makes First Court Appearance in Lawsuit," January 12, 1990, UPI Archives; Peter Moses, "Goetz in Court for $50m Injury Suit," *New York Post,* January 13, 1990, 7.
9. Associated Press, "New Light Shed on Goetz Shootings; Racist Comments Also Admitted," *The Record* (Woodland Park, NJ), September 27, 1990, A3, Papers of Ron Kuby.
10. Deposition of Bernhard Goetz, 84, September 26, 1990, Papers of Ron Kuby.
11. Ibid., 27–28.
12. Ibid., 30.
13. Associated Press, "New Light Shed on Goetz Shootings," A3.
14. William Kunstler and Ron Kuby, "Deposition of Bernhard Goetz, notes," Papers of Ron Kuby; Peter Moses, "Goetz Admits Firing 4th Shot at Cabey," *New York Post,* September 25, 1990, 8; Associated Press, "New Light Shed on Goetz Shootings," A3; Associated Press, "Goetz Flips His Version of Subway Shooting," *New York Post,* September 27, 1990, 3.
15. Notice of Motion, *Bernhard Goetz v. William Kunstler, Ronald Kuby, Darrell Cabey, Shirley Cabey, individually and in her capacity as legal guardian and conservator for Darrell Cabey, the Center for Constitutional Rights, Inc., and Attorneys X, Y and Z formerly or presently associated with that organization,* No. 586-90 (Sup. Ct. New York Cnty., March 5, 1990), Papers of Ron Kuby; Hal R. Lieberman, Chief Counsel for the Departmental Disciplinary Committee, New York Supreme Court, Appellate Division, First Judicial Department to William M. Kunstler, August 1, 1995, Papers of Ron Kuby.
16. Lieberman to Kunstler, August 1, 1995.
17. Complaint. *Bernhard Goetz v. William Kunstler, Ronald Kuby, Darrell Cabey, Shirley Cabey, individually and in her capacity as legal guardian and conservator for Darrell Cabey, the Center for Constitutional Rights. Inc., and Attorneys X, Y and Z formerly or presently associated with that organization,* No. 586-90 (Sup. Ct. New York Cnty. January 9, 1990), Papers of Ron Kuby.
18. Editorial Board, "The Man Who Said Enough!," *New York Post,* December 22, 1994, 36.
19. Complaint at 1, *Bernhard Goetz v. William Kunstler et al.,* No. 586-90 (Sup. Ct. New York Cnty., January 9, 1990), Papers of Ron Kuby.
20. Ibid.
21. Ibid.
22. Ibid.
23. Presiding Justice Beatrice Shainswit dismissed the suit against all lawyers. Order, *Bernhard Goetz v. William Kunstler, Ronald Kuby, Darrell Cabey, Shirley Cabey, individually and in her capacity as legal guardian and conservator for Darrell Cabey, the Center for Constitutional Rights. Inc., and Attorneys X, Y and Z formerly or presently associated with that organization,* No. 586-90 (Sup. Ct. New York Cnty., July 11, 1990), Papers of Ron Kuby; "Subway Gunman Goetz Sues Attorney," UPI Archives, October 4, 1994.
24. "Subway Gunman Bernhard Goetz Sues: Claims Kunstler Book Damaged His 'Good Name,'" press release from offices of Kunstler and Kuby, October 3, 1994, Papers of Ron Kuby.
25. Ibid.

37. Dirty Tricks

1. Carl J. Pelleck and Linda Stevens, "Goetz Takes Aim at 'Victims' Again," *New York Post,* April 25, 1988, 5.
2. Jim Nolan, "'Attorney' Goetz Wants to Face Off with His Accuser," *New York Post,* January 5, 1990, 7.
3. Alec D. B. McCabe, "Goetz Claims Youth He Shot No 'Vegetable,'" UPI, May 24, 1990, Papers of Ron Kuby.
4. Hal Davis, "Goetz: Victim Isn't a 'Mental Vegetable,'" *New York Post,* May 22, 1990, 19.
5. McCabe, "Goetz Claims Youth He Shot No 'Vegetable.'"

6. Affirmation in Support of Motion for Sanctions and in Opposition to Motion to Dismiss, *Darrell A. Cabey, by his legal guardian and proposed conservator, Shirley Cabey v. Bernhard Hugo Goetz,* No. 6747-1985 (Sup. Ct. Bronx Cnty., May 25, 1990), Papers of Ron Kuby.
7. Affidavit, *The People of the State of New York v. Darrell Cabey,* Ind. No. 4044/84 (Sup. Ct. Bronx Cnty., December 1, 1989), Papers of Ron Kuby.
8. Larry McShane, "For One Goetz Victim, Suffering Won't End," *Los Angeles Times,* January 8, 1995.
9. Darrell Cabey and Harry Katz, telephone conversation, December 19, 1989, audio recording, Papers of Ron Kuby.
10. Ibid.
11. Darrell Cabey and Harry Katz, "Darrell Cabey in Conversation with Harry Katz at the United Cerebral Palsy Association," taped December 27, 1989, United Cerebral Palsy Association, Papers of Ron Kuby.
12. Ibid.
13. Ibid.
14. Ibid.
15. Ibid.
16. Ibid.
17. Robert Gearty, "Goetz Says Cabey's No Vegetable," New York *Daily News,* May 25, 1990, 31.
18. Notice of Motion to Strike Plaintiff's Pleadings, *Darrell A. Cabey, by his legal guardian and proposed conservator, Shirley Cabey v. Bernhard Hugo Goetz,* No. 6747-1985 (Sup. Ct. Bronx Cnty., May 25, 1990), Papers of Ron Kuby; Gearty, "Goetz Says Cabey's No Vegetable," 31.
19. Chris Oliver, "Goetz Says 2nd Tape Proves Cabey Fit to Testify," *New York Post,* May 30, 1990, 16.
20. Jim Nolan, "Tapes Show Cabey Can Testify: Goetz," *New York Post,* May 25, 1990, 8; Oliver, "Goetz Says 2nd Tape Proves Cabey Fit to Testify," 16.
21. Don Broderick, "Judge Orders Goetz to Stay Away from Cabey," *New York Post,* May 26, 1990, 5.
22. Wayne A. Gordon to William M. Kunstler, May 10, 1990, Papers of Ron Kuby; "Judge Blocks Goetz's Access to Subway Victim," May 25, 1990, UPI Archives.
23. Wayne A. Gordon to William M. Kunstler, "Dr. Wayne Gordon Assess Cabey for Dep, P.1," May 10, 1990, Papers of Ron Kuby.
24. Ibid.
25. Ibid.
26. Ibid.
27. Motion for a Protective Order, *Darrell A. Cabey, by his legal guardian and proposed conservator, Shirley Cabey v. Bernhard Hugo Goetz,* No. 6747-1985 (Sup. Ct. Bronx Cnty., May 15, 1990), Papers of Ron Kuby.
28. Dr. Martin I. Lubin to Justice Barry Salman, June 26, 1990, Papers of Ron Kuby.
29. Ibid.
30. Ibid.
31. Ibid.
32. Ibid.
33. Ibid.
34. Ibid.
35. Esther Pessin, "Goetz Gets OK to Quiz Cabey in 50M Suit," *New York Post*, August 24, 1990, 8.
36. McCabe, "Goetz Claims Youth He Shot No 'Vegetable.'"
37. Dennis Hevesi, "Goetz Confronts Victim in Court in Suit Hearing," *New York Times,* September 27, 1990, B2.
38. Affidavit of Bernhard Goetz, *Darrell A. Cabey, by his legal guardian and proposed conservator, Shirley Cabey v. Bernhard Hugo Goetz,* No. 6747-1985 (Sup. Ct. Bronx Cnty., August 23, 1993), Papers of Ron Kuby.

38. *On the Offensive*

1. Shirley Cabey Deposition, *Darrell A. Cabey, by his legal guardian and proposed conservator, Shirley Cabey v. Bernhard Hugo Goetz,* No. 6747-1985 (Sup. Ct. Bronx Cnty., June 18, 1991), Papers of Ron Kuby.
2. Ibid., 3.
3. Ibid., 4, 8.
4. Ibid., 8.
5. Ibid., 9–10.
6. Ibid., 10.
7. Ibid., 33.
8. Ibid.
9. Ibid., 35.
10. Ibid., 37.
11. Ibid.
12. Ibid.
13. Ibid., 39–41.
14. Ibid., 40–41.
15. Ibid. 8.
16. Frank DiGiacoma and Joanna Malloy, "Stormy Day in Court for Goetz," *New York Post,* June 20, 1991, 6.
17. Jan Hoffman, "Fund Linked to N.R.A. Gave $20,000 for Goetz's Defense," *New York Times,* April 16, 1996, 1.
18. Jason W. Brown to Bernhard Goetz, June 26, 1992, Papers of Ron Kuby.
19. Ibid.
20. Ibid.
21. Ibid.
22. Ibid.
23. Darrell A. Cabey Deposition, 4–6, *Darrell A. Cabey, by his legal guardian and proposed conservator, Shirley Cabey v. Bernhard Hugo Goetz,* No. 6747-1985 (Sup. Ct. Bronx Cnty., June 9, 1993), Papers of Ron Kuby.
24. Ibid., 5.
25. Ibid.
26. The Goetz-sympathetic piece that Andrea Peyser would write about this the next day was Andrea Peyser, "Train Ride That Won't End," *New York Post*, Thursday, June 10, 1993, 3.
27. Darrell A. Cabey Deposition, 4–6.
28. Ron Kuby, conversation with author, July 29, 2024.
29. Peyser, "Train Ride That Won't End," 3.
30. Affidavit, 10, *Darrell A. Cabey, by his legal guardian and proposed conservator, Shirley Cabey v. Bernhard Hugo Goetz,* No. 6747-1985 (Sup. Ct. Bronx Cnty., August 26, 1993), Papers of Ron Kuby.
31. Ron Kuby, conversation with author, July 29, 2024.

39. *Old Wine, New Bottles*

1. The one before him, John Lindsay, would become a Democrat. Amanda Luz Henning Santiago, "How Rudolph Giuliani Became New York City's Mayor," *City and State New York,* October 15, 2019.
2. Dennison Young Jr. and Carolyn D. Simpson, "Result of Investigation Re B. Goetz; Establishment of Task Force Re Racial Violence," press release, February 25, 1985, Papers of Ron Kuby.
3. David R. Colburn and Jeffrey S. Adler, eds., *African-American Mayors: Race, Politics, and the American City* (Champaign: University of Illinois Press, 2002); Matthew J. Countryman, *Up South: Civil Rights and Black Power in Philadelphia* (Philadelphia: University of

Pennsylvania Press, 2007); Heather Ann Thompson, *Whose Detroit?: Politics, Labor, and Race in a Modern American City,* 2nd ed. (Ithaca, NY: Cornell University Press, 2017); Joshua Guild, George Derek Musgrove, Benjamin Talton, Keeanga-Yamahtta Taylor, and Leah Wright Rigueur, eds., "Introduction," Special Issue: The Black 1980s, *Journal of African American History* 108, no. 3 (Summer 2023).

4. Editorial Board, "The Man Who Said Enough!," *New York Post,* December 22, 1994, 36.
5. David Seifman interview, in Susan Mulcahy and Frank DiGiacomo, *Paper of Wreckage: The Rogues, Renegades, Wiseguys, Wankers, and Relentless Reporters Who Redefined American Media* (New York: Atria, 2024), 449.
6. Eric Fetterman interview, in Mulcahy and DiGiacomo, *Paper of Wreckage,* 449.
7. Gabriel S. Tennen, "Shattered Mosaic: David Dinkins, Rudolph Giuliani, and Social and Electoral Polarization in Late-20th Century New York City," PhD diss., City University of New York, 2016.
8. Laura Nahmias, "White Riot," Forgotten New York, *New York* online, October 4, 2021.
9. Celia W. Dugger, "2 Sides Seek More Police to Stymie Intimidation and Fraud at Polls," *New York Times,* November 1, 1993, B5.
10. Todd S. Purdum, "Giuliani Ousts Dinkins by a Thin Margin; Whitman Is an Upset over Florio," *New York Times,* November 3, 1993, A1.
11. Memorandum from Bruce Reed, Deputy Assistant to the President, and Jose Cerda III, Senior Policy Analyst, to President William J. Clinton, April 27, 1993, Folder: Crime Bill, Stack: S, Row: 106, Section: 3, William J. Clinton Presidential Library, Little Rock, AR.
12. Bureau of Justice Statistics, *Correctional Populations in the United States, 1990,* by Thomas P. Bonczar and Allen J. Beck, NCJ 134946 (Washington, DC: U.S. Department of Justice, November 1992); Bureau of Justice Statistics, "Prisoners in 2000," by Allen J. Beck and Paige M. Harrison, *Bureau of Justice Bulletin,* NCJ 188207 (Washington, DC: U.S. Department of Justice, August 2001). Between Reagan's election in 1980 and Clinton's final year in office in 2000, the nationwide incarceration rate increased more than 200 percent. Bureau of Justice Statistics, "Prevalence of Imprisonment in the U.S. Population, 1974–2001," by Thomas P. Bonczar, Bureau of Justice Statistics Special Report, NCJ 197976 (Washington, DC: U.S. Department of Justice, August 2003).
13. James Q. Wilson and George L. Kelling, "Broken Windows: The Police and Neighborhood Safety," *The Atlantic,* March 1982, 29.
14. Michael Goodwin, "Kyle Rittenhouse, Bernie Goetz Cases Share Similarities: Goodwin," *New York Post* online, November 20, 2021.
15. Bureau of Justice Assistance, *CompStat: Its Origins, Evolution, and Future in Law Enforcement Agencies* (Washington, DC: Police Executive Research Forum, 2013), v–40.
16. Steven D. Levitt, "Understanding Why Crime Fell in the 1990s: Four Factors That Explain the Decline and Six That Do Not," *Journal of Economic Perspectives* 18, no. 1 (Winter 2004): 163–90; Alfred Blumstein and Joel Wallman, eds., *The Crime Drop in America,* rev. ed. (New York: Cambridge University Press, 2006); Franklin E. Zimring, *The Great American Crime Decline* (New York: Oxford University Press, 2007); Barry Latzer, *The Rise and Fall of Violent Crime in America* (New York: Encounter Books, 2016); Peter Moskos, *Back from the Brink* (New York: New Press, 2025).
17. As Michael Tonry has pointed out, "Crime rates in major cities and in countries fell from the early nineteenth century until the middle of the twentieth. From the 1960s to the 1990s, rates for violent and property crimes rose in all wealthy Western countries. Since then, rates in all have fallen precipitously for homicide, burglary, auto theft, and other property crimes." Michael Tonry, "Why Crime Rates Are Falling Throughout the Western World," *Crime & Justice* 43, no. 1 (2014): 1–63.
18. Michael Meeropol, *Surrender: How the Clinton Administration Completed the Reagan Revolution* (Ann Arbor: University of Michigan Press, 1998); Jack Godwin, *Clintonomics: How Bill Clinton Reengineered the Reagan Revolution* (New York: AMACOM, 2009). For histories of the longer relationship between Democrats and liberals more generally and the politics of austerity and race, see: Lily Geismer, *Left Behind: The Democrats' Failed Attempt to Solve Inequality* (New York: PublicAffairs, 2022); and Brent Cebul, *Illusions of*

Progress: Business, Poverty, and Liberalism in the American Century (Philadelphia: University of Pennsylvania Press, 2023).

19. See Clinton's former assistant secretary of health and human services Peter Edelman's thoughts on welfare policy: Peter Edelman, "The Worst Thing Bill Clinton Has Done," *The Atlantic*, March 1997.
20. Kim Phillips-Fein, *Invisible Hands: The Businessmen's Crusade Against the New Deal* (New York: W. W. Norton, 2009), 241–78; Elizabeth Hinton, *From the War on Poverty to the War on Crime: The Making of Mass Incarceration in America* (Cambridge, MA: Harvard University Press, 2016), 267–310; Thomas Frank, *Listen, Liberal: Or, What Ever Happened to the Party of the People?* (New York: Metropolitan Books, 2016), 112–35; Jacob S. Hacker and Paul Pierson, *American Amnesia: How the War on Government Led Us to Forget What Made America Prosper* (New York: Simon & Schuster, 2016), 153–81; Gary Gerstle, *The Rise and Fall of the Neoliberal Order: America and the World in the Free Market Era* (New York: Oxford University Press, 2022), 187–205.
21. Duncan Lindsey, "The Welfare Reform Act of 1996 and the Dynamics of Child Poverty in the United States," *Children and Youth Services Review* 25, no. 1–2 (2003): 9–25; H. Luke Shaefer and Kathryn Edin, *$2.00 a Day: Living on Almost Nothing in America* (Boston: Houghton Mifflin Harcourt, 2015); Brenden D. Trisi, *Deep Poverty Among Children Rose in TANF's First Decade, Then Fell as Other Programs Strengthened* (Washington, DC: Center on Budget and Policy Priorities, February 27, 2020).
22. Marc Mauer and Meda Chesney-Lind, eds., *Invisible Punishment: The Collateral Consequences of Mass Imprisonment* (New York: New Press, 2003); Devah Pager, *Marked: Race, Crime, and Finding Work in an Era of Mass Incarceration* (Chicago: University of Chicago Press, 2007); Margaret Love and Nick Sibilla, *Access to SNAP and TANF Benefits After a Drug Conviction: A Survey of State Laws* (Washington, DC: Collateral Consequences Research Center, December 2023).
23. Tony August to President William CIinton, April 2, 1993, Records Management—Alpha Files, 16331, Trumana [Donald Trump] Folder, Clinton Presidential Records, William J. Clinton Presidential Digital Library, National Archives, Washington, DC.
24. Jane Mayer, "The Making of the Fox News White House," *New Yorker*, March 4, 2019.

40. *Going It Alone*

1. William Neuman, "Kunstler Dies at 76," *New York Post*, September 5, 1995, 3.
2. Eric Breindel, "What Makes Kunstler Run," *New York Post*, July 8, 1993, 25.
3. Ron Kuby, conversation with author, July 29, 2024.
4. Ibid.
5. Ibid.
6. Ronald L. Kuby to Hon. Bertram Katz, 1995, Papers of Ron Kuby.
7. Ibid.
8. *Dateline*, "Interview with Bernhard Goetz, 3/31/96," presented by Stone Phillips, aired March 31, 1996, NBC.
9. Ibid.
10. Ibid.
11. Ibid.
12. Ibid.
13. *Dateline*, "Interview with Bernhard Goetz, 3/31/96," presented by Stone Phillips, aired March 31, 1996, NBC.
14. U.S. Census Bureau, *American Community Survey 5-Year Estimates*, retrieved from Census Reporter page for "Tract 96, Bronx, NY," 2003.
15. Mary B. W. Tabor, "State Panel Decides to Censure Bronx Judge," *New York Times*, February 23, 1994, B3.
16. Ron Kuby, conversation with author, July 29, 2024.
17. Elizabeth A. Harris, "Darnay Hoffman Dies at 63; Lawyer with Notorious Clients," *New York Times* online, May 12, 2011.

18. John Lombardi, "Defending Joel Steinberg," *New York* online, August 6, 2004.
19. Ron Kuby, conversation with author, July 29, 2024.
20. "Hoffman's Planned Trial Strategy," n.d., Internal Notes, Papers of Ron Kuby.
21. Ibid.
22. Ron Kuby, conversation with author, July 29, 2024.
23. Ibid.

41. Relitigating the Past

1. Associated Press, "Civil Trial Empaneled in $50M Suit Against Goetz," *The Record* (Hackensack, NJ), April 11, 1996, 71.
2. *CNN Evening News,* "New York, New York / Goetz Suit #406556," reported by Ralph Begleiter, aired April 23, 1996, Vanderbilt Television Archives.
3. Jan Hoffman, "Goetz II: Race Card, Early and Often," *New York Times,* April 11, 1996, B3.
4. Ibid.
5. Ibid.
6. For more on how Black jurors, judges, and prosecutors addressed the rising crime rates of this period, and specifically their own tough-on-crime decisions and attitudes, see: James Foreman Jr., *Locking Up Our Own: Crime and Punishment in Black America* (New York: Farrar, Straus & Giroux, 2017).
7. Associated Press, "Civil Trial Empaneled in $50M Suit Against Goetz," 71.
8. "Opening Statements Begin in Goetz Trial," *Tucson Citizen,* April 11, 1996, 2.
9. Ibid.
10. Jorge Fitz-Gibbon, "Goetz New Day in Court," New York *Daily News,* April 12, 1996, 11.
11. Joseph A. Kirby, "The Trial of Hero Aims to Show He Is Racist," *Chicago Tribune,* April 12, 1996, 6.
12. "Goetz Jury Picked," *Newsday,* April 11, 1996, 7.
13. Ron Kuby, conversation with author, July 29, 2024.
14. Ibid.
15. Associated Press, "Civil Trial Empaneled in $50M Suit Against Goetz," 71.
16. Ron Kuby, conversation with author, July 29, 2024.
17. Jorge Fitz-Gibbon and Jane Furse, "Face to Face Again 12 Years Later," New York *Daily News,* April 13, 1996, 3.
18. Testimony of Bernhard Goetz, in Civil Trial Transcript, *Darrell A. Cabey, by his legal guardian and proposed conservator, Shirley Cabey v. Bernhard Hugo Goetz,* No. 6747-1985 (Sup. Ct. Bronx Cnty., April 12, 1996), Papers of Ron Kuby.
19. "Goetz Says Shooting Seen as a Public Service," *Elizabethton Star Sun* (TN), April 14, 1996, 6; Adam Nossiter, "Goetz Verdict Clears Injured Son, Mother Says," *New York Times,* April 25, 1996, B2.
20. Adam Nossiter, "A Gunman's Tale of Fear, Hatred and Drugs," *New York Times,* April 13, 1996, 1.
21. "Goetz Testifies at Civil Trial About Victim's Eyes," *Tipton County Tribune* (IN), April 12, 1996, 2.
22. Ibid.
23. Ibid.
24. Ibid.
25. *NBC Nightly News,* "New York, New York / Goetz Suit #612091," reported by Rehema Ellis and Brian Williams, aired April 23, 1996, Vanderbilt Television Archives.
26. "Goetz Testifies at Civil Trial," *Tipton County Tribune,* 2.
27. *NBC Nightly News,* "New York, New York / Goetz Suit #612091."
28. Ron Kuby, conversation with author, July 29, 2024.
29. Ibid.
30. Ibid.
31. Ibid.
32. Ibid.

33. Testimony of Claude Macaluso in Trial Transcript, 6553–6616, May 11, 1987, Folder 2, Box 10, Series III, Justice Stephen G. Crane Papers on the Bernhard Goetz Trial and Other Cases, MS 3152, The New York Historical, New York, NY.
34. Claude Macaluso, "History and Progress Notes," St. Vincent's Hospital and Medical Center of New York, February 8, 1985, Papers of Ron Kuby.
35. Ibid., February 11, 1985.
36. Ibid., March 8, 1985.
37. Ibid., March 12, 1985.
38. Ibid.
39. Nossiter, "A Gunman's Tale of Fear, Hatred and Drugs," 1.
40. Testimony of Peter Adams in Civil Trial Transcript, 1, *Darrell A. Cabey, by his legal guardian and proposed conservator, Shirley Cabey v. Bernhard Hugo Goetz,* No. 6747-1985 (Sup. Ct. Bronx Cnty., April 15, 1996), Papers of Ron Kuby.
41. Ibid., 8–11.
42. Ibid., 11–15.
43. Ibid., 26.
44. Ibid., 11–15.
45. Ibid., 28.
46. Ibid.
47. Ibid.
48. Ibid., 11–15.
49. Ibid., 32–33.
50. Ibid.
51. Ibid., 21–23.
52. Ibid., 39.
53. Ibid., 40.
54. Testimony of this doctor comes from information provided in Ron Kuby's trial notes about proposed questions for Macaluso, newspaper accounts of trial proceedings, and information provided to the court previously in the following document: Affidavit, *The People of the State of New York v. Darrell Cabey,* Ind. No. 4044/84 (Sup. Ct. Bronx Cnty., December 1, 1989). Affidavit and trial notes in Papers of Ron Kuby.
55. "Man Shot by Goetz 'Needs Help,'" *Des Moines Register,* April 17, 1996.
56. Affidavit, *The People of the State of New York v. Darrell Cabey,* Ind. No. 4044/84 (Sup. Ct. Bronx Cnty., December 1, 1989), Papers of Ron Kuby.
57. "Man Shot by Goetz 'Needs Help,'" *Des Moines Register.*
58. "Goetz Victim in Coma for Weeks," *Longview Daily News* (WA), April 16, 1996.
59. Affidavit, *The People of the State of New York v. Darrell Cabey.*
60. "Witness Recalls Man Paralyzed by Goetz," *Tucson Citizen,* April 16, 1996.
61. Adam Nossiter, "Mother of Man Goetz Shot Depicts Her Ordeal," *New York Times,* April 17, 1996, B3.
62. Ibid.; Jorge Fitz-Gibbons, "Mom Testifies at Trial vs. Goetz," New York *Daily News,* April 17, 1996, 4.
63. Nossiter, "Mother of Man Goetz Shot Depicts Her Ordeal," B3.
64. Ibid.
65. Ibid.
66. Ibid.
67. Ibid.
68. Fitz-Gibbons, "Mom Testifies at Trial vs. Goetz," 4.
69. Nossiter, "Mother of Man Goetz Shot Depicts Her Ordeal," B3.
70. Ibid.
71. Testimony of Charles Hirsch, in Civil Trial Transcript, *Darrell A. Cabey, by his legal guardian and proposed conservator, Shirley Cabey v. Bernhard Hugo Goetz.*
72. Ibid., 14.
73. Ibid., 14–15.
74. Ibid., 15.

75. Ron Kuby, conversation with author, July 29, 2024.
76. Curtis Sliwa, *Curtis Sliwa Show,* featuring Ron Kuby and Niger Innis, WABC 770 AM, New York, NY, April 20, 1996.
77. Ron Kuby, conversation with author, July 29, 2024.
78. Sliwa, *Curtis Sliwa Show*.
79. Ron Kuby, conversation with author, July 29, 2024.
80. Testimony of Jimmy Breslin in Civil Trial Transcript, 1–34, April 17, 1996, Folder 12, Box 10, Series III, Justice Stephen G. Crane Papers on the Bernhard Goetz Trial and Other Cases.
81. Ibid.
82. "Goetz Limits His Defense to Just Two Witnesses," *News Tribune* (Tacoma, WA), April 18, 1996, 4.
83. "Goetz Defense Attorney Fuels Criticism, Questions from Peers," *St. Cloud Times* (MN), April 22, 1996, 5.
84. Editorial Board, "Goetz: The 2nd Time as Farce," *New York Post,* April 13, 1996, 14.
85. Sliwa, *Curtis Sliwa Show*.
86. Ibid.
87. Ibid.
88. Ibid.
89. Ibid.
90. Ibid.
91. Ibid.
92. Ibid.
93. Joseph Kirby, "Subway Vigilante Case in Final Stage," *Chicago Tribune,* April 23, 1996, 52.
94. Ibid.
95. Leon Neyfakh, *Fiasco: Vigilante*, podcast transcript, episode 6, "Damages," Prologue Projects, Audible Originals, July 27, 2023.
96. Ibid.
97. Ibid.
98. Ibid.
99. Kirby, "Subway Vigilante Case in Final Stage," 52.
100. *Cabey v. Goetz*, No. 6747/85 4/2314, April 23, 1996, "As To Claims of Assault and Battery," "As To Claims for Intentional Infliction of Emotion Distress," and "Damages," Jury Sheet, 1–3, Papers of Ron Kuby.
101. *NBC Nightly News,* "New York, New York / Goetz Suit #612091."
102. Adam Nossiter, "Bronx Jury Orders Goetz to Pay Man He Paralyzed $43 Million," *New York Times,* April 24, 1996, A1.
103. Editorial, "The Goetz Verdict," *New York Times,* April 24, 1996, A20.

42. *Duck and Weave*

1. Adam Nossiter, "Goetz Verdict Clears Injured Son, Mother Says," *New York Times,* April 25, 1996, B2.
2. Ibid.
3. Leon Neyfakh, *Fiasco: Vigilante,* podcast transcript, episode 6, "Damages," Prologue Projects, Audible Originals, July 27, 2023.
4. Lynette Holloway, "Bankrupt, Goetz Still Owes Victim," *New York Times,* August 2, 1996, B3.
5. Neyfakh, *Fiasco: Vigilante,* episode 6, "Damages."
6. Ron Kuby, conversation with author, July 29, 2024.
7. Affidavit of Service, *Darrell A. Cabey, by his legal guardian and proposed conservator, Shirley Cabey v. Bernhard Hugo Goetz,* No. 6747-1985 (Sup. Ct. Bronx Cnty., December 29, 1998), Papers of Ron Kuby.
8. Ibid.
9. Notice of Commencement of Case under Chapter 7 of the Bankruptcy Code, Meeting of Creditors, and Fixing of Dates, Bernhard Hugo Goetz, 96B42293, United States Bankruptcy Court, Southern District. April 29, 1996, Ron Kuby Papers.

10. Garry Pierre-Pierre, "The Black and the Red of Goetz's Balance Sheet," *New York Times,* May 15, 1996, B3.
11. Ibid.
12. The so-called golden age of bankruptcy expanded, in fact, until the mid-1990s, but the spike in business bankruptcies was so high beginning in the early 1980s that it made headlines. As *The New York Times* noted in 1981, "Business bankruptcies are spreading through the nation's economy at a spectacular pace, largely because of last year's recession and current high interest rates. In the first 10 weeks of this year, business bankruptcy filings soared to 2,933, a gain of 63 percent from the comparable period last year and the highest number reported for the period since 1963. The gain early last year was already 53 percent above that for the similar period in 1979, according to data released last week by Dun & Bradstreet Inc." Kenneth B. Noble, "Bankruptcies Soaring as High Interest Rates Cause Cash Shortages," *New York Times,* March 30, 1981, A1.
13. Holloway, "Bankrupt, Goetz Still Owes Victim," B3.
14. Ron Kuby, conversation with author, July 29, 2024.
15. James B. Fishman to Ronald Kuby, November 13, 1998, Papers of Ron Kuby.
16. Tina Kelley, "Following Up; Still Seeking Payment from Bernard [*sic*] Goetz," *New York Times,* September 10, 2000, 39.
17. Ron Kuby, conversation with author, July 29, 2024.
18. Ibid.
19. Murdoch had "built a multibillion-dollar media empire" but he nevertheless "would be forced to sell the *Post* 11 years later due to an FCC cross-ownership ruling." In 1988, a new congressional bill had forced this sale because of prohibitions on owning television stations as well as newspapers in the same market. Two years earlier he had acquired WNYW-TV Channel 5 in New York. Murdoch, however, refused to accept the loss of this key paper and eventually, thanks to Governor Mario Cuomo, got a waiver so that he could buy it back in 1993. Antonia Felix and the Editors of the *New York Post,* eds., *The Post's New York: Celebrating 200 Years of New York City Through the Pages and Pictures of the New York Post* (New York: Harper Resource, 2001), 191.
20. For a longer history of this growing relationship between cable and the courting and marketing of an increasingly conservative political agenda, see: Kathryn Cramer Brownell, *24/7 Politics: Cable Television and the Fragmenting of America from Watergate to Fox News* (Princeton, NJ: Princeton University Press, 2023).
21. Ibid.; Greg Young, "The New York Post vs. the New York Daily News in 'America's Last Great Newspaper War,'" Bowery Boys Bookshelf, The Bowery Boys online, April 2, 2020.
22. Interview with Chris Ruddy, in Susan Mulcahy and Frank DiGiacomo, *Paper of Wreckage: The Rogues, Renegades, Wiseguys, Wankers, and Relentless Reporters Who Redefined American Media* (New York: Atria, 2024), 460.
23. Taylor K. Reade, *Sly Fox: The History of Fox News* (Monee, IL: Independently published, 2025), 6.

PART VI · THE REBIRTH OF WHITE RAGE IN AMERICA

1. Goetz's shooting spree might today be characterized as a mass shooting incident; more than 600 mass shootings were logged each year between 2020 and 2023, dropping to just over 500 in 2024. Refer to the Gun Violence Archive, an independent data collection and research group with no affiliation with any advocacy organization, for this data: "GVA—10 Year Review," Gun Violence Archive, January 8, 2025.
2. Billy Joel, "We Didn't Start the Fire," released September 18, 1989, track 2 on *Storm Front,* Columbia.

43. *Hearts and Minds*

1. Joyce Wadler, "Public Lives; Leftist Lawyer Reaches Right for Audience," *New York Times,* January 15, 1998, B2; Ron Kuby, email message to the author, October 13, 2024.

2. Larry McShane, "Kuby Miffed That Imus Is Taking His Slot," CBS News, November 5, 2007; Robert D. McFadden, "Don Imus, Radio Host Who Pushed Boundaries, Dies at 79," *New York Times,* December 27, 2019.
3. Ron Kuby, email message to the author, October 13, 2024.
4. Kuby would come back to cohost Sliwa's show but again would be let go, this time replaced by Eboni K. Williams, a Black woman who previously anchored at Fox News. Don Kaplan, "Ex-WABCer Ron Kuby: It's 'Zen' to Be Replaced by a Black Woman," New York *Daily News,* April 8, 2017; David K. Li, "Eboni Williams Will Replace Ron Kuby on WABC Radio Talk Show, *New York Post,* June 5, 2017.
5. "FOX News Channel Smashes Records with Highest-Rated Year in Cable News History Across Total Day and Primetime Viewership," *Business Wire,* December 16, 2020.
6. Ken Auletta, "Vox Fox," *New Yorker,* May 19, 2003; Nicole Hemmer, *Messengers of the Right: Conservative Media and the Transformation of American Politics* (Philadelphia: University of Pennsylvania Press, 2016); Taylor K. Reade, *Sly Fox: The History of Fox News (*Monee, IL: Independently published, 2025), 39.
7. "FOX News Channel Smashes Records," *Business Wire.*
8. Jane Mayer, "The Making of the Fox News White House," *New Yorker,* March 4, 2019.
9. "FOX News Channel Smashes Records," *Business Wire.*
10. Mayer, "The Making of the Fox News White House"; "FOX News Channel Smashes Records," *Business Wire.*
11. Mayer, "The Making of the Fox News White House."
12. Roy M. Cohn to Hon. Edwin Meese III, Hon. James A. Baker III, Hon. Michael K. Deaver, January 27, 1983, "White House Staff Memoranda" Folder, Box 4, James A. Baker Collection, Ronald Reagan Presidential Library, Simi Valley, California; Ronald Reagan to Rupert Murdoch, December 10, 1981, "White House Staff Memoranda" Folder, Box 4, James A. Baker Collection.
13. In 2017, only 10 percent of Fox viewers were Black and only 9 percent of them were poor. The overwhelming majority of them were both white and working- or middle-class. "Who's Watching?: A Look at the Demographics of Cable News Channel Watchers" (Alexandria, VA: Public Opinion Strategies, February 1, 2019).
14. Reade, *Sly Fox,* 90.
15. Nicole Hemmer quoted in Mayer, "The Making of the Fox News White House." For the history of conservative media in the twentieth-century United States, see: Hemmer, *Messengers of the Right*, and Kathryn Cramer Brownell, *24/7 Politics: Cable Television and the Fragmenting of America from Watergate to Fox News* (Princeton, NJ: Princeton University Press, 2023).
16. Elliott Ash et al., "From Viewers to Voters: Tracing Fox News' Impact on American Democracy," *Journal of Public Economics* 240 (2024): 1–9.
17. Reade, *Sly Fox,* 90.
18. "Climate Change Denial Dominates over 86% of Fox News Climate Segments," *Public Citizen,* August 13, 2019; Oliver Darcy, "How Fox News Misled Viewers About the Coronavirus," CNN, March 12, 2020; David Bauder et al., "Fox, Dominion Reach $787M Settlement over Election Claims," *AP News* online, April 18, 2023; Shannon Bond, "How Tucker Carlson Took Fringe Conspiracy Theories to a Mass Audience," NPR, April 25, 2023.

44. *Politics and Prejudice*

1. "Giuliani Approval, Satisfaction with City Hit New Highs, Quinnipiac College Poll Finds; Mayor's Lead over Messinger Nears 2–1" (Hamden, CT: Quinnipiac University, October 29, 1997).
2. Norimitsu Onishi, "Giuliani Goes After Voters in Messinger's Stronghold," *New York Times,* October 27, 1997, B4.
3. Justin Oppman, "Giuliani Wins with Ease," CNN, November 4, 1997.
4. ACLU of New York, "Stop-and-Frisk Data" (New York: NYCLU, May 27, 2025).
5. Laura Kurgan and Eric Cadora, "Architecture and Justice," Spatial Information Design

Lab, Columbia University Graduate School of Architecture, Planning and Preservation, September 15–October 28, 2006.

6. Nancy Gibbs, "Person of the Year 2001: Rudy Giuliani," *Time,* December 31, 2001; Lisa DePaulo, "Men of the Year: Maverick," *GQ Magazine* online, November 11, 2007.
7. Alex Heard, "Questions for: Bernard [*sic*] Goetz," *New York Times,* November 1, 1998, 25.
8. Ibid.; Denise Buffa, "Snickering Experts Take Potshots," *New York Post,* November 3, 1998, 7.
9. John M. Glionna, "New York City Mayoral Race Turns Squirrelly," *Los Angeles Times,* August 22, 2001, A9.
10. Heard, "Questions for: Bernard Goetz," 25.
11. Ibid.; Buffa, "Snickering Experts Take Potshots," 7.
12. Andrea Peyser, "You Got Someone Better in Mind than Bernie?," *New York Post,* November 3, 1998, 7.
13. Quote from Joseph Mercurio of National Political Services, in Buffa, "Snickering Experts Take Potshots," 7.
14. Peyser, "You Got Someone Better in Mind than Bernie?," 7.
15. Glionna, "New York City Mayoral Race Turns Squirrelly," A9.
16. "2001 General Election City of New York Statement and Return of the Votes for the Office of Mayor of the City of New York" (New York: Board of Elections in the City of New York, November 28, 2001).
17. Larry Celona, "'Subway Vigilante' Goetz Busted In Pot Sale," *New York Post,* November 1, 2013.
18. Ibid.
19. Laura Italiano, "Goetz Hit on Pretty Cop Who Busted Him for Pot," *New York Post,* November 2, 2013.
20. Ibid.
21. Celona, "'Subway Vigilante' Goetz Busted in Pot Sale."
22. Laura Italiano and Kevin Fasick, "Bernie Goetz: I Wasn't High in 1984," *New York Post,* November 3, 2013.
23. Rebecca Rosenberg and Kevin Fasick, "'Subway Vigilante' Goetz Rejects Plea Deal over Pot Bust," *New York Post,* December 18, 2013.
24. Leon Neyfakh, *Fiasco: Vigilante,* podcast transcript, episode 6, "Damages," Prologue Projects, Audible Originals, July 27, 2023.

45. *Saying Their Names*

1. Board of Governors of the Federal Reserve Board, *Monetary Policy Report to the Congress* (Washington, DC: Board of Governors of the Federal Reserve Board, February 24, 2009), 1.
2. For an interesting history of mortgage debt and financial speculation, see: Michael Glass, *Cracked Foundations: Debt and Inequality in Suburban America* (Philadelphia: University of Pennsylvania Press, 2025).
3. Sharada Dharmasankar and Bhash Mazumder, "Have Borrowers Recovered from Foreclosures During the Great Recession?," *Chicago Fed Letter,* No. 370 (Chicago: Federal Reserve Bank of Chicago, 2016); Carolina K. Reid, "Crisis, Response, and Recovery: The Federal Government and the Black/White Homeownership Gap," A Terner Center Report, Terner for Housing Innovation—University of California, Berkeley (March 2021): 2–24; Brian Goldstone, *There Is No Place for Us* (New York: Crown, 2025).
4. Kevin Warsh, "The Panic of 2008," April 6, 2009, Council of Institutional Investors 2009 Spring Meeting, Washington, DC.
5. Stephanie Hugie Barello, "Consumer Spending and U.S. Employment from the 2007–2009 Recession Through 2022," *Monthly Labor Review,* United States Bureau of Labor Statistics, October 2014.
6. Andrew Anthony, "'We Showed It Was Possible to Create a Movement from Almost Nothing': Occupy Wall Street 10 Years On," *The Guardian,* September 12, 2021.
7. Nikole Hannah-Jones, *The 1619 Project: A New Origin Story* (New York: One World, 2021).

8. John F. Timoney, *Beat Cop to Top Cop: A Tale of Three Cities* (Philadelphia: University of Pennsylvania Press, 2010), 31.
9. "65 Stories," *Say Their Names,* Green Library Exhibit, Stanford University, accessed June 28, 2025.
10. Two of the most dramatic killings of unarmed Black New Yorkers would come in 2004, when NYPD officers killed twenty-three-year-old Sean Bell, and in 2014, when they choked Eric Garner to death as he gasped, "I can't breathe." See: Valerie Bell, *Sean Bell Just 23: Thoughts from a Mother in Spoken Word* (Bloomington, IN: AuthorHouse, 2016) and Matt Taibbi, *I Can't Breathe: A Killing on Bay Street* (New York: Random House, 2018).
11. *Tennessee v. Garner,* 471 U.S. 1 (1985); Abraham N. Tennenbaum, "The Influence of the Garner Decision on Police Use of Deadly Force," *Journal of Criminal Law & Criminology* 85 (1994–1995): 241.
12. Michelle Jaffe, "Up in Arms over Florida's New 'Stand Your Ground' Law," *Nova Law Review* 30, no. 1 (2005): 155–81.
13. Caroline Light, *Stand Your Ground: A History of America's Love Affair with Lethal Self-Defense* (New York: Beacon, 2017).
14. *District of Columbia v. Heller,* 554 U.S. 570 (2008).
15. As quoted in Mark Obbie, "He Won the Supreme Court Case That Transformed Gun Rights. But Dick Heller Is a Hard Man to Please," *The Trace,* March 20, 2016.
16. John Roman, *Race, Justifiable Homicide, and Stand Your Ground Laws: Analysis of FBI Supplementary Homicide Report Data* (Washington, DC: Urban Institute, July 26, 2013), 8.
17. Donna Murch, "Ferguson's Inheritance," *Jacobin,* August 5, 2015.
18. Zimmerman, like Goetz almost thirty years earlier, came under legal scrutiny—in his case being arrested twice for domestic assault. (In both cases, charges were dropped when the alleged victim backed off of the accusations.) Greg Botelho and Carma Hassan, "George Zimmerman Arrested on Suspected Domestic Violence," CNN, January 13, 2015; Holly Yan, "George Zimmerman's Encounters with the Law and Public Spotlight," CNN, May 12, 2015.
19. Keeanga-Yamahtta Taylor, *From #BlackLivesMatter to Black Liberation* (Chicago: Haymarket Books, 2016); Donna Murch, *Assata Taught Me: State Violence, Racial Capitalism, and the Movement for Black Lives* (Chicago: Haymarket Books, 2022).
20. Kimberlé W. Crenshaw et al., *Say Her Name: Resisting Police Brutality Against Black Women* (New York: African American Policy Forum & Center for Intersectionality and Social Policy Studies, 2015).
21. "2008," The American Presidency Project, University of California, Santa Barbara, accessed June 28, 2025, https://www.presidency.ucsb.edu/statistics/elections/2008; "2012," The American Presidency Project, University of California, Santa Barbara, accessed June 28, 2025.
22. Julian E. Zelizer, ed., *The Presidency of Barack Obama: A First Historical Assessment* (Princeton, NJ: Princeton University Press, 2018).
23. David A. Skeel Jr., "The New Financial Deal: Understanding the Dodd-Frank Act and Its (Unintended) Consequences," *Faculty Scholarship at Penn Carey Law,* 2010; Arthur E. Wilmarth Jr., "The Dodd-Frank Act: A Flawed and Inadequate Response to the Too-Big-to-Fail Problem," *George Washington University Law School Public Law and Legal Theory Working Paper,* no. 516 (2011); Eric C. Chaffee, "The Dodd-Frank Act: A Failed Vision for Increasing Consumer Protection and Heightening Corporate Responsibility in International Financial Transactions," *American University Law Review* 60, no. 5 (2011): 1431–1500.
24. Fair Sentencing Act of 2010, Public Law No. 111–220, 124 Stat. 2372 (2010); Barack Obama, "The President's Role in Advancing Criminal Justice Reform," *Harvard Law Review* 130, no. 3 (January 2017): 811–66; Rachel E. Barkow and Mark Osler, "Designed to Fail: The President's Deference to the Department of Justice in Advancing Criminal Justice Reform," *William & Mary Law Review* 59, no. 2 (2017): 387–454; Alex Whiting, "Through Actions and Words, President Obama Has Promoted Criminal Justice Reform," *Harvard Law Record,* November 15, 2016, https://journals.law.harvard.edu/lpr/2016/11/15/alex-whiting-through-actions-and-words-president-obama-has-promoted-criminal-justice-reform/.

25. Glenn R. Schmitt et al., *An Analysis of the Implementation of the 2014 Clemency Initiative,* United States Sentencing Commission, Office of Research and Data (Washington, DC: United States Sentencing Commission, September 2017).
26. As Maya Schenwar and Victoria Law's important book *Prison by Any Other Name* shows, this approach met substantial concern that it would in fact only expand the footprint of the criminal justice system. Maya Schenwar and Victoria Law, *Prison by Any Other Name: The Harmful Consequences of Popular Reform* (New York: New Press, 2020). For more on the non-incarcerative but long reach of the carceral state see: Ben Austin, *Correction: Parole, Prison, and the Possibility of Change* (New York: Flatiron, 2023) and Reuben Jonathan Miller, *Halfway Home: Race, Punishment, and the Afterlife of Mass Incarceration* (New York: Little, Brown, 2021).
27. Krissah Thompson and Scott Wilson, "Obama on Trayvon Martin: 'If I Had a Son, He'd Look Like Trayvon,'" *Washington Post,* March 23, 2012.
28. E. J. Dionne Jr., "The Painful Paradoxes of Race: Obama, Booker, Problems & Progress," *Commonweal,* July 22, 2013.
29. Jamilas Lartey, "Obama on Black Lives Matter: They Are 'Much Better Organizers Than I Was,'" *The Guardian,* February 18, 2016.
30. Maya Rhodan, "Obama Defends Black Lives Matter: The Black Community Isn't 'Making This Up,'" *Time,* October 22, 2015.
31. National Police Foundation, *21st Century Policing Task Force Report: The First Five Years* (Arlington, VA: National Police Foundation, November 2021).
32. In Ferguson, the consent decree was a legally binding agreement between the U.S. Department of Justice and that city to reform the police department and municipal court system. Amended and Restated Consent Decree, *United States of America v. City of Ferguson,* No. 4:16-Cv-000180-Cdp, United States District Court, Eastern District of Missouri, Eastern Division, November 15, 2018.
33. William Jelani Cobb, *The Substance of Hope: Barack Obama and the Paradox of Progress* (New York: Walker Books, 2010).

46. *Referendum*

1. See: E. J. Dionne Jr., *Why the Right Went Wrong: Conservatism—from Goldwater to the Tea Party and Beyond* (New York: Simon & Schuster, 2016); Heather Cox Richardson, *How the South Won the Civil War: Oligarchy, Democracy, and the Continuing Fight for the Soul of America* (New York: Oxford University Press, 2020).
2. Donald Trump, *The America We Deserve* (New York: Macmillan, 2000).
3. Donald J. Trump, *Time to Get Tough: Making America #1 Again* (Washington, DC: Regnery, 2011).
4. "Trump Calls Obama 'Worst President,' 'a Disaster' After 'Unfit to Serve' Slam," *Fox News,* August 2, 2016.
5. Igor Bobic and Sam Stein, "How CPAC Helped Launch Donald Trump's Political Career," *HuffPost,* February 22, 2017.
6. David Freedlander, "'They Saw the World in This Dog-Eat-Dog, Manichaean Way': The Ugly '90s Roots of Rudy's Bond with Donald Trump," *Vanity Fair,* November 10, 2019.
7. Michael Barkun, *A Culture of Conspiracy: Apocalyptic Visions in Contemporary America* (Oakland: University of California Press, 2003); Nicole Hemmer, *Messengers of the Right: Conservative Media and the Transformation of American Politics* (Philadelphia: University of Pennsylvania Press, 2016); David Austin Walsh, *Taking America Back: The Conservative Movement and the Far Right* (New Haven, CT: Yale University Press, 2024); David Pakman, *The Echo Machine: How Right-Wing Extremism Created a Post-Truth America* (Boston: Beacon, 2025). For a study on the origins of public broadcasting as a political institution that would come to shape the rise of the commercial media industry in the late twentieth century, see: Josh Shepperd, *Shadow of the New Deal: The Victory of Public Broadcasting* (Champaign: University of Illinois Press, 2023).
8. David Neiwert, *Alt-America: The Rise of the Radical Right in the Age of Trump* (New York: Verso, 2017); Julian E. Zelizer, *The Presidency of Donald J. Trump: A First Historical*

Assessment (Princeton, NJ: Princeton University Press, 2022); David Neiwert, *The Age of Insurrection: The Radical Right's Assault on American Democracy* (New York: Melville House, 2023).

47. Fury Unfurled

1. *Historical U.S. Federal Corporate Income Tax Rates & Brackets, 1909–2025* (Washington, DC: Tax Foundation, January 1, 2025).
2. *Corporate Income Tax: Effective Rates Before and After 2017 Law Change*, GAO-23-105384 (Washington, DC: Government Accountability Office, December 14, 2022).
3. Karen L. Cox, "What Changed in Charlottesville," *New York Times*, August 11, 2019; Kathleen Belew, "White Power, White Violence," *The Atlantic*, May 16, 2022. For a study of white nationalism in historical perspective, see Kathleen Belew, *Bring the War Home: The White Power Movement and Paramilitary America* (Cambridge, MA: Harvard University Press, 2018). Also see: Karen L. Cox, *No Common Ground: Confederate Monuments and the Ongoing Fight for Racial Justice* (Chapel Hill: University of North Carolina Press, 2021).
4. Andrew Katz, "Clashes Over a Show of White Nationalism in Charlottesville Turn Deadly," *Time*, August 12, 2017.
5. George Lindbeck, "Lessons Learned from the 'Unite the Right Rally' of 2017," Tactical and Law Enforcement Medicine Section, American College of Emergency Physicians, March 19, 2021.
6. "Full Text: Trump's Comments on White Supremacists, 'Alt-Left' in Charlottesville," *Politico*, August 18, 2017.
7. Elizabeth Hinton, *America on Fire: The Untold History of Police Violence and Black Rebellion Since the 1960s* (New York: Liveright, 2021).
8. Steven A. Cook, "Yes, Lafayette Square Is Tahrir Square," *Foreign Policy*, June 4, 2020.
9. Evan Hill, "How George Floyd Was Killed in Police Custody," *New York Times*, May 31, 2020.
10. Sam Levin, "These US Cities Defunded Police: 'We're Transferring Money to the Community,'" *The Guardian*, March 11, 2021.
11. Alex Rogers, "Trump's Response to Police Killing Threatens to Further Deepen Unrest in America, Democrats and Republicans Say," *CNN*, May 31, 2020.
12. Alex Minna Stern, *Proud Boys and the White Ethnostate: How the Alt-Right Is Warping the American Imagination* (Boston: Beacon, 2019); Paola Ramos, *Defectors: The Rise of the Latino Far Right and What It Means for America* (New York: Pantheon, 2024).
13. Catrina Doxsee et al., "Pushed to Extremes: Domestic Terrorism amid Polarization and Protest," *CSIS Briefs* (Washington, DC: Center for Strategic and International Studies, May 17, 2022).
14. Federal Bureau of Investigation, "2020 FBI Hate Crimes Statistics" (Washington, DC: U.S. Department of Justice, last updated October 30, 2023).
15. Craig Timberg and Elizabeth Dwoskin, "Trump's Debate Comments Give an Online Boost to a Group Social Media Companies Have Long Struggled Against," *Washington Post*, September 30, 2020.
16. Christina Morales, "What We Know About the Shooting of Jacob Blake," *New York Times*, November 16, 2021.
17. Vanessa Romo and Sharon Pruitt-Young, "What We Know About the 3 Men Who Were Shot by Kyle Rittenhouse," *NPR*, November 20, 2021.
18. Julie Bosman, "Kyle Rittenhouse Acquitted on All Counts," *New York Times*, November 19, 2021.
19. "How Kyle Rittenhouse's Treatment and Trial Defied Norms," *PBS NewsHour*, November 20, 2021.
20. Michael Goodwin, "Kyle Rittenhouse, Bernie Goetz Cases Share Similarities: Goodwin," *New York Post*, November 20, 2021.
21. Ibid.
22. Brian Rokus, "Trump Says Rittenhouse Visited Him at Mar-a-Lago," *CNN*, November 23, 2021.

23. Daniel Nass and Champe Barton, "How Many Guns Did Americans Buy Last Month?," *The Trace,* August 3, 2020. Also quoted in Daniel de Visé, "Americans Bought Almost 60 Million Guns During the Pandemic," *The Hill,* April 21, 2023.
24. Goodwin, "Kyle Rittenhouse, Bernie Goetz Cases Share Similarities."
25. Zachary Parolin and Stefano Filauro, "The United States' Record-Low Child Poverty Rate in International and Historical Perspective: A Research Note," *Demography* 60, no. 6 (2023): 1665–73.
26. "Child Tax Credit," U.S. Department of the Treasury, accessed March 9, 2025.
27. Parolin and Filauro, "The United States' Record-Low Child Poverty Rate."
28. "Child Poverty More Than Doubled in 2022, Underscoring Need for Better Policy," press release, Center for Law and Social Policy, September 12, 2023, Washington, DC.
29. Matt Gertz, "Fox Has Run Nearly 1,000 Weekday Segments on 'Migrant Crime' in 2024. The GOP Turned That Bogus Narrative into a Convention Night Theme," *Media Matters for America,* July 16, 2024.
30. David Bauder et al., "Fox, Dominion Reach $787M Settlement over Election Claims," *AP News,* April 18, 2023.
31. Allison Murrow, "Fox Faces an 'Existential Threat' from Its Multibillion-Dollar Defamation Case," CNN, February 28, 2023.
32. Katie Robertson, "Newsmax Will Pay $67 Million to Settle Dominion Defamation Lawsuit," *New York Times,* August 18, 2025.
33. "What We Know About Truth Social, Donald Trump's Social Media Platform," *AP News,* March 22, 2024.
34. "Truth Social: Trump's Echo Chamber Masquerading as Free Speech," *CEO Today,* April 30, 2025.
35. John T. Psaropoulos, "Is Elon Musk a Nazi, and Can He Get European Far-Right Hardliners Elected?" *Al Jazeera*, January 31, 2025.
36. "Number of X (formerly Twitter) Users Worldwide from 2019 to 2024" (Hamburg, DE: Statistica, December 2022).

48. Reaping What Was Sown

1. Ali Vitali, "Trump Says He Could 'Shoot Somebody' and Still Maintain Support," NBC News, Jan. 23, 2016.
2. Joshua Nelken-Zitser, "Donald Trump Congratulates Kyle Rittenhouse on His Acquittal: 'If That's Not Self-Defense, Nothing Is,'" *Business Insider,* November 20, 2021.
3. Kathianne Boniello, "Daniel Penny's Prosecution Was 'BS' and a 'Political Trial,' Original NYC Subway Vigilante Bernie Goetz Says," *New York Post,* January 4, 2025.
4. Katie Puckrik and Tom Fordyce, *We Didn't Start the Fire: The History Podcast,* podcast, "Bernie Goetz," Crowd Stories, May 28, 2023.
5. Peter Senzamici, "Daniel Penny Demands Dismissal of Jordan Neely's Dad's Lawsuit in New Filing," *New York Post,* January 7, 2025.
6. Adriana Gomez Licon, "Daniel Penny Will Join Trump's Suite at Football Game After Being Acquitted in NYC Chokehold Case," *PBS NewsHour,* December 13, 2024.
7. Andrew Murray and Stephanie Pagones, "Kyle Rittenhouse Trial 'a Sham at Best,' Subway Vigilante Bernie Goetz Says: 'Satisfy a Mob,'" *Fox News,* November 11, 2021.
8. Ibid.
9. Helayne Seidman and Laura Italiano, "'Subway Vigilante' Bernie Goetz Is a Coronavirus Quarantine Denier," *New York Post,* May 1, 2020.
10. Boniello, "Daniel Penny's Prosecution was 'BS' and a 'Political Trial.'"
11. Ibid.

49. Requiem

1. Katie Puckrik and Tom Fordyce, *We Didn't Start the Fire: The History Podcast,* podcast, "Bernie Goetz," Crowd Stories, May 28, 2023.

2. Ibid.
3. Ibid.
4. Quoted in Monique Judge, "White Vigilantism Is American History," *Dame Magazine,* March 22, 2022.
5. Attendant to nationally recognized cases are more formal and official acts of vigilantism. Jon Michaels and David Noll, *Vigilante Nation: How State-Sponsored Terror Threatens Our Democracy* (New York: Simon & Schuster, 2024).
6. Georgett Roberts and Steve Janoski, "DA Bragg Drops Case Against Chinatown Landlord Who Beat Homeless Man After the Vagrant Attacked Him," *New York Post,* January 12, 2025.
7. Ibid.
8. *92Y American Conversation,* "Revisiting the Trial of Bernie Goetz—92nd Street Y," YouTube video, featuring Mark Lesly, Geraldo Rivera, Thane Rosenbaum, Barry Slotnick, and Gregory Waples, uploaded February 13, 2014, The 92nd Street Y, New York and Fordham University School of Law.
9. As one *New York Times* reporter noted in 2021, "While gun sales have been climbing for decades . . . Americans have been on an unusual, prolonged buying spree" that was "fueled" by "fears." Sabrina Tavernise, "An Arms Race in America: Gun Buying Spiked During the Pandemic. It's Still Up," *New York Times,* May 29, 2021.
10. Phillip Messing, "Bitter Dad: He'll Get Off Easy," *New York Post,* December 26, 1984, 2.
11. Carl Canty, conversation with author, March 26, 2024.
12. Interview with Barry Allen in prison, in *The Company You Keep,* written and directed by Adrian Liang (New York: Stone Age Films, 2018), animated documentary short.
13. Leon Neyfakh, *Fiasco: Vigilante,* podcast transcript, episode 3, "Four Teenagers," Prologue Projects, Audible Originals, July 27, 2023.
14. Ibid.
15. Ibid.
16. Carl Canty, conversation with author, March 26, 2024.
17. Ibid.
18. Charles Lachman et al., "'Death Wish' Victim Threatened in Hospital," *New York Post,* December 26, 1984, 2.
19. Laura Italiano and Kevin Fasick, "Bernie Goetz: I Wasn't High in 1984," *New York Post,* November 3, 2013.
20. John Saul, "One of Bernhard Goetz's Victims Kills Self on Anniversary of Subway Shooting," *New York Post,* December 23, 2011.
21. Leon Neyfakh, *Fiasco: Vigilante,* podcast transcript, episode 6, "Damages," Prologue Projects, Audible Originals, July 27, 2023.
22. Testimony of James Ramseur in Trial Transcript, 7033, May 19, 1987, Folder 5, Box 10, Series III, Justice Stephen G. Crane Papers on the Bernhard Goetz Trial and Other Cases, MS 3152, The New York Historical, New York, NY.
23. Charles Oliver and Leslie Gevirtz, "The Victims: We Wanted $5 to Play Video Game," *New York Post,* December 24, 1984, 3.
24. Bruce Weber, "James Ramseur, Wounded in '84 Subway Shooting, Dies at 45," *New York Times,* December 23, 2011.
25. Saul, "One of Bernhard Goetz's Victims Kills Self on Anniversary of Subway Shooting."
26. Adam Nossiter, "Mother of Man Goetz Shot Depicts Her Ordeal," *New York Times,* April 17, 1996, B3.
27. Ibid.
28. Raven Cabey, quoted in Neyfakh, *Fiasco: Vigilante,* episode 6, "Damages."
29. Ibid.
30. Ibid.
31. Ibid.
32. Heather Cox Richardson, *Democracy Awakening: Notes on the State of America* (New York: Viking, 2023).

Index

Page numbers in *italics* refer to photographs.

A NOTE ON THE TYPE

This book was set in Minion, a typeface produced by the Adobe Corporation specifically for the Macintosh personal computer and released in 1990. Designed by Robert Slimbach, Minion combines the classic characteristics of old-style faces with the full complement of weights required for modern typesetting.

Composed by North Market Street Graphics,
Lancaster, Pennsylvania

Designed by Cassandra J. Pappas